TRANSBOUNDARY ENVIRONMENTAL GOVERNANCE

Transboundary Environmental Governance

Inland, Coastal and Marine Perspectives

Edited by

ROBIN WARNER
University of Wollongong, Australia

SIMON MARSDEN
Flinders University, Australia

Routledge
Taylor & Francis Group
LONDON AND NEW YORK

First published 2012 by Ashgate Publishing

Published 2016 by Routledge
2 Park Square, Milton Park, Abingdon, Oxon OX14 4RN
711 Third Avenue, New York, NY 10017, USA

First issued in paperback 2017

Routledge is an imprint of the Taylor & Francis Group, an informa business

British Library Cataloguing in Publication Data
Transboundary environmental governance : inland, coastal and marine perspectives.
1. Environmental protection--International cooperation. 2. Coastal zone management--International cooperation. 3. Marine resources conservation--International cooperation. 4. Transboundary pollution--Case studies. 5. Environmental impact analysis--Case studies. 6. Environmental protection--Australia. 7. Environmental protection--Asia. 8. Environmental impact analysis--Law and legislation. 9. Transboundary pollution--Law and legislation.
I. Warner, Robin. II. Marsden, Simon, 1964-
344'.046-dc23

Library of Congress Cataloging-in-Publication Data
Transboundary environmental governance : inland, coastal and marine perspectives /
[edited by] Robin Warner and Simon Marsden.
p. cm.
"This book arose out of a seminar organised by the contributing editors, Robin Warner and Simon Marsden, which was held on 12 May 2011 ... at the University of Wollongong in Australia"--ECIP galley.
Includes bibliographical references and index.
ISBN 978-1-4094-4493-0 (hardcover) 1. Marine resources conservation--Law and legislation--Congresses. 2. Environmental management--Law and legislation--Congresses. 3. Coastal zone management--Law and legislation--Congresses. 4. Environmental impact analysis--Law and legislation--Congresses. 5. Transboundary pollution--Law and legislation--Congresses.
6. Convention on Environmental Impact Assessment in a Transboundary Context (1991) I. Warner, Robin. II. Marsden, Simon, 1964-
K3590.4.T73 2012
341.4'48--dc23

2012019364

ISBN 13: 978-1-138-11853-9 (pbk)
ISBN 13: 978-1-4094-4493-0 (hbk)

Contents

PART II: MARINE PERSPECTIVES

List of Figures

List of Tables

List of Contributors

Julie Davidson is a social scientist whose main research interest is environmental governance, particularly the governance of natural resources and marine biodiversity. She works with the National Climate Change Marine Biodiversity and Resources Adaptation Network, where she focuses on the resilience of marine social-ecological systems in the context of climate change and interdisciplinary approaches to adaptation. As a senior research fellow in the University of Tasmania's School of Geography and Environmental Studies, she is researching the adequacy of current governance and management arrangements for marine biodiversity conservation in the face of climate-induced changes in Australia's marine environment.

Brendan Grigg is a lecturer at Flinders Law School South Australia. He lectures in the areas of property, equity and trusts, environmental and land use planning law. He also teaches legal research and writing skills as part of the first year curriculum. Before joining the Flinders Law School he practised at a specialist planning and development law firm. He has also practised in native title law and in environmental law at the South Australian Crown Solicitor's Office. This included a role as in-house solicitor to the South Australian Environment Protection Authority.

Warwick Gullett is a Professor of Law and Deputy Director of the Australian National Centre for Ocean Resources and Security (ANCORS) at the University of Wollongong, NSW. His research interests focus on the law of the sea, legal protection of the marine environment and Australian and international fisheries law. He is the author of *Fisheries Law in Australia* (LexisNexis Butterworths, 2008) and editor (with Clive Schofield and Joanna Vince) of *Marine Resources Management* (LexisNexis Butterworths, 2011). Warwick holds an LLB and an honours degree in geography from Monash University and a PhD from the Australian National University.

Cameron Holley is a Senior Lecturer at the UNSW Law School and Research Affiliate at the National Centre for Groundwater Research and Training. Prior to joining UNSW, Cameron worked as a researcher and lecturer at the Centre for Legal Governance and the Centre for International & Environmental Law at Macquarie University and as a postdoctoral research associate at the Regulatory Institutions Network at the Australian National University. Cameron's research interests are in the areas of environmental law, natural resources law and water law, with a focus on regulation and governance.

Timo Koivurova is a research professor and has specialized in international law, in particular international environmental law. He leads the Northern Institute for Environmental and Minority Law. He has been involved as an expert in several international processes globally and in the Arctic region. Professor Koivurova was a co-leader of a global research project on the theory and practice of transboundary environmental impact assessment and is a member of the IUCN's Commission on Environmental Law (CEL). He is editor-in-chief of the *Yearbook of Polar Law* (Brill) and an editor of the *Nordic Journal of Environmental Law* and the *Nordic Journal of International Law*.

Lorne Kriwoken is an environmental scientist in the School of Geography and Environmental Studies, University of Tasmania, a Research Associate with the Antarctic Climate and Ecosystems Cooperative Research Centre, University of Tasmania and a lecturer at the Shanghai Ocean University, China. His research interests are interdisciplinary and include biodiversity protection, environmental planning and management and ocean and coastal governance. He has degrees in environmental science from Simon Fraser University, Dalhousie University and the University of Tasmania.

Michelle Lim is a researcher at the IHP-HELP Centre for Water Law, Policy and Science at the University of Dundee. Michelle's PhD research was conducted at the Australian Centre for Agriculture and Law at the University of New England. Michelle's PhD examined the legal and institutional requirements for effective biodiversity conservation across international boundaries. For her PhD research Michelle collaborated with national legal teams from Kyrgyzstan and Tajikistan on a United Nations transboundary project which covers the Pamir- Alai mountain ranges.

Michael Lockwood is a senior lecturer in the School of Geography and Environmental Studies at the University of Tasmania. He is internationally recognized for his work in the broad fields of environmental planning and management. His research focuses on understanding and improving environmental governance, contributing to our knowledge of the social and institutional dimensions of environmental conservation, identifying good-practice management for protected areas, and understanding people's values for nature.

Youna Lyons is a senior research fellow with the Centre for International Law at the National University of Singapore focusing on regional environmental governance in Southeast Asia. Her primary research areas are offshore oil and gas in Southeast Asia, the use of satellite imagery to inform maritime boundary disputes in the South China Sea, the protection of marine sensitive environments in the seas of Southeast Asia and the underlying legal and institutional governance framework, as well as integrated coastal management. Prior to her current position, she created and led the private international law practice of the Litigation and

Arbitration Group at Clifford Chance (Paris office) for more than 12 years. Youna trained in marine ecology and policy at the College of Ocean and Fisheries of the University of Washington, where she obtained a Masters in Marine Affairs.

Simon Marsden is an Associate Professor at Flinders Law School. He specializes in international and comparative environmental law and the relationship between legal systems. His research focuses on strategic and transboundary approaches to environmental impact assessment (EIA), terrestrial and marine protected areas, public participation and access to justice, and treaty based non-compliance procedures. Recent work considers comparative approaches to these matters in Europe, Asia and Australasia. Simon has published in a wide range of journals recently including *International and Comparative Law Quarterly, Nordic Journal of International Law, Review of European Community and International Environmental Law*, and *Chinese Journal of International Law.*

Karen Scott is an Associate Professor of Law at the University of Canterbury, New Zealand. She researches and teaches in the areas of law of the sea, international environmental law and Antarctic law and policy. Karen has published widely in these areas in journals such as the *International and Comparative Law Quarterly*, the *Yearbook of International Environmental Law* and the *Melbourne Journal of International Law*. She is the co-editor (with Alan D. Hemmings and Donald R. Rothwell) of *Antarctic Security in the Twenty-first Century: Legal and Policy Perspectives* (Routledge, 2012). Karen is the general editor of the *New Zealand Yearbook of International Law*.

Tim Stephens is Co-Director of the Sydney Centre for International Law at the Faculty of Law at the University of Sydney. An international lawyer and human geographer, Dr Stephens holds a PhD in international law from the University of Sydney, and an MPhil in geography from the University of Cambridge. He has published widely on issues of international environmental law and the law of the sea. His recent publications include *International Courts and Environmental Protection* (Cambridge, 2009), *The International Law of the Sea* with Donald R. Rothwell (Hart, 2010) and *Climate Change and Australia: Warming to the Global Challenge* with Ben Saul, Steven Sherwood, Jane McAdam and James Slezak (Federation, 2012).

Robin Warner is an Associate Professor at the Australian National Centre for Ocean Resources and Security, University of Wollongong. She holds a PhD in international law from the University of Sydney and a Master of International Law from the Australian National University. Her research interests include law of the sea, oceans governance, marine environmental law, climate law and transnational criminal law. She is the author of *Protecting the Oceans Beyond National Jurisdiction: Strengthening the International Law Framework* (Martinus Nijhoff, 2009) and editor (with Clive Schofield) of *Climate Change and the*

Oceans: Gauging the Legal and Policy Currents in the Asia Pacific (Edward Elgar Publishers, 2012) as well as many book chapters and journal articles on oceans law and policy.

Foreword

David Freestone

I am delighted to have been invited by the editors to write a short foreword for this timely and important volume. The linkage of the global governance agenda with perspectives on the development and evolution of environmental impact assessment is particularly timely as the world community is preparing for Rio+20, the UN Conference on Sustainable Development (UNCSD).

As the informal title of the UNCSD indicates, it is twenty years since the historic UN Conference on Environment and Development (UNCED) in Rio de Janeiro in June of 1992. Rio was itself twenty years on from the ground breaking 1972 Stockholm Conference on the Human Environment, which established the UN Environment Programme and, with the 1972 Stockholm Declaration, laid out the first principles of what we would now recognize as sustainable development. Many of the themes and aspirations of both the Stockholm Declaration and the Rio Declaration are captured in this volume, which also looks carefully and critically at the ways they have been implemented at national, regional and global level.

It is clear from the chapters of this book that this is still a developing regime – a work in progress. However it is a tribute to the journey of environmental law and governance to date, that at the time of the Stockholm Declaration there really was no discipline that could be usefully described as environmental law. In 1972, the US Environmental Protection Agency was first established, the same year that the European Community was expanded for the first time from the original six founding countries, and many countries in the Common Law tradition, such as the UK and Australia, had planning law but no mandatory environmental impact assessment (EIA) requirements. The development of environmental law in the UK, for example, was initially driven solely by European law requirements. Australian EIA requirements date from 1974 when the Environment Protection (Impact of Proposals) Act was passed by the Federal Government. The first World Bank policy on environmental impacts of Bank financed projects dates from 1984.

As well as endorsing Precaution in Principle 15, the Rio Declaration in its Principle 17 provides that 'Environmental impact assessment, as a national instrument, shall be undertaken for proposed activities that are likely to have a significant adverse impact on the environment ...'. And of course Principle 2 (echoing Principle 21 of the Stockholm Declaration) provides that 'States have the ... responsibility to ensure that activities within their jurisdiction and control do not cause damage to the environment of other States or of areas beyond the limits of national jurisdiction.' Although the implications are obvious in retrospect, the Rio Declaration does not 'join up these dots' to suggest that national EIA should also be undertaken for activities that pose the risk of having transboundary impacts, despite the fact that the Espoo Convention on Environmental Impact Assessment in a Transboundary Context was finalized in February 1991, some 16 months prior to Rio. Espoo is a UN Economic Commission for Europe Convention; there seemed to be little stomach however for adopting this as a global principle. Even in Europe the Convention did not enter into force until 1998. However, this is where – as this volume shows – treaty law and state practice have developed since 1992.

Europe has been the leader on this at a regional level with the EU adopting the Strategic Environmental Assessment Directive in 2001 (Directive 2001/42/EC) and Espoo following with its 2003 Kiev Protocol on Strategic Environmental Assessment, concluded at a time when a number of non-EU developed countries still do not have mandatory SEA. Nevertheless there are a number of important and interesting initiatives in this area from other regions which are dealt with in this volume, including voluntary arrangements under the innovative regional arrangements of PEMSEA (Partnerships in Environmental Management for the Seas of East Asia) and COBSEA (the Coordinating Body on the Seas of South Asia).

At the global level, the regulation of transboundary environmental impacts is still at a rudimentary stage. The most potent example of failure of this may perhaps be the continuing inability of the parties to the UN Framework Convention on Climate Change to agree a post 2012 regime for international climate change, now deferred to 2015. But the editors have put together a most useful collection of chapters in relation to the regime of the Law of the Sea Convention (LOSC), itself 30 years old this year. Although the LOSC does require that States undertake EA for 'planned activities under their jurisdiction and control' that they have reasonable grounds for believing 'may cause substantial pollution or significant and harmful changes to the marine environment' (Article 206), there is no international mechanism for monitoring observance of this requirement nor of the parallel requirement of publication (Article 205). The International Tribunal for the Law of the Sea, Seabed Disputes Chamber has however taken leadership on this in relation to seabed mining. In its historic February 2011 Advisory Opinion on *Responsibilities and Obligations of States Sponsoring Persons and Entities with Respect to Activities in the Area* (Case No. 17), the ITLOS Chamber recognized 'a trend towards making [the precautionary] approach part of customary international law' (para. 135), which it found in the ICJ 2010 *Pulp Mills* judgment. As I have written elsewhere, in its Advisory Opinion, the 'Chamber has unanimously set the highest standards of due diligence for sponsoring states and endorsed a legal obligation for them to apply precaution and best environmental practices, and to conduct environmental impact assessments' (105 *AJIL* 759, (2011)). Nevertheless as various chapters of this volume demonstrate, these normative statements still require a great deal of detailed implementation if they are to remain more than hortatory.

The editors have done an excellent job in pulling together the various and diverse themes in this volume. I am pleased to recommend this wide ranging and thoughtful work.

Chapter 1
Perspectives on Transboundary Environmental Governance

Robin Warner and Simon Marsden

Introduction

This book arose out of a seminar organized by the contributing editors, Robin Warner and Simon Marsden, which was held on 12 May 2011 and hosted by the Australian National Centre for Ocean Resources and Security (ANCORS) at the University of Wollongong in Australia. Inspired by shared interests in environmental impact assessment (EIA) and strategic environmental assessment (SEA) from different but complementary viewpoints, the seminar reviewed current transboundary environmental law and policy for inland, coastal and marine areas from global, regional and national perspectives, with examples and case studies drawn from Australia, Asia, Europe, Antarctica and marine areas beyond national jurisdiction (ABNJ). It also analysed the potential for developing and implementing additional transboundary environmental processes and mechanisms drawing on this experience. The keynote speaker, Timo Koivurova, addressed the question of whether the Espoo Convention on EIA in a Transboundary Context[1] (the Espoo Convention) could become a global treaty regime for EIA and SEA.

Themes examined at the seminar included: legal and policy frameworks for transboundary EIA and SEA; legal and policy frameworks for transboundary marine spatial planning (MSP) and marine protected areas (MPAs); collaborative planning and management arrangements between foreign and within federal States and in connection with non-State actors to protect marine, coastal and inland environments; global and regional developments related to protecting the marine environment beyond national jurisdiction. These and additional themes are addressed in the chapters that follow.

The editors of this book would like to express their sincere thanks to ANCORS and the Faculty of Law at the University of Wollongong, in particular to Warwick Gullett for supporting and hosting the seminar and to ANCORS Director Martin Tsamenyi for welcoming presenters and attendees and introducing the event. They

1 *Convention on Environmental Impact Assessment in a Transboundary Context*, opened for signature 25 February 1991, 30 ILM 802 (entered into force 14 January 1998) ('*Espoo Convention*').

would also like to extend their thanks to Professor David Freestone for kindly agreeing to prepare a Foreword to the book.

Rationale and Imperatives

Human activities in marine and coastal areas as well as inland waters are steadily growing in intensity and scope in response to the demand from all sectors for new resources and energy. Traditional uses of the sea such as fishing and shipping are now conducted on an industrial scale. Newer uses such as hydrocarbon exploitation, exploration for seabed minerals, wind and wave energy generation and bio-prospecting for marine genetic resources are proliferating in many offshore areas. The size and scale of these activities pose significant threats to the marine environment and its biodiversity, much of which is still undiscovered. Over exploitation of fish stocks across multiple jurisdictional boundaries can weaken the genetic diversity and resilience of target species and adversely affect associated and dependent species within the same ecosystem. Destructive fisheries practices such as bottom trawling, pelagic long line fishing and dynamite fishing have devastating consequences for non target species and habitats destroyed and damaged by heavy rollers, multiple hooks deployed across the ocean and toxic substances polluting the marine environment. Vessel source pollution, both accidental and deliberate, from the growing volume of international shipping traffic continues to cause significant harm to marine species, habitats and ecosystems across all ocean space.

The Deepwater Horizon disaster in the Gulf of Mexico in 2010 and the Montara disaster in the Timor Sea in 2009 highlight the continuing risk of catastrophic oil spills causing substantial transboundary pollution from offshore installations. They also emphasize the disconnection between (public) governance on the one hand, and the (private) technical capability to prevent and remediate the effects of such disasters on the other. The imminent exploitation of seabed minerals in Pacific jurisdictions will result in severe disturbance of the surrounding ocean floor habitats and destruction of much of the benthal fauna. The growth in bioprospecting expeditions for marine genetic resources continues to introduce alien elements of light and noise into sensitive ocean habitats, adversely affecting species and habitats. The damming of rivers for hydroelectric power, tidal barrages and the establishment of industrial installations on transboundary watercourses, and the dumping of dredging waste from port infrastructure development on the coast provide further examples of human activities with the potential for significant transboundary harm to species and ecosystems affected by polluted and degraded habitats, together with displaced communities who often rely on the resource.

Effective protection of marine, coastal and inland environments against these threats increasingly requires cooperation and decision making by a vast array of actors including neighbouring States, global and regional organizations, government and private sector entities and local communities within and across

State boundaries. All parts of the marine and coastal environment are interrelated and benefit from complementary global, regional and national strategies for environmental governance. EIAs and SEAs of human activities in marine, coastal and inland areas, across national boundaries and boundaries separating areas within national jurisdiction from the global marine commons are vital precautionary components of transboundary environmental governance, and are emphasized by several chapters in this book. Likewise, MSP systems and the establishment of MPAs are critical elements in integrating economic development with environmental protection in marine and coastal areas across national and international boundaries. The migratory patterns of numerous marine and bird species and the potential shifts in species distribution due to climate change impacts constitute further imperatives for strong and effective collaboration across boundaries in the conservation and management of living resources. With contributions by experienced scholars in these areas, this book explores the multiple dimensions of transboundary environmental governance with a particular focus on marine, coastal and inland areas and draws on examples from Asia, Australia and international areas such as the global marine commons.

What is Transboundary Environmental Governance?

Governance has been variously defined as a system of control, management or government of human activities.[2] Used in the transboundary environmental context, governance encompasses a wide spectrum of regulatory processes, both formal and informal, which seek to assess, mitigate and compensate for the transboundary impacts of particular human activities on the natural environment. Processes such as prior EIA and SEA, ongoing monitoring of environmental impacts, enforcement and judicial determination of liability for environmental damage are all key elements in transboundary environmental governance. Government institutions and non-governmental organizations (NGOs) which decide on, input to and implement these processes are also part of transboundary environmental governance.

The transboundary element in such governance is usually taken to refer to activities which cross, or have effects across, national boundaries, but it can also relate to activities which cross the boundary between areas within national jurisdiction and interactions with and between the global marine commons. The global marine commons is the best example of ABNJ, which also includes outer space and Antarctica, each of which is subject to a detailed regulatory regime. Transboundary environmental governance can also include considerations of

2 'Governance' is defined in the Macquarie Dictionary as: 'government; exercise of authority; control, method or system of government or management'. The Oxford Dictionaries online defines 'governance' as: 'the action or manner of governing a state or organization, etc.'.

how international and municipal law intersect, the relationship between law and policy, and between institutions at the executive, legislative and judicial levels within a State. More flexibly, it raises the question of learning across disciplines such as international law and international relations, and the relationship between environment, economy and society in exploring the concept of sustainable development.

Transboundary environmental governance typically involves States acting through and with global and regional organizations but non State actors are increasingly becoming important players in this arena as well. Marine industries such as fisheries, shipping, and the offshore mining industry are important stakeholders and implementing agents for transboundary environmental governance. Equally epistemic groups such as marine scientific researchers in particular fields have developed voluntary codes of conduct for environmental protection of marine areas within, between and beyond national jurisdictions. As noted, NGOs perform a critical role in advocating, developing, and in some instances, implementing transboundary environmental governance. Finally individuals and local and indigenous communities are essential catalysts and implementers of transboundary environmental governance in inland, coastal and marine areas.

Transboundary Environmental Governance at the Global Level

At the global level, there are a number of international instruments which relate directly to transboundary environmental governance and others that facilitate such governance. The Espoo Convention and its Protocol on Strategic Environmental Assessment (Kiev Protocol)[3] focus directly on transboundary EIA and SEA processes and how to implement these for both terrestrial and marine projects, plans, programmes and policies. Similarly the purpose of the Convention on Migratory Species (CMS)[4] is to protect threatened species throughout their migratory range. This is primarily achieved through a network of subsidiary agreements covering species such as albatross, petrels and cetaceans.[5] The Environmental Protocol to

3 *Protocol on Strategic Environmental Assessment to the Convention on Environmental Impact Assessment in a Transboundary Context*, opened for signature 21 May 2003 text at http://www.unece.org/env/pp/prtr/docs/prtrtext.html (entered into force 8 October 2009)('*Kiev Protocol*').

4 *Convention on the Conservation of Migratory Species of Wild Animals*, opened for signature 23 June 1979, 19 ILM 15 (entered into force 1 November 1983)('*CMS*').

5 *Agreement on the Conservation of Albatross and Petrels*, opened for signature 19 June 2001, http://www.acap.aq/Instruments (entered into force 1 February 2004)('*ACAP*'); *Agreement on the Conservation of Cetaceans of the Black Sea, Mediterranean Sea and Contiguous Atlantic Area*, opened for signature 24 November 1996, http://www.cms,int/species/accombams/acc_text.htm (entered into force 1 June 2001)('*ACCOBAMS*'); *Agreement on Small Cetaceans of the Baltic and North Seas*, opened for signature 13

the Antarctic Treaty[6] provides a suite of environmental protection mechanisms such as EIA and protected areas which cover an area of global significance and cross the boundaries of those Antarctic Treaty partners that have territorial claims in Antarctic territory as well as ABNJ. At one remove from these agreements is the Convention on the International Trade in Endangered Species (CITES),[7] which regulates global trade in endangered species and through this process affords a certain level of protection to these species. Through regulating the transboundary movement of hazardous wastes, the Basel Convention[8] assists in preventing potential marine and terrestrial pollution from toxic and hazardous substances.

Other international instruments have more general provisions providing for a duty of cooperation or urging cooperation in the protection of marine, coastal and inland environments. Article 5 of the Convention on Biological Diversity (CBD)[9] provides: 'Each Contracting Party shall, as far as possible and as appropriate, cooperate with other Contracting Parties, directly or, where appropriate, through competent international organizations, in respect of areas beyond national jurisdiction and on other matters of mutual interest, for the conservation and sustainable use of biological diversity.' This type of provision can provide the overarching authority and impetus for transboundary cooperation in environmental management, which often takes the form of non binding instruments. The CBD is currently developing draft Guidelines for Biodiversity Inclusive EIA and SEA in Marine and Coastal Areas including ABNJ.[10] The CBD has also developed criteria for identifying ecologically and biologically significant areas (EBSAs) in the marine environment.[11]

Similar provisions in the Law of the Sea Convention (LOSC)[12] have engendered binding and non binding instruments of transboundary environmental

---

September 1991, <http://www.cms.int/species/ascobans/asc_text.htm (entered into force 29 March 1994)('*ASCOBANS*').

6 *Protocol on Environmental Protection to the Antarctic Treaty*, opened for signature 4 October 1991, 30 ILM 1455 (entered into force 14 January 1998) ('*Madrid Protocol*')

7 *Convention on International Trade in Endangered Species of Wild Fauna and Flora*, opened for signature 3 April 1973, 993 UNTS 243 (entered into force 1 July 1975) ('CITES').

8 *Basel Convention on the Control of Transboundary Movements of Hazardous Wastes and their Disposal*, opened for signature 22 March 1989, 1673 UNTS 57 (entered into force 5 May 1992) ('*Basel Convention*').

9 *Convention on Biological Diversity*, opened for signature 22 May 1992, 31 ILM 822 (entered into force 29 December 1993)('*CBD*').

10 Report of the Tenth Meeting of the Conference of the Parties to the Convention on Biological Diversity, UNEP/CBD/COP/10/27, 20 January 2011, Annex, Decision X/29, paragraph 50, http://www.cbd.int/cop10/doc/.

11 CBD, *COP Decision IX/20 Marine and Coastal Biodiversity*, http://www.cbd.int/decision/cop/?id=11663.

12 *United Nations Convention on the Law of the Sea*, opened for signature 10 December 1982, 1833 UNTS 3 (entered into force 16 November 1994).

cooperation. Article 197 provides: 'States shall cooperate on a global basis and, as appropriate, on a regional basis, directly or through competent international organizations, in formulating and elaborating international rules, standards and recommended practices and procedures consistent with this Convention, for the protection and preservation of the marine environment, taking into account characteristic regional features.' This provision underpins the network of United Nations Environment Programme (UNEP) and non UNEP regional seas agreements and some non binding arrangements for the protection of the marine environment such as Partnerships in Environmental Management for the Seas of East Asia (PEMSEA)[13] and the Coral Triangle Initiative (CTI).[14]

There are also examples of voluntary global compacts among States, corporations and individuals to protect the marine environment which produce their own mechanisms of transboundary environmental governance. The InterRidge statement of commitment to responsible research practices at deep-sea hydrothermal vents,[15] which contains environmental protection provisions concerning marine scientific research at these significant deep sea features, and the International Marine Minerals Society (IMMS) Code for Environmental Management,[16] which recommends environmental safeguards relating to deep seabed mining, are cases in point. The International Union for the Conservation of Nature (IUCN) is an intergovernmental organization which has produced a variety of guidelines and principles relevant to transboundary environmental cooperation to protect marine coastal and inland environments. IUCN's 10 High Seas Principles[17] are an example of this type of collaborative environmental governance for ABNJ.

Key intergovernmental institutions involved in developing and implementing transboundary environmental governance for marine, coastal and inland areas at the global level are UNEP, the CBD, IUCN and the Committee on Environmental Protection under the Antarctic Treaty System. These organizations are augmented by a variety of NGOs such as World Wide Fund for Nature (WWF), Greenpeace, Natural Resources Defense Council and Sea Shepherd. International tribunals with jurisdiction to rule and advise on transboundary environmental matters related to marine, coastal and inland areas include the International Court of Justice (ICJ), the International Tribunal for the Law of the Sea (ITLOS), Annex VII and Annex VIII tribunals under Part XV of the LOSC and ad hoc arbitral tribunals whose members

13 PEMSEA, 'About PEMSEA,' http://www.pemsea.org/about-pemsea.

14 ARC Centre of Excellence, Coral Reef Studies, 'What is the Coral Triangle Initiative?' http://www.coralcoe.org.au/events/ctiworkshop/ctiinfo.html.

15 InterRidge, *InterRidge Statement of Commitment to Responsible Research Practices at Deep-sea Hydrothermal Vents*, http://www.interridge.org/IRStatement.

16 International Marine Minerals Society, *Code for Environmental Management*, http://www.immsoc.org/IMMS_code.htm.

17 IUCN, *10 Principles for High Seas Governance*, http://cmsdata.iucn.org/downloads/10_principles_for_high_seas_governance_final.pdf.

are appointed by parties to a dispute. Specific reference is made to experience in connection with these bodies in the chapters that follow this Introduction.

Transboundary Environmental Governance at the Regional Level

At the regional level there is a similar mix of binding and non binding instruments relating to transboundary environmental governance. The UNEP and non UNEP regional seas agreements[18] provide the foundation for transboundary environmental protection in many marine and coastal areas. In most cases they are supplemented by protocols on MPAs[19] and the prevention of pollution from various sources including dumping, oil, seabed mining and land based sources.[20] There are some

---

18 1978 *Kuwait Regional Convention for Cooperation on the Protection of the Marine Environment from Marine Pollution* 17 ILM 511 (Kuwait Convention); the 1981 *Convention for Cooperation in the Protection and Development of the Marine and Coastal Environment of the West and Central African Region* 20 ILM 46 (Abidjan Convention); the 1981 *Convention for the Protection of the Marine Environment and Coastal Areas of the South East Pacific* 33 International Digest of Health Legislation (1982) 96 (Lima Convention); the 1982 *Regional Convention for the Conservation of the Red Sea and Gulf of Aden Environment*, text at http://www.unep.ch/regional seas/main/persga/redconv.html (Jeddah Convention); the 1983 *Convention for the Protection and Development of the Marine Environment of the Wider Caribbean Region* (1983) 22 ILM 221(Cartagena Convention); the 1985 *Convention for the Protection, Management and Development of the Eastern African Region* (1986) Official Journal of the European Community, C253/10-58 (Nairobi Convention); the 1986 *Convention for the Protection of the Natural Resources of the South Pacific Region* (1987) 26 ILM 41 (Noumea Convention); the 1992 *Convention on the Protection of the Black Sea against Pollution* (1993) 32 ILM 1110 (Bucharest Convention); the 1995 *Convention for the Protection of the Marine Environment and Coastal Region of the Mediterranean* text at http://www.unep.ch/regional seas/regions/med/t_barcel.htm (Barcelona Convention); 1992 *Convention for the Protection of the Marine Environment of the Northeast Atlantic* (1993) 32 ILM 1069 (OSPAR Convention).

19 1995 *Protocol Concerning Specially Protected Areas and Biological Diversity in the Mediterranean*, UN Doc UNEP(OCA)MED IG.6/7, 10 June 1995 (SPAMI Protocol); 1990 *Protocol Concerning Specially Protected Areas and Wildlife to the Convention for the Protection and Development of the Marine Environment of the Wider Caribbean Region*, text reproduced at http://www.cep.unep.org/pubs/legislation/spaw.htm (*SPAW Protocol*); 1989 Protocol for the Conservation and Management of Protected Marine and Coastal Areas of the South-East Pacific, text reproduced at Internet Guide to International Fisheries Law, http://www.intfish.net/treaties/sepac.1989.htm at 16 April 2008 (Paipa Protocol)

20 1976 *Protocol Concerning Cooperation in Combating Pollution of the Mediterranean Sea by Oil and Other Harmful Substances in Cases of Emergency* (1976) 15 ILM 306 (Oil Pollution Emergency Response Protocol); 1995 *Protocol for the Prevention and Elimination of Pollution of the Mediterranean Sea by Dumping from Ships and Aircraft or Incineration at Sea*, text at http://www.unepmap.org/Archivio/All_Languages/WebDocs/BC&Protocols/Dumping95_eng.pdf (Anti Dumping Protocol); 1994 *Protocol for the Protection of the Mediterranean Sea against Pollution resulting*

specific regional instruments on transboundary EIA modelled on the Espoo Convention including the Draft Protocol and Guidelines on EIA in a Transboundary Context for the Caspian Sea[21] and the multilateral agreement among the countries of South-Eastern Europe for implementation of the Convention on Environmental Impact Assessment in a Transboundary Context (Bucharest, 2008).[22]

In some regions, States have tended to prefer non binding arrangements for the protection of transboundary marine and coastal areas. This is the preferred mode of transboundary environmental cooperation and governance in the South East Asian region with PEMSEA[23] and Coordinating Body on the Seas of East Asia (COBSEA)[24] emerging as regional alliances for environmental protection. The CTI[25] is a marine environmental protection programme which straddles South East Asian and Pacific seas and involves six States as members. In other regions such as the Arctic, transboundary environmental cooperation has occurred on a voluntary basis with the Arctic EIA Guidelines[26] being an example of such collaboration.

The primary institutional base for implementing transboundary environmental governance in marine and coastal areas is the regional seas network including UNEP and non UNEP organizations. Intergovernmental and non governmental organizations with marine environmental protection mandates are also active at the regional level in implementing transboundary environmental governance. Local and indigenous communities are more likely to exercise influence in transboundary

---

from Exploration and Exploitation of the Continental Shelf and the Seabed and its Subsoil, text at http://www.unepmap.org/Archivio/All_Languages/WebDocs/BC&Protocols/Offshore94_eng.pdf (Seabed Pollution Protocol); 1980 *Protocol for the Protection of the Mediterranean Sea against Pollution from Land Based Sources* (1980) 19 ILM 869 (Land Based Source Pollution Control Protocol); 1996 *Protocol on the Prevention of Pollution of the Mediterranean Sea by Transboundary Movements of Hazardous Wastes and their Disposal*, UN Doc UNEP(OCA)MED/IG.9/4. text at http://www.unepmap.org/Archivio/All_Languages/WebDocs/BC&Protocols/HazW96_eng.pdf (Transboundary Movement of Hazardous Wastes Protocol); 2002 *Protocol Concerning Cooperation in Preventing Pollution from Ships and in cases of Emergency Combating Pollution of the Mediterranean Sea*, text at http://www.unepmap.org/Archivio/All_Languages/WebDocs/BC&Protocols/Emergency02_eng.pdf (Ships Pollution and Emergency Response Protocol).

21 UNEP and Caspian Environment Programme, *Guidelines on Environmental Impact Assessment in a Transboundary Context in the Caspian Sea Region: Step by step procedures* (UNEP, 2003).

22 *Multilateral Agreement among the Countries of South-Eastern Europe for Implementation of the Convention on Environmental Impact Assessment in a Transboundary Context*, opened for signature 20 May 2008, 30 ILM 1455 (entered into force 25 February 2011) ('*Bucharest Agreement*'), http://www:unece.org/env/eia/bucharest_agreement.html.

23 See above note 13.

24 Coordinating Body on the Seas of East Asia (COBSEA), *About COBSEA*, http://www.cobsea.org/aboutcobsea/background.html.

25 See above note 14.

26 Arctic Environment Protection Strategy, *Guidelines for Environmental Impact Assessment in the Arctic*, 1997, http://ceq.hss.doe.gov/nepa/eiaguide.pdf.

environmental governance decision making at the regional and national levels due to their strong vested interests in the ecosystem services derived from the transboundary environment concerned.

Transboundary Environmental Governance at the National Level

Transboundary environmental governance at the national level is most apparent within federal States where a significant degree of autonomy is typically given by national constitutions to individual States within the federation to regulate matters such as the environment. In such cases there may need to be agreements reached with the national government to detail the precise allocation of powers, or grant the federal government powers which are not held under the national constitution.

Governance issues with transboundary dimensions for the environment may emerge in many different forms. Recent examples from Australia that have triggered the federal Environment Protection and Biodiversity Conservation (EPBC) Act 1999 (Cth) include the construction and operation of a pulp mill in Tasmania, an LNG port facility in Western Australia, and a coal port facility in Queensland.[27] Each concerns the export of natural resources or products sourced from them and has potential significant impacts upon the natural environment which have raised concerns of relevance to the international community, including Australia's national obligations under the CBD and the World Heritage Convention.[28]

Transboundary EIA is an example of a governance process that may be applicable in federal States. Like most, Australia does not require interstate transboundary EIA within the nation state. Belgium is an isolated exception to this, although in the USA legislative guidance recommends such assessment while the law is silent. In Canada, like Australia, coordination of inter-jurisdictional EIA is framed by bilateral agreements under intergovernmental accords. These sometimes include transboundary provisions, despite no statutory requirements.

Although it has rarely been applied within federal nations, transboundary EIA is potentially very relevant to promote better governance and improved environmental outcomes. As noted by Grigg in the second chapter of this book, in the Murray Darling Basin of Australia the Commonwealth, Queensland, New South Wales, Victoria and South Australia all have roles and responsibilities, yet reconciling economic, social and environmental issues and ensuring interstate cooperation have failed. Previous cooperative experiences in transboundary environmental governance are important background, including the Snowy Mountains Hydro-Electric Scheme and management of the Great Artesian Basin.

---

27 Department of Sustainability, Environment, Water, Population and Communities, http://www.environment.gov.au/epbc/notices/assessments.html.

28 *Convention for the Protection of the World Cultural and Natural Heritage*, opened for signature 16 November 1972, 1037 UNTS 151 (entered into force 17 December 1975).

Organization and Content

This book traverses the more highly articulated systems of transboundary environmental governance established in inland areas to the less well defined contours of transboundary environmental governance in the open ocean. The multiple dimensions of transboundary environmental governance are explored from its theoretical underpinnings to its diverse manifestations in inland watercourse management, coastal areas, semi-enclosed seas and marine ABNJ. Examination of current models of transboundary environmental management is leavened with discussion of global and regional initiatives for change and the extension of existing systems to frontier areas such as the open ocean and deep seabed.

In addition to this Introduction, the book contains twelve chapters and is divided into two parts. The first part focuses on inland and coastal areas with examples from Australia (Chapters 2–4) and Asia (Chapters 5–7) on transboundary environmental governance. The second part addresses the marine context of transboundary environmental governance, highlighting its evolutionary nature in remote areas such as Heard Island and McDonald Islands (HIMI) in Australia's sub-Antarctic, and global efforts to address the environmental impacts of new and emerging activities such as marine geo-engineering, and the use of dispute settlement mechanisms to resolve disputes between Australia and other States (Chapters 8–10). The role of transboundary EIA in marine areas, its application to deep seabed mining and bioprospecting in ABNJ, and the potential for a protocol to regulate ABNJ follow (Chapters 11–13).

The chapters in Part I can be summarized as follows: Brendan Grigg's chapter (2) provides a historical legal analysis into the complex governance arrangements applicable to Australia's Murray Darling Basin, which is subject to the jurisdiction of four States, one Territory and the Federal Government of Australia. It evaluates recent, ongoing attempts to plan the Basin in the interests of the environment, and the socio-economic interests of the communities that are dependent upon its water resources, in the light of the federal legal framework that underpins the operation of the collaborative institution known as the Murray Darling Basin Authority. The operationalization of this legal framework via the work of the Authority in planning and managing the water resource is the specific focus. The author finds that in meeting the challenge of integrating, or balancing, the needs of the environment, economy and society, the meaning of transboundary environmental governance beyond the cross-jurisdictional issues is considered in light of the concept of sustainable development, which is itself a 'transboundary' issue of some significance.

Cameron Holley's chapter (3) provides empirical insights from water and natural resource management in inland Queensland, Australia. Reviewing the collaborative environmental governance literature, the transboundary focus is upon governance arrangements at all levels, whether administrative boundaries within a federal State or between governments and civil society institutions that look to advance shared management of joint environmental resources. Regional Natural Resource

Management (NRM) is a partnership between governments and other stakeholders that is the basis for the author's analysis in this chapter. Two case studies are reported on, based on extensive interviews, to examine collaborative approaches taken to Regional NRM in inland Queensland. Policy recommendations are made concerning the conditions needed for successful collaboration in practice. Lessons learnt are grouped under four principal themes: the severity of environmental problems; trust; incentives; and structures for subsidising transaction costs. These provide significant insights into the relationship between traditional legal rules and new collaborative governance arrangements.

Lorne Kriwoken, Julie Davidson and Michael Lockwood's chapter (4) provides an international overview of MPA and cooperative federalism in Australia. The authors analyse the role of Australia's Oceans Policy, the National Representative System of Marine Protected Areas and State MPA systems before outlining two case studies from the Whitsundays in Queensland and Tweed Moreton in New South Wales. They evaluate relevant transboundary issues with respect to MPAs with a focus on the role of transboundary adaptive marine biodiversity conservation governance in the context of Australian MPAs. The chapter argues for a broadening of the concept of transboundary issues in the context of MPAs and the need for wider formal and informal arrangements to enhance adaptive capacity and effective marine biodiversity governance and management.

Michelle Lim's chapter (5) is a comparative study of legal and institutional requirements for biodiversity and water in relation to the management of transboundary resources in Central Asia. The chapter draws linkages between biodiversity conservation in the Pamir-Alai Land Management project (between the Kyrgyz Republic and the Republic of Tajikistan), and the management of transboundary watercourses in Central Asia. Transboundary governance criteria are applied to provide a framework for determining what complementary reforms are needed, in addition to suitable legal instruments, for effective management of the respective transboundary resources in this region. The comparison of water and biodiversity indicates that achieving the recommended transboundary criteria will differ depending on the resource that is being managed. The comparison also emphasizes the similarities between transboundary resource management issues in Central Asia and the opportunities for trans-sectoral learning and collaboration in the management of transboundary resources in the region.

Simon Marsden's chapter (6) reviews five agreements for TEIA and TSEA that apply in Asia, two cross-regional and three sub-regional. The cross-regional agreements, which apply in Europe and parts of Asia, are the Espoo Convention and the Helsinki Convention.[29] The sub-regional agreements are the Tehran,[30]

29 *Convention on the Protection and Use of Transboundary Watercourses and International Lakes*, opened for signature 17 March 1992, 1936 UNTS 269 (entered into force 6 October 1996) ('Helsinki Convention').

30 *Framework Convention for the Protection of the Marine Environment of the Caspian Sea*, opened for signature Tehran, 4 November, 2003, unreported (entered into

Mekong[31] and Tumen[32] agreements, which apply in the south-west (Caspian Sea), south-east, and north-east Asia. The chapter outlines and analyses the TEIA and SEA procedures in these agreements, giving examples of practice where possible. It evaluates the commonalities between them in an attempt to find similar ground to form the basis of a pan-regional agreement. This focuses on three aspects: overlapping membership, procedural similarities and the influence of and advocacy for the Espoo Convention, and the requirements of multilateral development banks.

The chapters in Part II can be summarized as follows. Youna Lyons' chapter (7) focuses on the environmental governance framework available to manage transboundary pollution from offshore oil and gas activities in some key marine areas of South East Asia including the South China Sea, the Gulf of Thailand, Indonesian archipelagic waters and offshore zones and the Sulu Celebes Sea. It reviews the location and extent of potential transboundary pollution risk from the over 1390 offshore platforms for hydrocarbon production in these areas. The pollution risks addressed are oil spills, drilling wastes, platform abandonment and invasive species through biofouling. The chapter discusses the applicability of relevant provisions in the LOSC and related global shipping and conservation treaties to offshore hydrocarbon production in these areas and the slow progress towards ratification of these treaties by coastal States in the region. Deficiencies and fragmentation in the regional legal and institutional framework to implement global instruments are explored. The regional preference for flexible and non binding arrangements for transboundary environmental governance which emphasize consensus and practical mechanisms for implementation is highlighted.

Simon Marsden's chapter (8) on coordinating SEA of terrestrial and marine plans draws on Australian experience in managing the environment of its sub-Antarctic territories, in particular HIMI. He analyses the potential application of SEA to the planning and management of HIMI as a marine reserve, and its actual application to the resource rich waters of the exclusive economic zone (EEZ) surrounding it, in particular the fishery. He begins with an examination of international experience in applying SEA to management plans and assessment tiering. This is followed by an analysis of the HIMI fishery management plan, which was subject to an SEA, and the Marine Reserve management plan for HIMI, which was not, and the implications of this inconsistent approach for the

---

force 12 August 2006) ('Tehran Convention').

31 *Agreement on the Cooperation for the Sustainable Development of the Mekong River Basin*, opened for signature Chiang Rai, 5 April 1995, unreported (entered into force 5 April 1995) ('Mekong Convention').

32 *Agreement on the Establishment of the Tumen River Area Development Coordination Committee*, opened for signature New York, 6 December 1995, unreported (entered into force 6 December 1995); and *Agreement on the Establishment of the Consultative Commission for the Development of the Tumen River Economic Development Area and Northeast Asia*, opened for signature New York, 6 December 1995, unreported (entered into force 6 December 1995).

environmental management of HIMI. He concludes by considering the benefits that a marine bioregional plan covering the whole of HIMI, including the marine reserve and the EEZ beyond the marine reserve, would bring to the environmental management of these islands and the surrounding offshore zones.

Karen Scott's chapter (9) approaches transboundary environmental governance through the prism of a new and emerging threat to the marine environment, geo-engineering, defined as 'the deliberate large-scale manipulation of the planetary environment to counteract anthropogenic climate change'. In discussing these activities, she asks the question whether they should be regulated through existing international regimes and institutions or whether a new regime should be developed for them. She describes selected geo-engineering techniques such as ocean fertilization and crop residue sequestration in the deep ocean, the potential threats they pose to the marine environment and the extent to which they are currently regulated by international regimes and institutions. This is followed by an analysis of the current initiatives by the London Convention/Protocol[33] to develop a risk assessment framework for ocean fertilization. She then examines a recent strategic development in international environmental governance which comprises the deliberate creation of institutional linkages and connections between international environmental regimes. These connections underpin the formation of cooperative relationships to more effectively address environmental threats. Three levels of connection are considered – basic cooperative agreements between regime administrations; integrated institutional management; and integrated political management. The chapter concludes by endorsing the value of such institutional linkages in addressing the threats posed to the marine environment by geo-engineering activities.

Tim Stephens' chapter (10) reviews Australia's record in international litigation involving environmental and natural resource issues with transboundary implications. He analyses the benefits and disadvantages of transboundary environmental litigation using the traditional methods of inter-State courts and tribunals. A number of international disputes involving marine activities are considered including the *Nuclear Tests* case,[34] the *East Timor* case,[35] the *Southern*

33 *Convention on the Prevention of Marine Pollution by Dumping of Wastes and Other Matter*, opened for signature 29 December 1972, 11 ILM 1294 (entered into force 30 August 1975) ('*London Convention*'); *Protocol to the Convention on the Prevention of Marine Pollution by Dumping of Wastes and Other Matter*, opened for signature 7 November 1996, 36 ILM 1 (entered into force 24 March 2006) ('*London Protocol*').

34 *Nuclear Tests (Australia v France) (Interim Measures)* [1973] ICJ Rep 99, *(Merits)* [1974] ICJ Rep 253.

35 *East Timor (Portugal v Australia) (Jurisdiction and Admissibility)* [1995] ICJ Rep 90.

Bluefin Tuna case,[36] the *Volga* case[37] and the pending *Scientific Whaling* case.[38] In all the decided cases, he notes the reluctance of the ICJ and ITLOS, as well as arbitral tribunals, to rely on international environmental law principles in their judgments and the tendency to revert to procedural rules in deciding cases or declining to exercise jurisdiction. He concludes that while the outcome of transboundary environmental litigation in tribunals such as the ICJ and ITLOS has not often produced clear and unequivocal resolution of environmental disputes, it has often been a catalyst for diplomatic or political resolution of the subject issues. He foresees a more definite role for such litigation in the twenty-first century as international environmental law evolves.

Warwick Gullett's chapter (11) provides a comprehensive perspective on the theoretical foundation for transboundary EIA in national and international law and the challenges involved in applying it to development activities in marine areas. The purpose and typical components of the EIA process are described. This is followed by a discussion of the origins of transboundary EIA in relevant international law principles such as the principle of State sovereignty, the duty to prevent transboundary harm or harm to ABNJ, the duty to cooperate and States' liability for transboundary harm. Gullett examines customary international law developments concerning the duty to conduct EIA of activities with the potential to cause transboundary harm and the rising customary international status of this principle. He analyses relevant treaty law, including the Espoo Convention and the LOSC, highlighting the rather nebulous and incomplete nature of the obligation to conduct EIAs of activities in marine areas. He finishes with a discussion of the application of EIA obligations to marine activities and the practical challenges involved in implementing these obligations to geographically dispersed projects and complex marine ecosystems. He concludes that while there is an international obligation to conduct transboundary EIA for marine activities, implementation of this obligation will continue to be difficult due to lack of specificity in its terms and limited institutional infrastructure.

Robin Warner's chapter (12) examines the scope of the current legal and institutional framework for EIA and SEA as it applies to ABNJ and its implementation in sectoral and regional contexts. She sets the regulatory framework for EIA and SEA in marine areas within the broader context of high seas governance and highlights the fact that the regulatory framework for environmental protection in ABNJ is at a much earlier stage of development as States grapple with the broader institutional and legal challenges posed by high seas governance. Gaps in the legal and institutional framework to implement EIA and SEA for activities affecting ABNJ are discussed as well as the initiatives being taken and the options available for the international community to develop a more comprehensive legal

36 *Southern Bluefin Tuna (New Zealand v Japan; Australia v Japan) (Provisional Measures)* (1999) 117 ILR 148, *(Jurisdiction and Admissibility)* (2000) 119 ILR 508.

37 *Volga (Russian Federation v Australia) (Prompt Release)* (2003) 42 ILM 159.

38 *Whaling in the Antarctic (Australia v Japan),* application filed 31 May 2010.

and institutional framework for EIA and SEA in these extensive areas of the ocean. In particular she examines the development by the CBD of voluntary biodiversity inclusive guidelines for EIA and SEA in marine and coastal areas including ABNJ. She concludes that this initiative represents an important step in articulating the peculiar characteristics of EIAs and SEAs related to activities affecting ABNJ and should provide a catalyst for more comprehensive implementation of these important tools in such areas across all regions and sectors.

Timo Koivurova's chapter (13) addresses the strategic question of whether the Espoo Convention should become a global regime for EIA and SEA and whether this would be a desirable development for environmental protection, particularly in the transboundary context. The principal focus of his chapter relates to whether the Espoo Convention could expand to cover EIA of activities affecting ABNJ. He begins by describing how the Espoo Convention is meant to function and how it has been implemented in practice, drawing on the Finnish experience and a case study involving the Baltic Sea gas pipeline project. He points to the escalation in normative expectations for EIA, including its ability to incorporate factors such as global biodiversity loss as a potential reason for extending the scope of the Espoo Convention to EIA of activities affecting ABNJ. In terms of EIA instruments he emphasizes the unique nature of the Espoo Convention, being the only binding international instrument dedicated to EIA and its twenty year evolution. He traces the decisions of international tribunals relating to EIA concluding that the duty to evaluate impacts on the environment of ABNJ is part of the corpus of general international law. Among the benefits he cites for the expansion of the Espoo Convention to activities affecting ABNJ is the extensive experience already gained in implementing transboundary EIA and the continuous improvement of the regime. He concludes that there appear to be no obstacles to the expansion of the Espoo regime to ABNJ but acknowledges that global political factors surrounding ABNJ will determine the outcome of this question.

Synergies and Themes

The following synergies and themes emerge from the chapters that form this book, making recommendations for reform of law and policy, and raising further questions for future research.

The first section of the book reflects the diverse arrangements for transboundary environmental governance which have been developed in national and regional contexts, drawing on examples from Australia and Asia. Transboundary watercourses and shared water resources feature in many chapters as a catalyst for the establishment of transboundary environmental governance mechanisms across national and sub-national boundaries. An underlying theme which emerges in many chapters is the tensions inherent in balancing a menu of stakeholder interests, including environmental protection, resource development and social cohesion, in effecting transboundary environmental governance. Brendan Grigg

(2) explores how these tensions have played out in a federal State context for a transboundary water course in Australia using the example of the Murray Darling Basin authority while Lorne Kriwoken et al. (4) examine comparable tensions between Federal and State governments, industry players and civil society in the marine bioregional planning process. Insights into how these tensions can be overcome using more flexible collaborative strategies are analysed in Cameron Holley's chapter (3) and Youna Lyon's chapter (7) on hydrocarbon production in South East Asian seas. The relatively sophisticated and multifaceted nature of transboundary environmental governance in the terrestrial context as compared to the marine context is demonstrated in Simon Marsden's description of multi-level arrangements for EIA and SEA in Central Asia (Chapter 6) and Michelle Lim's (Chapter 5) consideration of transboundary environmental governance for water and biodiversity in Central Asia.

The comparative immaturity of marine environmental governance and its implementation in transboundary contexts is a prominent motif in many of the chapters of the second section of the book including those of Warwick Gullett (11), Tim Stephens (10) and Robin Warner (12). The evolving nature of international environmental law obligations such as the precautionary approach and the lack of specificity in their content add to the challenges of implementation. Both Tim Stephens (Chapter 10) and Warwick Gullett (Chapter 11) also point to the tentative nature of engagement by international tribunals such as the ICJ and the ITLOS with international environmental law and their reliance on procedural outcomes. Karen Scott's chapter (9) explores the lack of integration between international environmental law regimes and institutions and benefits of promoting connections at different levels from flexible cooperative arrangements through to full political integration.

The complex challenges involved in implementing transboundary environmental governance in marine and coastal areas is a predominant theme across many of the chapters including those by Warwick Gullett (11), Robin Warner (12), Karen Scott (9), Simon Marsden (8) and Youna Lyons (7). Among the issues raised are the three dimensional nature of the marine environment in contrast to the two dimensional nature of the terrestrial environment, adding to the difficulties involved in implementing effective transboundary governance measures including EIAs, SEAs and marine spatial planning. These difficulties are compounded by the broad geographic scale and remote location of many activities, the technical complexity of projects such as deep seabed mining, the migratory nature of many marine species and the complex characteristics and interconnectedness across boundaries of marine ecosystems.

The dearth of institutional infrastructure and the fragmentary governance arrangements for ABNJ emerge as common themes in the chapters contributed by Timo Koivurova (13), Warwick Gullett (11), Robin Warner (12) and Karen Scott (9). The extension of existing international regimes to new areas and activities rather than the development of new regimes is explored in all these chapters. The sparse scientific knowledge of marine biodiversity, particularly in ABNJ, and the need to develop customs of practice for environmental governance of new and emerging activities are emphasized by Karen Scott (Chapter 9), Robin Warner (Chapter 12) and Warwick Gullett (Chapter 11). The need to apply EIA and SEA to activities, plans, policies and programmes affecting ABNJ is a shared theme in chapters contributed by Timo Koivurova (13), Warwick Gullett (11) and Robin Warner (12) while Timo Koivurova (Chapter 13) and Robin Warner (Chapter 12) explore the options available to do so. Both Simon Marsden (Chapter 8) and Robin Warner (Chapter 12) discuss the need for further development and implementation of SEA, particularly in marine areas.

The chapters comprising this book reflect the many dimensions of transboundary environmental governance, the continuum of its development from a relatively mature stage in many terrestrial environments to its more embryonic stage in marine environments. The perspectives from a range of legal, environmental and marine policy experts provide important insights into the theoretical foundations and practical application of transboundary environmental governance at global, regional and national levels. The shared themes and synergies between chapters indicate the significant challenges facing policymakers at all levels in achieving effective environmental governance across national boundaries and beyond national boundaries in the global marine commons.

PART I
Inland and Coastal Perspectives

Chapter 2
Transboundary Environmental Governance in the Murray Darling Basin

Brendan Grigg*

The Murray Darling Basin and the Objectives of Transboundary Environmental Governance

During the 1898 Constitutional Convention, held in Melbourne, to frame the constitution of the new Commonwealth of Australia, Joseph Carruthers, a delegate from the colony of New South Wales stated that: 'If the day is to come when the Darling and the Murrumbidgee are to be drained dry for irrigation purposes, Australia will be all the happier and all the better for that day having arrived.'[1]

This approach to the management of the resources of the Murray Darling Basin contrasts markedly with the approach of the Australian Aboriginal peoples for whom the Murray Darling Basin has been home for at least 40,000 years and in whose belief system it still plays a role.[2] The ways in which the Aboriginal peoples managed its resources have been described as follows: 'Our traditional management plan was don't be greedy, don't take any more than you need and respect everything around you. That's the management plan – it's such a simple management plan, but so hard for people to carry out.'[3] More than 100 years after Federation, the reality in the Murray Darling Basin corresponds more to the view expressed by Joseph Carruthers than that envisaged by the traditional owners: the Darling and Murrumbidgee Rivers, along with the Murray River and its other tributaries in the Murray Darling Basin have long been overtaxed with unsustainable levels of extractions that have had deleterious effects on both water quality and quantity.

---

* The author thanks Dr Simon Marsden, Dr Cameron Holley and Dr Laura Grenfell for their insightful and helpful comments on a draft of this chapter.

1 *Melbourne Debates*, n 1, 7 March 1898, p 1957 (Joseph Carruthers) cited in John M Williams and Adam Webster 'Section 100 and State water rights' (2010) 21 *Public Law Review* 267, 272.

2 John Scanlon, 'A hundred years of negotiations with no end in sight: Where is the Murray Darling Basin Initiative leading us?' (2006) 23 *Environmental and Planning Law Journal* 386, 387.

3 Tom Trevorrow, *Murrundi Ruwe Pangari Ringbalin 'River Country Spirit Ceremony: Aboriginal Perspectives on River Country'* (2010) cited in Commonwealth of Australia, *Proposed Basin Plan – a draft for consultation* (Murray Darling Basin Authority, November 2011) 1.

The Murray Darling Basin extends across more than one million square kilometres of eastern and south-eastern Australia. Its area is equivalent to 14% of Australia's land mass.[4] It covers a range of climatic conditions, ranging from rainforest and inland sub-tropical areas to mallee country and semi-arid land.[5] To the north it is characterized by ephemeral river systems while in the south the Murray Darling Basin features highly regulated river systems whose source lies in the Australian Alps.[6]

Socially, culturally and economically, the Murray Darling Basin is an area of national importance for Australia.[7] In 1996 it was home to 2 million people.[8] According to a census undertaken in 2006, 3.4 million people, whether living in or near the Murray Darling Basin, were 'directly reliant on Basin water'[9] including 1.06 million people in Adelaide, the capital city of South Australia.[10] The population of the nation's capital, Canberra, lives entirely within the Murray Darling Basin. In 2005/2006 an agricultural census found the following: that 84% of land in the Murray Darling Basin is owned by agricultural businesses;[11] that 67% of land in the Murray Darling Basin is used for agricultural purposes;[12] and that 70% of Australia's irrigated agriculture occurs within the Murray Darling Basin.[13] It has been estimated that it produces 'at least 40% of Australia's agricultural output'[14] and contributes $23 billion each year to the Australian economy.[15]

The Murray Darling Basin covers parts of four Australian states: Queensland, New South Wales, Victoria, and South Australia and it includes the entire area of the Australian Capital Territory.[16] It is subject to the regulation of those five jurisdictions as well as that of the Commonwealth of Australia. It is a manifest example of a transboundary environmental phenomenon within the Australian federation. Although some boundaries such as these jurisdictional boundaries

---

4 Brian Pink, *Water and the Murray Darling Basin – A statistical profile 2000–01 to 2005–06* (ABS Catalogue No 4610.0.55.007, Australian Bureau of Statistics, 2008) 1.

5 House of Representatives Standing Committee on Regional Australia, Parliament of Australia, *Of Drought and Flooding Rains: Inquiry into the impact of the guide to the Murray-Darling Basin Plan* (2011) 11.

6 Ibid.

7 Pink, above n 4.

8 William Blomquist, Brian Haisman, Ariel Dinar, Anjali Bhat, *Institutional Policy Analysis of River Basin Management: The Murray Darling River Basin, Australia* (World Bank Policy Research Working Paper No 3527, World Bank, February 2005) 6.

9 House of Representatives Standing Committee on Regional Australia, above n 6, 13.

10 Ibid.

11 Pink, above n 4, 7.

12 Ibid.

13 Scanlon, above n 2, 387; Blomquist et al, above n 8, 6.

14 Scanlon, above n 2, 387.

15 Ibid.

16 For a map of the Murray Darling Basin see http://www.environment.gov.au/water/publications/mdb/pubs/mdb-map.pdf.

bring benefits such as efficiency and accountability, the transboundary nature of environmental issues such as these highlight the need for cooperation and coordination at the very least.[17]

Water resources like those of the River Murray Darling Basin are valued in differing ways: they provide 'basic life-support functions such as for drinking, sanitation and food production, as well as for maintaining ecosystem health, a range of economic livelihoods and personal, cultural and spiritual wellbeing'.[18] These considerations suggest that there are, in addition to the jurisdictional boundaries referred to above, other, less physical and less legal, boundaries that present challenges to the management of these resources.[19] These competing values 'in a world of rapidly increasing population, environmental degradation and globalised telecommunications'[20] mean that the management of water in the Murray Darling Basin, as it is with the management of water resources generally, is 'an increasingly political process'.[21]

Douglas Fisher states that the way transboundary water resources are governed depends 'to a great extent upon the fundamental Grundnorms'[22] (or fundamental principles) that 'either underlie the system or are stated by it'.[23] This chapter explores the fundamental principles that underlie the system of governance in the Murray Darling Basin, their historical roots and their legacies. It considers what they mean for sound environmental governance in the Murray Darling Basin.

As has been widely noted, the environment of the Murray Darling Basin has suffered at the expense of economic development and, in particular, at the expense of irrigated agriculture.[24] For example, 20 mammal species in the Murray Darling Basin are extinct and there are at least 35 endangered bird species and 16 endangered mammal species in the Murray Darling Basin.[25] A 2001 assessment noted degradation in over 95% of the assessed river length and substantial modification from the original condition in 30%.[26] Against such a stark assessment it is important to consider that the Murray Darling Basin is home to 16 of Australia's

---

17 Peter Crabb, 'Straddling Boundaries: Inter-governmental Arrangements for Managing Natural Resources' in Stephen Dovers and Su Wild River (eds), *Managing Australia's Environment* (The Federation Press, 2003) 229.

18 Katherine Daniell, 'Enhancing Collaborative Management in the Basin' in Daniel Connell and R Quentin Grafton *Basin Future: water reform in the Murray-Darling Basin* (ANU E-Press, Canberra 2011) 413, 413.

19 Crabb, above n 17, 229.

20 Daniell, above n 18, 413.

21 Ibid.

22 Douglas Fisher, *The Law and Governance of Water Resources: The Challenge of Sustainability* (Edward Elgar, 2009) 145.

23 Ibid.

24 E.g. Scanlon, above n 2, 387.

25 Pink, above n 4, 19.

26 Blomquist et al, above n 8, 7.

64 wetlands of international significance listed under the *Ramsar Convention*.[27] The state of the environment in the Murray Darling Basin is therefore an issue of both international and national concern.

The scarcity of water in the Murray Darling Basin and the over allocation of the water resources that are available are particular management issues for the Murray Darling Basin. In October 2011 it was reported that the Premier of South Australia threatened Queensland, New South Wales and Victoria with legal action in the High Court of Australia for over use of the water resources of the Murray Darling Basin.[28] The prevalence of dryland salinity and the Murray Darling Basin's exposure to drought have also been persistent environmental issues confronting the Murray Darling Basin.

Public statements such as that of the Premier of South Australia are not new: the regulation of the resources of the River Murray has been one of the most pervasively difficult aspects of Australian political life. It was without doubt the subject of some of the most controversial debates of the Constitutional Conventions in the 1890s which led to the drafting of the *Australian Constitution* and the creation of the Commonwealth of Australia as a federal state.[29] It remains, as this chapter illustrates, a complex issue for Australian environmental regulation.

Despite the amount of time devoted to the question of how to regulate the resources of the Murray Darling Basin, the Convention Debates paid scant regard to the sustainability of those resources. Notwithstanding the fact that the concept of sustainable use has been noted in societies from ancient times,[30] the formalisation of the concept, scope and implications of sustainable use and sustainable development, which '[i]ntegrate[s] the social, economic and ecological aspects of the use and development of natural resources for present and future generations in making decisions about these resources and in undertaking operations in relation to them'[31] is of much more recent origin.[32]

---

27 *Convention on Wetlands of International Importance especially as Waterfowl Habitat* done at Ramsar, Iran, on 2 February 1971, ATS 1975 No 48 ('Ramsar Convention'); See Jamie Pittock, Max Finlayson, Alex Gardner and Clare McKay, 'Changing character: the Ramsar Convention on Wetlands and climate change in the Murray Darling Basin, Australia' (2010) 27 *Environmental and Planning Law Journal* 401, 409; See also Department of Sustainability, Environment, Water, Population and Communities, *Australian Ramsar* Wetlands, http://www.environment.gov.au/cgi-bin/wetlands/alphablist.pl.

28 Michael Owen, 'New premier's tough water talk returned' *The Australian*, 24 October 2011, 6.

29 Scanlon, above n 2, 386; Nicholas Kelly, 'A Bridge? The Troubled History of Inter-State Water Resources and Constitutional Limitations on State Water Use' (2007) 30 *University of New South Wales Law Journal* 639, 641.

30 See for example, the Separate Opinion of Vice President Weeramantry in *The Case Concerning the Gabcikvovo Nagymoros Project* (1998) 37 *International Legal Materials* 208.

31 Fisher, above n 22, 21.

32 Ibid.

Fisher notes that the concept of sustainable development lies 'at the apex of discourse about water resources governance'.[33] He observes that the concept of sustainable development is difficult to apply in certain circumstances: indeed he suggests, pessimistically, that it is 'perhaps impossible to create a set of legal arrangements for doing so effectively'.[34]

The concept of governance 'comprises the mechanisms, processes and institutions through which citizens and groups articulate their interests, exercise their legal rights, meet their obligations and mediate their differences'.[35] It thus speaks to more than just the legal and regulatory instruments of government. It comprises other instruments and institutions such as market-based economic and commercial instruments which are increasingly necessary components of water resource management, given that it is apparent governments now tend to lack the capacity 'to make and implement their own water-management decisions without the help of other stakeholders, as power and resources for managing water systems are increasingly distributed'.[36] Governance, in this sense, is a description of a dynamic process where the enterprise of steering a society towards certain goals is no longer the sole domain of government but is 'the common responsibility of a variety of agencies, representing governmental bodies, market agencies and civil society organisations'.[37]

Governance can be analysed qualitatively, by looking at how institutions perform in addition to what they perform.[38] Accordingly matters such as public participation, access to information and the justice system, transparency, responsiveness, accountability are all measures of good governance.[39]

Drawing on events associated with the release of the 2010 *Guide to the Proposed Basin Plan* his chapter will consider these qualitative measures to assess governance arrangements for the Murray Darling Basin. This document, and the Basin Plan which it foreshadowed, are key components of the *Water Act 2007* (Cth) ('*Water Act*') which represents the latest attempt by the Commonwealth to regulate the natural resources of the Murray Darling Basin in the national interest. The *Water Act*, a special arrangement for a particular transboundary natural resource, is characteristic of attempts worldwide to regulate transboundary water resources.[40] The *Water Act* illustrates most of the features that characterize environmental regulation and governance in Australia, such as

33 Ibid.

34 Ibid.

35 MC Cordonnier Segger, and A Khalfan, *Sustainable Development Law: Principles Practices and Prospects* (Oxford University Press, 2004) 166.

36 Daniell, above n 18, 414.

37 P Leroy and B Arts, 'Institutional dynamics in environmental governance' in P Leroy and B Arts (eds), *Institutional Dynamics in Environmental Governance* (Dordrecht: Springer) 1–20, 12 cited in Douglas Fisher, above n 22, 45.

38 Fisher, above n 22, 45.

39 Ibid.

40 Crabb, above n 19, 239.

the role of the States, the constitutional limitations on federal powers; and the role of co-operative federalism. This chapter will explore both its contributions to governance arrangements in the Murray Darling Basin, and the challenges that it faces in achieving them. Before doing so it will be necessary to consider constitutional foundations of the *Water Act* more broadly, given that these are crucial to the way in which water resources that are transboundary in nature are managed.[41]

The chapter begins with a consideration of 18th and 19th century colonial, political and legal institutions and practices that established the character of governance regimes, the legacies of which, today, still apply to the Murray Darling Basin. It then considers the role of the 1901 *Australian Constitution*; the constitutional provisions that apply to the Murray Darling system specifically; and the absence, in the *Australian Constitution*, of any provisions dealing with the environment generally. This chapter then considers two abiding features of federal environmental governance in Australia which have strengthened the ability of the Commonwealth Government to legislate in environmental matters, despite the presence of constitutional limitations that appear to restrict or prevent Commonwealth action on the environment. These features are first, the expansive role of the external affairs power contained in section 51(xxxix) of the *Australian Constitution* and, secondly, cooperative federalism. It examines how these two features of Australian environmental regulation have operated in the context of the Murray Darling Basin. This chapter endeavours to determine whether reliance on these governance structures, particularly in light of the *Water Act*, provides a sound basis for environmental management within the Murray Darling Basin, or whether the attempts to regulate these resources amount largely to a failed attempt to achieve sound environmental governance in a transboundary context within a federal state.

Transboundary Environmental Governance in the Murray Darling Basin: Historical and Constitutional Legacies

The roots of the transboundary context of the Murray Darling Basin lie in the way in which the British Crown colonized it in the late 1700s and 1800s.[42] When the First Fleet arrived in New South Wales on 26 January 1788, the Governor of New

41 Fisher, above n 22, 145.

42 These roots are deeper than simply the separation in 1851 of the colony of Victoria from the colony of New South Wales as asserted by Sandford Clark. See Sandford Clark, 'The River Murray Question: Part 1 – Colonial Days' (1971) 8(1) *Melbourne University Law Review* 11, 12. See also Sandford Clark, 'The River Murray Question: Part II – Federation, Agreement and Future Alternatives' (1971–1972) 8(1) *Melbourne University Law Review* 215 and Ian Renard, 'The River Murray Question: Part III – New Doctrines for Old Problems' (1971–1972) 8 *Melbourne University Law Review* 625.

South Wales exercised control over that part of the continent that lay to the east of the 135th meridian. At that time, the entire Murray Darling Basin was within the control of a single jurisdiction: colonial New South Wales. Over time, the boundaries of the colony of New South Wales were altered and new jurisdictions, in the form of new colonies, were established.

In 1836 South Australia was carved out of western New South Wales.[43] From that point on the Murray Darling Basin became a transboundary environmental issue and the ability for one political entity to regulate and protect the resources of the Murray Darling Basin was lost. Matters were complicated further when the Colony of Victoria was established on 1 July 1851. It was separated from New South Wales and the southern high water mark of the River Murray itself was used to define the border between the two colonies.[44] Later, three more jurisdictions were established and given control over parts of the Murray Darling Basin. In 1859 the Colony of Queensland, the uppermost riparian jurisdiction, was created out of part of the territory of New South Wales.[45] On 1 January 1901, the federation of the Australian colonies added a federal jurisdiction and confirmed the division of the Murray Darling Basin along artificial borders that ignored the reality of the hydrologically interdependent and holistic river systems that it contains.[46] Finally, in 1911 the area of the Australian Capital Territory, the home of the future federal capital, was created and formally transferred from New South Wales to the Commonwealth of Australia.[47]

Against the background of this process of incremental political fragmentation of the Murray Darling Basin, 19th-century technological advancements in irrigated agriculture, rail and river transport meant that the River Murray and its tributaries became a central focus of colonial expansion and development. By the 1850s the ways in which the colonies had developed and were using the River Murray and its tributaries led to heated disputes between New South Wales and Victoria, upstream, and South Australia, the lowest riparian State.

The disputes between New South Wales, Victoria and South Australia centred on the issue of whether the waters of the River Murray and its main tributaries were to be used for irrigation or for navigation. By the middle of the 19th century South Australia had established a thriving river trading network along the Murray, the Murrumbidgee and the Darling Rivers. The transported goods were off-loaded at river ports within South Australia and transferred to sea ports at Port Adelaide

---

43 Graeme Davison, John Hirst and Stuart Macintyre (eds), *The Oxford Companion to Australian History* (Oxford University Press, 2001) 467.

44 Clark, above n 42, 11–12.

45 Davison, Hirst and Macintyre (eds), above n 43, 541.

46 Paul Kildea and George Williams, 'The Constitution and the management of water in Australia's rivers' (2010) 32 *Sydney Law Review* 595, 597.

47 Geoscience Australia, *State and Territory Borders* http://www.ga.gov.au/education/geoscience-basics/dimensions/state-territory-borders.html.

or elsewhere in South Australia.[48] Accordingly, South Australia's prime interest in the waters of the River Murray and its tributaries was to maintain flows that permitted permanent navigation.[49] In contrast, New South Wales and Victoria were progressively developing irrigated agriculture.[50] Victoria, particularly, saw irrigation as a means of ensuring economic growth in arid areas and areas with low rainfall.[51]

South Australia sought to prevent Victoria from diverting water from various rivers and tributaries upstream and, in doing so, jeopardizing their navigability.[52] South Australia asserted that it enjoyed riparian rights in the River Murray since at least 1887 when it appointed a River Murray Waters Commission to investigate the issue.[53] Riparian rights require upstream users not to use the water in a way that deprives downstream users of its use.[54]

Victoria, having pioneered irrigated agriculture, claimed 'the right to divert water from the upper Murray and all tributaries within [Victoria]'.[55] As the border between the colony of Victoria and the colony of New South Wales had been established along the southern high water mark of the River Murray, New South Wales claimed 'exclusive use of the waters in the River Murray above the South Australian border and in its territorial tributaries, with no regard to the claims of Victoria and South Australia'.[56]

Over the course of the latter half of the 19th century South Australia made several unsuccessful attempts to secure an agreement on water sharing.[57] The federation movement, and the various Constitutional Conventions held to develop a constitution for the new Federation, provided South Australia with an alternative forum within which to advocate its claims.[58] This proved largely unsuccessful for South Australia. Nevertheless the federation of the Australian colonies under a new constitution marks an important point in the establishment of governance arrangements for the Murray Darling Basin. These are considered below.

---

48 Daniel Connell, *Water Politics in the Murray Darling Basin* (Federation Press, 2007) 12; Clark, above n 44, 24; Kildea and Williams above n 46, p 601.

49 Clark, above n 44, 24.

50 Ibid, 24–25.

51 Kildea and Williams above n 46, 601; Connell, above n 48, 12.

52 Clark, above n 44, 26.

53 Kelly, above n 29, 642.

54 Ibid.

55 Clark, above n 44, 26.

56 Ibid.

57 Kelly, above n 29, 641; Clark, above n 44, 26–30; Williams and Webster, above n 1, 268.

58 Kelly, above n 29, 641.

The Constitution, the Environment and the Murray Darling Basin

The *Australian Constitution* contains no express grant of power to the Commonwealth Parliament to pass legislation about the environment. The *Australian Constitution* confers only a limited number of specific legislative powers on the Commonwealth and leaves the residual powers to the States. Thus, traditionally, the legislative responsibility for land use and natural resources (including water resources) management lies with the States.[59] Notwithstanding the absence of an express power to regulate with respect to the environment, the Commonwealth does have a range of other legislative powers that enable it to enact environmental legislation.[60] These powers include those listed in section 51 of the *Australian Constitution*. These include, for example, the power to legislate with respect to:

- trade and commerce with other countries and among the States (section 51(i));
- astronomical and meteorological observations (section 51(viii));
- quarantine (section 51(ix));
- fisheries (section 51(x));
- external affairs (section 51(xxix));
- matters which are referred to the Commonwealth by parliaments of the States (section 51(xxxviii)) ('the referral power').

The use of these powers to support Commonwealth environmental legislation is manifestly evident today in the various pieces of Commonwealth legislation that protect and regulate the environment and natural resources. The *Water Act* is a classic example of how the Commonwealth can legislate with respect to the environment despite the fact that the *Australian Constitution* is silent about such matters. Indeed sections 9 and 9A of the *Water Act*, which set out its constitutional basis, cite a constitutional 'hotch-potch'[61] of nine specific heads of power in addition to the referral power.

It is important to understand two of these powers, the external affairs power and the referral power, because they are both fundamental elements in Australian environmental governance generally and play a significant role in the *Water Act*. The next section of this chapter considers these two powers as well as a

59 Gerry Bates, *Environmental Law in Australia*, 7th edn (LexisNexis Butterworths, 2010) 105.

60 Ibid; Hayden Opie, 'Commonwealth power to regulate industrial pollution' (1976) 10 *Melbourne University Law Review* 577, 613.

61 Paul Kildea and George Williams, 'The *Water Act* and the Murray Darling Basin Plan' (2011) 22 *Public Law Review* 3, 10; see also A Twomey, 'Aspirational Nationalism or Opportunistic Federalism?' *Quadrant* (October 2007) 40.

third constitutional provision, section 100, which is also a significant aspect of governance arrangements for the Murray Darling Basin.

The External Affairs Power

The external affairs power has developed into a major source of Commonwealth power to legislate with respect to environmental management largely as a result of the landmark 1983 High Court decision in the *Tasmanian Dam* case.[62]

In the *Tasmanian Dam* case, the State of Tasmania challenged Commonwealth legislation that purported to implement Australia's obligations under *The Convention for the Protection of the World Cultural and National Heritage* ('the *World Heritage Convention*'). The aim of the *World Heritage Convention* is to preserve natural and cultural areas of 'outstanding universal value'.[63] State parties to this convention, such as Australia, acknowledge a duty to ensure that areas of cultural and natural heritage situated on their territory are identified, protected, conserved, presented and transmitted to future generations.[64] The *World Heritage Convention* imposed various obligations upon States to take measures to fulfil this duty.[65]

The Commonwealth legislation in question prohibited the building of the proposed Franklin Dam in the Western Tasmanian Wilderness Area, which had been included on the World Heritage List, established under the *World Heritage Convention*. The High Court's decision upheld the validity of key parts of the legislation to prevent the construction of the Dam and effectively defined the scope of the external affairs power. The case held that the external affairs power will support Commonwealth legislation that is reasonably appropriate and adapted to the task of implementing an international treaty regardless of whether the subject matter of the treaty is inside or outside Australia.[66] The extensive scope of this power has enabled the Commonwealth to enact a range of domestic laws that give effect to the growing number of international treaties dealing with environmental concerns.[67] The *Water Act* is based, in part, on implementing both multilateral and bilateral obligations imposed by no less than eight international conventions.[68]

---

62 *Commonwealth v Tasmania (Tasmanian Dam Case)* (1983) 158 CLR 1.

63 Preamble to *The Convention for the Protection of the World Cultural and National Heritage* 151 UNTS 1037, opened for signature 23 November 1972, entered into force 17 December 1975.

64 *World Heritage Convention,* Article 4.

65 For example see *World Heritage Convention* articles 5 and 6.

66 *Tasmanian Dam Case* (1983) 158 CLR 1, 131–132 (Mason J); 172 (Murphy J); 232 Brennan J; 259 (Deane J).

67 D Fisher, 'The impact of international law upon the Australian environmental legal system' (1996) 16 *Environmental and Planning Law Journal* 372, 384.

68 *The Convention on Wetlands of International Importance especially as Waterfowl Habitat* done at Ramsar, Iran, on 2 February 1971, ATS 1975 No. 48 ('the Ramsar Convention'); *The Convention on Biological Diversity* done at Rio de Janeiro on 5 June 1992, ATS 1993 No. 32 ('The Convention on Biological Diversity'); *The United Nations*

Section 100 of the Constitution

In stark contrast to the treatment given to the topic of the environment generally, the 1890s Constitutional Conventions devoted much time to the issue of the River Murray and its resources. Indeed a Victorian delegate, Alfred Deakin, noted that the issue was of such importance that a resolution that was unsatisfactory to New South Wales could have jeopardized the chances of federation.[69]

The product of the lengthy and heated debates between 1891 and 1898 can be seen in sections 98 and 100 of the *Australian Constitution.* Section 98 states: 'The power of the Parliament to make laws with respect to trade and commerce extends to navigation and shipping, and to railways the property of any State.' While section 98 extends Commonwealth powers, section 100 is more of a prohibition. It states: 'The Commonwealth shall not, by any law or regulation of trade or commerce, abridge the right of a State or of the residents therein to the reasonable use of the waters of rivers for conservation or irrigation.'

The lack of any discernible concern for the environment and the sustainable use and management of the resources of the River Murray in these two sections reflects the level of scientific knowledge available to the framers of the *Constitution* at the close of the 19th century.[70] The debate surrounding sections 98 and 100 illustrates the economic interests each colony had in the ways it used the river systems of the Murray Darling Basin and fears about the extent to which a new federal authority may control or limit them. The outcome was essentially a compromise. South Australia, New South Wales and Victoria were unable to reach a conclusion on the question of the rights of any State.[71] The outcome, represented by sections 98 and 100, ostensibly confined the issue to the trade and commerce power and this meant

---

Convention to Combat Desertification in those Countries Experiencing Serious Drought and/or Desertification, Particularly in Africa done at Paris on 17 June 1994, ATS 2000 No. 18 ('the Desertification Convention'); *The Convention on the Conservation of Migratory Species of Wild Animals* done at Bonn on 23 June 1979 ('the Bonn Convention'); *The Agreement between the Government of Australia and the Government of the People's Republic of China for the Protection of Migratory Birds and their Environment* done at Canberra on 20 October 1986, Australian Treaty Series 1988 No. 22; *The Agreement between the Government of Australia and the Government of Japan for the Protection of Migratory Birds and Birds in Danger of Extinction and their Environment* done at Tokyo on 6 February 1981, Australian Treaty Series 1981 No. 6; *The Agreement with the Government of the Republic of Korea on the Protection of Migratory Birds* done at Canberra on 6 December 2006, Australian Treaty Series 2007 No. 24; *The United Nations Framework Convention on Climate Change* done at New York on 9 May 1992, Treaty Series 1994 No. 2 ('the Climate Change Convention').

69 Williams and Webster, above n 1, 273.

70 The term 'conservation' refers to the impounding or damming of water: see Alex Gardner, Richard Bartlett and Janice Gray, *Water Resources Law* (LexisNexis Butterworths, 2009) 93.

71 Kelly, see above n 29, 644.

that it would be left to the High Court to resolve future disputes and determine the rights of those involved.[72]

Shortly after federation an Inter-State Royal Commission was established to determine a regime for the equitable distribution of the waters of the River Murray.[73] Its final recommendations were equivocal, appearing to favour, but declining to acknowledge, the existence of riparian rights within the context of the Australian Federation.[74] As discussed below, the question about riparian rights has been noted, but never resolved, by the High Court.

Interpreting Section 100

The few decisions of the High Court that have dealt with section 100, in particular *Arnold v Minister Administering the Water Management Act 2000* ('*Arnold*'),[75] illustrate the difficult governance legacy brought about by the colonial wrangling at Federation and ultimately the compromise, represented by section 100. In the decisions in *ICM Agriculture Pty Ltd v Commonwealth* ('*ICM*')[76] and particularly in *Arnold* the High Court considered section 100 but ultimately did not, for various reasons associated with the particular issues in dispute, need to decide conclusively on its scope.

Both decisions concerned a claim that New South Wales had breached the *Constitution* when it acted pursuant to the Intergovernmental Agreement between the Commonwealth, New South Wales, Victoria, Queensland, South Australia and the Australian Capital Territory on a National Water Initiative ('the National Water Initiative'). In accordance with the National Water Initiative the National Water Commission was established by the *National Water Commission Act 2004* (Cth). A function of the Commission was to assist with the implementation of the National Water Initiative including the funding of particular water resource projects. The Commonwealth-funded water reform project for the Lower Lachlan Groundwater System was the subject of dispute in *ICM* while the Commonwealth-funded water reform project for the Lower Murray Groundwater System was considered in *Arnold*.

The Agreement between the Commonwealth and New South Wales required New South Wales to convert all water licences in the Lower Lachlan Groundwater System which had been granted under the *Water Act 1912* (NSW) into licences under the *Water Management Act 2000* (NSW) and to achieve a reduction of 56% in water entitlements in that resource by 1 July 2016. The Agreement also required New South Wales to implement water sharing plans pursuant to the *Water Management Act 2000* (NSW) so as to reduce the water entitlements of water

72 Ibid.
73 Ibid, 649.
74 Ibid.
75 (2010) 240 CLR 242.
76 (2009) 240 CLR 140.

licence holders in the Lower Murray Groundwater System to more sustainable levels. New South Wales was required to develop a package of ex gratia structural payments to assist licensees who held rights to extract groundwater to adjust to the impact of these reduced water entitlements. In due course the necessary administrative steps were taken to substitute existing aquifer access licences under the *Water Act 1912* (NSW) with arrangements under the *Water Management Act 2000* (NSW).

The appellants in both cases contended that the replacement of the licences issued under the *Water Act 1912* (NSW) with arrangements under the *Water Management Act 2000* (NSW) amounted to an acquisition of property contrary to the constitutional guarantee of just terms compensation contained in section 51(xxxi) of the *Constitution.* As the specific licences in the *Arnold* case related to the groundwater resources of the Lower Murray Groundwater System, the appellants in *Arnold* also argued that the funding agreement between the Commonwealth and New South Wales itself was a regulation of trade or commerce which contravened section 100 of the *Constitution.*

In *ICM*, the majority of the High Court held that there had been no acquisition of property in the sense contemplated by section 51(xxxi).[77] The constitutional just terms protection was not engaged. The High Court applied its decision in *ICM* to the facts in *Arnold.* The High Court in *Arnold* also dealt with the section 100 question by simply deciding that the groundwaters that were the subject of the substituted licences were not 'waters of rivers' for the purposes of section 100.[78] While this is an 'unexceptional and reasonable conclusion'[79] it leaves open several questions about the extent of section 100.

In *Arnold*, the High Court found it unnecessary to reopen another of its earlier decisions, *Morgan v Commonwealth*[80] ('*Morgan*') which had decided that the prohibition imposed by section 100 applied only to laws which were capable of being made under section 51(i) (the Commonwealth's trade and commerce power) and section 98 of the *Constitution* and, for example, did not apply to laws supported by other heads of power enumerated in section 51. The decision in *Morgan* was later described, in the *Tasmanian Dam* case, as artificial, given that it:

> confine[d] the restriction on legislative power to laws made, or capable of being made in exercise of one power when a somewhat similar effect in relation to the use of waters of rivers by a State and its residents for conservation or irrigation

---

77 *ICM Agriculture Pty Ltd v Commonwealth* (2009) 240 CLR 140 at 180 (French CJ, Gumow and Crennan JJ), 203 (Hayne, Kiefel and Bell JJ), Heydon dissenting.

78 *Arnold v Minister Administering the Water Management Act 2000* (2010) 240 CLR 242 at 258 (French CJ), 265 (Gummow and Crennan JJ), 269 (Hayne, Kiefel and Bell JJ).

79 Williams and Webster, above n 1, 280.

80 (1947) 74 CLR 421.

> might be achieved by the Commonwealth in the exercise of other legislative powers.[81]

The High Court in *Arnold* also found it unnecessary to determine whether the expression 'residents therein' in section 100 is confined to individuals and could not include corporate entities.[82] Equally, it was unnecessary for the Court to answer the riparian rights question. Gummow and Crennan JJ noted that it was unnecessary to rule on the question, left open in the *Tasmanian Dam* case, 'whether as between riparian States and their residents section 100 guarantees access to the use of the waters for the purposes mentioned, or does no more than impose a restriction upon the exercise of the power of the Commonwealth'.[83]

Other commentators have pointed out that even if section 100 is to be confined to laws made pursuant to the trade and commerce power in section 51(i) and not to other powers, section 100 may constitute a significant restriction on the ability of the Commonwealth to impose limits on water abstraction and trade in water allocations in the Murray Darling Basin due to the fact that such regulation would rely on the trade and commerce power in section 51(i).[84]

ICM and *Arnold* leave many questions unanswered.[85] These considerable uncertainties indicate that the constitutional provisions that are most applicable to the Murray Darling Basin, fail to provide a certain, stable or secure basis for sound transboundary environmental governance of the Murray Darling Basin.

Cooperative Federalism in the Murray Darling Basin 1914 – 2007, and Beyond?

Cooperative federalism is a second important mechanism which the Commonwealth has used to exert its power and influence in environmental matters. This cooperative exercise of powers between States and the Commonwealth in environmental matters generally is, in part, an expedient response to decisions of the High Court, such as the *Tasmanian Dam* case.[86] The significance of cooperative federalism in Murray Darling Basin governance, in particular, has been attributed, in part, to the potential restriction on Commonwealth power contained in section 100.[87] It is also a recognition that significant national environmental issues need to be dealt with on a national basis.[88] Many features of Commonwealth involvement in the

81 *Tasmanian Dam* case (1983) 158 CLR 1, 154 (Mason J).

82 *Arnold* (2010) 240 CLR 242, 264 (Gummow and Crennan JJ).

83 Ibid.

84 Gardner et al, above n 70, 93.

85 Williams and Webster, above n 1, 280.

86 Bates, above n 60, 136.

87 Gardner et al, above n 70, 100. See also Webster, A and Williams J 'Can the High Court save the Murray River?' (2012) 29 *Environmental and Planning Law Journal* 281, 294.

88 Bates, above n 59, 136.

Murray Darling Basin governance systems, including the *Water Act*, are examples of cooperative federalism.

The reliance on cooperative federalism is an abiding theme of environmental regulation in Australia generally. In Murray Darling Basin affairs in particular, it has led to a complex array of intergovernmental agreements that have established various regulatory and administrative bodies. The *Water Act* is the most recent instance of reliance on cooperative federalism, however the difficulties associated with enacting and implementing the *Water Act* demonstrate that it is a particularly fragile governance mechanism.

The pre-Federation disputes between New South Wales and Victoria and South Australia were not, as indicated above, resolved by federation. It was not until 1914 that an agreement was reached between the Commonwealth, New South Wales, Victoria and South Australia providing for the sharing of the water of the River Murray and its tributaries among the three States and for the sharing of the costs of infrastructure and maintenance.[89] The 1914 Interstate Agreement also established the River Murray Commission comprised of State-appointed Commissioners. It continued, with various alterations, until 1992 when the Commonwealth, New South Wales, Victoria and South Australia executed a new agreement which was ratified by legislation in each jurisdiction.[90] The 1992 Agreement reflected an intention to 'promote and co-ordinate effective planning and management for the equitable and sustainable use of the water, land and environmental resources of the Murray-Darling Basin'.[91] One of the major criticisms of the governance arrangements of the Murray Darling Basin Commission, however, was that it was comprised of State appointees and therefore lacked sufficient independence for decision-making appropriate to the entire Murray Darling Basin.[92]

In the late 1990s and early 2000s a number of national policy developments took place. The effects of these changes can be seen in the governance arrangements of the *Water Act*. In 1992 the Council of Australian Governments (CoAG) endorsed the National Strategy for Ecologically Sustainable Development, which highlighted the need for various reforms in relation to water resources. These included taking an integrated catchment management approach to regulation, effective public participation in developing allocation and pricing policies and management measures, and improved water markets.[93] This was followed in 1994 by the CoAG Water Reform Framework, which set out some fundamental principles for management of water resources, including within the Murray Darling Basin. These included:

89 Ibid, 127.

90 See e.g. *Murray-Darling Basin Act 1993* (Cth), Schedule 1.

91 *Murray-Darling Basin Act 1993* (Cth), Schedule 1, preamble.

92 Ibid.

93 Gardner et al, above n 70, 39.

- the creation of definable and transferable, water rights that were separate from land title;
- the creation of allocations of water for the environment as a legitimate user;
- addressing over allocation of water entitlements;
- interstate trade in water allocations; and
- integrated catchment management.[94]

The 2004 National Water Initiative renewed the commitment to the 1994 Water Reform Framework and refocussed attention on water allocations and entitlements.[95] At the same time the five jurisdictions finalized an Intergovernmental Agreement on Addressing Water Over-allocation and Achieving Environmental Objectives in the Murray-Darling Basin ('the Living Murray Agreement') pursuant to which the parties agreed to jointly fund measures to recover 500 gigalitres of water for environmental purposes at six ecological sites in the Murray Darling Basin.

These policy developments contributed to the criticism levelled at the governance arrangements under the 1992 Murray Darling Basin Agreement which, by that time, appeared dated.[96] To address criticisms such as these, the federal Government of Australia, led by Prime Minister John Howard, announced in 2007 a ten year National Plan for Water Security. This ten year plan included a range of measures, stating that it was 'in the national interest to secure the long-term economic and social returns to the Australian community afforded by sustainable access to the Basin's water resources'.[97] This was to be achieved through a number of methods:

- significant investments in water saving infrastructure and water resource monitoring and water use metering;
- addressing the problem of over-allocation by purchasing water entitlements and by providing funding for structural adjustments; and
- implementing new governance arrangements by replacing the Murray Darling Basin Commission with a Commonwealth government agency, the Murray Darling Basin Authority. [98]

Foreshadowing the *Water Act's* Basin Plan, which is considered in detail below, the National Plan for Water Security also proposed a 'strategic plan' that contemplated a revised cap on water diversions to be administered by the proposed Murray Darling Basin Authority.[99] The implementation of this plan in the Murray Darling

94 Ibid, 39–40.

95 Ibid, 41.

96 Ibid, 133.

97 Commonwealth of Australia, *A National Plan for Water Security* (25 January 2007) 12 http://www.nalwt.gov.au/files/national_plan_for_water_security.pdf.

98 Ibid, 13.

99 Ibid, 5.

Basin required a referral of powers to the Commonwealth as it otherwise lacked the constitutional power to implement such a comprehensive scheme. While New South Wales, Queensland and South Australia agreed to refer power to the Commonwealth and the Australian Capital Territory undertook to cooperate, Victoria refused to refer its legislative power to the Commonwealth. Victoria argued that the proposals rewarded States that had poor infrastructure and water efficiency and that more funding was required.[100] As a result of this, the Prime Minister acknowledged that the Commonwealth would be forced to proceed on the basis of the nine legislative powers that it did have under section 51 of the *Constitution*, noting that while that power was extensive it was 'not as extensive as to give [it] a close to ideal scheme'.[101] Thus the *Water Act* was enacted in August 2007 and it commenced in March 2008.[102] In July 2008 the newly elected Federal Labor Government signed the Agreement on Murray Darling Basin Reform with Queensland, New South Wales, Victoria, South Australia and the Australian Capital Territory (all of which had Labor governments). This conferred upon the Commonwealth the power to enact various amendments to the *Water Act* that strengthened some of the administrative elements of the scheme and the operation of the market for water rights.[103] These referrals did not make up for the lack of complete referral that characterized the initial enactment. Accordingly, sections 9 and 9A of the *Water Act*, which have been noted above, reveal the extent to which the Commonwealth, in the absence of a full referral of powers from the States, had to rely on a 'hotch-potch'[104] of its various constitutional powers, in particular the external affairs power and various international treaties, to enact the *Water Act.* The consequences of this became apparent in late 2010.

The *Water Act*

The *Water Act* represents the culmination of a century of federal involvement in the regulation of the resources of the Murray Darling Basin with the cooperation of the Murray Darling Basin States and territories. In summary it provides for the adoption and content of the Murray Darling Basin Plan, for its administration, implementation and enforcement, at a local level, through water resource plans for water resource plan areas and, consistent with notions of environmental governance that embrace the roles played by participants other than governments, it also provides for the rules for the trading of water rights based on the objectives and principles of the 2004 *National Water Initiative* referred to earlier.

100 Paul Kildea and George Williams, above n 62, 10.

101 J Howard, Press Conference (Perth, 24 July 2007) cited in Kildea and Williams, above n 62, 10.

102 *Water Act 2007* (Cth) section 2.

103 Gardner et al, above n71, 47.

104 Kildea and Williams, above n 62, 10.

The *Water Act* provides for considerable independence for the Murray Darling Basin Authority which replaced the Murray Darling Basin Commission. Rather than being comprised of State-appointed members like the Murray Darling Basin Commission, the Murray Darling Basin Authority is comprised of six members who are appointed for their expertise in areas relevant to the functions of the Authority.[105] This is a clearly positive feature of the *Water Act*.

One of the objects of the *Water Act* is to enable the Commonwealth, in conjunction with the Basin States, to manage the Basin water resources in the national interest. The *Water Act* does not, however, give the Commonwealth 'total, complete and comprehensive control of the water resources'[106] of the Murray Darling Basin due to the failure of the Commonwealth to achieve a full referral of the necessary powers from the States. Rather the *Water Act* can be characterized as a planning scheme that determines the way in which rights to access and use water resources in the Murray Darling Basin, as conferred by State or territory legislation, are to be exercised.[107]

Furthermore, section 3(b) of the *Water Act* states that an object is to give effect to international agreements that are relevant to the Murray Darling Basin and section 3(c) provides that in giving effect to those agreements another object is 'to promote the use and management of the Basin water resources in a way that optimizes economic, social and environmental outcomes'. Section 3(d)(i) provides that without limiting the objects set out in sections 3(b) or 3(c) that it is an object of the Act to ensure that water resources that are over allocated or overused are returned to an environmentally sustainable level of allocation or use. Another goal of the *Water Act* set out in section 3(d)(ii) is to protect, restore and provide for the ecological values and ecosystem services of the Murray Darling Basin. Section 3(d)(iii) sets out a further object: to maximize the net economic returns to the Australian community from the use and management of the Basin water resources. This object is, however, stated to be subject to the objects in sections 3(d)(i) and 3(d)(ii).

As explained earlier, these objects relate to the eight international agreements to which the use of the external affairs power is tied, thus empowering this legislation. The priority inherent in this hierarchy of objects hints at what has become a crucial question in relation to the Murray Darling Basin Plan: to what extent, if any, is the environment to be given preference over social and economic considerations? This key question is considered below.

The Basin Plan

The Basin Plan is a key component of the *Water Act*. The *Water Act* requires that the Murray Darling Basin Authority prepare this plan and that it is adopted by the

105 *Water Act 2007* (Cth), section 177.

106 Fisher, above n 22, 157.

107 Ibid.

Minister, as a legislative instrument.[108] The Basin Plan's purpose is to provide for the integrated management of the Basin's water resources in a way that promotes the objects of the Act. Section 20 contemplates that in order to achieve these objects, the Basin Plan is to:

a. give effect to relevant international agreements (to the extent to which those agreements are relevant to the use and management of the Basin water resources); and
b. establish and enforce environmentally sustainable limits on the quantities of surface water and ground water that may be taken from the Basin water resources; and
c. provide for Basin-wide environmental objectives for water-dependent ecosystems of the Murray Darling Basin and water quality and salinity objectives; and
d. provide for the use and management of the Basin water resources in a way that optimizes economic, social and environmental outcomes; and
e. provide for water to reach its most productive use through the development of an efficient water trading regime across the Murray Darling Basin; and
f. provide for requirements that a water resource plan for a water resource plan area must meet if it is to be accredited or adopted under Division 2; and
g. provide for improved water security for all uses of Basin water resources.

The Basin Plan must also address a number of mandatory matters, such as:

- the long-term average sustainable diversion limits ('the limits') for the water resources of the Basin;[109]
- an environmental watering plan;[110]
- provision for temporary diversion;[111]
- a water quality and salinity management plan;[112]
- water trading rules;[113]
- the requirements for the accreditation of State water resource plans.[114]

---

108 *Water Act 2007* (Cth), section 19.

109 *Water Act 2007* (Cth) section 22(1), Items 6 and 8; *Water Act 2007* (Cth) section 23.

110 *Water Act 2007* (Cth) section 22(1), Item 9; *Water Act 2007* (Cth) section 28–32.

111 *Water Act 2007* (Cth) section 22(1), Items 7 and 8; *Water Act 2007* (Cth) section 24.

112 *Water Act 2007* (Cth) section 22(1), Item 10; *Water Act 2007* (Cth) section 25.

113 *Water Act 2007* (Cth) section 22(1), Item 12; *Water Act 2007* (Cth) section 26.

114 *Water Act 2007* (Cth) section 22(1), Item 11, *Water Act 2007* (Cth) section 22(3).

The national scheme is given local effect by section 54 of the *Water Act* which contemplates that the Basin Plan limits will be implemented in local areas, termed 'water resource plan areas', through water resource plans that can either be accredited or adopted by the Minister. Water resource plans are required to 'provide for the management of the water resources of the water resource plan area' pursuant to section 55(1). They must, in accordance with section 55(2) also be consistent with the Basin Plan. Such consistency, crucially, is to include consistency with both the long-term average sustainable diversion limit determined (pursuant to section 23) for that water resource plan area by the Basin Plan and any other requirements set out in the Basin Plan itself. Sections 58 and 59 illustrate the importance of the Basin Plan because those two sections create broad obligations upon a number of Commonwealth Government officials and statutory bodies tasked with administering the *Water Act*, as well as their counterparts in the Basin States to comply with the water resource plan.

The significance of the link between the Basin Plan and its local counterparts was reflected in the recommendation of the *Independent Review of the Environment Protection and Biodiversity Conservation Act 1999* (Cth) ('the Hawke Report') that the Basin Plan prepared under the Water Act be subjected to a strategic review under the *Environment Protection and Biodiversity Conservation Act 1999* (Cth) ('the EPBC Act').[115] The Hawke Report noted that, while legislative amendment would be required, water plans required to comply with the Basin Plan could be excluded from the requirement for approval under the EPBC Act if the Basin Plan itself were subjected to a strategic review.[116] The benefits of strategic environmental assessment are well noted.[117] Strategic environmental assessment, which evaluates policies, plans and programmes with a view to contributing to ecologically sustainable development by integrating environmental considerations into the decision-making process, has the capacity to address environmental impacts earlier in the assessment process and in doing so seeks to avoid them at later stages of the process.[118] This would, in the view of the Hawke report, provide greater certainty, better environmental outcomes and reduce regulatory burden generally.[119] It would also, arguably, remove some of the jurisdictional limitations to which the Murray Darling Basin is subject.

---

115 Commonwealth of Australia, *The Australian Environment Act – Report of the Independent of the Environment Protection and Biodiversity Conservation Act 1999*, 30 October 2009.

116 Ibid, 110. This was reflected in Recommendation 9, see ibid, 111.

117 Simon Marsden, 'Strategic Environmental Assessment in Australia: An evaluation of Section 146 of the *Environment Protection and Biodiversity Conservation Act 1999*' (1999) 8 *Griffith Law Review* 394; Simon Marsden and John Ashe, 'Strategic Environmental Assessment legislation in Australian States and Territories (2006) 13 *Australasian Journal of Environmental Management* 205.

118 Marsden and Ashe, above n 117, 205.

119 Commonwealth of Australia, above n 115, 110.

The Commonwealth Government rejected this recommendation, turning its back on the opportunities to improve the quality of the Basin Plan. It stated that 'the Basin Plan is likely to be a high-level planning document supported by, and to a large extent implemented through, State-based water resource plans'.[120] It concluded that as a result, the Basin Plan was 'not likely to contain enough detail for strategic assessment'.[121]

The Commonwealth Environmental Water Holder

Part 6 of the *Water Act* establishes the office of the Commonwealth Environmental Water Holder to manage water acquired by the Commonwealth through its participation in water markets. It is to be used for protecting or restoring environmental assets both in and outside the Murray Darling Basin, so as to give effect to the relevant international agreements.[122] Significantly, it has been estimated that the Commonwealth Environmental Water Holder has the potential to have access to about 35% of all water entitlements in the Basin.[123]

This feature of the scheme has been described as a 'major break with the past'[124] given that it is not reliant on the consent of the States, but only on the size of its budget and self-imposed limitations governing its use.[125] Unlike the local water resource plan processes under section 54 of the *Water Act*, which are premised upon the finalisation of the Basin Plan, the use of the Commonwealth Environmental Water Holder's water has the potential to drive environmental flow targets, independently of the Basin Plan and regardless of State support.[126]

Striking the Balance

On 8 October 2010, the Murray Darling Basin Authority released its *Guide to the proposed Basin Plan* ('the *2010 Guide*') as a guide for discussions and debate on the development of the Basin Plan. The *2010 Guide* proposed that to achieve the objects of the *Water Act* the limits on the amount of water that could be

---

120 Department of Sustainability Environment Water Population and Communities, Australian Government response to the Report of the independent review of the Environment Protection and Biodiversity Conservation Act 1999 < *http://www.environment.gov.au/epbc/publications/epbc-review-govt-response.html*> 26.

121 Ibid.

122 *Water Act 2007* (Cth) section 105.

123 Mike Young, 'Improving the Basin Plan: Options for consideration' in Daniel Connell and R Quentin Grafton (eds), *Basin Future: Water reform in the Murray-Darling Basin* (ANU E-Press, 2011) 439, 444.

124 Daniel Connell, 'The Role of the Commonwealth Environmental Water Holder' in Connell and Quentin Grafton (eds) ibid, 327, 327.

125 Ibid, 328.

126 Ibid.

diverted would need to be reduced from between 3000 to 4000 gigalitres per year: equivalent to a reduction of between 22% and 29%.[127]

The day after the *2010 Guide* was released, the Murray Darling Basin Authority commenced a series of community information sessions within the Murray Darling Basin communities. While environmentalists welcomed the proposals, at these sessions, irrigators and various other members and representatives of the community expressed deep concern that the *2010 Guide* gave priority to environmental needs,[128] and at what such reductions meant for local economies and communities.[129]

From October 2010 onwards there was much political debate regarding the basis upon which the *2010 Guide* was drafted, including the legal question about the extent to which the *Water Act* and the Basin Plan required environmental concerns to be given priority over economic and social concerns. In response to public statements by officers of the Murray Darling Basin Authority that the *Water Act* required priority to be given to environmental considerations, the Commonwealth Minister sought and publicly released a legal opinion on the question that provided a basis for the Minister to express contrary views.[130] The *Water Act* and the Basin Plan also became the subject of three Commonwealth Parliamentary Inquiries.[131]

The House of Representatives Standing Committee on Regional Australia Inquiry reported serious failures in the consultation and communication processes adopted by the Murray Darling Basin Authority at the time. For example, the Standing Committee's report noted that neither the role of the *2010 Guide* nor the purpose of these community discussions was explained to the communities.[132] It also noted that where information sessions were held only days after the release

---

127 Kildea and Williams, above n 61, 11.

128 For example see Bronwyn Herbert 'Murray-Darling cuts "could spark riots"' *ABC News Online*, 10 October 2010, http://www.abc.net.au/news/2010-10-08/murray-darling-cuts-could-spark-riots/2290068; *ABC NewsOnline*, 'Angry Crowd Burns Copy of Murray-Darling Report', 13 October 2010, http://www.abc.net.au/news/2010-10-13/angry-crowd-burns-copy-of-murray-darling-report/2296638; See also Kildea and Williams, above n 62, 11.

129 Kildea and Williams, above n 61, 11.

130 Australian Government Solicitor, 'The Role of Social and Economic Factors in the Basin Plan' (25 October 2010); See also Kildea and Williams, above n 61, 11.

131 House of Representatives Standing Committee on Regional Australia, Parliament of Australia, *Of drought and flooding rains: Inquiry into the impact of the Guide to the Murray Darling Basin Plan* (May 2011) http://www.aph.gov.au/house/committee/ra/murraydarling/report.htm; Senate Legal and Constitutional Affairs References Committee, Parliament of Australia, *A Balancing Act: provisions of the Water Act 2007* (June 2011). http://www.aph.gov.au/senate/committee/legcon_ctte/provisionswateract2007/report/index.htm; A third inquiry, *The Inquiry into the Management of the Murray-Darling Basin* by the Senate Rural Affairs and Transport References Committee remains, at the time of writing, an ongoing inquiry.

132 House of Representatives Standing Committee on Regional Australia, above n 131, 4.

of the *2010 Guide*, communities were not given an adequate opportunity to read and digest the contents of the various components of the *2010 Guide* which it described as 'unduly complex to many readers'.[133] The Standing Committee observed that these factors were symptomatic of a broader governance malaise, which it termed reform fatigue, to describe the feelings of many in Murray Darling Basin communities who had been through the instability of an almost perpetual process of reforms without having the need for such reforms explained.[134] These findings suggest that quality governance processes in the development of the Basin Plan, such as public participation, access to information, transparency and government responsiveness, had been compromised.

The terms of reference of the Senate Legal and Constitutional Affairs References Committee ('the Senate Committee') required it to inquire into and report on the *Water Act* with particular reference to the direction it gives to the development of the Basin Plan. Among the matters it was asked to look at were:

- any ambiguities or constraints that prevented the economic, social and environmental considerations being given equal weight in the Basin Plan and any amendments necessary to ensure that equal weight could be given to these considerations;
- the constitutional power for the Commonwealth to legislate in the area of water resources;
- the role of the relevant international agreements that the Basin Plan is required to give effect to.[135]

The majority report of the Senate Committee was critical of the *Water Act's* ability to provide stable and sustainable management of the Murray Darling Basin's water resources.[136] In its view, this was due to the fact that the *Water Act* was 'uncertain and ambiguous'[137] and required urgent amendment.[138] It noted that this uncertainty, which had become acutely apparent in October 2010, threatened the community-wide acceptance of the Basin Plan and, as a result, its ability to constitute a long-term solution.[139]

The majority report blamed the absence of a clear constitutional power for the Commonwealth to legislate over water resources in Australia and the adequacy of trying to do so by relying on the external affairs and referral powers.[140] While the

133 Ibid.

134 Ibid, 23.

135 The Senate Legal and Constitutional Affairs References Committee, above n 131, [1.2].

136 Ibid, [4.2].

137 Ibid, [4.1].

138 Ibid, [4.1].

139 Ibid [4.5].

140 Ibid [4.11].

majority report noted that there was some scope for discretion in the balancing of economic, social and environmental considerations, it felt that the use of the external affairs power: 'in conjunction with international agreements for the protection of the environment, has created a legislative framework in the *Water Act* for the development of the Basin Plan where environmental considerations can be, and are, given substantially more "weight" than social and economic considerations'. The majority report of the Senate Committee adopted the view of the Standing Committee, which in its report argued that '[n]o society can wantonly destroy the essential balance between social, environmental and economic outcomes'.[141] Accordingly the majority of the Senate Committee considered that the *Water Act* needed to give more discretion to policy makers in balancing the three objectives and that this discretion needed to be articulated clearly in the *Water Act*.[142]

The Senate Committee majority report noted that no legislation is immune from the risk of legal challenge, but noted that legislation that is dependent on the external affairs power is particularly prone to challenge in the High Court.[143] Accordingly the Senate Committee majority report recommended that the *Water Act* be amended as a matter of urgency and that the government take all necessary measures to 'strengthen the constitutional validity of the *Water Act*'.[144]

In a dissenting report government Senators indicated that the longstanding reliance on the eternal affairs and referral power was a justification for relying on them to enact the *Water Act*.[145] Government Senators noted and relied on the Australian Government Solicitor's legal opinion that the Basin Plan could consider social and economic factors in giving effect to the international agreements through the Basin Plan.[146] They also felt that to amend the *Water Act* would lead to further confusion and uncertainty in Murray Darling Basin communities.[147] A dissenting report was also written by federal Greens Senator, Sarah Hanson-Young. That report stated that legal advice provided to the Inquiry was: '... clear that, given the reliance on the external affairs power as well as the stated objects of the Water Act, the Murray Darling Basin Authority (MDBA) and the Minister are required to give environmental considerations precedence in developing the Basin Plan'.[148] These contrasting views confirm that water resource management issues are inherently political and that it is not easy to separate the legal question from the political debate on appropriate governance in the Murray Darling Basin.

Heated debates in Canberra and in other Murray Darling Basin communities throughout 2010 and early 2011 led to resignations of key actors. The Chair of the

141 Ibid [4.9].
142 Ibid [4.10].
143 Ibid [4.12].
144 Ibid, ix.
145 Ibid, [1.3].
146 Ibid [1.16].
147 Ibid [1.21].
148 Ibid [1.16].

Murray Darling Basin Authority resigned, citing differences with the Government about the approach to the weight to be given to environmental, social and economic considerations.[149] The Chief Executive Officer of the Murray Darling Basin Authority also resigned a few months later.[150]

The *2010 Guide* was abandoned. Ultimately, in November 2011, the Murray Darling Basin Authority released a revised plan, *The Proposed Basin Plan* ('the 2011 Plan') for consultation. The 2011 Plan proposed a lower level of reductions on the amount of water, namely 2700 gigalitres per year, that can be diverted from the resources of the Murray Darling Basin.[151] While the 2011 Plan has been more palatable to some, but not all, irrigators, these changes do not alter any of the fundamental governance problems associated with the constitutional validity of the *Water Act* highlighted, for example, by the Senate Committee majority report. The 2011 Plan has been criticized by environmental groups, including Green Senators who have threatened to disallow the Basin Plan, if adopted in this form, when it is laid before the Commonwealth Parliament.[152] The South Australian Government responded to the 2011 Plan by threatening a legal challenge to the validity of the Basin Plan and media reports about the proposed legal challenge have referred to the possibility that South Australia may seek, once again, as it has done repeatedly since at least the late 1880s, to assert its riparian rights as part of its claims[153] though the reason for doing so is no longer to protect upstream navigation but to protect flows for downstream users generally.

In early February 2012 the Hon. Tony Windsor, an influential and independent Member of Parliament who headed the House of Representatives Standing Committee on Regional Australia's Inquiry, warned that the attitudes of community leaders in New South Wales and South Australia could lead to a failure to finalize the Basin Plan.[154] In August 2012, before being forwarded, as part of

149 Emma Rodgers, 'Murray-Darling boss resigns' *ABC News*, 7 December 2010 http://www.abc.net.au/news/2010-12-07/murray-darling-boss-resigns/2365224; Emma Rodgers, 'Basin plan "in crisis" as water boss quits' *ABC News*, 7 December 2010 http://www.abc.net.au/news/2010-12-07/basin-plan-in-crisis-as-water-boss-quits/2365614.

150 'Murray-Darling authority chief resigns' *ABC News*, 12 May 2011, http://www.abc.net.au/news/2011-05-12/murray-darling-authority-chief-resigns/2709160.

151 Murray Darling Basin Authority, above n 3, 24 and Schedule 2; See also Commonwealth of Australia, *Plain English summary of the Proposed Basin Plan – including explanatory notes* (Murray Darling Basin Authority, November 2011) 79–80.

152 http://www.theaustralian.com.au/national-affairs/climate/greens-threaten-to-pull-plug-on-murray-darling-basin-plan/story-e6frg6xf-1226208636022, 13 January 2012. For an overview on this process, see Gardner, A, 'An overview of the historical legal background to the "Proposed Basin Plan"' (2012) 29 Environmental and Planning Law Journal 263, 267.

153 Gardner, A, above n 152; Kelly, above n 29, 650.

154 Lanai Vasek, 'States could "kill" Murray Darling basin plan, warns Tony Windsor', *The Australian*, 6 February 2012 http://www.theaustralian.com.au/in-depth/murray-darling-crisis/states-could-kill-murray-darling-basin-plan-warns-tony-windsor/

the formal consultation process, to the relevant ministers in each jurisdiction, the 2011 Plan was amended again. The amendment, proposes a water recovery target of 2750 gigalites per year.[155] This amendment has done little to allay the concerns expressed in relation to the 2011 Plan. Deadlines for the development of the plan have again been extended,[156] and thus, it is not completely clear, at the time of writing, what form the final Basin Plan will take or whether the Basin Plan will be finalized at all. However, what is apparent is that striking an acceptable balance between competing State interests, and between the demands of irrigators and environmentalists, remains an enormous political challenge.

Where Does the Balance Lie for the Basin Plan?

The provisions relating to the regulation of the water resources of the Murray Darling Basin, contained in Part 2 of the *Water Act*, fall outside the scope of matters which were the subject of referral by all the required States to the Commonwealth.[157] This means that in this part of the *Water Act*, there is little room for manoeuvre as these provisions rely predominantly, if not exclusively, on the external affairs power. Accordingly, the primary purpose of the Basin Plan is to implement the aspects of international environmental agreements that are relevant to the management of the resources of the Murray Darling Basin. There is a direct link between these international agreements and the Basin Plan itself. Section 21(1) of the *Water Act* states that: 'The Basin Plan ... must be prepared so as to provide for giving effect to relevant international agreements (to the extent to which those agreements are relevant to the use and management of the Basin water resources.)' In this regard, section 21(2) and 21(3) provides further particulars, all of which are stated expressly to be interpreted as not limiting section 21(1). The Basin Plan must:

- be prepared having regard to the fact that the use of the Basin water resources has had, and is likely to have, significant adverse impacts on the conservation and sustainable use of biodiversity;[158]

---

story-e6frg6px-1226263611449; see also Greg Kelton, 'Premier Jay Weatherill to pressure federal MPs for action on River Murray plan', *The Advertiser*, 6 February 2012, http://www.adelaidenow.com.au/premier-jay-weatherill-to-pressure-federal-mps-for-action-on-river-murray-plan/story-e6frea6u-1226264143845.

155 Murray Darling Basin Authority, *Proposed Basin Plan Consultation Report*, http:// http://www.mdba.gov.au/proposed-basin-plan/consultation-report/.

156 Ken McGregor, 'States fail to meet consensus deadline on Murray-Darling Basin Plan, *The Advertiser, 27 August 2012* http://www.adelaidenow.com.au/news/south-australia/states-fail-to-meet-consensus-deadline-on-murray-darling-basin-plan/story-e6frea83-1226459348400.

157 *Water Act 2007* (Cth), section 9.

158 *Water Act 2007* (Cth), section 21(2)(a)(i).

- be prepared having regard to the fact that the Basin water resources require, as a result, special measures to manage their use to conserve biodiversity;[159]
- promote sustainable use of the Basin water resources to protect and restore the ecosystems, natural habitats and species that are reliant on the Basin water resources and to conserve biodiversity;[160]
- promote the wise use of all the Basin water resources;[161]
- promote the conservation of declared Ramsar wetlands in the Murray-Darling Basin;[162]
- take account of the ecological character descriptions of:
  - all declared Ramsar wetlands within the Murray-Darling Basin; and
  - all other key environmental sites within the Murray-Darling Basin.[163]

The provisions of section 21(4) require the Murray Darling Basin Authority and the Minister to take into account the principles of ecologically sustainable development and to have regard to various matters such as the consumptive and other economic uses of the Basin's water reserves, and to social, cultural, Indigenous and other public benefit issues. These provisions are all stated expressly to be subject to section 21(1), 21(2) and 21(3).[164] These factors are clearly, therefore, secondary to the primary obligation of the Basin Plan: to give effect to the various relevant international agreements.[165]

Commonwealth legislation based upon the external affairs power must be 'reasonably capable of being considered appropriate and adapted to implementing the treaty'.[166] Nevertheless, there is considerable discretion in the way the Commonwealth can implement an international obligation: it does not have to be implemented in full.[167] Indeed, the High Court has stated that the compromises associated with the negotiation and conclusion of international treaties mean that their terms can be expressed in 'indeterminate language [and are often] more aptly described as goals to be achieved, rather than rules to be obeyed'.[168] There is a potential, therefore, for there to be a discord between Australia's obligations under international law and Australian domestic law.

As the Australian Government Solicitor noted in its October 2010 legal opinion on the role of social and economic factors in the Basin Plan, it would be misguided

159 *Water Act 2007* (Cth), section 21(2)(a)(iii).

160 *Water Act 2007* (Cth), section 21(2)(b).

161 *Water Act 2007* (Cth), section 21(3)(a).

162 *Water Act 2007*(Cth), section 21(3)(b).

163 *Water Act 2007* (Cth), section 21(3)(c).

164 See *Water Act 2007* (Cth), section 21(4).

165 Kildea and Williams, above n 61, 12.

166 *Victoria v Commonwealth* (*Industrial Relations Act Case*) (1996) 187 CLR 416 at 34 per Brennan CJ, Toohey, Gaudron, McHugh and Gummow JJ.

167 Ibid.

168 *Project Blue Sky v Australian Broadcasting Authority* (1998) 194 CLR 355 at 392 per McHugh, Gummow Kirby and Hayne JJ.

to assume that the international agreements upon which the *Water Act* is based were 'concerned with "purely" environmental objectives as opposed to social and economic considerations'.[169] Indeed, the *Ramsar Convention*, for example, states that the inclusion of a wetland in the Ramsar Convention's List of Wetlands of International Importance does not prejudice the exclusive sovereign rights of the State in whose territory the wetland is situated.[170]

Nevertheless, it is incorrect to state that the *Water Act* provides that environmental, social and economic considerations are all to have equal weight in the Basin Plan.[171] Doing so obscures the primacy of the requirement of the Basin Plan to implement the international agreements. It may be more accurate to say, drawing on the language of section 3(c) of the *Water Act*, that in giving effect to the international agreements, the Basin Plan must promote the use and management of the Basin water resources in a way that *optimizes*, economic, social and environmental outcomes.[172]

As the Australian Government Solicitor has stated, the *Water Act* creates 'a discretionary choice'[173] between a number of options, adding: 'there is scope for consideration of how economic, social and environmental outcomes should be optimised'.[174] However, the first task is to implement the relevant international environmental agreements, noting the potential for there to be a difference between the obligations under public international and municipal law.

In this regard it is necessary to ask whether the pursuit of the goal of optimization of economic, social and environmental outcomes is in fact the goal contemplated by many of the international conventions upon which the *Water Act* is based. Ecologically sustainable development which is a fundamental principle of many of these conventions does not necessarily seek to optimize these outcomes, rather it seeks their integration into the environmental policy agenda.[175] Article 6(b) of the *Convention on Biological Diversity* is an example of this: it commits States, among other things, to: 'Integrate, as far as possible, and as appropriate, the conservation and sustainable use of biological diversity into relevant sectoral or cross-sectoral plans, programmes and policies'.[176]

---

169 AGS, The Role of Social and Economic Factors in the Basin Plan, Discussion [28].

170 *Ramsar Convention*, above n 68, art 2(3).

171 Kildea and Williams, above n 61, 13.

172 Ibid (emphasis added).

173 AGS, above n 169, Summary [4].

174 Ibid, Summary [5]; See also R Kelly, 'Getting the Balance Right: Why the Murray Darling Basin Plan can implement the "triple bottom line" approach' (2011) 10(3) *Canberra Law Review* 178.

175 Douglas Fisher, above n 22, 21; See also Stephen Dovers, 'Processes and Institutions for Resource and Environmental Management: Why and How to Analyse?' in Stephen Dovers and Su Wild River *Managing Australia's Environment* (The Federation Press, 2003) 3.

176 *The Convention on Biological Diversity*, above n 68, art 6(b).

It remains to be seen how the final version of the Basin Plan, should it be adopted, navigates its course through these complex requirements – both international and domestic. It is clear, however, that had all Murray Darling Basin jurisdictions referred a full range of powers to the Commonwealth, the federal government would have been able to regulate the resources of the Murray Darling Basin in a much more comprehensive, straightforward and unlimited way.[177]

Conclusion

Fisher has asserted that the efficacy of transboundary environmental governance structures depends on the fundamental principles that underlie them. This assertion applies to environmental governance in the Murray Darling Basin which, as this chapter described at its outset, is an extremely important feature of the Australian environment and economy and which is subjected to the jurisdiction of four Australian States, as well as the Australian Capital Territory and the Commonwealth of Australia.

This chapter has analysed the fundamental constitutional provisions that, since federation, have been the basis of environmental governance in the Murray Darling Basin. In particular, it has analysed the Commonwealth's reliance on two mechanisms, the external affairs power and cooperative federalism.

This chapter has traced the historical and legal roots of these two mechanisms. While the founders of the *Australian Constitution* gave little, if any, thought to the environment, they devoted a considerable amount of time to debating how and by whom the waters of the River Murray should be used and how such issues should be enshrined in the *Australian Constitution.* The result was a constitutional text that is silent about the environment, leaving its regulation in the domain of the States. The text also contains the compromise, section 100, which the High Court is yet fully to delineate. The complexities and uncertainties that attend section 100 have, in part, led to the use of cooperative federalism in the Murray Darling Basin.

Cooperative federalism is an abiding feature of Australian environmental governance generally and it has been a particularly crucial component of governance arrangements in the Murray Darling Basin for a century. An agreement on water sharing in the Murray Darling Basin was not reached until 1914, after decades of colonial disputes between New South Wales, Victoria and South Australia. Various amendments to that intergovernmental agreement and further policy developments were still unable to secure governance of the Murray Darling Basin in the national interest, to end the regulatory fragmentation of the resource, or to halt the over allocation of its water resources and the degradation of its environment. The Commonwealth Government came close to securing that aim with the enactment of the *Water Act*. The opportunity was not fully realized, however, as Victoria refused to refer to the Commonwealth the full range of powers

177 Kildea and Williams, above n 61, 12.

necessary for legislation that was most suited to the task. This refusal revealed the particular fragility of this governance arrangement.

The external affairs power has become a prominent source of environmental legislative power for the Commonwealth Parliament since the 1980s when the expansive limits of the power were determined by the High Court in the *Tasmanian Dam* case. The external affairs power offers a fundamental basis for constitutional validity to the *Water Act* as both the *Water Act* and the Basin Plan are required to give effect to a number of international agreements relating to the environment and natural resources of the Murray Darling Basin.

Without this link to those international agreements, the constitutional validity of at least Part 2 of the *Water Act* falls away. It is for this reason, therefore, that the question about whether the Basin Plan can treat economic, social and environmental considerations equally takes on a particularly crucial constitutional and governance dimension. This chapter has noted that while the constitutional framework within which the Murray Darling Basin Authority and the Minister must operate will not permit each factor to be given equal weight, the international conventions themselves do contain economic and social considerations. Social and economic considerations therefore do play a part in the discretion available to the Minister in finalizing the Basin Plan.

In some respects the *Water Act* is an example of modern water resource governance, drawing as it does on market-based approaches to water regulation to supplement the role of government. This chapter has argued, however, that in addition to the structural hurdles to comprehensive environmental governance in the Murray Darling Basin as a result of the structure of the Constitution and the federal distribution of powers, some of the more qualitative indicators of good environmental governance have been compromised in the development of the Basin Plan. As was evident in late 2010, Murray Darling Basin communities have not felt that they were given access to the full range of relevant information in order to properly participate in the consultation process. The uncertainties surrounding threatened legal challenges to the Basin Plan by States such as South Australia mean that an end to the process may not be in sight, if at all. Delays of this kind decrease the quality of the outcome. Recommendations such as those by the Senate Legal and Constitutional Affairs References Committee that the *Water Act* be amended in fundamental respects, including strengthening its constitutional and legal foundations, leave further room for doubt and uncertainty about the fundamentals and stability of the scheme upon which the livelihoods of many depend.

As noted, at the time of writing, the Basin Plan is yet to be finalized. There are questions about whether it will take the form of the 2011 Plan. Indeed there are doubts about whether it will be finalized at all. In the context of the Murray Darling Basin, therefore, it would appear that the management of the Murray Darling Basin's natural resources, subject as they are to a range of different concurrent and competing values, in the national interest is a goal that is still a long way off. This suggests that the participants in the process (including the

States) do not share a sense of common purpose about the goals and objectives of transboundary governance in the Murray Darling Basin. These goals and objectives remain clouded in States' rights arguments and advocacy for sectoral interests. The co-operation upon which transboundary governance hinges is lacking. The lack of clarity here about the goals and objects of transboundary governance in the Murray Darling Basin is reflected in the fact that the *Water Act* itself, given its constitutional limitations, has as its essential objective not the pursuit of environmental objectives per se but rather, due to constitutional necessity, the objective of implementing a number of international treaties.

The process has become a deeply political one. This has meant that the Commonwealth Government and the instruments of the *Water Act* have not been able to overcome the problem of distributed powers and resources that characterize water resource management in general, and the management of transboundary water resources in particular. It is now hoped that the market-based operations of the Commonwealth Environmental Water Holder will offer a way to transcend this problem.

The concept of sustainability lies at the heart of water resources governance; as long as the resources are used unsustainably, there cannot be good environmental governance. Fisher's pessimistic observation that it may well be impossible to create sound legal arrangements for effectively applying the concept of sustainability in certain situations may, in the case of the Murray Darling Basin, be warranted.

Chapter 3
Transboundary Environmental Governance, Collaboration and the Law: Empirical Insights from Water and Natural Resource Management in Inland Queensland, Australia

Cameron Holley*

Introduction

Biodiversity loss, climate change and diffuse pollution of freshwater and marine environments are some of the most pressing environmental problems facing the globe. Yet, the capacities of sovereign nation States and subnational States have proven largely inadequate for solving such complex environmental problems, whether they occur within a State's territorial boundaries, or partially beyond them.[1] As a result, numerous governance 'experiments' have emerged at both domestic and international levels, which seek to address these environmental challenges through new mechanisms that supplement, and in some cases supplant, conventional State centred regimes.[2] Rather, the aim of international and domestic

* This chapter is based on research partially funded by a UNSW Early Career Researcher Start Up Grant, Macquarie University CORE and New Staff Grants, the National Centre for Groundwater Research and Training, and an Australian Research Council Discovery Grant, through the ANU Regulatory Institutions Network. I am grateful for the comments of an anonymous reviewer and the editors of this book. Some elements of this chapter first appeared in Cameron Holley, 'Removing the Thorn from New Governance's Side: Examining the Emergence of Collaboration in Practice & the Roles for Law, Nested Institutions & Trust' (2010) 40(7) *Environmental Law Reporter* 10, 656; Cameron Holley, Neil Gunningham and Clifford Shearing, *New Environmental Governance* (Earthscan, 2011).

1 Bradley Karkkainen, 'Managing Transboundary Aquatic Ecosystems: Lessons from The Great Lakes' (2006) 19 *Pacific McGeorge Global Business and Development Law Journal* 209, 209–210.

2 Cameron Holley and Neil Gunningham, 'Natural Resources, New Governance and Legal Regulation: When Does Collaboration Work?' (2011) 24 *New Zealand Universities Law Review* 309, 309–310.

lawmakers is to manage complex environmental problems through new regional transboundary collaborations.[3]

These new approaches are commonly referred to as 'collaborative environmental governance' (CEG). The CEG literature does not derive from a single legal or governance theory but rather has a diversity of intellectual foundations, as can be illustrated by the different terms that have been used to describe it.[4] Prominent amongst these are 'experimentalism', 'new governance', 'transboundary environmental governance', 'post sovereign environmental governance', 'earth systems governance', 'soft law', 'modular regulation', 'collaborative ecosystem governance', 'multilevel governance' and 'regionalism'.[5] Although these ideas have diverse theoretical bloodlines, they share significant commonalities, including an emphasis on collaboration, integration, participation, place based management, and multilevel decision-making. Thus, while there is no single CEG model per se, the term collaborative environmental governance is increasingly used to refer to governance approaches that encompass some or all of these principles.[6]

CEG could equally be described as a 'polycentric' vision of governing, with decision-making involving the totality of interactions between public and private actors, and the State no longer necessarily playing the central role in decision-making.[7] For example, a variety of non-State actors may assume administrative, regulatory, managerial and mediating functions previously undertaken by sovereign nation States.[8]

Perhaps more importantly from the perspective of this chapter, the new CEG vision signifies a shift from a system of exclusive territorial sovereignty,

---

3 Orly Lobel, 'The Renew Deal: The Fall of Regulation and the Rise of Governance in Contemporary Legal Thought' (2004) 89 *Minnesota Law Review* 342, 343.

4 Holley and Gunningham, above n 2. David Hess, 'Social Reporting and New Governance Regulation: The Prospects of Achieving Corporate Accountability through Transparency' (2007) 17(3) *Business Ethics Quarterly* 453, 454.

5 For discussion and references see Bradley Karkkainen, '"New Governance" in Legal Thought and in the World: Some Splitting as Antidote to Overzealous Lumping' (2004) 89 *Minnesota Law Review* 471; Michael Lockwood et al, 'Governance Principles for Natural Resource Management' (2010) 23(10) *Society and Natural Resources* 986; Cameron Holley, 'Facilitating Monitoring, Subverting Self-Interest and Limiting Discretion: Learning from "New" Forms of Accountability in Practice' (2010) 35 *Columbia Journal of Environmental Law* 127; Frank Biermann et al, 'Earth System Governance: A Research Framework' (2010) 10(4) *International Environmental Agreements: Politics, Law and Economics* 277.

6 Karkkainen, above n 5, 473; Neil Walker, 'EU Constitutionalism and New Governance' in Gráinne De Búrca and Joanne Scott (eds), *Law and New Governance in the EU and the US* (Hart Publishing, 2006) 15, 22; Holley and Gunningham, above n 2.

7 Michael McGinnis (ed), *Polycentric Governance and Development* (University of Michigan Press, 1999).

8 Elinor Ostrom, 'Beyond Markets and States: Polycentric Governance of Complex Economic Systems' (2010) 100 *American Economic Review* 641, 643; Vincent Ostrom et al, 'The Organization of Government in Metropolitan Areas: A Theoretical Inquiry' (1961) 55(4) *American Political Science Review* 831.

characterized by politically defined jurisdictional boundaries, toward transboundary collaborative governance processes. In this chapter, the term 'transboundary' is used to refer to governance arrangements that cross administrative regions at all levels, not only across sovereign State boundaries.[9] Indeed, CEG itself creates and governs through new regional jurisdictions matched not to administrative or politically based jurisdictions, but to the spatial and temporal scales of natural ecological units, such as ecosystems, bioregions and catchments.[10] Such 'post-territorial' arrangements effectively decentre sovereign national and subnational arrangements by focusing environmental governance around new regional jurisdictions. These jurisdictions in turn encompass new transboundary coalitions between governments and institutions of civil society that are typically held together via guidelines, plans and non-binding agreements that seek to achieve effective joint management of shared ecological resources.[11]

Much of the focus in reshaping environmental governance from a unicentric to a polycentric approach has been on designing and implementing new systems of transboundary governance on the international stage.[12] Prominent CEG examples have included regional strategies and governance mechanisms that encourage cooperation between nation States and civil society stakeholders in terrestrial biodiversity management in transboundary protected areas in Asia and Africa,[13] collaborative regional efforts to protect various regional seas and lakes,[14] and collaboration under the Water Framework Directive in Europe.[15]

---

9 Xia Yu, 'Transboundary Water Pollution Management: Lessons Learned from River Basin Management in China, Europe and the Netherlands' (2011) 7(1) *Utrecht Law Review* 188, 189.

10 Karkkainen, above n 1.

11 Bradley Karkkainen, 'Post-Sovereign Environmental Governance' (2004) 4(1) *Global Environmental Politics* 72, 77.

12 Ibid; Ken Conca, *Governing Water* (MIT Press, 2006); Chukwumerije Okereke, Harriet Bulkeley and Heike Schroeder, 'Conceptualizing Climate Governance Beyond the International Regime' (2009) 9(1) *Global Environmental Politics* 58.

13 See e.g. Nathan Badenoch, *Transboundary Environmental Governance Principles and Practice in Mainland Southeast Asia* (World Resources Institute, 2002) 4–5; Ngendakumana Serge et al, *Transboundary Landscape Management to Improve Livelihoods and Biodiversity Conservation: Case of Guinea and Sierra Leone* (USAID, The World Agroforestry Centre and The Centre for International Forestry research, 2009) http://www.worldagroforestry.org/downloads/publications/PDFs/RP16486.PDF.

14 See e.g. Baltic Sea Helsinki Commission http://www.helcom.fi/helcom/en_GB/aboutus; Bradley C Karkkainen, 'Collaborative Ecosystem Governance: Scale, Complexity, and Dynamism' (2002) 21 *Virginia Environmental Law Journal* 189, 192. Karkkainen, above n 1.

15 Andrea M Keessen, Jasper van Kempen and Helena van Rijswick, 'Transboundary River Basin Management in Europe Legal Instruments to Comply with European Water Management Obligations in Case of Transboundary Water Pollution and Floods' (2008) 4(3) *Utrecht Law Review* 35; David Trubek and Louise Trubek, 'New Governance and Legal Regulation' (2006) 13 *Columbia Journal of European Law* 540, 541.

But there has also been increasing interest in comparable domestic CEG initiatives that have emerged in response to a host of threats that human action has caused primarily at the regional or local, rather than the international level: challenges, such as diffuse water pollution of large rivers and aquatic ecosystems in the United States, China and Europe, as well as a loss of terrestrial habitat and biodiversity connectivity within various nations across the globe.[16] Such problems do not respect traditional domestic boundaries, any more than they do international ones. As a result, the governance response is frequently of a transboundary character,[17] and necessitates the kind of multistakeholder, regional collaborative focus typical of CEG.

It is within this context, and with an interest in promoting effective collaborative environmental governance for transboundary environmental problems that this chapter is situated. To date, the CEG literature has tended to focus more on theory than practice.[18] The limited empirical research has primarily focused on emerging experiments in Europe and the United States.[19] It is, however, in the Federal State of Australia, that some of the most interesting CEG experiments can be found and where empirical study can provide substantial insights for lawyers and policymakers.

Under international law, the Federal Australian government has responsibilities for meeting international environmental obligations under treaties. However, as a matter of Australian constitutional law, subnational State governments could equally be considered sovereign or quasi-sovereign entities, as the Federal government is understood to have limited, enumerated powers with respect to the environment.[20] In both theory and practice, some environmental matters fall within the exclusive competence of the States, while other responsibilities are exclusive

16 Yu, above n 9; Alejandro E Camacho, 'Can Regulation Evolve? Lessons from a Study in Maladaptive Management' (2007) 55 *UCLA Law Review* 293; Bradley Karkkainen, 'Toward Ecologically Sustainable Democracy?' in Archon Fung and Erik Olin Wright (eds), *Deepening Democracy* (Verso, 2003); Karkkainen, n 11.

17 Jón Geir Pétursson1, Pål Vedeld and John Kaboggoza, *Transboundary Biodiversity Management Challenges: Case Of Mt. Elgon In Uganda And Kenya* http://www.landbunadur.is/landbunadur/wgsamvef.nsf/0/a3a279aa3fd7b53900257102005467cb/$FILE/83.pdf.

18 Biermann et al, above n 5; Karkkainen, above n 1, 212.

19 See e.g. Susan Baker and Katarina Eckerberg (eds), *In Pursuit of Sustainable Development: New Governance Practices at the Sub-national Level in Europe* (Routledge, 2008); Tanya Heikkila and Andrea Gerlak, 'The Formation of Large-scale Collaborative Resource Management Institutions: Clarifying the Roles of Stakeholders, Science, and Institutions' (2005) 33(4) *Policy Studies Journal* 583, 586; Paul Sabatier et al, *Swimming Upstream: Collaborative Approaches to Watershed Management* (MIT Press, 2005).

20 For further on the interplay between international environmental law and domestic Australian law see Cameron Holley, 'International Environmental Law and Australia and New Zealand' in Shawkat Alam, Jahid Hossain Bhuiyan, Tareq MR Chowdhury and Erika J Techera (eds), *Routledge Handbook of International Environmental Law* (Routledge, 2012). Karkkainen, above n 11, 85–86.

to the Federal government (or broadly shared with the States, with the federal role paramount in the event of conflict).[21] Given this 'dual sovereign' role of the States, the legal and policy attempts of Australian Federal and State governments to manage shared environmental resources provides a ripe context for exploring new CEG models for managing transboundary environmental problems.[22]

This chapter focuses on one of the most far-reaching CEG approaches in Australia's history, which is known as Regional Natural Resource Management (NRM). This program contributes in part to Australia's delivery of its obligations under the Convention on Biological Diversity,[23] and to the management of Word Heritage sites such as the Great Barrier Reef.[24] In practice, Regional NRM has involved billions of Australian dollars being invested in 'partnerships' between Federal, State, and local governments, regional communities, farmers, and industry bodies in an attempt to regionally manage natural resource problems.[25] Inherent to this Regional NRM approach is an aspiration for Federal and State governments to willingly surrender and recombine crucial elements of their traditional sovereign powers to forge a new problem-solving hybrid arrangement. This arrangement also seeks to embrace other non-State actors as active partners in the environmental governance process, at an ecologically defined scale that seeks to decentre and in some cases supersede conventional territorially defined jurisdictional boundaries.[26] Drawing on 57 interviews from two Queensland Regional NRM case studies, the chapter draws lessons from their achievements and shortcomings in living up to this aspiration and sheds light on two crucial and under researched issues in the CEG literature.

The first is concerned with the fundamental issue of collaboration. It is essential for good transboundary governance that all parties collaborate, and that they do so

---

21 Karkkainen, above n 11, 85–86.

22 Other emerging Australian CEG experiments not discussed in this paper include the Murray Darling Basin, on which see Daniel Connell and R Quentin Grafton, *Basin Futures: Water Reform in the Murray-Darling Basin* (ANU E-Press, 2011). Karkkainen, above n 11, 85–86; and Grigg, Chapter one.

23 *Convention on Biological Diversity*, opened for signature 5 June 1992, 1760 UNTS 79, 31 ILM 818 (entered into force 29 December 1993). Natural Resource Management Ministerial Council, *Australia's Biodiversity Conservation Strategy 2010–2030* (Australian Government, 2010).

24 *Convention for the Protection of the World Cultural and Natural Heritage (Paris)*, opened for signature 16 November 1972, 1037 UNTS 151 (entered into force 17 December 1975). State of Queensland (Department of the Premier and Cabinet), *Reef Water Quality Protection Plan 2009* (RWQPP Secretariat, 2009).

25 Marcus Lane, Bruce Taylor and Cathy Robinson, 'Introduction: Contested Country – Regional Natural Resource Management in Australia' in M Lane, C Robinson and B Taylor (eds), *Contested Country* (CSIRO, 2009) 1.

26 Karkkainen, above n 11, 86; Brian Head, 'Assessing Network-Based Collaborations' (2008) 10(6) *Public Management Review* 733; Richard Margerum, 'A Typology of Collaboration Efforts in Environmental Management' (2008) 41(4) *Environmental Management* 487.

in a genuine way.[27] The analysis explores how to imagine and promote effective transboundary coalitions at different scales and reveals a number of practical and policy insights with regard to a range of under-examined issues including: the roles and forms of government intervention and institutional design conditions that might best overcome transaction costs (that is, the personal time, resources, and travel expenses associated with participating in the interactive process) to produce a successful collaborative processes;[28] and when and under what conditions collaborations are likely to deliver effective environmental outcomes.[29]

The chapter also evaluates an issue that has been the subject of vigorous debate by legal scholars at both an applied and theoretical level, namely whether, to what extent, and in what ways to blend polycentric elements with State-centric governance understandings and practices so as to better govern human impacts on the environment.

This is a significant issue because the gradual move to CEG has not resulted in the unicentric vision of State control being relinquished, but rather in the development of approaches that seek to relate these two governance ideals in a variety of ways. Of particular concern at both a domestic and international level has been the specific relationship between traditional 'hard' legal rules and 'softer', often non-binding, collaborative approaches to governance. In this context, the chapter evaluates the so called 'gap' thesis, a hypothesized relationship between conventional legal regulation and collaborative governance, which is thought to be detrimental to achieving effective CEG, and is somewhat lacking in rigorous empirical exploration and validation.[30]

The analysis proceeds in five sections. The first section introduces CEG theory and its defining collaborative features. The next outlines the Regional

---

27 Keessen et al, above n 15, 55.

28 Eric Orts and Cary Coglianese, 'Collaborative Environmental Law: Pro and Con, Debate' (2007) 156 *University of Pennsylvania Law Review* 289, 302–303, 309; K Floress et al, 'Constraints to Watershed Planning: Group Structure and Process' (2009) 45(6) *JAWRA* 1352, 1352–1353; Carole Menkel-Meadow, 'Getting to "Let's Talk": Comments on Collaborative Environmental Dispute Resolution Processes' (2008) 8 *Nevada Law Journal* 835, 850.

29 Annecoos Wiersema, 'A Train without Tracks: Rethinking The Place Of Law And Goals In Environmental And Natural Resources Law' (2008) 38 *Environmental Law* 1239, 1243–44; Thomas M Koontz and Craig W Thomas, 'What Do We Know and Need to Know about the Environmental Outcomes of Collaborative Management' (2006) 66 *Public Administration Review* 111, 113–14.

30 Joanne Scott and David Trubek, 'Mind the Gap: Law and New Approaches to Governance in the European Union' (2002) 8 *European Law Journal* 1; Gráinne De Búrca and Joanne Scott, 'Introduction: New Governance, Law and Constitutionalism' in Gráinne De Búrca and Joanne Scott (eds), *Law and New Governance in the EU and the US* (Hart Publishing, 2006) 1, 4; Michael Wilkinson, 'Three Conceptions Of Law: Towards A Jurisprudence Of Democratic Experimentalism' (2010) *Wisconsin Law Review* 673; Holley and Gunningham, above n 2.

NRM program, followed by an examination of the two case studies to identify the conditions under which CEG was able to achieve successful collaborative approaches to manage transboundary environmental problems. The final section explores these conditions and provides recommendations for policy and theory regarding the conditions under which successful collaboration is likely to be achieved in practice. These lessons are grouped under four principal themes: the severity of environmental problems; trust, incentives; and structures for subsidising transaction costs. The section also offers important insights for CEG theory and practice regarding the relationship between traditional legal rules and new forms of collaborative governance.

CEG Theory, Collaboration and Legal Regulation

There are various bodies of work on 'collaboration', which makes it important to explain how the term is used in this chapter.[31] At the core of CEG collaborations are 'consensus' processes, which seek to move towards some level of agreement among parties.[32] For present purposes it can be defined broadly as a process where two or more stakeholders agree to share power and pool knowledge, and/or tangible resources (e.g. information, money, labour) to reach agreement and solve a set of shared problems.[33]

Proponents of CEG have claimed that such forms of collaboration are capable of (1) reducing conflict and increasing cooperation; (2) enhancing democracy and civic engagement; and (3) contributing to a rich understanding of and capacity to solve 'wicked' transboundary problems.[34]

Notwithstanding this enthusiasm, there is no shortage of concerns and questions regarding CEG's collaborative approach. Some, for example, argue that collaborative efforts, which inevitably involve many different government and non-government parties, will come up against extensive transaction costs, and

31 Robert Axelrod, *The Evolution of Cooperation* (Basic Books, 1984); Robert Putnam, Robert Leonardi and Raffaella Nanetti, *Making Democracy Work: Civic Traditions in Modern Italy* (Princeton UP, 1993); RAW Rhodes, 'Understanding Governance: Ten Years On' (2007) 28 *Organization Studies* 12431; Holley and Gunningham, above n 2.

32 Karkkainen, above n 14, 240; Holley and Gunningham, above n 2.

33 Barbara Gray, *Collaborating: Finding Common Ground for Multiparty Problems* (Jossey-Bass, 1989) 10; Brian Head, 'Participation or Co-Governance? Challenges for Regional Natural Resource Management' in R Eversole and J Martin (eds), *Participation and Governance in Regional Development* (Ashgate, 2005) 137, 146.

34 Alejandro Camacho, 'Beyond Conjecture: Learning about Ecosystem Management from the Glen Canyon Dam Experiment' (2008) 8 *Nevada Law Journal* 942, 961; Karkkainen, above n 1, 212, 228–229; Julia Wondolleck and Steven Yaffee, *Making Collaboration Work: Lessons From Innovation in Natural Resource Management* (Island Press, 2000) 23–41; Holley and Gunningham, above n 2.

other well-known 'cooperation dilemmas' that may be intractable in practice.[35] An associated problem here is volunteer fatigue, as CEG collaborations depend heavily on ongoing engagement from non-government organizations (NGOs) and community volunteers to maintain successful collaboration.[36]

Yet, despite these challenges, a diversity of legal and political science literatures have suggested that such cooperation dilemmas may be overplayed and that more sanguine possibilities for cooperation exist under certain conditions.[37] For example, alternative dispute resolution approaches claim that successful collaborative agreements are more likely to occur and be implemented where, *inter alia*, trust is built between parties and a process of negotiation, facilitated by a neutral party, is followed to reach consensus outcomes.[38]

Elinor Ostrom's research on sustainable co-management of common pool resources has likewise identified a range of conditions (such as trust, severe environmental problems, and autonomy from external authorities) associated with an increased likelihood of successful collaboration in common pool resource contexts.[39]

In addition to the work of Ostrom and others on collaboration, a range of conditions have been suggested in the CEG literature as necessary or desirable for successful collaboration. For example, some CEG authors suggest nested collaborative structures (that is, developing institutions at different scales/levels) may be used to overcome transaction costs.[40] Examples of such approaches can be

35 See, for example, Orts and Coglianese, above n 28, 298; Wondolleck and Yaffee, above n 34, 48–49. For further see Garrett Hardin, 'Tragedy of the Commons' (1968) 162 (3859) *Science* 1243, 1244; Mancur Olson, *The Logic of Collective Action Public Goods and the Theory of Groups* (Harvard UP, 1965).

36 Archon Fung and Erik Olin Wright, 'Thinking about Empowered Participatory Governance' in Archon Fung and Erik Olin Wright (eds), *Deepening Democracy* (Verso, 2003) 3, 38; Rena I Steinzor, 'The Corruption of Civic Environmentalism' (2000) 30(10) *Environmental Law Reporter* 909.

37 Donald Hornstein, 'Complexity Theory, Adaptation, and Administrative Law' (2005) 54 *Duke Law Journal* 913, 951–952; Karkkainen, above n 14, 226–233.

38 Lawrence Susskind, Alejandro E Camacho, and Todd Schenk, 'Collaborative Planning and Adaptive Management in Glen Canyon: A Cautionary Tale' (2010) 35(1) *Columbia Journal of Environmental Law* 1, 37–43; Rosemary O'Leary, Tina Nabatchi and Lisa B Bingham, 'Environmental Conflict Resolution' in Robert F Durant, Daniel J Fiorino and Rosemary O'Leary (eds), *Environmental Governance Reconsidered* (MIT Press, 2004) 338; Holley and Gunningham, above n 2.

39 Elinor Ostrom, *Governing the Commons: The Evolution of Institutions for Collective Action* (Cambridge UP, 1990); Elinor Ostrom, 'The Danger of Self Evident Truths' (2000) 33(1) *Political Science and Politics* 33, 39–40.

40 DeWitt, John, 'Civic Environmentalism' in Robert F Durant, Daniel J Fiorino and Rosemary O'Leary (eds), *Environmental Governance Reconsidered* (MIT Press, 2004) 219, 236–37; Karkkainen, above n 1, 221, 235–36; Richard Margerum, 'Overcoming Locally Based Collaboration Constraints' (2007) 20 *Society and Natural Resources* 135, 144–46; Ostrom, above n 39.

found in a variety of transboundary CEG experiments at domestic and international levels, such as the Chesapeake Bay and Great Lakes programs. These programs commonly involve basin- or ecosystem-wide institutions (e.g., a multi-agency collaborative body) that addresses system-wide problems and coordinates efforts across the ecosystem as a whole, while other levels of more localized institutional arrangements manage locally varying conditions (e.g., government and non-government partnerships managing specific tributaries).[41]

Such nested arrangements are claimed to be effective both where geographic scale is larger (by allowing multi-party collaborative organizations to divide a region into smaller areas and thus reduce the costs and time associated with collaborating across the whole region),[42] and at more local levels (allowing local groups to operate at regional scales to share information and interact with higher level agencies in a more structured single forum rather than in an ad hoc, once off manner).[43]

While this nested approach is thought to have the potential to reduce transaction costs greatly, on the other hand, a nested model, with its many levels, necessarily involves greater total costs in cooperating than collaboration at a single local level.[44] Indeed, various parts of this structure may impose additional challenges, such as achieving power sharing between agencies/governments at higher regional-ecosystem, national or international scales.[45] Different governments and agencies are notoriously unwilling to share authority and funds and if their cooperation is not forthcoming the consequences may be devastating for lower levels that depend on government for guidance and support.[46] How much conflict and cooperation is actually evident between different agencies and levels of government in CEG accordingly remains an important focus for research.[47]

Beyond nested institutions, some CEG authors suggest that the existence of external and institutional triggers can open the way to successful collaboration.

---

41 Karkkainen, above n 1, 235.

42 Joseph E Bonnell and Tomas M Koontz, 'Stumbling Forward: The Organizational Challenges of Building and Sustaining Collaborative Watershed Management' (2007) 20 *Society & Natural Resources* 153, 161, 163; Graham R Marshall, 'Can Community-based NRM Work at the Scale of Larger Regions? Exploring the Roles of Nesting and Subsidiarity' in M Lane, C Robinson and B Taylor (eds), *Contested Country* (CSIRO, 2009) 50–54.

43 Margerum, above n 40, 144–146.

44 Ibid.

45 Bonnell and Koontz, above n 42, 161, 163; Marcus Lane, *Critical issues in Regional Natural Resources Management* (prepared for the Australian State of the Environment Committee, 2006) 5–6.

46 Sarah Ewing, 'Catchment Management Arrangements' in Stephen Dovers and Su Wild River (eds), *Managing Australia's Environment* (Federation Press, 2003) 405, 406; Megan Farrelly, 'Regionalisation of Environmental Management: A Case Study of the Natural Heritage Trust, South Australia' (2005) 43 *Geographical Research* 393, 400; Margerum, above n 40, 144–146, 149.

47 Head, above n 33, 145.

These include economic and regulatory incentives (e.g., the shadow of the law) or the existence of severe environmental problems (especially the perception of a crisis) that can bring parties to the 'collaborative table'.[48] Others emphasize the need for a strong governmental role, including the use of funding and/or in kind assistance to offset transaction costs.[49]

Another pressing but under-researched issue concerns the extent to which conventional legal rules facilitate (as opposed to frustrate) new forms of collaborative governance in practice. This issue has attracted theoretical attention as part of debates concerned with the relation of collaborative forms of governance and traditional 'hard' law.[50] In this context (although a range of configurations between law and CEG systems are also being explored) one of the more challenging for collaborative governance is the gap thesis.[51]

The gap thesis argues that conventional legal regulation remains blind to the practice and presences of CEG, effectively ignoring, resisting and even impeding developments which do not conform to the traditional legal and regulatory structures of State centred domestic or international law. This resistance, it is argued, arises because the 'softness' and multiparty nature of collaborative governance lacks the legitimacy mechanisms that the statist institutional legacy is able to provide (i.e., centralized lawmaking bodies that are representative, democratically accountable, and subject to a hierarchical rule of law).[52]

For present purposes, what is significant about the gap hypothesis is that the blindness of conventional legal rules to CEG may in fact serve to curtail and inhibit the success of CEG approaches by maligning and downplaying cooperative efforts, as well as sidelining or at worst overriding their outputs and functions. Certainty scholars in Europe and elsewhere have identified such problems in the context of employment law, where the EU Constitution has served to impede rather than to foster the emergence of transnational civil society governance.[53]

Given the obstacles that 'the gap' thesis may pose to achieving effective CEG, there is considerable merit in further exploring the conditions where such gaps arise in practice and how they may be avoided.[54] The gap thesis, the challenge of achieving successful collaboration and when and whether CEG is a viable

48 Menkel-Meadow, above n 28. Holley and Gunningham, above n 2.

49 Lane, above n 45, 4–5. Floress et al, above n 28.

50 Trubek and Trubek, above n 15, 543; Lisa Alexander 'Stakeholder Participation in New Governance: Lessons from Chicago's Public Housing Reform Experiment' (2009) 16 *Georgetown Journal on Poverty Law and Policy* 117, 178–184.

51 Wilkinson, above n 30; Trubek and Trubek above n 15; De Búrca and Scott, above n 30, 4–9; Holley and Gunningham, above n 2.

52 Wilkinson, above n 30, 692–693.

53 De Búrca and Scott, above n 30. Wilkinson, above n 30.

54 Jason Solomon, 'Law and Governance in the 21st Century Regulatory State' (2008) 86(4) *Texas Law Review* 819, 833–834; Trubek and Trubek, above n 15, 539, 558, 564; De Búrca and Scott, above n 30, 4–9.

and credible approach to governing transboundary water and natural resources problems will each be addressed in the following sections.

Collaboration in a CEG Policy Context – Regional NRM

Before examining the experience of the case studies, it is necessary to understand the CEG policy context within which they operate.

Background on Regional NRM Arrangements

The evolution of Regional NRM has been considered in detail elsewhere and so can be succinctly described here.[55] Its antecedents emerged during the late 1980s and 1990s and included the National Landcare Program, State based Integrated Catchment Management programs[56] and the Federal government's competitive grants scheme known as the Natural Heritage Trust.[57] Despite some successes, numerous reviews pointed to substantial shortcomings with these respective endeavours.[58]

In response, the Federal government developed a more 'strategic' approach to NRM between 2000 and 2008.[59] The Regional NRM program was premised on the assumption that a CEG approach is better suited to governing complex, severe and increasingly urgent transboundary natural resource problems than more traditional regulatory approaches, because CEG can better deal with 'the differing and cascading responsibilities for natural resource management: from the national level, to the State and territory and local government levels, to regional, catchment, local and property levels'.[60] As one policy document described the collaborative nature of the Regional NRM approach: 'the active involvement and participation of rural and regional communities is the cornerstone of this Plan … we seek to

55 Cameron Holley and Darren Sinclair, 'Collaborative Governance and Adaptive Management: (Mis)Applications to Groundwater, Salinity and Run-Off' (2011) 14(1) *Australasian Journal of Natural Resources Law and Policy* 37.

56 Allan Curtis, 'The Landcare Experience' in Dovers and Wild River, above n 46, 442; Ewing, above n 46.

57 *Natural Heritage Trust Act 1997* (Cth); Kate Crowley, 'Effective Environmental Federalism? Australia's Natural Heritage Trust' (2001) 3 *Journal of Environmental Policy & Planning* 255.

58 ANAO, Commonwealth Natural Resource Management and Environment Programs (Australian Government, Canberra, Audit Report No. 36, 1996–97); ANAO, Performance Information for Commonwealth Financial Assistance under the Natural Heritage Trust (Australian Government, Canberra, Audit Report No. 43, 2000–01).

59 National Natural Resource Management Taskforce (NNRMTF), *Managing Natural Resources in Rural Australia for a Sustainable Future* (DAFF, Canberra, 1999). Holley and Sinclair, above n 55.

60 Ibid, 27.

enable communities to take responsibility for planning and implementing natural resource management strategies, in partnership with all levels of government, that meet their priorities for sustainable development and ongoing viability'.[61]

This approach was rolled out via two key programs: the National Action Plan for Salinity and Water Quality (NAP) in 2000/2001, followed by a revised second phase of the Natural Heritage Trust program (NHT2) in 2001/2002.[62] A primary emphasis of these programs was regional 'place based' NRM solutions,[63] linked to nationally agreed goals, including preventing, stabilizing and reversing salinity; improving water quality for human use and the environment; biodiversity conservation and sustainable use of natural resources.[64] Regional NRM arrangements were subject to individually negotiated Bilateral Agreements between the Federal government and the States/Territories, with some supported by State level legislation, with the remainder taking a non-statutory path (which include the Queensland cases that are the subject of this chapter).[65] Under these arrangements, almost $3 billion of investment was delivered via 56 community/stakeholder regional bodies (14 of which were in Queensland).

Although there is no single form that a regional organization must take, in Queensland they were required to meet several criteria so as to be 'designated' as regional bodies – these included incorporation as a not for profit body, having community members constitute a majority of the body, and appropriate stakeholder representation (including both indigenous groups and local government).[66] Once established, the body, in consultation with the regional 'community', was responsible for developing and implementing a consensus-based non-statutory plan and an investment strategy. The former sets targets and actions to improve

61 Commonwealth of Australia and State of Queensland, *An Agreement between the Commonwealth of Australia and the State of Queensland for the Implementation of the Intergovernmental Agreement on a National Action Plan for Salinity and Water Quality* (2001) ('Queensland NAP Bilateral') 2; Commonwealth of Australia and the State of Queensland, *Bilateral Agreement between the Commonwealth of Australia and the State of Queensland to Deliver the Natural Heritage Trust* (2004) ('Queensland NHT2 Bilateral') cls 1, 13 Attachment E, 57, 62.

62 Commonwealth of Australia, *Our Vital Resources: A National Action Plan for Salinity and Water Quality* (Council of Australian Governments, 2000). Natural Resource Management Ministerial Council (NRMMC), *Framework for the Extension of the Natural Heritage Trust* (NRMMC, 2002).

63 Natural Heritage Trust investment also occurred at national/State and local levels. NRMMC, above n 62.

64 Ibid; Cwth, NSW, Vic, Qld, WA, SA, Tas, NT, and ACT, *Intergovernmental Agreement on a National Action Plan for Salinity and Water Quality* (Australian Government, Canberra, 2001) cl 5.

65 L Robins and S Dovers, 'Community-based NRM Boards of Management: Are they Up to the Task?' (2007) 14 *Australasian Journal of Environmental Management* 111, 113; Holley and Sinclair, above n 55.

66 *Queensland NHT2 Bilateral,* above n 61, cl 68(b); *Queensland NAP Bilateral,* above n 61, cl 7.1(b).

natural resources, while the latter provides a prospectus of government financial support required to support this agenda.[67]

By June 2007, over half of the administered funds allocated to NHT2 and NAP had been spent through the 56 Regional NRM bodies across Australia.[68] However, following audits, various national evaluations,[69] and a change of political leadership at the Federal level, the delivery of NHT2, NAP and other Federal NRM programs was integrated into a new program known as Caring for our Country in 2008. Approximately $2 billion was invested over five years and it was designed to be an integrated package that achieved an overarching goal of a healthy and better protected environment.[70] It focused on six national priorities (e.g. building Australia's National Reserve System; biodiversity and natural icons; coastal environments and critical aquatic habitats; sustainable farm practices) and proposed to improve Regional NRM accountability via a new centralized and competitive grant system[71] based around 24 outcomes for each of the national priorities.[72] Importantly, Caring for our Country continues an emphasis on partnerships between the Federal Government and both States and Territories (under transitional arrangements)[73] and regional bodies. The latter in particular, is expected to 'play a central role in delivering Caring for our Country at the regional scale'.[74]

---

67 *Queensland NHT2 Bilateral,* above n 61, cls 87 and 93; *Queensland NAP Bilateral,* above n 61, cl 13.1.

68 ANAO, Regional Delivery Model for the Natural Heritage Trust and the National Action Plan for Salinity and Water Quality (Australian Government, Canberra, Audit Report No. 21, 2007–08), 14, 19.

69 Ibid; ANAO, *The Administration of the National Action Plan for Salinity and Water Quality* (Australian Government, Canberra, Audit Report No. 17, 2004–05). For national evaluations see Commonwealth Government, *Publications and Resources* http://nrm.gov.au/publications/index.html.

70 For an overview see L Robins and P Kanowski, '"Crying for our Country": Eight Ways in Which "Caring for our Country" has Undermined Australia's Regional Model for Natural Resource Management' (2011) 18(2) *Australasian Journal of Environmental Management* 88.

71 In its most significant departure from NHT2 and NAP, Caring for Our Country established a new competitive grant system to increase opportunities for NGOs, as well as regional bodies, local, State, Territory and Commonwealth government agencies, to access a greater proportion of its funds to achieve the national priorities.

72 Commonwealth of Australia, *Caring for our Country Outcomes* (Australian Government, 2010).

73 Commonwealth of Australia and the State of Queensland (Qld), *Transitional Arrangement and Financial Agreement between the Australian Government and the State of Queensland for Implementation of Caring for our Country* (Australian Government, Canberra 2008) cls 5.2(d), 5.2(e).

74 Commonwealth of Australia, *Caring for our Country Business Plan 2010–11* (Australian Government, 2010) 12–16; Commonwealth of Australia and the State of Queensland (Qld), *Transitional Arrangement and Financial Agreement between the*

Fostering Collaborative Environmental Governance: The Design of Regional NRM

Although aspiring to wide-ranging collaboration, Regional NRM was likely to face problems of free riding, fear of future defection, and high transaction costs in practice.[75] Nevertheless, while potentially fatal, these challenges can often be overcome or at the very least, mitigated.[76] Designers and program implementers, aware of these potholes on the road to collaboration, sought to develop mechanisms that would avoid or minimize them.

Mechanisms 1 and 2 Funding and Incentives A central concern of the Regional NRM program was to design relevant incentives to bring parties to the table. In contrast to many prominent CEG initiatives,[77] Regional NRM in Queensland relies solely on positive economic incentives as opposed to 'negative' inducements such as legal regulation and the shadow of the law. It does this by offering access to significant pots of government funding, which may act as an important inducement for interested actors to collaborate on regional bodies and through this mechanism, advance their natural resource management initiatives. Further, the regional bodies are expected to liaise, engage, work with and oversee timely implementation of government funded projects by other regional stakeholders (such as farmers or NGOs in the region).[78] The Regional NRM program may succeed in such broader collaboration because access to and use of government funding is likely to act as a key benefit in return for the time and costs of otherwise reluctant collaborators' efforts.[79]

Australian Government and the State of Queensland for Implementation of Caring for our Country (Australian Government, Canberra, 2008) cls 7.1, 7.4.

75 Leigh Raymond, 'Cooperation without Trust: Overcoming Collective Action Barriers to Endangered Species Protection' (2006) 34 *Policy Studies Journal* 37, 39; Heikkila and Gerlak, above n 19, 583–584.

76 Gary Libecap, *Contracting for Property Rights* (Cambridge UP, 1994); Axelrod, above n 31.

77 See Cameron Holley and Neil Gunningham, 'Environment Improvement Plans: Facilitative Regulation in Practice' (2006) 23 *Environmental and Planning Law Journal* 448; Bradley Karkkainen, 'Information – Forcing Regulation and Environmental Governance' in Gráinne De Búrca and Joanne Scott (eds), *Law and New Governance in the EU and the US* (Hart Publishing, 2006) 293.

78 Depending on the arrangements developed by a given regional community, the body's relationships with these lower level implementers may take on a number of different forms. For example, some may involve close collaboration between regional bodies and 'sub regional' groups, while others may involve a service provider style of relationship where projects are sub-contracted out by the body to individuals. Other bodies may employ a mix of these or other strategies. Despite such variation, all these relationships are central to the success of Regional NRM in the long term and for the purposes of this discussion they are all considered to fall under Regional NRM's broad idea of 'cooperative partnerships'; *Queensland NHT2 Bilateral*, above n 61, Attachment E, 62–63.

79 Sabatier et al, above n 19, 184.

Regional NRM also utilizes its substantial funds to offset transaction costs and offer support to volunteer collaborators,[80] to assist them in meeting the costs of their consultative obligations.[81] The support provided for in the Regional NRM program included:

- a rebate (e.g. $1000 to $5000 per annum) for volunteer collaborators on the regional body (covering costs, such as time and travel);
- 'foundational' and 'priority' funding to support the process of establishing regional bodies, and consultation to involve stakeholders in plan development under NHT2/NAP;[82] and
- base-level funding for regional organizations' core operations (e.g. employing staff and paying rent) during NHT2/NAP and Caring for Our Country.[83]

Mechanism 3 – Nested Design As with many transboundary arrangements internationally, the scale, complexity and number of responsible stakeholders involved in managing natural resource problems led Regional NRM to be administered through a nested model of collaboration which was thought to reduce transaction costs. At the national level, the overarching body was the Natural Resource Management Ministerial Council comprised of Federal and State representatives.[84] At the Queensland State level, a number of key multiagency organizations were formed to: (i) oversee implementation of regional and State arrangements in Queensland;[85] (ii) foster strong community–government

---

80 John, above n 40, 230–242; Jody Freeman and Daniel A Farber, 'Modular Environmental Regulation' (2005) 54 *Duke Law Journal* 795, 890.

81 *Queensland NHT2 Bilateral*, above n 61, cl 80-93; *Queensland NAP Bilateral*, above n 61, cl 12.7.

82 *Queensland NHT2 Bilateral*, above n 61, cl 95; *Queensland NAP Bilateral*, above n 61, cl 9.24. Farrelly, above n 46, 396. In-kind support can also be provided by government officers.

83 Burdekin Dry Tropics Natural Resource Management (BDTNRM), *Regional Investment Strategy* (BDTNRM, 2005) 8–9, 57. Under Caring for Our Country, regional bodies continued to receive a secure, albeit reduced share of funding to that received under NTH2/NAP, with the shortfall arguably recouped through the new competitive grant system. Regions also received funding to assist in adjusting to the new arrangements. Commonwealth of Australia, above n 74.

84 Although the responsibilities of the Natural Resource Management Ministerial Council (NRMMC) were recently withdrawn amidst national environmental reforms, this body had comprised the Commonwealth and State ministers and oversaw the development and implementation of national natural resource management programs, including regional NRM. In addition to the NRMMC, a Ministerial Board had responsibility for administering the regional NRM funding account (*Natural Heritage Trust of Australia Act 1997* (Cth), s 40).

85 See for example, the Joint Strategic Investment Panel (previously Joint Steering Committee), which is predominantly comprised of multiple representatives from different

partnerships; (iii) coordinate a whole of government processes; and (iv) resolve policy inconsistencies at the regional level.[86]

Nested below these State-level arrangements were regional bodies and more localized stakeholders, such as local-level farmers, community groups or other subregional collaborative bodies.

As discussed above, these types of nested arrangements are argued to reduce transaction costs by creating opportunities for interaction that might otherwise have required considerable investment of time and resources.[87] At the same time, however, the nested model, with its many levels, necessarily involves collaboration costs. In particular, a major challenge for nested models is achieving collaboration between different agencies and governments.[88] The chapter returns to consider Regional NRM's success in this regard below.

Empirical Insights into Collaborative Environmental Governance

The Case Studies

The analysis examines two regional bodies in Queensland that were chosen as case studies to examine whether, and under what conditions, successful transboundary collaboration was achieved. The case studies were both located in northern Queensland. The first, referred to as Case Study One (CS1), was examined in 2005/2006 under NHT2/NAP. The data collected from this study is reinterrogated in light of a more recent case referred to as Case Study Two (CS2), which was examined in 2009/2010 under Caring for Our Country.[89]

Queensland and Federal Government agencies. *Queensland NHT2 Bilateral*, above n 61, cl 37-43; *Queensland NAP Bilateral*, above n 61, cl 22.

86 This was tasked to Regional Coordination Groups (RCGs), composed of senior management-level representatives from State governmental agencies. The groups had responsibility for one of four areas into which Queensland is divided. For further see State of Queensland, *Regional Coordination Groups*, http://www.regionalnrm.qld.gov.au/about_new/who_does_what/rcgs.html.

87 For example, structured collaborative forums at the State level like RCG may reduce the time spent by agencies consulting each other. Similarly, local-level groups gain from nested arrangements because they can interact within a single regional forum.

88 Margerum, above n 40, 144–147; Freeman and Farber, above n 80, 900–901; Farrelly, above n 46, 400; Head, above n 33, 145.

89 Guided by advice from key agency officials in each program, the selection of these cases followed a non random, purposive approach designed to select 'information rich' cases (e.g. groups that had substantially implemented their plan of action and faced some of the most difficult natural resource problems in the State, including rural, coastal and highly urbanized areas). The earlier regional NRM case study was conducted as a part of a broader empirical based research project concerned with exploring collaborative approaches to environmental governance. The project was conducted between 2004 and 2008. It asked the question: under what conditions can we achieve 'good' collaborative

Both cases involved large regions (approximately 100000 km^2 and 20000 km^2) that addressed a broad range of natural resource and social and cultural issues. For example, both case studies sought to manage the quality of multiple small and large scale groundwater aquifers across their regions. Both regional bodies also addressed sediment/nutrient run-off into large rivers that crossed multiple regional and local jurisdictional boundaries, and flowed into the Federally managed Great Barrier Reef Marine Park. Further, the cases both aimed to manage biodiversity, which existed at different scales (regional diversity, ecosystem diversity, species diversity and genetic diversity) and was impacted upon by pressures such as grazing, urbanization, invasive species and pollution that occurred across multiple local government boundaries and across multiple State and Federal administrative jurisdictions.[90] In assessing the success of collaboration to manage such transboundary problems, the case studies drew on 57 respondents' opinions[91] and documentary evidence as to whether the collaborative processes included relevant stakeholders, and whether these stakeholders were able to combine their power, capacity, resources and knowledge to improve the condition of the regions' natural resources.[92]

---

governance. To answer this question it examined a range of defining characteristics of 'collaborative environmental governance', including collaboration, participation, deliberation, accountability and learning and adaption. This chapter reinterrogates the data collected on the 'collaborative approach' of the Regional NRM case study in light of the more recent case study data collected in 2009. For further see Cameron Holley, Neil Gunningham and Clifford Shearing, *New Environmental Governance* (Earthscan, 2011).

90 State of Queensland, Biodiversity, http://www.derm.qld.gov.au/wildlife-ecosystems/biodiversity/index.html.

91 Interviewees were selected to capture some of the main forms of diversity across the types of stakeholders involved in the programs, including regional body, farmers, Federal, State and local governments and non government bodies. Specific interviewee numbers were as follows: 30 for Case Study 1, 27 for Case Study 2.

92 As with most social research, the ethical and confidentiality requirements of the research require the anonymity of specific interviewees to be preserved, save for a general description of their stakeholder category. The interview questions sometimes varied between interviewees to allow for individual experiences and meanings to emerge. However all interviews involved in-depth conversations, utilizing a semi structured interviewing technique that was guided by a standard protocol of largely open-ended questions. The primary questions asked were as follows: How was the collaborative group formed? Are the stakeholders involved sufficient for the tasks at hand? What are the main ways the group achieves its goals? Have the plan's actions been implemented? Is the collaboration sustainable over the longer term? How do the decision making processes operate? Is there equal influence from partners? How representative is the group? Does the process account for/interact with broader legal requirements? Has the collaboration delivered environmental improvements?; Alexander Conley and Margaret A Moote, 'Evaluating Collaborative Natural Resource Management' (2003) 16 *Society & Natural Resources* 371.

The Findings – Regional NRM

As with all transboundary environmental governance processes, the Regional NRM program sought to form cooperative structures that crossed traditional jurisdictional levels. Collaboration was to occur between (i) Federal and State governments to negotiate bilateral agreements that develop joint policies and rules for regional focused governance; (ii) State government agencies to support regional delivery; and (iii) local and regional government and non-government stakeholders to negotiate and cooperatively agree upon governing regional plans.[93]

The findings below reveal that stakeholders achieved substantial cooperation at all of these levels, and had agreed to plans and implemented a number of actions. However, at each level problems were reported. These included drawn out conflicts between Federal and State governments; agency 'turf wars' at the State level; vague guidance and insufficient support for regional bodies; and State agency resistance to integrating statutory programs with regional NRM plans. None of these problems were fatal to collaborative arrangements. Nonetheless, they served to diminish their overall success as a transboundary governance endeavour.

This section first examines the challenges confronting collaboration at the higher levels of the nested model of Regional NRM. It then describes how that model was rolled out despite the challenges, and managed to gain buy-in from a substantial range of rural stakeholders, although questions about inclusiveness and balance of interests remain. Finally, it shows how some of the obstacles to collaboration, whilst demonstrably not insurmountable, nevertheless served to limit its success in a number of ways.

A central issue for Regional NRM's nested approach was State and Federal governments agreeing to provide the strategic framework for Queensland's Regional NRM. Consistent with suspicions of some Regional NRM commentators and CEG authors,[94] conflict rather than cooperation was evident at all major stages of program design. This meant that the transaction costs of negotiating bilateral agreements proved to be extremely high – negotiations were problematic, lengthy, and repeatedly stalled.[95] This was particularly the case regarding the more expansive NHT2 and Caring for Our Country programs (NAP being limited to only four 'priority' regions in Queensland). Indeed, following announcements that NHT and NAP would be implemented together,[96] the NAP Agreement was reached relatively quickly in 2002, but negotiations continued on the NHT2 Bilateral Agreement until 2004. Four years later in 2008, as both NHT2 and NAP approached expiration, the

93 Head, above n 33, 144.

94 Margerum, above n 40, 149.

95 Interview with 3210, Science (Queensland, July 2005).

96 Brian Head and Neil Ryan, 'Can Co-Governance Work? Regional Natural Resource Management in Queensland, Australia' (2004) paper presented at *International Symposium on Public Sector Management VIII*, Budapest, 31 March–2 April 2004, Akademiai Kiado, Budapest, 16–17.

State and Federal governments were unable to reach agreement on a new bilateral framework for Caring for Our Country, and Regional NRM currently operates under transitional arrangements, even some three years later.

Three main factors contributed to these difficulties. First, respondents from both CS1 and CS2 pointed to State/Federal conflicts and the lack of trust between the two sovereign actors:[97] 'the State continues to blame the Federal government and the Federal government continues to blame the State government. Whatever is or isn't happening, it's the other one's fault if it's not. It doesn't seem to change.'[98]

Second was a lack of adequate incentives to encourage the State to meaningfully share its power and resources with the Federal government. During the NHT2 and NAP years, the Federal government had reportedly assumed that the State would see resource benefits arising from Regional NRM collaboration and would willingly participate for this reason. This proved to be incorrect since the Federal resources available were reportedly too little to motivate Queensland to change their stance. As one respondent in CS1 put it: '[the federal government] think they've so much money to run this [Regional NRM] that the State will click and dance. Well it started to click and dance and then it decided well no, get nicked ... there's not enough money ... so you had a failed system to start off with'.[99]

This dilemma was only augmented with the shift to Caring for Our Country, which centralized funding priorities and accordingly reduced State access to resources. As one CS2 respondent explained, the Federal government 'lost the leverage over the States' and stymied any incentive for Queensland to come to the table and engage in substantial and meaningful cooperation.[100]

As we will see below, this inter-governmental conflict not only substantially weakened the foundation of transboundary collaboration, but significantly reduced its overall success at the regional management level.

Exacerbating this problem was an ongoing conflict within the Queensland government. Similar to the turf warfare among administrative departments that had plagued earlier collaborative experiments,[101] State agencies reportedly struggled

97 Interview with 334, Regional Body (Queensland, July 2005).

98 Interview with 442, Peak Industry Body (Queensland, May 2009).

99 Interview with 3210, Science (Queensland, July 2005). One respondent referred to a previously ongoing debate about agreeing to core funding arrangements under NHT 2: 'a big debate going on between us and Commonwealth, cause there is a view particularly in the central agencies that this model was foist on Queensland and as a result the Commonwealth should pay for the administrative cost, particularly the NHT groups'; Interview with 323, Government Agency (Queensland, July 2005).

100 Interview with 4312, Regional Body (Queensland, November 2009) noting that 'the way it was before they said, 'Look we're going to do this but before we give you the dough what are you going to do?' Now that's the argy bargy between State and Commonwealth that you've got to have otherwise State will just use it as cost shifting exercises as best they can and fund their core functions and they're very good at doing that and dressing it up as something else'.

101 Ewing, above n 46, 406.

to reach agreement regarding their collective approach to Regional NRM. While some agencies with direct responsibility for Regional NRM reportedly wished to pursue a collaborative and 'whole of government' approach, others were resistant to sharing their power, leading to a 'disintegrated government system'. As one respondent put it, this uncertainty and conflict 'was a tragedy because … the whole of government solidarity sort of fell apart'.[102]

With government solidarity at a low point, a number of independent reviews of Queensland's Regional NRM system were instigated by the State government, including a public options paper on the future of Regional NRM for the State.[103] Although there was overwhelming support for the current system, the outcome led to little improvement in State agency partnerships or support. Indeed, even after the transition to Caring for Our Country and the recent development of a Queensland NRM funding program (that is, Q2 Coasts and Country),[104] key agencies were still reportedly providing only 'begrudging support … [as] the State government [remained] very equivocal about, NRM bodies'. [105]

Beyond government collaboration across State and Federal levels, the central challenge was establishing and then maintaining regional ecosystem-focused governance of key transboundary environmental issues.

In its early years, this initially involved governments' defining regions and establishing regional bodies, often based on pre-existing community groups.[106] This process typically involved numerous meetings with the regional community, and government officers facilitating the development of collaborative regional bodies across the State. Consistent with regional experimentation encouraged under Regional NRM, both regional body case studies adopted slightly different representative structures.[107] However, each achieved a wide range of local stakeholder involvement, including subregional catchment interests, indigenous,

102 Interview with 334, Regional Body Staff (Queensland, July 2005); Charles Zammit et al, *A Review of the NRM Arrangements in Queensland* (Department of Natural Resources and Mining, 2004).

103 Department of Natural Resource Management (DNRM), *Options for Future Community Engagement in Regional Natural Resource Management* (Queensland State Government, 2005) 7.

104 Queensland Government, *Q2 Coasts and Country* http://www.regionalnrm.qld.gov.au/policies_plans_legislation/policies_strategies/q2_coasts_country.html.

105 Interview with 421, Government Agency (Queensland, May 2009). This lack of coordination was exemplified by an apparent failure of individual agencies to commit both in kind and funding support for multi-agency organizations at the State level, including some Regional Coordination Groups, which were described as 'almost dysfunctional'. Interview 411, Government Agency (Queensland, May 2009).

106 Head and Ryan, above n 96, 16–17.

107 In Case Study 1 this included 5 subregional groups, and 2 science local government and indigenous interests respectively.

production, local government, as well as many other (although as discussed below far from all) relevant interests (e.g., science and World Heritage).[108]

Why did these stakeholders want to collaborate? At the broadest level, they were interested in participating because they were concerned about the regions' severe natural resource problems. Indeed, since the early 1990s, there had been growing community concern and mobilization (e.g., through voluntary catchment groups) to try and manage diverse natural resources that were reportedly threatened and degraded by competing and interconnected resource uses, such as grazing, cane farming, and urban development.[109] Further, some stakeholders, particularly representatives from existing voluntary catchment groups, were motivated by an additional incentive for participation – the potential for voluntary groups to obtain and/or control government funding. Put simply: 'they nominated these people to make sure that they got some money for their organizations'.[110]

Although valid questions exist about the inclusiveness and balance of interests on the regional bodies (not least that a number of stakeholder groups were not represented there as discussed further below), the membership went some way toward bringing a diverse mix of key stakeholders into the regional collaboration to make decisions, set strategic direction and manage staff and partnerships regarding implementation.

A particularly beneficial feature of both CS1's and CS2's regional structure was their specific attempts to involve and foster links with existing subregional groups (e.g., community catchment management bodies) in a nested design approach that took account of the distribution of natural resources and problems across both local political and smaller scale ecological boundaries. To do this, the regional bodies divided the region into smaller areas and utilized their funding to hire coordinators for specific collaborative subregional groups in each area.[111] These coordinators in turn ensured regional and local capacities were linked via a two way flow of communication between the regional body and the subregional groups and their wider local networks.[112]

---

108 In Case Study 2, this included a representative from each of the following interests: Catchment/Community, Industry, Conservation, Coastal; Indigenous; Local Government; World Heritage and any significant geographic regions not otherwise represented on the board.

109 Burdekin Dry Tropics NRM (BDTNRM), *Burdekin Dry Tropics Natural Resource Management Plan 2005–2010* (BDTNRM, 2005) 1, 8, 29–33.

110 Interview with 341, Regional Body (Queensland, July 2005).

111 BDTNRM, above n 109, 15; P Gilbey, (2002) *Rights and Duty of Care: A Queensland Perspective*, http://www.clw.csiro.au/lbi/publications/ANCID2002paper-Gilbey.pdf.

112 Interview with 342, Subregional Body (Queensland, July 2005). These networks also fed up to the coordinating regional bodies, where the remaining funding was vital in enabling it to rent an office and employ support and planning staff to complete and support regional planning documents and coordinate the implementation of subsequent actions. BDTNRM, above n 109, 197.

This nested arrangement accordingly helped reduce transaction costs in ways broadly consistent with suggestions in the literature. For example, the regional bodies' each provided a forum that reduced the costs of disseminating government information, funding and guidance down to the multiple subregional groups.[113] As one respondent explained: 'prior to the regional body the smaller catchment groups, received direct funding from the government ... now the regional body is an asset for them because they have to do less of the going out and getting the money and there's someone there to lobby at a policy level for them to bring more money into the region for action on the ground'.[114]

Simultaneously, the nested structure also benefited the regional bodies by dividing the workload among these groups and reducing the time and resources spent by the regional bodies in consulting and networking with various local governments, farmers and other actors within the wider region. Indeed, local groups and their coordinators were reportedly vital to consulting and bargaining regarding critical NRM assets and targets, and carrying out actions in each subregion.[115]

This nested approach was particularly important to achieving relatively wide ranging stakeholder agreement on regional plans and supporting documents.[116] Repeated interactions and consensus-orientated negotiations to develop these – while far from conflict free – helped build stronger relationships, reduce mistrust and ensured agreements were reached with greater ease: 'trust is the biggest thing … the only way you can get through all the planning and legislation and decisions is just to keep the dialogue going and to actually demonstrate that, yes, something will come out the end of this'.[117]

Having built trust over time, the parties in both CS1 and CS2 reached agreement on planning documents. The regional planning documents that emerged contained several ambitious targets. These included biodiversity issues (e.g., by 2015, ensure 90 per cent of all threatened flora and fauna species in the region will be represented in conservation reserves or under voluntary conservation agreements; and no net loss of the area of native vegetation across the region by 2008) and surface and groundwater resources (e.g., improve water quality by reducing sediment and nutrient loads in all [regional] waterways; progressive improvement in condition of coastal, estuarine and marine ecosystems by 2014; by 2015, the health and

113 BDTNRM, above n 109, 187.

114 Interview with 432, Regional Body (Queensland, May 2009).

115 As the following respondent illustrated: '[the subregional] coordinator makes sure information is disseminated properly… [they're] needed because farmers or landholders, they don't know how to connect [to the regional body]', Interview with 342, Subregional Body (Queensland, July 2005).

116 BDTNRM, above n 109, 66, 197.

117 Interview with 351, Regional Body (Queensland, July 2005) noting that 'successfully facilitating multiple planning forums and technical workshops at the local and regional level actually allowed people and allowed our facilitators to work much more closely with the landholders and it allows them to basically develop a relationship with that community'.

diversity of 25 per cent of poor condition key groundwater dependent ecosystems is improved to good condition; and allocation of regional water resources including underground water will demonstrably not exceed sustainable levels by 2015).[118]

Over time, the bodies' implementation of these plans had reportedly led to a number of significant outputs and outcomes, both social and to a lesser extent, environmental. Although the data on outcomes was more limited in terms of the early CS1 research, government investment for implementation had reportedly allowed the regional collaboration to make substantial progress on the ongoing implementation of around 100 projects even a few short years after agreeing to the plan. This included a number of tangible results, including 25 property management plans, 23,000 ha of native riparian vegetation protected, and 25.7 km of divisional fencing built and 90 ha of wetlands cleared of weeds.[119]

Although admittedly a different body, the data available for the more recent CS2 study suggested this early progress had been extended and consolidated overtime. This included delivering significant behavioural change, such as increased awareness and attitude in the region regarding natural resource management.[120] Furthermore, the data revealed important (albeit limited) rehabilitation to creeks, parks and river areas.[121] There was also data on positive trends in aquatic life and water quality in freshwater and inshore-reef environments, however at present these changes remained small and it was unclear to what extent these improvements were attributable to Regional NRM as opposed to other public interventions or natural changes.[122]

The above were all undoubtedly very positive achievements in the Regional NRM program. However, the collaboration was limited in a number of ways that seriously constrained the success of Regional NRM and its achievement of wide-ranging and significant improvements to transboundary natural resource issues. First, because of the ongoing bickering between State and Federal governments over the Bilateral Agreements, government guidance was often vague and changing. As one government advisor from CS1 explained: 'the regional bodies have been evolving at the same time as the infrastructure has been [evolving] ...

118 BDTNRM, above 109; FNQ NRM Ltd & Rainforest CRC, *Sustaining the Wet Tropics: A Regional Plan for Natural Resource Management 2004–2008* (FNQ NRM, 2004).

119 Cameron Holley, 'Aging Gracefully? Examining the Conditions for Sustaining Successful Collaboration in Environmental Law and Governance' (2009) 26(6) *Environmental and Planning Law Journal* 457.

120 Interview with 4312, Regional Body (Queensland, November 2009). Interview with 434, Regional Body (Queensland, May 2009) pointing out that 'I think they've raised the profile of environmental issues. I do think they've achieved that.'

121 See, for example, Interview with 438, Regional Body (Queensland, May 2009).

122 Interview 443, Peak Body (Queensland, November 2009). Interview with 444, Science (Queensland, May 2009) noting that 'in some instances, we've had trends that have shown declines in organic phosphorus, declines in some of the nitrate and total in levels in those areas ... but no we cannot attribute it at the moment'.

the administrative arrangements [and] the guidelines … we haven't necessarily provided them with the framework or the support to be able to achieve what we want them to achieve'.[123]

This did little to offset transaction costs, and may have even amplified them, as regional bodies continually had to adapt and readapt to changing requirements (e.g. the form of their organizational structure). The findings suggest this lack of firm guidance was detrimental to the overall success of fostering transboundary cooperation, with regional bodies often failing to connect effectively with key stakeholders across the region. As one respondent reflected: 'We have got some major coal and gold mines in the area. Not one of the mining industries has even been talked to.'[124]

The second issue that undermined the success of transboundary collaboration was reported delays in government funding to mitigate transaction costs. As with the above issues, this delay was created by the ongoing disagreement between Federal and State governments. This increased the time it took to complete plans and take actions and made it more difficult to engage local stakeholders. As one CS1 respondent explained: 'I see the [Queensland]–[Federal] crunch as incredibly negative. It's stopped us getting funding when we needed our funding … and then that flows through to the community … so there is all this negative stuff that comes out of friction at the top end.'[125]

Third, the lack of effective ongoing cooperation between different levels of government and government agencies unsurprisingly led to a disjointed delivery framework.[126] Indeed, not only were Federal and State funding priorities sometimes unaligned (creating 'multiple masters' for the regional bodies),[127] but there was often little integration across the actions of individual government stakeholders, who themselves were unwilling to relinquish and share their power to achieve coordinated action on transboundary resources. As one CS2 respondent explained:

> Yeah I don't think there's much alignment really from Federal, State and regional objectives on the myriad of natural resource stuff. You get local government doing its bit, you get the State doing its bit, you get one agency doing a bit and the other agency not knowing about it, and then Feds funding something, it's a terribly fragmented system.[128]

---

123 See also Farrelly, above n 46, 399; Interview with 327, Government Agency (Queensland, July 2005).

124 Interview with 341, Regional Body (Queensland, July 2005).

125 Interview with 342, Subregional Group (Queensland, July 2005).

126 Interview 431, Regional Body (Queensland, May 2009) describing the arrangements as 'a shemozzle'.

127 Holley and Sinclair, above n 55.

128 Interview with 4312, Regional Body (Queensland, November 2009).

Over and above the lack of coordination across government jurisdictional boundaries, there was a significant lack of integration between targets and actions contained in regional plans and the more conventional regulatory tools under State legislation (e.g., *Vegetation Management Act 1999 (Qld)*). This fourth weakness was evidenced in both case studies, with the findings suggesting State statutory instruments remained on parallel rather than integrated paths with Regional NRM. As one respondent explained:

> The tension lies in this issue of statutory delivery tools that government has their hands on and the outcome that the community through the regional bodies want to achieve. That's where the jury is out in lots of ways and the partnership, the alliance if you like between regions and government legislation they haven't achieved it yet.[129]

In theory, this gap between the decisions and actions made under existing legal regulation and new collaborative forms of Regional NRM is not in itself problematic. Both governance approaches could perform separate functions but contribute to a common goal of managing natural resource issues.[130] However, according to respondents, this was not the case in practice. As the interviewees portrayed it, there was an 'unhealthy disconnect between the [State] departments and their statutes and the regions and their non statutory plans' that limited their combined ability to achieve optimal natural resource goals for the region, State and the nation.[131] As another respondent illustrated:

> Look let's use a very simple example, the regional plans identify an area that is a hot spot that needs a lot of work. Does the State government say 'well you look at that and we'll go over there' – that is in recognition of the regional plan … or does the government set their own statutory work programs … we haven't yet begun to complement their program.[132]

In part, the tendency for agencies to overlook Regional NRM plans stemmed from the conflict and lack of whole of government approach at the State government level. However the findings suggested that this problem was also attributable to a perceived lack of regional body legitimacy in the eyes of State agencies.

129 It is important to note that regional bodies were required to ensure the targets and actions within the regional plans were consistent with existing statutory processes. Even so, active State support in delivering on these targets still appeared to be lacking. Interview with 323, Government Agency (Queensland, July 2005).

130 Trubek and Trubek, above n 15.

131 Interview with 421, Government Agency (Queensland, May 2009).

132 Interview with 323, Government Agency (Queensland, July 2005); Interview with 424, Government Agency (Queensland, May 2009) stating 'I don't think that our regional arrangements have for example been used to identify where we should be putting the new protective areas, saving critical parts of the landscape'.

According to many State agency respondents, regional bodies were the 'poor cousins' of government, which had, at best, only dubious authority and weak capacities. As one respondent described it, many agencies had: 'a jaundice[d] view … that these groups [were] made up of well meaning amateurs who [had] replaced the local tennis club'.[133] Although this view was not held by all State agencies, it was sufficiently widespread that one respondent suggested regional bodies 'almost existed in spite of Queensland agencies'.[134] This enmity and lack of State agency support for integration was similarly confirmed by regional bodies:

> I've got a very low opinion on State government involvement … when we were trying to do the [water project] we couldn't get State engagement … and very rarely do you get a Department of Primary Industries person up here, Environment Protection Agency we don't see ... and then the Department of Natural Resources didn't want to be involved, and so I don't have much respect for them.[135]

Beyond the challenges posed by this gap between Regional NRM and State statutory tools, the fifth challenge for Regional NRM was the more fundamental issue of a lack of government resourcing. As one respondent frankly stated: 'the biggest deficiency is that it is hopelessly underresourced'.[136] This underresourcing limited the success of Regional NRM's collaborative processes in a number of ways. One of these was the failure to adequately offset the sheer cost and task of collaborating across large regional scales.[137] Challenges of scale are, of course, not unique to Regional NRM. There are many large transboundary institutions across the globe. However, on all accounts there were significant insufficiencies in the funding.

In CS1, even with volunteers putting in 'thousands of hours',[138] government funding did not sufficiently equip the subregional groups to overcome transaction costs and cooperative barriers that arose. Indeed, respondents reported that they lacked the time and resources to engage with a range of peak industry bodies.

---

133 Interview with 323, Government Agency (Queensland, July 2005).

134 Interview with 424, Government Agency (Queensland, May 2009).

135 Interview with 437, Regional Body (Queensland, May 2009).

136 Interview with 337, Government Body (Queensland, October 2005).

137 Certainly, research into early stages of regional NRM suggests that at least some regional bodies have had some noted success in utilizing government funding to reduce transaction costs and provide an incentive to bringing together a range of relevant stakeholders to plan and deliver projects. However, many others, including the cases studied in this chapter, appeared to struggle to bring the range of relevant stakeholders to the table. See generally M Lockwood et al, 'Multilevel Environmental Governance: Lessons from Australian Natural Resource Management' (2009) 40(2) *Australian Geographer* 169, 177–178; Marcus Lane et al, 'Will Regionalisation Achieve Integrated Natural Resource Management? Insights from Recent South Australian Experience' in Marcus Lane, Cathy Robinson and Bruce Taylor (eds), *Contested Country* (CSIRO, 2009).

138 Interview with 342, Subregional Group (Queensland, July 2005).

Even more problematic was the failure to 'tap into all of the farming structures' in the region – in particular 'average' farmers as opposed to those who were already involved in existing subregional catchment bodies.[139] As one respondent put it: 'we have had a group of most probably 30 landholders, commercial beef property people, who have been involved fairly heavily in doing all this consultation process for the planning, but the majority haven't engaged'.[140]

CS2 respondents also reported similar challenges and gaps, with a number of key partners remaining isolated from the regional collaborative arrangements. These included some of the main representative bodies of marine and reef tourism interests in the region, as well as key environmental organizations. As one peak marine tourism group put it: 'the regional bodies … there's been no real engagement with us at all … when you're not engaging the main end user, there's something inherently wrong in your consultation process'.[141]

Certainly CS2 was aware of these gaps, and had taken some steps to develop relationships, including leaving positions open for tourism and environmental interests on various consultative and advisory committees. However with only scarce resources, the body had few incentives to actively promote and support the benefits of collaborative partnership with these non-agricultural stakeholders.[142] This lack of engagement from key stakeholders appears likely to have reduced the overall success of the collaborative process and the effectiveness of the plan and actions that were produced.

Finally, and perhaps most importantly, many respondents questioned the capacity of Regional NRM to actually achieve its goals to improve environmental conditions, not least because there were major inadequacies in funding for collaborative implementation.[143] Although bodies had increasingly been encouraged and had some success in accessing external non-government resources, public funds remained central to the operation of Regional NRM. Yet, respondents suggested this funding was not commensurate with the responsibilities and outcomes to be delivered by regional bodies. As they pointed out: 'our budget is a few million a year. Now what we are expected to do with a few million dollars is make sustainable land use, protect all the biodiversity and fix the water quality out to the reef, all within 10 years. That's a pretty big ask.'[144]

While outcomes in natural resource contexts can take decades to emerge, to date this lack of investment was reportedly the main reason that neither case study

139 Interview with 314, Industry Body (Queensland, July 2005).

140 Interview with 344, Subregional Body (Queensland, July 2005).

141 Interview with 413, Peak Body (Queensland, May 2009).

142 Interview with 4310, Regional Body (Queensland, May 2009).

143 Interview with 334, Regional Body (Queensland, July 2005).

144 Interview with 337, Regional Body (Queensland, July 2005); Interview with 411, Government Agency (Queensland May 2009) stating 'I mean look on a comparative basis 200 million for saving the reef, the Queensland government spends that on one piece of road infrastructure when it's upgraded … so you just, you can't help but think that we still have a well, a fair path to travel'.

had yet achieved any major strategically directed improvements in water and natural resource conditions. As one respondent bluntly summed up the situation: 'This is going to sound a bit unkind – I'd be hard pressed to say "here's something that the regional body did that's really good, that's made a real positive difference to the environment", I'd have a hard time saying that'.[145]

Discussion and Conclusion

The research set out in this chapter has investigated attempts to foster collaboration between different domestic sovereign powers and non-government actors across different jurisdictional and administrative levels. In Queensland it did so through an analysis of two Regional NRM case studies and the subsequent findings yield a number of insights into the effective implementation and operation of collaborative approaches to environmental governance in practice.

Any successful transboundary governance approach will require cooperation, and Regional NRM was no exception. Although collective action barriers remained a significant obstacle for this CEG approach, the findings revealed that under the appropriate conditions collaboration was possible. These findings make clear that it is a gross oversimplification to rely on 'tragedy of the commons' arguments to conclude that cooperative solutions within CEG are impossible.[146]

Indeed, the above analysis revealed that Regional NRM had considerable success in fostering processes that engaged diverse stakeholders and that achieved some key outcomes. The program has been successful in enabling Federal, State and a range of regional and local government and non-government stakeholders to come together in a web of regional transboundary cooperation and interpenetration through a nested set of collaborative arrangements.[147] The findings suggested that what encouraged this success were several key conditions – a community concern about pressing natural resource problems, monetary incentives to engender interest from key regional and local stakeholders, government support (albeit insufficient) to offset transaction costs and trust-building via negotiation and consensus orientated decision-making.

Nevertheless, it is also clear that achieving *successful* collaboration was far from easy. Realizing collaboration is both time and resource intensive and provision for this (including significant sums of government money) has to be built into CEG processes if they are to be successful.[148] The findings also revealed only limited success by processes designed to enhance collaboration. Indeed, the

145 Interview with 421, Government Agency (Queensland, May 2009).

146 Sanford E Gaines, 'Reflexive Law as a Legal Paradigm for Sustainable Development' (2002/2003) 10 *Buffalo Environmental Law Journal* 1, 15–16; Steinzor, above n 36; Karkkainen, above n 14, 231, 233.

147 Karkkainen, above n 11.

148 Orts and Coglianese, above n 28; Lane, above n 45; Karkkainen, above n 14, 225.

success of Regional NRM was qualified by a host of weaknesses and difficulties in securing key stakeholders' input into the planning and implementation process. While nested arrangements certainly assisted in reducing transaction costs, given the regions' size, conflict and uncertainty at higher levels created an unstable foundation for the Regional NRM program, delayed financial support, created fragmented and poorly coordinated delivery systems and reduced effective guidance from government to regional bodies. Further, the fissure between Regional NRM and traditional statutory programs stymied productive working relationships, and limited integration vital to effective transboundary cooperation and implementation.

What broader lessons can be gleaned from this study? While there are inherent dangers in generalizing from this type of research,[149] nevertheless, a number of insights can be drawn from the findings across the contexts and institutional arrangements of the two cases. They suggest some key lessons with regard to the conditions that increase the likelihood of successful collaboration in CEG.[150] These lessons can be grouped under four principal themes: the severity of environmental problems; trust; incentives; and structures for subsidising transaction costs. For each, the findings provide important lessons for CEG theory and for policymakers in transboundary contexts.

Commencing with the issue of problem severity, Regional NRM dealt with urgent natural resource problems that were perceived to be severe by key stakeholders. This created personal stakes and strong motivation for many non-government actors to actively collaborate and participate in efforts to solve them. Such an approach is also broadly consistent with emerging research in other medium to large collaborative settings that found successful collaboration is more likely to emerge where problems are perceived to be severe.[151]

In terms of trust, the CEG and related literatures have often argued that building trust will make it easier for stakeholders to cooperate and achieve successful collaboration.[152] The research set out in this chapter also found this to be broadly true. Trust, and trust-building through regular negotiations and consensus oriented decision-making were vital to facilitate working relationships among

---

149 In particular, the findings offer only a snapshot of these evolving processes. Time is, in fact, a vital issue from the perspective of successful collaborative approaches as many of the impacts of governance efforts are only experienced over the longer term. JB Ruhl, 'The Pardy-Ruhl Dialogue on Ecosystem Management, Part IV: Narrowing and Sharpening the Questions' (2007) 24 *Pace Environmental Law Review* 25.

150 Cameron Holley, 'Removing the Thorn from New Governance's Side: Examining the Emergence of Collaboration in Practice and the Roles for Law, Nested Institutions and Trust' (2010) 40(7) *Environmental Law Reporter* 10654, 10683–10684.

151 Heikkila and Gerlak, above n 19, 586; Mark Lubell et al, 'Watershed Partnerships and the Emergence of Collective Action Institutions' (2002) 46(1) *American Journal of Political Science* 146, 148.

152 Jenny Stewart and Grant Jones, *Renegotiating the Environment* (Federation Press, 2003); Fung and Wright, above n 36, 15; John, above n 40, 232, 235.

non-government actors engaged in Regional NRM. Certainly, building such trust will not always be easy. This is particularly so in circumstances where there is entrenched mistrust between parties, as was the case between Federal and State governments. In such instances, other tools, such as incentives, may be needed to shift a party's motivation and willingness to work cooperatively with actors, despite such mistrust.

In this regard, the findings provided insights into the use of incentives to increase the likelihood of successful collaboration.[153] It is widely acknowledged in the regulatory literature that the strategic use of government funding and/or authority (or even harnessing pressure from third parties) can be an effective spur to cooperation and affirmative self-regulatory behaviour.[154] A key question for CEG in terms of incentives is what is likely to shift the cost–benefit calculation of stakeholders? The findings revealed that 'positive economic incentives' are vital to successful collaboration (as was the case in encouraging the regional body membership and local stakeholders to engage in actions).

The findings also suggest incentives such as federal funding programs can be vital to engaging other sovereign actors (like subnational State governments) in transboundary cooperation.[155] Yet, it is clear from the experience of State and Federal relations in Regional NRM that when incentives are used, they will need to be tailored to offer sufficient inducement to spur the desired participants to not only contract into CEG, but also to 'compel' them to take affirmative action that they are otherwise disinclined to pursue.[156] This was acutely evident from the begrudging and ultimately minimal support provided by the State government to the Regional NRM program. In short, their position as a relatively powerful and well resourced government meant they saw little gain or benefit to be achieved from cooperating with the Federal government in return for a comparatively minimal (and in the case of Caring for Our Country, nonexistent) Federal monetary inducement.

In addition to incentives, the findings also shed light on the issue of transaction costs. Many authors in the literature have suggested that sufficient support for collaborators to enable them to offset transaction costs is vital to successful collaboration.[157] The findings strongly support these claims.[158] In addition to transaction costs, the findings suggest it is also crucial to provide for the costs of facilitation in the form of funding for a coordinator.

Importantly, the findings suggest that the above support may need to be quite substantial to be effective.[159] Indeed, the costs of CEG and the importance of

153 Karkkainen, above n 14, 241.
154 Ibid, 229; Karkkainen, n 77, 296.
155 Wondolleck and Yaffee, above n 34, 224.
156 De Búrca and Scott, above n 30, 9; Karkkainen, n 77, 298.
157 John, above n 40, 230–242; Sabatier et al, above n 19, 181.
158 Ibid.
159 Farrelly, above n 46, 402; Head, above n 33, 145.

resources to cover these costs were starkly evident across the large regional areas of the two case studies. More often than not, inadequacies were found in funding that caused some of the most fundamental weaknesses. In particular, inadequate funding from government undermined successful engagement, constraining the contribution of time and cash-strapped volunteers and constrained the commitments and actions necessary to improve environmental conditions on the ground.[160]

The adverse effects of inadequate funding expose a crucial contradiction that is evident in many CEG programs. Governments find CEG and similar collaborative governance approaches attractive in part because of their perceived promise to reduce State expenditure by engaging other actors and their resources.[161] But governments' preoccupation with minimizing expenditure often results in such programs being denied the very resources that are essential to their success.

Of course, pleas for 'more funding' are hardly new in environmental law and governance. Government funds are invariably in short supply and there will always be difficult trade-offs to be made in their deployment.[162] Nevertheless, the harsh reality is that CEG can rarely work effectively without resources to cover core costs, especially transaction costs. Certainly, CEG may attract investments from other stakeholders that can be added to government investments, but they can rarely, if ever, replace them. To imagine that CEG programs will relieve governments of funding pressures is not only mistaken, but counterproductive. If governments see advantages in CEG programs and want them to work, they must also fund them adequately.

The research set out in this chapter also found evidence to suggest that appropriate institutional design at large regional transboundary scales, can mitigate transaction costs, particularly through the use of nested structures. While this is clearly no 'magic bullet', it can reduce transaction costs by tapping into existing institutional resources to divide and conquer collaborative tasks at lower local levels, while receiving guidance from government in a structured manner through higher regional fora.[163]

Indeed, as we saw in Regional NRM, large regional collaboration was relatively successful because it had worked simultaneously at comparatively 'easier' smaller scales. It did so by dividing the large regions into small areas, at which level collaborative processes faced fewer transaction costs and were more closely connected to local actors. Yet important benefits also arose from Regional NRM operating at the higher regional and State levels as well. While this can create power-sharing problems, collaborating at high scales may help reduce *overall* transaction costs of interactions between local collaborators, help pool resources, and foster information sharing.[164]

160 Bonnell and Koontz, above n 42, 165.

161 Adam Crawford, *The Local Governance of Crime* (Clarendon Press, 1997).

162 Holley and Sinclair, above n 55.

163 Bonnell and Koontz, above n 42, 161, 163; Margerum, above n 40, 144–146.

164 Margerum, above n 40, 141; Karkkainen, above n 1, 235–236.

However, the potential of nested designs can be undermined where guidance is ineffective and uncertain, and where funding support is not forthcoming. One cause of this found in Regional NRM was a desire to 'get on' with programs before fully overcoming the resistance of agencies and governments to share power.[165] This suggests that achieving cooperation at these higher levels poses one of the greatest challenges to the effectiveness of nested collaborative models and their potential to reduce transaction costs. Indeed, it will be fundamentally important to ensure future nested institutional designs in transboundary contexts employ credible incentives and support to overcome these challenges, and the findings above offer a number of directions in this regard.

Beyond these specific policy lessons, the findings provide significant insights for collaborative governance practice and theory with regard to CEG's interaction with State centred legal rules,[166] especially as regards the fraught question of the gap hypothesis. The gap thesis attests to the imperviousness of traditional legal rules in the face of CEG, and to the existence of a gap between formal law and the practice of new forms of collaborative governance.[167]

At a descriptive level, the experience of Regional NRM and State legislative frameworks appeared very similar to the gap hypothesis, with Regional NRM plans and statutory controls effectively operating in different worlds.[168] Regional NRM is not alone in this gap, with others recognizing similar examples at domestic[169] and international levels.[170]

As we saw, this gap in the Regional NRM context stemmed from a lack of a 'whole of government' approach at the State level, and an enmity held by many State agencies towards community based regional arrangements. In the eyes of these State government actors, regional bodies lacked the skills, authority and legitimacy otherwise bestowed on agencies and legal regulation.

This enmity and subsequent 'gap' between legislative tools and Regional NRM plans had significant consequences for the effectiveness of collaboration. In particular, the resulting lack of policy integration and jointly delivered or supported actions appeared to impede the delivery of significant natural resource outcomes.

At a normative level these findings suggests that transboundary collaborative approaches are unlikely to be successful where policy makers overlook the need for productive combinations and relationships between CEG and conventional legal administration and regulation. Focusing solely on collaborative approaches,

165 Head, above n 33, 145; Margerum, above 40, 144–146; Freeman and Farber, above n 80, 900–901.

166 De Búrca and Scott, above n 30, at 3–10.

167 Ibid, 4.

168 Wilkinson, above n 30, 692–693.

169 Orly Lobel, 'Beyond Experimentation: Governing Occupational Safety in the United States' in Gráinne De Búrca and Joanne Scott (eds), *Law and New Governance in the EU and the US* (Hart Publishing, 2006).

170 Scott and Trubek, above n 30.

and effectively treating other policy instruments and their relationships to CEG as afterthoughts, can clearly be counterproductive to the success of transboundary governance and the outcomes achieved. Such a conclusion suggests the value of designing complementary and hybrid combinations of governance instruments. This must occur not only in terms of aspirations, but also in terms of institutional designs.[171]

For example, policy makers could look to actively develop hybrid relationships between legally binding rules and CEG, and a number of relationships have already been canvassed in the literature.[172] Perhaps the most relevant for present purposes would involve closing 'the gap' between law and CEG by conferring legal backing on collaborative regional arrangements (e.g., community based regional bodies). This would effectively make regional cooperative relationships adopt a more formal statutory backed arrangement, replete with the legal mandate and powers that bestows. There is clearly no guarantee that legally backed regional arrangements would be any better equipped at achieving integration of programs and cooperation between stakeholders (for as we saw, State agencies often struggle to work together in practice).[173] However, at the very least, such an approach may confer a level of perceived credibility and legitimacy on CEG approaches, so as to facilitate productive interaction between statutory tools and regional transboundary frameworks.[174] Certainty there has been evidence in Australia that legal backing to regional bodies can improve relationships between conventional legislative tools and CEG.[175]

While these insights are important in their own right, they also raise a number of significant issues that warrant further inquiry by legal and governance

171 Tabatha Wallington, Geoffrey Lawrence and Barton Loechel, 'Reflections on the Legitimacy of Regional Environmental Governance: Lessons from Australia's Experiment in Natural Resource Management' (2008) 10(1) *Journal of Environmental Policy and Planning* 1.

172 Lisa Blomgren Bingham, 'The Next Generation of Administrative Law: Building the Legal Infrastructure for Collaborative Governance' (2010) *Wisconsin Law Rev* 297; Trubek and Trubek, n 15, 543; Alexander, n 50, 178–84.

173 Such a proposal would not be without trade-offs, however, as the shift to legally backed State-sponsored forums would arguably undo the very purpose for which CEG is pursued – to provide flexibility and deeper forms of democracy that are seen to be better at addressing complex transboundary issues – which has proven to be beyond simply replicating cumbersome bureaucracies and instrumental State instruments. Wallington et al, above n 171.

174 Wallington et al, above n 171, 13.

175 Susan A Moore and Susan F Rockloff, 'Organizing Regionally for Natural Resource Management in Australia: Reflections on Agency and Government' (2006) 8 *Journal of Environmental Policy and Planning* 259. Even so, it is important to recognize that their statutory status may mean that regional arrangements will need to simultaneously develop strategies that emphasize a separation from government in order to establish community (earned) legitimacy with NGOs and other civil society actors. Lockwood et al, above n 137.

scholars, so that we can better understand the nature and extent of gaps between conventional law and CEG. This inquiry could include an empirical analysis to clarify the range of potential causes of such 'gaps' and how they can be overcome to foster more effective cooperative and integrated governance arrangements. Further, the findings in this chapter have only focused on domestic transboundary issues in one Australian State, and further studies would be warranted to examine whether similar gaps exist in other Australian States, in other federations, or at the international level.[176] Furthermore, at a more general level, scholars could examine additional institutional examples of CEG in practice to better identify and understand both the constructive and destructive roles that legal regulation may play in CEG approaches.[177]

Finally, it must also be recognized that the conclusions and implications drawn in this chapter are limited to the cases and program from which they were drawn. While the comparative and empirical analysis of multiple cases has allowed the chapter to explore collaborative transboundary approaches in practice, research into other manifestations and experiments in CEG is still vital to test and confirm whether or to what extent the findings and implications drawn here hold for other CEG institutions and contexts. This chapter cannot resolve these questions, but it may add to the knowledge base that will assist both policymakers and legal scholars when debating and redesigning CEG institutions to ensure that this novel approach to solving transboundary environmental problems will be a success.

176 Kakkrainen, above n 1, 221.

177 Trubek and Trubek, above n 15, 564; Wiersema, above n 29, 1294–1299; De Búrca and Scott, above n 30, 6–9; Holley, above n 5, 159–172.

Chapter 4
Marine Protected Areas and Transboundary Governance

Lorne Kriwoken, Julie Davidson and Michael Lockwood

Introduction

Marine protected areas (MPAs) are a widely accepted management tool that protect marine biodiversity and support the sustainable use of marine resources. Australia is considered one of the international leaders in developing a representative MPA system. The Australian, state and territory governments broadly support the development of a national system of MPAs with the designation of representative samples of Australia's marine ecosystems. The governance framework that underpins the national system of MPAs means that in many cases cooperative and transboundary management arrangements must be developed and recognized. This is especially true for those cases where MPAs straddle the 3 nautical mile (nm) boundary between national and state/territory marine jurisdictions.

The aim of this chapter is to explore the role of transboundary marine biodiversity conservation governance in the context of Australian MPAs. International instruments and institutions relevant to MPA governance are first introduced including an examination of how MPAs are implemented, categorized and zoned. The Australian governance framework of national, state, regional, local and non-state arrangements specific to MPAs is then described. The role and relevance of the regional marine planning process, the National Ocean Policy and the National Representative System of Marine Protected Areas are presented. Cooperative federalism in the marine environment provides the current context for MPA planning and management. Two case studies (Whitsundays and Tweed-Moreton) are used to illustrate the challenges facing transboundary governance arrangements for MPAs. These case studies variously illustrate transboundary issues associated with increasing and compounding pressures of coastal development, fishing and climate change[1] impacts on the marine environment. In light of the multiplicity and

---

1 See: E M P Madin, N C Ban, Z A Doubleday, T H Holmes, G T Pecl and F Smith, 'Socio-economic and Management Implications of Range-shifting Species in Marine Systems' (2011) 22 *Global Environmental Change* 137–146. P R Last, W T White, D C Gledhill, A J Hobday, R Brown, G J Edgar and G Pecl, 'Long-term Shifts in Abundance and Distribution of a Temperate Fish Fauna: A Response to Climate Change and Fishing Practices' (2011) 20(1) *Global Ecology and Biogeography* 58–72. E S Poloczanska, R C

complexity of the issues confronting transboundary MPA governance, we argue for a broader consideration of transboundary issues and the need to enhance adaptive capacity for effective marine biodiversity governance.

In developing the case for an expanded appreciation of transboundary issues, we first draw on work undertaken with stakeholders to identify the key issues confronting marine biodiversity conservation in the case study regions.[2] Then as a framework for discussion, we deploy a set of themes around adaptive governance requirements for marine biodiversity.[3] We use these themes to analyse current transboundary MPA governance regimes for our case studies. We conclude by highlighting the lessons for more strategic, integrated and adaptive approaches to transboundary marine governance.

MPA Governance

In 1972 the United Nations Conference on the Human Environment, commonly known as the Stockholm Conference, established the World Heritage Convention.[4] The Convention came into force in 1975 and encourages States Parties to nominate sites for inclusion on the World Heritage List. These sites must be of outstanding universal value and can include both natural and cultural elements. Listed sites must support long-term conservation and support appropriate legislative, regulatory and institutional protection.[5] The Convention does not specifically outline the role of MPAs. However, important international world heritage area designations have included the marine environment. The most famous is the Australian Great Barrier Reef World Heritage Area.

More specific references to the role of MPAs came about in the early 1990s. One of the agreements adopted at the 1992 Rio Earth Summit was the Convention on Biological Diversity (CBD), which came into force in 1993. The CBD is considered one of the most significant global environmental agreements on the conservation and sustainable use of biodiversity. Australia signed the CBD

Babcock, A Butler, A J Hobday, O Hoegh-Guldberg, T J Kunz, R Matear, D A Milton, T A Okey and A J Richardson, 'Climate Change and Australian Marine Life' (2007) 45 *Oceanography and Marine Biology: An Annual Review* 407–478.

2 M G Haward and J Davidson, *Scenarios (Phase 1), Report Number 2, Changing Currents in Marine Biodiversity Governance and Management: Responding to Climate Change* (School of Geography and Environmental Studies, University of Tasmania, 2012).

3 M Lockwood, J Davidson, M Hockings, M Haward, L Kriwoken and R Allchin, *Requirements for Marine Biodiversity Conservation Governance and Management in a Changing Climate Change* (School of Geography and Environmental Studies, University of Tasmania, 2012).

4 Formally known as the *Convention Concerning the Protection of the World Cultural and Natural Heritage 1972*, 1037 UNTS 151 (entered into force 16 November 1972).

5 See: M Lockwood, G L Worboys and A Kothari (eds), *Managing Protected Areas: A Global Guide* (Earthscan, 2006).

on World Environment Day (5 June 1992) and ratified on 18 June 1993.[6] The agreement covers all ecosystems, species and genetic resources. Article 6 of the CBD states that parties shall undertake the following:

a. develop national strategies, plans or programs for the conservation and sustainable use of biological diversity or adapt for this purpose existing strategies, plans or programs which shall reflect, *inter alia*, the measures set out in this convention relevant to the contracting Party concerned; and
b. integrate, as far as possible and as appropriate, the conservation and sustainable use of biological diversity into relevant sectoral or cross-sectoral plans, programs and policies.

The CBD supports the establishment of guidelines for the selection, establishment and management of MPAs. One of the most important protected area concepts to emerge from the Convention was the phrase 'comprehensive, adequate and representative' (CAR) reserves.[7] In addition, the CBD outlines a program of works specifically for marine and coastal areas.[8] Operational objectives and priority activities within five key program elements were identified in order to ensure action at national and local levels. Each program element sets a goal and a number of operational objectives.

Agenda 21[9] also makes specific reference to the role of MPAs. Chapter 17[10] of Agenda 21 acknowledges the requirements to address critical uncertainties for

---

6 L K Kriwoken, 'Australian Biodiversity and Marine Protected Areas' (1996) 33 *Ocean and Coastal Management* 113.

7 The Australian National Reserves System defines 'comprehensive' as the aim of including samples of the full range of regional ecosystems recognizable at an appropriate scale across bioregions. 'Adequacy' refers to how much of each ecosystem should be sampled to provide ecological viability and integrity of populations, species and ecological communities. 'Representativeness' is comprehensiveness at a finer scale and recognizes that the regional variability within ecosystems is sampled within the reserve system. See Commonwealth of Australia, *Australia's Strategy for the National Reserves System 2009–2030* (National Reserves System Task Force convened under the Natural Resource Policies and Program Committee, 2009) 10 and G Wescott, 'The Long and Winding Road: The Development of a Comprehensive, Adequate and Representative System of Highly Protected Marine Protected Areas in Victoria, Australia' (2006) 49 *Ocean and Coastal Management* 905.

8 *Convention on Biological Diversity*, 1760 UNTS 79 (signed 5 June 1992 and entered into force 29 December 1993). Program of works include: integrated marine and coastal area management; marine and coastal protected areas; sustainable use of coastal and marine living resources; mariculture; and alien species.

9 Agenda 21 is the United Nations sustainable development action plan resulting from the Rio Earth Summit in 1992.

10 Chapter 17 is entitled: Protection of the Oceans, All Kinds of Seas, Including Enclosed and Semi-Enclosed Seas, and Coastal Areas and the Protection, Rational Use and Development of Their Living Resources.

the management of the marine environment and climate change. It supports the United Nations Convention on the Law of the Sea[11] (LOSC) and marine scientific research. Seven program areas are outlined in the Chapter.[12] Recent additions specific to the marine environment were made at the 9th CBD Conference of Parties (COP) in 2008. The Parties to the Convention adopted a set of seven scientific criteria to identify ecologically or biologically significant areas in the global marine realm.[13] The COP recognized the importance of MPAs and their critical role in achieving conservation and sustainable use of biodiversity within and beyond national jurisdictions.

Significant support for protecting biodiversity has also been made at a nongovernment level. There has been very strong international leadership from the International Union for the Conservation of Nature (IUCN). The IUCN, established in 1947, is the world's largest and most influential conservation network. The World Commission on Protected Areas (WCPA), one of the six expert commissions established by the IUCN, promotes the establishment and effective management of a worldwide representative network of terrestrial and marine protected areas. The IUCN has published a number of influential guidelines for protected areas including the *Guidelines for Protected Area Management Categories*[14] and the recent *Guidelines for applying the IUCN Protected Area Management Categories to Marine Protected Areas*.[15] The 2008 *Guidelines for Applying Protected Area*

---

11 *United Nations Convention on the Law of the Sea,* 1833 UNTS 396 (signed 10 December 1982 and entered into force 16 November 1994).

12 (1) integrated management and sustainable development of coastal and marine areas, including exclusive economic zones; (2) marine environmental protection; (3) sustainable use and conservation of marine living resources of the high seas; (4) sustainable use and conservation of marine living resources under national jurisdiction; (5) addressing critical uncertainties for the management of the marine environment and climate change; (6) strengthening international, including regional, cooperation and coordination; and (7) sustainable development of small islands.

13 Uniqueness or rarity; special importance for life history of species; importance for threatened, endangered or declining species and/or habitats; vulnerability, fragility, sensitivity, slow recovery; biological; biological diversity; and naturalness. See: Global Ocean Biodiversity Initiative, *Identify EBSAs in the World's Oceans* (2010) http://www.cbd.int/cop/cop-10/doc/gobi-briefing-contribute-expertise-en.pdf.

14 IUCN, *Guidelines for Protected Area Management Categories* (IUCN, 1994), which was updated in *Guidelines for Applying Protected Area Management Categories* (Dudley, 2008).

15 Category Ia areas strictly protect biodiversity and possibly geological/ geomorphological features, where human visitation, use and impacts are strictly controlled and limited to ensure protection of the conservation values. Category Ib areas are usually large unmodified or slightly modified areas, retaining their natural character and influence, without permanent or significant human habitation. Category II areas are large natural or near natural areas set aside to protect large-scale ecological processes, along with the complement of species and ecosystems characteristic of the area, which also provide a foundation for environmentally and culturally compatible spiritual, scientific, educational,

Categories state that: 'a protected area is a clearly defined geographical space, recognized, dedicated and managed, through legal or other effective means, to achieve the long-term conservation of nature with associated ecosystem services and cultural values'. The six categories for protected areas are internationally recognized and used to identify management responses and a range of zoning applications. These guidelines adopt management categories ranging from strict protection through to multiple use.[16] Assignments of IUCN categories are reported to the UNEP World Conservation Monitoring Centre, so that this information can be included in the World Database on Protected Areas and the UN List of Protected Areas.

For instance, Australia's Great Barrier Reef Marine Park (GBRMP), which is one of the most widely known MPAs, has a range of relevant IUCN categories that make up the protected area (Table 4.1). Zone types within the GBRMP are assigned IUCN categories that are in turn used to determine activities allowed in the MPA (Table 4.2). In the GBRMP Preservation zones are 'no go' areas and make up less than 1%. Marine National Park zones of around 33% are 'no take' zones where extractive activities including fishing or collecting require a permit, yet anyone may enter the zone and participate in recreational activities including swimming, boating, snorkelling and sailing. Conservation Park zones allow for most extractive activities including limited line fishing, trolling, limited spearfishing, bait netting, limited crabbing and limited collecting, while other activities such as research and aquaculture require a permit. Habitat Protection zones, which make up 28% of the area, prohibit trawling but allow most other fishing activities. General Use zones allow for all fishing activities but require a permit for harvesting aquarium fish and tropical rock lobster and research activities. Scientific research zones allow research usually around scientific research facilities. Buffer zones provide protection of areas in a natural state yet allow the public to enjoy the area.

---

recreational and visitor opportunities. Category III areas protect a specific natural monument, which can be a landform, sea mount, submarine cavern, geological feature such as a cave or even a living component such as a specific coralline feature. Category IV areas protect species or habitats and may need interventions to address the requirements of a species or to maintain habitats. Category V areas are where the interaction of people and nature has produced an area of distinct character with significant ecological, biological, cultural and scenic value. Category VI areas conserve ecosystems and habitats, together with associated cultural values and traditional natural resource management systems. They are generally large, with most of the area in a natural condition, where a proportion is under low-level non-industrial sustainable natural resource management and where such use of natural resources compatible with nature conservation is one of the main aims. Adapted from: WCPA, *Guidelines for applying the IUCN Protected Area Management Categories to Marine Protected Areas (supplementary to the 2008 Guidelines)* (IUCN, 2011).

16 See: IUCN, *Guidelines for Applying Protected Area Management Categories* (Dudley, 2008).

Table 4.1 Zone types within the Great Barrier Reef Marine Park[17]

Zone name	Equivalent IUCN category	Area (km²)	Area (ha)	% of GBRMP
Preservation Zone	Ia	710	71,000	<1
Marine National Park Zone	II	114,530	11,453,000	33
Scientific Research Zone	Ia	155	15,500	<1
Buffer Zone	IV	9,880	988,000	3
Conservation Park Zone	IV	5,160	516,000	2
Habitat Protection Zone	VI	97,250	9,725,000	28
General Use Zone	VI	116,530	11,653,000	34
Commonwealth Islands	II	185	18,500	<1
Total		344,400	34,440,000	100

17 The Great Barrier Reef Marine Park does not include Queensland State islands, intertidal waters, Queensland internal waters, or port areas.

Table 4.2 Matrix of IUCN categories and activities permitted in an MPA

Activities that may be permitted in an MPA	**Ia**	**Ib**	**II**	**III**	**IV**	**V**	**VI**
Habitation	N	N*	N*	N*	N*	Y	N*
Untreated waste discharge	N	N	N	N	N	Y	Y
Mining (seafloor as well as sub-seafloor)	N	N	N	N	N	Y*	Y*
Commercial fishing/collection	N	N	N	N	*	Y	Y
Recreational fishing/collection	N	N	N	N	*	Y	Y
Aquaculture	N	N	N	N	*	Y	Y
Works (e.g. harbours, ports, dredging)	N	N	N	N	*	Y	Y
Research: extractive	N*	N*	N*	N*	Y	Y	Y
Renewable energy generation	N	N	N	N	Y	Y	Y
Restoration/enhancement for other reasons (e.g. beach replenishment, fish aggregation, artificial reefs)	N	N	N*	N*	Y	Y	Y
Problem wildlife management (e.g. shark control programmes)	N	N	Y*	Y*	Y*	Y	Y
Shipping (except as may be unavoidable under international maritime law)	N	N	Y*	Y*	Y	Y	Y
Commercial tourism	N	N	Y	Y	Y	Y	Y
Non-extractive recreation (e.g. diving)	N	*	Y	Y	Y	Y	Y
Traditional fishing/collection in accordance with cultural tradition and use	N	Y*	Y	Y	Y	Y	Y
Non-extractive traditional use	Y*	Y	Y	Y	Y	Y	Y
Research: non-extractive	Y*	Y	Y	Y	Y	Y	Y
Restoration/enhancement for conservation (e.g. invasive species control, coral reintroduction)	Y*	*	Y	Y	Y	Y	Y

Note: Key: N = No; Y = Yes

* = Variable; depending on the management plan for the MPA demonstrating their compatibility with the MPA's objectives

N* = Generally no, unless special circumstance apply

Y* = No alternative exists and therefore special approval is needed

Transboundary protected areas can also play an important role in biodiversity protection and are defined as:

> an area of land and/or sea that straddles one or more borders between states, sub-national units such as provinces and regions, autonomous areas, and/or areas beyond the limit of national sovereignty or jurisdiction, whose constituent parts are especially dedicated to the protection and maintenance of biological diversity, and of natural and associated cultural resources, and are managed cooperatively through legal or effective means.[18]

The Waterton-Glacier International Peace Park, declared in 1932, is often cited as a successful example of Canadian–US transboundary protected area partnership. Recognizing the importance of this arrangement in general, an expert group of the IUCN WCPA was convened in 2004. The Task Force on Transboundary Protected Areas devised a typology for transboundary conservation initiatives.[19] The typology addressed areas such as: jurisdiction, land use, peace and cooperation, and migratory processes. Whilst this represents a significant development in transboundary conservation and development initiatives, it has largely focussed on terrestrial areas. Little work has been carried out on transboundary conservation on a large marine ecosystem scale.

Australian MPA Governance

Under the LOSC, Australia has sovereign rights to manage the natural resources of the Exclusive Economic Zone (EEZ) (extending up to 200 nm from the territorial sea baseline), and sovereignty over its territorial sea (up to 12 nm from baselines). Under an agreement with the Australian Government, known as the Offshore Constitutional Settlement, Australian states and the Northern Territory generally have legal responsibility for the waters in the 3 nm of the territorial sea immediately offshore.[20] This settlement is implemented through a number of Acts and covers management of oil and gas exploration and extraction, the GBRMP and other MPAs, historic shipwrecks, shipping, marine pollution and fishing. With the third largest marine environment in the world, it is not surprising that the complexities associated with Australia's marine jurisdiction mean that there are significant economic, cultural, social and scientific transboundary issues associated with managing this area in an ecologically sustainable manner.

---

18 T Sandwith and M Lockwood, 'Linking the Landscape' in M Lockwood, G L Worboys and A Kothari (eds), *Managing Protected Areas: A Global Guide* (Earthscan, 2006) 574–602.

19 Ibid, 589.

20 M G Haward, 'The Australian Offshore Constitutional Settlement' (1989) 13 *Marine Policy* 334.

Australia's ecological responsibilities were developed in parallel with international environmental developments discussed above. The 1992 Australian National Strategy for Ecologically Sustainable Development[21] supported the establishment of a comprehensive system of protected areas. This system includes representative samples of both terrestrial and marine ecosystems. The 1996 National Strategy for the Conservation of Australia's Biological Diversity specifically recognized the wealth of the nation's marine and terrestrial biodiversity. It included the broad goal of protecting biological diversity and maintaining ecological processes and systems.[22] The establishment of a CAR system of ecologically viable protected areas integrated with other resource production systems was supported.

Specific national interest in managing the marine estate for conservation began in the late 1990s. In 1997 the Commonwealth Government released a consultation paper entitled *Australia's Oceans: New Horizons.*[23] The Government committed to undertaking marine resource planning and management. A series of background and issues papers were released describing Australia's maritime areas, sectoral issues and management principles.[24] The Commonwealth Government's *Australia's Ocean Policy* was then released in 1998.[25] The policy set in place the 'framework for integrated and ecosystem-based management of Australia's marine jurisdictions'.[26] The policy called for the development of regional marine plans (RMPs) supported through the concept of multiple use, large marine ecosystems and the precautionary principle.[27]

The use of RMPs was introduced at the April 2000 National Oceans Forum, and the first RMP to be developed was the South-East Regional Marine Plan (SERMP) which includes waters off Tasmania, (and sub-Antarctic Macquarie

---

21 Commonwealth of Australia, *National Strategy for Ecologically Sustainable Development* (Council of Australian Governments, 1992).

22 Commonwealth of Australia, *National Strategy for the Conservation of Australia's Biological Diversity* (Department of Environment, Sport and Territories, 1996) available at: http://www.environment.gov.au/biodiversity/publications/strategy/index.htm.

23 Commonwealth of Australia, *Australia's Oceans, New Horizons, Oceans Policy Consultation Paper* (Australian Government Publishing Service, 1997).

24 See for example: K Sainsbury, M Haward, L K Kriwoken, M Tsamenyi and T Ward, *Multiple Use Management in the Australian Marine Environment: Principles, Definitions and Elements: Issues Paper 1* (Environment Australia, 1997).

25 See: J Vince, 'Managing Australia's Oceans through the Oceans Policy Process' in W Gullett, C Schofield and J Vince (eds), *Marine Resources Management* (LexisNexis Butterworths, 2011) 77–89.

26 Commonwealth of Australia, *Australia's Ocean Policy* (Environment Australia, 1998) 2.

27 L K Kriwoken, L Fallon and D R Rothwell, 'Australia and the Precautionary Principle: Moving from International Principles to Domestic and Local Implementation' in D R Rothwell and D VanderZwaag (eds), *Towards Principled Oceans Governance: Australian and Canadian Approaches and Challenges* (Routledge, 2006) 181–202.

Island), Victoria and parts of New South Wales and South Australia. A discussion paper was released and a draft plan for the region completed in July 2003. At that time, details on how an MPA system would be supported in the SERMP were not apparent. However, the Ocean Policy recognized the importance of ecologically sustainable development and the accelerated development of improved management of marine reserves, and advocated an expansion of MPAs through the establishment of the National Representative System of Marine Protected Areas (NRSMPA).

The Ocean Policy recognized that cooperative marine management was required and identified that the primary means of consultation between the Commonwealth and States would be the Australian and New Zealand Environment and Conservation Council (ANZECC). The ANZECC Task Force on MPAs was set up to provide an opportunity for the Australian Government, states and the Northern Territory to coordinate MPA activities and collaborate on policy development and related projects. ANZECC operated between 1991 and 2001. It was replaced by the Natural Resource Management Ministerial Council and the Environment Protection and Heritage Council. These Ministerial Councils consist of Australian, state, territory and New Zealand government ministers responsible for primary industries, natural resources, environment and water policy.

ANZECC released the Guidelines for Establishing the NRSMPA in 1998.[28] The Guidelines supported a national system of MPAs with representative samples of Australia's marine ecosystems.[29] The goal of the system was to 'establish and manage a comprehensive, adequate and representative system of MPAs to contribute to the long-term ecological viability of marine and estuarine systems, maintain ecological processes and systems, and protect Australia's biological diversity at all levels'.[30] The Guidelines set out how MPAs are to be established, the roles and responsibilities of the NRSMPA and the criteria for identification and selection of MPAs. Secondary goals of the NRSMPA have also been established. These are to promote integrated ecosystem management; management of human activities; provision for the needs of species and ecological communities; and for the recreational, aesthetic, cultural and economic needs of Indigenous and non-indigenous peoples.

In parallel with these arrangements, new Commonwealth environment legislation was developed in the latter part of the 1990s. The *Environment*

---

28 Commonwealth of Australia, *Guidelines for Establishing the National Representative System of Marine Protected Areas* (Australian and New Zealand Environment and Conservation Council Task Force on Marine Protected Areas, Environment Australia, 1998). Available at: http://www.environment.gov.au/coasts/mpa/publications/pubs/nrsmpa-establishing-guidelines.pdf.

29 See: L K Kriwoken, 'Charting a Course for Marine Protected Areas' in W Gullett, C Schofield and J Vince (eds), *Marine Resources Management* (LexisNexis Butterworths, 2011) 171–181.

30 Commonwealth of Australia, above n 28.

Protection and Biodiversity Conservation Act 1999 (Cth) (EPBC Act) represented the most significant reform of Australian environmental legislation since the first suite of environmental legislation was introduced in 1974. Chapter 4 of the Act regulates actions that have or are likely to have a significant impact on matters of national environmental significance[31] (MNES)[32] through the federal environmental impact assessment process. A number of these MNES include specific reference to marine environments, species or communities. The Act sets out the management of Commonwealth reserves (including MPAs). MPAs are the responsibility of the Director of National Parks, and are managed on behalf of the Director by Parks Australia, which is an agency within the Department of Sustainability, Environment, Water, Population and Communities (SEWPAC). All MPAs require a management plan that sets out objectives for protection and conservation. Reserves are managed in accordance with the Australian IUCN Reserve Management Principles and the EPBC Regulations 2000, which set out the Australian IUCN Reserve Management Categories and Principles (Part 10.04).[33] These principles were derived from the 1994 IUCN Guidelines for Protected Area Management Categories.[34] The development of management plans involves public consultation and an assessment of the impact on existing businesses with a marine focus.

Marine bioregional planning is established under section 176 of the EPBC Act and is the responsibility of SEWPAC. The planning process involves Commonwealth waters only and there is no provision to include state waters. Five marine bioregional planning regions have been identified and the first completed was the above-mentioned South-East Region.[35] The plans are seen as a means to fulfil the Australian Government commitment to the NRSMPA. Conservation values and key ecological features are identified for each regional assessment. Once that occurs, regional priorities and pressures are identified. After extensive public consultation the plan and associated marine reserve network for each region are released.

---

31 Available at http://www.environment.gov.au/epbc/publications/pubs/nes-guidelines.pdf.

32 Matters of national environmental significance were identified as direct triggers that invoke the EPBC Act. Significant impact guidelines have been developed that provide guidance on whether a development action would likely have a significant impact on a matter protected under national environmental law. They include: listed threatened species and communities; listed migratory species; Ramsar wetlands; national heritage places; nuclear actions; Great Barrier Reef Marine Park; and Commonwealth marine areas.

33 Commonwealth of Australia, *Australian IUCN Reserve Management Principles for Commonwealth MPAs* (Environment Australia, 2002).

34 Department of the Environment, Water, Heritage and the Arts, *Australian Government and IUCN Protected Area Categories* (2010) http://www.environment.gov.au/parks/iucn.html.

35 South-East, South-West, North-West, North and East. See: http://www.environment.gov.au/coasts/mbp/publications/north-west/fs-north-west.html#what.

Part 10 of the EPBC Act allows for the strategic assessment of impacts of actions under a policy, plan or program. This can include a regional-scale development or policy, industry sector policies, resource management plans, programs or policies of large-scale industrial development. For instance, a strategic assessment for the Browse Basin[36] liquefied natural gas precinct was undertaken to address alternatives to prevent ad hoc developments from individual companies operating on the northwest shelf of Western Australia. The application of part 10 of the Act has recently been adopted for the Great Barrier Reef World Heritage Area (GBRWHA). The Great Barrier Reef Marine Park Authority (GBRMPA), which is the Australian Government agency responsible for the management of the GBRMP, and the Commonwealth Minister for SEWPAC entered into an agreement to conduct a strategic assessment on 16 February 2012.[37] The draft terms of reference (TOR) for the GBRMP strategic assessment and the Queensland coastal zone strategic assessment have been released.[38] The draft TOR requires that potential impacts on MNES from the implementation of the GBRMPA management arrangements will be addressed. The draft TOR makes specific reference to addressing cumulative impacts. The assessment will identify and analyse potential impacts, including cumulative impacts, on relevant MNES and will examine measures to avoid, mitigate and offset likely impacts. The marine component will be undertaken by the GBRMPA and will address management arrangements to protect the GBRMP and GBRWHA. In concert, the Queensland Government will lead the coastal component. This will include specific reference to coastal development and planning for urban, industrial and port development.

The *Great Barrier Reef Marine Park Act 1975 (Cth)* establishes the GBRMPA and sets out its powers and functions. The Act details the implementation of zoning arrangements, the preparation of plans of management as well as offences and enforcement provisions. In addition the Act introduces the collection of an environmental management charge, and compulsory pilotage on regulated ships of the GBR Region and administration and financial reporting provisions. The GBRMPA makes recommendations to the Minister with regard to matters relating

---

36 A site selection process was undertaken by the Western Australian Government in 2008 to identify a common-user liquefied natural gas precinct and associated activities in the Browse Basin. See: http://www.environment.gov.au/epbc/notices/assessments/kimberley.html.

37 Great Barrier Reef Marine Park Authority, *Strategic Assessment of the Impacts of Actions on the Values of the Great Barrier Reef World Heritage Area, Other Relevant Matters of National Environmental Significance, and the Management Arrangements to Deal with such Impacts under the Jurisdiction of the GBRMPA* (Great Barrier Reef Marine Park Authority, 2011) http://www.gbrmpa.gov.au/__data/assets/pdf_file/0018/15183/GBRMPA-Draft-ToR-Strategic-Assessment-17022012.pdf.

38 Great Barrier Reef Marine Park Authority, *Draft Terms of Reference* (2012) http://www.gbrmpa.gov.au/outlook-for-the-reef/strategic-assessment/draft-terms-of-reference.

to the Marine Park, including research and investigations, zoning and management planning, educational, advisory and informational services.[39]

The GBRMPA has adopted an Environmental Impact Management Policy (EIMP)[40] to manage major developments in the park. The EIMP includes four phases: scoping, assessment, implementation and audit. Cumulative impacts associated with proposed developments are considered in the process. A range of tools are supported in the policy. The GBRMPA allocates projects to one of four levels of assessment ranging from minor projects with a transient impact through to complex or large-scale projects with significant public interest and irreversible and/or major impact. The process is run by the GBRMPA Environmental Assessment Management team. Whilst the EIMP is recognized in the planning and management of the GBRMP, this is not typical of other MPAs more generally. In MPAs outside the GBRMP the use of environmental impact assessment is not widely adopted and institutional frameworks do not usually support its application.

In addition, the states and territories have an important role in establishing and managing MPAs. The Australian states have jurisdiction to the 3 nm boundary and most have established networks of marine reserves of varying sizes and levels of protection. However, there is increasing recognition that activities occurring in hinterland catchments and along the coastline have implications for the marine environment. In Australia, the relevant decision-making actors are the regional or catchment-based natural resource management (NRM) authorities and local government. Since 2002, regional NRM has been the main mechanism for addressing issues of environmental degradation although there is considerable variation in structure both among and within states and territories. Structural variation is influenced by the degree of legislative standing and statutory functions conferred on regional NRM organizations. Queensland NRM bodies are community based and lack statutory responsibility while the NSW catchment management authorities are structured as statutory authorities. Land use planning and development approval is generally undertaken in the first instance by local governments, with subsequent oversight of these decisions by state governments or associated state-level statutory planning authorities. Although coastal urban development is acknowledged to be a significant factor in the health of the marine environment, coastal planning and management is not yet a pressing priority for many Australian local governments[41] so that, on the whole, marine park management is not well integrated with local government land use planning.

---

39 Great Barrier Reef Marine Park Authority, Legislation http://www.gbrmpa.gov.au/about-us/legislation-regulations-and-policies/legislation.

40 Great Barrier Reef Marine Park Authority, *Environmental Impact Management Policy* (2004) http://www.gbrmpa.gov.au/__data/assets/pdf_file/0004/3847/gbrmpa_EnvironmentalImpactManagementPolicy_2004.pdf.

41 M Nursey-Bray, 'Learning and Local Government: The Local Government Coastal Management Strategy, South Australia, *20th NSW Coastal Conference* (2011).

MPA Case Studies in Transboundary Governance

The following section presents two case studies of MPAs located on the east coast of Australia. These case studies enable us to explore a range of transboundary issues that influence MPA governance and highlight the need for new models of governance and a broadening of both formal and informal arrangements. They also highlight the challenges presented by climate change and variability for MPA governance. For each case study, a short introduction is followed by a discussion of the main issues (identified through stakeholder workshops[42]) driving the condition of marine biodiversity, an outline of current state-level MPA arrangements, and a summary of transboundary challenges. The main issues for the Whitsundays region include growth in port-related infrastructure and other coastal development, land-based impacts on reef water quality, and climate change. For the Tweed-Moreton region, the key issues with transboundary implications are similar. They involve the pressures of population growth and associated coastal development, pressures from fishing, land-based impacts on water quality and climate change impacts on marine ecosystems.

Whitsundays

Background The Whitsundays case study area encompasses a 100 km stretch of water from Cape Edgecumbe to Cape Hillsborough, Queensland and extends eastward to the edge of the GBRMP.[43] The region is characterized by complex jurisdictional arrangements involving both the Australian Government and the State of Queensland.

The Commonwealth is responsible for the GBRMP, which generally incorporates Queensland state waters, as well as Commonwealth islands. The remainder of the islands are under Queensland jurisdiction. Queensland is responsible for the management of the Great Barrier Reef Coast Marine Park. This area is contiguous with the GBRMP and covers the area between the low and high water mark and any waters within Queensland jurisdiction.[44] Queensland is responsible for the management of fisheries and recreational fishing found in the 200 nm EEZ. However, the Commonwealth Australian Fisheries Management Authority manages the Eastern Tuna and Billfish Fishery, and the Southern Bluefin Tuna Fishery, in accordance with the *Fisheries Management Act 1991*, subject to provisions of the *Great Barrier Reef Marine Park Act 1975*.

42 Haward and Davidson, above n 2.

43 R Allchin and J Davidson, *Whitsundays Case Study Background Report, Changing Currents in Marine Biodiversity Governance and Management: Responding to Climate Change* (School of Geography and Environmental Studies, University of Tasmania, 2012).

44 Great Barrier Reef Marine Park Authority, *Great Barrier Reef Outlook Report* (GBRMPA, 2009).

Infrastructure and Port Development The region faces a number of transboundary issues associated with poor water quality in inner reef areas and development pressure along the Queensland coast. This is associated with the expansion of port infrastructure to service coal and coal seam gas exports and an increase in the volume of cruise ships. Concern has also been raised regarding the extent of growth and development along the Queensland coast. The prospect of an increasing incidence of marine accidents and oil spills that damage the reef has implications for marine biodiversity and for tourism and fishing sectors.

The World Heritage Committee had concerns in 2011 about the approval of the Liquefied Natural Gas developments on Curtis Island near Gladstone in the GBRWHA. A Committee visit to the GBRWHA in 2012 voiced reservations about the scale and expansion of coal terminals along the coast. As a result the Committee requested that Australia undertake a comprehensive strategic assessment of the GBRWHA that will identify planned and potential future development that could impact on WHA values. A strategic assessment under Part 10 of the EPBC Act will be used to examine new proposals or developments (actions) over a much larger scale and timeframe.[45] The process includes an assessment and endorsement of a policy, plan or program.

Catchment-based Impacts A synthesis of new and existing knowledge[46] on GBR water quality was recently undertaken as a means to reinvigorate the Reef Water Quality Protection Plan. Freshwater discharged from rivers into the GBR continues to be of poor water quality in many locations. The health of freshwater ecosystems is impaired by agricultural land use, hydrological change, riparian degradation and weed infestation. Land-derived contaminants, including suspended sediments, nutrients and pesticides/herbicides are present in the GBR at concentrations likely to cause environmental harm. Increasing evidence suggests the causal relationship between water quality and coastal and marine ecosystem health.

Studies have investigated various aspects of land-based impacts on the GBR including nearshore water quality, and coral and other reef species. Land-based pollutants exacerbate climate change impacts such as bleaching and storm disturbance. Herbicides, for example, compound the effects of bleaching by reducing the ability of coral to take up energy, which leads to reductions in

---

45 Open Lines Environmental Consulting, *A Guide to Undertaking Strategic Assessments* (Department of Sustainability, Environment, Water, Population and Communities, 2011). See: http://www.gbrmpa.gov.au/__data/assets/pdf_file/0018/15183/GBRMPA-Draft-ToR-Strategic-Assessment-17022012.pdf.

46 J E Brodie, J Binney, K Fabricius, I Gordon, O Hoegh-Guldberg, H Hunter, P O'Reagain, R Pearson, M Quirk, P Thorburn, J Waterhouse, I Webster, S Wilkinson, *Synthesis of Evidence to Support the Scientific Consensus Statement on Water Quality in the Great Barrier Reef* (Intergovernmental Operations Committee and the RWQP Management Committee, 2008).

reproductive output.[47] Herbicides are frequently detected in inshore waters of the GBR and the highest concentrations occur during flood plumes associated with the monsoon season, coinciding with rising ocean temperatures. These flood plumes also transport high levels of suspended solids and dissolved nutrients and can significantly reduce salinity, all of which may interact with high sea surface temperatures to threaten corals and other sensitive organisms.

Climate Change With warming sea temperatures, areas of the GBR subject to coral bleaching are expected to expand. The fast growing reef building coral *Acroporidae* are severely impacted by bleaching. While they can recover, under the expected disturbance regime of increased bleaching and more severe cyclones, this species may struggle to be resilient to climate change impacts.[48] Global warming and acidification will likely result in less diverse reef communities. Acidification and bleaching eventually drive coral reefs to become dominated by macroalgae and non-coral communities. Reef-building corals can only adapt slowly and are unlikely to adapt to present acidification levels.[49] The intertidal location of mangroves, salt marshes and salt flats makes them particularly vulnerable to changes in sea level. Mangrove-dominated offshore islands are highly vulnerable to sea level rise given the low position in the intertidal zone and limited sediment supply to the islands. Rainfall changes will also impact directly on biodiversity of GBR islands. It is likely there will be more intense rainfall events interspersed with longer periods of low rainfall or drought.[50]

Current State-level MPA Arrangements Marine parks are declared under the Queensland *Marine Parks Act 2004*, and provisions including zoning are made under the *Marine Parks Regulations 2006*. Zoning plans are used to establish the level of protection for certain areas and include general use, habitat protection, conservation park and marine national park. One of the three state marine parks – the Great Barrier Reef Coast Marine Park – is in part located in the Whitsundays region.

---

47 See: S E Lewis, J E Brodie, Z T Bainbridge, K W Rohde, A M Davis, B L Masters, M Maughan, M J Devlin, J F Mueller and B Schaffelke, 'Herbicides: A New Threat to the Great Barrier Reef' (2009) 157(8–9) *Environmental Pollution* 2470–2484. A P Negri, F Flores, T Röhig and S Uthicke, 'Herbicides Increase the Vulnerability of Corals to Rising Sea Surface Temperature' (2011) 56(2) *Limnology and Oceanography* 471–485.

48 A Thompson and A Dolman, 'Coral Bleaching: One Disturbance too many for Near-shore Reefs of the Great Barrier Reef' (2010) 29(3) *Coral Reefs* 637–648.

49 O Hoegh-Guldberg, *Likely Ecological Impacts of Global Warming and Climate Change on the Great Barrier Reef by 2050 and Beyond* (Queensland Land and Resources Tribunal, 2007).

50 M Turner and G N Batianoff, 'Vulnerability of Island Flora and Fauna in the Great Barrier Reef to Climate Change' in J E Johnson and P A Marshall (eds), *Climate Change and the Great Barrier Reef: A Vulnerability Assessment* (Great Barrier Reef Marine Park Authority and Australian Greenhouse Office, 2007) 622–666.

In Queensland, the land–sea connection is acknowledged in an injunction from the state's Environmental Protection Agency (EPA) that '[w]here coastal management issues are relevant to regional NRM plans, the NRM plans must ensure consistency with and support State and Regional Coastal Management Plans'.[51] Regional NRM is linked to State and Regional Coastal Management Plans through consistency in desired outcomes, and NRM resource condition targets, management action targets and management actions that are consistent with state and regional policies relevant to water quality management, storm water management, groundwater quality, and acid sulphate soils. Regional NRM is linked to marine park planning – boundaries declaration, zoning plans and management plans – through the identification of environmental values, resource condition targets and management action targets, respectively.

A particularly relevant initiative concerning the risks from declining quality of water entering the GBR is the *Reef Water Quality Protection Plan*, which provides coordinated action on chemical, sediment and nutrient pollutants arising from land use activities. This is a joint initiative between the Queensland and Australian Governments and requires regional NRM bodies to undertake actions on developing appropriate resource condition targets, partnerships, research projects and education programs under the Plan. Land use planning relevant to the marine environment occurs at the regional level and focuses on coastal planning and management through State and Regional Coastal Management Plans (EPA 2004).[52]

Tweed-Moreton Bay

Background The Tweed-Moreton case study is delineated by the boundaries of the Tweed-Moreton Bioregion from the waters north of Nambucca Heads, NSW in the south to the northern boundary of Moreton Bay Marine Park, Queensland. It excludes waters in the bioregion north including the Great Sandy Marine Park. The case study crosses the state jurisdictions of both NSW and Queensland within the 3 nm territorial sea and includes Commonwealth waters from 3 nm to the edge of the continental shelf, the 200 m isobath.[53]

Due to the cross-jurisdictional characteristics of the region, there are three different zoning schemes offering various levels of protection. Within the case study there are one Commonwealth marine reserve, three state marine parks, one aquatic reserve and 12 national park marine extensions. In total these MPAs cover approximately 4,500 km^2.

51 Environmental Protection Agency, 'Integrating coastal and marine park management into regional NRM plans' (2004) www.regionalnrm.qld.gov.au/policies_plans_legislation/planning_guidance_docs/coastal.pdf.

52 Ibid.

53 Allchin and Davidson, above n 43.

Catchment-based Impacts and Coastal Development With respect to water quality impacts, there are significant differences between the Moreton Bay and Tweed sub-regions. Moreton Bay is the fastest growing region in the country. It is expanding to the north and south rather than to the west. The main driver is land capable of development for residential purposes. The result is almost continual coastal urban development from the Gold Coast to Brisbane to the Sunshine Coast. The large and growing population around Moreton Bay creates high volumes of storm water that transports a large amount of sediment into the bay. Seagrass mapping shows a significant change in species following flooding events on the scale of tens of square kilometres. This has meant dramatic changes as a result of recent flooding events, including loss of species. Changes in the Brisbane Valley through forest removal for grazing are one of the sources of sedimentation in Moreton Bay.[54]

Problems of water quality in NSW are more a legacy of history associated with flood mitigation efforts and acid sulphate soil problems as opposed to more recent development. As well, flood management is not as well developed as in the Great Barrier Reef area. Water quality problems particularly affect estuaries, many of which are currently under significant stress. Water quality is influenced by agricultural practices of water and chemical use and cultivation practices. Around Coffs Harbour, for example, changes in agricultural practices as farmers shift from bananas to blueberries have resulted in changes in sediment runoff. In part, this is the result of the banana leaf debris no longer left on the ground to hold down the soil. Property development resulting from the influx of population is adding to the sediment and pollutant loads of storm water.[55]

Climate Change With climate change, the East Australian Current (EAC), the main oceanographic influence in this region, is anticipated to strengthen and warm and this will have flow on effects associated with weather patterns and species distribution.[56] Results from global climate models suggest that changes in the EAC will maintain increases in volume transport, warming of sea surface temperatures, particularly in the southern regions, increases in sea surface salinity and increased cloud cover and rainfall.[57]

It is likely that the EAC will have a range of transboundary impacts on MPAs throughout the case study. The EAC has a variable influence on the waters of the Solitary Islands Marine Park (see below), one of the high marine biodiversity

54 Haward and Davidson, above n 2.

55 Ibid.

56 A J Hobday, J W Young, C Moeseneder and J M Dambacher, 'Defining Dynamic Pelagic Habitats in Oceanic Waters off Eastern Australia' (2011) 58(5) *Deep Sea Research Part II: Topical Studies in Oceanography* 734–745.

57 K Ridgway and K Hill, 'The East Australian Current' in E S Poloczanska, A J Hobday and A J Richardson (eds), *A Marine Climate Change Impacts and Adaptation Report Card for Australia 2009* (NCCARF Publication, 2009).

regions in this area of tropical-temperate overlap. The southward flowing tropical EAC exerts a greater influence on the offshore parts of the park while inshore areas are influenced by temperate inshore currents that flow northward or are generated locally. Due to the variable influence of the EAC from inshore to offshore, strong cross-shelf differences in reef assemblages have been recorded for a range of taxa. The combination of extensive reef, offshore islands, and a stronger EAC offshore provides an opportunity for a higher diversity and stronger cross-shelf patterns in the SIMP than would be expected elsewhere in NSW.[58]

The pattern of increasing ocean temperatures is likely to be variable in the SIMP, because there is considerable variation in sea temperatures, spatially and temporally. The EAC more frequently influences the outer islands than mid and inner islands and the North Solitary Island is more frequently influenced than South Solitary Island.[59] The sea-temperature patterns are also strongly influenced by localized intrusions of colder water. Patterns over seasonal scales were found to be the most consistent, with stronger EAC influence covering larger areas of shelf occurring mostly in summer. This is an important observation which is likely to have a strong influence on recruitment and larval dispersal and resulting biotic patterns.

A stronger EAC may flood the inner shelf more frequently and for longer periods, which may result in an increase in ambient temperatures and wider and more frequent dispersal of tropical larvae across the shelf. This could strongly influence the composition of reef communities by displacing a number of species that are endemic or have temperate or subtropical distributions. A stronger EAC could also increase cold-water intrusions through upwelling mechanisms. Inshore macroalgae species may contract southwards while coral communities may experience more bleaching events. In addition to changes in the EAC, climate change is also expected to affect the region through coastal erosion and degradation, extreme events and storm surges.[60]

Current State-level MPA Arrangements Due to the cross-jurisdictional characteristics of the region, there are three different zoning schemes offering various levels of protection. Within the case study area there are one Commonwealth Marine Reserve, three state marine parks, one aquatic reserve and 12 national park marine extensions. In total these MPAs cover approximately 4,500km^2.

The 160 km^2 Commonwealth Solitary Islands Marine Reserve was declared in 1993. It abuts the NSW Solitary Islands Marine Park and extends from the 3 nm state limit seaward to the 50 m depth contour.[61] There are two marine parks

58 Allchin and Davidson, above n 43.

59 H A Malcolm, S D A Smith and A Jordan, 'Using Patterns of Reef Fish Assemblages to Refine a Habitat Classification System for Marine Parks in NSW, Australia' (2010) 20(1) *Aquatic Conservation: Marine and Freshwater Ecosystems* 83–92.

60 Allchin and Davidson, above n 43.

61 Department of Sustainability, Environment, Water, Population and Communities, *Solitary Island Marine Reserve (Commonwealth waters)* (DSEWPC, 2011). See: http://

in NSW waters. The Solitary Islands Marine Park covers 722 km^2 and includes all waters to the 3 nm boundary including estuaries to their tidal limits.[62] Within Queensland waters is the Moreton Bay Marine Park which comprises 3400 km^2, taking in the waters in a 125 km stretch from Caloundra to the southern tip of Stradbroke Island.[63]

The NSW marine parks are divided into zones that allow different sustainable levels of commercial and recreational activities. Moreton Bay Marine Park is a multi-use marine protected area zoned for general use, habitat protection, conservation park, and marine national park. The Marine Parks (Moreton Bay) Zoning Plan 2008 applies restrictions on classes of users (e.g., tourism operators), mooring and anchorage, material extraction and disposal, navigation speeds, and on certain types of fishing. Under the Zoning Plan, if there is any inconsistency between local government law and a zoning plan, then whichever instrument provides the most stringent protection prevails.[64]

The lack of integration between marine park management, catchment management and land use planning is one of the key insights from a recent audit report of marine management in NSW.[65] The report notes that threats from land-based contaminants, nutrients and sediments are highest in estuarine environments, especially those that are receiving waters for urban drainage or rivers with significant areas of agricultural development and human settlement in their basins. The threats posed by pollution, habitat loss and introduced species are the main consequences of urban development for marine biodiversity recognized in the report.

The South East Queensland Regional Plan 2009–2031 is the main land use planning instrument applying to Moreton Bay Marine Park. The Plan charges that land use and infrastructure plans are consistent with the Moreton Bay Marine Park zones, fish habitat zones and management plans for the region.[66]

---

www.environment.gov.au/coasts/mpa/solitary/index.html.

62 NSW Marine Parks Authority, *Cape Byron Marine Park Operation Plan* (NSW Marine Parks Authority, 2010).

63 Department of Environment and Resource Management, *Moreton Bay Marine Park* (DERM, 2010).

64 NSW Marine Parks Authority, Marine Parks (Moreton Bay) Zoning Plan 2008, Subordinate Legislation 2008 No. 343, *Marine Parks Act 2004.*

65 R J S Beeton, C D Buxton, G C Cutbrush, P G Fairweather, E L Johnston and R Ryan, *Report of the Independent Scientific Audit of Marine Parks in New South Wales* (NSW Department of Primary Industries and Office of Environment and Heritage, 2012) 1–124.

66 Queensland Government, *South East Queensland Regional Plan 2009–2031* (Queensland Government, 2009).

Challenges for Case Study Regimes to Address Transboundary MPA Issues

Systems Understanding, Networks and Learning

Systems understanding[67] can enhance capacity for collaboration, shared decision making and more effective management planning and implementation for transboundary MPAs. Stakeholders who understand the importance of a systems approach and acknowledge the linkages between social and ecological dimensions are more likely to understand and work with the complexity of governance arrangements in the marine and coastal zone rather than managing within a more limited sectoral or disciplinary context. The imperative to take a systems approach to planning and management is heightened when the need to adapt to climate change impacts on MPAs is considered.

Building shared understanding at the science–policy interface is a particular concern in the context of climate change. Networks affect social processes associated with resource governance such as knowledge transfer, information sharing, consensus building and power relations. Boundary organizations that can bridge different scales of governance and management or mediate the relationship between science and policy are also helpful in providing necessary communication and brokerage services and supporting adaptive capacity.[68] Boundary organizations can function as 'convenors', bringing stakeholder parties together for face-to-face contact to foster trust building and mutual understanding, which is the foundation of effective information production, transfer and ultimate use. For example, the Australian Government's Oceans Policy Science Advisory Group promotes coordination among marine scientists, as well as providing advice and support to marine governance agencies. This has helped connect scientists with policy and decision makers in the GBRMP and other Australian MPAs. Nonetheless, factors such as divergent stakeholder views and priorities, as well as the level of resources and lengthy time frames required to produce good science, continue to challenge the effective integration of science into MPA governance and management processes.

Learning is a key component of adaptation and a key element of managing system resilience.[69] This involves experimentation and innovation to develop and

---

67 R Margoulis, C Stem, N Salafsky and M Brown, 'Using Conceptual Models as a Planning and Evaluation Tool in Conservation' (2009) 32 *Evaluation and Program Planning* 138–147.

68 See: T Hahn, P Olsson, C Folke and K Johansson, 'Trust-building, Knowledge Generation and Organizational Innovations: The Role of a Bridging Organization for Adaptive Co-management of a Wetland Landscape around Kristianstad, Sweden' (2006) 34 *Human Ecology* 573–592.

69 B H Walker, L H Gunderson, A P Kinzig, C Folke, S R Carpenter and L Schultz, 'A Handful of Heuristics and some Propositions for Understanding Resilience in Social-ecological Systems' (2006) 11(1) *Ecol. Soc.* http://www.ecologyandsociety.org/vol11/iss1/art13/.

test knowledge and understanding for coping with change and uncertainty. The learning approach to management – adaptive management – is predicated on the fact that social-ecological systems are managed with incomplete knowledge and that there is an imperative to monitor management outcomes and adjust management strategies and activities based on the results of the assessment. Implementation of monitoring and evaluation systems in transboundary MPA management requires an institutional culture that encourages an adaptive approach to management as a basis for learning and improvement. Again, the GBRMPA is leading the way in adopting adaptive approaches, informed by systems analyses – a key instance of this commitment is their Climate Change Adaptation Planning Framework, which incorporates vulnerability assessments, resilience analyses and adaptation planning.

World Views and Engagement

The broad attitudes and values of an individual shape how actors make and respond to policy options and decisions used to address transboundary MPA issues. Underlying individuals' environmental responses are a fundamental set of values and associated attitudes.[70] Orientations, or collections of attitudes and values, are sometimes referred to as 'world views'.[71] World views that support an adaptive approach to transboundary MPA management require all actors – decision makers and stakeholders – to be open to change and new ideas. They must also accept the value and legitimacy of diverse knowledge forms such as scientific, local and indigenous. Effective deployment of this knowledge demands openness to change and new ideas, as well as a willingness to confront and deal with complex decision contexts.

There is an evident tension between the world views of stakeholders of the Solitary Islands Marine Park in the Tweed-Morton study area. In a survey of 407 local residents, almost two-thirds named the preservation of the environment for future generations as the main benefit of having marine parks, and indicated that there were no drawbacks in having such parks. However, one-third of respondents appeared not to accept the legitimacy of MPAs, citing fewer areas to fish, fewer opportunities for recreation, and loss of commercial benefits as the main reasons.[72] This suggests that resistance to change and the introduction of new governance approaches will be an impediment to resolving these divergent views in the context of MPA establishment and management.

---

70 P Stern and T Dietz, 'The Value Basis of Environmental Concern' (1994) 50(3) *Journal of Social Issues* 65–84.

71 See: R E Dunlap, K D Van Liere, A Mertig and R E Jones, 'Measuring Endorsement of the New Ecological Paradigm: A Revised NEP Scale' (2000) 56 *Journal of Social Issues* 428.

72 McGregor Tan Research, *Solitary Islands Marine Park Community Survey Final Report* (NSW Marine Parks Authority, 2008).

This challenge is made particularly compelling by the likely impacts of climate change and sea level rise on MPAs. Management techniques and stakeholder responses that have worked in the past may not be appropriate indicators of successful approaches for the future. While there is no direct empirical evidence of MPA stakeholders' openness to change, responses to property damage caused by extreme weather events on the eastern seaboard suggest strong resistance to, for example, relocating away from vulnerable coastal areas. This reflects an inflexible world view that relies on potentially high-impact and high-cost engineering solutions and ignores more environmentally sustainable options such as staged retreat. Such views constrain the ability of decision makers to explore and trial new and innovative processes and methods, including responses to difficult transboundary MPA issues.

Engagement and decision making are central in considering the requirements for transboundary MPAs. Even without the threat of climate change, MPA governance and management can be fraught with conflict due to sharp differences in power and values across interested parties. As illustrated above in the relation to the Solitary Islands Marine Park, this is particularly evident in the tensions between biodiversity protection and resource use. When this conflict is overlain by conditions of uncertainty and complexity, the level of conflict may become particularly intense, leading to significant challenges for MPA governors to undertake inclusive engagement.

In the context of a rezoning process, and despite a survey indicating strong support for GBRMP management, the level of trust of GBRMPA among recreational fishers was found to be low. This is a barrier to building and maintaining productive relationships between resource managers and the recreational fishing community.[73] A significant number of recreational fishers considered that they were treated unfairly in the rezoning process, and believed they were not properly consulted. Furthermore, many were dissatisfied with traditional engagement methods such as public meetings and wanted theadoption of more locally appropriate methods to be used.[74]

Cohesion and Direction

Institutional fragmentation is a key issue in managing transboundary MPAs. The consequences of this fragmentation are particularly acute for marine biodiversity, given that the resilience of marine systems is threatened by multiple, interactive, and cumulative stressors, including climate change. There is the need for MPA

73 S G Sutton, *Recreational Fishers' Perceptions about the Costs and Benefits of the 2004 Great Barrier Reef Marine Park Zoning Plan* (Reef and Rainforest Research Centre Limited, 2008).

74 D M De Freitas, *The Role of Public Participation, Spatial Information and GIS in Natural Resource Management of the Dry Tropical Coast, Northern Australia*, PhD thesis (James Cook University, 2010).

governance structures to function across multiple scales and levels, from local, sub-national, national and global.[75],[76] Alignment between organizations and across boundaries (jurisdictional, sectoral and geographic) is required for system coherence in purpose, strategy and action. Strategic connectivity is important in building shared recognition of interdependencies among transboundary MPA issues. It allows actors to address shared problems in a concerted fashion.

In the case of Australian natural resource management, governance and management approaches vary across a complex of national and sub-national institutions, from governments, to regional authorities. Occasionally, regional or local groups become dysfunctional but this has not caused system-wide impacts because the units and subunits are sufficiently modularized. On the other hand, informal links among key decision makers are strong enough for information from the diverse approaches and experiences to be transmitted among the organizations, and so building the resilience of MPAs in a transboundary context. In well-connected polycentric governance systems, local, sub-national, national and international actors possess the mutual respect, trust and cohesion to collectively work through conflicts and difficulties, and thereby properly represent and address the full range of conservation values and issues. Establishing such connectivity for MPAs may involve coordination of information and knowledge, joint mobilization of resources, cooperative compliance and enforcement arrangements, and attempts to align multiple interests and priorities. These approaches can help to transcend the limitations of legally binding jurisdictional boundaries[77] that are often applied without reference to system relationships.

In the Whitsundays, governance arrangements between the Australian and Queensland governments are generally well developed and coordinated. However, regional planning frameworks and mechanisms for coordination of guidelines for the GBRWHA and adjacent regions are more recent and are not expected to lead to significant improvement in reef water quality for some years. Current arrangements are being overtaken by the rush to develop and export hinterland mineral resources to a rapidly industrializing China. Maintaining an integrated approach to MPA governance under these pressures will be a major challenge for governing authorities associated with the Whitsundays.

Moreton Bay's proximity to a large and growing urban area means that ongoing water quality, climate change and habitat loss issues will require further maturation of the state's integrated governance arrangements. While Queensland MPA governance and planning arrangements encourage integrated approaches

---

75 B Cicin-Sain and S Belfiore, 'Linking Marine Protected Areas to Integrated Coastal and Ocean Management: A Review of Theory and Practice' (2005) 48 *Ocean and Coastal Management* 847–868.

76 R Mahon, L Fanning, P McConney and R Pollnac, 'Governance Characteristics of Large Marine Ecosystems' (2010) 34(5) *Marine Policy* 919–927.

77 B Karkkainen, 'Marine Ecosystem Management & "Post-Sovereign" Transboundary Governance' (2004) 6 *San Diego International Law Journal* 113–142.

to land-based pollution, it is clear from the NSW audit report that the kind of cooperation between marine and land-based managers required to address threats to marine biodiversity needs significant development. Vertical and horizontal coordination among governing authorities over a range of issues is a continuing challenge.

The governability of transboundary MPAs depends in large part on what happens outside their borders, so that interactions and relationships between marine and land-based management authorities are critical for effective management outcomes. Interdependencies between marine and terrestrial values necessitate greater interaction between protected area governors and colleagues from resource-based sectors such as fisheries and nature-based tourism, as well as authorities responsible for land use planning and management in adjacent catchments. Policy networks and partnerships are needed to coordinate policy direction, conservation planning and transboundary management. Marine biodiversity conservation needs to be undertaken as part of an integrated approach to coastal and ocean management. Again, strong vertical and horizontal relationships are required, for example, to link MPAs with coastal and marine institutions and planning processes through coordination and harmonization of policies, plans and programs.

Among the political and jurisdictional factors that are currently driving marine biodiversity conservation in the Tweed-Moreton region are jurisdictional fragmentation, overlapping zoning, and cross-jurisdictional requirements in particular areas that result in confusion over the responsible authority. The necessary degree of integration among the three regulatory authorities – two states and the Commonwealth – is lacking. Cross-border coordination between Queensland and NSW is problematic when the two states have different management approaches, as, for example, in relation to the shared crab fishery, where one state allows the taking of female crabs but not the other. Coordination between local and higher levels of government is also unsatisfactory, particularly in relation to lack of integration between land use planning and the consequences of such planning decisions for marine environments. In both case study areas, dredging also presents challenges in coordinating local governments and multiple government departments.

Lessons for MPA Transboundary Governance

An MPA governance and management regime that effectively addresses transboundary issues is one that is oriented towards a systems perspective and embraces diversity and change. Requirements in such a systems orientation need to address governance of marine ecosystems and biodiversity across sectoral, jurisdictional and related boundaries. This is particularly important under climate change scenarios as boundaries and impacts shift. If the system is managed under traditional sectoral divisions then both the understanding of change and the capacity for adaptation are likely to be hampered by the constrained conceptualization of management.

Transboundary MPA governance must work across diverse environments, sectors and jurisdictions, stakeholder values and perspectives, as well as information types and sources. This orientation requires decision makers who have skills, knowledge and capacity to work with this diversity, are comfortable in interacting with a range of stakeholders and are able to build trust between decision makers and these diverse constituencies. Agencies operating in MPA governance are likely to require staff with skills and capacities across biophysical and social science disciplines, experience across relevant sectors (land use and marine planning, catchment management, fisheries, biodiversity conservation), and a history of engagement with diverse stakeholders.

This chapter has outlined elements of an MPA governance regime founded on a broadened approach to transboundary issues. To be more effective in coping with environmental change, including a changing climate, such a regime would incorporate key elements of an adaptive approach to governance that includes systems understanding, flexible institutional forms, inclusive engagement that addresses a variety of world views, and cohesion between a multiplicity of marine governance organizations.

Chapter 5

Effective Governance across Central Asian Boundaries: What Lessons does the Central Asian Transboundary Watercourse Management Experience Provide for Mountain Biodiversity Conservation across the Kyrgyz-Tajik Boundary?

Michelle Lim*

Introduction

Major transitional challenges confront the former Soviet republics of Central Asia. These challenges include the withdrawal of subsidies from a centralized Soviet government, moves towards privatization and the conversion of administrative boundaries to international boundaries all within a short timeframe. The dissolution of the Soviet Union and emergence of independent States in its territory meant that many internal problems concerning the use, distribution and protection of natural resources have assumed a transboundary character.[1] Transboundary strategies are

---

* Special thanks to Prof Paul Martin (Australian Centre for Agriculture and Law) for many helpful comments on various drafts of this chapter; also gratefully acknowledged is the support and encouragement of Dr Simon Marsden and Dr Robin Warner. Further thanks to Dr Marsden and an anonymous reviewer for helpful comments on the chapter. Thanks also to Dr Ian Hannam for facilitating the practical component of the research; and to Maksatbek Anarbaev (National Centre of Mountain Regions Development of the Kyrgyz Republic) for invaluable assistance in all aspects of field work. I also acknowledge the contribution of PALM project Legal Task Forces from Tajikistan and the Kyrgyz Republic in the analysis of the law and institutions of the Kyrgyz Republic and Tajikistan and thank them for their hospitality. Many thanks also to the Mountain Societies Development Support Program (MSDSP) of the Aga Khan Development Network for assisting field visits to the Tajik side of the PALM project area. This study was carried out in the context of this project, see n 4 below. The chapter reflects only the author's views.

1 Iulia Trombitcaia et al, *River Basin Commissions and Other Institutions for Transboundary Water Cooperation – Capacity for Water Cooperation in Eastern Europe, Caucasus and Central Asia* (Economic Commission for Europe – Convention on the

therefore required to address the multiple resource use and protection issues in Central Asia.

Globally, the practice of transboundary watercourse management is significantly more developed than transboundary biodiversity conservation.[2] Since 1948, 295 international water agreements have been recorded.[3] In contrast there are few agreements aimed specifically at conserving biodiversity across an international boundary. The situation in Central Asia reflects global trends with the degree of attention given to the issue of transboundary water management eclipsing that of transboundary biodiversity conservation. While challenges remain for the transboundary management of Central Asian watercourses, the institutions, legal instruments and associated commentary and analysis are far more extensive than those for biodiversity conservation.

This chapter will look to the experience of Central Asian transboundary water resource management to identify pitfalls and develop strategies for addressing the challenges to transboundary biodiversity conservation in the Pamir-Alai Land Management (PALM)[4] transboundary project. The chapter first highlights the threats to the unique biodiversity in the PALM project area and the importance of transboundary approaches and then sets out the complexities of transboundary water resource management in Central Asia. Existing regional agreements and institutions and the influence of Soviet era policies are explained as well as the main points of contention between upstream and downstream states.

A summary of transboundary governance criteria and a comparison of the relative ease of fulfilling each criterion in the case of biodiversity conservation and freshwater management is provided. Following this, five criteria that have particular relevance in the comparison of transboundary water resource management in Central Asia and the PALM project are used to identify the areas for inter-sectoral learning in the management of Central Asian transboundary resources. The trans-sectoral comparison in the Central Asian context focuses on the importance of political buy-in; the equitable distribution of costs and benefits; effective legal and institutional frameworks; and dispute resolution mechanisms.

Protection and Use of Transboundary Watercourses and International Lakes, United Nations, 2009) 5.

2 The Food and Agricultural Organization of the United Nations (FAO) has documented more than 3600 international water treaties dating from AD 805 to 1984 (UNEP, *Atlas of International Freshwater Agreements* (UNEP, 2002), 6).

3 Aaron T Wolf, 'Transboundary Waters: Sharing Benefits, Lessons Learned' (Paper presented at the International Conference on Freshwater, Bonn, 2001), at 2.

4 The PALM project is a transboundary initiative of the Central Asian countries of Tajikistan and the Kyrgyz Republic. The full project name is the 'GEF/UNEP/UNU Sustainable Land Management in the High Pamir and Pamir-Alai Mountains (PALM) Project (Project Number: IMIS: GFL-2328-2770-4984)'. GEF, UNEP and UNU refer respectively to the Global Environment Facility, the United Nations Environment Programme and the United Nations University.

The PALM project

The PALM project is an integrated transboundary initiative of the governments of the Kyrgyz Republic and the Republic of Tajikistan. The project aims to address the interlinked problems of land degradation and poverty within one of Central Asia's key freshwater sources and an identified biodiversity hotspot. The overall goal of the PALM project is to 'restore, sustain, and enhance … the transboundary ecosystems of the High Pamir and Pamir-Alai Mountains, of Tajikistan and Kyrgyzstan, to improve the social and economic well-being of the rural communities of the region …'.[5] The PALM project area encompasses the High Pamir mountains in Tajikistan and the Pamir-Alai mountain ranges in the Kyrgyz Republic. This area is located at altitudes which range from 2000 to 7495 m above sea level and contains some of the world's highest peaks (Ismoil Somoni Peak (7495 m), Ibn Sina Peak (formerly Lenin Peak) (7134 m)). The area is also renowned for its unique biodiversity.[6]

Each of the two PALM countries contains high levels of biodiversity. The temperate, continental climate and large elevational variation of the Kyrgyz Republic has resulted in high species diversity and a large number of endemics for its land area.[7] Despite only taking up 0.13% of the world's land mass the country contains nearly 1% of all known species.[8] The Kyrgyz Republic also contains populations of rare or endangered vertebrates.[9] The Republic of Tajikistan has similarly high levels of biodiversity with its mountain landscapes containing 0.66% of the world's animal species and 1.8% of its plant species, which include the wild relatives of domestic animals and cultivated plants.[10]

5 'Full Project Brief: Sustainable Land Management in the High Pamir and Pamir-Alai Mountains – an Integrated and Transboundary Initiative in Central Asia' (United Nations Environment Programme Global Environment Facility).

6 Thomas Breu and Hans Hurni, 'High Mountain Areas: A Wildlife Habitat' in Thomas Breu and Hans Hurni (eds), *The Tajik Pamirs – Challenges of Sustainable Development in an Isolated Mountain Region* (2003) 28, 28.

7 V Nifadiev, Y Ogurstsov, G Desyatkov and V Levelken, 'State of the Kyrgyz Environment Report 1998', Bishkek, The Kyrgyz Republic. Kyrgyz –Russian Slavic University 1999' cited in Joel T Heinen, Emil Shukurov and Chinara Sadykova, 'Legislative and Policy Initiatives in Biodiversity Conservation in The Kyrgyz Republic' (2001) 42 *Post-Soviet Geography and Economics* 519, 519.

8 Kyrgyz Ministry of Environmental Protection (MEP), 'Kyrgyz RepublicBiodiversity Strategy and Action Plan' (November 1998) http://www.cbd.int/doc/world/kg/kg-nbsap-01-en.pdf, 7.

9 V Krever, O Pereladova, M Williams and H Jungius (eds), *Biodiversity Conservation in Central Asia* cited in Joel T Heinen, Emil Shukurov and Chinara Sadykova, 'Legislative and Policy Initiatives in Biodiversity Conservation in the Kyrgyz Republic' (2001) 42 *Post-Soviet Geography and Economics* 519, 520.

10 Republic of Tajikistan, 'National Strategy and Action Plan on Conservation and Sustainable Use of Biodiversity' (2003) http://www.cbd.int/doc/world/tj/tj-nbsap-01-p01-en.pdf, 31.

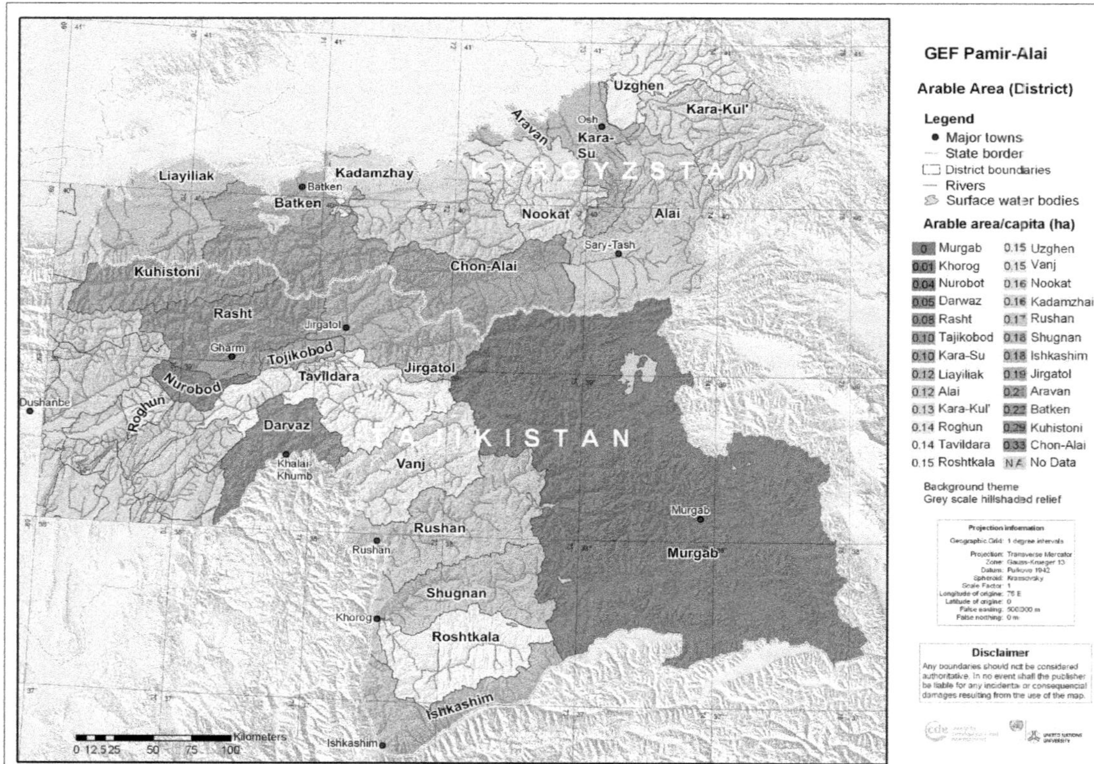

Figure 5.1 PALM project area map showing project districts and arable land per capita at district level

Source: http://www.ehs.unu.edu/palm/file/get/3454.

The National Biodiversity Strategy and Action Plans (NBSAPs)[11] of both countries highlight the urgent need to address biodiversity issues in each country. The Kyrgyz NBSAP points to recent declines in many species with 9.5% of bird species and 18.1% of mammal species considered to be at risk of extinction.[12] The Kyrgyz NBSAP also indicates that a number of rare and valuable ecosystems are highly threatened and the extent of forest cover has halved in the last 50 years.[13] The Tajik NBSAP states that 226 plant taxa and 162 animal species have become rare or endangered and are listed in the Red Data Book of Tajikistan. Ten vertebrate species are listed in the Red Data Book of the IUCN.[14] The NBSAP indicates that reptiles and mammals are the most vulnerable with 50% of Tajikistan's mammals and 44.7% of its reptiles on the Tajik Red List.[15]

Reflecting trends in the two PALM countries, the unique biodiversity of the PALM region is also under threat. Larger mammals are affected by over-hunting, interference from livestock and humans and habitat degradation caused by livestock.[16] Many species such as the snow leopard and Marco Polo sheep are listed as vulnerable[17] and most populations of Siberian ibex are at risk of reduced numbers or local extinction in many parts of their range.[18]

Transboundary approaches in the PALM project area are of particular importance. The Pamir and Alai mountain ranges have been traditionally used as an integrated geographic unit. The 270 km-long border separating Tajikistan and the Kyrgyz Republic constrains the movement of goods, services, livestock and people across the mountain ranges and the collection and exchange of information on migrating wildlife species.[19] Access to markets and resources from national capitals is limited by remoteness and under-developed transport infrastructure.

---

11 National Biodiversity Strategies and Action Plans (NBSAPs) are the principal instruments for implementing the *Convention on Biological Diversity* at the national level (Article 6). The Convention requires countries to prepare a national biodiversity strategy (or equivalent instrument) and to ensure that this strategy is mainstreamed into the planning and activities of all those sectors whose activities can have an impact (positive and negative) on biodiversity: http://www.cbd.int/nbsap/. *Convention on Biological Diversity* ('*CBD*') opened for signature 5 June 1992, 1760 UNTS 142 (entered into force 29 December 1993).

12 Kyrgyz MEP, above n 8.

13 Ibid.

14 Republic of Tajikistan, above n 10.

15 Ibid, 75.

16 Ibid, 29.

17 Ibid, 28.

18 DM Shackleton and IUCN/SSC Caprinae Specialist Group, 'Wild Sheep and Goats and their Relatives' (1997), cited in Breu and Hurni, above n 6, 29.

19 AS Shanazarov et al, 'Strategy and Action Plan for Sustainable Land Management in the High-Pamir and Pamir-Alai Mountains' (GEF/UNEP/UNU Project, 'Sustainable Land Management in the High Pamir and Pamir-Alai Mountains – Integrated and Transboundary Initiative in Central Asia', 2011) 12.

Transboundary Watercourses of Central Asia

The problems within each Central Asian basin differ and issues present themselves differently across the basins.[20] While it may not be accurate to 'generalize about a crisis of water in the region',[21] the way states approach the management of transboundary watercourses follows certain trends. The common Soviet history of Central Asian states, patterns in the transboundary watercourse governance and state positions are explored below.

Soviet Watercourse Management History

Once Russian control was established in Central Asia in the mid-nineteenth century, agricultural policies encouraged the expansion of irrigated areas and the production of cotton.[22] In 1924, Stalin nationalized Soviet water resources by decree.[23] From 1925 to 1936 the former Tsarist administrative units of Central Asia were divided into five republics.[24] The desire for central control of Central Asian watercourses, which crossed the boundaries of the five republics, led to water management in Central Asia being directed by central planning organizations and ministries in Moscow.[25]

The Soviet allocation regime favoured downstream cotton production in the downstream states of Uzbekistan and Turkmenistan.[26] Benefits were shared in the former Soviet Union at the expense of the two upstream states, Tajikistan and the Kyrgyz Republic. The upstream countries received payments for forgone hydropower generation and provided upstream storage.[27] Large dams and reservoirs were constructed in the mountainous areas of Tajikistan and the

20 Kai Wegerich, 'Water Resources in Central Asia: Regional Stability or Patchy Make-up' (2011) 30(2) *Central Asian Survey*, 275.

21 Ibid.

22 Ibid, 276.

23 Olaf Caroe, *Soviet Empire: Turks of Central Asia and Stalinism* (1954) 153 cited in A Dan Tarlock, 'Changing Currents: Perspectives on the State of Water Law and Policy in the 21st Century: Four Challenges for International Water Law' (2010) 23 *Tulane Environmental Law Journal* 369, 399.

24 Bakhiyor Mukhamadiev, 'Application of the "Benefits Sharing" Concept to the Case of Transboundary Water Resources Politics in the Aral Sea Basin' (unpublished manuscript) cited in Tarlock, above n 23, 399.

25 Tarlock, above n 23, 399; Daene C McKinney, 'Cooperative Management of Transboundary Water Resources in Central Asia' in D Burghart and T Sabonis-Helf (eds), *In the Tracks of Tamerlane - Central Asia's Path into the 21st Century* (National Defence University Press, 2003) 187, 187.

26 Tarlock, above n 23, 399.

27 A Dan Tarlock and Patricia Wouters, 'Are Shared Benefits of International Waters an Equitable Apportionment?' 18 *Colorado Journal of International Environmental Law & Policy* 523, 532.

Kyrgyz Republic.[28] The development of irrigated lands in Tajikistan and the Kyrgyz Republic was limited. Region-wide Basin Water Organizations (BVOs) were established in 1986 in the Amu Darya and Syr Darya Basins. The BVOs were created to manage water resources according to plans approved by the Soviet Ministry of Water Management and to ensure compliance with inter-republican water allocations.[29]

Post-Soviet Challenges

The Central Asian republics recognized the urgency of stabilizing transboundary water relations on independence due to the heavy dependence of their economies on irrigated agriculture.[30] Downstream riparians, still utilizing generous water allocations, immediately became dependent on their upstream neighbours for water. This increased both the possibility for conflict as well as the need for cooperation in the region.[31]

On 12 September 1991, the water ministers of the five Central Asian Republics (the Kyrgyz Republic, Tajikistan, Kazakhstan, Turkmenistan, Uzbekistan) declared that joint water resources management would be established on the basis of equity and mutual benefit.[32] The following month, a regional water resources management mechanism was developed to replace the centralized system of the Soviet period. The *Agreement on Cooperation in the Field of Joint Management and Conservation of Interstate Water Resources* was concluded in Almaty (Kazakhstan) on 18 February 1992.[33]

---

28 Shavkat Rakhmatullaev et al, 'Facts and Perspectives of Water Reservoirs in Central Asia: A Special Focus on Uzbekistan' (2009) 2(2) *Water* 1, 2.

29 McKinney, above n 25, 187.

30 Ibid.

31 Ariel Dinar et al, 'Case Study 4: The Aral Sea Basin' in Ariel Dinar et al (eds), *Bridges Over Water – Understanding Transboundary Water Conflict, Negotiation and Cooperation*, World Scientific Series on Energy and Resource Economics (World Scientific Publishing, 2007) Vol 3, 291–2.

32 Viktor Dukhovny and Vadim Sokolov, 'Lessons on Cooperation Building to Manage Water Conflicts in the Aral Sea Basin' (Scientific-Information Center of the Interstate commission for Water Coordination in Central Asia, 2003) http://waterwiki.net/images/2/26/PCCP_Aral_Sea_Basin_case_study.pdf.

33 *Agreement on Cooperation in the Field of Joint Water Resources Management and Conservation of Interstate Sources* ('*Almaty Agreement*'), (signed and entered into force 18 February 1992).

Figure 5.2 Map of Central Asia showing major rivers

Source: Map no 3763, Rev 7, December 2011, United Nations Cartographic Section

Article 7 of the Agreement established the Interstate Coordinating Water Commission (ICWC). The ICWC was created for the control, rational use and protection of interstate water resources and was responsible for the management of water allocation.[34] The ICWC was responsible for the development of regional water management polices to ensure the rational utilization of water resources. The ICWC also governed the activities of the two regional BVOs (the Amu Darya and Syr Darya BVOs) created in 1986. From 1992 onwards, the ICWC and the two regional BVOs were responsible for water development and allocation planning, water quality control, conservation and environmental protection.[35]

Under the 1992 Agreement Central Asian states agreed to maintain the basic principles of water allocation that prevailed in Soviet times. The agreement acknowledged the equal rights of member states to use the interstate water resources of Central Asia and their responsibility to protect these resources.[36] The agreement affirmed the continuation of existing Soviet structures and principles of interstate water allocation and was approved by the Presidents of the Central Asian Republics.[37]

The inheritance of Soviet water allocation regimes is the main reason for transboundary water disputes in present-day Central Asia. The inherited Soviet water management rules prioritize irrigated agriculture and do not take into account the current power generation needs of the upstream states of the Kyrgyz Republic and Tajikistan. These upstream states often claim that water allocation based on Soviet era rules limits the development of irrigation on their lands. Downstream countries, on the other hand, complain that poor water quality in the middle and lower reaches of the Basins is reducing agricultural production and damaging public health.[38]

Seasonal demands for water among Central Asian states differ. Low precipitation in parts of Central Asia makes downstream countries in the plains and deserts dependent on spring thaw off snow and glaciers of the high mountains of the Tian-Shan and Pamirs.[39] Peak demand for power generation in the upstream mountain states of Tajikistan and Kyrgyzstan, however, occurs in the cold winter months. In summer, the upstream countries store runoff from the Pamir glaciers

---

34 *Almaty Agreement*, art 8.

35 Sergei Vinogradov and Vance PE Langford, 'Managing Transboundary Water Resources in the Aral Sea Basin: in Search of a Solution' (2001) 1(3/4) *International Journal of Global Environmental Issues* 345, 351.

36 Almaty Agreement, art 1.

37 Ibid, preamble.

38 McKinney, above n 25, 187.

39 Down to below 70 mm annually in the lowland areas, with 338 mm average in the region as a whole (The United Nations Food and Agriculture Organization (FAO), *Irrigation in the Countries of the Former Soviet Union in Figures* (Rome, 1997), available at http://www.fao.org/docrep/W6240E/w6240e00.htm (accessed autumn 2000)) cited in Necati Polat, *Boundary Issues in Central Asia* (Transnational Publishers, 2002) 99; Rakhmatullaev et al, above n 28, 1.

in reservoirs to ensure adequate winter water supplies for power generation. This conflicts with peak demand of downstream countries that require water for irrigated agriculture in the dry summer months.[40]

The main points of contention among Central Asian states are that upstream countries insist on revising the Soviet water quotas and pursue increased use of water for hydroelectric purposes.[41] The Kyrgyz Republic and Tajikistan also feel that the Soviet allocation regime stunted their development of irrigated agriculture and therefore call for the reassessment of their future water share.[42] These states insist on schedules of release from main reservoirs that are favourable to them and compensation in the alternative. Downstream states push for preserving existing agreements and quotas to maintain Soviet allocations for irrigated agriculture.[43]

Climate change is likely to have a significant impact on water resources in Central Asia. The 1°C rise in average global temperature in the last 35 years has led to a 22% reduction in the size of Pamiro-Alai glaciers. It is predicted that by 2020 the annual decrease in the volume of water will be at the rate of 6–20 km^3/year (5–15% of total regional water resources).[44] Conflicting national water management and planning approaches could exacerbate the consequences of already limited water resources. Effective interstate cooperation is essential.[45]

Areas for inter-sectoral learning in the management of transboundary resources in Central Asia

Elsewhere the author has developed criteria for effective transboundary biodiversity conservation. The criteria provide a framework for determining what complementary reforms may be needed, in addition to suitable legal instruments, for effective management of the respective transboundary resources. The author has demonstrated that similar criteria are broadly applicable to the management of transboundary freshwater resources and thus calls for greater inter-sectoral learning in the transboundary management of natural resources.[46]

---

40 Vinogradov and Langford, above n 35, 358.

41 Darya Pushkina, 'EU Crisis Management Role in Water Conflict in Central Asia: Open Opportunities or Lost Causes?' (2009) 7–8 *Historical Processes and Peace Politics* 105, 117.

42 Dukhovny and Sokolov, above n 32, 34; McKinney, above n 25, 187.

43 Pushkina, above n 41, 117; Rakhmatullaev et al, above n 28, 1.

44 Dukhovny and Sokolov, above n 32.

45 Ibid.

46 Michelle Lim, 'Is Water Different From Biodiversity? Governance Criteria for the Effective Management of Transboundary Resources' (Paper presented at the 9th Annual Colloquium of the IUCN Academy of Environmental Law, Water and the Law: Towards Sustainability, Eastern Cape, South Africa, 3–7 July 2011) (on file with author); Michelle Lim, 'Transboundary Conservation of Mountain Biodiversity in a Climate Change Impacted World – Governance Perspectives from Central Asia and the Island of Borneo'

While the transboundary governance principles remain largely unchanged for biodiversity conservation and water resource management, meeting each criterion faces unique challenges in the distinct natural and management environments of each resource. The comparative study of governance principles for the transboundary management of water and biodiversity examined how the relative ease with which each of the criteria can be fulfilled differs according to the resource that is being managed.

Table 5.1 lists the criteria that are common to transboundary water resource management and transboundary biodiversity conservation. A summary of the criteria is provided below. Five of the criteria have particular relevance in the comparison of transboundary biodiversity conservation and water management in the Central Asian context. Drawing on the experience of transboundary watercourse management in Central Asia the potential challenges to achieving the criteria in the PALM project as well as possible ways forward for transboundary resource management in the region are identified.

Governance Criteria for Transboundary Water Resource Management and Transboundary Biodiversity Conservation

Table 5.1 Governance criteria common to transboundary water resource management and transboundary biodiversity conservation

1	Engages Each Level of Political Organization
2	Has Political Buy-in
3	Costs and Benefits are Equitably Distributed
4	An Integrated Approach which Incorporates Available Science is Applied
5	Has Clear Objectives and Common Goals
6	Good Governance is Practised
7	Adaptive Management is Practised and there Exist Clear Success Indicators for Ongoing Monitoring and Evaluation
8	Existence of Rules and Legal Instruments that Enable the Process
9	Designated Institutions are Identified at Each Level of Organization and Vertical and Horizontal Linkages are Established Across All Levels
10	Operates in Consideration of Capacity
11	Complexity Recognized and Appropriate Funding is Secured
12	Dispute Resolution Mechanisms Exist

in *Proceedings of the 8th Annual Colloquium of the IUCN Academy of International Environmental Law* (Edward Elgar, forthcoming).

Criterion 1: Engages Each Level of Political Organization The transboundary context creates an additional layer of institutional complexity and a unique power structure. The principle of sovereignty means that transboundary level authority is dependent on the endorsement of national level powers. Though transboundary initiatives need not operate from every level of political organization the involvement of each level is desirable. Though the levels of organization differ for water and biodiversity, as with biodiversity, the meaningful engagement of stakeholders at all levels of political organization is a necessary component of transboundary water resources management.

Criterion 2: Has Political Buy-in Endorsement of transboundary initiatives by authorities and stakeholders at each level of political organization is one of the most important components of the transboundary process. Maintaining genuine political support facilitates the effective operation of transboundary initiatives and gives these initiatives the best chance of long-term sustainability.

Political interest is easier to develop for transboundary water management than it is for biodiversity conservation. This is because the importance of water resources for sustaining life and livelihoods is more easily observed in the case of water. The challenges for collaborative management that can arise from the intense political interest in water resources should however be acknowledged. Any call on countries to improve water allocation and management must therefore take into account the highly sensitive and politicized nature of water.[47]

Criterion 3: Costs and Benefits are Equitably Distributed People are likely to manage the environment when the benefits of management are perceived to exceed its costs and if they have the means to meet these costs.[48] Systems should be developed which ensure the equitable sharing of benefits and costs among stakeholders at all levels of political organization.[49]

Criterion 4: An Integrated Approach which Incorporates Available Science is Applied Integrated holistic approaches are essential for the effective management of transboundary resources. The 5th Conference of the Parties to the CBD defined the ecosystem approach as 'a strategy for integrated management that provides

---

47 Sabine Brels, David Coates and Flavia Loures, *Transboundary Water Resources Management: The Role of International Watercourse Agreements in Implementation of the CBD*, CBD Technical Series No. 40 (Secretariat of the Convention on Biological Diversity, 2008), 14.

48 Marshall W Murphree (ed), *Communities as Resource Management Institutions*, Gatekeeper Series No. 36 (Sustainable Agriculture and Rural Livelihoods Programme, International Institute for Environment and Development, London, 1991).

49 Yemi Katerere, Ryan Hill and Sam Moyo, *A Critique of Transboundary Natural Resource Management in Southern Africa*, IUCN Series on Transboundary Natural Resource Management (2001), 119.

conservation and sustainable use in an equitable way'.[50] The WSSD Implementation Plan emphasizes the importance of integrated natural resources management and calls on countries to prepare plans and programmes for the integrated management of river basins and aquifers.[51] The ecosystem approach and IWRM are similar approaches which focus on integrating human and environmental needs.

Holistic approaches to environmental protection pose considerable legal difficulties. Integrated action is effective but more difficult to achieve than the narrower sectoral or source-based approach of prior decades.[52] Many international instruments contain vague directives calling for integrated participatory action but lack specific implementation provisions.[53] Though the specific challenges for transboundary biodiversity conservation and transboundary water management differ, coordinating integrated approaches is difficult for both resources.

A common theme of successful conservation initiatives is the use of appropriate science in the decision-making process.[54] The CBD's Principles 11 and 12 for the implementation of the ecosystem approach advocate the use of science to give effect to the approach.[55] The incorporation of science should be an important component of integrated approaches in the management of all transboundary resources. The use of science in determining allocation and flows is familiar to water managers. In the implementation of integrated measures for water management, managers should heed the lessons learnt regarding the use of science to implement the ecosystem approach in biodiversity conservation initiatives.

Criterion 5: Has Clear Objectives and Common Goals In the biodiversity conservation context it is essential that the objective of conservation is not overlooked in the integration of multiple values and sectors. Biodiversity conservation and poverty alleviation objectives often conflict and are themselves highly complex. Where the goals of biodiversity conservation and livelihood enhancement are pursued simultaneously, care should be exercised to ensure that conservation is not neglected.

The existence of multiple issues in the implementation of integrated approaches means that it is still important to identify priorities and to have clear objectives and

---

50 Convention on Biological Diversity, Conference of the Parties, *Ecosystem Approach*, UNEP/CBD/COP/5/6 (2000) [2].

51 Brels et al, above n 47, 15.

52 Dinah Shelton, 'International Cooperation on Shared Natural Resources' in Sharelle Hart (ed), *Shared Resources: Issues of Governance* (World Conservation Union, 2008) 12.

53 Ibid.

54 Carolyn J Lundquist and Elise F Granek, 'Strategies for Successful Marine Conservation: Integrating Socioeconomic, Political and Scientific Factors' (2005) 19 *Conservation Biology* 1771, 1774.

55 Convention on Biological Diversity, Conference of the Parties, *Ecosystem Approach*, UNEP/CBD/COP/5/6 (2000), Principle 11, Implementation Guideline 11.3; Principle 12, Implementation Guideline 12.4.

common goals for the management of a transboundary basin. Clear objectives will also prevent immediate economic benefits being prioritized at the expense of long-term sustainable use.

To be effective, institutions should provide clear allocation schedules and water quality standards. Riparian states may consider prioritizing uses throughout the basin. The establishment of catchment-wide priorities could avert inter-riparian conflicts over water use and protect the environmental health of the basin as a whole.[56]

Criterion 6: Good Governance is Practised Good governance must be practised regardless of the resource being managed. Successful transboundary management requires good governance at all levels of political organization. The Rio Declaration's principles of transparency and access to information; participation; and accountability are of particular importance for securing good governance.[57] To give effect to these principles administrative systems that are just, transparent and based on accountability to stakeholders should be created.[58]

Criterion 7: Adaptive Management is Practised and there Exist Clear Success Indicators for Ongoing Monitoring and Evaluation Ongoing monitoring and evaluation play a vital role in adaptive management. The guidance of value-based standards is essential for the delivery of good governance so as to achieve intended outcomes for natural resource management.[59] Clear success indicators provide an objective framework for evaluation and facilitate the iterative process of adaptive management towards meeting set goals.

The desire for certainty and secure property rights is a challenge for the adaptive management of both water and biodiversity. Adaptive management in the case of biodiversity will often be easier as this concept has always been a component of ecosystem management. Where large investment has been committed to infrastructure such as dams there is more likely to be resistance to adaptive management practices.

The shared management of water resources requires the existence of stringent and continuing environmental assessment and monitoring duties that meet the international standards.[60] The development of clear success indicators at the start of the project and periodical review of the choice of indicators are key components of adaptive management.

56 UNEP, above n 2 at 8.

57 Nathan Badenoch, *Transboundary Environmental Governance – Principles and Practice in Mainland Southeast Asia* (World Resources Institute, 2002) at 23.

58 Katerere et al, above n 49, 117.

59 Michael Lockwood et al, *Governance Principles for Natural Resource Management*, Report for Land and Water Australia (2009) 2.

60 Tarlock, above n 26, 404.

Criterion 8: Existence of Rules and Legal Instruments that Enable the Process Legal instruments articulate rules and create the enabling framework within which stakeholders interact. Such instruments can provide the mechanisms through which regulatory and control measures are exercised.[61] At the transboundary level, formal and informal agreements are an important means to declare common interests; agree on objectives; state guiding principles; and determine and ensure levels of commitment from parties.[62] In most cases it will be necessary to amend each state party's laws and develop harmonized rules.[63]

Criterion 9: Designated Institutions are Identified at Each Level of Organization and Vertical and Horizontal Linkages are Established across All Levels Regardless of the instrument/s chosen to regulate the environment, all require efficient institutional backing and adequate implementation resources.[64] It is important to develop institutional systems that link transboundary planning to planning at national and local levels.[65] Transboundary watercourse law urges riparians to found a 'joint management mechanism'[66] or 'joint body'[67] for each body of water. International basins with water institutions generally demonstrate greater levels of cooperation than basins without treaties or other cooperative management mechanisms.[68] The presence or absence of institutions is one of the most important factors influencing co-riparian water relations.[69]

---

61 Ann Majchrzak, 'Focus of Information Inquiry' in her *Methods for Policy Research* (Sage Publications, 1984) 24, 25.

62 Trevor Sandwith et al, *Transboundary Protected Areas for Peace and Co-operation*, Best Practice Protected Area Guidelines Series No. 7 (IUCN, 2001) 41.

63 Clare Shine, 'Legal Mechanisms to Strengthen and Safeguard Transboundary Protected Areas' (Paper presented at the Parks for Peace – International Conference on Transboundary Protected Areas as a Vehicle for International Cooperation, Somerset West, South Africa, 16–18 September 1997) 1.

64 Paul V Martin et al, 'Developing a Good Regulatory Practice Model for Environmental Regulations Impacting on Farmers' (Australian Farm Institute, 2007) ix.

65 Jennifer Mohamed-Katerere, *Review of the Legal and Policy Framework for Transboundary Natural Resource Management in Southern Africa*, The IUCN-ROSA Series on Transboundary Natural Resources Management (IUCN Regional Office for Southern Africa, 2001) 113.

66 *United Nations Convention on the Law of the Non-Navigational Uses of International Watercourse*, adopted by the General Assembly of the United Nations 21 May 1997, UNGA Res 51/229, 55th sess, UN Doc A/51/49, (not in force) art 24.

67 *Convention on the Protection and Use of Transboundary Watercourses and International Lakes* (*United Nations Economic Commission for Europe Water Convention, 'UNECE Water Convention')*, opened for signature 17 March 1992, 1936 UNTS 269 (entered into force 6 October 1996), art 9.2.

68 Wolf, Aaron T, Shira B Yoffe, and Mark Giordano, 'International Waters: Identifying Basins at Risk' in UNEP above n 2, 4.

69 Ibid.

The success or failure of transboundary initiatives does not however hinge on whether an overarching transboundary institution exists. There are valid arguments for and against establishing such an institution. What matters is that corresponding government bodies are identified within each participating country and responsible institutions are allocated at each level of authority. Institutions should be linked horizontally at each level across the international boundary as well as vertically across each scale of organization from the local to the transboundary.

Criterion 10: Operates in Consideration of Capacity Capacity deficits can be a severe constraint to environmental action. Building capacity is an obvious and important strategy for addressing this issue. This criterion stresses however the importance of evaluating existing capacity from the outset then designing transboundary initiatives and the reform of legal instruments and institutions in consideration of existing capacity. Implementation strategies should also be structured to match available resources at each level of authority involved in the transboundary process.

Capacity is just as important for water management as it is for biodiversity conservation. Experience in transboundary water management demonstrates that transboundary collaboration is most successful when immediate need is combined with appropriate human, financial and technical capacity.[70] The WSSD Implementation Plan highlights the importance of strengthening capacity at local, national and regional levels.[71] As with biodiversity conservation, transboundary water initiatives should evaluate existing capacity at the start of collaboration and incorporate capacity building into project design.

Criterion 11: Complexity Recognized and Appropriate Funding is Secured Initiatives must be resourced appropriately. Many transboundary initiatives are aimed at the management of multiple resources.[72] The management of multiple resources is more complicated in the transboundary context. It is important to secure flexible and multiple source funding bases.[73] The incorporation of 'transboundary thinking' into normal management operations and the opportunistic use of existing funds can go a long way to achieving funding sustainability.[74] The transboundary context can also provide opportunities for

70 LA Swatuk, and LL Wirkus, 'Transboundary Water Governance in Southern Africa: An Introduction', in *Transboundary Water Governance in Southern Africa – Examining Underexplored Dimensions*, BICC/DCAF series on Sustainable Peace and Global Security Governance No. 2, LA Swatuk and LL Wirkus eds, 2009) in Ruth Vollmer et al, *Institutional Capacity Development in Transboundary Water Management* (United Nations Education, Scientific and Cultural Organization (UNESCO), 2009) 4.

71 Vollmer et al, above n 70, 3.

72 Ibid, 18.

73 Harry van der Linde et al, *Beyond Boundaries: Transboundary Natural Resource Management in Sub-Saharan Africa* (2001), 59.

74 Sandwith et al, above n 62, 31.

securing funding through the establishment of cooperative budgets, joint revenue generation and joint project proposals.[75]

Securing appropriate resources for the management of transboundary water resources is likely to be easier than for transboundary biodiversity conservation. This again is due to the greater importance attributed to the management of water over biodiversity. Managers of transboundary biodiversity resources could benefit from an understanding of the funding mechanisms for transboundary water management such as incorporation of transboundary issues into national budgets.

Criterion 12: Dispute Resolution Mechanisms Exist International experience in the management of transboundary water resources indicates that clear mechanisms for dispute resolution are essential for effective, long-term basin management.[76] The importance of dispute resolution mechanisms is also recognized in the main international water law instruments.[77] The existence of dispute resolution mechanisms is equally important for the management of other transboundary resources.

Evaluation of Central Asian Transboundary Natural Resource Management against Five Criteria

Criterion 2: Has Political Buy-in The political support for the PALM project itself is greater than that for transboundary biodiversity conservation in the project area. Project documents often cite the unique biodiversity of the PALM area as one of the key justifications for the project. There does not however appear to be genuine political commitment to biodiversity conservation from either country or any level of political organization. While there is political support for the project at the local level there appears to be a growing disenchantment as the project has yet to meet local-level expectations. Within the PALM project there appears to be much stronger political support from the country that was closely involved with the initiation of the project. The national legal teams from this country demonstrate much greater willingness to contribute to the project development process.

The experience of transboundary basin management indicates that success depends above all on the long-term political will and commitment of member States.[78] McKinney indicates that while the capacity for the shared management

75 Ibid.

76 UNEP, above n 2, 8.

77 The UNECE Convention dedicates a full article to the issue of dispute settlement (art 22). The UN Watercourse Convention describes mechanisms of dispute settlement in Article 33. The Berlin Rules draw on the previous UN Convention and address the settlement of international water disputes in Chapter XIV. Vollmer et al, above n 70, 5.

78 International Lake Environment Committee Foundation (ILEC), 'Managing Lakes and Their Basins for Sustainable Use, A Report for Lake Basin Managers and Stakeholders' (Shiga, Japan, 2005) 34 cited in Charles E Di Leva, 'Transboundary Management of

of water resources exists in Central Asia its effectiveness is hampered by the lack of high-level political will.[79] The range of treaties, agreements and declarations on water issues in Central Asia belie the fact that political will has yet to be mobilized to give effect to the commitment to water reform apparently evidenced in these instruments. Sievers suggests that the conclusion of agreements is often merely a gesture for the donor community. He cites the Nukus Declaration[80] as an example where parties did not follow through with drafting a promised convention when donors did not proffer rewards for developing an international instrument.[81]

Political commitment from Central Asian governments is a necessary condition for the implementation of environmental protection measures in the region.[82] There are common ethnic, religious and customary frameworks in all Central Asian countries.[83] This could facilitate the development of trust and subsequently political will to address transboundary resource governance issues. Communal activity in the Soviet period inculcated an understanding that problematic conditions can be addressed only through collaboration and cooperation.[84] These are reasons to be optimistic about the possibilities of developing true commitment to resolving transboundary issues.

While political interest may be easier to generate in the context of transboundary watercourses, the less politicized nature of biodiversity may mean that securing genuine political commitment for transboundary biodiversity conservation may be relatively easier, especially if the benefits of collaboration are shared equitably. The lesson for the PALM project that emerges from the transboundary water experience is that the quantity of international agreements is an inadequate indicator of the extent of political commitment.

Criterion 3: The Costs and Benefits of Transboundary Conservation are Equitably Distributed The lack of equitable distribution of costs and benefits is an issue common to the PALM project and the management of Central Asian water resources. What differs is the level of political organization where this issue arises.

Natural Resources: A Brief Overview of World Bank Policies and Projects' in Sharelle Hart (ed), *Shared Resources: Issues of Governance* (IUCN, 2008) 50–1.

79 McKinney, above n 25, 187.

80 *Nukus Declaration Among the Heads of States Of Central Asia to Provide All Possible Assistance And Extend Trust to the Organizations Of The International Aral Sea Fund,* signed 20 September 1995. Nukus, Uzbekistan, Kazakhstan-Tajikistan, Kyrgyz Republic, Uzbekistan-Turkmenistan. See Eric W Sievers, 'Water, Conflict and Regional Security in Central Asia' (2002) 10 *New York University Environmental Law Journal* 356, 392.

81 Ibid, 388.

82 Gulnara Roll et al, 'Aral Sea – Experiences and Lessons Learned Brief' (IW: Science, United Nations University-Institute for Water, Environment and Health (UNU-INWEH), 2006), 10.

83 Dukhovny and Sokolov, above n 32.

84 Ibid.

In the Central Asian water context the existing agreements do not facilitate the equitable distribution of water resources among upstream and downstream states. In the PALM project the concern is that a few national elites benefit from the use of biodiversity. Both cases highlight the importance of equity in the distribution of costs and benefits.

In the context of the PALM project more needs to be done to ensure equitable distribution of benefits to the local level. Trophy-hunting and hunting-tourism often result in profits accumulated by a few with little if any gain for local communities. Nevertheless, community-based tourism is under-developed but is emerging in the Kyrgyz Republic. Local cooperatives and families provide home-stays, accommodation and guides. The income from this practice feeds into the local economy.

The PALM project includes community-based components. The main activities under these components are micro-projects at project pilot sites.[85] The Biodiversity and Forestry Action Plan of the project includes activities such as changing the system of distribution of returns from hunting to ensure an increased share to local communities; and establishing a fund to provide financial incentives for local people to combat poaching. These are notable objectives. More is needed to implement these activities.

Interstate disputes over water allocation occur every year between Central Asian states.[86] One of the key reasons for this is that states feel that the existing agreement on annual water allocation is inconsistent with principles of equity and sustainable development.[87] Another source of contention is that countries have not shared equitably in the financial obligations of joint water management and development of the ICWC. Only Turkmenistan and Uzbekistan have met their obligations for operation and maintenance works and Uzbekistan is the only state that has met the obligation to provide funds for research.[88]

The full project brief of the PALM project recognizes the importance of mountain ecosystem resources of Central Asia and that the costs of maintaining these resources are unequally borne by Tajikistan and the Kyrgyz Republic. By protecting the ecosystem function of the Pamir, Pamir-Alai system Tajikistan and the Kyrgyz Republic provide essential ecological goods and services to neighbouring countries. The inhabitants of these mountain areas currently bear all the costs for the management of the upper watershed areas and receive no financial or technical support from the downstream beneficiaries.[89]

---

85 *Micro-Projects in Sub District Units (SDUs) of The Kyrgyz Republic and Tajikistan* (2010–2011) http://www.ehs.unu.edu/palm/file/get/8638.

86 Roll et al., above n 82, 5.

87 Ibid.

88 McKinney, above n 25, 187.

89 *GEF/UNEP/UNU Project 'Sustainable Land Management in the High Pamir and Pamir-Alai Mountains – Integrated and Transboundary Initiative in Central Asia – Full Project Brief.*

Countries have traditionally considered water separately from other transboundary issues. Internationally there have been increased calls to shift the focus of transboundary water management from allocation to benefit sharing throughout the basin.[90] There are examples where a range of benefits have been identified so as to increase the potential to develop win-win solutions.[91]

In the transboundary governance criteria, the author advocates an integrated approach to the management of the transboundary resources.[92] An integrated approach which incorporates multiple sectors may assist Central Asian states in identifying an increased range of benefits that can be gained from transboundary collaboration. A shared benefits approach could lead to a more equitable distribution of transboundary resources among Central Asian states. Many resources, in addition to freshwater and biodiversity, would benefit from a transboundary approach to their management. Access to winter energy sources and markets in downstream states are just two areas where collaboration would be beneficial for Tajikistan and the Kyrgyz Republic.

It was recognized above that integrated action is more difficult to achieve than narrower sectoral or source-based approaches.[93] While there is growing evidence of the many crucial ecosystem services provided by biodiversity[94] there is as yet insufficient political acknowledgement of the economic value of these services. Recognizing the importance of biodiversity as a regional resource would be a vital first step to the implementation of the shared benefits approach in Central Asia and the equitable resolution of costs and benefits between states.

The concept of 'Green Economy', one of the two themes of the Rio +20 summit, has the potential to enhance incorporation of natural capital and ecological services in the assessment of national wealth. However, as Central Asian states are still

90 The history of the shift from rights to needs is traced in Aaron T Wolf, 'Criteria for Equitable Allocations: The Heart of International Water Conflict' (1999) 23 *Natural Resources Forum* 3 cited in Tarlock, above n 27, 397.

91 UNEP, above n 2, at 7.

92 See Table 5.1 above, Criterion 4.

93 Shelton, above n 52, 12.

94 The Millennium Ecosystem Assessment (Millennium Ecosystem Assessment, *People and Ecosystems: A Framework for Assessment* (2003)) identifies the most crucial ecosystem services provided by biodiversity as: *Supporting Services* e.g. Soil formation, and retention, nutrient cycling, primary production, pollination and seed dispersal, production of oxygen, provision of habitat; *Regulating Services* e.g. Air quality maintenance; climate regulation; water regulation; flood control; erosion control; water purification; waste treatment; detoxification; human disease control; biological control of agriculture and livestock pest and disease; storm protection; *Provisioning Services* e.g. Food; wood fuel; fibre; biochemicals; natural medicines; pharmaceuticals; genetic resources; ornamental resources; fresh water; minerals, sand and other non-living resources; *Cultural Services* e.g. Cultural diversity and identity; spiritual and religious values; knowledge systems; educational values; inspiration; aesthetic values; social relations; sense of place; cultural heritage; recreation and ecotourism; communal; symbolic.

striving to meet Millennium Development Goals,[95] the extent to which the 'green economy' concept can be influential in Central Asian discussions will be limited at least in the short term. Further, and as seen in the PALM example, reform within national systems is needed to achieve equity between various stakeholders in the distribution of transboundary resources.

Criterion 8: Rules and Legal Instruments that Enable the Process to Exist In Tajikistan and the Kyrgyz Republic the development of rules and legal instruments for transboundary biodiversity conservation is in infancy at all levels from the transboundary to the local. An improved enabling legal and regulatory framework is one of the planned outputs of the PALM project.[96] Kyrgyz and Tajik Legal Task Forces (LTFs) of the PALM project analysed the institutions and legal instruments that exist within each country. This work provided a valuable means to identify conflicts, overlaps and duplication within and between national systems and a positive basis for future action. The LTFs found that existing legislation is often internally inconsistent and as a result of a lack of coordination often conflicts with other legislation. There is also a lack of clear principles of hierarchy between existing laws. By-laws also often conflict with primary legislation.[97]

The *Agreement on Basic Intergovernmental Relations between Republic of Tajikistan and Kyrgyz Republic*[98] defines interstate relations between the republics. Article 7 states that the republics shall engage in mutually advantageous cooperation and Article 8 expresses the desirability of joint efforts in a number of areas. These areas include a joint economic zone and joint environmental management. The LTFs used the basic intergovernmental agreement as the foundation to develop the PALM MoU which is aimed at enabling the implementation of the PALM project.

---

95 *The MDGs in Europe and Central Asia: Achievements, Challenges and the Way Forward* (2010). This report prepared jointly by the regional offices for Europe and Central Asia of 14 United Nations agencies and the UNECE finds that substantial progress towards achieving the Millennium Development Goals (MDGs) in Central Asian countries risks being interrupted or even reversed with the surge of the economic and financial crisis. The report also highlights rising inequalities, setbacks in social protection, comparatively low life expectancy and unprecedented migration flows accompanied by regional tensions and large scale conflicts. The report finds that actively pursuing institutional reforms according to the principles of a participatory political and social system, and a market economy are major challenges for these countries.

96 United Nations Environment Programme Global Environment Facility (GEF) Grant Request, *Draft Full Project Brief* (2006); *Inception Report*, June 2008, GEF/UNEP/UNU, Sustainable Land Management (SLM) in High Pamir and Pamir-Alai Mountains (PALM), An Integrated and Transboundary Initiative in Central Asia, Phase I: Strengthening of the Enabling Environment for SLM.

97 Shanazarov et al, above n 19, 40.

98 *Agreement on Basic Intergovernmental Relations between Republic of Tajikistan and Kyrgyz Republic*, signed 12 July 1996 2015 UNTS 139 (entered into force 16 October 1997).

The initial work of the LTFs is commendable. It is important however that this work is recognized as merely a starting point. As the LTFs have acknowledged,[99] further development of appropriate national and local-level instruments is essential. The MoU may assist in enabling the operation of the project and pave the way for future agreements. The non-binding provisions of the MoU are too vague to be implemented in a meaningful way. The MoU does not prescribe specific actions or responsibilities. The development of complementary institutions in combination with necessary institutional and capacity building and adequate funding are fundamental to ensuring the effectiveness of any legal instruments that are developed.

Kraska indicates that in the South Asian experience the existence of transboundary river agreements has helped to strengthen political ties. He attributes positive ripple effects on the regional security environment to the process and results of concluding these agreements.[100] Central Asian practice illustrates however that agreements alone are insufficient. Despite the numerous bilateral and regional agreements that concern watercourse management in Central Asia[101] these arrangements are highly strained in practice. This is due to complications in implementation followed by frequent unilateral breaches and suspensions of the agreements.[102]

Existing legal instruments are often inadequate to deal with the complexity of Central Asian water issues.[103] There is a lack of interstate coordination of national water policies and laws of Central Asian states[104] and existing international instruments do not ensure proper use and control of the transboundary water

99 See Shanazarov et al, above n 20, 40–42.

100 James Kraska, 'Sustainable Development is Security: the Role of Transboundary River Agreements as Confidence Building Measure (CBM) in South Asia' (2003) 28 *Yale Journal of International Law* 465, 492.

101 Central Asian water agreements include: *Agreement between the Government of the Russian Federation and the Government of the Republic of Kazakhstan Concerning the Joint Use and Protection of Transboundary Wate*rs (1992); *Agreement between the Republic of Kazakhstan, the Kyrgyz Republic, the Republic of Uzbekistan, the Republic of Tajikistan and Turkmenistan on Cooperation in Joint Management of Use and Protection of Water Resources of Interstate Sources* (1992); *Agreement between the Government of the Republic of Uzbekistan and the Government of Turkmenistan concerning Cooperation on Water Management Issues* (1996); *Agreement between the Government of the Republic of Kazakhstan, the Government of Kyrgyz Republic, the Government of the Republic of Tajikistan, and the Government of the Republic of Uzbekistan Concerning Use of Water and Energy Resources in Syr Darya River Basin* (1998); *Agreement between the Government of the Republic of Kazakhstan and the Government of Kyrgyz Republic on the Use of Water Management Facilities of Intergovernmental Status on the Rivers Chu and Talas* (2000) (see Trombitcaia et al, above n 1 5–6).

102 Polat, above n 39, 101; Pushkina, above n 41, 114.

103 Vinogradov and Langford, above n 35, 414.

104 McKinney, above n 25, 187.

resources.[105] In addition, existing framework agreements do not cover all the issues of joint water management in Central Asia[106] and none of the agreements direct state action in a meaningful way.[107] Water use is inefficient, flows to the Aral Sea are not secured,[108] and none of the interstate agreements for the Aral Sea address the responsibilities of cost sharing or information exchange.[109] These inadequacies of existing instruments result in difficulties in coordinating water governance and planning.[110]

International law appears to have a subordinate role in the transboundary water management positions of Central Asian states.[111] The 1998–2003 Syr Darya Framework Agreement, for example, has had little impact in preventing states involved from taking positions that threaten to defeat the purposes of the agreement.[112] Furthermore states rarely refer to the treaty when accusing each other of wrongdoing.[113] Central Asian republics agreed to continue with the principles of water allocation that existed in the Soviet era.[114] Many interstate policies are still determined by practices in the former Soviet Union.[115]

From 1991 to 1996 Central Asian countries focused on multilateral agreements on water sharing. These agreements were under-funded and often not implemented.[116] By the second half of the 1990s additional agreements had to be made in all transboundary basins that contained transboundary infrastructure.[117] Central Asian countries are increasingly resorting to bilateral agreements to address water issues. These too are regularly broken. Since 2006 Tajikistan and the Kyrgyz Republic have been pushing for a legally binding regional water-sharing framework. Such a framework still does not exist.[118]

These issues highlight the need for new, more appropriate legal arrangements between and within Central Asian states, which are better suited to the situation

---

105 Dukhovny and Sokolov, above n 32, 21.

106 Ibid.

107 Sievers, above n 80, 385.

108 Dukhovny and Sokolov, above n 32, 21.

109 A draft agreement containing provisions on cost sharing and information exchange was prepared under WARMAP project in 1999 (SIC-ICWC/IWMI 2002), but countries have still not approved it for operational use (see Roll et al, above n 84, 5).

110 Roll et al, above n 84, 5.

111 Vinogradov and Langford, above n 35, 414.

112 Sievers, above n 80, 385. Further Arts 18 and 58 *Vienna Convention on the Law of Treaties* ('*VCLT*') open for signature 23 May 1969, 1155 UNTS 33, (entered into force 27 January 1980) require parties to a treaty to refrain from action that would defeat the object and purpose of the treaty. Tajikistan acceded to the VCLT on 6 May 1996 and the Kyrgyz Republic on 11 May 1999.

113 Sievers, above n 80, 385.

114 Wegerich, above n 20, 286.

115 Vinogradov and Langford, above n 35, 414.

116 Pushkina, above n 41, 117.

117 Wegerich, above n 20, 286.

118 Pushkina, above n 41, 117.

of water management that faces these now independent states. Vinogradov and Langford indicate that the framework for regional cooperation in Central Asia should be established in well-drafted agreements with unambiguous legal status in combination with a logical and well-defined institutional structure. Procedures for needs assessments, project planning, implementation and review must be clear, consistent and supported by effective dispute resolution and enforcement mechanisms. Financial responsibilities and reporting procedures must also be clarified and are fundamental to the credibility of the cooperative regional framework.[119]

Despite the limitations of Central Asian water agreements there are examples where these legal instruments can play a role in relieving tensions over water and energy use in the basin.[120] The signing of the 1998 *Syr Darya Agreement*[121] has provided the impetus for basin countries to conduct earnest annual negotiations.[122] Sievers points to the many agreements that exist for the Syr Darya basin. He indicates that while these agreements have not been effective they have helped focus attention on the seriousness of the disagreements that exist between states, thus forcing them to recognize the complexity of water allocation problems. He suggests that these short-term tensions may be a necessary evil to convince states to resolve issues which could otherwise explode into unmanageable conflict in the longer term.[123]

Shortcomings in the legal framework for Central Asian watercourse management provide important lessons for transboundary biodiversity conservation in the region. The Central Asian water experience illustrates that while legal instruments can be a significant catalyst for collaborating on transboundary issues, strong political commitment to the implementation of any agreements and the necessary resources and infrastructure are essential. It is important too not to underestimate the significance of the content of legal instruments from international level agreements to national legislation. The methods for legislative evaluation (MRGs)[124] used in the PALM project enabled national legal teams to objectively assess existing legal instruments and identify areas of overlap. This provides an important platform for legislative reform and

---

119 Vinogradov and Langford, above n 35, 346.

120 McKinney, above n 25, 187.

121 *Agreement Between the Governments of the Republic of Kazakhstan, the Kyrgyz Republic, and the Republic of Uzbekistan on the Use of Water and Energy Resources of the Syr Darya Basin*, signed 17 March 1998 (Article XI states that the Agreement enters into force from the date the Parties forward the notification of depository) http://ocid.nacse.org/tfdd/tfdddocs/591ENG.pdf.

122 McKinney, above n 25, 187.

123 Sievers, above n 80, 388.

124 University of New England, *Methodological Research Guidelines for Legal Task Forces, for Analysing the Capacity of Legal, Policy and Institutional Aspects of Sustainable Land Management in the High Pamir and Pamir-Alai Mountain Environment*, GEF/UNEP/UNU Sustainable Land Management in the High Pamir and Pamir-Alai Mountains (2009).

collaboration on transboundary issues in the PALM area. The challenge in the PALM context is moving forward with the implementation of the LTF findings. Legislative reform based on the LTFs' report appears to have stagnated.

Criterion 9: Designated Institutions are Identified at Each Level of Organization and Vertical and Horizontal Linkages are Established Across All Levels At the national level the LTF analysis found that mechanisms and procedures for the implementation of laws and by-laws in Tajikistan and the Kyrgyz Republic are either inadequate or non-existent. They also point to lack of control over the mechanisms for implementing statutory laws and that this situation leads to frequent infringements of the law and the inadequate management of natural resources.[125]

At the transboundary level both countries indicate a preference for working within existing institutions (i.e. the Committee on Environment Protection in Tajikistan and the National Centre for Mountain Regions Development in the Kyrgyz Republic) to address transboundary issues rather than establishing a new joint body. The MoU however indicates that a joint commission may be created to implement the strategy and action plan. In addition the *Agreement on Basic Intergovernmental Relations between Republic of Tajikistan and Kyrgyz Republic* contains a *Protocol on the Establishment of a Tajik-Kyrgyz Intergovernmental Commission for the Integrated Consideration of Bilateral Issues*.[126] The LTFs recommend that this Intergovernmental Commission assumes significant authority and functions with regard to monitoring the implementation of the PALM Strategy and Action Plan and that the Commission should play a key role in achieving the objectives of the PALM project. What this illustrates is that the PALM parties have yet to adopt a position on the type of institution/s needed to realize the objectives of the project. Without a clear understanding of the type of institution that is required this could lead to a new series of institutions with uncoordinated and conflicting responsibilities.

The lessons for the PALM project from the Central Asian water experience is that the identification or creation of responsible institutions is not enough in itself. This highlights the importance of also realizing the other governance criteria presented in Table 5.1. The institutions responsible for water management in Central Asia are the ICWC and the two regional BVOs of the Amu Darya and

125 Shanazarov et al, above n 19, 40.

126 *Protocol on the Establishment of a Tajik-Kyrgyz Intergovernmental Commission for the Integrated Consideration of Bilateral Issues* (signed and entered into force 12 July 1996) 2015 UNTS 139. Article 12 of the Protocol states that the Protocol is concluded for a period of five years from its signature on 12 July 1996 and is automatically extended for a further five-year period, unless one of the parties indicates in writing an intention to terminate the agreement before this time. That time has lapsed but the Commission continues operation de facto.

Syr Darya basins.[127] The ICWC lacks legal authority, political support, financial resources and capacity and sufficient linkages among the various levels of political organization. Though the foundation documents of the BVOs provide that all main structures for the management of transboundary waters on the Syr Darya and Amu Darya rivers should be transferred to the control of the BVOs, the reality is that the only structures currently under BVO control are the main interstate canal structures in Uzbekistan.[128] As the BVOs do not actually control the critical structures in the basins this creates uncertainty in the role of the BVOs and subsequently in water resource management in the region.[129]

Trombitcaia et al indicate that transboundary watercourse institutions could improve their activities by strengthening institutional mechanisms. Their recommendations echo components of the criteria presented above. Trombitcaia et al recommend better representation of national authorities in the joint body and improving national level coordination; greater financial commitments from riparian States; the establishment of executive and working organs; and the introduction of mechanisms for public participation and access to information.[130] Further principles which can increase the efficiency of transboundary watercourse institutions and contribute to improving cooperation include clearly defined powers; an organizational structure that allows for developing, adopting and implementing decisions; and effective mechanisms for cooperation between the joint body and the national authorities.[131]

Transboundary-level institutions (whether in the form of a designated transboundary institution or the identification of a responsible body within national authorities) are vital to the effective management of transboundary resources. The Central Asian water experience demonstrates that similar to the case for legal instruments discussed in Criterion 8 above, without the presence of other governance elements these institutions will be ineffective.

Criterion 12: Dispute Resolution Mechanisms Exist Dispute resolution is important at all levels from the transboundary to the local. One of the responsibilities of the Kyrgyz and Tajik national LTFs was to evaluate the extent to which dispute resolution is provided for in national and international legal instruments.[132] The LTFs' findings point to a general lack of dispute resolution mechanisms at all levels

127 Vinogradov and Langford, above n 35, 351.

128 McKinney, above n 25, 187.

129 Ibid.

130 Trombitcaia et al, above n 1, 2–3.

131 Ibid.

132 The role of the LTFs was to analyse the legal, policy and institutional basis for Sustainable Land Management in the region. The LTFs prepared their analysis based on the Methodological Research Guidelines (MRGs) developed by Component 1.2 leader Dr. Ian Hannam. Dispute resolution was one of the 17 essential elements of legislative design set out in the MRGs. For a full version of the MRGs see University of New England, above n 124.

of political organization. Where dispute resolution is provided for the provisions are vague and incomplete and therefore difficult if not impossible to implement.[133]

Central Asian water agreements also lack adequate provisions for dispute resolution. Conflict resolution in the region is further obstructed by the lack of information, transparency and communication among the various levels of stakeholders.[134] The 1992 agreement refers water disputes to the Ministers of Water Resources of the five republics[135] but does not cover situations where the Ministers are unable to resolve the dispute. There is consequently a need for a dispute settlement mechanism that clarifies the type of tribunal, the applicable law and procedure, and the authority of the dispute settlement body.[136] A draft international convention produced at a session of the ICWC in 1994 provides that any intentional violation within a basin state of water withdrawal limits, regimes and schedules that causes damage or affects the interests of other basin states leads to a penalty and to liability for compensation. Such cases are to be heard by an arbitral court composed of three nationals of third states.[137] There do not appear to be any further developments in the implementation of the draft convention.

The absence of adequate dispute resolution mechanisms is evident in both the water context and PALM project. The Central Asian water experience highlights that dispute resolution mechanisms need to be specific and include the necessary political commitment and financial support to ensure their implementation and enforcement.

Conclusions

This chapter has examined the effectiveness of transboundary water resource management in Central Asia and the PALM project within the framework of a set of governance criteria. The author drew on the experiences of Central Asian transboundary water resource management to identify pitfalls and develop strategies for addressing the challenges to transboundary biodiversity conservation in the PALM project.

The analysis of particular governance criteria in the context of the PALM project and Central Asian transboundary water resource management emphasized the interconnected nature of the criteria and that fulfilling one criterion often

---

133 PALM Project Kyrgyz and Tajik Legal Task Forces, 'Integrated Report – Analysis of legislative, political and institutional systems of the Kyrgyz Republic and Republic of Tajikistan, GEF/UNEP/UNU Project "Sustainable Land Management in the High Pamir and Pamir-Alai Mountains – Integrated and Transboundary Initiative in Central Asia"' (2010) see pp 28, 37, 64, 72.

134 Dukhovny and Sokolov, above n 32, 35.

135 *Almaty Agreement*, art 13.

136 Vinogradov & Langford, above n 35, 353.

137 Ibid.

depended on simultaneously meeting one or more of the other governance criteria. The analysis underscored the essential nature of political will and commitment. In both the PALM and transboundary water contexts integrated approaches which identify shared benefits have the potential to improve political support for the project and contribute to more equitable distribution of the costs and benefits of transboundary collaboration. The preliminary legal and institutional analysis by the LTFs of the PALM project is a commendable starting point. However, the Central Asian transboundary water experience demonstrates that without other governance components in place, agreements and institutions are insufficient. A similar conclusion was reached in the examination of dispute resolution mechanisms.

Transboundary strategies are needed in many parts of the world to effectively manage shared natural resources. The development of such strategies is particularly urgent in post-Soviet Central Asia. The governance criteria point to the necessity of aligning a variety of legal, institutional and managerial factors to create effective transboundary management. This chapter has demonstrated the utility of the governance criteria in the assessment of transboundary initiatives and the identification of solutions and trans-sectoral synergies. This suggests that the governance criteria could be a valuable tool for achieving effective transboundary natural resource management in other regions and sectors.

Chapter 6
Developing Agreements for Transboundary Environmental Impact Assessment and Strategic Environmental Assessment in Asia

Simon Marsden

Introduction

Transboundary environmental impact assessment (TEIA) is a process generally applied by one or more states to evaluate potentially significant environmental effects from proposals within their own territory or which physically cross territorial borders, and which may impact upon the territory of another state or states.[1] Proposals usually concern individual projects (EIA), although they may also be strategic in nature, relating to policies, plans or programs. The evaluation process for these latter proposals is known as strategic environmental assessment (SEA), which can also be applied in a transboundary context (TSEA).[2] Proposals may result in impacts within enclosed areas such as inland waters,[3] and beyond the territory of individual states, such as on the high seas.[4] In Asia, both project and strategic proposals are subject to TEIA and/or TSEA and may be located in any of these areas. This is common with experiences elsewhere, especially in Europe.[5]

---

1 Kees Bastmeijer and Timo Koivurova (eds), *Theory and Practice of Transboundary Environmental Impact Assessment* (Martinus Nijhoff, 2008); Neil Craik, *The International Law of Environmental Impact Assessment: Process, Substance and Integration* (Cambridge University Press, 2008); Charles Kersten, 'Rethinking Transboundary Environmental Impact Assessment' (2009) 34 *Yale Journal of International Law* 173.

2 Simon Marsden, *Strategic Environmental Assessment in International and European Law: A Practitioner's Guide* (Earthscan, 2008); Simon Marsden, 'Assessment of Transboundary Environmental Effects in the Pearl River Delta Region: Is There a Role for Strategic Environmental Assessment?' (2011) 31 *Environmental Impact Assessment Review* 593.

3 See Timo Koivurova and Ismo Pölönen, 'Transboundary Environmental Impact Assessment in the Case of the Baltic Sea Gas Pipeline' (2010) 25 *The International Journal of Marine and Coastal Law* 121.

4 See Robin Warner, *Protecting the Oceans beyond National Jurisdiction: Strengthening the International Law Framework* (Martinus Nijhoff, 2009) 14–15.

5 Simon Marsden and Timo Koivurova (eds), *Transboundary Environmental Impact Assessment in the European Union: The Espoo Convention and its Kiev Protocol on*

In a few parts of the world regional agreements for TEIA have been established, again notably in Europe and related areas under the *Espoo Convention*,[6] and further to the *Nordic Environmental Protection Convention*.[7] The *Helsinki Convention*,[8] which applies in Europe and Asia, also contains obligations for this, and there is potential for such an agreement under frameworks in North America[9] and Central America,[10] although neither has yet been developed.[11] What agreements do exist give force to the general international principle of no-harm, which has been examined by the International Court of Justice (ICJ) in the *Pulp Mills on the River Uruguay*,[12] *Danube Dams*[13] and *Nuclear Tests*[14] cases. Most recently in the *Pulp Mills* case, the ICJ gave particular emphasis to the role of TEIA in relation to shared resources, such as inland lakes bordered by several states and international rivers, which are often found within the sub-regions of continents. Both of these types of resources are common in the sub-regions of Asia, and include the Caspian Sea and Mekong river basin. The Court comments: '... it may now be considered a requirement under general international law to undertake an environmental impact assessment where there is a risk that the proposed industrial activity may have a significant adverse impact in a transboundary context, in particular, on a shared resource'.[15]

Strategic Environmental Assessment (Earthscan, 2011).

6 Convention on Environmental Impact Assessment in a Transboundary Context, opened for signature 25 February 1991, 1989 UNTS 3029 (entered into force 27 June 1997) ('Espoo Convention').

7 Nordic Environmental Protection Convention, opened for signature 19 February 1974, 13 ILM 511 (entered into force 5 October 1976).

8 Convention on the Protection and Use of Transboundary Watercourses and International Lakes, opened for signature 17 March 1992, 1936 UNTS 269 (entered into force 6 October 1996) ('Helsinki Convention'); note Arts 3(1)(h) and 9(2)(h) and (j) in particular.

9 North American Agreement on Environmental Cooperation, opened for signature 14 September 1993, 32 ILM 1480 (entered into force 1 January 1994).

10 Agreement on the Strengthening of the Environmental Impact Assessment System in Central America, opened for signature 4 July 2002, unreported (not in force).

11 Neil Craik, 'Transboundary Environmental Impact Assessment in North America: Obstacles and Opportunities', and Marianela Cedeño, 'Assessment of Transboundary Environmental Impacts in Developing Countries: The Case of Central America', both in Bastmeijer and Koivurova (eds), above n 1, 93 and 119.

12 *Pulp Mills on the River Uruguay (Argentina v. Uruguay)* (request for provisional measures by Argentina) (2006) 45 ILM 1025, para 204.

13 *Gabčíkovo-Nagymaros Project (Hungary v. Slovakia)* [1997] ICJ Rep. 7.

14 *Nuclear Tests (New Zealand v. France)* (merits) [1974] ICJ Rep. 457; Request for an Examination of the Situation in Accordance with Paragraph 63 of the Court's Judgment of 20 December 1974 in the *Nuclear Tests (New Zealand v. France)* [1995] ICJ Rep. 288.

15 For discussion, see Jan De Mulder, 'Case Note' (2010) 19 *Review of European Community and International Environmental Law* 263; Owen McIntyre, 'Analysis: The

The purpose of this chapter is to evaluate experiences with cross-regional (Europe/Asia) and Asian sub-regional agreements for the development of a pan-regional agreement for TEIA/TSEA in relation to the Asian continent as a whole. While in other parts of Asia there has been some informal experience with TEIA and TSEA, this has largely been outside a legal framework, in particular in the Pearl River Delta concerning the relationship between Hong Kong and China.[16] There have also been suggestions that TEIA should be applied to the marine environment of the Bay of Bengal in South Asia.[17] For the purposes of this chapter, and driven by the developing jurisprudence of the ICJ, significant state practice with the *Espoo Convention* and the coming into force of its *SEA Protocol*,[18] the application of the *Helsinki Convention* in Central and East Asia,[19] and the development of and experience with the *Tehran*,[20] *Mekong*,[21] and *Tumen*[22] sub-agreements, the practicalities of an Asian pan-regional agreement will be examined.

The second part will comprehensively outline and analyse the procedures of, and where possible give examples of practice under, the cross-regional and sub-regional agreements. The third part will then briefly evaluate the commonalities between them in an attempt to find similar ground to form the basis of a pan-regional agreement. This will focus on three aspects: overlapping membership, procedural

---

Proceduralisation and Growing Maturity of International Water Law' (2010) 22 *Journal of Environmental Law* 475.

16 Marsden (2011), above n 2; Simon Marsden, 'Developing Approaches to Transboundary Environmental Impact Assessment in China: Cooperation through the Greater Tumen Initiative and in the Pearl River Delta Region' (2011) 9 *Chinese Journal of International Law* 393; and Simon Marsden, 'Environmental Impact Assessment in Hong Kong: An Evaluation of Principles, Procedures and Practice Post-1997' (2010) 13 *Asia Pacific Journal of Environmental Law* 115.

17 Daud Hassan, 'Environmental Impact Assessment in the Bay of Bengal Sub Region of South Asia' in Bastmeijer and Koivurova (eds), above n 1, 135.

18 Protocol on Strategic Environmental Assessment to the Convention on Environmental Impact Assessment in a Transboundary Context, opened for signature Kiev, 21 May 2003, unreported (entered into force 11 July 2010) ('SEA Protocol').

19 For activities in Central Asia, see: http://www.unece.org/env/water/centralasia.htm.

20 Framework Convention for the Protection of the Marine Environment of the Caspian Sea, opened for signature Tehran, 4 November, 2003, unreported (entered into force 12 August 2006) ('Tehran Convention').

21 Agreement on the Cooperation for the Sustainable Development of the Mekong River Basin, opened for signature Chiang Rai, 5 April 1995, unreported (entered into force 5 April 1995) ('Mekong Convention').

22 Agreement on the Establishment of the Tumen River Area Development Coordination Committee, opened for signature New York, 6 December 1995, unreported (entered into force 6 December 1995); and Agreement on the Establishment of the Consultative Commission for the Development of the Tumen River Economic Development Area and Northeast Asia, opened for signature New York, 6 December 1995, unreported (entered into force 6 December 1995).

similarities and the influence of and advocacy for the *Espoo Convention*, and the requirements of multilateral development banks, including the Asian Development Bank.[23] A conclusion then follows.

Cross-regional and Sub-regional Agreements: Procedure and Practice

There are five agreements of relevance in Asia: two cross-regional (applying to Europe and Asia), and three sub-regional (within Asia). Central Asia (CA) is a core region of the Asian continent from the Caspian Sea in the west to China in the east, Afghanistan in the south, and Russia in the north. The first cross-regional agreement, and the only one of the five which deals exclusively with TEIA, is the *Espoo Convention*.[24] In CA this agreement is applied by Kazakhstan and Kyrgyzstan as Parties, and by Tajikistan, Turkmenistan and Uzbekistan who are members of the treaty sponsor, the UNECE. None of these states are currently Parties or signatories to the *SEA Protocol*. The second cross-regional agreement, the *Helsinki Convention*,[25] also applies to a number of CA states, including Azerbaijan, Kazakhstan, Kyrgyzstan, Uzbekistan and Russia. It is however neither limited to a sub-region (as with the *Mekong*, *Tumen* and *Tehran* Agreements), nor has it specific application to a group of neighbouring states (as with the *Espoo Convention* in CA).[26]

The first of the sub-regional agreements examined is the *Mekong Agreement*, which is made up of the South East Asian states of Cambodia, Laos, Thailand and Vietnam; China and Myanmar became Dialogue Partners in 1996. The second, the *Tumen Agreements*, were originally signed by North Korea, China and Russia, and later by South Korea and Mongolia. The third, the *Tehran Convention*, applies to the 'Caspian Littoral States': Azerbaijan, Iran, Kazakhstan, Turkmenistan and

---

23 As distinct from these government supported institutions are the global private financiers which increasingly apply the 'Equator Principles', a set of statements of social and environmental principles, to project finance operations. See David M Ong, 'From "International" to "Transnational" Environmental Law? A Legal Assessment of the Contribution of the "Equator Principles" to International Environmental Law' (2010) 79 *Nordic Journal of International Law* 35.

24 Wiecher Schrage, 'The Convention on Environmental Impact Assessment in a Transboundary Context' in Bastmeijer and Koivurova (eds), above n 1, 29.

25 Angela Z Cassar and Carl E Bruch, 'Transboundary Environmental Impact Assessment in International Watercourse Management' (2003) 12 *New York University Environmental Law Journal* 169 at 194–195; Eric W Sievers, 'Transboundary Jurisdiction and Watercourse Law: China, Kazakhstan, and the Irtysh' (2002) 37 *Texas International Law Journal 1*; Kersten, above n 1, 179.

26 See however the following, which indicates that despite not being a Party to the Helsinki Convention, Kyrgyzstan has cooperated with Kazakhstan in a similar manner to that under the Espoo Convention: http://www.unece.org/env/water/centralasia.htm.

Russia; all of these are 'South West'[27] or CA states or have territory that extends into North or East Asia (Russia).

The Espoo Convention *and* SEA Protocol *(Central Asia)*

The *Espoo Convention* is concerned with harm prevention and cooperation, with the objective to 'ensure environmentally sound and sustainable development' and 'enhance international cooperation'.[28] Article 1 defines 'Party of origin', 'affected Party', 'proposed activity', 'environmental impact assessment', 'impact', 'transboundary impact', 'competent authority' and 'public'. Article 2 contains general provisions for the management of effects, legal measures required, anticipation and notification, consultation and participation, exemptions and requirements for more stringent measures. Article 2(10) confirms the relationship of the Convention with other international law. The objective of the *SEA Protocol* is to: 'provide for a high level of protection of the environment, including health'. Definitions in Article 2 of the Protocol follow the Convention where possible. Although related to the Convention, the Protocol addresses environmental effects from plans and programmes developed and required by government, primarily in a national context, which set the framework for development consent.

The application of the Convention in CA derives from its membership and Decisions reached at the Second and Third Meetings of the Parties in Sofia and Cavtat. In Sofia in February 2001, Decision II/8 entitled 'Strengthening subregional cooperation' emphasized the need to encourage the development of bilateral and multilateral agreements through subregional cooperation to better implement the Convention.[29] Building on pilot workshops in the Balkan and Black Sea regions, subregional cooperation was aimed at countries in transition, in particular those formerly part of the Soviet Union, including the CA states, with a view to improving the ratification process. In Cavtat in June 2004, Decision III/5 also entitled 'Strengthening subregional cooperation', developed this further, following experience gained in Central and Eastern Europe and South Eastern Europe, as detailed in associated guidance.[30]

Procedure The specific procedures of the *Espoo Convention* are found in Articles 3 (notification), 4 (documentation), 5 (consultation), 6 (final decision), 7 (post-project analysis) and 8 (bilateral and multilateral cooperation). These and

27 The geography of the Middle East has connections both with Africa and Asia and appears unsettled.

28 Given the detailed analysis of the Espoo Convention and practice in a Finnish context by Koivurova in this volume, this section comprises a summary only, as linked with practice in Central Asia.

29 See ECE/MP.EIA/4, Annex VIII, 128–130.

30 See ECE/MP.EIA/6, Annex V, 76–91.

other procedures have been elaborated in the literature.[31] The process is designed to provide better information for decision-makers, and involve public and government stakeholders in the process. The terms 'Party of origin' and 'affected Party' are used under the *Espoo Convention* to differentiate the obligations and rights of each. The procedure that applies in all instances for TEIA is very similar to that for domestic EIA, although there are differences based on the underlying agreement between the Parties.

Determinations of harm significance are first made in order to trigger the procedure (Article 2(3), 2(5)), which may be in accordance with a list approach of major activities (Appendix I) or through a general determination based on criteria such as location or scale (Appendix III). An inquiry procedure is available for Appendix 1 activities, where there is a strong presumption that the screening threshold is exceeded. The latter may be combined with the former under the Convention (Article 2(5)). Once the notification, documentation and consultation processes have been completed, Article 6(1) stipulates the substantive obligation to give 'due account' to the outcome of the EIA and Article 6(2) requires reasons and other considerations on which the decision is based to be given.

Contextualizing the Convention in CA are the *Guidelines on Environmental Impact Assessment in a Transboundary Context for Central Asian Countries* (the *Guidelines*).[32] The objective is to detail the procedural mechanisms, although they are only recommendatory. Any legal basis is hence derived from national EIA laws unless, in the case of the two CA Parties to the Convention, they have also ratified its provisions and deposited their instruments of ratification. The *Guidelines* consist of five independent but interrelated parts: review of national EIA legislation and practice; recommendations for the country or Party of origin; recommendations for the affected country or Party; recommendations for the project proponent; and other matters, which include SEA. Most of the *Guidelines* in the first part detail the steps taken by the CA Parties and others up to mid-2005 to implement the Convention where applicable.

In relation to the *SEA Protocol*, despite the national focus of its procedures, Article 10 provides for transboundary consultations where significant transboundary effects are expected, and Article 11 factors this consultation into the decision-making process. 'Party of origin' is used to refer to the contracting party responsible for the strategic decision, and 'affected Party' refers to the contracting

31 See Wiek Schrage and Nick Bonvoisin, 'Transboundary Impact Assessment: Frameworks, Experiences and Challenges' (2008) 26 *Impact Assessment and Project Appraisal* 234.

32 See ECE, MOP to the Espoo Convention, Working Group on EIA, Tenth Meeting, Geneva, May 2007, Activities related to the Convention listed in the workplan (Decision III/9), Capacity-building in Eastern Europe, Caucasus and Central Asia (EECCA), Guidelines on Environmental Impact Assessment in a Transboundary Context for Central Asian Countries, Prepared by Kazakhstan, Kyrgyzstan, Tajikistan, Turkmenistan and Uzbekistan. See ECE/MP.EIA/WG.1/2007/6, 12 March 2007.

party whose environment may be impacted upon by the proposal. General provisions are contained in Article 3. The *SEA Protocol Resource Manual* explains the legal obligations that determine whether SEA is required and the procedures to be followed, including transboundary consultation.[33]

Practice While only two CA states are Convention Parties (Kazakhstan and Kyrgyzstan), others have decided to follow its procedures in relation to the development of proposals with potential transboundary significance. Together with these Parties, Tajikistan has passed domestic implementing legislation,[34] and Uzbekistan is preparing to ratify the Convention.[35] To demonstrate the application of the *Guidelines*, a UNECE pilot project was begun soon afterwards.[36] It proceeded between 2006 and 2009, and involved international as well as local experts. The objective was to demonstrate effective implementation of the Convention in Kazakhstan and Kyrgyzstan through conducting a full TEIA procedure on a specific planned project in Kyrgyzstan, with the involvement of Kazakh authorities and the public.

The project was a new copper and gold mining operation proposed by a mining company which required a licence in Kyrgyzstan, and was situated very close to the Kazakh border. Downstream water pollution was a significant potential impact. On the basis of this experience, national implementation mechanisms were developed and human capacities increased through training sessions in Kazakhstan and Kyrgyzstan. Two major EIA laws were also amended to clarify procedures and include public participation. The later phases of the project concentrated on updating the 2005 *Guidelines*.

Most recently, a series of capacity building workshops were held in 2010 and 2011 in the CA states.[37] These have included an expert workshop to enhance understanding of the Convention and Protocol with a focus on domestic land-use and sectoral planning in Uzbekistan.[38] The objective was to raise awareness of what would be involved if Uzbekistan chose to accede to the Protocol, and the workshop was designed to improve the actors' capacities to transpose and

33 UNECE, Resource Manual to Support Application of the UNECE Protocol on Strategic Environmental Assessment (United Nations and Regional Environment Centre for Central and Eastern Europe, 2012, 2nd edition) 89–90.

34 Tajikistan ratified the Espoo Convention in 2004 but has still to deposit its instrument of ratification with the UN, which is needed for it to become a Party. See *Guidelines* para 39.

35 For the latest information, see: http://www.unece.org/env/eia/subregions/central_asia.html#Caguide. None of the CA states are signatories or Parties to the SEA Protocol.

36 Organization for Security and Cooperation in Europe/UNECE, Environmental Impact Assessment in a Transboundary Context: Pilot Project in Central Asia Project Report (Vienna, 2009).

37 http://www.unece.org/env/eia/subregions/central_asia.htm.

38 http://www.unece.org/index.php?id=27140.

implement international principles, standards and good practice in SEA based on practical exercises.

The Helsinki Convention *(Central and East Asia)*

The *Helsinki Convention* is also concerned with harm prevention and cooperation, specifically in connection with transboundary watercourses and international lakes. As with the *Espoo Convention* it also applies in CA, and as a result of Russian membership in East Asia also.[39] The Preamble emphasizes the role of the UNECE in 'promoting international cooperation for the prevention, control and reduction of transboundary water pollution and sustainable use of transboundary waters'. Article 1 contains definitions of 'transboundary waters', 'transboundary impact', 'Party', 'riparian Parties', 'joint bodies', 'hazardous substances' and 'best available technology'. The Convention is divided into two parts: Part I applying to all Parties, and Part II applying to riparian Parties.

Article 2 contains general provisions applying to all. These include obligations to 'take all appropriate measures to prevent, control and reduce any transboundary impact', including pollution and 'with the aim of ecologically sound and rational water management, conservation of water resources and environmental protection'. Reasonable and equitable use, and conservation and restoration of ecosystems are also objectives. In taking these measures, the Parties must be guided by the precautionary, polluter-pays and intergenerational equity principles. Joint monitoring and assessment obligations further to Article 11 provide information to guide action. As with the *Espoo Convention* Parties may adopt and implement more stringent measures.

Procedure EIA is part of the procedures stipulated under the *Helsinki Convention.* Article 3(1)(h), applying to all Parties, requires EIA as part of the approach to prevention, control and reduction of transboundary impact. Further provision is found in Part II in relation to the obligations of riparian Parties, although given the broader focus of the Convention this does not detail components of the EIA process. Article 9(2) provides for the establishment of joint bodies between the riparian Parties under the Convention, one of the purposes of which (j) is 'to participate in the implementation of environmental impact assessments relating to transboundary waters, in accordance with appropriate international regulations'.

---

39 Note that the UNECE Convention on the Transboundary Effects of Industrial Accidents, opened for signature 17 March 1992, 2105 UNTS 457 (entered into force 19 April 2000), also applies to three CA states (Kazakhstan, Azerbaijan and Armenia) and Russia. It was also adopted in Helsinki, requires a TEIA procedure (Annex III), includes the possibility of an inquiry commission (Annex II), and makes specific reference to the related Espoo Convention (Article 4(4)). Because of the specific focus of the Industrial Accidents Convention, it is not considered in the text.

To discover the meaning of the Convention obligations, reference should be made to the *Draft Guide to Implementing the Convention*,[40] (the '*Guide*'), prepared by the Legal Board. In regard to Article 3(1)(h) the *Guide* devotes four pages to discussing the requirement for EIA, which it refers to as 'an important element within the whole range of the "appropriate measures"', because it 'enhances public participation and transparency in the authorization of projects' 'and enables public authorities to adopt better informed decisions implementing the substantive obligations of prevention'.[41] It furthermore comments that the adoption of national legislation requiring EIA 'is a necessary condition for the implementation of EIA also at the international level'.[42]

In respect of Article 9(2)(j) the *Guide* emphasizes that the Convention does not require a joint body to conduct an EIA, rather to 'participate in its implementation'. As to the 'international regulations' deemed appropriate, the *Guide* makes specific reference to the *Espoo Convention* and comments:

> The Espoo Convention provides a parameter for reference for the implementation of EIA which is directly legally binding for those Parties of the Water Convention that are also Parties to it. It can nonetheless provide legal guidance in the field also for those Parties of the Water Convention that are not Parties to the Espoo Convention. Such guidance is likely to become indirectly binding also for non-Parties to the Espoo Convention insofar as its standards become general practice customarily followed, at least at the pan-European level.[43]

With regard to SEA, the *Guide* makes reference to the *SEA Protocol*, and opines correctly that SEA is relevant for the implementation of Article 3(1)(h) of the *Helsinki Convention* as it falls within the scope of the expression 'other means of assessment'. The relationship between this Article and Article 9(2)(j) and (h) is also considered by the *Guide.* The participation of joint bodies in the implementation of EIA relating to transboundary waters must therefore be read in the light of the earlier obligation. Article 9(2)(h) provides that joint bodies shall serve as a 'forum for the exchange of information on existing and planned uses of water and related installations that are likely to cause transboundary impact'.

The *Guide* furthermore considers the minimum requirements needed to comply with the EIA provision in the Convention in paras 201–205. A legislated

40 United Nations Economic and Social Council, Economic Commission for Europe, Meeting of the Parties to the Convention on the Protection and Use of Transboundary Watercourses and International Lakes, Fifth session Geneva, 10–12 November 2009, Item 5(a) of the provisional agenda, Integrated Management of Water and Related Ecosystems, Draft Legal Guide to Implementing the Convention, draft guide by the Chairperson of the Legal Board, ECE/MP.WAT/2009/L.2, 31 August 2009.

41 Ibid, para 197.

42 Ibid.

43 Para 198.

national consent regime for activities likely to cause harm to transboundary waters is required, with EIA a precondition before any authorizations. SEA should also be considered as part of any such regime in respect of plans and programmes relevant to the *Helsinki Convention*. Annex II of the *SEA Protocol* makes reference to water-specific projects for which plans and programmes may set the context. Designation of competent authorities is needed for such a regime and documentation considered should comply with minimum content and standard requirements, as outlined by the relevant Annexes in the *Espoo Convention* and *SEA Protocol*. Notification and consultation should follow the procedures of these agreements and information and public participation obligations should also be informed by the *Aarhus Convention*.[44]

Practice The Article 11 obligation enables the collection of baseline data to evaluate practice, which includes 'the effectiveness of measures taken for the prevention, control and reduction of transboundary impact' (Article 11(3)). In relation to the second assessment of the condition of transboundary rivers, lakes and groundwaters in CA, two working groups under the Convention recommend the following:

> Joint environmental impact assessments of planned transboundary projects should be carried out. This is particularly relevant considering further flow regulation ... There is a need for transparency in the work of the joint commissions and for co-riparian(s) to be better informed about development plans for transboundary rivers that could have a significant impact upon their water resources, so that costs and benefits of various development plans can be analysed.[45]

In East Asia assessments have also been completed for the Amur River Basin, shared between China, Mongolia and Russia; and the Tumen River Basin, shared between China, North Korea and Russia. In relation to the latter, regulation of which overlaps to an extent with the *Tumen Agreements* (below), the assessment comments: 'The drawing up of a multilateral agreement between China, the Democratic People's Republic of Korea and the Russian Federation is of utmost importance. It should provide for joint measures on monitoring and assessment ...

44 Convention on Access to Information, Public Participation in Decision-Making and Access to Justice in Environmental Matters, opened for signature Aarhus, 25 June 1998, 2161 UNTS 447 (in force 30 October 2001) ('Aarhus Convention').

45 United Nations Economic and Social Council, Economic Commission for Europe, Meeting of the Parties to the Convention on the Protection and Use of Transboundary Watercourses and International Lakes, Working Group on Integrated Water Resources Management, Sixth meeting Geneva, 4–5 May 2011; Working Group on Monitoring and Assessment, Twelfth meeting, Geneva, 2–4 May 2011; Finalization of the second Assessment of transboundary rivers, lakes and groundwaters in the UNECE region: Major findings of the assessment for Central Asia; ECE/MP.WAT/WG.1/2011/4; ECE/MP.WAT/WG.2/2011/4, 27 April 2011, para 83, p 19.

in order to decrease the overall human impact on the waters in the Tumen River basin.'[46]

The *Guide* also makes reference to practice in several sections, some of which is relevant to EIA. This includes development of the Rogun hydroelectric dam by the Tajikistan Government, a major concern of Uzbekistan's. The dam was begun during Soviet times, although it was halted in the 1990s. Neighbouring Uzbekistan's withdrawal from the regional power grid in 2009 ended Tajikistan's electricity supply from Russia, which prompted its need for hydroelectricity. As the downstream state, Uzbekistan is concerned about its water supply for irrigation of its cotton industry. The project is to be assessed under World Bank procedures, as the Bank is the major financier.[47] This will include riparian issues and cross-border impacts.[48] The Environmental-Social Assessment to be undertaken includes consideration of riparian issues and cross-border impacts. This is subject to a consultancy tender at present.[49]

Since Tajikistan is a member neither of the *Espoo Convention* nor the *Helsinki Convention* it does not have to comply with either, so the application of the Bank's procedures is significant.[50] Tajikistan is also planning to construct a reservoir and hydropower station in the upper reaches of the Zeravshan River which may affect the quantity of water downstream, again impacting upon Uzbekistan. To attempt to deal with these matters and more, an ambitious *Environmental Framework Convention* is being considered with the objective of providing a legal basis for cooperation between CA states on a broad range of issues. TEIA is included in rudimentary form in Articles 4(6) and 6(2) with Article 3 providing that:

> The purpose of this Convention is to ensure the effective protection of the environment for sustainable development in Central Asia, including the improvement of ecological environment, rational use of natural resources, as

---

46 United Nations Economic and Social Council, Economic Commission for Europe, Meeting of the Parties to the Convention on the Protection and Use of Transboundary Watercourses and International Lakes, Working Group on Monitoring and Assessment, Eighth meeting, Helsinki, 25–27 June 2007, Preliminary assessment of transboundary rivers discharging to Pacific Ocean and their major transboundary tributaries, ECE/MP.WAT/WG.2/2007/14, para 25, pp 7–8.

47 See generally Salman Salman, *The World Bank Policy for Projects on International Waterways: An Historical and Legal Analysis* (The World Bank, 2009).

48 Rayhan Demytrie, 'Tajikistan looks to solve energy crisis with huge dam' BBC News (London), 23 March 2010, http://news.bbc.co.uk/2/hi/asia-pacific/8580171.stm.

49 See World Bank E2476 V5, Terms of Reference for the Preparation of an Environmental and Social Impact Assessment.

50 Compare the experience of two other CA states in their relations with the European Bank for Reconstruction and Development; see Mehrdad M Nazari, 'The Transboundary EIA Convention in the Context of Private Sector Operations Co-Financed by an International Financial Institution: Two Case Studies from Azerbaijan and Turkmenistan' (2003) 23 *Environmental Impact Assessment Review* 441.

well as reduce and prevent transboundary environmental damage through the harmonization and coordination of environmental policies and actions of the Contracting Parties and by establishing reciprocal rights and responsibilities.[51]

The Mekong Agreement *(South East Asia)*

The *Mekong Agreement* is a framework agreement which requires the Mekong River Commission (MRC) to adopt rules and procedures to carry out its work through its Joint Committee (JC). Article 24 sets out the functions of this Committee. Key activities include the formulation of a Basin Development Plan (Article 2), a program for the protection of the environment and ecosystems (Article 3), and reasonable and equitable programming, utilization and protection of water resources and the environment for the member countries (Article 5). In 1999, the MRC and member countries adopted a Water Utilization Program funded by the Global Environmental Fund and executed by the World Bank to develop rules for water utilization. Of most relevance to TEIA, however, are the *Procedures for Notification, Prior Consultation and Agreement* ('the *Procedures*').[52]

Chapter III of the Agreement, entitled 'Objectives and Principles of Cooperation', contains the substantive operative provisions and includes those cited above. Article 1 outlines the areas of cooperation 'in all fields of sustainable development, utilization, management and conservation of the water and related resources of the Mekong River Basin … to optimize the multiple-use and mutual benefits of all riparians and to minimize the harmful effects that might result …'. Article 7 is concerned with the prevention and cessation of harmful effects.

Procedure The *Procedures* are explained in related *Guidelines on Implementation*, which provide practical assistance in relation to their content and application. The objectives of the *Procedures* are to 'provide steps for the MRC member states

51 Framework Convention for the Protection of the Environment for Sustainable Development in Central Asia, opened for signature 22 November 2006, unreported (not in force).

52 These were approved pursuant to the MRC Council Resolution of 18 October 1999 on the Water Utilization Programme and its subsequent approval by the Joint Committee on 13 November 2003 at its 10th Meeting. For a general overview of the background to these procedures, see Worawan Sukaroek, 'The MRC Policy Framework on Transboundary EIA: A Better Cooperation will be Enhanced in the Lower Mekong Basin', paper presented to conference entitled Role of Water Sciences in Transboundary River Basin Management, Thailand, 2005; and J Horberry, 'Transboundary Environmental Assessment: The Experience of the Mekong River Commission', presentation to the third Meeting of the Parties to the Espoo Convention, 2004. For comparison with international procedures, see Li Xikun and Shu Min, 'Transboundary Environmental Impact Assessment of Hydroelectric Resources Exploitation in [an] International River: A Case Study of Lancang-Mekong River', paper presented to the GMSARN International Conference on Sustainable Development: Issues and Prospects for GMS, 6–7 December 2006.

to support the establishment of the Rules for Water Utilization and Inter-Basin Diversions' (Article 26), and to 'promote better understanding and cooperation among the MRC member countries …'. With respect to notification, intra-basin use or diversion on the tributaries or mainstream during the wet season require notification to the MRC JC in a timely manner (section 4).

Provisions for prior consultation are the closest to TEIA requirements (section 5). These require timely notification to the JC and provision of additional data and information, to allow the other member riparians to discuss and evaluate the impact of the proposed use. They are needed in three circumstances: inter-basin diversion from the mainstream during the wet season, intra-basin use on the mainstream during the dry season, and inter-basin diversion of surplus water during the dry season. Proposed uses are proposals for a definite use of waters by a riparian, excluding domestic and minor uses not having a significant impact. Prior consultation attempts to balance the interests of the Parties. The *Procedures* also provide for a Specific Agreement to be approved by all members in relation to any inter-basin diversion projects during the dry season from the mainstream. The notification and prior consultation procedures apply also to these.

The provisions for prior consultation are far more detailed than those for notification, and have different institutional mechanisms, adding a role for National Mekong Committees (NMCs) to the MRC JC. The MRC Secretariat and Council also have roles to play. NMCs are established in each of the member Parties to act on behalf of the notifying or notified states, the 'origin' and 'affected' Parties under the terminology of the *Espoo Convention*. The NMC of the notifying state must put together the information to send via the Mekong Secretariat to the JC and hence to the other NMCs of the notified states. The JC evaluates potential significant environmental effects, and can establish a Working Group following an evaluation of the information from the notifying state by each of the other notified states.

Decisions by the JC on the proposed use should contain any agreed conditions. The notifying state must 'not implement the proposed use without providing the opportunity for the other member states to discuss and evaluate the proposed use'. One of the weaknesses of the Procedures is the absence of any obligations for public participation.[53] The MRC does have a public participation strategy, but in practice it is distant from the public. This needs to change so that the NMCs 'can engage with civil society and the Basin public within each country'.[54] A legal basis for TEIA in relation to proposed inter-basin and intra-basin diversions

53 Jona Razzaque, 'Public Participation in Water Governance' in JW Dellapenna and J Gupta (eds), *The Evolution of the Law and Politics of Water* (Springer, 2009) 353, 359.

54 See Philip Hirsch and Kurt Mørck Jensen *with* Ben Boer, Naomi Carrard, Stephen FitzGerald and Rosemary Lyster, *National Interests and Transboundary Water Governance in the Mekong* (Australian Mekong Resource Centre, University of Sydney, Danish International Development Assistance, 2006), in particular chapter 3: 'Legal and institutional framework for Mekong Water Governance', 26, 122.

(number 7), and mandatory requirements for public participation (number 8), are recommended:

> A further issue in the context of formulating binding procedures and rules under the Agreement concerns transboundary environmental impact assessment. While basin-wide environmental and social impact assessment processes have been in place since 1998, there appear to be no legally-based standards for conducting those assessments. It would be desirable to formulate such standards and include them in rules or in a protocol to the Agreement. An important starting point for drafting such mechanisms would be the *Convention on Environmental Impact Assessment in a Transboundary Context*, which obliges signatories to 'take all appropriate and effective measures to prevent, reduce and control significant adverse transboundary environmental impact from proposed activities' and to take legal and administrative measures to implement these provisions.[55]

Practice Hydropower development in the Mekong region continues to be the primary concern.[56] The flexibility of the MRC rules and their weakness in dealing with this has been noted.[57] While Article 3 concerning environmental protection is a partial exception, there remains an absence of enforcement provisions.[58] Informal procedures, which include the *Procedures*, are used extensively to operationalize the Agreement. The exact nature of these 'obligations' is however uncertain,[59] and many are not binding. These include the procedures for water utilization and inter-basin diversion developed under the Agreement, which should be transformed into enforceable rules pursuant to Article 26.[60] As a result it has been said: 'The fact that the Joint Committee has not carried out the clear legal obligations to formulate such rules in the 10 years since the Agreement came into force seems to indicate that there is neither the motivation to do so on the part of the MRC executive nor the requisite political will on the part of the member governments.'[61]

Four controversial case studies illustrate the failure of the MRC to play a prominent mediating role in achieving better governance. The first concerns the

---

55 Ibid, 31.

56 See generally François Molle, Tira Foran and Mira Käkönen (eds), *Contested Waterscapes in the Mekong Region: Hydropower, Livelihoods and Governance* (Earthscan, 2009); in respect of China's role, see Phua Peipei, 'China's Collaboration with Indochina Countries in Hydropower Development in the Mekong Region: How Far Can It Go?' in Mingjiang Li and Chong Guan Kwa (eds), *China–ASEAN Sub-Regional Cooperation* (World Scientific/Imperial College Press, 2011) 95.

57 See F Johns, B Saul, P Hirsch, T Stephens and B Boer, 'Law and the Mekong River Basin: A Socio-Legal Research Agenda on the Role of Hard and Soft Law in Regulating Transboundary Water Resources' (2010) 11 *Melbourne Journal of International Law* 154.

58 Above n 54, 27.

59 Above n 54, 30–31.

60 Above n 54, 23.

61 Above n 54, 24.

Sesan dispute. Here, Vietnam began construction of a dam in 1993 with significant environmental effects downstream in Cambodia, yet the downstream areas were not included in the EIA. Later involvement by the MRC in 2000 failed to resolve the matter, primarily because of the national interests at stake.[62] In the second, Thailand and Laos came to terms in relation to planned water transfers in 2004 outside the framework of the MRC, ostensibly because it better ensured their national interests were upheld. Despite opposition and impact upon the other MRC states, transboundary considerations were not reviewed by the MRC, with no TEIA being conducted.[63]

The third concerns the Laos hydropower dam on the Thuen River. While the World Bank was involved as financier, there has been significant opposition. The approval of the dam by Laos failed to take into account the interests of downstream nations, apparently because the tributary concerned was not explicitly transboundary, and as a result the MRC was not involved.[64] The fourth relates to Chinese development on the upper Mekong.[65] In this case Chinese actions were unilateral and motivated by economic interests. Not being a member of the MRC it had no obligations to notify or consult with downstream states.[66]

Most recently, the MRC deferred a decision on the Xayaburi hydropower plant in Laos, a blow to Laos' hydropower ambitions and its efforts to raise foreign revenue through exporting electricity to Thailand. This would have been the first dam on the mainstream of the Lower Mekong Basin. Vietnam recommended deferring all hydropower development on the Mekong mainstream for at least ten years, and although Thailand concurs with the delay, it supports the dam as Thai companies will build it and Thailand will benefit from the electricity. Although agreement was expected, member states were unable to agree, which was hailed as a partial reprieve by conservationists for the fisheries of the river. The matter is likely to be determined at a ministerial-level meeting at a later date.[67]

---

62 Above n 54, 145–146. See also Andrew B Wyatt and Ian G Baird, 'Transboundary Impact Assessment in the Sesan River Basin: The Case of the Yali Falls Dam' (2007) 23 *International Journal of Water Resources Development* 427.

63 Above n 54, 150–151. See: http://www.guardian.co.uk/environment/2009/mar/13/laos-hydroelectric-dam?INTCMP=SRCH.

64 Above n 54, 153.

65 Joint Experts Group on EIA of China, Laos, Myanmar and Thailand, Report on the Environmental Impact Assessment: The Navigation Channel Improvement Project of the Langcang-Mekong River from China-Myanmar Boundary Marker 243 to Ban Houei Sai of Laos, 2001; Carl Bruch, Mikiyasu Nakayama, Jessica Troell, Lisa Goldman and Elizabeth Marunma Mrema, 'Assessing the Assessments: Improving Methodologies for Impact Assessment in Transboundary Watercourses' (2007) 23 *Water Resources Development* 391, which highlights the weaknesses in the MRC regimes; and Cassar and Bruch, above n 25, 236.

66 Above n 54, 156.

67 Jonathon Watts, 'Mekong River Nations Defer Dam Decision', *The Guardian* (London), 20 April 2011. This was expected to be December 2011 following consultation, see:

The status and application of SEA in the Greater Mekong Subregion (GMS) has been supported by the Asian Development Bank (ADB), as part of the GMS Core Environmental Program.[68] Most recently, the Final Report on SEA of Hydropower on the Mekong Mainstream has now been published by the MRC.[69] This reflects a proactive effort on the part of the MRC to deal with 12 hydropower schemes being studied by private sector developers for the mainstream of the Mekong, eight in Laos. At the time of publication one of these had reached the stage of notification and consultation, and the underlying reason for the SEA was to provide a broader understanding of the opportunities and risks involved in the development, in support of the wider basin development planning process.

Again with ADB support, infrastructural linkages and cross-border trade have recently been improved as a result of a transboundary road connecting two marginalized areas, which has encouraged environmentally and socially sound investments. This North–South Economic Corridor is currently in its second phase, with investment opportunities to be laid out in a strategy and action plan. This targets the ecologically and culturally sensitive border area between China's Yunnan Province, Northern Lao, and Thailand. A transboundary, cross-sectoral SEA was conducted to support the respective governments in assessing potential environmental and social impacts, developing alternatives and mitigation options, and in feeding the findings back into the planning process.[70]

The Tumen Agreements *(North East Asia)*

The Greater Tumen Initiative (GTI) is the name given to the inter-governmental co-operation mechanism under the *Tumen Agreements*.[71] There are two main bodies. The Consultative Commission is composed of government representatives of the five GTI member states and it is the core decision-making institution. At its 8th Meeting the governments agreed to extend the 1995 agreements for a decade. The role of the Coordination Committee is to consult and coordinate in relation

---

http://www.mrcmekong.org/news-and-events/consultations/proposed-xayaburi-hydropower-project-prior-consultation-process/.

68 International Centre for Environmental Management, Strategic Environmental Assessment in the Greater Mekong Subregion – Status Report, Greater Mekong Subregion (GMS) Core Environment Program (Asian Development Bank, 2006). Further study has recently also been approved, see: http://www.mrcmekong.org/news-and-events/news/further-study-on-impact-of-mekong-mainstream-development-to-be-conducted-say-lower-mekong-countries/.

69 International Centre for Environmental Management, Strategic Environmental Assessment of Hydropower on the Mekong Mainstream: Final Report (Mekong River Commission, 2010).

70 Pavit Ramachandran and Lothar Linde, 'Integrating Spatial Support Tools into Strategic Planning – SEA of the GMS North–South Economic Corridor Strategy and Action Plan' (2011) 31 *Environmental Impact Assessment Review* 602.

71 North Korea has chosen not to participate since 2010.

to social, legal, environmental and economic issues raised by any of the Parties. TEIA procedures are detailed in a *Memorandum of Understanding* ('the *MoU*') agreed between the Parties, which was signed by all five contracting parties at the same time as the original two agreements.[72]

The *MoU* affirms the overall goal of the parties 'to attain environmentally sound and sustainable development of Northeast Asia and the Tumen River Economic Development Area' in accordance with '(b) the international consensus reached at the United Nations Conference on Environment and Development; (c) the requirements of national laws and regulations and of bilateral and multilateral environmental agreements; and (d) the environmental requirements of the multilateral development banks of which the Contracting Parties are members'. The Contracting Parties also 'affirm their intention to cooperate and coordinate with each other to protect and enhance the environment of the Region and to conduct all development activities in the Region in a manner that does not damage the environment of any Contracting Party, of any other state or of areas beyond the limits of national jurisdiction'.[73]

Procedure The first section of the *MoU* is entitled 'Environmental Assessment, Mitigation and Management'. Article 1.3 states that Contracting Parties will prepare and adopt national laws and policies and bilateral and multi-lateral environmental agreements where 'required to attain environmentally sound and sustainable development of the Region'. Article 1.5 contains the EIA obligation for environmentally significant national and transboundary projects, although it fails to detail this other than requiring an EIA report and an Environmental Mitigation and Management Plan (EMMP) to deal with any anticipated effects. Participation by experts in the affected state is also a specific requirement, but not public participation.

Article 1.2 requires plans to be assessed and in its reference to the joint conduct of regional environmental assessment, Article 1.2 provides for TSEA. There is a general screening obligation for all contemplated development plans and all 'local, national, regional and global implications', regardless of significance. More general environmental obligations are set out in Articles 1.6–2.5, which affect the obligations for both SEA and EIA. Access to environmental information and public participation is a general requirement in Article 2.4. Article 1.6 makes further reference to the effect of the SEA and EIA in decision-making, so Contracting Parties are obliged to co-ordinate and co-operate with each other so that the results of each 'are taken into account in development planning activities for the Region, and to implement the regional and project-specific EMMPs'.

---

72 Memorandum of Understanding on Environmental Principles Governing the Tumen River Economic Development Area and North East Asia, 1995.

73 For discussion, see Marsden, *Chinese JIL*, above n 16.

Practice Initiated by South Korea, workshops for TEIA in the Northeast Asia Region have been held annually since 2004. The purpose has been to standardize procedure and enhance co-operation in relation to the projects planned. It also recommended that an SEA/EIA Committee be established to consult on alternatives and mitigation methods, together with a Monitoring Commission to ensure activities comply with implementation conditions. One of the significant environment projects approved is the GTI Environmental Cooperation, which focuses on TEIA and environmental standardization in Northeast Asia. There is no elaboration of the TEIA procedure although the other approved projects to which TEIA must presumably be applied indicate that most are infrastructure projects which physically cross the borders of the member states.

These include: the Mongolia–China Railway Feasibility Study, which is a proposal for a railway line linking Mongolia with the seaports in the region; the Road and Harbour Project on the China–DPRK border, which includes reconstruction of a trans-border road into a new road and bridge. Potential application of TSEA is also something that could be considered, notably in connection with the Northeast Asia Ferry Route Border Infrastructure Framework, which is analogous to a transport program; similarly, Capacity Building on GTI Energy and GTI Tourism at the regional level has potential for a broader strategic assessment to be applied to them.

In 2010, the 7th Annual TEIA Workshop was held in Korea, as a platform for discussing the issues of establishing a TEIA system for Northeast Asia. Current issues are the reasons for the need of an assessment system, as well as the role of the region's governments in implementing a system. A TEIA system would, if implemented, provide common measurements and data for the region's governments and scientific community about the environmental impact that each region has on the neighbouring regions. This is an important project for promoting stability in the region as currently there is no agreed-upon system for measuring environmental impact on a multi-regional scale. If completed, an assessment impact system will provide reliable information and common standards for analysing impacts, and aid the progress towards more sustainable and less environmentally destructive development practices among all countries in the area.

The Tehran Convention *(Caspian Sea, South West and Central Asia)*

The Caspian Sea, the subject of the *Tehran Convention*, is the largest inland body of water on earth. Its isolation, climate and salinity have resulted in a unique ecology that is threatened by the economic development of the sub-region, in particular oil and gas exploration and exploitation. In 2003 Azerbaijan, Iran, Kazakhstan, Russia and Turkmenistan (the 'Caspian Littoral States') signed the Convention following the earlier 1994 adoption of the *Almaty Declaration on Cooperation of the Environmental Protection of the Caspian Sea Region*. Reflecting the strategic importance of the area, the international community played a significant role in the development of the Convention, in particular through the combined efforts of the UNECE, UNEP, UNDP, the World Bank, and others.[74]

The Convention has the stated objective in Article 2 of 'the protection of the Caspian environment from all sources of pollution including the protection, preservation, restoration and sustainable and rational use of the biological resources of the Caspian Sea'. The Convention applies specifically to the marine environment (Article 3). General obligations are found in Article 4 and include taking measures to prevent, reduce and control pollution; and to protect, preserve and restore the environment. Principles guiding action include the precautionary principle, the polluter-pays principle and the principle of access to information (Article 5). Parties also have a duty to cooperate in the development of protocols and other measures to implement the Convention (Article 6).

Procedure Procedures for EIA are briefly enumerated in the Convention, with *Guidelines on Environmental Impact Assessment in a Transboundary Context* ('the *Guidelines*') providing more detail.[75] These contain the requirement of Article 13, which deals with environmental emergencies and requires EIA in relation to hazardous activities, and also Article 17(1), which requires them for 'any planned activity that are likely to cause significant adverse effect on the marine environment'. Results of any EIA are to be disseminated to the other Parties to the Convention further to Article 17(2). Article 18 is also relevant to the development of TEIA, as it requires Parties to cooperate in 'formulating, elaborating and harmonising rules, standards, recommended practices and procedures consistent with this Convention and with the account of requirements, commonly used in international practice ...'. The reference to international practice suggests the role of the *Espoo Convention* in the establishment of an EIA Protocol further to Article 6. Other relevant reference to international practice in the Convention is found in Article 21(2) in relation to access to information, which suggests the treaty has close associations with the *Espoo Convention* and the *Aarhus Convention.*

At the same time as the *Tehran Convention* was being considered by the Caspian Littoral States, the *Guidelines* were being developed by the Littoral States with the support of the UNEP, UNDP, the World Bank and others. Reflecting its ratification by two of the five Littoral States (Azerbaijan and Kazakhstan), signature by a third (Russia) and the stated aspirations of a fourth (Iran, not a UNECE member), the *Guidelines* were explicitly based on the *Espoo Convention.* They reflect the need for TEIA to be harmonized in the sub-region. The *Guidelines*

74 Although focused on the Eastern part of the region, for detailed background and analysis of the recent situation, see UNEP, UNECE, UNDP, NATO, REC, OSCE, *Environment and Security in Europe, Transforming Risks into Cooperation: The Case of the Eastern Caspian Region* (2008).

75 UNEP and Caspian Environment Programme, Guidelines on Environmental Impact Assessment in a Transboundary Context in the Caspian Sea Region: Step by step procedures (UNEP, 2003).

were agreed in October 2003, and the *Tehran Convention* was signed a month later. They follow the *Espoo Convention* closely, contextualizing it to the needs of the Caspian Littoral States.[76]

Soon after the approval of the *Guidelines* in 2004 the development of a draft *TEIA Protocol* was begun, in part because the *Guidelines* are not binding, in part because not all of the Littoral States are Parties to the *Espoo Convention*, and in part because private companies are subject to a range of legal requirements, which include those for project financing. Tsutsumi and Robinson outline these drivers and background to the *Tehran Convention* and development of the *Guidelines*, which they believe form a solid basis for any protocol. They comment:

> The draft Protocol seeks to establish a set of clear, detailed and legally binding procedures for the implementation of transboundary EIA in the Caspian Sea region and to contribute to the prevention of adverse impacts on the Caspian environment. The development of the draft Protocol also contributes to prevent unnecessary delay and promote transparency, particularly in terms of administrative procedures.[77]

In relation to screening, the draft *Protocol* proposes to begin with Appendix I of the *Espoo Convention*, and add further activities of importance to the Littoral States. In relation to the main elements of EIA, again Appendix II of the *Espoo Convention* is proposed as the starting point, reflecting the weight of experience with TEIA under this treaty.

Practice Tsutsumi and Robinson discuss two case studies in relation to TEIA.[78] The first was led by Dragon Oil, Turkmenistan and British Petroleum (BP) in Azerbaijan for offshore oil development. While Turkmenistan was neither a Party nor signatory to the *Espoo Convention*, the financier, the European Bank for Reconstruction and Development (EBRD) together with Dragon Oil requested the Turkmen authorities to begin the Espoo procedure, which didn't however continue further.[79] In the second case study, the Azerbaijan International Operating Company and BP collaborated in an oilfield development project and prepared an EIS and scoping report, although again the procedure didn't continue further. In both cases, poor communication between the stakeholders would appear to be the major problem, and as in other regions (such as the Tumen), training workshops were subsequently organized to trial and develop the procedures (including for public participation) and the draft *Protocol*.

---

76 Rie Tsutsumi and Kristy Robinson, 'Environmental Impact Assessment and the Framework Convention for the Protection of the Marine Environment of the Caspian Sea' in Bastmeijer and Koivurova (eds), above n 1, 53.

77 Ibid, 57.

78 Ibid, 65–69.

79 For background, see Nazari above n 50.

A Pan-Regional TEIA Agreement for Asia?

Based on a summary evaluation of the cross- and sub-regional experiences above, this section examines the potential for a pan-regional TEIA agreement in Asia. In this regard, three things are immediately apparent: first, the overlap between the Parties to several of the sub-regional agreements; second, the sharing of procedures between a number of the agreements and related reach of the *Espoo Convention* into the other agreements; and third, the key relationship between the regulation of proposals by international agreements and the requirements imposed by international lending organizations. These are discussed briefly below, before the conclusions follow.

Overlapping Membership

Membership of more than one of the conventions by the Parties is common and has the advantage of cross-fertilization of procedures; the *Helsinki Convention* benefits from potentially utilizing the detailed procedures on TEIA in the *Espoo Convention* for example. The advantages of building synergies between the treaties were highlighted in a recent seminar held in CA on the *Helsinki Convention.*[80] The status of ratification of selected international agreements relevant to transboundary water management by the countries in CA has also been summarized.[81]

Kazakhstan is an example of a state with overlapping membership of more than one agreement, and has experience in relation to the *Espoo Convention, Helsinki Convention* and the *Tehran Convention.* It has also raised concerns with China in relation to a breach of customary international law in relation to equitable use and sustainable development.[82] Given the limitation on membership of the UNECE treaties to ECE states, it is also advantageous in an Asian context that membership is being opened to non-ECE states, many of which are in Asia.[83] However until the entry into force of the amendments to both ECE treaties, Afghanistan, China, Iran and Mongolia cannot accede to either, and are therefore not bound by their obligations. The question therefore arises of the status of TEIA in customary international law in connection with the no-harm principle (as considered by the ICJ), and in particular that of the *Espoo Convention* as evidence of state practice in regard to due diligence.

---

80 UNECE, Report of the national seminar 'UNECE Water Convention and its Role in International Law', Almaty, Kazakhstan, 18–19 October 2010. See session 3: Building synergies with other legal instruments, 7.

81 Above n 45, Annex III, 26. This includes the Espoo Convention and SEA Protocol, Helsinki Convention and Tehran Convention.

82 Sievers, above n 25.

83 See proposed amendments to Articles 25–26 of the Helsinki Convention, and Article 17 of the Espoo Convention.

Procedural Similarities: Influence of and Advocacy for the Espoo Convention

TEIA/TSEA procedure adds an inter-territorial dimension to domestic EIA/SEA procedure, hence the need for a Party of origin and affected Party(ies) to be identified. This generally occurs with respect to the agreements discussed; in the *Mekong Agreement* these are referred to as the 'notifying' or 'notified' states for example. In regard to outlining detailed procedures, it is clear that the *Mekong* and *Tumen Agreements*, with the weakest link to the *Espoo Convention*, fail to do this in several respects, for example public participation obligations. With respect to the others, the *Tehran Convention Guidelines* explicitly follow the *Espoo Convention*, and the *Helsinki Convention* draft *Guide* also recommends following the *Espoo Convention* procedures. As noted, independent analysis of experience with the *Mekong Agreement* also recommends adhering to the *Espoo Convention* procedures, and future elaboration of the *Tumen Agreement* procedures is very likely to do this, strengthening the case for the *Espoo Convention* representing state practice in international law.

Consideration has already been given in the literature to the potential for a global agreement on TEIA. Although there are acknowledged political challenges with this, Knox, and Bastmeijer and Koivurova point to the *Espoo Convention* as the most likely candidate.[84] In 2008 Bastmeijer and Koivurova indicated that only nine parties had ratified the first amendment to the *Espoo Convention*. There are now 21 Parties to the first amendment and three-quarters of the Parties to the Convention (there are 45 presently) are needed. Ratification of this amendment is therefore progressing rapidly. Given the procedural similarities between the *Espoo* and *Tehran Conventions* and recommendations that the *Helsinki Convention* and *Mekong Agreement* follow the *Espoo* procedures, there is therefore strong evidence of its reach beyond Europe and into Asia. When the first amendment to the *Espoo Convention* comes into force, and when the *Helsinki Convention* is also extended to non-ECE states, this reach into Asia will be enhanced.

Requirements of International Financiers

The relationship between TEIA/TSEA and international lending organizations is an important one. The World Bank, ADB and EBRD have all been involved in the region and have their own requirements. The World Bank integrates environmental assessment into its funding procedures to governments of developing countries, which include a range of approaches including TEIA and TSEA. Sectoral environmental assessments or country environmental assessments are often

84 John H Knox, 'Assessing the Candidates for a Global Treaty on Transboundary Environmental Impact Assessment' 12 (2003) *New York University Environmental Law Journal* 153; and Kees Bastmeijer and Timo Koivurova, 'Conclusions: Globalisation of Transboundary Environmental Impact Assessment' in Bastmeijer and Koivurova (eds), above n 1, 376.

required.[85] Similarly, the ADB operates a comprehensive Country Safeguards System (CSS) to determine the suitability of borrower countries. The focus of the CSS on the legal and institutional framework of potential borrower countries raises the prospect of legal reform in relation to EIA/SEA, and requirements to mitigate involuntary resettlement require the application of social impact assessment.[86] The EBRD also plays a prominent role in this area, and has committed itself to amending its environmental policy to see compliance with the *Espoo Convention*.[87] As noted, where the *Espoo Convention* does not bind states in the region, the requirements of these lenders are the only way to ensure compliance with best practice for TEIA/TSEA.

Conclusions

This chapter reviews procedures for TEIA and TSEA in Asia further to a number of regional agreements. It highlights a wide range of approaches to TEIA in relation to the cross-regional and sub-regional experiences discussed. Experience in CA in particular benefits from the supporting framework of the *Espoo Convention*, the most broadly applicable of the TEIA agreements which has been applied elsewhere hundreds of times to a broad range of project proposals. This is the case regarding the application of the *Espoo Convention* itself in CA and the *Tehran Convention*, which is heavily influenced by it. It is recommended that the *Tumen* and *Mekong Agreements* follow the procedures under the *Espoo Convention* if at all possible to benefit from this developing state (best) practice.

Moving from a series of cross- and sub-regional agreements to a pan-regional agreement for the whole of Asia is of course another matter entirely. While treaty and customary international law in relation to TEIA has developed significantly in the last decade, existing arrangements are likely to remain, and there is unlikely to be such an agreement in the short or medium term. What can be foreseen is the potential expansion of the *Espoo Convention,* application to water related proposals under the *Helsinki Convention*, and improvements to procedure in the sub-regional agreements. Looking at a map of Asia, it is not difficult to see why. The position of China and India in particular, which border so many states in the region, suggests that without their involvement, a pan-regional agreement will never be achieved. Instead efforts should be made to harmonize procedures further

85 Jean-Roger Mercier, 'The World Bank and Environmental Impact Assessment' in Bastmeijer and Koivurova (eds), above n 1, 291.

86 Asian Development Bank, *Safeguard Policy Statement* (Asian Development Bank, 2009), see appendix 1 (environment).

87 Elizabeth Smith, 'Implementing the Espoo Convention: An International Financial Institutions Perspective' in Bastmeijer and Koivurova (eds), above n 1, 313; see also Nazari, above n 50.

to take advantage of the best practice emerging from implementation of the *Espoo Convention* and, in time, the *SEA Protocol*.

PART II
Marine Perspectives

Chapter 7
Transboundary Pollution from Offshore Oil and Gas Activities in the Seas of Southeast Asia

Youna Lyons

The seas of Southeast Asia, which include the South China Sea (SCS), the Gulf of Thailand, the Indonesian Sea and the Sulu-Celebes Sea,[1] host 1390 offshore platforms for hydrocarbon production. While this represents more than double the number of platforms in the North Sea,[2] they are spread over the many meanders in the seas of Southeast Asia. However, these seas are semi-enclosed and shared among several coastal States, increasing the risk that initially domestic pollution events would transform into transboundary pollution. Another type of potential transboundary maritime pollution is one that would arise from offshore activities taking place in an area subject to maritime boundary disputes between two or more States. Many current and prospective offshore oil and gas activities in the SCS are in this situation.

This chapter focuses on the environmental governance framework available to manage transboundary pollution from offshore oil and gas activities at international and regional levels. It reviews the location and extent of potential transboundary pollution risk before discussing the application of the United Nations Convention on the Law of the Sea (UNCLOS),[3] the applicability of international shipping and conservation treaties, and the impact of the fragmentation in the legal and

1 These four seas correspond to four Large Marine Ecosystems (LME) of Southeast Asia, the boundaries of which are based on four linked ecological criteria: bathymetry, hydrography, productivity and trophic relationships. The map of the 64 LMEs of the world is the result of a collaborative effort led within the Regional Seas' program of the United Nations Environmental Program involving the United States National Oceanographic and Atmospheric Administration and other UN agencies <http://www.lme.noaa.gov/index.php?option=com_content&view=article&id=178&Itemid=62>. Unlike the other seas, the Indonesian Sea is primarily composed of Indonesia's archipelagic waters.

2 Located in the North of Europe, the North Sea is a hydrocarbon rich semi-enclosed sea. It opens on to the Atlantic Ocean in the north and is surrounded by Norway, Denmark, Germany, the Netherlands, Belgium, France and the United Kingdom (from east to west).

3 *United Nations Convention on the Law of the Sea*, opened for signature 10 December 1982, 1833 UNTS 3 (entered into force 16 November 1994) http://cil.nus.edu.sg/1982/1982-united-nations-convention-on-the-law-of-the-sea/. To date *UNCLOS* has

institutional regional policy framework. The emphasis is on international and regional relevant law and institutional organization flowing from relevant international and regional instruments rather than on customary international law.[4]

The pollution risks focused on are oil spills, drilling wastes, platform abandonment and invasive species through biofouling.

Location and Extent of Transboundary Pollution Risks

Offshore Oil and Gas Activities in the Seas of Southeast Asia

The Seas of Southeast Asia Among the four seas of Southeast Asia,[5] the SCS and the Indonesian Sea are the largest and the densest in offshore oil and gas activities. However, the latter comprises only ocean areas under Indonesian jurisdiction. Furthermore, the Indonesian Sea is connected to the Sulu-Celebes Sea and the SCS through narrow straits, making transboundary pollution less likely. This chapter thus focuses primarily on transboundary pollution in the SCS and the western area of the Celebes Sea where prospective offshore activities are ongoing despite competing maritime claims from Indonesia and Malaysia.

Physical geography defines the SCS as a semi-enclosed sea, as it is separated from other surrounding seas by shallow straits. UNCLOS gives the same definition from a legal perspective.[6] The Sulu-Celebes Sea is also a semi-enclosed sea.

When considering the environmental impact of offshore oil and gas activities in the seas of Southeast Asia, it is informative to compare them to other sea basins that are subject to high hydrocarbon activities. With surface area of more than double that of the Gulf of Mexico (itself double the North Sea),[7] they hold under

---

been ratified by all coastal States in the SCS but for Cambodia who only signed (see below Table 7.1).

4 In particular, the applicability and relevance of the precautionary principle to offshore pollution in Southeast Asia is not discussed due to the difficulties in establishing a clear and agreed content for the precautionary principle in the context.

5 The South China Sea is a semi-enclosed sea surrounded by China, the Philippines, Malaysia, Brunei Darussalam, Indonesia, Vietnam, Cambodia and Thailand. Although it is ecologically a distinct large marine ecosystem, the Gulf of Thailand is often included in the reference made to the SCS. The Sulu-Celebes Sea is also a large marine ecosystem composed of two linked sub-seas, the Sulu Sea (north), bordered mostly by the Philippines, except the west corner along Sabah (Malaysia), and the Celebes Sea bordered by Indonesia, Malaysia and the Philippines.

6 Both criteria set out in *UNCLOS*, art 122 are met for the SCS as it is a sea 'surrounded by two or more States and connected to another sea or the ocean by a narrow outlet or consisting entirely or primarily of the territorial seas and exclusive economic zones of two or more coastal States'.

7 The SCS alone covers 3.6 million km^2. Wu Shicun and Hong Nong, 'The Energy Security of China and Oil and Gas Exploitation in the South China Sea' in Myron H

half of the 4000 platforms located in the Gulf of Mexico, while the North Sea contains less than 550 platforms. The Gulf of Mexico is thus where the presence of offshore platforms is the densest. However, unlike the Gulf of Mexico, the seas of Southeast Asia are still generally considered as holding promising and underexploited hydrocarbon basins.[8]

When considering the profile of the offshore activities in the SCS, the bathymetry of the basin is also informative.[9] More than half of the SCS is a shallow basin located over the Sunda Shelf with a depth not exceeding 100m. The rest is a deep basin with a maximum depth of 5000m.[10] This geographical characteristic explains that most of the now obsolete platforms are located in less than 100m of water, even occasionally more than 100nm from the coast. It is also the reason why deep-water drilling can only occur in a limited number of places.

Nordquist, John Norton Moore and Kuen-Chen Fu (eds), *Recent Developments in the Law of the Sea and China* (Martinus Nijhoff Publishers, Koninklijke Brill NV, 2005) 149.

8 It is noted that ideas on the size of the hydrocarbons reservoirs in the SCS vary. Wu Shicun and Hong Nong reported that, according to decades of research, there are 13 large and medium sediment bancs in the SCS containing over 172 millions barrels of oil and 10 trillion cubic metres of natural gas (*Ibid*). Recent press articles from China report a much higher quantity of 366.5 billion barrels of oil and 20 trillion cubic metres of gas: Zou Lee, 'Oil bonanza in South China Sea', *Global Times* (online), 19 April 2011, http://special.globaltimes.cn/2011-04/645909.html.

9 See Map 7.1 below.

10 See NOAA website on Large Marine Ecosystems http://www.emecs.or.jp/guidebook/eng/pdf/18southchina.pdf.

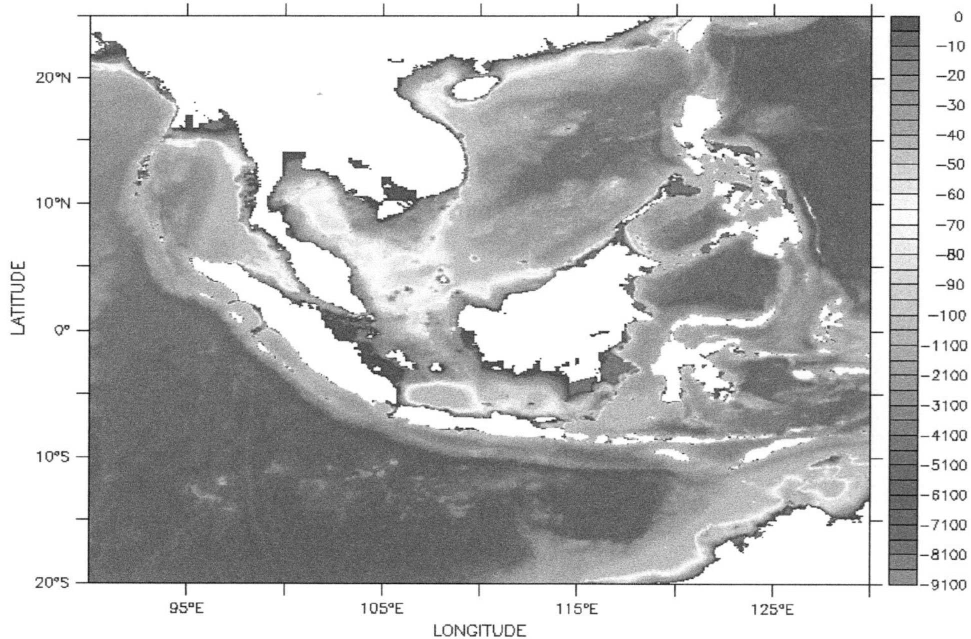

Figure 7.1 Offshore oil and gas activities in the SCS

Oil and Gas Activities Offshore: An Overview Oil and gas production plays a critical role in Southeast Asia's economic and social development. While all coastal States of the SCS have some oil and gas production, the proportion of offshore production varies. It is estimated that today there are a minimum of 1350[11] platforms in the SCS and adjacent seas. Indonesia has by far the greatest number of platforms, followed by Malaysia and Thailand. Together, these three countries have 74% of offshore installations in the SCS, and this rises to 86% with Brunei. However, they are not all positioned in places where transboundary pollution is likely. Indonesia has for instance a large number of platforms located within its archipelagic waters in locations where pollution incidents can only affect its own coastlines. This chapter focuses primarily on oil and gas activities which may lead to transboundary environmental damage. Such activities can be divided into two categories: (i) activities located close enough to the maritime boundary with another coastal State; and (ii) activities located in areas subject to overlapping maritime claims.

In the SCS, the current risk of transboundary pollution from offshore oil and gas platforms is generally confined to boundaries between contiguous coastal States rather than the continental shelf boundary between opposite States.[12] Developments in deeper basins located on the outskirts of continental shelves under national jurisdiction are a more recent occurrence. Although the number of offshore oil and gas installations in areas subject to overlapping claims remains limited, the risk of occurrence and the potential magnitude of pollution may be increased by the absence of one responsible coastal State on these areas. Further, the risk of transboundary pollution will also increase as the need for energy triggers new developments despite unresolved disputes on maritime claims.

In the SCS and in the Sulu-Celebes Sea, another type of transboundary pollution may occur in areas that are subject to offshore oil and gas activities despite disputed territorial claims from several States. The largest area believed to hold large hydrocarbon reservoirs and under overlapping claims is the Spratly Archipelago. It covers an area of 410,000km^2, which is currently subject to

---

11 1288 of these are fixed to the seabed, generally small and light (compared to installations in the Gulf of Mexico or the North Sea) and positioned in shallow waters (50% appear to be located in less than 50m and close to 75% in 75m or less). It is noted that the number of platforms will vary according to data availability, the classification adopted (e.g. whether several platforms connected together are counted as one or several and/or whether they are counted by reference to their mode of attachment or mooring to the seafloor), and the date of assessment (temporary installations or new installations). Brian Twomey, 'Study Assesses Asia-Pacific Offshore Decommissioning Costs' (2010) 15 March, *Oil and Gas Journal* 51–55; OPL, *World Offshore Field Development Guide Database*, Vol 2: Asia, India, Australasia & Far East, 2010.

12 As oil and gas activities extend further offshore, the depth at which operations are taking place generally increases as does its complexity and difficulty. These are linked to water pressure, which increases with water depth and adds constraints and tensions on the building of offshore installations, their maintenance and their use.

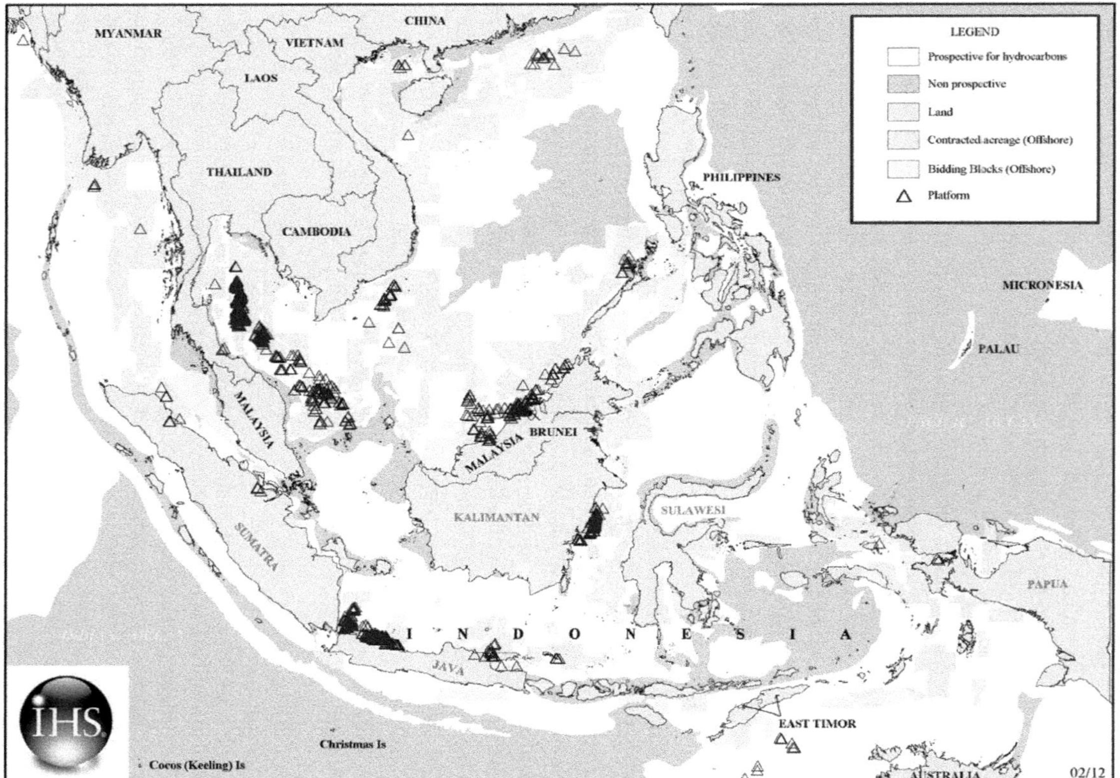

Figure 7.2 Bathymetry of the Seas of Southeast Asia

overlapping claims of maritime boundaries from six coastal States: China, Taiwan, Philippines, Brunei Darussalam, Malaysia and Vietnam.

Offshore Activities Close to Maritime Boundaries

Exploratory drilling and offshore production taking place in the vicinity of maritime boundaries between contiguous States are an obvious source of potential transboundary pollution which may be resolved through bilateral measures.[13] In Southeast Asia, however, this concerns a substantial yet minor part of offshore developments along the maritime borders between Malaysia and Brunei, Malaysia and Indonesia and Vietnam and Malaysia south of the Gulf of Thailand. Pollution from many of the hydrocarbon fields currently in production close to maritime boundaries is likely to involve more than two States. Pollution from production sites in the Gulf of Thailand could for instance involve more than two coastal States due to the geographical characteristics of the respective borders.[14] The same is true of pollution from hydrocarbon sites located Northeast of Sabah, where the Philippines coast can be affected as well as Indonesia and Malaysia.

Given the number of countries potentially involved, clear global and regional rules and regulations are thus necessary to establish a transnational regime aimed at preventing pollution from offshore oil and gas activities and if pollution does occur to mitigate the impact on the marine environment and ensure compensation for the victims of prejudice suffered and to remediate the environment. Worth noting are specific rules which already exist for the development of hydrocarbon resources in areas subject to joint-development agreements. The Gulf of Thailand is an area where such regimes have been agreed and apply to small areas under joint development.[15]

Offshore Activities in Disputed Areas

Many exploratory drilling or production sites are located within China's nine-dashed line[16] and the oil and gas industry is accustomed to disturbances in their

13 The Montara incident in the Timor Sea is an example of pollution from a drilling rig, which is being resolved on a bilateral basis between Indonesia and Australia. For an overview of the Montara oil spill, see Australian Government, Department of Sustainability, Environment, Water, Population and Communities http://www.environment.gov.au/coasts/oilspill.html.

14 A common feature of oil and gas activities in the Gulf of Thailand and in Brunei is that offshore installations are in less than 90 metres of water.

15 Malaysia has for instance signed two joint-development agreements in the Gulf of Thailand, one with Thailand and the other one with Vietnam. See section entitled 'Bilateral and Multilateral Agreements on Hydrocarbon Resources' below for further details on these.

16 For the history of the infamous nine-dashed boundary claim by China, see Robert Beckman, 'China, UNCLOS and the South China Sea' (2011) *Asian Society of International Law Third Biennale Conference*, Beijing, China 27–28 August 2011, 11 [32] http://cil.nus.

prospecting or development. However, three areas have been the subject of more public controversies: the first two in the Spratly Archipelago[17] (the Reed Bank and the western part of the Spratly Archipelago, off the coast of Vietnam) and the third one in the south part of the Sipadan and Ligitan islands, south of the Sulu-Celebes Sea. They also have in common their proximity to coral reefs, fishing grounds and areas of high biodiversity. It must also be noted that while the Reed Bank and west of the Spratly Archipelago are two current 'hot spots' of offshore oil and gas activities creating contests between the claimants to parts or all of the Spratly Archipelago, eight of the 13 sedimentary basins expected to hold promising reservoirs of oil and gas[18] are located in the Spratly Islands Archipelago. New 'hotspots' may therefore develop in the future given Vietnam's and the Philippines' choice to continue granting oil and gas concessions and seismic surveys being carried out in the area.

The Reed Bank Surveys carried out in the eastern part of the Spratly Archipelago revealed that the Reed Bank might be very rich in natural gas reserves. The Sampaguita gas field claimed by the Philippines as a result of this is expected to hold more than the Malampaya gas field, located to the south-west of it.[19] Despite an incident with China in March 2011 where exploratory drilling initiated by the Philippines was interrupted by two Chinese vessels threatening to ram the drilling ship,[20] the Philippines recently reiterated its intention to develop the Sampaguita gas reserves, which created further diplomatic incidents with China.[21] While the operator in charge of the development of the concession is expected to follow the rules and standards provided for in Philippines law on environmental law, monitoring of compliance and enforcement is also unlikely for several reasons. First, the area is more than 100nm away from the Philippines archipelagic

edu.sg/wp/wp-content/uploads/2009/09/AsianSIL-Beckman-China-UNCLOS-and-the-South-China-Sea-26-July-2011.pdf.

17 The Spratly Archipelago is an area of 410,000km^2, which is currently subject to overlapping claims of maritime boundaries from 6 coastal States: China, Taiwan, Philippines, Brunei Darussalam, Malaysia and Vietnam.

18 Wu and Hong, above n 7, 148.

19 Edison Investment Research, *Outlook Forum Energy* (online) 14 April 2010, http://www.forumenergyplc.com/DocumentLibrary/ForumOutlook140410.pdf.

20 Ian Storey, 'China and the Philippines: Implications of the Reed Bank Incident', *Institute of Southeast Asia China Brief* 11(8), 6 May 2011, http://web1.iseas.edu.sg/?p=3512.

21 On 2 March 2011, the Philippines sent two military observation planes in response to reports of harassment from Chinese patrol boats, which allegedly threatened to ram the Research Vessel M/V Venture if it continued seismic survey in the Reed Bank area. See for instance on this, Dow Jones Newswire, 'China Warns Against South China Sea Oil Exploration', *Rigzone* (online), Thursday 24 March 2011, http://www.rigzone.com/news/article.asp?a_id=105427; BBC Mobile, 'Philippines halts tests after China patrol challenge', *News, Asia-Pacific* (online), 8 March 2011, http://www.bbc.co.uk/news/world-asia-pacific-12672889.

baselines; secondly, the security issues created by the tensions between China and the Philippines may distract from the importance of respecting environmental standards; and thirdly, the Philippines' government may prefer to not send an enforcement vessel which may be misconstrued by China, the other main claimant to this part of the Spratly Archipelago.

West SCS, off Vietnam In 1992, China granted the Wan'an Bei 21 block (a.k.a. WAB 21) off Vietnam to Crestone Energy Corporation, a US oil and gas company. The difficulties this created with Vietnam led Crestone Energy Corporation to forgo its right to this block. It was replaced by Harvest Natural Resources in 1996. Vietnam's position is that the WAB 21 block, which is located within 200nm of its baseline, is located on its continental shelf and thus under its jurisdiction. Based on this, Vietnam has also granted concessions on and around WAB 21. Talisman Energy is jointly exploring blocks 133 and 134 with its partner PetroVietnam[22] while Exxon Mobil has been granted the three blocks located east of these, which include the most part of WAB 21. While Talisman is currently proceeding with exploratory drilling with PetroVietnam, Harvest Natural Resources[23] appears to be waiting for some solution to the dispute between China and Vietnam prior to proceeding.[24] Exxon's position is unknown at this stage. Different corporations adopt different positions on these boundary disputes and the degree of risk they are prepared to undertake varies. A common trait of offshore oil and gas activities in areas subject to overlapping concessions by two claimant States is that companies engaged in developing resources under a concession granted by a coastal State are expected to comply with the national environmental rules and standards of that coastal State and the treaties ratified by that State.

Sulu-Celebes Sea In 2002, the International Court of Justice (ICJ) determined that the Sipadan and Ligitan islands (South of Sabah) are under Malaysian sovereignty.[25] While this decision did not solve the disputed overlapping claims of Indonesia and Malaysia to the Ambalat block located south of these islands,

22 Talisman Energy, *Investor Open House, May 2010 – Southeast Asia Operations* http://www.talisman-energy.com/upload/oh_presentation/19/02/southeast_asia_operations.pdf or Talisman Energy, *Annual Information Form for the year ended December 31, 2010, February 28, 2011* http://www.talisman-energy.com/upload/editor/File/Annual Information Form.PDF.

23 See website of Harvest Natural Resources http://www.harvestnr.com/operations/china.html.

24 Daniel Ten Kate, 'South China Sea oil rush risks clashes as U.S. bolsters Vietnam' (27 May 2011) *Bloomberg Businessweek* http://www.globalsecurity.org/org/news/2011/110527-south-china-sea.htm.

25 *Indonesia v Malaysia (Judgement) (International Court of Justice*, Judgment of 17 December 2002, in ICJ Reports (2002) 625 the sovereignty over Pulau Litigan and Pulau Sipadan http://www.icj-cij.org/docket/index.php?p1=3&k=df&case=102&code=inma&p3=4.

it pushed the Malaysian boundary southward, prompted Indonesia to review its baselines and in that way strengthened Malaysia's overlapping claim to the Ambalat. The presence of oil in the Ambalat area led to minor military clashes in 2009 between Indonesia and Malaysia. The countries have since tried to settle the dispute and agreed on joint military exercises in order to avoid clashes. However, the disputed claims to this area remain unresolved.[26] Indonesia's intentions to start exploratory drillings in this area nevertheless remain unchanged.[27]

The Compounded Impacts from Conflicting Uses of the Seas of Southeast Asia
The oil and gas industry's investigation of the unexploited hydrocarbon reservoirs in the seabed of the Southeast Asian seas is set against a backdrop of multiple uses of these seas, abundant marine resources and a sensitive marine environment. These seas host among the most biodiverse ecosystems of the world, one-third of the world's maritime trade in volume, half of the world's supertanker traffic,[28] and more than 40% of the world's total fish catch.[29] The latter relies on productive coral reefs (almost half globally).[30] mangrove areas (37% of the world's) and seagrass (72% of the world's)[31] which are very vulnerable to oil spills as well as to many disturbances to the water flow, such as diversion of water, dredging or

---

26 Ali Nur Yasin and Sorta Tobing, 'Ambalat's huge oil and gas reserves' (2 June 2009) *Tempointeractive* http://www.tempo.co.id/hg/nasional/2009/06/02/brk,20090602-179380,uk.html.

27 Reuters, 'Indonesia says Japan's inpex wins Babar Selaru oil/gas block' (21 September 2011) *Jakarta Globe* http://www.thejakartaglobe.com/business/minister-stands-firm-on-keeping-eni-in-ambalat/311791.

28 80% of the crude oil supplies for Japan, South Korea and Taiwan flow through the SCS from the Middle East, Africa and other coastal States of the SCS. (DG Wiencek, 'Energy Issues in the South China Sea Region' in JC Baker and DG Wiencek (eds), *Cooperative Monitoring in the South China Sea* (Praeger, 2002). 90% of the world's trade is estimated to be carried on ship (Opening session welcome address H.E. Mr Raymond Lim S.K. Minister for Transport and second minister for foreign affaires, Singapore, transcribed on the website of the Marine Port Authorities of Singapore http://www.mpa.gov.sg/sites/global_navigation/news_center/speeches/speeches_detail.page?filename=sp040907g.xml). Furthermore, the forecast increase in import of oil and gas (fuelled by development) implies substantially increased tanker traffic in the future. This is due to the fact that the promising reserves held in the SCS cannot be put into production early enough to meet the energy demand from development because of the development time required and the unresolved maritime disputes.

29 FAO (Food and Agriculture Organization of the United Nations), 'Review of the State of the World Marine Capture Fisheries Management: Pacific Ocean' (2007) *FAO fisheries technical paper* T488/1.

30 CR Wilkinson, *Status of Coral Reefs of the World: 2008* (Australian Institute of Marine Science, 2008).

31 For a map of coral, seagrass and mangrove biodiversity showing the SCS's relatively high biodiversity, refer to http://maps.grida.no/go/graphic/distribution-of-coral-mangrove-and-seagrass-diversity.

drainage.[32] This rich biodiversity also attracts a growing coastal tourism, which, paradoxically, is itself the source of environmental degradation and generally losses in ecosystem services. Coastal and marine resources are reported to be responsible for 40% of the GDP of the less developed economies of the region.[33] Furthermore, these conflicting uses and competing values lead to a race for resources and unsustainable practices such as overfishing, destructive fishing, oil spills and pollution from offshore exploitation to name but a few. Finally, climate change is yet another stressor projected to compound the pressures on natural resources and the environment,[34] especially with respect to coral reefs and mangroves.[35]

ASEAN's energy demand is expected to nearly double by 2020 (compared to 2005) and more than triple by 2030.[36] These figures, which do not include China's increase in energy demand although it is now the second energy consumer in the world, a major importer and an important stakeholder in the seas of Southeast Asia, demonstrate the unique opportunity created by the oil and gas resources in the seas of Southeast Asia and the inevitable pressure to scale up production.

However, given the value of the ecosystems surrounding these oil and gas reserves and the intensity of anthropogenic stressors to which they are already subject, the sustainable exploitation of oil and gas resources would need to take into account the combined impact of oil and gas production with environmental stressors from other sources. To some extent, this could be achieved through the implementation of the many relevant international treaties.

---

32 The productivity of the mangroves system depends on a dynamic balance among water flows, sedimentation, erosion and species composition. See IUCN, *Oil and gas exploration and production in mangroves areas* (1993) Gland, Switzerland and Cambridge, UK http://www.ogp.org.uk/pubs/184.pdf.

33 Chou Loke Ming and COBSEA Secretariat (eds), *State of the Marine Environment Report for the East Asian Seas 2009* (UNEP/COBSEA, 2010).

34 IPCC, *Climate Change 2007: Synthesis Report* (Cambridge University Press, 2007).

35 IPCC, *Asia. Climate Change 2007: Impacts, Adaptation and Vulnerability* (Cambridge University Press, 2007). Of note are the repercussions for fisheries from loss of coral reefs and mangroves.

36 ASEAN, 'The 2nd ASEAN Energy Demand Outlook' (March 2009) http://www.energycommunity.org/documents/SecondASEANEnergyOutlook.pdf.

A Fragmented International Framework for Environmental Impacts from Seabed Activities

UNCLOS Sets General Rules and Standards for Activities from Seabed Activities and their Environmental Impact

The UNCLOS grants exclusive sovereign rights to coastal States for the purpose of exploring and exploiting their natural resources of their continental shelves,[37] namely non-living and sedentary living resources.[38] The continental shelf extends to 200nm from the coastal State's territorial sea baseline or a maximum of 350nm from the coastal State's territorial sea baseline or 100nm from the 2500m isobath in cases where the physical continental shelf extends beyond 200nm.[39] As for the territorial sea, it may be viewed as an extension of a coastal State's land territory extending to a maximum limit of 12nm from the coastal State's baseline.[40]

With respect to pollution of the marine environment, UNCLOS creates an overarching and general obligation on coastal States to protect and preserve the marine environment.[41] More specifically in the context of pollution from seabed activities, coastal States have an obligation to adopt national laws and take measures to prevent, reduce and control pollution of the marine environment arising from or in connection with seabed activities subject to their jurisdiction[42] and from

37 *UNCLOS*, art 77(1).

38 *UNCLOS*, art 77(4).

39 *UNCLOS*, art 76(4) and (5).

40 *UNCLOS*, arts 2(1) and 24.

41 *UNCLOS*, art 192 and 194. UNCLOS contains several other provisions applicable in the context of transboundary pollution, including the obligation to notify imminent or actual damage to the marine environment. This obligation applies to any State who would be aware of such occurrence (art 198). UNCLOS also provides for the obligation to monitor and report the risks or effect of pollution (art 204 and 205). However, while any transboundary pollution could theoretically qualify, the degree of pollution required to trigger the application of these provisions is not specified. Of note also is article 206 which provides for an obligation to assess potential effects of activities when States have reasonable grounds for believing that activities under their jurisdiction may cause substantial pollution.

42 *UNCLOS*, art. 208. This provision on legislative authority falls within the obligation to protect the marine environment, including pollution from installations and devices used in exploration or exploitation of the natural resources of the seabed and subsoil, provided for in *UNCLOS* art 194(3)(c).

dumping[43] within their jurisdiction.[44] UNCLOS provides that these national laws and measures adopted to prevent, reduce and control pollution shall be no less effective than the 'global rules and standards' on dumping by pollution[45] and not less effective than 'international rules, standards and recommended practices and procedures'[46] on pollution from seabed activities. The wording seems to place on parties to UNCLOS an obligation to adopt rules and standards in other conventions to which they might not and need not be a party. The difficulty, however, is that such a reading of UNCLOS' provisions, which implies that the parties are deemed to have incorporated future instruments by reference, might be considered as an unacceptable intrusion on the sovereignty of States.[47] On the other hand, any other construction would deprive the provision of any '*effet utile*' or effectiveness.[48] Furthermore, the reference to 'global rules and standards' and 'international rules, standards and recommended practices and procedures' depending on pollution sources creates confusion in the determination of the international instruments concerned.

Many non-binding guidelines relevant to offshore activities have been adopted by the International Maritime Organization (IMO).[49] Although they are not binding

43 The term 'dumping' includes any deliberate disposal of waste or other matter from a vessel, platform or other manmade structure at sea, as well as disposal of vessel, platform or other manmade structure at sea themselves. However, disposals that are incidental to or derived from the normal operation of the vessel (or platform, or other manmade structure) or amount to an intentional placement rather than a disposal do not constitute 'dumping' (*UNCLOS* art 1-1(1)(a)).

44 Enforcement powers are granted to coastal States for pollution of the marine environment occurring in their territorial sea, exclusive economic zone or on the continental shelf from seabed activities (*UNCLOS*, art 208) and by dumping (*UNCLOS*, art 210). These assume that the violation to be sanctioned has been implemented into the national laws of coastal States.

45 *UNCLOS*, art 210(6).

46 *UNCLOS*, art 208(3) for pollution from seabed activities.

47 Alan Boyle, 'Marine Pollution under the Law of the Sea Convention' (1985) 79 *American Journal of International Law* 356 (pro) and CG Timagenis, *The International Control of Marine Pollution* (Oceana Publications, 1979).

48 The fundamental principle of *effet utile* is that a treaty interpreter is not free to adopt a meaning that would reduce parts of a treaty to redundancy or inutility. This principle is implied in the *Vienna Convention on the Law of Treaties*, opened for signature 23 May 1969, 1155 UNTS 331 (entered into force 27 January 1980), arts 31 and 32.

49 Of direct relevance to pollution from offshore hydrocarbon activities are the International Maritime Organization 1989 Guidelines and Standards for the Removal of Offshore Installations and Structures on the Continental Shelf and in the Exclusive Economic Zone, (IMO Resolution A.672 (16), adopted on 19 October 1989). The IMO has adopted many other circulars, resolutions, guidelines and standards applicable to offshore activities, especially with Floating Production Storage and Offloading Unit or Vessel (FPSO) and Floating and Storage Units (FSU), some of which are indirectly relevant to

on their own standing,[50] it may be argued that they are setting a minimum mandatory standard by virtue of application of articles 208 and 210 of UNCLOS.[51] The legal strength of the standards set in the 1996 Protocol to the London Convention is subject to the same question. Can they be considered as establishing a global rule or, better, a global standard although it has only been ratified by a small number of countries? Or would the 1972 London Convention[52] be preferred based on the fact that it is widely ratified? Can the standards set by either of them be mandatory on non-signatories by virtue of UNCLOS? This is of particular relevance in the context of pollution from offshore oil and gas in Southeast Asia where neither the London convention nor the 1996 London Protocol[53] are widely ratified.

The UNCLOS provisions on pollution from dumping and seabed activities are in contrast to the UNCLOS provisions on pollution from vessels where coastal States have no obligation to implement nationally global rules and standards unless they have ratified the respective treaties.[54] With respect to pollution from vessels, flag States (not coastal States) have the primary legislative and enforcement powers.[55] This difference in coastal States' obligations with respect to pollution from vessels and from dumping and seabed activities is the source of additional uncertainty with respect to the regime of pollution from offshore oil and gas activities, particularly where shipping treaties contain provisions designed to control pollution from seabed activities. The wording of article 208 UNCLOS must be noted here, as it is not limited to pollution arising from seabed activities[56] but it includes in its scope pollution 'arising from or in connexion with' seabed activities. One circumstance which comes to mind where it is unclear which of (i) article 208 (pollution from seabed activities), (ii) article 210 (pollution from dumping); or (iii) article 211 (pollution from vessel) of UNCLOS should apply is where an international shipping treaty contains provisions relating also to pollution

---

offshore pollution, especially those relating to safety of navigation through safety zones and routing measures, construction rules or decommissioning.

50 This is the IMO's own approach. See 'Implications of the United Nations Convention on the Law of the Sea for the International Maritime Organization, Study by the Secretariat of the International Maritime Organization' LEG/MISC.6, 10 September 2008 http://www.imo.org/ourwork/legal/documents/6.pdf.

51 See Boyle, above n 47, 536.

52 *Convention on the Prevention of Marine Pollution by Dumping of Wastes and Other Matter*, opened for signature 29 November 1972, 1046 UNTS 120 (entered into force 30 August 1975).

53 *1996 Protocol to the 1972 London Convention on Prevention of Marine Pollution by Dumping of Wastes and other Matter*, opened for signature 7 November 1996, 2006 ATS 11 (entered into force 24 March 2006).

54 *UNCLOS*, arts 211(4) and (5).

55 *UNCLOS*, art 211(2).

56 An earlier version of this provision was so limited (M Nordquist (editor-in-chief), *United Nations Convention of the Law of the Sea 1982, a Commentary* (Center for Ocean Law and Policy, University of Virginia, Martinus Nijhoff Publishers, 1985–) Vol IV [208.7].

from seabed activities. This observation is of particular relevance in the context of the seas of Southeast Asia where all shipping pollution treaties have not been widely ratified but they include aspects of offshore oil and gas activities in their scope. Where an IMO shipping treaty containing provisions relating to pollution from seabed activities has been widely ratified globally but not in Southeast Asia,[57] a strict construction of UNCLOS would impose national implementation insofar as it relates to pollution from seabed activities by virtue of article 208 of UNCLOS.

IMO's Treaties Applicable to Offshore Oil and Gas Activities

The only international treaties and guidelines specifically applicable to offshore oil and gas activities have been adopted or negotiated through the IMO. Although the core mandate of this UN specialized agency is to promote shipping safety and to protect the marine environment from international shipping activities,[58] offshore oil and gas activities have fallen within the scope of its responsibility in so far as the activities involve ships and/or interfere with shipping safety (as do installations, structures and platforms). Many shipping treaties and guidelines also apply to offshore installations where the definition of 'ship' includes offshore platform or parts thereof such as Mobile Drilling Units (MODU), Floating, Storage and Offloading Unit or Vessel (FSO) or Floating Production Storage and Offloading Unit or Vessel (FPSO) or Floating and Storage Unit (FSU). The general view of the IMO appears to be that while it will continue to contribute to the regulation of offshore activities, as it has done to date, the pollution directly arising from exploration and exploitation of the seabed is deemed to fall outside its mandate.[59] Furthermore, as the focus of the IMO lies with shipping, national delegations generally comprise shipping regulators and rarely include representatives of national oil and gas regulatory bodies. This situation would need to be addressed if the IMO were to embrace a more comprehensive regulatory role with respect to seabed activities and implement article 208 of UNCLOS.[60]

This situation results in a fragmented international legal regime for offshore oil and gas activities based on a confusing set of rules derived from many different instruments. Furthermore, the scope of application of each set of rules is dependent on definitions such as whether the given installation or part thereof is a permanent installation or a disconnectable installation or whether it is self-

57 For instance, the 1972 London Convention with regard to decommissioning of offshore platforms. See discussion in section entitled 'Platform Decommissioning' below.

58 *Convention on the International Maritime Organization*, opened for signature 6 March 1948, 9 UST 621 (entered into force 17 March 1958) and *Charter of the United Nations*, opened for signature 26 June 1945, ATS 1 (entered into force 24 October 1945) art 57.

59 IMO, above n 49.

60 Alan Spackman, 'Environmental Standards for Offshore Drilling', *Touch Oil and Gas* (online) (2003) http://www.touchoilandgas.com/environmental-standards-offshore-drilling-a101-1.html.

propelled or non-propelled. The IMO has acknowledged this difficulty and sought to clarify some issues in its 2010 Guidance for the application of safety, security and environmental protection provisions to FPSOs and FSUs where it insists on the importance of distinguishing non-disconnectable FPSOs and FSUs (designed to be permanently moored) as opposed to disconnectable ones, and self-propelled craft as opposed to non-propelled craft while operating in location.[61] These key criteria determine the sovereign rights and obligations that a coastal State has over given offshore installations located on its continental shelf and the legal regime which is applicable.

Transboundary pollution from underwater pipelines (used primarily for the transport of gas from offshore installations) is another existing pollution risk in the SCS. As the production of natural gas is growing in the SCS, so too does the pipeline network, which already covers several thousand kilometres.[62] However, there is no international or regional framework determining rights and obligations in relation to environmental standards to be met in the laying and maintenance of pipelines. Conversely, deepwater drilling is currently limited in the seas of Southeast Asia. However, it is a developing activity with higher environmental risks and no international or regional environmental safeguards exist other than industry standards.[63]

61 IMO, Marine Environment Protection Committee and Maritime Safety Committee, MSC-MEPC.2/Circ.9, 25 May 2010.

62 Youna Lyons, 'Offshore Oil and Gas in the SCS and the Protection of the Marine Environment – Part 1 A Review of the Context and Profile of Offshore Activities (2011) 25[5.2.3] 28[5.3.5] http://cil.nus.edu.sg/wp/wp-content/uploads/2010/10/OOG_SCS-YounaLyons-Part1.pdf.

63 Deepwater drilling is currently located mostly off China's southern coast around the hydrocarbon fields of the Pearl River Delta (off Hong Kong, some fields average 1500m depth). However, based on the number of planned developments of deepwater fields and specialized press coverage, deepwater drilling is due to increase rapidly in the coming five years. In addition to China's deepwater fields, the SCS today holds 26 deepwater fields (over 500m depth) granted for exploration and development, where production has started in the last eight years or is due to start within the coming two to five years (as at 2010). With two new deepwater fields in production since 2003 (West Seno is 976m), Indonesia has another 11 deepwater fields (two of which are 600m deep, nine are more than 800m deep or more) forecast to come into production in the coming five years. Malaysia's 12 current deepwater fields are located off Sabah. Two are in development and production (respectively Gumusut-Kakap, 1000m and Kikeh, 1342m), the other nine are 1000m deep to 1465m on average (except one, 800m) and development is planned within the coming five years. The Philippines' Malampaya gas field is also located at 800 to 1200m water depth. Finally, blocks CA1 and CA2 located off Brunei and jointly managed under a joint commercial arrangement between Brunei and Malaysia are 1000 to 2720m deep.

Oil Spills from Offshore Oil and Gas Activities

This section investigates the applicability of shipping treaties on oil pollution to oil spills from offshore oil and gas activities prior to transfer and transportation for export.

Preventative Measures Oil discharge from ships is regulated by numerous international treaties and technical publications.

Annex I to the 1973 International Convention for the Prevention of Pollution from Ships as amended by the Protocol of 1978 (MARPOL 73/78) which applies to pollution by oil contains special requirements for fixed or floating platforms including drilling rigs, FPSOs used for the offshore production and storage of oil, and FSUs used for the offshore storage of produced oil.[64]

When they are engaged in the exploration, exploitation and associated offshore processing of sea-bed mineral resources and other platforms, such offshore installations must comply with requirements applicable to ships of 400 gross tonnage and above other than oil tankers. Other requirements include maintaining a record of all operations involving oil or oily mixture discharges, and complying with the prohibition on discharge into the sea of oil or oily mixtures except when the oil content of the discharge without dilution does not exceed 15 parts per million.[65]

The MARPOL Convention Annex I has been unanimously ratified in Southeast Asia and thus binds all coastal States in the region in respect of its provisions applicable to offshore installations.

---

64 MARPOL operates through six technical annexes, each addressing a different kind of pollution. Annex I regulates pollution by oil (Revised Annex I adopted by resolution MEPC.117(52) on 15 October 2004). Annex II regulates pollution by noxious substances in bulk; Annex III pollution by harmful substances in packaged form; Annex IV pollution by sewage from ships; Annex V pollution by garbage from ships and Annex VI prevention of air pollution from ships http://treaties.un.org/doc/Publication/UNTS/Volume 1340/volume-1340-I-22484-English.pdf. All the annexes and amendments are also available http://cil.nus.edu.sg/1978/1973-international-convention-for-the-prevention-of-pollution-from-ships-as-amended-by-the-protocol-of-1978-marpol-7378/. It must be noted that annexes only apply to pollution from offshore oil and gas activities if there is a special provision to that effect in the annex, because the general convention excludes as a matter of general principle 'the release of harmful substances directly arising from the exploration, exploitation and associated off-shore processing of seabed minerals resources' from the definition of 'discharge' under the Convention.

65 Revised Annex I *ibid*; Guidelines for the Application of the Revised MARPOL Annex I requirements to Floating Production, Storage and Offloading Facilities (FPSOs) and Floating Storage Units (FSUs), IMO, Marine Environment Protection Committee, Resolution MEPC.139(53), adopted 22 July 2005. See also Paragraphs 6.13 and 6.14 of IMO, Marine Environment Protection Committee, MEPC 59/24 (July 2009) on the interpretation of the requirements of MARPOL Annex I Regulation 15 as regards discharge of oil and oily waste from fixed and floating platforms.

Oil Spill Response This section focuses on oil spills directly occurring from an offshore installation and in the course of export from the installation.

The only international convention specifically addressing liability for offshore exploration and exploitation for hydrocarbons is the 1976 Convention on Civil Liability for Oil Pollution Damage Resulting from Exploration and Exploitation of Sea Bed Mineral Resources (CLEE Convention)[66] which has never entered into force. One of the difficulties faced was the lack of a competent international organization to host the convention and act as secretariat.

Despite the lack of a comprehensive international treaty on pollution from seabed activities, pollution incidents from offshore platforms, either nationally or in co-operation with other countries, fall within the scope of the 1990 International Convention on Oil Pollution Preparedness, Response and Cooperation (the OPRC Convention), which entered into force in 1995.[67] Under this convention, operators of offshore units (either floating or fixed) located within the jurisdiction of States Parties must have an oil pollution emergency plan or similar arrangements which must be coordinated with national systems in order to respond promptly and effectively to oil pollution incidents.[68] Similarly, ships flying the flag of a State Party must carry a shipboard oil pollution emergency plan.[69] The OPRC Convention also requires that specific tools be developed and equipment be used, including oil spill combating equipment, training programmes and exercises, detailed plans and communication capabilities as well as a mechanism or arrangement to coordinate the response to an oil pollution incident.[70] To date, Malaysia, the Philippines, Singapore and Thailand have ratified the OPRC Convention. However, Vietnam and Cambodia, which are not parties to the OPRC Convention, signed a Joint Statement on Partnership in Oil Spill Preparedness and Response in the Gulf of Thailand with Thailand in January 2006.[71] At regional level, an MOU was also signed between the ASEAN countries on 24 January 1994 for the creation of OSRAP (oil spill response action plan).[72]

Responsibilities in Oil Spill Ship-owners at the time of an incident (including the registered owner, bareboat charterer, manager and operator of the ship) are liable

---

66 The initial signatories were the Netherlands, Norway, Sweden, the United Kingdom, Germany, and Ireland http://sedac.ciesin.org/entri/register/reg-092.rrr.html.

67 *International Convention on Oil Pollution Preparedness, Response and Co-operation*, opened for signature 30 November 1990 1891 UNTS 51 (entered into force 13 May 1995) (OPRC) http://cil.nus.edu.sg/1990/1990-international-convention-on-oil-pollution-preparedness-response-and-co-operation/ (last accessed on 29 July 2011).

68 *OPRC*, art 3(1)(c).

69 *OPRC*, art 3(1)(b).

70 *Ibid* arts 6(1) and (2).

71 P Charlebois et al, 'Steering the Course towards Safer Shipping and Cleaner Seas' (2010) 16 *Tropical Coasts* 8.

72 See section entitled 'Regional Governance in Southeast Asia: The ASEAN Way, below.

for pollution damage according to the 2001 International Convention on Civil Liability for Bunker Oil Pollution Damage (2001 Bunker Convention)[73] which entered into force in 2008, and has been ratified by China, Malaysia, Singapore and Vietnam to date[74]. This Convention is applicable to pollution from parts of offshore installations, which can be considered to be a ship under the Convention. Given the definition of bunker oil as 'hydrocarbon mineral oil, including lubricating oil, used or intended to be used for the operation or propulsion of the ship, and any residues of such oil', it includes crude oil.[75] The pollution incident must involve bunker oil on board or originating from a ship,[76] defined as any seagoing vessel or seaborne craft, of any type.[77] The 2001 Bunker Convention may thus apply to oil pollution from FSU, FPSO and drilling units and more generally to any floating platforms without distinction as to whether they are self-propelled or not, nor engaged in an international voyage. However, the 2001 Bunker Convention deals primarily with the principle of liability, and compensation for damage.[78] It does not envisage other remedies to address pollution nor duties on ship-owners to repair and mitigate. This is of particular concern in the context of transboundary pollution where a framework is necessary to ensure coordination and consistency between the respective domestic rules of the States involved. Furthermore, these conventions do not apply to oil pollution from fixed platforms. The Legal Committee of IMO has expressed its support for the inclusion of a new item in the Committee's work programme to consider liability and compensation issues connected with transboundary pollution damage resulting from offshore oil exploration and exploitation activities. This may go some way toward resolving the current patchy regime.[79]

Only a few States have so far ratified the 2001 Bunker Convention. The question of the application of article 208 of UNCLOS to the standard set by this convention thus arises. If the view is taken that article 208 must be applied literally,[80] provisions which relate to pollution connected to seabed activities should be implemented into

---

73 *International Convention on Civil Liability for Bunker Oil Pollution Damage* opened for signature 23 March 2001 UKTS No 8 (2005) (entered into force 21 November 2008) (2001 Bunker Convention) http://cil.nus.edu.sg/rp/il/pdf/2001 International Convention on Civil Liability for Bunker Oil Pollution Damage-pdf.

74 See below Table 7.1.

75 *2001 Bunker Convention*, art 1(5).

76 *Ibid* arts 3 and 4.

77 *Ibid* art 1(1).

78 The 2001 Bunker Convention also contains important provisions on compulsory insurance and financial security certificate and liability limitation.

79 IMO Legal Committee, 97th Session, 15–19 November 2010, 'IMO Legal Committee supports follow-up to deep-water Horizon and Montara' http://www.imo.org/MediaCentre/MeetingSummaries/Legal/Pages/LEG-97th-Session.aspx.

80 See section entitled 'UNCLOS Sets General Rules and Standards for Activities from Seabed Activities and their Environmental Impact' above for discussion on the application of *UNCLOS* art 208.

the national legislation of coastal States insofar as they qualify as 'international rules, standards and recommended practices and procedures'.[81] The same would be true for the implementation of relevant provisions the OPRC Convention in the legislation of coastal States which may not have ratified them.[82] To this extent, these conventions would be considered as setting minimum requirements under UNCLOS with respect to pollution connected to seabed activities.

Drilling Wastes

Drilling Muds and Other Liquid Wastes Drilling wastes include drilling fluids or muds, drill cuttings and produced water, the disposal of which vary depend on environmental standards being complied with. Drilling muds (which assist in removing cuttings from the hole and cool the drill bit) get mixed with rock and sediment fragments to form the drill cuttings. Following treatment of the drill cuttings on site to separate as much of the muds as possible, used muds and drill cuttings are generally treated differently as the toxicity of the latter (per volume) is decreased. Production water consists primarily of relatively warm water from oil and gas reservoirs containing dissolved and dispersed oils and has a varying chemistry depending on the site. Drilling fluids can also contaminate these waters.[83] The legal framework available for the disposal of drill cuttings is reviewed in the following section.

Drilling fluids can be oil or water based. Non-oily components of drilling fluids include produced water and offshore processing drainage and displacement water. MARPOL Annex II, which addresses pollution by noxious liquid substances, would be applicable to these fluids. However, this Annex does not include specific provisions allowing for its application to offshore oil and gas operations. This means that discharges occurring directly from offshore platforms do not fall within the scope of Annex II. Nonetheless, the transport and handling of hazardous and noxious liquid substances in bulk on offshore support vessels fall within the scope of this Annex.[84] If noxious substances other than oil and oily mixtures are handed

81 For a full discussion on this topic, see section entitled 'UNCLOS Sets General Rules and Standards for Activities from Seabed Activities and their Environmental Impact' above.

82 For instance Brunei Darussalam, Cambodia, Indonesia, the Philippines and Vietnam (see below Table 7.1).

83 Sandra Kloff and Clive Wicks, *Environmental Management of Offshore Oil Development and Maritime Oil Transport*, A background document for stakeholders of the West African Marine Eco Region (October 2004) http://cmsdata.iucn.org/downloads/offshore_oil_eng.pdf; Jonathan Wills, 'Muddied Waters: A Survey of Offshore Oilfield Drilling Wastes and Disposal Techniques to Reduce the Ecological Impact of Sea Dumping', 25 May 2000, Ekologicheskaya Vahkta Sakhalina (Sakhalin Environment Watch) http://www.alaskaforum.org/other/muddiedwaters.pdf.

84 IMO Assembly Resolution A.673(16) adopted 19 October 1989, as amended by the Resolutions of the Maritime Safety Committee MSC 184(79) and MSC.236.

over from the oil or gas rig to an offshore vessel for disposal, the prohibitions included in Annex II are applicable.

The 2000 Protocol on Preparedness, Response and Co-operation to Pollution Incidents by Hazardous and Noxious Substances (HNS 2000) to the 1990 OPRC Convention provides for similar rules to those applicable to oil spills.[85] However, to date, it has only been ratified by China and Singapore.

Pollution from produced water currently falls outside the scope of existing international instruments. In contrast, drilling fluids can fall within the scope of MARPOL, depending on the composition of the fluids, and within the scope of HNS 2000 in the event of the spill of drilling fluids.

Disposal of Drill Cuttings Drill cuttings are generally disposed of in large piles located in the vicinity of the platforms if not just under. The environmental impact of drill cutting piles in Southeast Asia is not well understood at this point though some scientific publications[86] and the recent *ad hoc* Drilling Fluids and Cuttings Management Asia Forum held in Bangkok on 22–24 February 2011[87] demonstrate a growing attention to these issues and a regional awareness that some regional standard practice would be desirable.

MARPOL Annex V on pollution by garbage specifically applies to the disposal of garbage from fixed or floating platforms engaged in the exploration, exploitation and associated offshore processing of seabed minerals. Given the wide scope of the definition of garbage, it might include drill cuttings as well all other solid waste gathered during construction and operations. Disposal is forbidden within 500m of the platforms.

Aquatic Invasive Species through Ballast Water and Biofouling

Marine ecosystems surrounding offshore platforms and installations are particularly exposed to invasive species due to the volume of shipping traffic they attract to load or unload people, material or other cargo. Ballast movements surrounding offshore installations can be similar to that of a busy port, depending on the size of the operations. Biofouling is also recognized as a major pathway for the transfer of species from one location to another.[88] Furthermore, they can

85 See section entitled 'Oil Spill Response' above.

86 Hock Lye Koh and Su Yean, 'Simulation of Drill Cuttings Dispersion and Deposition in the South China Sea' 2011 *Proceedings of the International MultiConference of Engineers and Computer Scientists*, IMECS 2011, Hong Kong, 16–18 March 2011 http://www.iaeng.org/publication/IMECS2011/IMECS2011_pp1501-1506.pdf.

87 This event brought together representatives of Thailand, Indonesia, the Philippines and Vietnam. They discussed updates in regulations and the possibility of creating a regional standard for effluent guidelines governing drilling fluids and cuttings management. See http://www.prtoday.com/news/84916/ or http://www.free-press-release.com/news-top-asian-drilling-regulators-converge-in-bangkok-1297068614.html.

88 Biofouling is biological growth on manmade structures in the aquatic environment.

be located in the proximity of remote, sensitive, biodiverse and/or commercially important marine systems, although the magnitude of the potential impact will vary according to the local condition (including physical and biological oceanography).

Ratification of the 2004 International Convention for the Control and Management of Ships' Ballast Water and Sediments[89] is not widespread in Southeast Asia, but as it is a relatively recent convention which has not yet entered into force, it is too early to take any view on the position adopted by respective coastal States in that respect. Although this convention is not in force, the oil and gas industry has prepared guidelines for the prevention, containment and management of aquatic invasive species (AIS) in onshore and offshore projects and operations.[90] They include a list of species that are identified as potentially particularly invasive and set out pathways for travel of AIS within oil and gas activities. Of note is also the approval of the IMO biofouling guidelines at the MEPC 62nd session in July 2011.[91]

Platform Decommissioning[92]

The need for platform decommissioning is of great relevance in the SCS given that (i) 50% of the platforms are over 20 years old; (ii) 80% are in 75m of water or less; and (iii) 78% weigh 40,000 tons or less.[93] Yet, there have to date been very few decommissionings of offshore platforms in this region.

Increasing international concern in the last 20 years over the issue of offshore abandonment of oil and gas installations and facilities prompted the IMO to adopt Guidelines and Standards for the removal of offshore installations and structures on the continental shelf and in the exclusive economic zone in 1989,[94] before UNCLOS came into force in 1994. These IMO guidelines reflect article

89 2004 *International Convention for the Control of Management of Ships' Ballast Water and Sediments*, opened for signature 13 February 2004 IMO Doc BMW/CONF/36 (not yet in force) http://cil.nus.edu.sg/2004/2004-international-convention-for-the-control-and-management-of-ships-ballast-water-and-sediments/.

90 IPIECA/OGP, *Alien Invasive Species and the Oil and Gas Industry – Guidance for Prevention and Management*, 2010 Report Number 436 http://www.ogp.org.uk/pubs/436.pdf.

91 2011 IMO guidelines for the control and management of ships' biofouling to minimize the transfer of invasive aquatic species (Res. MEPC 207(62)).

92 For a detailed review of the topic, see Morakinyo Adedayo Ayoade, *Disused offshore installations and pipelines: towards sustainable decommissioning* (Kluwer Law International, 2002).

93 Lyons, above n 62, 7–10.

94 IMO Assembly Resolution A.672(16), adopted 19 October 1989 http://cil.nus.edu.sg/1989/1989-guidelines-and-standards-for-the-removal-of-offshore-installations-and-structures-on-the-continental-shelf-and-in-the-exclusive-economic-zone-imo-resolution-a-672-16-adopted-on-19-october-198/.

60 of UNCLOS, which prescribes that any installations or structures which are abandoned or disused shall be removed to ensure safety of navigation and that removal shall take into account fishing, protection of the marine environment and the rights and duties of other States.

While reiterating the obligation to remove platforms, the guidelines define conditions in which non-removal or partial removal can be acceptable. However, as a rule, installations of less than 4000 tons[95] have to be removed if either they are in less than 75m of water or are in less than 100m and have been emplaced after 1 January 1998.[96] Installations or structures which may interfere with navigation through straits or routes used for international navigation (even through territorial or archipelagic waters) must also be removed. Partial or total removal requires a 'case-by-case evaluation', i.e. an assessment of impact including an environmental impact assessment as well as a weighing of cost and feasibility. Standards are also set;[97] in relation to effects on the marine environment, the guidelines specify that the assessment must be based on scientific evidence taking into account the effect on water quality, geological and hydrographic characteristics, the presence of endangered or threatened species, existing habitat types, local fishery resources, and the potential for pollution or contamination of the site by residual products from, or deterioration of, the offshore installation structure. An official authorization from the coastal State is necessary to maintain an installation on the seabed and monitoring afterwards of accumulation and deterioration of material left on the seabed. These guidelines and standards are sometimes criticized for allowing partial removal only in cases of extreme cost or unacceptable risk. It should also be noted that the coastal State must ensure that legal title to installations and structures which have not been entirely removed is unambiguous and that responsibility for maintenance and the financial ability to pay future damages are clearly established.

The issue of offshore abandonment of oil and gas platforms also prompted the parties to the 1972 London Convention[98] to adopt:

---

95 Excluding the deck and superstructure.

96 Unless the entire removal is not technically feasible or would involve extreme cost, or an unacceptable risk to personnel or the marine environment (IMO Resolution A.672(16), art 3.5, *ibid*).

97 This analysis must include potential effects on the safety of subsurface navigation or other uses of the sea, the rate of deterioration of the material and future effects on the marine environment, the potential effect on the marine environment, the risk that the material will shift from its position, the costs, feasibility and risk of injury associated with removal, and the determination of a new use or other reasonable justification for allowing the installation to remain on the seabed.

98 The 1972 London Convention is the *Convention on the Prevention of Marine Pollution by Dumping of Wastes and Other Matter*, opened for signature 29 November 1972, 1046 UNTS 120 (entered into force 30 August 1975). It regulates dumping, i.e. the deliberate disposal at sea of wastes and other material of any kind, which includes any deliberate waste at sea from offshore oil and gas installations (art III 1(a)(i)) but not if

i. the new 1996 Protocol,[99] which explicitly includes within its scope 'abandonment or toppling at site of platforms or other man-made structures at sea, for the purpose of deliberate disposal,'[100] and which adopts a precautionary approach, and the polluter pays principle;[101]
ii. general guidelines for the assessment of wastes or other matter that may be considered for dumping, which include guidelines for waste prevention audit, consideration of waste management options and dump-site selection and are applicable to the disposal of offshore oil and gas installations or platforms;[102] and,
iii. specific guidelines for assessment of platforms or other manmade structures at sea.[103] These latter guidelines are also part of a series of specific guidelines. However, the London Convention has, in the SCS, only been ratified by the Philippines and China and the 1996 Protocol only by the latter.[104]

Conservation Treaties Relevant to Oil and Gas Activities

While they do not directly apply to oil and gas activities, conservation treaties, many of which have been widely ratified by the coastal States of Southeast Asia[105] may set goals that are relevant to the planning for offshore oil and gas activities. Adequate planning will ensure that offshore oil and gas developments do not compromise the wise use of wetlands of international importance as directed by the 1971 Ramsar Convention on Wetlands of International Importance,[106] nor the migratory routes of species protected under the 1979 Convention on

---

they are a by-product of the exploration, exploitation and associated processing of seabed mineral resources (art III 1(c)). Thus it only regulates the dumping of oil and gas platforms that are no longer in operation.

99 For more on this topic see Zhiguo Gao, *Environmental Regulation of Oil and Gas* (Kluwer Law International, 1998).

100 *1996 Protocol*, art 1(4.1)(4), above n 53.

101 *1996 Protocol*, arts 3.1 and 3.2, above n 53.

102 Adopted at the 22nd Consultative Meeting of the Contracting Parties to the London Convention in 2000.

103 Adopted at the 23rd Consultative Meeting of the Contracting Parties to the London Convention in 2001.

104 For a discussion on the applicability of the London Convention to coastal States which have not ratified, see section entitled 'Aquatic Invasive Species through Ballast Water and Biofouling'.

105 See below table of ratification (Table 7.1).

106 1971 *Convention on Wetlands of International Importance, especially as Waterfowl Habitat* (the Ramsar Convention), opened for signature 2 February 1971, 14583 UNTS 996 (entered into force 21 December 1975) http://www.ramsar.org/cda/en/ramsar-documents-texts/main/ramsar/1-31-38_4000_0.

the Conservation of Migratory Species of Wild Animals,[107] or areas of marine biodiversity protected under the 1992 Convention on Biological Diversity.[108]

The risk of conflict with conservation treaties is of particular relevance when very large offshore concession blocks are granted by coastal States. In the SCS, they range between 4000 and 10,000 km^2.[109] The largest blocks are often located on the outer limits of the continental shelf.[110]

Transboundary Environmental Governance at Regional Level

Regional Governance in Southeast Asia: The ASEAN Way

UNCLOS requires States bordering enclosed or semi-enclosed seas to cooperate with each other when exercising their rights and performing their duties under the Convention.[111] The duty to cooperate includes an obligation to coordinate the management, conservation, exploration and exploitation of the living resources of the sea and the implementation of the rights and duties of States with respect to the protection and preservation of the marine environment.

With respect to pollution from seabed activities, coastal States must endeavour to harmonize their policies at the appropriate regional level[112] and establish global and regional rules, standards and recommended practices and procedures to prevent, reduce and control pollution of the environment from these activities.[113] Many coastal States have entered into regional agreements establishing rules, standards and procedures for the protection of the marine environment, to supplement rules established at international level.[114] The Mediterranean Region

---

107 1979 *Convention on the Conservation of Migratory Species of Wild Animals* (the CMS Convention), opened for signature 23 June 1979, 1459 UNTS 362 (entered into force 1 November 1983) http://www.cms.int/documents/index.htm.

108 1992 *Convention on Biological Diversity* (CBD), opened for signature 5 June 1992, 1760 UNTS 79 (entered into force 23 December 1993) http://www.cbd.int/convention/text/.

109 Some are smaller. The rationale behind the map of concession blocks drawn by each coastal State has not been investigated.

110 The surface area of the concession blocks is based on Map Vietnam General, Global Exploration and Production Service by HIS (May 2008) Ref. VN08E1GEN, and South China Sea Map 803425AI (G02257) 1–10.

111 *UNCLOS*, art 123.

112 *UNCLOS*, art 208(4).

113 *UNCLOS*, art 208(5).

114 The UNEP Regional Seas Programme, initiated in 1974, assumes that the seas of the world include 13 regional seas: Mediterranean Sea, Baltic Sea, Black Sea, Red Sea and Gulf of Aden, West and Central African Sea, East African Seas, Caribbean Region, South Asian Seas, East Asian Seas, South Pacific, South East Pacific and North West Pacific Oceans.

is often presented as providing the leading model of regional seas agreements. It is the oldest and most frequently revised convention[115] of this type supplemented by an extensive range of protocols specific to an issue or the implementation of a particular convention. Of note in the context of pollution from seabed activities is the 14 October 1994 Protocol for the Protection of the Mediterranean Seas against Pollution resulting from Exploration and Exploitation of the Continental Shelf and the Seabed and its subsoil.[116]

Although the coastal States of the seas of South East Asia (or South Asian seas) have not entered into such a binding regional agreement, they have, on numerous occasions, stressed the importance and necessity of sustainably managing their marine environment.[117] Recently, the 2004 ASEAN Vientiane Action Programme,[118] the 2007 ASEAN Singapore Declaration on Environmental Sustainability[119] as well as the Roadmap for an ASEAN Community 2009–2015[120] emphasized the need for

115 The 1976 *Convention for the Protection of the Mediterranean Sea against Pollution* (1976 Barcelona Convention) now replaced by the 1995 *Barcelona Convention for the Protection of the Marine Environment and the Coastal Region of the Mediterranean* opened for signature 10 June 1995 UNEP (OCA)/MED IG.6/7 (entered into force 9 July 1994) aims to protect the marine environment of the region from pollution. Other examples of conventions include the 1992 *Convention for the Protection of the Marine Environment of the North Atlantic* (OSPAR Convention), the 1978 *Regional Convention for Cooperation of the Protection of the Marine Environment from Pollution* (1978 Kuwait Convention) and the 1989 *Kuwait Protocol*. For more details on these, see for example Zhiguo Gao, 'Environmental Regulation of the Oil and Gas Industries' (2000) 2(11) *Journal for the Centre for Energy, Petroleum and Mineral Law and Policy* http://www.dundee.ac.uk/cepmlp/journal/html/vol2/article2-11.html; M Kashubsky, 'Marine Pollution from the Offshore Oil and Gas Industry: Review of Major Conventions and Russian Law (Part I)' (2006) *Maritime Studies* 151, 1–11.

116 The Protocol was opened for signature on 14 October 1994, and came into force 24 March 2011 http://195.97.36.231/dbases/webdocs/BCP/ProtocolOffshore94_eng.pdf.

117 The 1994 Strategic Plan of Action on the Environment (1994–1998) was signed by the ASEAN Environment Ministers. It was designed to implement Agenda 21 in the ASEAN's member States http://www.aseansec.org/8950.htm. It includes the development of a framework for the integrated management of regional coastal zones as part of a strategy to promote the protection and management of coastal zones and marine resources. Milestones on this path included three agreements between the Environment Ministers of ASEAN in 2002 for a first set of criteria for National Marine Protected Areas, see 'ASEAN Criteria for National Marine Protected Area' http://www.aseansec.org/cme/ASEAN%20Criteria%20for%20National%20MPAs.pdf, for marine water quality for aquatic life and human health protection see 'Marine Water Criteria for the ASEAN Region' http://www.aseansec.org/cme/Marine%20Water%20Quality%20Criteria%20for%20the%20ASEAN%20Region.pdf and for marine heritage areas'ASEAN Criteria for Marine Heritage Areas' http://www.aseansec.org/cme/ASEAN%20Criteria%20for%20Marine%20Heritage%20Areas.pdf.

118 See http://cil.nus.edu.sg/2004/2004-vientiane-action-programme-2004-2010-signed-on-29-november-2004-in-vientiane-laos-by-the-heads-of-stategovernment-vap/.

119 See http://www.aseansec.org/21060.htm.

120 See http://www.aseansec.org/publications/RoadmapASEANCommunity.pdf.

coordination in the management and protection of the marine environment. More specialized, the ASEAN Cooperation Plan on Transboundary Pollution includes shipborn pollution in its scope but not offshore activities. The emphasis is on setting the basis for regional cooperation through the implementation of the 1994 OSRAP,[121] the ratification of the MARPOL conventions, the promotion of reception facilities for oil wastes and capacity building.[122] However, no coordination mechanisms or entities are created or designated to fulfil this mission.[123] The OSPAR plan is supported by the ASEAN-OSPAR project, funded by the Ministry of Transport of Japan and started in 1993. It focuses on the improvement of the capability of the ASEAN countries to deal with oil spill incidents and includes the purchase of equipment and materials for combating oil spills.[124]

The absence of a regional framework and/or of institutional mechanisms for regional coordination for marine environmental protection in Southeast Asia may be attributed to a lack of institutional and political maturity or as an expression of the 'ASEAN way'. Consistently with the interpretation adopted in other fields, the 'ASEAN Way' would translate to a preference for cooperative mechanisms following issue-specific declarations.[125] From this perspective, the recent transformation of the Partnerships in Environmental Management for the Seas of East Asia (PEMSEA)[126] into a self-sustained regional mechanism makes it the natural champion to develop such regional policy, in collaboration with other relevant institutions, be they international or regional, private or public, depending on the issues being considered.[127] However, it is noted that the member States of

---

121 See section entitled 'Oil Spills from Offshore Oil and Gas Activities' above.

122 See http://www.aseansec.org/8938.thm. It is noted that the implementation of this plan is placed under the purview of the ministries of environment who, as a general rule, have little impact on decisions from the shipping industry.

123 The ASEAN-OSPAR project can be compared with the Northwest Pacific Action Plan (NOWPAP) which binds China, Korea, Japan and Russia. It is an example of development of agreed guidelines (for instance in the use of dispersants in case of an oil spill) and cooperation mechanisms without a binding treaty. See http://dinrac.nowpap.org/about_NOWPAP.php.

124 See http://www.nmc.sg/asean-ospar.html.

125 On this topic, see Koh Kheng-Lian and Nicholas A Robinson, 'Strengthening Sustainable Development in Regional Intergovernmental Governance: Lessons from the ASEAN' (2002) 6 *Singapore Journal of International and Comparative Law* 640–682.

126 The 11 signatories are Cambodia, China, the Democratic People's Republic of Korea, Indonesia, Japan, Lao, the Philippines, Korea, Singapore, Timor-Leste and Vietnam. The SDS-SEA defines steps to be taken towards the goals of key international agreements and action plans related to coasts, islands and oceans, including in respect of subregional mechanisms to combat transboundary environmental threats such as pollution from offshore platforms http://pemsea.org/pdf-documents/sds-sea/SDSSEA-Full.pdf, 64.

127 The 2009 Manila Declaration on Strengthening the Implementation of Integrated Coastal Management for Sustainable Development and Climate Change Adaptation in the Seas of East Asia Region also calls on PEMSEA, as the regional mechanism for the implementation of the Sustainable Development Strategy for the Seas of East-Asia (SDS-

PEMSEA include the coastal States of the East Asian Sea, China, the Democratic People's Republic of Korea, Japan, Korea, in addition to most States of Southeast Asia. Furthermore, the States of Brunei Darussalam, Malaysia and Thailand, without which no successful marine environmental policy can be concluded, are not members yet.

A Fragmented Regional Governance Framework

The governance of the seas of Southeast Asia is, at this stage, characterized by an array of decentralized bilateral or multilateral treaties, agreements, declarations and programmes of varying scope organized around a diversity of international and regional bodies or initiatives.

Bilateral and Multilateral Agreements on Hydrocarbon Resources There are currently a large and diverse number of development agreements or arrangements between coastal States or national oil and gas companies aimed at exploring and/or producing hydrocarbon resources in areas subject to disputed maritime claims or the development of oil or gas fields straddling an agreed boundary.[128] They range from short agreements, geographically bound and limited in use and time (such as joint seismic surveying subject to a specified duration and area[129]), to ambitious agreements including boundary setting and joint development of the resources under set rules.[130] Until now, arrangements have been signed on a bilateral and occasionally tripartite basis. This has resulted in a patchwork of agreements throughout the SCS with varied rules and geographic scope and a disparity in the activities covered by the agreements. Some of these agreements designate the law applicable to the area being developed, which would include rules relating to pollution from these activities, but not necessarily enforcement mechanisms,

---

SEA), to undertake the development of the Implementation Plan for the SDS-SEA in 2010. The Manila Declaration was signed on 26 November 2009 http://pemsea.org/eascongress/section-support-files/manila_declaration.pdf. The Declaration follows the signed 2003 Putrajaya Declaration of Regional Cooperation for the Sustainable Development of the Seas of East Asia and the Manado Ocean Declaration reportedly adopted by acclamation on 14 May 2009.

128 The conclusion of provisional Joint Development Agreements of mineral resources located in areas subject to overlapping claims is encouraged by *UNCLOS* art 74(3) pending a boundary agreement.

129 Three years tripartite Agreement for Joint Marine Seismic Undertaking (JMSU) signed on 14 March 2005 between CNOOC, PNOC and PetroVietnam. See Lyons above n 62, Part 1 (4.3) 20 [3].

130 The 2000 Agreements in the Gulf of Tonkin are an example of an agreement on boundary as well as joint management of the resources, with respect to living resources. Agreements entered into between national oil companies appear to be particularly popular for the flexibility they offer. However, their wording and modalities are generally not available for public scrutiny.

especially in the case of transboundary pollution. Such choice of law clauses may allow for direct recourse against the enterprise causing the damage, provided that such a mechanism is embedded in the domestic law designated in the clause. Furthermore, these agreements cover a relatively small part of the overall disputed area, and thus a small proportion of hydrocarbon reservoirs under development.

In the Gulf of Thailand, Malaysia has signed two JDAs with Thailand and Vietnam respectively.[131] The most ambitious and legally complex of the two JDAs is the first one,[132] the instruments of ratification of which were exchanged on 30 May 1990. It creates a Joint Authority[133] and its scope extends beyond hydrocarbon exploration and exploitation to recognize the rights of both States with respect to fishing, navigation, hydrographic and oceanographic surveys and to the prevention of pollution in the overlapping area.[134] The cumulative application of national laws in the agreed 'Joint Development Area' provided for in the agreement could technically also apply to pollution and create an obligation of conservation attached to the rights dealt with in the agreement. In contrast the 1992 Malaysia–Vietnam agreement, which deals with a smaller overlapping area (the 'Defined Area'), is limited to joint exploration for and development of hydrocarbons. It also employs a different and arguably more pragmatic and flexible management model in which national oil and gas companies are the primary actors.[135] Petronas[136] and PetroVietnam[137] agreed on the application of the laws of Malaysia to the Defined Area for petroleum operations. Malaysian law thus applies to the determination of obligations and liabilities relating to the environmental impact of oil and gas activities in the Defined Area.[138]

---

131 Tara Davenport, 'Joint Development in Asia: Lessons for Sustainable Peace in the South China Sea' (2011) *Asian Journal of Comparative Law* 11 (personal copy from the author).

132 It stems from a Memorandum of Understanding (MoU) agreed between Malaysia and Thailand in 1972, which is valid for 50 years or indefinitely if no agreement is reached on boundaries. The first agreement, signed in 1972, was only a partial agreement as the countries could not agree on the application of delimitation rules over the islet of Ko Los, a Thai islet standing 1.5 metres high above sea level and supporting no economic life of its own. See Nguyen Hong Thao, 'Joint Development in the Gulf of Thailand' 1999 (Autumn), *IBRU Boundary and Security Bulletin* 79–88 http://www.dur.ac.uk/resources/ibru/publications/full/bsb7-3_thao.pdf.

133 The chairmanship of the Authority alternates between the two countries every two years.

134 Nguyen Hong Thao, above n 132.

135 In a commercial arrangement signed in 1993, Petronas and PetroVietnam (with agreement of the respective governments) established a Coordination Committee composed of eight members, with an equal number of nominees appointed by each company, responsible for decisions for the management of the Defined Area.

136 The national oil company of Malaysia.

137 The national oil company of Vietnam.

138 The first exploitation under the MoU occurred in July 1997 in the Bunga Kekwa field. While the 1990 agreement between Malaysia and Thailand is generally viewed as

In the Gulf of Tonkin (or Gulf of Beibu) the agreements on Maritime Boundary Delimitation and on Fisheries Resources signed by China and Vietnam in 2000[139] set the basis for the 2005 Framework Agreement on Oil and Gas Cooperation between China National Offshore Oil Corp (CNOOC) and PetroVietnam but contain no provision on hydrocarbon resources or pollution from such activities, or any choice of law clause.[140]

In the Southern SCS, following the signature of a Tripartite Cooperation Agreement in November 2000, PetroVietnam, Petronas and Pertamina[141] entered into several production sharing contracts in disputed areas as well as in undisputed areas between the respective coastal States.[142] These successful collaborations are said to be paving the way for a new era of intra-ASEAN knowledge and information sharing designed to upgrade skills and expertise.[143] However, there is no indication that these agreements, which all concern areas covering waters under the jurisdiction of two or more States, contain provisions relating to environmental damage from such activities.

The common element in the Joint Development Arrangements referred to above is that they are temporary solutions which allow for oil and gas extraction to be undertaken despite overlapping claims to the continental shelf.[144] Sustainable exploration and extraction and management of pollution of the seabed from oil

---

an especially successful example of a comprehensive joint-development agreement, the speed of implementation of the 1992 MoU between Malaysia and Vietnam deserves particular attention. Unlike the 1979 MoU, it has been very quickly implemented. The behind the scenes involvement of Petronas and PetroVietnam in the 1992 MoU may explain this dynamism in implementation as well as the 2000 tripartite arrangement (extending this relationship to Pertamina) reviewed below. As with the MoU between Malaysia and Thailand, sharing of all costs, expenses, liabilities and benefits from petroleum operations are key principles.

139 Zou Keyuan, 'Cooperative Development of Oil and Gas Resources in the South China Sea' in Sam Batement and Ralf Emmers (eds), *Security and International Politics in the South China Sea: Towards a Cooperative Management Regime* (Routledge, 2009).

140 Zou Keyuan, 'The Sino-Vietnamese Agreement on Maritime Boundary Delimitation in the Gulf of Tonkin' (2005) 36(1) *Ocean Development and International Law* 13–24.

141 The national oil company of Indonesia.

142 The first contract was concluded in 2001 over Blocks 10 and 11.1 located off Vietnam. Another contract was entered into in 2003 over block SK305 off Sarawak; see Robert Piepul, 'PetroVietnam, Petronas, Pertamina to explore two blocks off Vietnam' 9 January 2001 *PennEnergy* http://www.pennenergy.com/index/petroleum/display/131688/articles/oil-gas-journal/exploration-development/petrovietnam-petronas-pertamina-to-explore-two-blocks-off-viet-nam.html and http://rigzone.com/news/article.asp?a_id=7027.

143 For more recent news coverage see http://www.ethiopianreview.com/news/48192.

144 Note that this comment concerns primarily the agreements between Malaysia and Thailand, Malaysia and Vietnam and Brunei and Malaysia. It does not apply to agreements reached over areas stretching over delimited boundaries, namely the agreement between China and Vietnam for the Gulf of Tonkin.

and gas activities are not built into the agreements nor implied. Compared with the US, Europe or the Persian Gulf, exploitation of hydrocarbon in the SCS is at an earlier stage of development, both from an industry and a regulatory perspective. While Malaysia's petroleum legislation, developed over years, is today regarded as one of the most sophisticated in the region, the national legislation of some other coastal States remains rudimentary and the subject of ongoing developments.[145]

Regional and Sub-Regional Programmes The seas of Southeast Asia have been the subject of a large diversity of independent marine conservation initiatives at regional and sub-regional level that are often focused on a specific habitat (mangroves or coral reefs) within a given geographical area or on whole ecosystems.[146] However, pollution from oil and gas activities does not appear to be integrated in these programmes, except on a very local scale, in the Sulu-Sulawesi Sea.[147] The SCS, where most of the risks of transboundary pollution from offshore oil and gas activities are located, falls outside the geographic scope of many of these ongoing marine environmental programmes.[148]

Of note is the ASEAN Council on Petroleum (ASCOPE),[149] the mission statement of which includes the promotion of collaboration and mutual assistance

---

145 Eleodoro Mayorga Alba (study managed by), 'Environmental Governance in Oil-producing Developing Countries – Findings from a Survey of 32 Countries' 2010 (June) 17 *Extractive Industries for Development Series, World Bank* (available online) http://siteresources.worldbank.org/EXTOGMC/Resources/336929-1266963339030/eifd17_environmental_governance.pdf.

146 Anna Tengberg, 'Overview of Regional Transboundary Initiatives, Projects and Programmes for the Seas of East Asia: Status and Funding Opportunities' (Paper presented at the United Nations Development Programme, EAS Congress, Manila, 23–27 November 2009).

147 The Sulu-Sulawesi Seascape Project is a cooperative project including NGO, public and private partners that includes environmental impacts from offshore oil and gas activities within its geographic scope. Launched in 2005 by Conservation International to protect critical species and habitats in the marine biodiversity conservation corridors of Verde Passage, Cagayan Ridge, Balabac Strait and the Tri-National Sea Turtle Corridor, it involves partnerships with major stakeholders, including oil and gas companies in Indonesia, Malaysia and the Philippines. Evangeline FB Miclat and Romeo B Trono, 'One Vision, One Plan, Common Resources, Joint Management Conserving the Sulu-Sulawesi Sea' (2008) 15(1) *Tropical Coasts* 4–10.

148 For a review of programmes in place, see John W McManus, Kwang-Tsao Shao and Szu-Yin Lin, 'Towards Establishing a Spratly Islands International Marine Peace Park: Ecological Importance and Supportive Activities with an Emphasis on the Role of Taiwan' (2010) 41(3) *Ocean Development and International Law* 270–280; Aldo Chircop, 'Regional Cooperation in Marine Environmental Protection in the South China Sea: A Reflection on New Directions for Marine Conservation' (2010) 41(4) *Ocean Development and International Law* 334–356.

149 It was established on 15 October 1975 by the then member States of the ASEAN and joined in 2006 by all the other members.

in the development of petroleum resources in the region through joint endeavours and facilitating exchange of information. The national oil company or public agency in charge of supervising oil and gas activities represents their country within ASCOPE. Current projects include the crafting of regional decommissioning guidelines tailored to the ASCOPE countries with full concurrence and mutual approval by the relevant national oil companies in accordance with international laws and regulations and complying with the national legislation of each member country.[150] This could potentially set the basis for the regional framework necessary to manage transboundary pollution from decommissioning of offshore installations.

Conclusion

This chapter reviews the risk of different types of transboundary pollution from offshore oil and gas activities in the seas of Southeast Asia and the fragmentation and gaps in the governance framework in place to manage them, both at international and regional levels. However, it also emphasizes that despite some gaps and inconsistencies (linked to the legal regimes of different types of offshore platforms), some international treaties set rules and guidance applicable to different types of pollution from these offshore activities. Where such treaties have been ratified, the issue lies rather in the consistency in interpretation, compliance and enforcement. Marine ecologists and international organizations involved in marine environmental management in the region call for better coordination between programmes in the region and many argue that a binding treaty is needed for this, as has been done in other regional seas. However, the ASEAN way might prefer a more empirical and cooperative approach where transnational and specialized groups agree on guidelines for the region. To be successful, this method would require sufficient coordination among such groups. However, the proposal made in this chapter is that the priority should go towards the implementation of ratified treaties, ratification of treaties which have not yet been ratified, and regional coordination to that end, rather than towards the drafting of a new treaty for the region. With regard to the management of pollution from offshore oil and gas activities, the outcome of ASCOPE's endeavour to set decommissioning guidelines for the region will help identify the best path forward.

This chapter also emphasizes the particular challenges created by the competing and increasing uses of the seas of Southeast Asia. The environmental rules adopted with respect to each use must take into account the combined impact from all of them.

150 ASCOPE website http://ascope.org/.

Table 7.1 International treaties relevant to offshore oil and gas activities and the protection of the marine environment: status of ratification by coastal States of the SCS[1]

	International Treaties	Adoption/Ratification/Accession (1)								
		Brunei Darussalam	Cambodia	China (7)	Indonesia	Malaysia	Philippines	Singapore	Thailand	Viet Nam
UNCLOS	**United Nations Convention on the Law of the Sea 1982 (UNCLOS) and Agreement on Part XI**	1996	signed in 1983	1997	1986	1996	1984	1994	2011	1994
Safety	**Convention on the International Regulation for Preventing Collision at Sea, 1972 (as amended in 1981, 1987, 1989, 1993, 2001, 2007)**	1987	1994	1980	1979	1980	1987	1977	1979	1990
	International Convention for the Safety of life at Sea, 1974, 1978 Protocol, 1988 Protocol	1986/1986/N	1994/1994/ 2001	1982/1982/ 1995	1981	1983	1981	1981	1984	1990
Oil only	**International Convention for the Prevention of Pollution from Ships 73/78 and Annex I (MARPOL)**	1986	1994	1983	1986	1997	2001	1990	2007	1991
	International Convention on Oil Pollution Preparedness, Response and Co-operation 1990 (OPRC)	N	N	1998	N	1997	signed in 1995	1999	2000	N
	International Convention on Civil Liability for Oil Pollution Damage (CLC) 1969, 1976 Protocol, 1984 Protocol, 1992 Protocol and 2000 Amendments	1976/1976/ 1992/ 1992	1969/1976/ 1992/1992	1999/1999/ 1999/1999	1969/1992/ 1992/1992/1992	1992/1992/ 1992/1992/1992	1992/1992/ 1992/1992/199?	19761976/ 1992/1992	N	1992/1992/ 1992/1992/1992
	International Convention on the Establishment of an International Fund for Compensation for Oil Pollution Damage Protocol 1992 (IOPC-FUND)	1992	1992	1999 (HK only)	N	1992	1992	1992	N	N
	International Convention on Civil Liability for Bunker Oil Pollution Damage 2001 (Bunkers Convention)	N	N	2008	N	2008	N	2006	N	2010

	International Treaties	Adoption/Ratification/Accession (1)								
		Brunei Darussalam	Cambodia	China (7)	Indonesia	Malaysia	Philippines	Singapore	Thailand	Viet Nam
	1976 Convention on the Limitation of Liability for Maritime Claims and 1996 Protocol (1996 LLMC)	N	N	1997	N	N	N	2005	N	N
Solid and liquid waste	Convention on the Prevention of Marine Pollution by Dumping of Wastes and Other Matter 1972 and 1996 Protocol (London Convention)	N	N	1985/2006	N	N	1973	N	N	N
	International Convention for the Prevention of Pollution from Ships 73/78 and Annexes II to V (MARPOL)	Annex II	Annex II-V	Annex II-V	Annex II	Annex II-V	Annex II-V	Annex II-V	Annex II	Annex II
		No Annex III to V			No Annex III to V				No Annex III to V	No Annex III to V
	Nairobi International Convention on the removal of Wrecks 2007(Nairobi WRC) NYF (8)	N	N	N	N	N	N	N	N	N
	Hong Kong International Convention for the safe and environmentally sound recycling of ships 2009 (SRC) – NYF(8)	N	N	N	N	N	N	N	N	N
Toxic substances	Basel Convention on the Control of Transboundary Movements of Hazardous Wastes and their Disposal 1989 and Amendment 1995 (not yet into force)	2002	2001/N	1991/2001	1993/2005	1993/2001	1993/N	1996/N	1997/N	1995/N
	Protocol on Preparedness, Response and Co-operation to pollution Incidents by Hazardous and Noxious Substances 2000 (HNS 2000), 2010 Protocol	N	N	2009/N	N	N	N	2003/N	N	N
	International Convention on the Control of Harmful Anti-fouling Systems on Ships 2001 (AFS)	N	N	2011	N	2010	N	2009	N	N

International Treaties		Adoption/Ratification/Accession (1)								
		Brunei Darussalam	Cambodia	China (7)	Indonesia	Malaysia	Philippines	Singapore	Thailand	Viet Nam
Air pollut.	**International Convention for the Prevention of Pollution from Ships 73/78 and Annexes VI (MARPOL)**	N	N	2006	N	2010	N	2000	N	N
	Montreal Protocol on Substances that Deplete the Ozone Layer 1987 (Montreal Protocol) under the 1985 Vienna Convention for the Protection of the Ozone Layer	1993	2001	1989	1992	1989	1991	1989	1989	1994
Inv. Species	**International Convention for the Control and Management of Ships' Ballast Water and Sediments 2004 (BWM) - NYF (8)**	N	N	N	N	2010	N	N	N	N
Conservation	**Convention on Wetlands of International Importance 1971 (Ramsar Convention), Paris Protocol (1982), Regina Amendment (1987)**	N	1999	1992	1992	1994/1995/N	1994/1994/N	N	1998/1998/N	1988/1989/N
	Convention concerning the World Cultural and Natural Heritage 1972 (World Heritage Convention)	N	1991	1985	1989	1988	1985	N	1987	1987
	Convention on International Trade in Endangered Species of Wild Fauna and Flora 1973 (CITES), Bonn Amendment (1979) and Gaborone Amendment (1983)	1990	1997	1981/1997/1988	1978/1987/N	1977/N/N	1981/1981/1988	1986/1986/N	1983	1994
	Convention on the Conservation of Migratory Species of Wild Animals 1979 (CMS), Agreement on the conservation of albatrosses and petrels 2001, MoU on the conservation of marine turtles 2001, MoU on the conservation of dugongs 2007, MoU on the conservation of migratory sharks 2010	N/N.A./N/N.A./N	N/N.A./2002/N/N	N/N/N/N/N	N/N/2005/N/N	N/N.A./N/N/N	1994/N.A./2001/2010/2010	N/N.A./N/N/N	N/N.A./2004N/N	N/N.A./2001/N/N
	Convention on Biological Diversity 1992	2008	1995	1992	1994	1994	1993	1995	2004	1994
	Convention on the Protection of the Underwater Cultural Heritage 2001	N	2006	N	N	N	N	N	N	N

Notes to Table 7.1

(1) according to the information available as at March 2011.
(2) N.A. stands for Not Applicable.
(3) N. stands for No Adoption/Ratification/Accession.
(4) Y. stands for Adoption/Ratification/Accession.
(5) This table does not include all IMO Convention relating to safety at sea.
(6) d. stands for denounced.
(7) The change of Hong Kong's status in 1997 has translated in the denunciation of several treaties and, often, later re-accession following China's policy.
(8) Not Yet in Force.

Chapter 8

Coordinating Strategic Environmental Assessments of Marine and Terrestrial Plans: Australian Experience in the Sub-Antarctic

Simon Marsden

Introduction

The International Union for the Conservation of Nature (IUCN), also known as the World Conservation Union, identifies six types of protected area (PA), from a strict nature reserve and wilderness area to a managed resource PA, the difference between each largely depending upon on the degree of human activity present.[1] To date classifications have been focused on terrestrial areas and there is a need to classify in the marine context to take account of key differences.[2] The number and types of PA in or between any country or countries have expanded greatly over recent years. This has resulted in great complexity; the case of the United Kingdom as affected by European law is but one example.[3] Whether terrestrial or marine, PAs are also managed in a variety of ways.[4] Yet conventional approaches

---

1 International Union for the Conservation of Nature (IUCN), *Guidelines for Protected Areas Management Categories* (IUCN, 1994). The definition of protected areas was revised by the IUCN World Commission on Protected Areas (WCPA) in 2008, and is affected by the definition in the *Convention on Biological Diversity*, opened for signature 22 May 1992, 31 ILM 822 (entered into force 29 December 1993) ('CBD'). See N Dudley (ed), *Guidelines for Applying Protected Areas Management Categories* (IUCN, 2008). For explanation see Barbara Lausche and Francoise Burhenne, *Guidelines for Protected Areas Legislation* (IUCN, 2011) 11–14; the categories however remain the same, 147–149.

2 Dalal Abdulrazzak and Stephen Trombulak, 'Classifying Levels of Protection in Marine Protected Areas' (2011) 36 *Marine Policy* 576. The revised 2008 definition by the IUCN WCPA is intended to apply to marine protected areas (MPAs) and aims to clarify the distinction between conservation-focused sites and others, where for example fisheries management is the objective.

3 K Bishop, A Phillips and LM Warren, 'Protected Areas for the Future: Models from the Past' (1997) 40 *Journal of Environmental Planning and Management* 81.

4 Michael Lockwood, Graeme Worboys and Ashish Kothari (eds), *Managing Protected Areas: A Global Guide* (Earthscan, 2006).

through management plans and environmental impact assessment (EIA) remain the most common.[5]

There remains a need to link PAs and non-PAs,[6] develop and expand marine protected areas (MPAs) in areas within,[7] between and beyond national jurisdiction[8] in the context of marine spatial planning (MSP),[9] and further ecosystem based approaches including to fisheries management.[10] Evidence of strategic environmental assessment (SEA) being applied to management plans for PAs is growing,[11] although the potential has yet to be fully explored.[12] It has been completely absent in management planning and EIA under the Antarctic Treaty System (ATS),[13] although the Committee for Environmental Protection, (established under the Madrid Protocol[14] to the ATS), had in a recent Five Year Work Plan for the first time recommended considering the application of SEA as part of improving and implementing the EIA Annex to the Protocol.[15] The

5 J Leitmann, 'Options for Managing Protected Areas: Lessons from International Experience' (1998) 41 *Journal of Environmental Planning and Management* 129.

6 Roger Crofts, 'Linking Protected Areas to the Wider World: A Review of Approaches' (2004) 6 *Journal of Environmental Policy and Planning* 143.

7 Lorne Kriwoken, 'Australia's Marine Protected Areas: Charting a Course towards a Representative System' in Warwick Gullett, Clive Schofield and Joanna Vince (eds), *Marine Resources Management* (Lexis Nexis Butterworths, 2011) 171.

8 Alexander Gillespie, *Protected Areas and International Environmental Law* (Martinus Nijhoff, 2007) 109–111.

9 Frank Maes, 'The International Legal Framework for Marine Spatial Planning' (2008) 32 *Marine Policy* 797.

10 Mitsutaku Makino, Hiroyuki Matsuda and Yasunori Sakurai, 'Expanding Fisheries Co-Management to Ecosystem-Based Management: A Case in the Shiretoko World Natural Heritage Area, Japan' (2009) 33 *Marine Policy* 207.

11 JG Carter, CM Wood and M Baker, 'The Environmental Appraisal of National Park Management Plans in England and Wales' (2003) 46 *Journal of Environmental Planning and Management* 271; Suzanne Therrien-Richards, 'SEA of Parks Canada Management Plans' in MR Partidario and R Clark (eds), *Perspectives on Strategic Environmental Assessment* (CRC-Lewis, 2000).

12 Lockwood at al, above n 4, emphasize the application of EIA to policies and programs but not plans (p 230). They recognize the relationship of management planning with other strategic proposals, but fail to discuss assessment of management plans or assessment tiering in this context (see their chapter 11).

13 *Antarctic Treaty*, opened for signature 1 December 1959, 402 UNTS 71 (entered into force 23 June 1961). For discussion, see Ricardo M Roura and Alan D Hemmings, 'Realising Strategic Environmental Assessment in Antarctica' (2011) 13 *Journal of Environmental Assessment Policy and Management* 483.

14 *Protocol on Environmental Protection to the Antarctic Treaty*, opened for signature 4 October 1991, 30 ILM 1461 (entered into force 14 January 1998) ('Madrid Protocol').

15 Committee for Environmental Protection, *Report of the Committee for Environmental Protection* (CEP XII), Baltimore, April 6–9, 2009, Appendix I. For discussion, see Simon Marsden, 'Introducing Strategic Environmental Assessment to the Madrid Protocol: Lessons from International Experience' (2011) 1 *The Polar Journal* 36.

area covered by the Convention on the Conservation of Antarctic Marine Living Resources (CCAMLR),[16] a part of the ATS, includes Australia's sub-Antarctic External Territory, Heard Island and McDonald Islands (HIMI), which is the focus of this chapter. As a sub-Antarctic external territory of Australia, HIMI is beyond the jurisdiction of the ATS generally (which does not extend this far north), however, the Parties to CCAMLR, (which extends as far north as the Antarctic Convergence), work in close connection with the Parties to the Madrid Protocol, and many of them are in fact the same.[17]

The chapter considers the potential application of SEA to the planning and management of HIMI as a marine reserve, and the actual application to the resource rich waters of the Exclusive Economic Zone (EEZ) surrounding it, in particular the fishery. As such, it examines the relationship between an MPA and related but unprotected waters. It is argued that the planning and assessment processes undertaken to date have been hindered by inconsistent law and unimplemented policy which have failed to effectively plan and manage the ecosystem as a whole.[18] It first examines international experience with SEA of management plans and assessment tiering, before outlining the planning and management regime of HIMI. The SEA of the HIMI Fishery Management Plan and preparation of the Marine Reserve Management Plan (which was not assessed) is then discussed, and the HIMI experience analysed. In the light of the development of Australian Marine Bioregional Plans,[19] recommendations that these be extended,[20] and work

---

16 *Convention on the Conservation of Antarctic Marine Living Resources*, opened for signature 1 August 1980, 19 ILM 837 (entered into force 7 April 1982) ('CCAMLR'). See Gail L Lugten, 'Net Gain or Net Loss? Australia and Southern Ocean Fishing' in Lorne Kriwoken, Julia Jabour, and Alan Hemmings (eds), *Looking South: Australia's Antarctic Agenda* (Federation Press, 2007) 100.

17 For examples of the relationship between these international instruments of relevance to PAs, see Decision 9 (2005) – ATCM XXVIII – CEP VIII, Stockholm – *Marine Protected Areas* (adopted 17 June 2005), and Resolution 2 (2011) – ATCM XXXIV – CEP XIV, Buenos Aires – *Revised Guide to the Preparation of Management Plans for Antarctic Specially Protected Areas* (adopted 1 July 2011). The first requires that prior approval from the Commission of CCAMLR be obtained for proposals for Antarctic Specially Protected Areas or Antarctic Specially Managed Areas (under the Madrid Protocol) which contain marine areas. The second updates a previous guide to reflect best practice, although there is no reference to SEA.

18 The overlap between international resource management regimes has also been noted in respect of the sub-Antarctic. See Donald Rothwell, 'Conservation and Management Frameworks for Sub-Antarctic International Waters' (2007) 141 *Papers and Proceedings of the Royal Society of Tasmania* 1, 4.

19 Department of Environment, Water, Heritage and the Arts, *Australian Government, Fact Sheet – Marine Bioregional Planning – the Process* (March 2010), see http://www.environment.gov.au/mbp.

20 In the legislative review of the environment protection law known as the *Environment Protection and Biodiversity Conservation Act 1999* (EPBC Act). See Department of the Environment, Water, Heritage and the Arts, *Independent Review of the*

by CCAMLR for bio-regionalization, the next section considers the advantages that a Marine Bioregional Plan for both HIMI and the marine area beyond the Reserve and EEZ may bring. In the final section, recommendations and concluding comments suggest how to overcome the anomalies and failings of past assessment approaches.

International Experience with SEA of Management Plans and Assessment Tiering

There are many benefits that come from applying SEA to proposals focused on environmental protection, including avoidance of unforeseen and cumulative effects; such a process recognizes that environmental effects may be positive or negative depending on the target.[21] Applying a transparent process including report production, review and monitoring by varied stakeholders is also an important attribute to gain support for the process. It is particularly important for management plans for strict nature reserves and wilderness areas, which may also be listed under the World Heritage[22] and Ramsar[23] Conventions. Because of their extreme isolation, such areas should be managed in such a way that maximum protection is afforded to them. Similar governance principles for decision making also apply to environmental planning and management processes, whether SEA is applied to them or not.[24]

Environment Protection and Biodiversity Conservation Act 1999 (DEWHA, 2009), Chapter 10, Strategic Assessments and Bioregional Planning: http://www.environment.gov.au/epbc/review/publications/pubs/interim-report.pdf.

21 Both the European SEA Directive and SEA Protocol define environmental effect broadly with this in mind: Directive Annex I, note 1; Protocol Article 2(7). See *Directive 2001/42/EC of the European Parliament and of the Council of 27 June 2001 on the assessment of the effects of certain plans and programmes on the environment* [2001] OJ L197/30; *Protocol on Strategic Environmental Assessment to the Convention on Environmental Impact Assessment in a Transboundary Context*, opened for signature Kiev, 21 May 2003, unreported (entered into force 11 July 2010) ('SEA Protocol').

22 *Convention Concerning the Protection of the World Cultural and Natural Heritage*, opened for signature 16 November 1972, 11 ILM 1358 (entered into force 17 December 1975) ('World Heritage Convention'). For relevance and relationship with protected areas, see Lausche and Burhenne, above n 1, 50–54.

23 *Convention on Wetlands of International Importance, especially as Waterfowl Habitat*, opened for signature 2 February 1971, 11 ILM 963 (entered into force 21 December 1975) ('Ramsar Convention'). For relevance and relationship with protected areas, see Lausche and Burhenne above n 1, 54–56.

24 See Lausche and Burhenne above n 1, 40–46, with notable reference to the importance of the *Convention on Access to Information, Public Participation in Decision-Making and Access to Justice in Environmental Matters*, opened for signature 25 June 1998, 2161 UNTS 447 (entered into force 17 May 2005) ('Aarhus Convention').

The Ramsar Convention Secretariat and the IUCN have been exploring the importance of impact assessment to the biodiversity conventions for some time, including the Ramsar,[25] and World Heritage Conventions.[26] This may extend to the application of SEA to management plans.[27] As many World Heritage Areas comprise both terrestrial and marine elements,[28] it has been argued that SEA should be applied to the ecosystem as a whole in MSP processes, to determine policy and planning priorities and avoid cumulative effects.[29] HIMI at first appears unusual within the Antarctic sphere of influence for having World Heritage status, because Article IV of the Antarctic Treaty prevents further territorial claims to the continent; however, the fact that HIMI lies outside the ATS area and that Australian sovereignty has not been contested explains why.[30] General trends in MSP have

25 Ramsar Strategic Plan Action 2.54 calls for the application of SEA together with integrated environmental management when assessing impacts from development proposals or change in land or water use. Found at http://www.ramsar.org. Note also the Handbook on EA (2006), Chapter 6, 6, and see A Bagri and F Vorhies, 'The Ramsar Convention and Impact Assessment', paper presented to the 7th Meeting of the Conference of the Contracting Parties to the Convention on Wetlands, San Jose, Costa Rica, 1999.

26 Article 5 contains provisions that have the potential to set the framework for and also to require SEA without making it explicit. Note also the Operational Guidelines 2005, Chapter 6, 8; see Simon Marsden, 'An International Overview of Strategic Environmental Assessment, with Reference to World Heritage Areas Globally and in Australian Coastal Zones' (2002) 4 *Journal of Environmental Assessment Policy and Management* 31. Note also the *Convention on Migratory Species Convention on the Conservation of Migratory Species of Wild Animals*, opened for signature 23 June 1979, 19 ILM 15 (entered into force 1 November 1983)('CMS'), and Article 14 of the CBD (above n 1), which are also relevant.

27 Countryside Council for Wales, English Nature, Environment Agency, Royal Society for the Protection of Birds, *Strategic Environmental Assessment and Biodiversity: Guidance for Practitioners* (2004) 15 and 19; Helen Byron and Joanna Treweek, 'Guest Editorial: Strategic Environmental Assessment – Great Potential for Biodiversity?' (2005) 7 *Journal of Environmental Assessment Policy and Management* v.

28 See Rosamunde Codling, 'Aspects of Environmental Planning in the Antarctic' (2001) 44 *Journal of Environmental Planning and Management* 129, at 132; Tim Stephens and Ben Boer, 'Enforcement and Compliance in the Australian Antarctic Territory: Legal and Policy Dilemmas' in Kriwoken et al, above n 16, at 56.

29 Intergovernmental Oceanographic Commission, *Marine Spatial Planning – A Step by Step Approach towards Ecosystem-Based Management* (UNESCO, 2009), 79–80.

30 Two other parts of the sub-Antarctic are also World Heritage listed: Macquarie Island, jurisdictionally part of the Australian State of Tasmania (the planning and management of which is contrasted with HIMI below), and the New Zealand Sub-Antarctic Islands.

been extensively reported on,[31] and examples of SEA being applied to resource development in coastal areas are growing.[32]

With respect to HIMI, SEA should include assessment of Australia's overarching Oceans Policy, any policy for the sub-Antarctic territories, relevant marine plans, and potentially also the relationship between Australian and French conservation and management policies[33] (the neighbouring Kerguelen Islands under French sovereignty share straddling fish stocks with the waters around HIMI as well as potential habitat for many species that reside in and around HIMI).[34] Such an assessment approach may better protect the overall integrity of the region, as without it there is likely to be a greater risk of cumulative impacts and other impacts that escape recognition.[35]

Assessment tiering, whereby higher level proposals are assessed before and related to lower level ones, has been found to be essential for successful SEA,[36] but it is often hindered by the presence of distinct legal and policy requirements. In Europe, where the law is most developed, the SEA, Habitats, Water Framework and Public Participation Directives all contain provisions for or of relevance

31 Fanny Douvere, 'The Role of Marine Spatial Planning in Implementing Ecosystem-Based, Sea Use Management' (2008) 32 *Marine Policy* 762; N Schäfer, 'Maritime Spatial Planning: About the Sustainable Management of the Use of Our Seas and Oceans' in Timo Koivurova, Aldo Chircop, Eric Franckx, Eric Molenaar and David VanderZwaag (eds), *Understanding and Strengthening European Union-Canada Relations in Law of the Sea and Ocean Governance* (University of Lapland, 2009) 89.

32 In relation to the Bay of Fundy, a marine national park, see Meinhard Doelle, 'The Role of Strategic Environmental Assessments in Energy Governance: A Case Study of Tidal Energy in Nova Scotia's Bay of Fundy' in Koivurova et al above note 31, 191. In regard to Scotland, see Freedom-Kai Phillips, 'Ocean Renewable Energy in the European Union: Understanding and Strengthening EU–Canada Relations in Law of the Sea and Oceans Governance', also in Koivurova et al above note 31, 151.

33 This is recognized in Australia's Oceans Policy; see Commonwealth of Australia, *Australia's Oceans Policy* (Commonwealth of Australia, 1998), 38–40. For recent discussion, see Joanna Vince, 'Managing Australia's Oceans through the Oceans Policy Process' in Warwick Gullett et al, above note 7, 77.

34 Note the *Treaty between the Government of Australia and the Government of the French Republic on cooperation in the Maritime Areas Adjacent to the French Southern and Antarctic Territories, Heard Island and the McDonald Islands, Australia–France*, signed 24 November 2003, 2438 UNTS 253 (entered into force 1 February 2005). Other than encouraging cooperative scientific research into marine living resources, the Treaty does not have relevance for this chapter.

35 For examples, see Emma James, Paul Tomlinson, Vicki McColl and Chris Fry, *Final Report – Literature Review/Scoping Study on Cumulative Effects Assessment and the Strategic Environmental Assessment Directive*, Unpublished Project Report (TRL Limited/ Environment Agency, 2003).

36 Thomas Fischer, *Theory and Practice of SEA – Towards a More Systematic Approach* (Earthscan, 2007).

to SEA, which should link closely with provisions in the EIA Directive.[37] Yet the relationship is not always as clear as it should be. A number of studies have considered this,[38] and consolidation may eventually be required.[39]

Overview of the Management of Heard Island and McDonald Islands

HIMI is an external territory of Australia located in the Antarctic Convergence approximately 4000 km south-west of Perth (see Figure 8.1). It is the only unmodified example of a sub Antarctic island ecosystem globally, and the Marine Reserve is one of the world's largest MPAs.[40] Both the Islands and the territorial sea are closed to fishing as they are managed as a Wilderness Reserve by the Australian Antarctic Division (AAD). The EEZ waters from the 12 nautical mile limit to the 200 nautical mile limit are managed by the Australian Fisheries Management Authority (AFMA) as part of the Australian Fishing Zone (see Figure 8.2). The Islands and the 12 nautical mile territorial sea around them are on the World Heritage List and form part of the Heard Island Wilderness Reserve. In recognition of the Islands' importance, fishing is prohibited to 13 nautical miles offshore, providing an additional buffer zone for the islands of one nautical mile. The fishery extends from 13 nautical miles offshore to the edge of the 200 nautical mile Australian EEZ around the Islands, which does not have PA status, with the exception of the north-west because of the Kerguelen Islands.

Haward indicates that the establishment of the management plan regime for Commonwealth managed fisheries has given increased roles and responsibilities to the fishing industry, and as such has introduced a more cooperative approach to fisheries management. New forms of property right have been created to access the fishery, although overall limits are imposed by way of a total allowable catch (TAC) that can be varied according to the viability of the stock.[41] Kriwoken and Holmes consider the emerging issues related to HIMI are commercial fishing,

---

37 For details, see Simon Marsden, *Strategic Environmental Assessment in International and European Law: A Practitioner's Guide* (Earthscan, 2008).

38 William Sheate, Helen Byron, Suzan Dagg and Lourdes Cooper, *The Relationship between the EIA and SEA Directives: Final Report to the European Commission* (Imperial College Consultants, 2005); J Carter and J Howe, 'The Water Framework Directive and the Strategic Environmental Assessment Directive: Exploring the Linkages' (2006) 26 *Environmental Impact Assessment Review* 287.

39 European Commission, *Study Concerning the Report on the Application and Effectiveness of the SEA Directive (2001/42/EC)* Final Report (European Commission, 2009).

40 See Jane Harris, Marcus Haward, Julia Jabour and Eric J Woehler, 'A New Approach to Selecting Marine Protected Areas (MPAs) in the Southern Ocean' (2007) 19 *Antarctic Science* 189.

41 Marcus Haward, 'The Ocean and Marine Realm' in Stephen Dovers and Sue Wild River (eds), *Managing Australia's Environment* (Federation Press, 2003) 38. See also

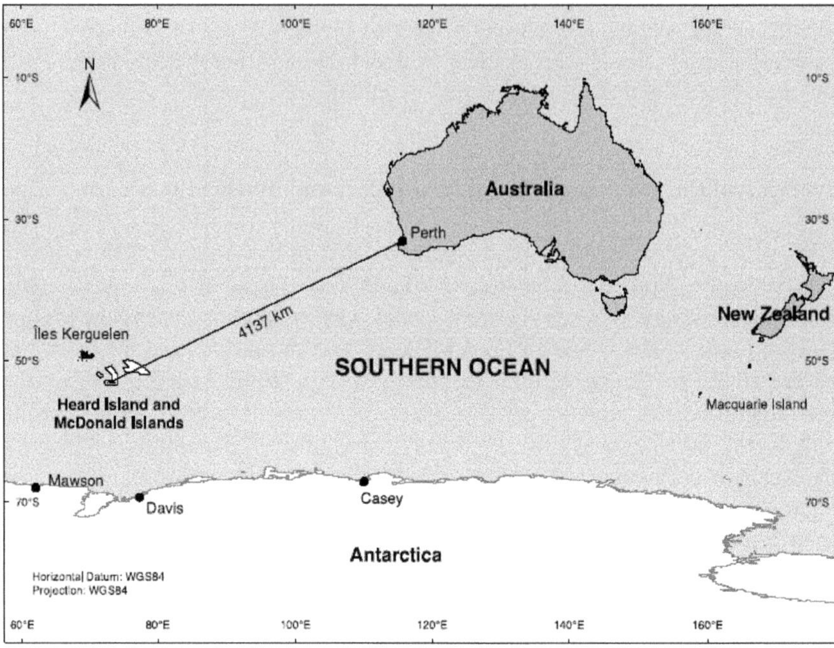

Figure 8.1 Location of HIMI, with Macquarie Island to the East

tourism, science and management, quarantine, disease and introduction of alien species. Governance arrangements in relation to these issues are identified as key to successful environmental planning and management.[42]

The HIMI Marine Reserve that forms part of these waters was declared for the purpose of 'protecting the conservation values of HIMI and the adjacent unique and vulnerable marine ecosystems'.[43] It is of outstanding national and international conservation significance; the islands themselves provide important breeding locations for seabird and seal populations,[44] and the surrounding waters

---

Marcus Haward, 'Australian Marine Resources and Environmental Policy and Politics' in Gullett et al, above n 7, 147.

42 Lorne Kriwoken and Nick Holmes, 'Emerging Issues of Australia's Sub-Antarctic Islands: Macquarie Island and Heard Island and McDonald Islands' in Kriwoken et al, above n 16, 162–163.

43 This was set out in the Declaration of the HIMI Marine Reserve in 2002 under s 351(3)(c) *Environment Protection and Biodiversity Conservation Act* 1999 (Cth). The Proclamation of the Reserve that year is due to be amended to reflect the inclusion of additional areas of conservation significance; see Department of Sustainability, Environment, Water, Population and Communities, *Heard Island and McDonald Islands: Marine Reserve Amendment Proposal* (Australian Government, 2011).

44 Protection is afforded for albatrosses and petrels under the *Agreement on the Conservation of Albatross and Petrels*, opened for signature 19 June 2001 (entered into

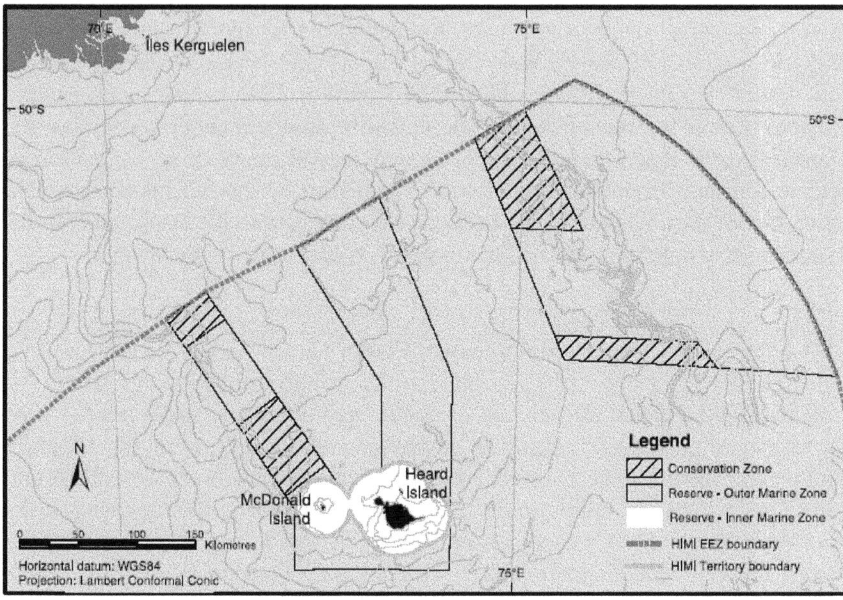

Figure 8.2 Management Zones, including current Conservation Zones, with the Kerguelen Islands in the North West

provide valuable foraging grounds for land-based marine predators. The marine areas also provide important habitats for many species. HIMI was inscribed on the World Heritage List in 1997 in recognition of many of these values and has been nominated as a wetland of international importance under the Ramsar Convention. Of particular significance to HIMI is the fact that the extreme isolation and severe climate of the islands has ensured that human visitation and associated disturbance has been minimal, resulting in the Islands being one of the most biologically pristine areas in the world.[45]

Fisheries management is subject to mandatory SEA requirements in Australia's national environmental protection law,[46] which means plans approved under the related fisheries law are accredited under the environmental protection law so

force 1 February 2004)('ACAP').

45 Australian Antarctic Division on behalf of Director of National Parks, *Heard Island and McDonald Islands Marine Reserve Management Plan 2005–2012* (Commonwealth of Australia, 2005). The Plan is currently under review and is likely to be completed and implemented in late 2012; this will include the boundary changes that incorporate the additional areas of conservation significance, see above n 43.

46 Simon Marsden, 'Strategic Environmental Assessment and Fisheries Management in Australia: How Effective is the Commonwealth Legal Framework?' in Simon Marsden and Stephen Dovers (eds), *Strategic Environmental Assessment in Australasia* (Federation Press, 2002) 47.

there is no further need for approval. Related discretionary SEA provisions that apply in a terrestrial context have similar effect,[47] but have only been applied a few times.[48] Under the fisheries law, AFMA must produce management plans of Commonwealth managed fisheries, and under the environment protection law the plans are to be assessed first by AFMA and second (more of an evaluation or review forming part of the advice to the Minister) by the federal environment department.[49] Fishing permits are issued in accordance with the plans; fisheries for export must also be assessed under Australian wildlife protection law.[50]

SEA of the HIMI Fishery Management Plan

In April 2002 the first *Assessment of the Heard Island and McDonald Islands Fishery* was published,[51] detailing environmental impacts from the fishery.[52] The management regime is considered sufficiently precautionary by AFMA and capable of controlling, monitoring and enforcing the fishery, whilst ensuring stocks are fished sustainably. Of most concern are impacts on by-catch species[53] and the illegal, unreported and unregulated (IUU) fishing for Patagonian toothfish, which extends beyond the boundaries of the HIMI fishery. An investigation of the extent to which HIMI and the Kerguelen Islands share a single or straddling stock was recommended and is ongoing (see Figure 8.2 for location) because if confirmed,

---

47 Simon Marsden, 'Strategic Environmental Assessment in Australia: An Evaluation of s 146 of the *Environmental Protection and Biodiversity and Conservation Act* 1999' (1999) 8 *Griffith Law Review* 394.

48 It has been applied to Offshore Petroleum Exploration and Appraisal Activities, and Environmental Management Processes, Procedures and Systems for the Conduct of Major Military Training Exercises. See Department of Industry, Tourism and Resources, *Draft Strategic Assessment of Offshore Petroleum Exploration and Activities* (2005) and Department of Defence, *Draft Terms of Reference for the Strategic Assessment of the Environmental Management Processes, Procedures and Systems for the Conduct of Major Military Training Exercises* (2005).

49 W Gullett, *Fisheries Law in Australia* (LexisNexis Butterworths, 2008) 141–147.

50 See Part 13A, *Environment Protection and Biodiversity Conservation Act* 1999 (Cth).

51 Australian Fisheries Management Authority, *Heard Island and McDonald Islands Fishery Management Plan* (Australian Fisheries Management Authority, 2002).

52 The relevant documents can be accessed via the AFMA website: http://www.afma.gov.au/fisheries/antarctic/himi/publications/default.htm.

53 AFMA Bycatch Action Plans and progress reports prepared by the Sub-Antarctic Fisheries Management Advisory Committee provide data on this. For the former see Australian Fisheries Management Authority, *Antarctic Fisheries – Bycatch Action Plan* (Australian Fisheries Management Authority, 2001 and 2003). For the latter, see Sub-Antarctic Fisheries Management Advisory Committee, *Six-Monthly Bycatch Action Plan Progress Reports* (2005 and 2008).

there is a clear need to coordinate assessments.[54] Joint projects have since been developed with France,[55] as well as cooperative treaties to enhance surveillance of and enforcement against illegal fishing activity.[56]

Concerns were also expressed over the impact of trawling on benthic communities and it was recommended that a Category 1A MPA be established to protect the ecological sustainability of the fishery; this was done when the HIMI Marine Reserve was established in October 2002 (see below), which protects these communities together with land-based predators and other protected species. This MPA was foreshadowed as long ago as 1998 in accordance with the National Representative System of MPAs but it took a considerable time before a formal recommendation was made following the Final Report to the federal environment department on the Conservation of Marine Habitats in the Region of Heard Island and McDonald Islands,[57] and the issues raised in the Sub-Antarctic Fisheries Bycatch Action Plan in 2001. The Australian government therefore considered that the actions of the fishery would not have an unacceptable or unsustainable impact on the marine environment and the Fishery Management Plan was approved.

Although the assessment confirmed the fishery had minimal interaction with protected species, monitoring of seal interactions with fishing vessels was recommended, together with an evaluation of the effects of introducing long-line fishing methods on seabird populations. A Threat Abatement Plan for the Incidental Catch (or By-Catch) of Seabirds during Oceanic Long-line Fishing Operations was developed,[58] which required suitable and effective seabird by-catch mitigation measures to be in place before long-lining is introduced. These methods were trialled for toothfish in the HIMI EEZ during the 2002/03 season and long-lining was introduced in November 2005. The concerns about the effects of long-lining

---

54 Department of the Environment and Water Resources, *Assessment of the Heard Island and McDonald Islands Fishery* (Commonwealth of Australia, 2007) Recommendation 1.

55 Sub-Antarctic Fisheries Assessment Group, *Antarctic Fisheries Strategic Research Plan 2003–2008* and *2008–2013.*

56 See n 34. For discussion, see Marcus Haward, Rob Hall and Aynsley Kellow, 'Setting and Implementing the Agenda: Australian Antarctic Policy' in Kriwoken et al, above note 16, 21, at 32; W Gullett and C Schofield, 'Pushing the Limits of the Law of the Sea Convention: Australian and French Cooperative Surveillance and Enforcement in the Southern Ocean' (2007) 22 *International Journal of Marine and Coastal Law* 545; and Cameron Moore, 'Maritime Regulation and Enforcement', in Rachel Baird and Donald R Rothwell (eds), *Australian Coastal and Marine Law* (The Federation Press, 2011) 331–332.

57 L Meyer, A Constable and R Williams, *Conservation of Marine Habitats in the Region of Heard Island and McDonald Islands* (Australian Antarctic Division, Department of the Environment and Heritage, 2000).

58 Environment Australia, Department of Environment and Heritage, *Threat Abatement Plan for the Incidental Catch (or bycatch) of Seabirds during Oceanic Longline Fishing Operations* (1998). See also Department of Environment and Heritage, *Sub-Antarctic Fur Seal and Southern Elephant Seal Recovery Plan* (2004). See Gullett, above n 49, 165–166.

relate to the protection for the islands and territorial sea, and are of particular concern because there was no SEA for the HIMI Marine Reserve Management Plan. The report comments:

> [A]lbatross and giant-petrel species typically forage within a few hundred kilometers of the colony during the early chick-rearing (brooding) period. This area has *significant overlap with the fishery area, making the likelihood of interaction with fishing vessels potentially high.* Interactions between seabirds and trawl fisheries elsewhere have resulted in significant mortalities.[59] (emphasis added)

The proximity of the fishery to the World Heritage Area, together with the high conservation value of the islands' flora and fauna, was instrumental in the introduction of strategies to minimize the impact of the fishery on the islands, related waters and biota. Although the establishment of the Marine Reserve significantly enhances precautionary management, priority was given to the fishery above other concerns and inevitably impacts have occurred. Haward et al comment that the development of the HIMI fishery 'was a significant milestone in Australian Antarctic policy ... [which has] subtly shifted Australia's interests in CCAMLR',[60] effectively giving more weight to commercial interests.[61]

The Fishery Management Plan was reviewed in 2007 and the authors concluded that there has been a significant decline in the estimate of IUU catches (attributed to enforcement activity), and that there remains 'a high level of confidence [i]n the reliability of information collected on protected species interactions in the HIMI Fishery'.[62] Since the 2002 Assessment Report, 27 seabird and 24 seal deaths have

---

59 Environment Australia, Marine and Water Division, Assessment of the Heard Island and McDonald Islands Fishery for the Purposes of Part 10, Part 13 and Part 13A of the Environment Protection and Biodiversity Conservation Act 1999 (Commonwealth of Australia, 2002). Ecological risk assessments are becoming a more common feature in relation to protected species, see Cleo Small, Susan M Waugh and Richard A Phillips, 'The justification, design and implementation of Ecological Risk Assessments of the effects of fishing on seabirds', Paper presented to the Agreement on the Conservation of Albatrosses and Petrels, Sixth Meeting of Advisory Committee, Guayaquil, Ecuador, 29 August–2 September 2011.

60 Above n 56, 31. Since the Fishery falls within the CCAMLR Convention area, it is managed by AFMA (in cooperation with the AAD) in accordance with CCAMLR Conservation Measures.

61 Certification of Southern Ocean toothfish fishery by the Marine Stewardship Council may mitigate the worst of such incidents; see 'Helping save albatrosses and petrels through Marine Stewardship Council certification of Southern Ocean toothfish fisheries', Agreement on the Conservation of Albatrosses and Petrels, 23 June 2011, http://www.acap.aq/2011-news-archive/helping-save-albatrosses-and-petrels-through-marine-stewardship-council-certification-of-southern-ocean-toothfish-fisheries.

62 Above n 54, 8.

been reported,[63] including an incident in March 2005 regarded as 'unprecedented' as it occurred in a mid-water trawl with no previous incidents; measures were immediately put in place to deal with this, and new technologies were trialled to mitigate the risk of seal deaths.[64]

With respect to the Marine Reserve, although the fishery continues to be excluded in the territorial sea, further research is ongoing concerning possible ecological risks. Although it is concluded that actions taken by individual fishers in accordance with the Plan would not be expected to have significant impacts upon World Heritage matters, whether *any* impacts are acceptable, with a recorded history of only two visitations and no introduced species, should perhaps be asked in conjunction with the need to apply SEA to World Heritage Areas.[65]

Overview of the HIMI Marine Reserve Management Plan

The Marine Reserve Management Plan includes measures to ensure that the Reserve's values are identified, protected and communicated to the public. In particular it includes comprehensive measures designed to prevent the introduction of alien species from human activities, to ensure protection of important terrestrial and marine species, habitats and ecosystems, and to interpret the cultural heritage values associated with nineteenth-century sealing activities and the earliest Australian Antarctic Research Expedition.[66] The Plan was prepared by the AAD, with sections containing an 'Aim' or list of 'Aims' that describe the desired results of Reserve management activity, and a series of 'Prescriptions' that control activities in the Reserve and strategies for managing the Reserve to meet the aim(s). One of the sections deals with EIA and approval,[67] although there is no recognition that the Plan itself could have been a suitable candidate for assessment. The section concerning research and monitoring is of particular interest. One of the stated aims

63 For a recent evaluation of the effects of long-lining on seabirds, see SM Waugh, GB Baker, R Gales and JP Croxall, 'CCAMLR Process of Risk Assessment to Minimise the Effects of Longline Fishing Mortality on Seabirds' (2008) 32 *Marine Policy* 442.

64 More up to date data is available, including interactions with protected species and on the ecosystem. See Australian Fisheries Management Authority, *Annual Status Report – Heard Island and McDonald Islands Fishery* (Australian Fisheries Management Authority, 2009) 22–23.

65 Marsden, above n 26.

66 The key conservation values of the HIMI region were documented in the report, Conservation of Marine Habitats in the Region of Heard Island and McDonald Islands. See Meyer et al, above n 57.

67 The administrative guidelines for the project EIA process in HIMI are modelled on those applied to activities in Antarctica under the *Antarctic Treaty (Environment Protection) Act* 1980 (Cth), which implements the Madrid Protocol. See LK Kriwoken and DM Rootes, 'Tourism on Ice: Environmental Impact Assessment and Antarctic Tourism' (2000) 18 *Impact Assessment and Project Appraisal* 138.

is to 'contribute to the effective management of the Reserve and the surrounding region', which recognizes the close relationship between the Islands and the EEZ:

> Research within the Reserve is required to contribute to the integrated and ecologically sustainable management of the *HIMI region as a whole*. Studies into the condition of fish stocks, the foraging ranges and diets of land-based marine predators, and the composition and condition of benthic communities are essential *if informed decisions are to be made for the adjacent HIMI fishery and the CCAMLR region in which the Reserve is located.*[68]

There is no doubt that the relationship between the Reserve and the fishery is vital to the maintenance of the values of both, and that reference should be made to CCAMLR where appropriate. Despite this, the Reserve Management Plan was not assessed either individually or in conjunction with the AFMA Fisheries Plan, the assumption being that there is no need to do so because the former is designed to avoid environmental impacts.[69] The Reserve Management Plan should also be subject to SEA, and a more integrated, higher level assessment may be the best approach to providing comprehensive protection, as the author has argued elsewhere.[70]

Is a Bioregional Plan Needed to Coordinate the Two Plans?

Recent research has highlighted the need for MPAs to be coordinated via broader MSP processes.[71] In the light of this, the development of a Regional Marine Plan (RMP) for Australia's sub-Antarctic zone may be the most practical way to integrate the different legislative requirements and provide for a multi-purpose management area. RMPs were originally forecast to be established as part of Australia's Oceans Policy 1998 which made a commitment to integrated ecosystem-based management of the Australian EEZ.[72] They were designed to integrate sectoral commercial interests and conservation requirements to prevent conflict between

68 Above n 45, at 58.

69 Ewan McIvor, Senior Environment Officer, Environmental Policy and Protection Section, AAD, personal communication, 11 April 2005.

70 Simon Marsden, 'Strategic Environmental Assessment and Protected Areas Management in the Sub-Antarctic: Are Some Areas Better Protected than Others?', Paper presented to the International Association for Impact Assessment Conference, International Experience and Perspectives on SEA (Prague, 2005); John Ashe and Simon Marsden, 'SEA in Australia' in Barry Sadler et al, (eds), *Strategic Environmental Assessment Handbook* (Earthscan, 2011) 26–27.

71 Tundi Agardi, Giuseppe Notarbartolo di Sciara and Patrick Christie, 'Mind the Gap: Addressing the Shortcomings of Marine Protected Areas through Large Scale Marine Spatial Planning' (2011) 36 *Marine Policy* 226.

72 Commonwealth of Australia, above n 33.

resource access and allocation. They were to be binding on all Commonwealth agencies, including AFMA and AAD and to be prepared by the National Oceans Office, providing for coordination across and between governments.[73] If such an overarching plan to the Fishery and Reserve Plans were prepared and assessed, it may be possible to achieve the integration required.

Australia's Oceans Policy foreshadowed the application of SEA to RMP prior to the enactment of the federal environment protection law in the following terms:

> The Environment Protection and Biodiversity Conservation Bill before Parliament identifies the marine environment as one of a range of matters of national environmental significance ...
>
> The Environment Protection and Biodiversity Conservation Bill also provides for strategic assessments of the impacts of actions arising from policies, plans and programmes, allowing for recommendations from the Minister for the Environment and Heritage and subsequent endorsement of the policies, plans and programmes by the Minister.
>
> - The Government will, as appropriate, use strategic environmental assessment as a key mechanism in the development, endorsement and implementation of Regional Marine Plans.
>
> The Government will:
>
> - Foster strategic regional environmental assessment, to improve efficiency for industry clients and enhance capacity to identify potential risks and protect the marine environment from cumulative impacts.[74]

One of the proposed RMPs was concerned with the Kerguelen area comprising the HIMI territory, yet distinct from the Kerguelen Island group, under French sovereignty. Despite the significance attached to RMPs under the Oceans Policy and the requirement for performance assessment of the Policy,[75] no plan was prepared for this area, and the approval of the Reserve Management Plan accorded HIMI a lower priority in terms of further integrated planning;[76] the outstanding issue of the EEZ surrounding HIMI was believed to have been 'largely if not wholly addressed

---

73 Haward (2003), above n 41. The South East Regional Marine Plan was issued under this original blueprint from the Oceans Policy; see Ashe and Marsden, above n 70, 28.

74 Commonwealth of Australia, above n 33, Volume 2, 7 and 9 (note slightly different wording used on p 9, including the addition of 'where appropriate').

75 An initial review of effectiveness was to be undertaken within the first two years of the policy and thereafter comprehensive reviews at least every five years. (Commonwealth of Australia, above n 33, 31 and 43.)

76 Barbara Musso, Director Planning (South), National Oceans Office Branch, DEH, personal communication, 30 August 2005.

though the designation of the HIMI Marine Reserve'.[77] Although amendments to the environmental protection law gave RMPs statutory force which could mean that an obligation to carry out SEA of such plans is created given the nature of the language used in the Oceans Policy,[78] this is irrelevant if a plan is not prepared for the area.

Under the new Australian planning approach, Marine Bioregional Plans are currently being drafted for Australian waters which are designed to provide new impetus to the implementation of the Oceans Policy as well as to bring the MPAs program within the broader regional marine planning program.[79] These are to be key documents guiding the government, sectoral managers and industry, to ensure that notice is given about activities that may need approval. The plans set out the various statutory obligations such as those relating to recovery planning for threatened species. Despite Australia's other sub-Antarctic island, Macquarie Island (see Figure 8.1) being part of the South East Regional Marine Plan, because jurisdictionally it is part of the state of Tasmania, there is no plan in preparation to include HIMI in any of the marine bioregional plans.

Kriwoken and Holmes highlight the inconsistency between the much greater size of the Macquarie Island Marine Park, with a 200 nautical mile buffer zone compared with the HIMI Marine Reserve with a 13 nautical mile buffer zone, and argue that consideration should be given to extending the boundaries of the World Heritage Areas of both.[80] The issue of buffer zones for World Heritage Areas is supported by UNESCO, which produced an information document on this following an international expert meeting in 2008.[81] Supporting the argument put here, Kriwoken and Holmes comment:

> It might be prudent to investigate a regional marine planning process for HIMI to integrate these two plans and possibly subject the Marine Reserve Management Plan to a SEA process. A regional marine plan could integrate

77 Sandra Potter, Territories and Environment Team, AAD, personal communication, 21 October 2009; confirmed by Ewan McIvor, Senior Environmental Policy Advisor, Territories Environment and Treaties, AAD, personal communication, 26 October 2009.

78 The changes were announced in a media release by the Minister for the Environment and Heritage on 13 October 2005. See http://www.deh.gov.au/minister/env/2005/mr13oct305.html. See also Department of Environment, Water, Heritage and the Arts, *Marine Bioregional Planning*, Fact Sheet (2009).

79 See Matthew Osborne, 'Commonwealth and State Marine Environmental Management' in Rachel Baird and Donald R Rothwell (eds), *Australian Coastal and Marine Law* (The Federation Press, 2011) 89–90; and Donald Rothwell, 'Environmental Integration and Coastal and Marine Law' in Rachel Baird and Donald R Rothwell (eds), *Australian Coastal and Marine Law* (The Federation Press, 2011) 356–363.

80 Above note 42, 163.

81 Oliver Martin and Giovanna Piatti (eds), *World Heritage and Buffer Zones: International Expert Meeting on World Heritage and Buffer Zones*, Davos, Switzerland, 11–14 March 2008 (UNESCO, 2009).

> sectoral commercial fisheries interests and conservation requirements and would be binding on all [Australian] Commonwealth agencies.[82]

Further support for a bioregional plan comes from the Parties to the ATS, and in particular CCAMLR, which has been working towards developing an MPAs system in the Southern Ocean within the ATS/CCAMLR area.[83] A broad scale bioregionalization has been carried out to date and 11 priority areas of interest have been highlighted, one of which is for the Kerguelen Plateau region.[84] Although a work program is yet to be agreed to identify and designate candidate MPAs, which has been strongly advocated by interested groups within the context of the ATS/CCAMLR without delay,[85] the process has a substantial chance of influencing the Australian government to consider a Marine Bioregional Plan under domestic law.

Recommendations and Conclusions

This chapter argues for planning and management to be better coordinated in sub-Antarctic marine and terrestrial areas, and for SEA to be applied more comprehensively if environmental planning and management at HIMI and in the surrounding EEZ are to provide effective protection. Why there is no Kerguelen Regional Marine Plan nor any intention to prepare a Marine Bioregional Plan for this area while Macquarie Island is part of the SE planning processes, why national buffer zones are different for these two sub-Antarctic island groups, why one relevant management plan has been assessed but not another, and why there is no tiered framework for assessment are all key questions that need to be addressed.

---

82 Above note 42, 163.

83 United Kingdom, *Proposed Approach for the Identification of Important Marine Areas for Conservation.* Information Paper submitted by UK, Agenda Item CEP 7(e), Antarctic Treaty Consultative Meeting, Kyiv, Ukraine 2–13 June 2008. As a follow-up to this, the UK plans to undertake further work for a pilot study region in the South Atlantic sector and comments: 'Similar studies by other Members in other regions would contribute to the development of "best practice" guidance for systematic conservation planning, which could then be employed in the selection and designation of areas to conserve marine biodiversity.' (p 5).

84 I am grateful to Ewan McIvor for information on this point; see personal communication, 26 October 2009. See also Report of the Committee for Environmental Protection (2009, 21–24), and in particular paragraph 173 where France in thanking the Antarctic and Southern Oceans Coalition for its paper (2008), notes the progress being made under other international regimes for MPAs and argues that it is time for the ATS to make similar progress in the Southern Ocean.

85 Antarctic and Southern Oceans Coalition, *A System of Comprehensive Marine Protection – Some Policy Considerations.* Paper for XXVI Meeting of CCAMLR, October–November 2007, 2; Antarctic and Southern Oceans Coalition, *Furthering Implementation of Networks of MPAs in Antarctica and the Southern Ocean.* Paper for XXVII Meeting of CCAMLR, Agenda item 7, October 2008, 1.

While the assessment of the HIMI Fishery Management Plan has been largely positive for the fishery in the EEZ as reflected in the second assessment, this does not mean that there have been no effects on the Marine Reserve, as evidenced by the seabird and seal fatalities from among those that transit the islands as well as the Southern Ocean. The absence of an assessment of the Marine Reserve Management Plan is a failure to comprehensively plan and manage the World Heritage Area which includes its surrounding waters. As others have also argued, compartmentalized approaches to PAs should be avoided and ecosystem approaches to MSP taken, which if applied may have concluded that the economic benefits of the fishery are not worth the potential impact on the conservation interests of the MPA and protected species.[86]

Because of the relationship between the fishery and the Marine Reserve, the spatial planning process for the Fisheries Management Plan should have been coordinated with that of the Marine Reserve Management Plan, (which, as part of its current review, which will also extend the boundaries of the Reserve (see Figure 8.3)), and should also be subject to an SEA.[87] Preparation and assessment of an overarching plan (for Kerguelen), or any future revision of Australia's Oceans Policy should also be considered and taken forward in the context of the CCAMLR bio-regionalization process. Preparation and assessment of a prospective Kerguelen Plan can however occur under Australian domestic law, and if so, coordination of regulatory requirements, (domestic and international), is highly recommended.

As a World Heritage Area of special significance for its isolation and inherent difficulties in data collection, precaution should determine all approaches to MSP at HIMI, and the most complete environmental protection arrangements should be secured to attain this. Given the cyclical nature of environmental planning and management, the deficiencies identified in the current planning and management arrangements and recommendations to address them can and should be considered in future legislative, policy and planning reviews. Given political will it is entirely possible for a prospective Kerguelen RMP / Marine Bioregional Plan to deal with these issues, which could later be applied in subsequent revisions of the HIMI Fishery and Reserve Management Plans. The application of SEA to planning processes in a transboundary context, while emerging, has much to recommend it in improving environmental governance in Australia's sub-Antarctic and globally.

---

86 It should be noted that only the second of these is satisfied by a provision in Australia's domestic environmental protection law (the *Environment Protection and Biodiversity Conservation Act* 1999 (Cth)) however, with independent oversight and compliance monitoring required by the fisheries legislation.

87 See above nn 43 and 45.

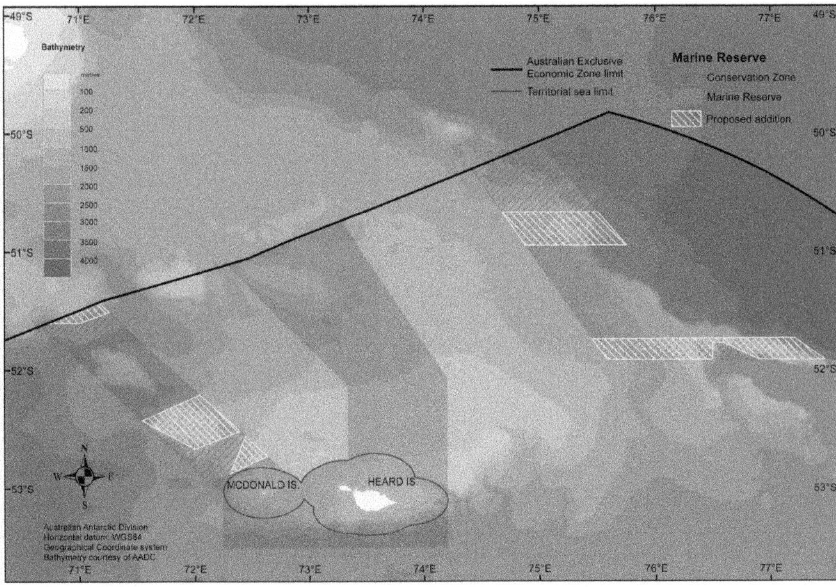

Figure 8.3 Additional Conservation Zone Areas proposed for the Marine Reserve with HIMI indicated in white

Chapter 9
Transboundary Environmental Governance and Emerging Environmental Threats: Geo-engineering in the Marine Environment

Karen N. Scott

Introduction

This chapter will explore the concept of transboundary environmental governance in the context of a new and emerging threat to the marine environment: geo-engineering. Defined as 'the deliberate large-scale manipulation of the planetary environment to counteract anthropogenic climate change',[1] over half of geo-engineering strategies proposed to date are designed to be deployed in, or otherwise significantly impact upon, the marine environment. Despite the fact that geo-engineering technologies are as yet largely confined to the research stage of development, questions have already been raised within national, regional and international fora as to whether and how geo-engineering should be regulated.[2] As with any new activity that poses a risk to the marine environment, the principal governance dilemma is whether that activity can be regulated or controlled through existing regulatory instruments or whether a new regime must be developed. This chapter argues that a recent strategic development in international environmental governance supports the regulation of geo-engineering technologies through existing instruments and institutions and renders the creation of a new regime superfluous. This development comprises the deliberate creation of institutional connections and relationships between treaty regimes, which permit the formation of cooperative arrangements between international environmental institutions designed to more effectively address environmental threats.[3] In short, the central thesis of this chapter is that in responding to geo-engineering as a new threat to the

1 The Royal Society (UK), *Geoengineering the climate: Science, governance and uncertainty* (RS Policy Document 10/09, 2009) at 1 (hereinafter, Royal Society, *Geoengineering the climate*).

2 See the discussion in the section entitled 'Geo-engineering and the Marine Environment' below.

3 This chapter draws on the ideas and work developed in Karen N Scott, 'International Environmental Governance: Managing Fragmentation through Institutional Connection' (2011) 12 *Melbourne Journal of International Law* 177.

marine environment, policy makers should draw from the experiences of certain multilateral environmental agreements (MEAs) and their associated institutions and begin to govern geo-engineering technologies using tools and institutions from across multiple regimes through the development of cooperative networks between those regimes.

This chapter will begin by briefly describing selected geo-engineering technologies designed to be deployed within the marine environment, the potential risk they pose to marine biodiversity and ecosystems and the extent to which they are currently regulated under existing regimes and institutions. It will then turn to the nature of international environmental governance and focus on one aspect of that governance: the creation of institutional linkages and connections between international environmental regimes. In particular, this chapter will identify and briefly explore three levels of institutional linkages and connections: basic cooperative agreements between regime administrations; integrated institutional management; and integrated political management. This section will draw on a number of examples from the field of international environmental law to illustrate the nature and extent of these cooperative and integrated arrangements, and will explore whether these governance strategies might be successfully developed in order to regulate and manage geo-engineering. Finally, this chapter will conclude with a number of observations as to the benefits and risks associated with this approach to international environmental governance both generally and, more particularly, within the context of geo-engineering.

Geo-engineering and the Marine Environment

Once confined to the realms of science fiction, geo-engineering is rapidly entering the category of science fact. The term 'geo-engineering' was coined by Cesare Marchetti in 1977 in connection with what he referred to as the CO_2 problem,[4] but more broadly, geo-engineering can be defined to mean 'the intentional large scale manipulation of the environment'.[5] The history of geo-engineering dates back to at least the 1840s when James Pollard Espy, the first US government meteorologist (and former lawyer) proposed burning vast areas of forest in order to create columns of heated air which, in his opinion, would trigger precipitation.[6] Seeding clouds for the purpose of generating rainfall has been carried out since the late 1940s, and continues to be used today. Cloud seeding has also been used to lessen the intensity of hurricanes, to improve air quality and, less benignly, by the US as

4 C Marchetti, 'On Geo-engineering and the CO_2 Problem' (1977) 1 *Climate Change* 59.

5 J Virgo, 'International Governance of a Possible Geo-engineering Intervention to Combat Climate Change' (2009) 95 *Climate Change* 103.

6 James R Fleming, 'The Climate Engineers' (2007) 31 *The Wilson Quarterly* 46, 51.

so-called 'weather warfare' in Vietnam.[7] In fact, concern that a very real 'weather-warfare race' was developing between the US and the (then) USSR led directly to the negotiation and adoption of the UN Convention on the Prohibition of Military or any other Hostile Use of Environmental Modification Techniques (ENMOD) in 1976.[8] More recently, however, the term geo-engineering has become closely associated with climate change mitigation and this raison d'être – climate change mitigation – is now ubiquitously central to its modern definition.

Although first formally proposed as a means of addressing climate change in 1965 in a policy assessment provided to the US President Lyndon Johnson,[9] until very recently, geo-engineering was regarded as something of a fringe topic. As a climate change mitigation strategy, geo-engineering benefited from only a couple of paragraphs in the entire IPCC's Fourth Assessment Report released in 2007[10] and was not mentioned at all in the *Stern Review Report on the Economics of Climate Change* released by the British government in 2006.[11] David Victor commented in 2009 that the entire 'scientific literature on the subject could be read during the course of a transatlantic flight'.[12] However, more recently geo-engineering technologies and strategies have migrated from marginal to mainstream science and policy making. The first signs of this migration occurred in 2003 with the release of two high profile reports in the US by the Pentagon[13] and the National Research Council.[14] Both reports recommended that further research into geo-engineering as a climate change mitigation measure should be carried out. On the other side of the Atlantic, a report published by the British Royal

---

7 Ibid, 55–56. For an engaging introduction to the history of geo-engineering see David W Keith, 'Geoengineering the Climate: History and Prospect' (2000) 25 *Annu. Rev. Energy Environ.* 245. See also James Rodger Fleming, *Fixing the Sky: The Checkered History of Weather and Climate Control* (Columbia University Press, 2010) and Jeff Goodell, *How to Cool the Planet: Geoengineering and the Audacious Quest to Fix Earth's Climate* (Houghton Mifflin Harcourt, 2010).

8 *Convention on the Prohibition of Military or any other Hostile Use of Environmental Modification Techniques*, opened for signature 10 December 1976, 1108 UNTS 151 (entered into force 5 October 1978).

9 Keith, above n 7, 254.

10 B Metz et al, *Contribution of Working Group III to the Fourth Assessment Report of the Intergovernmental Panel on Climate Change* (Cambridge University Press, 2007) at para. 11.2.2.

11 The full report is available online at: http://webarchive.nationalarchives.gov.uk/+/http://www.hm-treasury.gov.uk/stern_review_report.htm.

12 David G Victor et al, 'The Geoengineering Option: A Last Resort against Global Warming?' (2009) 88 *Foreign Affairs* 64, 73.

13 Peter Schwartz and Doug Randall, *An Abrupt Climate Change Scenario and its Implications for United States National Security* (October 2003) Available online at: http://www.edf.org/documents/3566_AbruptClimateChange.pdf.

14 National Research Council, *Critical Issues in Weather Modification Research* (The National Academies Press, 2003) available online at: http://www.nap.edu/catalog.php?record_id=10829#toc.

Society in 2009 entitled *Geo-engineering the Climate: Science, Governance and Uncertainty*[15] gained worldwide attention. Two Parliamentary Committees have recently published reports on issues associated with geo-engineering in the UK[16] and the US House of Representatives Committee on Science and Technology published a report in 2010 on research needs and strategies for international coordination on climate remediation.[17] At the international level, geo-engineering or, more particularly, one geo-engineering strategy – ocean fertilization – has received attention from the UN General Assembly[18] and is currently under serious consideration by the parties to at least two international instruments: the 1996 Protocol to the 1972 London (Dumping) Convention[19] and the 1992 Convention on Biological Diversity (CBD).[20] This upward trend of interest in geo-engineering as a climate change mitigation measure is likely to increase in the future; the economics of geo-engineering are, as described by Scott Barrett, 'incredible'[21] and thus potentially provide an attractive alternative to emissions reductions as a response to climate change. Acknowledging this, the Fifth Assessment Report due

15 Royal Society, above n 1. For commentary on the Report see Geoff Brumfiel, 'Climate Control Plans Scrutinized' (September 2009) 461 *Nature* 19; John A Glaser, 'Climate geo-engineering' (2010) 12 *Clean Technologies and Environmental Policy* 91.

16 House of Commons, Innovation, Universities, Science and Skills Committee, *Engineering: turning ideas into reality: Government Response to the Committee's Fourth Report* (Fifth Special Report of Session 2008–2009) (June 2009) available online at: http://www.publications.parliament.uk/pa/cm200809/cmselect/cmdius/759/759.pdf; House of Commons Science and Technology Committee, *The Regulation of Geoengineering* (Fifth Report of Session 2009–2010) (March 2010) available online at: http://www.publications.parliament.uk/pa/cm200910/cmselect/cmsctech/221/221.pdf.

17 Chairman Bart Gordon, Committee on Science and Technology, US House of Representatives, *Engineering the Climate: Research Needs and Strategies for International Coordination Report* (111 Congress, Second Session, October 2010. See also Kelsi Bracmort, Richard K Lattanzio and Emily Barbour, *Geoengineering: Governance and Technology Policy* (Congressional Research Service Report for Congress, R41371, 2010).

18 See for example, UNGA Resolution 62/215 *Oceans and the Law of the Sea* (2007) (para. 98) and UNGA Resolution 64/17 *Oceans and the Law of the Sea* (2009) (paras. 132 and 133). See also the 2009 *Report of the Secretary General on the Law of the Sea* (A/65/69, 2009) at para. 86.

19 *1996 Protocol to the Convention on the Prevention of Marine Pollution by Dumping of Wastes and Other Matter of 29 December 1972*, opened for signature 7 November 1996, [2006] ATS 11 (entered into force 24 March 2006).

20 *Convention on Biological Diversity*, opened for signature 5 June 1996, 1760 UNTS 79 (entered into force 29 December 1993).

21 Scott Barrett, 'The Incredible Economics of Geo-engineering' (2008) 39 *Environ. Resource Econ.* 45, 49. Nevertheless, it should be noted that few proposals have been demonstrated or costed. For one attempt to estimate the costs of geo-engineering see J Eric Bickel and Lee Lane, 'Climate Engineering' in Bjørn Lomborg, *Smart Solutions to Climate Change. Comparing Costs and Benefits* (Cambridge University Press: 2010) 9–51 and Roger A Pielke, Jr, 'Climate Engineering: Alternative Perspective' in Bjørn Lomborg, ibid, 52–61.

to be published by the IPCC in 2014 will include, for the first time, a chapter on geo-engineering in the context of climate change mitigation.

Geo-engineering for climate change mitigation purposes[22] is designed to either: manipulate the Earth's solar radiation budget through enhancing its albedo (or reflectivity) by, for example, injecting sulphur or other reflective particles into the atmosphere[23] or placing sunshades or strategically positioned mirrors in outer space;[24] or to alter the balance of carbon dioxide between the atmosphere and ocean or terrestrial carbon sinks.[25] Although a small number of – largely speculative – proposals have been developed to enhance the Earth's albedo using ocean-based technologies, such as marine cloud brightening[26] or the creation of reflective microbubbles in the sea,[27] most marine geo-engineering technologies are designed to draw down carbon dioxide from the atmosphere into the oceans. The oceans comprise a natural sink for carbon dioxide and hold about 38,000 gigatonnes of carbon dioxide, representing 55 times the amount of carbon dioxide present in

---

22 For an excellent overview of geo-engineering strategies and technologies see Naomi E Vaughan and Timothy M Lenton, 'A Review of Climate Geoengineering Proposals' (2011) 109 *Climatic Change* 745.

23 Paul J Crutzen, 'Albedo Enhancement by Stratospheric Sulfur Injections: A Contribution to Resolve a Policy Dilemma?' (2006) 77 *Climatic Change* 211; Robert E Dickinson, 'Climate Engineering: A Review of Aerosol Approaches to Changing the Global Energy Balance' (1996) 33 *Climatic Research* 279; Alan Robock et al, 'Regional Climate Responses to Geoengineering with Tropical and Arctic SO_2 Injections' (2008) 113 *Journal of Geophysical Research* D16101. See also G Bala et al, 'Impact of Geoengineering Schemes on the Global Hydrological Cycle' (June 3 2008) 105 *PNAS* 7664; B Govindasamy et al, 'Impact of Geoenginnering Schemes on the Terrestrial Biosphere' (2002) 29 *Geophysical Research Letters* No. 22, 20, doi:10.1029/2002GL015911.

24 CR McInnes, 'Space-based Geoengineering: Challenges and Requirements' (2010) 224 *Proc. IMechE Vol. 224 Part C: J. Mechanical Engineering Science* 571. See also Takanobu Kosugi, 'Role of Sunshades in Space as a Climate Control Option' (2010) 67 *Acta Astronautica* 241 and DJ Lunt et al, '"Sunshade World": A Fully Coupled CGM Evaluation of the Climatic Impacts of Geoengineering' (2008) 35 *Geophysical Research Letters* L12710.

25 See for example, Leonard Ornstein, Igor Aleinov and David Rind, 'Irrigated Afforestation of the Sahara and Australian Outback to End Global Warming' (2009) 97 *Climatic Change* 409; KS Lackner, 'Capture of Carbon Dioxide from Ambient Air' (2009) 176 *The European Physical Journal, Special Topics* 93; John H Martin, 'Glacial-Interglacial CO_2 Change: The Iron Hypothesis' (1990) 5 *Paleoceanography* 1; V Smetacek and SWA Naqvi, 'The Next Generation of Iron Fertilization Experiments in the Southern Ocean' (2008) 366 *Phil. Trans. R. Soc. A.* 3947; S Zhou and P Flynn, 'Geoengineering Downwelling Ocean Currents: A Cost Assessment' (2005) 71 *Climatic Change* 203.

26 See John Latham et al, 'Global Temperature Stabilization via Controlled Albedo Enhancement of Low-level Maritime Clouds' (2008) 366 *Phil. Trans. R. Soc. A* 3969 and Stephen Slater, Graham Sortino and John Latham, 'Sea-going Hardware for the Cloud Albedo Method of Reversing Global Warming' (2008) 366 *Phil. Trans. R. Soc. A* 3989.

27 Russell Seitz, 'Bright Water: Hydrosols, Water Conservation and Climate Change' (2011) 105 *Climatic Change* 365.

the atmosphere and 20 times the carbon dioxide contained in the biosphere and soils.[28] Carbon dioxide is transferred from the surface of the ocean to deep water by means of the biological and solubility pumps and ocean circulation.[29] Scientists and, increasingly, engineers have postulated that if either or both of these pumps could be enhanced, in order to draw down greater quantities of carbon dioxide, this would operate as an effective climate change mitigation measure. There are nevertheless significant risks associated with increasing the level of carbon dioxide in the oceans including increased ocean acidity,[30] diminished phytoplankton productivity and damage to ecosystems.[31]

The technologies and strategies of marine based geo-engineering proposed to date include: the use of vertical ocean pipes to pump deep water to the surface in order to increase the supply to nutrients at the surface with a view to enhancing the biological pump;[32] crop residue oceanic permanent sequestration – the disposal of baled crop residues in the deep ocean;[33] so-called weathering techniques which seek to increase the alkalinity of the oceans in order to reduce acidification and enhance the solubility pump;[34] modification and enhancement of sea-ice designed to enhance down-welling ocean currents;[35] and the building of strategic dams in order to isolate key bodies of water such as the Arctic Ocean or the Mediterranean.[36] The marine geo-engineering method which has thus far received the greatest scientific and, consequently, regulatory attention, seeks to enhance the ocean's

28 CBD, *Scientific Synthesis of the Impacts of Ocean Fertilization on Marine Biodiversity* (CBD Technical Series No. 45) (2009) 11.

29 Ibid.

30 H Damon Matthews et al, 'Sensitivity of Ocean Acidification to Geoengineered Climate Stabilization' (2009) 36 *Geophysical Research Letters* L10706 doi: 10.1029/2009/GL037488.

31 Tom Garrison, *Essentials of Oceanography* (5th edition) (Brooks/Cole Cengage Learning, 2009) 379.

32 See J Lovelock and C Rapley, 'Ocean Pipes Could Help the Earth to Cure Itself' (27 September 2007) 449 *Nature* 403; A Yool et al, 'Low Efficiency of Nutrient Translocation for Enhancing Oceanic Uptake of Carbon Dioxide' (2009) 114 *Journal of Geophysical Research* 114.

33 S Strand and G Benford, 'Ocean Sequestration of Crop Residue Carbon: Recycling Fossil Fuel Carbon Back to Deep Sediments' (2009) 43 *Environ. Sci. Technol.* 1001.

34 L Harvey, 'Mitigating the Atmospheric CO_2 Increase and Ocean Acidification by Adding Limestone Powder to Upwelling Regions' (2008) 113 *Journal of Geophysical Research* 113; K House et al, 'Electrochemical Acceleration of Chemical Weathering as an Energetically Feasible Approach to Mitigating Anthropogenic Climate Change' (2007) 41 *Environ. Sci. Technol.* 8464; H Kheshgi, 'Sequestering Atmospheric Carbon Dioxide by Increasing Ocean Alkalinity' (1995) 20 *Energy – The International Journal* 915.

35 Zhou and Flynn, above n 25, 203.

36 See for example R Shutterhelm, *Diomede Crossroads: Saving the North Pole? Thoughts on Plausibility* available online at: http://www.cleverclimate.org/art/uploads/Diomede_Crossroads(1).pdf.

biological pump, through the utilization of so-called fertilization techniques.[37] This strategy exploits the fact that particular regions, most notably the Southern Ocean and the Equatorial Pacific, are relatively unproductive in biological terms. Within these regions biological production is limited by the low availability of one or more nutrients such as iron, nitrogen or phosphate. Theoretically, if the missing nutrient such as iron is added to the ocean this will facilitate an increase in the biological productivity in the region and, as a consequence, enhance the draw-down of carbon dioxide into the deep ocean. As John Martin memorably stated in 1990: '[g]ive me half a tanker of iron and I will give you an ice-age'.[38] More than a dozen iron fertilization experiments have been carried out over the last decade mostly in the Southern Ocean.[39] The results of this research are inconclusive. For example, it is not clear how large the fertilized area needs to be in order to draw down a meaningful quantity of carbon dioxide[40] and it is uncertain as to how long the sequestration of carbon dioxide lasts for, compromising its potential effectiveness as a climate change mitigation measure.[41] Moreover, this deliberate attempt to modify an ecosystem may well have negative impacts on the existing food chain of that ecosystem,[42] could potentially induce the growth of toxic algae[43] or cause the suffocation of that ecosystem or it could even make climate change worse by initiating the release of large quantities of methane and nitrous oxide from the ocean.[44]

The Regulatory Regime for Marine Based Geo-engineering

Whilst no regime specifically regulates geo-engineering and there are few legal obligations developed with the particular purpose of constraining these

---

37 See generally, A Strong et al, 'Ocean Fertilization: Science, Policy and Commerce' (2009) 22 *Oceanography* 236; Theme Section – 'Implications of Large-scale Iron Fertilization of the Oceans' (2008) 364 *Marine Ecology Progress Series* 213.

38 Martin, above n 25, 10.

39 CBD, *Scientific Synthesis of the Impacts of Ocean Fertilization on Marine Biodiversity* (CBD Technical Series No. 45) (2009) at 24.

40 K Buesseler et al, 'The Effects of Iron Fertilization on Carbon Sequestration in the Southern Ocean' (2004) 304 *Science* 417.

41 S Blain, 'Effect of Natural Iron Fertilization on Carbon Sequestration in the Southern Ocean' (2007) 446 *Nature* 1070; P Boyd et al, 'A Mesocale Phytoplankton Bloom in the Polar Southern Ocean Stimulated by Iron Fertilization' (2000) 407 *Nature* 695; K Caldeira and P Duffy, 'The Role of the Southern Ocean in Uptake and Storage of Anthropogenic Carbon Dioxide' (2000) 287 *Science* 620.

42 A Strong, 'Ocean Fertilization: Time to Move On' (2009) 461 *Nature* 347.

43 Q Schiermeier, 'The Oresmen' (2003) 421 *Nature* 109, 110.

44 J Furhman and D Capone, 'Possible Biogeochemical Consequences of Ocean Fertilization' (1991) 36 *Limnology & Oceanography* 1951; M Lawrence, 'Side-effects of Ocean Iron Fertilization' (2002) 297 *Science* 1993.

technologies, marine based geo-engineering activities do not take place in a legal vacuum.[45]

The 1982 United Nations Convention on the Law of the Sea (UNCLOS)[46] establishes a basic set of rights and obligations which undoubtedly provide at least the bones of the framework for any governance regime. States are entitled to exercise the freedoms of the seas on the high seas subject to the interests of other users, the provisions of UNCLOS and other, notably environmental, obligations. Marine scientific research – including research relating to geo-engineering – is classified as a high seas freedom[47] and, since geo-engineering is not currently prohibited, it may be argued that geo-engineering itself constitutes a freedom of the high seas.[48] Nevertheless, the obligation to have due regard to the interests of other users[49] may limit the deployment of geo-engineering technologies where they, for example, involve placing objects into the sea such as pipes which hinder navigation or where fertilization activities have a negative impact on fish stocks or other biological resources. Similarly, whilst coastal states undoubtedly have exclusive jurisdiction in connection with both scientific research in the territorial sea and exclusive economic zones and, arguably, the exploitation of these waters for marine geo-engineering purposes,[50] they too must exercise their jurisdiction with due regard to the rights of other states including the navigational rights of foreign flag vessels.[51]

Moreover, marine scientific research must be carried out in accordance with Parts XII and XIII of UNCLOS and, in particular, with the principles set out in Article 240 of the Convention. Specifically, states must comply with principles related to the publication and dissemination of information connected to proposed major projects and the promotion of transfer of data, information and knowledge

45 See Daniel Bodansky, 'May We Engineer the Climate?' (1996) 33 *Climate Change* 301; W Davis, 'What Does Green Mean? Anthropogenic Climate Change, Geoengineering and International Law' (2009) 43 *Georgia Law Review* 901; J Michaelson, 'Geoengineering: A Climate Change Manhatten Project' (1988) 17 *Stanford Environmental Law Journal* 73; Philomene Verlaan, 'Geo-engineering, the Law of the Sea, and Climate Change' (2009) 4 *Carbon and Climate Law Review* 446; David G Victor, 'On the Regulation of Geo-engineering' (2008) 24 *Oxford Review of Economic Policy* 322; D Victor et al, above n 12; J Virgo, 'International Governance of a Possible Geoengineering Intervention to Combat Climate Change' (2009) 95 *Climate Change* 103.

46 *United Nations Convention on the Law of the Sea*, opened for signature 10 December 1982, 1833 UNTS 396 (entered into force 16 November 1994) ('UNCLOS').

47 *1982 UNCLOS*, Article 87(1)(f).

48 This is based on the prevailing view that unless an activity is specifically excluded by a rule of international law then it should be regarded as a high seas freedom. See RR Churchill and AV Lowe, *The Law of the Sea* (3rd edition) (Manchester, 1999) 206.

49 *1982 UNCLOS*, Article 87(2).

50 *1982 UNCLOS*, Article 56(1).

51 *1982 UNCLOS*, Article 56(2).

to developing states,[52] ensure that geo-engineering activities undertaken in the Area[53] are for the benefit of mankind[54] and, most importantly, comply with the environmental safeguards as set out in Part XII of UNCLOS and developed further under international law. Article 194 of the Convention requires states to take all measures to prevent, reduce and control pollution of the marine environment from *any* source. More specifically – and of particular relevance to geo-engineering – Article 196 of UNCLOS requires parties to 'take all measures necessary to prevent, reduce and control pollution of the marine environment resulting from the use of technologies under their jurisdiction or control'. 'Pollution of the marine environment' is defined in Article 1(4) of UNCLOS as:

> the introduction by man, directly or indirectly, of substances or energy into the marine environment, including estuaries, which results or is likely to result in such deleterious effects as harm to living resources and marine life, hazards to human health, hindrance to marine activities, including fishing and other legitimate uses of the sea, impairment of quality for use of sea water and reduction of amenities.

However, although certain geo-engineering technologies – such as iron fertilization – might be characterized as polluting, or at least creating a risk of pollution as defined by UNCLOS, others may not. The placement of pipes in the ocean designed to transfer nutrients from its depths to its surface, for example, would not appear to constitute 'pollution' in the sense of Article 1(4). Nevertheless, Article 192 of UNCLOS establishes a more general obligation to protect and preserve the marine environment, and this is supported by Article 194(5), which requires states to take measures to protect rare and vulnerable ecosystems and habitats. Furthermore, Part XII of UNCLOS establishes a number of obligations associated with environmental impact assessment, monitoring, contingency planning and notification in the event of an environmental emergency,[55] all of which are applicable to geo-engineering related activities.

These provisions under UNCLOS are supported and, in many cases, strengthened by obligations under numerous other environmental instruments aimed at the prevention of climate change or the protection of species, habitats, ecosystems and biodiversity. Examples include, but are not limited to, the 1992 United Nations Framework Convention on Climate Change (UNFCCC),[56] the

52 *1982 UNCLOS*, Article 245.

53 The Area is defined as 'the seabed and ocean floor and subsoil thereof, beyond the limits of national jurisdiction' (*1982 UNCLOS*, Article 1(1)(1)) and is subject to the regime established under Part XI of *UNCLOS* and the Part XI Implementation Agreement.

54 *1982 UNCLOS*, Article 140.

55 *1982 UNCLOS*, Articles 198, 199, 204 and 206.

56 *United Nations Framework Convention on Climate Change*, opened for signature 4 June 1992, 1771 UNTS 107 (entered into force 21 March 1994) ('*UNFCCC*').

1992 CBD and the 1979 Migratory Species Convention.[57] The CBD has, in fact, directly addressed the issue of geo-engineering and, in Decision 10/33 adopted at the tenth Conference of the Parties in 2010, called upon parties to:[58]

> Ensure, in line and consistent with decision IX/16 C, on ocean fertilization and biodiversity and climate change, in the absence of science based, global and transparent and effective control and regulatory mechanisms for geo-engineering, and in accordance with the precautionary approach and Article 14 of the Convention, that no climate-related geo-engineering activities that may affect biodiversity take place, until there is an adequate scientific basis on which to justify such activities and appropriate consideration of the associated risks for the environment and biodiversity and associated social, economic and cultural impacts, with the exception of small scale scientific research studies that would be conducted in a controlled setting in accordance with Article 3 of the Convention, and only if they are justified by the need to gather specific scientific data and are subject to a thorough prior assessment of the potential impacts on the environment.

Although not legally binding, this decision effectively creates a moral moratorium on geo-engineering outside of small-scale scientific research. This approach has received recent support from the European Parliament, which expressed its opposition to 'proposals for large scale geo-engineering' in a 2011 resolution setting out the EU common position ahead of the United Nations Conference on Sustainable Development (Rio+20).[59]

It is also worth noting that a number of general principles of international law, including the no-harm duty, the precautionary approach, environmental impact assessment and state responsibility, also comprise important components of the current regulatory framework for geo-engineering. In light of the risks associated with geo-engineering, the precautionary principle is of particular significance. No longer confined to individual treaty regimes, the precautionary principle now merits recognition as a principle of customary international law. Support for this status can be found in the decision of the International Court of Justice (ICJ) in the 2010 *Pulp Mills on the River Uruguay* Case, where the Court concluded that the precautionary approach may be relevant in the interpretation of the statute in

---

57 *Convention on the Conservation of Migratory Species of Wild Animals*, opened for signature 23 June 1979, 1651 UNTS 333 (entered into force 1 November 1983).

58 *Convention on Biological Diversity*, Decision X/33 *Biodiversity and Climate Change* (2010), para. 8(w).

59 *European Parliament resolution of 29 September 2011 on developing a common EU position ahead of the United Nations Conference on Sustainable Development (Rio+20)*, P7_TA-PROV(2011)0430, B7-0522/2011 at para. 90.

a dispute between Argentina and Uruguay.[60] Arguably, the ICJ acknowledged the status of the precautionary approach through its implicit reference to Article 31(3)(c) of the 1969 Vienna Convention on the Law of Treaties.[61] This interpretation has recently been confirmed by the Seabed Disputes Chamber of the International Tribunal for the Law of the Sea (ITLOS) in its 2011 advisory opinion on the *Responsibilities of States Sponsoring Persons and Activities in the Area*, which also confirmed the trend towards recognizing the precautionary approach as a principle of customary international law:[62]

> The Chamber observes that the precautionary approach has been incorporated into a growing number of international treaties and other instruments, many of which reflect the formulation of Principle 15 of the Rio Declaration. In the view of the Chamber, this has initiated a trend towards making this approach part of customary international law. This trend is clearly reinforced by the inclusion of the precautionary approach in the Regulations and in the 'standard clause' contained in Annex 4, section 5.1 of the Sulphides Regulations. So does the following statement in paragraph 164 of the ICJ judgment in *Pulp Mills on the River Uruguay* that 'a precautionary approach may be relevant in the interpretation and application of the provisions of the Statute' (ie the environmental bilateral treaty whose interpretation was the main bone of contention between the parties). This statement may be read in light of article 31(3)(c) of the Vienna Convention, according to which the interpretation of a treaty should take into account not only the context but 'any relevant rules of international law applicable in the relations between the parties'.

Similarly, the obligation to conduct an environmental impact assessment of activities with the potential for significant and harmful changes to the marine environment was also endorsed as a principle of general international law to be applied in both a transboundary and a commons context by the ICJ[63] and the ITLOS Seabed Disputes Chamber respectively.[64] Far from operating within a legal vacuum, marine-related geo-engineering is consequently governed by a complex set of treaty provisions and general principles from the early stages of research and development to the deployment and operation of specific technologies. These

---

60 *Case Concerning Pulp Mills on the River Uruguay* (Argentina v. Uruguay) (2010), para. 164.

61 *Vienna Convention on the Law of Treaties*, opened for signature 22 May 1969, 1155 UNTS 331 (entered into force 17 January 1980). Article 31(3)(c) permits parties to take into consideration 'any relevant rules of international law applicable in the relations between the parties' in the interpretation of treaties.

62 *Responsibilities and Obligations of States Sponsoring Persons and Entities with Respect to Activities in the Area*, Advisory Opinion No. 17, Seabed Disputes Chamber of the International Tribunal for the Law of the Sea (2011), para. 135 ('*Advisory Opinion No. 17*').

63 *Case Concerning Pulp Mills on the River Uruguay*, para. 204.

64 *Advisory Opinion No. 17*, paras. 145 and 148.

provisions and principles are, in all but one case, nevertheless general in nature, and have not been developed with geo-engineering in mind.

A limited exception to the general nature of geo-engineering governance is found in the evolving management programme for legitimate and small scale experiments on ocean fertilization in the process of being developed by the IMO under the auspices of the 1996 Protocol to the 1972 London Dumping Convention. The parties to the 1996 Protocol issued a statement of concern in respect of iron fertilization of the oceans in 2007[65] and, in 2008, adopted a resolution affirming that the scope of the Convention and the Protocol includes ocean fertilization activities.[66] The parties agreed that in order to provide for legitimate scientific research, those research activities should be regarded as placement for a purpose other than the mere disposal thereof under Article III.1(b)(ii) of the Convention and Article 1.4.2.2 of the Protocol.[67] A twin-track process was subsequently initiated under the Protocol whereby the parties agreed to develop a risk assessment framework designed to guide decision makers authorizing (or otherwise) ocean fertilization experiments and to identify a series of options for formal or informal regulation of ocean fertilization.[68] The Risk Assessment Framework was adopted in 2010 and applies to scientific research involving ocean fertilization only.[69] Pursuant to the Framework, parties must carry out an initial assessment in order to determine whether the activity proposed constitutes an ocean fertilization experiment. Parties must then undertake a full environmental assessment of the activity, including consideration of the site of the proposed experiment, the likely environmental impact of the experiment and the risks (both known and unknown) associated with it. Where experiments are authorized, the Framework requires parties to put in place procedures to permit monitoring and, where appropriate, facilitate adaptive management in respect of the experiment. Significantly, the Framework requires parties to act with caution, and stipulates that where adverse effects are predicted, projects should be abandoned.[70] The Framework is a model of precautionary and adaptive management although it remains to be seen how it is implemented by parties in respect of individual proposed activities.

The process of developing a regulatory regime for ocean fertilization has thus far proven more taxing and has yet to be completed. Led by Canada, an Intersessional Working Group was established in order to explore regulatory

---

65 *Statement of concern regarding iron fertilization of the oceans to sequester CO_2* (13 July 2007), LC-LP.1/Circ.14.

66 *Resolution LC-LP.1 (2008) on the Regulation of Ocean Fertilization* (adopted on 31 October 2008), para. 1.

67 Ibid, para. 3.

68 See the *Report of the Thirtieth Consultative Meeting and the Third Meeting of the Contracting Parties*, 27–31 October 2008 (LC30/16, 16 December 2008) at paras. 4.1–4.18.

69 *Resolution LC.LP.2 (2010) on the Assessment Framework for Scientific Research Involving Ocean Fertilization* (adopted on 14 October 2010).

70 Ibid.

options[71] and, by the end of 2011, four options appear to remain on the table: an amendment to the 1996 Protocol adding one additional annex for the purpose of regulating ocean fertilization; an amendment to the 1996 Protocol adding two additional annexes, separating out the principles permitting or prohibiting ocean fertilization from the Risk Assessment Framework, the latter being located in the second annex; the adoption of an interpretive resolution, which may or may not be binding; and the implementation of and gathering experience from the Risk Assessment Framework without the adoption of further regulatory steps.[72] Whilst a number of delegations declared themselves in favour of options one or two[73] and the US indicated that it endorsed option four,[74] no consensus was achieved at the 2011 meeting of the parties. Nevertheless, the terms of reference of the Intersessional Working Group on Ocean Fertilization were revived and revised and the question of regulation will be revisited in 2012.[75] What this process does demonstrate is that the task of devising a complex assessment framework would appear to be significantly less challenging than deciding on the mechanism of regulating geo-engineering.

Governance Challenges and Marine Based Geo-engineering

As might be anticipated there are a wide range of governance challenges associated with geo-engineering. To begin with, geo-engineering technologies and strategies have been described by the IPCC in their Fourth Assessment report as largely 'speculative' and 'unproven'.[76] Moreover, the risks associated with these technologies are essentially unknown and potentially significant. In short, this potential cure for global warming could be worse than the disease.

In light of these unknowns the question arises as to how the risks associated with geo-engineering can be managed without stifling or inhibiting research altogether. What role should the precautionary approach play in the governance of geo-engineering? Concern over stifling research and innovation led the British House of Commons Science and Technology Committee in their 2010 report on *The*

---

71 See the *Report of the 3rd Meeting of the Intersessional Working Group on Ocean Fertilization* (20 June 2011), LC33/4 submitted to the Thirty-Third Consultative Meeting of Contracting Parties to the London Convention and Sixth Meeting of Contracting Parties to the London Protocol, 17–21 October 2011.

72 See the *Report of the Thirty-third Consultative Meeting of Contracting Parties to the London Convention & Sixth Meeting of Parties to the London Protocol*, 17–21 October 2011, LC33/15 (8 November 2011), para. 4.3.

73 Ibid, para. 4.11.

74 Ibid.

75 Ibid, para. 4.13.

76 B Metz et al, *Contribution of Working Group III to the Fourth Assessment Report of the Intergovernmental Panel on Climate Change* (Cambridge University Press, 2007), para 11.2.2.

Regulation of Geo-engineering to deliberately exclude the precautionary principle from their proposed list of governance principles,[77] but the emphatic endorsement of the principle in the Risk Assessment Framework for ocean fertilization noted above suggests that the principle is likely to prove not only relevant but central to international regulation of geo-engineering.

The third challenge arises from the fact that certain geo-engineering technologies are relatively inexpensive[78] and the decision to deploy these technologies could potentially be undertaken unilaterally by individual states, corporations or even wealthy individuals.[79] Private corporations are already engaged in ocean fertilization activities: the most well known is the US-based Climos corporation,[80] but the Ocean Nourishment Corporation has recently conducted urea fertilization experiments in the Sulu Sea[81] and Atmocean – also a US venture – has undertaken experiments with the use of wave driven pumps to transfer nutrient rich deep water to the surface.[82] Who gets to decide if and how we should engineer our planet?

The fourth challenge focuses on how geo-engineering relates to other climate change mitigation strategies including emissions reductions. Although even proponents of geo-engineering argue that these technologies do not represent a silver bullet and should form part of a wider portfolio of climate change mitigation strategies, geo-engineering risks being viewed by some as an *alternative* to emissions reductions; essentially as a get-out-of-jail-free card. The reluctance of states to commit to significant reductions in emissions was demonstrated in Copenhagen in 2009 and not entirely ameliorated by the qualified success of the climate change negotiations in Durban in 2011. The so-called moral hazard argument against geo-engineering is self evident: if states or indeed individuals view these technologies as providing a quick fix for global warming they will feel no imperative to make the necessary lifestyle changes that are inevitably necessary in order to address climate change in the longer term.

---

77 House of Commons, Science and Technology Committee, *The Regulation of Geo-engineering* (5th Report of Session 2009–10) (UK)) at para. 86.

78 See further Barrett, above n 21.

79 For example, Bill Gates has apparently contributed US$4.5 million to geo-engineering research over the last three years. See Clive Hamilton, *The Return of Dr Strangelove: The Politics of Climate Engineering as a Response to Global Warming* (June 2010) available online at: http://www.clivehamilton.net.au/cms/media/documents/articles/dr_strangeloves_return.pdf.

80 In 2009 Climos announced plans to fertilize 40,000 square km of the Southern Ocean with iron for the sale of carbon offset credits. See Strong, above n 42, 348. These plans are on hold for the time being.

81 J Mayo-Ramsay, 'Environmental, Legal and Social Implications of Ocean Urea Fertilization; Sulu Sea Example' (2010) 34 *Marine Policy* 831. Further trials by the Ocean Nourishment Corporation have also been put on hold.

82 R Warner, 'Preserving a Balanced Ocean: Regulating Climate Change Mitigation Activities in Marine Areas beyond National Jurisdiction' (2007) 14 *Australian International Law Journal* 99, 104.

The final governance challenge is connected to the relationships between international regimes and institutions in respect of their response to geo-engineering. For example, although the IMO through the 1996 Protocol to the London Convention is undoubtedly leading the international regulatory response to ocean fertilization for scientific purposes, the parties to the 1992 CBD have also contributed to the debate over governance. Taking a more cautious approach to ocean fertilization proposals, the CBD adopted Decision IX/16 in 2008 whereby they called upon parties 'in accordance with the precautionary approach, to ensure that ocean fertilization activities do not take place until there is an adequate scientific basis on which to justify such activities, including assessing associated risks, and a global, transparent and effective control and regulatory mechanism is in place for these activities'.[83] Notably, the parties to the 1996 Protocol have yet to determine whether a distinct regulatory mechanism will be developed in respect of ocean fertilization activities. Without a recognized forum within which geo-engineering can be addressed it is likely that other institutions and regimes will also begin to debate and ultimately respond to geo-engineering proposals. This probability represents a challenge to geo-engineering governance; the development of competing and potentially conflicting international standards would undoubtedly create confusion and potentially undermine all of the institutions and regimes involved with respect to geo-engineering. However, the involvement of multiple regimes and institutions in developing geo-engineering governance also represents a significant opportunity, and it is this regulatory opportunity that will be explored in the remainder of this chapter.

Environmental Governance and Institutional Interaction: A Typology

With over 500 global and regional MEAs in force today international environmental law is correctly characterized as fragmented. Whilst the concept of fragmentation is neither inherently positive nor negative, the question of how to manage multiple and fragmented environmental regimes has come to dominate the various environmental governance reform processes that have been initiated by the United Nations over the last decade.[84] Equally dominant is the common response to this question: the creation and strengthening of linkages and institutional connections between MEAs and other environmental regimes.[85] Moreover, the conceptualization of linkage and connection as a significant environmental governance strategy has

83 *Decision IX/16 Biodiversity and Climate Change* (adopted on 9 October 2008), para. C.4.

84 At least four major environmental governance reform processes have been initiated by the United Nations over the last decade in addition to several MEA initiated processes. See Scott, above n 3, 182–184.

85 Ibid.

also been developed by a number of academic commentators, most notably by Oran Young, Thomas Gehring and Sebastian Oberthür.[86]

Institutional interaction or linkage, as it is commonly referred to in international relations literature, operates on a number of different levels: arising as a mere consequence of ecological, sociological or functional interdependence or as a deliberate governance strategy.[87] Ultimately all international legal regimes and institutions are linked or 'embedded', to use the terminology developed by Oran Young,[88] by the fact that they all operate within the realm of public international law. The parameters of interaction between these regimes are necessarily facilitated and limited by international law, including the rules relating to treaties, international organizations and state responsibility. Where the subject matter of regimes overlaps or intersects in functional terms, linkages are created but this may not necessarily lead to deliberate interaction between those regimes.[89] The linkage between the 1992 UNFCCC and the 1982 UNCLOS with respect to geo-engineering might be described as functional or overlapping at this stage. Similarly, 'behavioural' linkage or 'interaction through commitment' – terms developed by Thomas Gehring and Sebastian Oberthür[90] – describe the relationship between treaty regimes where obligations undertaken in respect of one instrument impact on the commitments incurred under the auspices of a separate regime. In the context of geo-engineering, climate change mitigation measures undertaken pursuant to commitments under the climate change regime may impact positively or negatively on obligations to protect marine biodiversity and vulnerable ecosystems under the 1982 UNCLOS or the 1992 CBD. Whilst these categories of linkage arise naturally as a result of overlaps in function or the common use of legal tools to promote treaty objectives, other forms of interaction may be intentionally pursued as a deliberate governance strategy. Cognitive interaction, for example, occurs when information or ideas

86 See in particular, Oran R Young, 'Institutional Linkages in International Society: Polar Perspectives' (1996) 2 *Global Governance* 1; Thomas Gehring and Sebastian Oberthür, 'Interplay: Exploring Institutional Interaction' in Oran Young, Leslie A King and Heike Schroeder (eds), *Institutions and Environmental Change: Principal Finds, Applications and Research Frontiers* (MIT Press, 2008) 187; Sebastian Oberthür and Thomas Gehring, 'Conceptual Foundations of Institutional Interaction' in Sebastian Oberthür and Thomas Gehring (eds), *Institutional Interaction in Global Environmental Governance: Synergy and Conflict among International and EU Policies* (MIT Press, 2006) 19; Sebastian Oberthür, 'Interplay Management: Enhancing Environmental Policy Integration among International Institutions' (2009) 9 *International Environmental Agreements: Politics, Law and Economics* 371; Oran Young, 'Institutions and the Growth of Knowledge: Evidence from International Environmental Regimes' (2004) 4 *International Environmental Agreements: Politics, Law and Economics* 215.

87 Scott, above n 3, 184.

88 Young (1996), above n 86, 8.

89 This level of linkage is described as 'functional' by Thomas Gehring and Sebastian Oberthür, above n 86, 197 and 'overlapping' in Young (1996) above n 86, 8.

90 Gehring and Oberthür, above n 86, 204 and Oberthür and Gehring, above n 86, 35.

generated by one institution or regime are used or developed by another regime;[91] essentially, when regimes 'learn from one another'.[92] A deeper level of interaction is achieved where regimes actively choose to coordinate their activities through the development of joint work programmes or the creation of joint rules or institutions. Referred to as 'clustering'[93] or 'joint interplay management',[94] this form of interaction characterizes the North-East Atlantic environmental protection regime,[95] and is in the process of being developed within the areas of wildlife, fisheries and pollution prevention and control governance.[96] The final and most extensive example of interaction or linkage occurs where regimes are formally connected or 'nested' to use the term developed by Oran Young.[97] The Antarctic Treaty system is an example of a nested regime.

To date, few if any examples of deliberate linkage or institutional interaction can be found between international regimes and institutions within the context of geo-engineering. Nevertheless, the creation of formal linkages and interaction between interested regimes and institutions provides one mechanism through which the governance of geo-engineering could be initiated in the absence of a designated treaty regime that applies to these technologies. A survey of the extent of cooperation between MEAs and other international environmental institutions reveals three basic levels of interaction although it should be noted that these categories are not mutually exclusive. At the first level of interaction, MEAs enter into basic cooperative agreements with one another that are primarily focused on sharing information and permitting mutual representation at meetings and other events. The second level of cooperation requires a deeper level of interaction and enables regimes to actively coordinate programmes of work or aspects of procedure and administration. This level of cooperation is referred to as integrated institutional management for the purposes of this chapter. The third level of interaction integrates political as well as institutional management and requires high level, political cooperation between regimes in managing joint issues or areas. This level of political cooperation falls short of formal institutional nesting.

91 Oberthür and Gehring, above n 86, 35.

92 Oberthür, above n 86, 378.

93 Sebastian Oberthür, 'Clustering of Multilateral Environmental Agreements: Potentials and Limitations' (2002) 2 *International Environmental Agreements: Politics, Law and Economics* 317; Young (1996), above n 86, 5.

94 Oberthür, above n 86, 376.

95 See JBSkjaeseth, 'Protecting the Northeast Atlantic: One Problem, Three Institutions' in Sebastian Oberthür and Thomas Gehring (eds), *Institutional Interaction in Global Environmental Governance: Synergy and Conflict among International and EU Policies* (MIT Press, 2006) 103.

96 See further below and Scott, n 3, 192–207.

97 Young (1996), n 86, 3–4.

Basic Cooperative Agreements between Regimes and Institutions

At the most basic level of cooperation, an ever increasing number of MEAs are negotiating formal agreements, commonly referred to as Memoranda of Understanding or Cooperation (MOU or MOC), with an ever growing range of partners. For example, the Biodiversity Convention secretariat has concluded 157 agreements to date with partners that include eighteen MEAs, international organizations, universities, non-governmental organizations (NGOs) and botanical gardens. Such agreements are by no means confined to the field of biodiversity protection and can be found in the areas of fisheries management and pollution prevention and control.[98] Normally adopted on the basis of overlapping subject matter, a small number of these agreements also exploit synergies in function. For example, the 2002 MOU among the secretariats of the 1973 Convention on International Trade in Endangered Species of Wild Fauna and Flora (CITES),[99] the 1987 Protocol on Substances that Deplete the Ozone Layer (Montreal Protocol)[100] and the 1989 Convention on the Control of Transboundary Movements of Hazardous Wastes and their Disposal (Basel Convention)[101] exploits the common legal tool – management of international trade – used by all three instruments to govern respectively the transfer of wildlife, ozone depleting substances and hazardous waste.[102]

Most of these cooperative agreements have common aims and objectives but vary with respect to the mechanisms they deploy in order to achieve those aims and objectives. The principal purpose of all of these agreements is the establishment of a procedure for the exchange of information between treaty regimes, commonly in the form of mutual representation at meetings. Some of the more dynamic agreements, such as the 1998 MOC between the secretariats of the 1992 CBD and the 1996 Desertification Convention[103] go beyond this and provide

98 For a more extensive survey of these cooperative agreements see Scott, n 3, 188–200.

99 *Convention on International Trade in Endangered Species of Wild Fauna and Flora*, opened for signature 3 April 1973, 993 UNTS 243 (entered into force 1 July 1975) ('CITES').

100 *Montreal Protocol on Substances that Deplete the Ozone Layer*, opened for signature 16 September 1987, 1522 UNTS 3 (entered into force 1 January 1989) ('*Montreal Protocol*').

101 *Basel Convention on the Control of Transboundary Movements of Hazardous Wastes and their Disposal*, opened for signature 22 March 1989, 1673 UNTS 57 (entered into force 5 May 1992) ('*Basel Convention*').

102 2002 Memorandum of Understanding: http://www.cites.org/common/disc/sec/CITES-BASEL-OZONE.pdf.

103 *United Nations Convention to Combat Desertification in Those Countries Experiencing Serious Drought and/or Desertification, Particularly in Africa*, opened for signature 14 October 1994, 1954 UNTS 3 (entered into force 26 December 1996) ('*UNCCD*').

for joint liaison positions, procedures for joint representation at external meetings and mechanisms for joint reporting.[104] Others provide for joint work programmes to be developed by the participating regimes; this is a particular feature of the cooperative arrangements entered into by the secretariats of the Basel Convention, the Convention on the Prior Informed Consent Procedure for Certain Hazardous Chemicals and Pesticides in International Trade (Rotterdam Convention)[105] and the Convention on Persistent Organic Pollutants (Stockholm Convention)[106] (the 'Chemical Conventions').[107] All provide for – at least in principle – opportunities for cognitive interaction; for the exchange of ideas and experiences with a view to improving the effectiveness of environmental governance. A feature common to all of these agreements is that they are driven by administrative bodies within the regime, such as a secretariat, rather than by the parties themselves. The success and indeed the very negotiation of such arrangements are therefore dependent upon the existence of a dynamic secretariat[108] and the legal capacity or personality of that secretariat to enter into cooperative alliances.[109]

In the context of geo-engineering, the creation of formal cooperative agreements between regimes and institutions with an interest in the management of geo-engineering technologies and strategies represents one path towards developing a coherent governance regime for geo-engineering. Obvious candidates for such an agreement include the IMO, the secretariats to the 1992 UNFCCC, the 1992 CBD, the 1982 UNCLOS and interested regional organizations such as the OSPAR Commission.[110] Given that many geo-engineering proposals are not marine based

---

104 1998 Memorandum of Understanding: http://www.cbd.int/doc/agreements/agmt-unccd-1998-07-31-moc-web-en.pdf.

105 *Rotterdam Convention on the Prior Informed Consent Procedure for Certain Hazardous Chemicals and Pesticides in International Trade*, opened for signature 10 September 1998, 2244 UNTS 337 (entered into force 24 February 2004).

106 *Stockholm Convention on Persistent Organic Pollutants*, opened for signature 22 May 2001, 2256 UNTS 119 (entered into force 17 May 2004).

107 See Ad Hoc Joint Working Group on Enhancing Cooperation and Coordination among the Basel, Rotterdam and Stockholm Conventions, *Chronology of the Consideration by Parties to the Basel, Stockholm and Rotterdam Conventions on Cooperation and Coordination between the Three Conventions*, UN Doc BC-RC-SC/AHJWG.1/INF/4 (13 February 2007) http://ahjwg.chem.unep.ch/documents/1stmeeting/i04e.pdf (Decision VIII/8 on Cooperation and Coordination between the Basel, Rotterdam and Stockholm Conventions; Decision SC-2/15 on Synergies; Decision RC-3/8 on Cooperation and Coordination between the Rotterdam, Basel and Stockholm Conventions).

108 See Steffan Bauer, Per-Olf Busch and Bernd Siebenhüner, 'Treaty Secretariats in Global Environmental Governance' in Frank Bierman, Bernd Siebenhüner and Anna Schreyögg, *International Organisations in Global Environmental Governance* (Routledge, 2009) 174.

109 For a discussion of the legal capacity of secretariats to enter into cooperative agreements see Scott, n 3, 189 – 190.

110 *Convention for the Protection of the Marine Environment of the North East Atlantic*, opened for signature 22 September 1992, 2354 UNTS 67 (entered into force 25

it would be sensible to include other interested institutions such as the secretariat of the 1979 Convention on Long-range Transboundary Air Pollution (LRTAP)[111] and the UN Committee on the Peaceful Uses of Outer Space. The adoption of such an agreement would facilitate the exchange of information between these institutions and regimes and facilitate a wider discussion on how these technologies should be developed and regulated. Such an agreement would also provide a platform from which to develop joint or at least mutually supportive work programmes and political cooperation.

Integrated Institutional Management

A more ambitious level of linkage and interaction characterizes the arrangements described here as integrated institutional management. Unsurprisingly, there are relatively few arrangements that can be placed in this category. The Biodiversity Liaison Group and the joint activities of the five tuna Regional Fisheries Management Organizations (RFMOs) (known as the Kobe process) probably represent the clearest examples to date of integrated institutional management. The Biodiversity Liaison Group (BLG), formally established in 2006,[112] comprises six biodiversity conventions: the 1992 CBD; CITES; the 1971 Ramsar Convention;[113] the 1979 Convention on Migratory Species; the 1972 World Heritage Convention;[114] and the 2001 International Treaty on Plant Genetic Resources for Food and Agriculture.[115] The BLG developed two priority areas of focus during its first five years of operation: the 2010 Biodiversity Target and the Global Partnership on Biodiversity. However, to date the BLG has emphasized strengthening joint participation within existing projects rather than developing new initiatives.[116] This emphasis is set to continue in the future with its new priorities, established in 2011, comprising collaboration in order to support the early entry into force of the

March 1998) ('*OSPAR Convention*').

111 *United Nations Economic Commission for Europe Convention on Long-range Transboundary Air Pollution*, opened for signature 13 November 1979, 1302 UNTS 217 (entered into force 16 March 1983) ('*LRTAP*').

112 *Memorandum of Cooperation between Agencies to Support the Achievement of the 2010 Biodiversity Target* (15 September 2006) http://www.cbd.int/doc/agreements/agmt-hoatf-cites-2006-10-15-moc-web-en.pdf.

113 *Convention on Wetlands of International Importance Especially as Waterfowl Habitat*, opened for signature 2 February 1971, 996 UNTS 245 (entered into force 21 December 1975).

114 *Convention for the Protection of the World Cultural and Natural Heritage*, opened for signature 16 November 1972, 1037 UNTS 151 (entered into force 17 December 1975).

115 *International Treaty on Plant Genetic Resources for Food and Agriculture*, opened for signature 3 November 2001, 2400 UNTS 303 (entered into force 26 June 2004).

116 See Scott, n 3, 201–203.

2010 Nagoya Protocol on Access and Benefit Sharing[117] and cooperation intended to promote the United Nations Decade on Biodiversity.[118] The most significant achievement of the BLG thus far has been the adoption by all six conventions of common guidelines[119] designed to flesh out the *Addis Ababa Principles and Guidelines for the Sustainable Use of Biodiversity*.[120]

The cooperative arrangement entered into by the five tuna RFMOs as part of the Kobe process has a rather more ambitious suite of objectives and aims to go beyond the work of the individual RFMOs in order to address issues of implementation and compliance at a global rather than a regional level.[121] The RFMOs have met three times since 2007, established a joint website providing access to a central list of IUU vessels, and are in the process of developing common methodologies for the presentation of stock assessments and evaluation of performance.[122] In a very recent development, the OSPAR Commission initiated, in 2011, a collective arrangement between itself and four international institutions[123] for the management of selected areas beyond national jurisdiction in the North-East Atlantic. This collective arrangement is designed to facilitate information exchange, to promote cooperation with respect to environmental and strategic environmental impact assessments and to improve knowledge about the ecosystems subject to the arrangement.[124] Although it is too early to engage in any form of assessment as to the success of this arrangement, the

---

117 *Nagoya Protocol on Access to Genetic Resources and the Fair and Equitable Sharing of Benefits Arising from their Utilization to the Convention on Biological Diversity*, opened for signature 29 October 2010, UNEP/CBD/COP/DEC/X/1 of 29 October 2010 (not yet in force).

118 Liaison Group of the Biodiversity Related Conventions, 'Special Meeting of the Liaison Group of the Biodiversity Related Conventions, Geneva, 13 April 2011' http://www.cbd.int/cooperation/doc/blg-07-02-en.pdf.

119 The agreed guidelines are available on CD-Rom and online. See United Nations Environment Programme, Convention on Biological Diversity, *Sustainable Use of Biodiversity* (16 December 2010) http://www.cbd.int/blg/.

120 See Conference of the Parties to the Convention on Biological Diversity, *Sustainable Use (Article 10)*, UN Doc UNEP/CBD/COP/DEC/VII/12 (Decision VII/12 adopted at the Seventh Meeting of the Conference of the Parties to the Convention on Biological Diversity, 13 April 2004) http://www.cbd.int/doc/decisions/cop-07/cop-07-dec-12-en.pdf.

121 See Tuna Regional Fisheries Management Organizations, 'Report of the Second Joint Meeting of Tuna Regional Fisheries Management Organizations (RFMOs)' (Report, Joint Tuna RFMOs, 23 June–3 July 2009) http://www.tuna-org.org/trfmo2.htm.

122 For further discussion of the Kobe Process see Scott, above n 3, 203–205.

123 The four institutions comprise the North East Atlantic Fisheries Commission (NEAFC), the IMO, the International Seabed Authority and the International Atomic Energy Agency.

124 Information on the Collective Arrangement for Management of Selected Areas of the North East Atlantic can be found in IMO Document MEPC 63/INF.3 (25 November 2011).

mechanisms and principles designed to achieve the aims and objectives of the collective arrangement undoubtedly constitute an ambitious example of integrated institutional management.

The creation of an integrated institutional management arrangement in respect of geo-engineering between institutions such as the IMO and regimes including UNCLOS, UNFCCC and the CBD, for example, has considerable appeal. Although at a very early stage of development, international institutions are already taking steps towards governing geo-engineering technologies. As noted above, the IMO, through the London Protocol, has developed a risk assessment framework in respect of ocean fertilization research activities and is currently exploring regulatory options. Given the interest of other institutions in these activities – most notably the CBD – there is a strong argument for broadening the forum within which these debates, work programmes and other developments take place. Nevertheless, integrated institutional management arrangements are still largely driven by treaty institutions rather than by the parties themselves, and in the case of geo-engineering – an undoubtedly controversial activity – higher level, political cooperation is likely to be required in order to move the governance agenda forward.

Integrated Political Management

The final level of linkage and interaction incorporates high-level political as well as administrative cooperation and is referred to here as integrated political management. The best example of such an arrangement is the so-called chemicals conventions cluster.[125] This remarkable arrangement has its origins in a series of decisions adopted in 2006 by the Rotterdam, Stockholm and Basel Conventions designed to improve both administrative and political cooperation between the regimes.[126] It culminated in the decision to convene an extraordinary meeting of the parties of all three conventions in February 2010 under the auspices of which a series of decisions were taken to integrate much of the administration of the conventions and to promote the creation of joint work programmes in respect of cross-cutting activities.[127] Whilst preserving the autonomy of the three conventions, the initiatives taken in 2010 are clearly designed to improve the implementation

125 For further discussion of the chemicals conventions cluster arrangement see Scott, above n 3, 205–207.

126 Decision VIII/8 on Cooperation and Coordination between the Basel, Rotterdam and Stockholm Conventions; Decision SC2/15 on Synergies; Decision RC-3/8 on Cooperation and Coordination between the Rotterdam, Basel and Stockholm Conventions, UN Doc BC-RC-SC/AHJWG.1/INF/4.

127 *Report of the Simultaneous Extraordinary Meetings of the Conferences of the Parties to the Basel, Rotterdam and Stockholm Conventions,* UN Doc UNEP/FAO/CHW/RC/POPS/EXCOPS.1/8 (7 April 2010) annex I ('*Omnibus Decision Adopted by the Conference of the Parties to the Basel Convention*').

and enforcement of the regimes through mutual support, cognitive interaction, efficiency savings and, ultimately, joint management.

It is not suggested here that a similar arrangement should be entered into by institutions and regimes with an interest in geo-engineering governance. In contrast to the chemicals conventions cluster, whilst geo-engineering is an issue in common for a number of institutions and regimes (such as, but not limited to, the IMO, UNFCCC, CBD and UNCLOS), the aims and objectives of these institutions and regimes are quite different. Nevertheless, the point is that where political interaction is combined with administrative linkages, the opportunities for improving environmental governance are greatly enhanced. This is demonstrated by the chemicals conventions cluster arrangement, which is undoubtedly more extensive and possesses considerably more potential for improved environmental governance in the area of chemicals management than any of the other cooperative arrangements identified above. Consequently, a joint meeting between interested regimes at the political level on the topic of geo-engineering, in additional to cooperation at the administrative level, has considerable potential to move the governance agenda forward notwithstanding the absence of a designated management regime for geo-engineering.

Concluding Observations: The Benefits and Risks Associated with Developing Geo-engineering Governance through Institutional Connection

The crucial question is: why should we begin to address the management and regulation of geo-engineering through cooperative mechanisms between existing institutions? An alternative strategy is to negotiate a free-standing instrument to govern geo-engineering or adopt a protocol on geo-engineering to the UNFCCC.[128] At the other end of the spectrum, some commentators have suggested that these technologies should be self-regulated through a consortium of scientists and technical institutions.[129] However, the risks associated with geo-engineering and the capability of states or even individuals to deploy these technologies mean that self-regulation is an unattractive long-term strategy. Whilst in principle a specialist regulatory instrument has significant appeal, the resources required to successfully adopt such an instrument would be considerable. Negotiation would likely prove challenging on account of the significant disagreements between states on ethical and other policy issues associated with geo-engineering and the response to

128 Karen N Scott, 'The Legal and Policy Implications of Geoengineering' paper presented at *Problems of Adaptation to Climate Change*, Russian Academy of Sciences, Moscow, 7–9 November 2011.

129 Barrett, above n 21, 51; Victor, above n 45, 325. Precedents for such a consortium include the European Organization for Nuclear Research (CERN), the Human Genome Project and InterRidge, a non-profit organization established to promote the study, use and protection of mid-ocean ridges.

climate change more generally. By contrast, cooperative action taken by existing interested institutions and regimes to facilitate the exchange of information, to provide a forum for discussion and to promote and manage work programmes connected to geo-engineering research would require only a low level of resources and could avoid some of the more contentious political issues, at least in the interim stages of cooperation. Such an arrangement could, nevertheless, provide the basis for further political cooperation and the development of a governance regime for geo-engineering.

However, there are governance-related risks associated with increased cooperation and linkages between regimes. First, where institutional cooperation is driven by treaty institutions rather than by parties, states and other participants risk becoming unwillingly drawn into regimes which they are not party to or affiliated with, and implicitly become subject to concepts, principles and even obligations under those regimes by virtue of a cooperative agreement. In the context of geo-engineering, states may get drawn into an evolving management regime with little actual control over how that regime develops. Secondly, cooperating regimes or institutions risk overreaching their regulatory mandate and acting in a manner which might be categorized as *ultra vires* through their participation in a cooperative arrangement. For example, this may occur where an institution such as the IMO with responsibility in one area – the oceans and shipping in particular – incurs responsibility in another area – climate change – through a cooperative arrangement. Thirdly, any cooperative arrangement risks being dominated by one or a small group of institutions and their priorities and interests. This risk has been demonstrated with the Biodiversity Liaison Group, which is undoubtedly dominated by the CBD.[130] Finally, closer cooperation in respect of controversial issues – and geo-engineering is indubitably controversial – may achieve little more than simply transferring a problematic issue from one regime to another without resolving that problem and with potentially serious consequences for the effectiveness of that other regime.

Nevertheless, whilst acknowledging the existence of risks to both the legitimacy and the effectiveness of environmental regimes and institutions arising from closer cooperation, the deliberate creation of institutional connections between regimes is an increasingly important component of international environmental governance. Moreover, in the context of a new and emerging threat to the marine environment – geo-engineering – formal cooperation between institutions and regimes provides an opportunity to begin managing and, ultimately, governing that threat.

130 Scott, above n 3, 213.

Chapter 10

A Model Litigant? Australia's Record in Transboundary Environmental Litigation

Tim Stephens*

Introduction

In May 2010 Australia commenced proceedings in the International Court of Justice (ICJ) against Japan in the *Scientific Whaling* case[1] challenging the legality of Japanese 'scientific' whaling in the Southern Ocean. This is but the latest in a string of international environmental cases in which Australia has participated since the 1970s. Environmental and natural resource issues have featured prominently in the international disputes to which Australia has been a party. This is despite the relative isolation of the Australian environment from that of other states. The Australian mainland shares no land frontiers[2] and few maritime boundaries with other states where transboundary pollution issues may arise, no freshwater basins with other states where there is a need to share water resources,[3] and few maritime boundaries where there are strained relations over fisheries and other natural resource issues.[4]

---

* The author acknowledges the fruitful research collaboration with Natalie Klein and Jacqueline Peel that this chapter draws from.

1 *Whaling in the Antarctic (Australia v Japan)*, application filed 31 May 2010.

2 However Australia's largest external territory, the Australian Antarctic Territory (AAT), borders areas of Antarctica claimed by France, New Zealand and Norway. For the life of the 1959 *Antarctic Treaty*, opened for signature 1 December 1959, [1961] ATS 12 (entered into force 23 June 1961), which places sovereign claims on hold, the prospect of litigation against or by a neighbouring claimant for damage to or originating from the AAT is remote.

3 It is presumably for this reason that Australia has not become a party to the *United Nations Convention on the Law of the Non-Navigational Uses of International Watercourses,* opened for signature 21 May 1997, (1997) 36 ILM 700 (not yet in force), notwithstanding that aspects of the Convention are relevant to the sustainable management of non-international rivers.

4 See generally Stuart Kaye, *Australia's Maritime Boundaries* (Centre for Maritime Policy, University of Wollongong, 2nd edn, 2001). The obvious exception is Australia's northern maritime boundaries with Indonesia and Timor Leste, with the latter still to be permanently resolved. For discussion of litigation in Australian courts which has engaged with the international implications of resource management in Australia's maritime zones see Natalie Klein and Nikolas Hughes, 'National Litigation and International Law:

Given this it is significant that the international cases in which Australia has participated have had environmental elements of one type or another. Australia was an applicant in the first case in the ICJ relating to transboundary environmental harm (the *Nuclear Tests* cases[5]), a respondent in two later natural resources cases (*Certain Phosphate Lands in Nauru*[6] and the *East Timor* case[7]), and more recently has been a party in three disputes involving marine living resources. Australia was an applicant in the *Southern Bluefin Tuna* case[8] and the respondent in the *Volga* case,[9] both of which were brought under the 1982 United Nations Convention on the Law of the Sea (LOSC),[10] and in 2010 Australia began proceedings against Japan in the ICJ in the *Scientific Whaling* case.[11] This record indicates that Australia can be regarded in many respects as a model litigant on matters of environmental protection and natural resources. Not only has Australia actively engaged in litigation in international courts against several states, but it is also prepared to have its own behaviour subjected to international judicial examination.

Indeed with the tremendous growth of multilateral environmental agreements in the latter part of the twentieth century, most of which Australia has supported and become a party to,[12] the opportunities for international environmental litigation involving Australia as an applicant or respondent have increased considerably. A number of key environmental regimes contain systems for dispute settlement, including by compulsory means (see Tables 10.1 and 10.2, below). Most commonly this is to be by arbitration or conciliation, however judicial settlement through the ICJ or the International Tribunal for the Law of the Sea (ITLOS) is also a possibility. Increasingly important institutions for dispute settlement within environmental regimes are non-compliance committees, which are designed to provide a more targeted response to compliance problems than classic inter-state dispute settlement systems. Such committees have been established for a number of regimes in which Australia participates, including the 1997 Kyoto Protocol[13]

Repercussions for Australia's Protection of Marine Resources' (2009) 33 *Melbourne University Law Review* 163.

5 *Nuclear Tests (Australia v France) (Interim Measures)* [1973] ICJ Rep 99, *(Merits)* [1974] ICJ Rep 253.

6 *Certain Phosphate Lands in Nauru (Nauru v Australia)* [1992] ICJ Rep 240.

7 *East Timor (Portugal v Australia) (Jurisdiction and Admissibility)* [1995] ICJ Rep 90.

8 *Southern Bluefin Tuna (New Zealand v Japan; Australia v Japan) (Provisional Measures) (1999)* 117 ILR 148, *(Jurisdiction and Admissibility)* (2000) 119 ILR 508.

9 *Volga (Russian Federation v Australia) (Prompt Release)* (2003) 42 ILM 159.

10 Opened for signature 10 December 1982, [1994] ATS 31 (entered into force 16 November 1994).

11 *Whaling in the Antarctic (Australia v Japan)*, application filed 31 May 2010.

12 See generally Greg Rose, 'Australian Approaches to International Environmental Law during the Howard Years' (2008) 27 *Australian Year Book of International Law* 115.

13 Opened for signature 11 December 1997, (1998) 37 ILM 22 (entered into force 16 February 2005).

to the 1992 United Nations Framework Convention on Climate Change.[14] Australia is also a participant in a number of non-environmental regimes in which environmental issues have been raised, or could be raised in the future. An example is the World Trade Organization (WTO) dispute settlement system which has been used by several states to challenge quarantine measures imposed by Australia. In the recent *New Zealand-Apples* dispute,[15] the WTO Appellate Body found that the measures were not based on a proper risk assessment and were inconsistent with the 1995 WTO Sanitary and Phytosanitary Agreement.[16]

Against this background this chapter considers Australia's experience in international litigation on transboundary environmental issues and the benefits and pitfalls of this technique for advancing environmental foreign policy objectives through the use of international courts and tribunals. To this end, the first section of the chapter examines the environmental disputes to which Australia has been a party including the pending *Scientific Whaling* case, and draws some lessons from this history of environmental disputation. It is seen that environmental disputes have seldom been resolved through international litigation, with the relevant court or tribunal in most cases seeking to broker what was in effect a diplomatic outcome. Having regard to Australia's participation in many and varied environmental regimes, the second section of the chapter considers the prospects for future international environmental litigation involving Australia.

14 Opened for signature 9 May 1992, 1771 UNTS 165 (entered into force 21 March 1994).

15 Panel Report, *New Zealand-Apples*, WTO Doc WT/DS367/11 (9 August 2010). On 10 August 2010 it was announced that Australia would appeal the panel's decision to the Appellate Body: Stephen Smith, Minister for Foreign Affairs, 'Australia to Appeal WTO Apples Decision' (Media Release, 10 August 2010) www.foreignminister.gov.au/releases/2010/fa-s100810.html.

16 Sanitary and Phytosanitary Agreement (Marrakesh Agreement Establishing the World Trade Organization, opened for signature 15 April 1994, 1869 UNTS 190, annex 1A (entered into force 1 January 1995)).

Table 10.1 Australia's membership of environmental regimes having a compulsory dispute settlement system

Regime title	Method of dispute settlement
1973 Convention on International Trade in Endangered Species of Wild Fauna and Flora [1976] ATS 29 (Resolution 14.3 (2007))	Compliance procedure (otherwise non-compulsory conventional means: Art 18)
1982 United Nations Convention on the Law of the Sea (see Pt XV)	Compulsory arbitration or judicial settlement
1986 Convention on Assistance in the Case of a Nuclear Accident or Radiological Emergency [1987] ATS 15, (Art 13)	Compulsory arbitration or judicial settlement in the ICJ
1987 Montreal Protocol on Substances that Deplete the Ozone Layer [1989] ATS 18	Compliance procedure
1991 Protocol on Environmental Protection to the Antarctic Treaty [1998] ATS 6 (see Arts 18–20)	Compulsory arbitration
1992 Convention on Biological Diversity [1993] ATS 32 (Art 27)	Compulsory conciliation
1992 United Nations Framework Convention on Climate Change [1994] ATS 2 (Art 14)	Compulsory conciliation
1994 International Tropical Timber Agreement [1997] ATS 2 (Art 31)	Compulsory review by International Tropical Timber Council
1995 Agreement for the Implementation of the Provisions of the United Nations Convention on the Law of the Sea of 10 December 1982 Relating to the Conservation and Management of Straddling Fish Stocks and Highly Migratory Fish Stocks [2001] ATS 8 (see Pt VIII)	Compulsory arbitration or judicial settlement via procedures under LOSC, Pt XV
1996 Protocol to the Convention on the Prevention of Marine Pollution by Dumping of Wastes and Other Matter of 29 December 1972 [2006] ATS 11 (Art 15)	Compulsory ad hoc arbitration or via procedures under LOSC, Pt XV
1997 Kyoto Protocol to the 1992 UN Framework Convention on Climate Change (see Decision 24/CP.1 (2002))	Compliance procedure
2000 Convention on the Conservation and Management of Highly Migratory Fish Stocks in the Western and Central Pacific Ocean [2004] ATS 15 (Art 31)	Compulsory arbitration or judicial settlement via procedures under FSA, Pt VIII and LOSC, Pt XV
2001 Agreement on the Conservation of Albatrosses and Petrels [2004] ATS 5 (Art 14)	Technical arbitration

Table 10.2 Australia's membership of environmental regimes having a non-compulsory dispute settlement system

Treaties in force
1959 Antarctic Treaty [1961] ATS 12, Art 11
1978 Treaty between Australia and the Independent State of Papua New Guinea concerning Sovereignty and Maritime Boundaries in the area between the two Countries, including the area known as Torres Strait, and Related Matters [1985] ATS 4
1979 Agreement on Fisheries between the Government of Australia and the Government of Japan [1979] ATS 12
1979 Convention on the Conservation of Migratory Species of Wild Animals [1991] ATS 32, Art 13
1980 Convention on the Conservation of Antarctic Marine Living Resources [1982] ATS 9, Art 25
1985 Vienna Convention for the Protection of the Ozone Layer [1988] ATS 26, Art 11
1989 Basel Convention on the Control of Transboundary Movements of Hazardous Wastes and their Disposal [1992] ATS 7
1990 Convention for the Protection of the Natural Resources and Environment of the South Pacific Region [1990] ATS 31, Art 26
1993 Agreement to Promote Compliance with International Conservation and Management Measures by Fishing Vessels on the High Seas [2004] ATS 26
1993 Convention for the Conservation of Southern Bluefin Tuna [1994] ATS 16, Art 16
1993 Convention on the Prohibition of the Development, Production, Stockpiling and Use of Chemical Weapons and on their Destruction [1997] ATS 3
1994 Convention on Nuclear Safety [1997] ATS 5, Art 29
1994 United Nations Convention to Combat Desertification in those Countries Experiencing Serious Drought and/or Desertification, particularly in Africa [2000] ATS 18, Art 28
1995 Convention to Ban the Importation into Forum Island Countries of Hazardous and Radioactive Wastes and to Control the Transboundary Movement and Management of Hazardous Wastes within the South Pacific Region [2001] ATS 17, Art 20
1997 Joint Convention on the Safety of Spent Fuel Management and on the Safety of Radioactive Waste Management [2003] ATS 21, Art 38
1998 Rotterdam Convention on the Prior Informed Consent Procedure for Certain Hazardous Chemicals and Pesticides in International Trade [2004] ATS 22, Art 20
2001 Stockholm Convention on Persistent Organic Pollutants [2004] ATS 23, art 18

Treaties not yet in force
2009 Agreement on Port State Measures to Prevent, Deter and Eliminate Illegal, Unreported and Unregulated Fishing [2010] ATNIF 41
2004 International Convention for the Control and Management of Ships' Ballast Water and Sediments [2005] ATNIF 18
2001 International Convention on the Control of Harmful Anti-fouling Systems on Ships [2008] ATS 15

Australia's Participation in International Environmental Litigation

Nuclear Tests *cases (1973–1995)*

In 1973 Australia was an applicant alongside New Zealand in the *Nuclear Tests* cases in the ICJ contesting the legality of French nuclear testing in the Pacific, and was an intervener in proceedings in 1995 when New Zealand sought to reactivate the case against France following the announcement of a new round of tests.[17]

The Australian and New Zealand arguments were inventive, pressing at the then boundaries of international environmental law to hold France to account for its atmospheric, and later underground, nuclear testing programmes. Australia's case was distinctive by virtue of its implicit reliance on the principle in the *Trail Smelter* case,[18] which provides that states are under an obligation to prevent transboundary environmental harm to other states, and to areas beyond national jurisdiction.[19] It was argued that France's testing caused a type of international trespass, in that the deposit of even very small amounts of radioactive material on Australian soil violated Australian territorial sovereignty. Second, it was argued that the testing interfered with Australian 'decisional sovereignty', by limiting 'Australia's independent right to determine what acts shall take place within its territory and in particular whether Australia and its people shall be exposed to radiation from artificial sources'.[20]

As is well known, these arguments were never considered by the Court, since it determined that the case had been rendered moot because of the unilateral

17 *Request for an Examination of the Situation in Accordance with Paragraph 63 of the Court's Judgment of 20 December 1974 in Nuclear Tests (New Zealand v France)* [1995] ICJ Rep 288.

18 *Trail Smelter (Canada/United States)* (1938 and 1941) 3 *RIAA* 1911.

19 See further Tim Stephens, *International Courts and Environmental Protection* (Cambridge University Press, 2009) 123–136, 139–151.

20 'Application by Australia', *Nuclear Tests (Australia v France)* [1973] I ICJ Pleadings 3, 14.

announcement by the French government that it would cease atmospheric testing.[21] The 1995 proceedings also failed to produce a decision on the merits, with the ICJ again finding a justification for avoiding the substantive legal issues, on the basis that the original proceedings concerning atmospheric nuclear testing and that the 1995 case instead related to planned underground tests.

The *Nuclear Tests* cases demonstrate that the prospects of successful international litigation on environmental (and other matters) are likely to be compromised if the respondent has not given its full support to the process. The competence of the ICJ derived from the 1928 General Act of Arbitration for the Pacific Settlement of Disputes,[22] to which the applicants and the respondent were parties. However France was caught by surprise by the proceedings, never acknowledged or accepted the jurisdiction of the Court, and declined to participate in the case. In this context it was understandable that the Court reached the conclusion that it did.

The litigation also illustrates the potential value in pursuing compliance with environmental obligations of a procedural rather than substantive character. The original 1973 applications focussed on substantive obligations under international law, however these were of a somewhat nebulous character, because of the then embryonic nature of international environmental law. After all the case was brought just a year after the 1972 Stockholm Declaration on the Human Environment[23] had set out the key developing principles of international environmental law, and well before most of the major multilateral environmental agreements had been negotiated. By contrast, the 1995 case was able to draw upon significant developments in substantive and procedural international environmental law. Hence in 1995 Australia and New Zealand contended not only that the underground testing would result in unlawful transboundary pollution, but also that it would be unlawful if it were conducted without a thorough environmental impact assessment.[24] However, although the legal arguments against the tests were stronger in 1995 than they were in 1973, the fact remained that the litigation was highly controversial, and with France's ongoing refusal to participate, the Court managed once again to avoid a decision on the merits.

Certain Phosphate Lands in Nauru *(1989–1993)*

In 1989 Australia was the respondent in proceedings in the ICJ brought by Nauru, in which it was argued that the Pacific microstate, while under Australian

---

21 *Nuclear Tests (Australia v France)* [1974] ICJ Rep 253, [52].

22 Opened for signature 26 September 1928, [1975] ATS 49 (entered into force 16 August 1929).

23 UN Doc A/CONF.48/14/Rev. 1 (1973).

24 *Request for an Examination of the Situation in Accordance with Paragraph 63 of the Court's Judgment of 20 December 1974 in Nuclear Tests (New Zealand v France)* [1995] ICJ Rep 288, [6].

administration as a United Nations Trust territory, was stripped of its phosphate mineral resources, with little benefit accruing to the Nauruan people.

While not invoking international legal rules of an environmental character, Nauru did point to environmental concerns in formulating its allegations of Australian maladministration, pointing out that this had resulted in Nauru's island environment being severely degraded such that the 'land was ... rendered completely useless for habitation, agriculture, or any other purpose'.[25]

The case was not considered on its merits because in 1993 the two disputants reached a settlement agreement,[26] in which Nauru obtained a cash payment of AU$107m from Australia. However the litigation does illustrate the potentially unexpected ways in which environmental issues can arise in international litigation, and the need for appropriate attention to be given to sound environmental policies even in areas of international relations where environmental concerns are not prominent.

Certain Phosphate Lands in Nauru also demonstrates the value of litigating environmental matters on the basis of established rules of international law rather than seeking to make arguments on the basis of emerging and amorphous norms of an environmental character.

East Timor *case (1991–1995)*

Natural resource issues were implicated in the *East Timor* case commenced against Australia in the ICJ by Portugal in 1991. The Portuguese application presented the case as raising not only Australia's duties to Portugal as the administering power for East Timor, and the right of the East Timorese to self-determination, but also the related rights of the East Timorese to territorial integrity and unity, and permanent sovereignty over natural wealth and resources.[27]

As with the *Nuclear Tests* cases, the merits of the case were not broached by the Court for reasons of jurisdiction and admissibility. In the *East Timor* case the ICJ accepted Australia's argument that the Court could not determine the matter because Indonesia was an indispensable third party, and was not a party to the proceedings.[28] The Court observed that all of the claims of Portugal turned on a common question, namely whether Indonesia's entry into East Timor in 1975 and subsequent presence was lawful, and Indonesia was not present to address this issue.

---

25 'Application by Nauru', *Certain Phosphate Lands in Nauru (Nauru v Australia)*, International Court of Justice, General List No 80, 19 May 1989, 14.

26 *1993 Settlement of the Case in the International Court of Justice Concerning Certain Phosphate Lands in Nauru*, opened for signature 10 August 1993, (1993) 32 ILM 1471 (entered into force 10 August 1993).

27 'Application by Portugal', *East Timor (Portugal v Australia)*, International Court of Justice, General List No 84, 22 February 1991, 3.

28 *East Timor (Portugal v Australia) (Jurisdiction and Admissibility)* [1995] ICJ Rep 90, [35].

In the *East Timor* case Portugal challenged the legality of a resource agreement, the 1989 Treaty between Australia and the Republic of Indonesia on the Zone of Cooperation in an Area between the Indonesian Province of East Timor and Northern Australia (Timor Gap Treaty).[29] Portugal argued that Australia should not have entered into this agreement, as Portugal remained the administering power for East Timor, with authority over matters concerning the exploration, exploitation and delimitation of the continental shelf in the Timor Gap area.[30] Portugal placed particular emphasis on a legal issue of a procedural character, namely the failure of Australia to comply with its obligation to negotiate with Portugal.[31]

On Timor Leste gaining independence there was a need to revisit the continental shelf boundary issues that had been addressed in the Timor Gap Treaty and canvassed in the *East Timor* case. Several new treaties were concluded, including the 2002 Timor Sea Treaty between the Government of Australia and the Government of East Timor,[32] which in broad terms adopts the same approach as the Timor Gap Treaty, although it provides a more favourable split in the sharing of petroleum production for East Timor (90:10) than that for Indonesia (50:50) under the Timor Gap Treaty. A signal feature of the negotiations between Australia and Timor Leste is that they have not proceeded under the shadow of litigation, the possibility of which is largely ruled out by Australia's revised declarations under Article 36(2) of the *Statute of the ICJ*[33] and Article 298(1)(a) of the LOSC.[34] These have the effect of withdrawing maritime boundary disputes involving Australia from the jurisdiction of the ICJ and the dispute settlement system of the LOSC.[35]

These new declarations were justified by the Australian Government on the grounds that Australia's 'strong view' was 'that any maritime boundary dispute is best settled by negotiation rather than litigation'.[36] The more general point

29 Opened for signature 11 December 1989, [1991] ATS 9 (entered into force 9 February 1991).

30 'Application by Portugal', *East Timor (Portugal v Australia)*, International Court of Justice, General List No 84, 22 February 1991, [20].

31 Ibid [25], [31].

32 Opened for signature 20 May 2002, [2003] ATS 13 (entered into force 2 April 2003).

33 See International Court of Justice, *Declarations recognizing the jurisdiction of the Court as compulsory* (22 March 2002) www.icj-cij.org/jurisdiction/index.php?p1=5&p2=1&p3=3&code=AU.

34 See United Nations Treaty Collection (22 March 2002) http://treaties.un.org/Pages/ViewDetailsIII.aspx?&src=TREATY&mtdsg_no=XXI~6&chapter=21&Temp=mtdsg3&lang=en#EndDec.

35 See further Gillian Triggs and Dean Bialek, 'Australia Withdraws Maritime Disputes from the Jurisdiction of the ICJ and ITLOS' (2002) 17(3) *International Journal of Marine and Coastal Law* 423.

36 Alexander Downer, Minister for Foreign Affairs, and Daryl Williams, Attorney-General, *Changes to International Dispute Resolution* (Media Release, 25 March 2002) www.foreignminister.gov.au/releases/2002/fa039j_02.html.

was made that while the ICJ and other dispute settlement mechanisms 'play an important role in the settlement of disputes', Australia's preference was for 'every endeavour [to] be made to reach an agreed resolution of disputes'.[37]

Southern Bluefin Tuna *case (1999–2000)*

The *Southern Bluefin Tuna* case was the first fisheries dispute involving Australia to be taken to an international court or tribunal, notwithstanding that the history of disputation between Australia and other states, including Japan, over fisheries matters stretches back well over a century.

The case arose out of a breakdown in the effective functioning of the fisheries commission established by the 1993 Convention for the Conservation of Southern Bluefin Tuna (CCSBT),[38] and was brought via the compulsory dispute settlement mechanism supplied by Part XV of the LOSC. Australia and New Zealand challenged the legality of an experimental fishing programme for the tuna species undertaken by Japan without the approval of the Commission, and were successful in obtaining provisional measures in ITLOS. Subsequently the arbitral tribunal established to determine the merits of the dispute found that it did not have jurisdiction, on the grounds that its competence was ousted by Article 281(1) of the LOSC which gave priority to the dispute settlement system of the CCSBT.[39]

The *Southern Bluefin Tuna* case is an example, alongside the *Nuclear Tests* case, of the respondent being an unwilling participant in the litigation, and this feature of the case goes some way to explaining the strained reasoning of the arbitral panel on the jurisdictional point. Japan had initially expressed its willingness to have the dispute submitted to mediation, an offer that was refused by Australia and New Zealand because it was not accompanied by an undertaking to suspend the experimental fishing programme. Japan had also suggested arbitration, pursuant to Article 16(2) of the 1993 Convention, but again, because it would not put the programme on hold while the matter was arbitrated, Australia and New Zealand considered that they should pursue the unilateral option of litigating under Part XV of the LOSC. This latter option carried the apparent benefit, among other things, of the potential for interim measures. However given the substantial economic interest that Australia has in the fishery it is not surprising that an outcome was pursued through the 'hard' option of litigation under the LOSC. In economic

37 Ibid.

38 Opened for signature 10 May 1993, [1994] ATS 16 (entered into force 20 May 1994).

39 *Southern Bluefin Tuna (New Zealand v Japan; Australia v Japan)* (jurisdiction and admissibility) (2000) 119 ILR 508, [59]. Article 281 provides that if the 'parties to a dispute concerning the interpretation or application of [the LOSC] have agreed to seek the settlement of the dispute by a peaceful means of their own choice, the procedures provided for in [the LOSC] apply only where no settlement has been reached by recourse to such means…'.

terms, Southern Bluefin Tuna is the most significant of Australia's international fisheries, generating very significant economic returns estimated in 2004 to be in the order of AU$450m per annum.[40]

From an Australian and New Zealand standpoint the loss in this litigation was disappointing for two reasons. Not only did it mean that there was no ruling on the specific complaints levelled against Japan, but it also raised the prospect that the arbitral award would be a precedent in future cases, thereby greatly reducing the opportunities for the fisheries conservation provisions of the LOSC to be enforced. It is impossible to say whether a different result would have been achieved by Australia and New Zealand had the negotiations continued, or had an agreed method of dispute settlement such as mediation or arbitration under the 1993 Convention been utilized. While Australia and New Zealand were on the losing side in the litigation, it did nonetheless bring some benefits, encouraging the parties to return to serious negotiations within the Commission, resulting in greater levels of cooperation to manage and protect the fishery.[41] As with the *Nuclear Tests* cases the litigation therefore had some broader educative or informational effects in bringing international attention and publicity to a chronic problem of overfishing.

Another feature of the litigation is the lengths to which both ITLOS and the arbitral tribunal went to arrive at a mutually acceptable compromise. The ITLOS provisional measures order, which did not find a breach by Japan, was couched in very even-handed terms requiring all parties to refrain from an experimental fishing programme (when clearly only the respondent, Japan, was engaged in such a programme). This attracted the criticism of Judge ad hoc Shearer, who remarked in his separate opinion that the Tribunal had 'behaved less as a court of law and more as an agency of diplomacy' in seeking to assist the parties in resolving the dispute.[42] Others have been complimentary of ITLOS's approach, such as Johnston who argued that this is precisely the conciliatory tactic that courts should take, and that the 'facilitative function of modern international adjudication should in no way be relegated to a lower position than the more traditional resolutive and declaratory functions'.[43]

Koskenniemi has contended that this type of pragmatic resolution of disputes is an inevitable feature of international environmental disputation, because of the inherent nature of international environmental law.[44] He has argued that

40 See Natalie Klein, 'Whales and Tuna: The Past and Future of Litigation between Australia and Japan' (2009) 21 *Georgetown International Environmental Law Review* 143, 151–154, 163.

41 Bill Mansfield, 'The Southern Bluefin Tuna Arbitration: Comments on Professor Kwiatkowska's Article' (2001) 16 *International Journal of Marine and Coastal Law* 361.

42 *Southern Bluefin Tuna (New Zealand v Japan; Australia v Japan)* (*Provisional Measures*) (1999) 38 ILM 1624, [14] (Judge ad hoc Shearer).

43 Douglas M Johnston, 'Fishery Diplomacy and Science and the Judicial Function' (1999) 10 *Yearbook of International Environmental Law* 33, 38.

44 Martii Koskenniemi, 'Peaceful Settlement of Environmental Disputes' (1991) 60 *Nordic Journal of International Law* 73.

international environmental law is often highly non-specific and aspirational because it engages with controversial issues of ecological limits in response to which states cannot be brought to impose fetters on their economic development. As a result there is agreement on vague values or motherhood statements, with controversies apparently neutralized and 'proceduralized' in the hope that any disputes that may arise will be determined in further negotiations, or through dispute settlement bodies. 'Proceduralization' is therefore the price that is paid to attract the broadest possible participation in multilateral environmental treaties.

This analysis is relevant to the *Southern Bluefin Tuna* case given the nature of the provisions of the LOSC that Australia and New Zealand relied upon, which are some of the more ambiguous and open-ended provisions of the Convention. It was argued, among other things, that Japan had violated its duty under Article 118 'to co-operate … in the conservation and management of living resources in the areas of the high seas' and the requirement in Article 117 that in relation to their nationals all states should take such conservation measures 'as may be necessary for the conservation of the living resources of the high seas'.

If litigation is to be pursued to secure a clear finding of breach and strong accompanying remedies then evidently it will have the best chances of success where the norms relied upon are fairly certain in their application and not bound up with large questions of policy on which international courts will be reluctant to pronounce. Koskenniemi presented his critique of international environmental litigation in 1991, at a relatively early stage in the development of international environmental law. Since that time there have emerged a number of environmental regimes that are highly prescriptive, and several existing regimes have been transformed through amendments and protocols to include clear and readily enforceable rules. Nonetheless there remain many regimes, old and new, that are an amalgam of strict and precise with relaxed and general standards, the LOSC being a case in point.

A further lesson of this analysis is that international environmental litigation may be most effective when it is administrative in character in focussing on procedural obligations. In such circumstances the 'proceduralization' strategy adopted at the negotiation stage in the formation of a regime can potentially yield benefits at the time of enforcement. This is because while there may not be agreement on the content of general principles such as 'sustainable development' or 'precaution', there may be a willingness on the part of states, in lieu of this, to accept new rules to improve the processes of environmental decision-making, such as by imposing requirements upon states to share information, and to undertake environmental impact assessment (EIA).

The recent *Pulp Mills* case[45] in the ICJ supports this conclusion. That case concerned the operation of two paper pulp mills on the banks of the River Uruguay, forming the boundary between Argentina and Uruguay. Argentina argued that

45 *Pulp Mills on the River Uruguay (Argentina v Uruguay) (Judgment)* (International Court of Justice, General List No 135, 20 April 2010).

the mills would cause damage to the riverine environment, contrary to the 1975 Statute of the River Uruguay[46] (1975 Statute) concluded by the two states which set out a range of obligations and established a commission for the management of the river.

While making generic reference to sustainable development,[47] the ICJ did not rely upon the concept or any other general norm of environmental law. In relation to the 1975 Statute, the Court found that Uruguay had breached several procedural obligations to notify the river commission of planned works before their authorization, and to notify Argentina of its environmental impact assessment, but had not violated any substantive obligations in the agreement such as the obligation under Article 41 to prevent pollution and preserve the river environment. Significantly, the Court held that the proper performance of the 1975 Statute required an EIA,[48] a position both parties accepted. It was found that EIA had 'gained so much acceptance among States that it may be considered a requirement under general international law' to undertake such an assessment 'where there is a risk that the proposed industrial activity may have a significant adverse impact in a transboundary context'.[49]

Also relevant to understanding the prospects for international environmental litigation on procedural obligations is the recent advisory opinion of the ITLOS Seabed Disputes Chamber in *Responsibilities and Obligations of States Sponsoring Persons and Entities with Respect to Activities in the Area (Seabed Mining Advisory Opinion).*[50] The International Seabed Authority Council sought the opinion to clarify the rights and duties of states that sponsor exploration of minerals on the deep seabed or the 'Area'. In relation to EIA, the Chamber held that sponsoring states were bound by an obligation to conduct an EIA. The Chamber noted that this was not only required by the LOSC, but also by customary international law, and the Chamber referred with approval to the decision of the ICJ in the *Pulp Mills* case.

Volga *Case*

The *Volga* case is one of a string of cases brought before ITLOS by flag states seeking the prompt release of fishing vessels and their crew on the payment of a reasonable bond, a procedure established under Articles 73 and 292 of the LOSC. The *Volga* case was preceded by four prompt release cases in ITLOS through which the Tribunal had developed a substantial body of jurisprudence upon which

46 Opened for signature 26 February 1975, 1296 UNTS 340 (entered into force 18 September 1976).

47 *Pulp Mills on the River Uruguay (Argentina v Uruguay) (Judgment)* (International Court of Justice, General List No 135, 20 April 2010), especially [75], [177].

48 Ibid [203].

49 Ibid [204].

50 (2011) 50 ILM 458.

to base its response to Russia's argument that the vessel and its crew should be released on the payment of a minimal bond.

ITLOS concluded that the bond and the conditions set by Australia were not reasonable, but nonetheless set the bond at a substantial figure of AU$1.92m, equal to the agreed value of the vessel and almost four times the amount submitted by Russia to be reasonable. This litigation represented a significant 'win' for Australia, given the modest amounts that had previously been determined by ITLOS to be reasonable bonds. However Australia did not receive all that it asked for, as it had also argued that it was entitled to set a AU$1m 'good behaviour bond' to guarantee non-repetition of future illegal fishing by the vessel. Australia also sought to impose as a condition of release the installation of a Vessel Monitoring System on the vessel. Neither of these measures was accepted.

The decision in the *Volga* case reveals some reticence on the part of the Tribunal to engage with the underlying environmental problem of which the prompt release proceedings were a symptom; the fact that the *Volga* was one of a fleet of vessels engaged in extensive illegal fishing operations in the Southern Ocean, threatening the viability of the targeted species (Patagonian toothfish) and by-catch species (including seabirds). In his dissenting opinion Judge ad hoc Shearer was critical of the narrow focus of the Tribunal, holding that the reasonableness of the bond could not be determined in isolation from the 'grave allegations of illegal fishing in a context of the protection of endangered fish stocks in a remote and inhospitable part of the seas'.[51]

Scientific Whaling *Case*

The history of Australia's international environmental litigation, particularly in the *Southern Bluefin Tuna* case, throws considerable light on the current case in which Australia is an applicant in the ICJ, the *Scientific Whaling* case, which was commenced unilaterally by application on 31 May 2010. The *Scientific Whaling* case makes good the 2007 pre-election commitment of the Australian government to seek an end to Japanese whaling in the Southern Ocean through international litigation if diplomatic efforts to resolve the matter are unsuccessful.

Since 1987 Japan has taken large numbers of minke whales in the Southern Ocean through successive research programmes (JARPA I and JARPA II). Japan began its special permit whaling in the Antarctic shortly after the moratorium on commercial whaling adopted by the International Whaling Commission established by the 1946 International Convention for the Regulation of Whaling (ICRW)[52] came into effect. Under JARPA II, which commenced in 2004, Japan plans to take up to 850 minke whales, 50 fin whales, and 50 humpback whales per

---

51 *Volga (Russian Federation v Australia) (Prompt Release)* (2003) 42 ILM 159, 194 (Judge ad hoc Shearer).

52 Opened for signature 2 December 1946, [1948] ATS 18 (entered into force 10 November 1948).

annum. While on average around 500 minke whales have been taken each year, and a total of 14 fin whales have been taken since JARPA II began, no humpback whales have yet been caught.

Australia's application advances five legal arguments, and invokes three international environmental agreements. The primary contention is that Japan has breached and is continuing to breach the ICRW. It is argued that Japan has violated the obligation under paragraph 10(e) of the Schedule to the ICRW to observe in good faith the moratorium. It is also contended that Japan is in breach of the obligation under paragraph 7(b) of the Schedule to act in good faith to refrain from undertaking commercial whaling of fin and humpback whales in the Southern Ocean Sanctuary (this is in recognition that Japan has lodged a reservation in respect of the coverage of minkes by the sanctuary). It is argued further that the scale of the JARPA II programme and the lack of any relevance of the programme for the conservation and management of whales, takes it outside Article VIII of the ICRW, which allows the taking of whales for scientific research purposes.

The second environmental instrument raised by Australia is the 1973 Convention on the International Trade in Endangered Species of Wild Fauna and Flora (CITES).[53] CITES prohibits trade in endangered species including whales listed in Appendix I to the Convention. JARPA II may be said to be 'trade' within the meaning of CITES, because it involves the 'introduction from the sea' of a listed specimen other than in 'exceptional circumstances'.[54] The argument relating to CITES applies only to humpback whales, as Japan has entered reservations for minke and fin whales. The obvious difficulty that Australia will face in making its CITES argument is that Japan has not yet taken any humpback whales, although it may be possible to argue that Japan has breached CITES by the mere grant of permits to take humpbacks to the Institute for Cetacean Research, the Japanese body responsible for the scientific whaling programme.

The third environmental instrument relied upon by Australia is the 1992 Convention on Biological Diversity (CBD).[55] It is argued that Japan has violated the obligation under Article 3 to ensure that activities within its jurisdiction or control do not cause damage to the environment of other states or of areas beyond the limits of national jurisdiction; that Japan has not cooperated as required by Article 5 with other parties directly or through a competent international organization in respect of areas beyond national jurisdiction and on other matters of mutual interest, for the conservation and sustainable use of biological diversity, and has not adopted measures as demanded by Article 10(b) to avoid or minimize adverse impacts on biological diversity.

---

53 Opened for signature 3 March 1973, [1976] ATS 29 (entered into force 1 July 1975) ('*CITES*').

54 *CITES* arts II(1) and III(5).

55 Opened for signature 5 June 1992, [1993] ATS 32 (entered into force 29 December 1993).

Particulars for each of the allegations concerning breaches of the CBD are not found in the application, so the legal basis upon which each will be advanced will remain unclear until the memorial filed by Australia is made public by the Court.[56] By comparison with the arguments concerning the ICRW and CITES, the points made in relation to the CBD are the most general, and for that reason probably the least likely to succeed given the past experience. Rather than finding a breach of Articles 3, 5, or 10(b) the ICJ may well conclude that the parties are under an obligation to continue to cooperate in order to find a mutually acceptable outcome.

A further difficulty that Australia may encounter in relation to both CITES and the CBD is the potential jurisdictional argument that Japan is entitled to rely on Australia's reservation in its declaration under Article 36(2) of the *Statute of the ICJ*, which excludes from the ICJ's jurisdiction disputes in relation to which 'the parties have agreed ... to have recourse to some other method of peaceful settlement'. Both CITES and the CBD include provisions for dispute settlement (unlike the ICRW which is entirely silent on the matter). If jurisdictional issues are hard fought, and close run, then the history of international environmental litigation would suggest that the likelihood of a strong decision finding for either party is greatly reduced.

Future Prospects for International Environmental Litigation Involving Australia

Australia's Participation in Environmental Regimes

Australia's ecological profile generally inclines Australia towards cooperation on an array of global environmental issues. The Australian continent is megadiverse, supporting about 10 per cent of the world's biological diversity, and this in large part explains Australia's participation in bilateral and multilateral environmental agreements addressing species and ecosystem protection, most notably the CBD. Australia has also joined most regimes addressing other environmental issues of regional and global importance.

There is a substantial element of self-interest in Australia's involvement in most environmental regimes, with Australia pursuing the conclusion of environmental treaties that minimize detrimental environmental impacts upon Australian citizens and the Australian environment. An example is Australia's early and continued support for the regime to prevent the depletion of the ozone layer, for strong public health and other reasons.[57] Australia has shown far less support for the

---

56 On 13 July 2010 the Court fixed 9 May 2011 for the filing of the Australian Memorial and 9 March 2012 for the Counter-Memorial of Japan. The written submissions may only be made public by the ICJ on the commencement of the oral hearings.

57 Detlef Sprinz and Tapani Vaahtoranta, 'The Interest-Based Explanation of International Environmental Policy' (1994) 48 *International Organization* 77, 87–90.

international climate regime, despite most analyses finding that Australia is among the states likely to be most seriously affected by rising global temperatures. The climate change example illustrates that environmental foreign policy-making is seldom a straightforward process, and that there is a two-level game in play in which domestic political considerations may constrain the government's capacity to support international environmental regimes. Hence although there is broad and enduring public support in Australia for national and international action to address climate change, the policy process has been strongly influenced, some would say corrupted, by industry lobbying with the effect that the government is hamstrung in the emissions reduction commitments it can make.

Another area where there has been some divergence from the pattern of international environmental cooperation by Australia is in the area of biosafety. Australia has not ratified the 2000 Cartagena Protocol on Biosafety to the CBD,[58] which promotes the safe handling, transfer and use of genetically modified organisms, because of the concern that the Protocol may prevent Australia from becoming a centre for research and development in modern biotechnology.[59] Consistent with this approach, in the *Biotech Products* case[60] in the WTO, Australia intervened in support of the United States, Argentina and Canada, which were successful in challenging the legality of European Union measures to restrict the importation of genetically modified organisms.

Litigation Opportunities in Environmental Regimes

A search of the Australian Treaties Database[61] indicates that Australia is a party to over a dozen multilateral environmental agreements that include provision for the compulsory settlement of disputes (see Table 10.1). Most of these provide for arbitration or judicial settlement, with several establishing systems of compulsory conciliation. The only one of these regimes under which Australia has sued or been sued is the LOSC. Significantly, the remaining environmental regimes rely upon a relatively new institution for dispute settlement, non-compliance committees.

Although non-compliance procedures are usually described as being radically different from adjudicative systems of dispute settlement (which in many respects is the case), many have quasi-judicial characteristics. Because they are generally able to be invoked more readily than inter-state dispute settlement mechanisms (because rules of standing are more relaxed or non-existent), the likelihood of

---

58 Opened for signature 29 January 2000, [2000] ATNIF 4 (entered into force 11 September 2003).

59 See Statement by Australia, Final Plenary Session, Second Meeting of the Parties to the Cartagena Protocol, 3 June 2005.

60 Panel Report, *European Communities – Measures Affecting the Approval and Marketing of Biotech Products* WTO Docs WT/DS291/r, WT/DS292/R, WT/DS293/R (29 September 2006).

61 See http://www.dfat.gov.au/treaties/index.html.

proceedings involving Australia is relatively strong. Australia could, for instance, be taken to task under the Kyoto Protocol's compliance procedure, which can be activated by regime institutions, should it fail to meet its greenhouse gas reporting obligations or its quantified emissions limitation target during the 2008–2012 first commitment period. It must be noted, however, that the future of the Kyoto regime as a whole is under a cloud given the lack of clear international support for a second commitment period.

Generally it can be expected that Australia is more likely to be an applicant than a respondent in future international environmental litigation, for the reasons that Australia has an interest in supporting environmental regimes, and in ensuring that there are no defections from regime rules by other states. The effective operation of environmental regimes is an objective that Australia pursues primarily through diplomacy, through participation in conferences and meetings of parties and in the other institutions operating within environmental regimes. Litigation remains an option where diplomacy fails, as can be seen from the *Scientific Whaling* case which is no doubt inspired by a hope, perhaps forlorn, that it will lead to a gestalt-shift, in which issues of whale conservation can be looked at afresh by Japan. Yet by contrast with the laborious process of working through regime institutions to detect compliance problems and resolve them, litigation involves significant costs and risks of failure, particularly when it comes to regimes protective of global environmental goods where a litigator may be hard pressed to identify a discernible impact upon its interests which places it above any other state.

Although it is less likely that Australia will be a respondent than an applicant in international environmental litigation, it is not entirely out of the question, as shown by events in the Timor Sea in 2009. The oil spill from the West Atlas rig in the Montara oil field in the Timor Sea in late 2009, which polluted the marine environment around the islands of Sumba and Timor, may provoke a claim by neighbouring states.[62] Both Indonesia and Timor Leste have indicated that they will seek compensation from the operator of the oil rig, PTTEP Australasia,[63] although neither has stated that in the event that such compensation is inadequate, they will pursue an international claim against Australia.

As Indonesia, like Australia, is a party to the LOSC, it could make a case based on the provisions of Part XII of the Convention, including Article 194(2) which requires states to 'take all measures necessary to ensure that activities under their jurisdiction or control are so conducted as not to cause damage by pollution

62 The West Atlas leak was the subject of a Commission of Inquiry established by the Australian Government: Montara Commission of Inquiry (5 November 2009) www.montarainquiry.gov.au. The report of the Commission was provided to the Government in July 2010.

63 'Indonesia seeks Montara leak compensation' *United Press International*, 22 July 2010; 'East Timor wants compo for oil spill fallout', *Australian Broadcasting Commission*, 5 November 2009. PTTEP Australia is the Australian subsidiary of PTTEP, Thailand's national petroleum exploration and production company.

to other States …'. There is a history of litigation of this type under the LOSC, as seen in the *MOX Plant* case[64] concerning potential pollution affecting Ireland from a reprocessing plant in the United Kingdom, and the *Straits of Johor* case[65] concerning pollution affecting Malaysia as a result of land-reclamation activities being carried out by Singapore.

Timor Leste, not being a party to the LOSC, would have to rely on customary international law, which is reflected in Article 194 of the LOSC, and which is also set out in general terms in the International Law Commission's Draft Articles on the Prevention of Transboundary Harm from Hazardous Activities,[66] and the Draft Principles on the Allocation of Loss in the Case of Transboundary Harm Arising out of Hazardous Activities.[67] However as Timor Leste has not made a declaration under Article 36(2) of the *Statute of the ICJ* accepting as compulsory the jurisdiction of the ICJ, any litigation against Australia would have to proceed via ad hoc arrangement.

Australia is also a party to a large number of environmental regimes that include no system for dispute settlement (see Table 10.3). If Australia is to litigate in respect of breaches of these regimes it cannot therefore rely on any endogenous, treaty-based, dispute settlement machinery, and must instead look to exogenous, general systems for dispute settlement such as that provided for in the *Statute of the ICJ* under Article 36(2). Importantly, this system can also be used in situations where the regime itself possesses a dispute settlement system, although such use may be complicated by jurisdictional issues.

---

64 *MOX Plant (Ireland v United Kingdom) (Provisional Measures)* (2002) 41 ILM 405 *(Suspension of Proceedings)* (2003) 42 ILM 1187.

65 *Land Reclamation by Singapore in and around the Straits of Johor (Malaysia v Singapore)* (*Provisional Measures*) (International Tribunal for the Law of the Sea, Case No 12, 8 October 2003).

66 Report of the International Law Commission, 53rd Session, UN Doc A/56/10 (2001).

67 Report of the International Law Commission, 56th Session, UN Doc A/59/10 (2004).

Table 10.3 Australia's membership of environmental regimes having no dispute settlement system

1946 International Agreement for the Regulation of Whaling [1946] ATS 10
1963 Treaty banning Nuclear Weapon Tests in the Atmosphere, in Outer Space and Under Water [1963] ATS 26
1971 Convention on Wetlands of International Importance especially as Waterfowl Habitat [1975] ATS 48
1971 International Convention on the Establishment of an International Fund for Compensation for Oil Pollution Damage [1995] ATS 2
1972 Convention for the Conservation of Antarctic Seals [1987] ATS 11
1972 Convention for the Protection of the World Cultural and Natural Heritage [1975] ATS 47
1973 Protocol Relating to Intervention on the High Seas in Cases of Pollution by Substances Other than Oil [1984] ATS 5
1974 Agreement between the Government of Australia and the Government of Japan for the Protection of Migratory Birds in Danger of Extinction and their Environment [1981] ATS 6
1976 Convention on Conservation of Nature in the South Pacific [1990] ATS 41
1977 Convention on the Prohibition of Military or any other Hostile Use of Environmental Modification Techniques [1984] ATS 22
1982 Agreement between the Government of Australia and the Government of Japan concerning Japanese Tuna Long-Line Fishing [1982] ATS 18
1985 South Pacific Nuclear Free Zone Treaty [1986] ATS 32
1986 Agreement between the Government of Australia and the Government of the People's Republic of China for the Protection of Migratory Birds and their Environment [1988] ATS 22
1986 Protocol Concerning Co-operation in Combating Pollution Emergencies in the South Pacific Region [1990] ATS 32
1989 Convention for the Prohibition of Fishing with Long Driftnets in the South Pacific [1992] ATS 30
1990 Agreement between the Government of Australia and the Government of the Union of Soviet Socialist Republics on Cooperation in the Field of Protection and Enhancement of the Environment [1990] ATS 10
1990 International Convention on Oil Pollution Preparedness, Response and Co-Operation [1995] ATS 12
2001 International Convention on Civil Liability for Bunker Oil Pollution Damage [2009] ATS 14
2006 Agreement Between the Government of Australia and the Government of the Republic of Korea on the Protection of Migratory Birds and Exchange of Notes [2007] ATS 24

Conclusion

None of the international environmental disputes that Australia has litigated have resulted in the legally clear outcome that would be expected in comparable domestic court proceedings. Not only has Australia in all cases failed to secure the formal relief that it has sought, but there has been no real consideration of the substantive questions of environmental law and policy implicated in the disputes. International courts and tribunals have preferred to avoid these questions altogether, where possible in favour of a compromise result broadly acceptable to the parties. Hence in the *Nuclear Tests* case, the Court turned to unilateral declarations and to rules of admissibility, in the *East Timor* case to the indispensable third party doctrine, in the *Southern Bluefin Tuna* case to the trumping of the LOSC by the CCSBT, and in the *Volga* case to the procedural provisions of the LOSC relating to prompt release of vessels. A similar Solomonic outcome may well be expected in the *Scientific Whaling* case, at least in respect of several of the central arguments made by the Australian government.

However it would be a mistake to conclude from this review of Australia's experience in transboundary environmental disputes that international litigation will always lead to indeterminate results, or that other arenas of international disputation are inherently better suited to litigation than environmental cases. All of the environmental cases in which Australia participated raised a host of legal issues besides purely environmental ones and these were often left equally unresolved. And the cases in which Australia has been involved must also be understood in their historical context; most were decided before international environmental law came to resemble in specificity and clarity most other fields of international legal regulation and well before the use of international courts became more commonplace. We might therefore reasonably expect environmental litigation to be more successful in the twenty-first century than in the twentieth. Moreover, it must also be recognized that none of the cases discussed in this chapter produced zero-sum outcomes; while Australia did not emerge clearly victorious in any cases, nor was it clearly defeated either. The litigation often constituted an important step towards the resolution of the dispute, even if it did not achieve the solution in and of itself. Indefinite and inconclusive litigation may be a source of consternation for lawyers, but it is one tool among a range of others that can be used to advance Australian foreign policy goals in transboundary environmental governance.

Chapter 11
Transboundary Environmental Impact Assessment in Marine Areas

Warwick Gullett

Introduction

One of the clearest messages to emerge from the wealth of environmental literature that has been generated since the late 1960s is that environmental degradation does not respect jurisdictional borders. Although many international and intrastate borders lie along geographical 'divides' such as mountain ridges and rivers, these natural features do not break physical and biological linkages of ecosystems. These linkages are often more pronounced where human-selected borders bisect especially fluid environments, such as the ocean in which there is constant movement of water, energy and marine life. Transboundary environmental problems are generally the result of planned human activities. They may be caused by specific development projects within one State or by activities in areas beyond national jurisdiction (ABNJ), such as the high seas. Environmental impact assessment (EIA) has largely proven to be a successful tool for understanding and minimizing the environmental impacts of specific development projects or activities since it was adopted in numerous States from the early 1970s. There is extensive, worldwide, experience in conducting EIAs for large scale land-based projects. However, the application of EIA to developments and activities in the marine environment is of more recent origin and often more challenging because of the large geographical and temporal scale of potential environmental impacts, as well as the increased likelihood that environmental harm might be caused to neighbouring States. Degradation of marine environments also tends to be more difficult to monitor than terrestrial environments and ecosystems.

This chapter examines the obligation and challenge of conducting EIA for developments and activities in the marine environment which have the potential to cause transboundary environmental harm. The process of EIA is first reviewed followed by an examination of developments in international law which reveal the emergence of a clear yet insufficiently detailed obligation on States to conduct EIA for projects and activities which might cause significant environmental harm in areas outside their jurisdiction, as well as an obligation to cooperate with adjacent States, including in the provision of information about planned development activities. The discussion then turns to the application of these obligations to marine activities. It is suggested that the nature and variety of activities at sea, coupled with the complexity of jurisdictional rights in different maritime zones, merits attention being given to the development of marine activity or marine area-specific transboundary EIA agreements to facilitate the implementation of the general international law obligation to conduct transboundary EIA.

Environmental Impact Assessment

On 1 January 1970 the *National Environmental Policy Act* 1969[1] (NEPA) became law in the United States. NEPA has often been referred to as the Magna Carta of environmental law.[2] It was the first legislative EIA procedure in the world. Numerous States observed its implementation in the 1970s before adopting their own EIA systems. Australia, for example, drew heavily on the NEPA model when it formulated its EIA procedures in 1974.[3]

NEPA contains a number of ambitious provisions aimed at promoting 'efforts which will prevent or eliminate damage to the environment'.[4] To ensure that the federal government considered the environmental consequences of its actions adequately, an 'action-forcing' section was included. Thus the cornerstone of NEPA is its requirement that all federal agencies shall – 'to the fullest extent possible' – accompany 'major Federal actions significantly affecting the quality of the human environment' with a detailed environmental impact statement (EIS).[5] The stated purpose of the EIA process is that it: 'shall provide full and fair discussion of significant environmental impacts and shall inform decisionmakers and the public of the reasonable alternatives which would avoid or minimize adverse impacts or enhance the quality of the human environment'.[6] NEPA set a benchmark standard for EIA which has since been implemented in more than 100 States[7] as well as being adopted by many international agencies.[8]

---

1 42 USC §§4321–4375.

2 Bruce S Manheim, 'NEPA's Overseas Application' (1994) 36 *Environment* 43–45, 43.

3 *Environmental Protection (Impact of Proposals) Act* 1974 (Cth) (replaced in 2000 by the *Environment Protection and Biodiversity Conservation Act* 1999 (Cth)). Australian States also developed EIA in the 1970s. See, eg, *Environment Effects Act* 1978 (Vic).

4 42 USC §4321. See John V Cardone, 'Substantive Standards and NEPA: Mitigating Environmental Consequences with Consent Decrees' (1991) 18 *Boston College Environmental Affairs Law Review* 159–184, 159.

5 42 USC §4332(2)(c). NEPA does not actually use the phrase 'Environmental Impact Statement'; rather, it requires a 'detailed statement'.

6 Council on Environmental Quality, *Regulations for Implementing the Procedural Provisions of the National Environmental Policy Act, 1978*, §1502.1.

7 Neil Craik, *The International Law of Environmental Impact Assessment: Process, Substance and Integration* (Cambridge University Press, 2008) 4.

8 For eg, the World Bank and the UN Environment Program. See Carole Klein-Chesivoir, 'Avoiding Environmental Injury: The Case for Widespread Use of Environmental

Purpose of EIA

The rationale for EIA is that optimal development decisions will result if the short- and long-term environmental effects of a project or activity are assessed in conjunction with a study of and comparison with feasible alternatives. The object of EIA is to ensure that matters affecting the environment are fully examined and taken into account so that development activities avoid or minimize anticipated adverse environmental effects. The hallmark of the process is its institutionalization of foresight. It introduces consideration of environmental factors as a condition precedent to planning decisions.

EIA has become an established component in the planning process for most major developments in many States. It is the only legislative process by which environmental considerations are studied in a systematic and detailed manner, and then expressly taken into account in developmental decision-making. Yet typically there is a limited mandate for EIA. Often when legislative EIA measures are introduced their importance is qualified by statements by their proponents that they are not a panacea for environmental ills, and that their objective is not to prevent projects being undertaken which are harmful to the environment but to ensure that decisions about such projects are taken in the knowledge of their environmental consequences. For example, it is simply stated in the legislation which provides the legal framework for Australia's federal EIA process that the Act 'adopts an efficient and timely Commonwealth environmental assessment and approval process that will ensure activities that are likely to have significant impacts on the environment are properly assessed'.[9] The focus of EIA processes is thus to provide a procedure to consider possible adverse environmental consequences of certain activities, but not necessarily to avoid them. However, although a proposed project might not be prohibited following the preparation of an EIA that reveals the potential for it to cause environmental harm, other avoidance measures (such as changes in project location, scale and design) may be taken to minimize harm, thus improving the environmental performance of the project.

EIA Process

There is no uniform or universal EIA process. The method by which environmental assessments are conducted vary from one State to another and also across sub-national jurisdictions. This is due to differences in public administration, cultural

---

Impact Assessments in International Development Projects' (1990) 30 *Virginia Journal of International Law* 517–551; Nicholas A Robinson, 'International Trends in Environmental Impact Assessment' (1992) 19 *Boston College Environmental Affairs Law Review* 591–619 and Jean-Roger Mercier, 'The World Bank and Environmental Impact Assessment' in Kees Bastmeijer and Timo Koivurova (eds), *Theory and Practice of Transboundary Environmental Impact Assessment* (Martinus Nijhoff, 2008) 291–311.

9 *Environment Protection and Biodiversity Conservation Act* 1999 (Cth) s 3(2)(d).

values, legislative procedures and institutional capacity across jurisdictions.[10] Nevertheless, a general EIA framework can be identified which most jurisdictions adopt notwithstanding variations in detail, commitment and capacity to undertake certain elements. The main steps of EIA are outlined in Table 11.1.

Table 11.1 EIA process

EIA steps	Content
Screening	The first step is to determine the threshold that a project or activity must meet for the process to be triggered. To assist screening, some procedures include a list of activities for which the conduct of an EIA is mandatory. Where an activity is not included on such a list, a decision needs to be made concerning whether the proposed activity warrants the undertaking of an EIA. Internal guidelines are often prepared to assist this determination. Typically the threshold set is whether the activity is 'likely' to cause 'significant' environmental impacts. Some jurisdictions have tiered assessments which incorporates flexibility into the process by allowing different levels of assessment depending on the environmental significance of the proposal.[a]
Scoping	The second step is to determine what issues need to be addressed in the environmental assessment. The magnitude, extent and significance of impacts need to be identified with focus being on the most potentially significant impacts. Ideally public consultation and participation is part of this stage. Three broad types of impacts should be considered: *direct* (caused by the project or activity in proximate location and time); *cumulative* (caused by incremental impacts of the project or activity when added to other activities or reasonably foreseeable activities); and *indirect* (caused by the project or activity but distant in space or in time). The scoping phase should be conducted early so that alternative activities (including the 'no action' option) can be considered and projects can incorporate mitigation measures identified. Scoping also requires determining appropriate methods for assessment (these may include checklists, matrices, overlays, environmental indices, cost-benefit analysis and computer modelling). Most EIA processes include scoping requirements, although the level of detail varies.

10 Alexandre S Timoshenko, 'The Problem of Preventing Damage to the Environment in National and International Law: Impact Assessment and International Consultations' (1988) 5 *Pace Environmental Law Review* 475–486, 481.

Content	It is common for jurisdictions to have different standards concerning the level of detail required in EIAs. However, the normal requirements for EIAs is that they contain a description of the project as well as reasonable alternatives; a baseline study of the area prior to development so that impacts can be evaluated; an evaluation and quantification (where possible) of impacts identified in the scoping phase; a consideration of alternatives including comparison of predicted impacts; and a consideration of mitigation measures. As EIA studies are normally comprehensive studies of numerous different issues, it is common for all the various impact studies to be summarized in an easily readable report. This report is commonly called the environmental impact statement (EIS).
Decision-making	Once the EIS has been prepared, it is normally reviewed by the government agency responsible for approving the development as well as by the public. Advanced processes also require that the EIS be reviewed by an independent body to determine whether it is adequate in terms of the issues addressed and the depth of analysis. Finally, a decision is made as to whether, and on what grounds, the project or activity should proceed. In theory EIA should lead to the selection of the most suitable project option, although in practice the proposed project is normally selected rather than other investigated options. The EIA may also set conditions for project approval aimed at minimizing predicted environmental impacts.
Post-decision monitoring and auditing	EIA procedures also normally include a requirement that monitoring systems are established after the project is completed to determine whether the actual impacts of the projects correspond with those that were predicted during the EIA process. This also enables verification of the effectiveness of mitigation measures and the ability to determine whether further mitigation measures are necessary.

Notes: [a] For eg, in the Australian federal context, s 87(1) of the Environment Protection and Biodiversity Conservation Act 1999 (Cth) provides for the selection of one of six levels of assessment.

International Environmental Law Obligations

EIAs are conducted within States or sub-national jurisdictions in accordance with domestic laws and policies. Additionally States are obliged under public international law to assess, consider and avoid possible environmental impacts to neighbouring States of their developments and activities. This international obligation seeks to balance the entrenched concept of State sovereignty with the potentially competing principle of the need to avoid environmental harm to other States.

State Sovereignty

States have a number of rights concerning their territory which they can exercise freely. This collection of rights is referred to as national or State sovereignty. States are considered to be equal and autonomous actors on the world stage with virtually unfettered power over internal decision-making. However, a few important limits to this right have emerged. The general principle is that a State may not exercise its rights beyond the point where they interfere with the capacity of another State to exercise equivalent rights. In the environmental context, this means, for example, that a State may not exploit its own natural resources if this unduly impinges on the interests of other States.

The overarching framework of State sovereignty presents problems for the development of international standards for the assessment, planning, monitoring and conduct of activities that have transboundary environmental implications. Cooperation among States and the harmonization of their environmental protection policies can be hampered by the continual reaffirmation of the concept of State sovereignty in international environmental treaties and policy documents. This is because the continued acceptance of the notion of State sovereignty can be used by States to justify controversial developments that may be in their national interests but are a cause of concern to other States. The commitment to State sovereignty is seen for example, in the United Nations Law of the Sea Convention (LOSC)[11] – as well as the two most significant international documents dealing with environmental matters – the 1972 UN Stockholm Declaration and the 1992 UN Rio Declaration – both of which entrench States' commitment to sovereignty, although tempered by statements of environmental responsibility. Principle 21 of the Stockholm Declaration states that:

> States have, in accordance with the Charter of the United Nations and the principles of environmental law, the sovereign right to exploit their own resources pursuant to their own environmental policies and the responsibility to ensure that activities within their jurisdiction or control do not cause damage to the environment of other States or of areas beyond the limits of national jurisdiction.

This principle was reiterated virtually verbatim in Principle 2 of the Rio Declaration. However, there has been some further erosion of the concept of sovereignty since the 1970s due to developments in international environmental law. This is

11 United Nations Convention on the Law of the Sea, opened for signature 10 December 1982, 1833 UNTS 3 (entered into force generally 16 November 1994) art 193: 'States have the sovereign right to exploit their natural resources pursuant to their environmental policies and in accordance with their duty to protect and preserve the marine environment.' See also United Nations Convention on Biological Diversity, opened for signature 5 June 1992, 1760 UNTS 79 (entered into force 29 December 1993) art 3.

principally due to developing rules of customary international law brought about by improvements in States' environmental practices and the proliferation of multilateral environmental agreements.

Developments in International Law

Through a growing body of State practice, decisions of international courts and tribunals, the work of the International Law Commission and several treaties, there is now a core framework in international law regulating transboundary environmental harm. This framework is now reviewed.

Liability for Transboundary Harm The proposition that States are responsible for transboundary environmental harm was articulated in 1941 in the landmark *Trail Smelter Arbitration*[12] decision. At issue was whether Canada was liable for the transboundary effects of sulphur dioxide emissions from a copper smelter in British Columbia. The emissions had, over a period of 12 years, caused damage to farmlands and crops in the United States. The Tribunal awarded the United States compensation and stated: '[N]o State has the right to use or permit the use of its territory in such a manner as to *cause injury* by fumes in or to the territory of another or the properties or persons therein, when the case is of *serious* consequence and the injury is established by *clear and convincing* evidence' (emphasis added).[13] This formulation of State liability was extended beyond air pollution to other injurious acts by the decision eight years later of the International Court of Justice (ICJ) in the *Corfu Channel case.*[14] This case is authority for the proposition that every State has an obligation 'not to allow knowingly its territory to be used for acts contrary to the rights of other states'. A further responsibility incumbent on States, established in the 1957 *Lac Lanoux Arbitration,*[15] is the obligation to cooperate with other States to mitigate any transboundary harm which has been caused. Importantly, the arbitral and judicial determinations make no distinction between lawful and unlawful activities occasioning harm. The responsibility placed on the State is an obligation to prevent harm from being caused, either directly from its own activities, or by persons or entities within its territory, jurisdiction or control. It is the transboundary harm itself that is prohibited, not the activity in question, which caused the harm. Moreover only significant or serious harm is to be avoided, rather than lower level damage.

A limitation in international law is that the standard of liability for harm caused to the territory of another State turns on discharging the rather general obligation of 'due diligence'. That is to say that only harm that results from negligence or

12 *Trail Smelter Arbitral Tribunal Decision* (United States v Canada) (1941) 35 *American Journal of International Law* 684.

13 Ibid 716.

14 *Corfu Channel Case* (United Kingdom v Albania) [1949] ICJ Reports 4.

15 *Lac Lanoux Arbitration* (France v Spain) [1957] *International Law Reports* 101ff.

other failure to act with due diligence will give rise to liability.[16] 'Due diligence' is generally understood as imposing an obligation on States to promote 'good governance', which, in the environmental arena, is interpreted as requiring action to abate or prevent further transboundary harm. It may also require the taking of 'reasonably appropriate' domestic legal measures[17] from State to State depending, among other things, on the availability of resources.[18] The due diligence concept and the liability gap was a focus of the International Tribunal for the Law of the Sea's (ITLOS) recent advisory opinion. It stated:

> The content of 'due diligence' obligations may not easily be described in precise terms. Among the factors that make such a description difficult is the fact that 'due diligence' is a variable concept. It may change over time as measures considered sufficiently diligent at a certain moment may become not diligent enough in light, for instance, of new scientific or technological knowledge. It may also change in relation to the risks involved in the activity.[19]

Although States must restrict the use of their territory so as not to harm other States, the concept of 'due diligence' means that if harm does occur, a State will only be required to pay compensation where the harm was brought about through a lack of proper care. This standard falls far short of imposing strict liability for harm. For example, if diligent regulation and control over resources is exercised (such as where a State has introduced legislative and administrative controls considered sufficient to prevent transboundary harm), but nevertheless harm is caused to another State (such as where it was not reasonably foreseeable), the harm will be regarded as lawful and the injured State will have no legal redress in the absence of a breach of a specific treaty provision.[20] This allows a State to conduct a hazardous activity in a reasonable manner and derive the economic benefits from it, while avoiding responsibility to pay compensation at a later time should harm occur to another State.[21]

---

16 Alan E Boyle, 'State Responsibility and International Liability for Injurious Consequences of Acts not Prohibited by International Law: A Necessary Distinction?' (1990) 39 *International and Comparative Law Quarterly* 1–26, 15.

17 *Responsibilities and Obligations of States Sponsoring Persons and Entities with Respect to Activities in the Area* (Advisory Opinion) (2011) ITLOS Case no 17, [120].

18 Malgosia Fitzmaurice, 'International Responsibility and Liability' in Daniel Bodansky, Jutta Brunnée and Ellen Hey (eds), *The Oxford Handbook of International Environmental Law* (Oxford University Press, 2007) 1010–1035, 1014.

19 *Responsibilities and Obligations of States Sponsoring Persons and Entities with Respect to Activities in the Area* (Advisory Opinion) (2011) ITLOS Case no 17, [117].

20 See Thomas Gehring and Markus Jachtenfuchs, 'Liability for Transboundary Environmental Damage: Towards a General Liability Regime?' (1993) 4 *European Journal of International Law* 92–106, 93.

21 René Lefeber, *Transboundary Environmental Interference and the Origin of State Liability* (Kluwer Law International, 1996) 15.

The United Nations International Law Commission (ILC) proceeded on the basis of the distinction between activities which are or are not prohibited by international law in its codification and progressive development of the rules of international liability for harmful consequences of lawful activities in its attempt to remedy the situation where States are not liable to compensate for harm caused by activities it regulated diligently. The object of the project is to enable States to agree on rules for prevention and adopt them in treaties, thus creating obligations prior to any consideration of the lawfulness of an activity. In its deliberations, the ILC was guided by three overarching principles:

1. every State must have the maximum freedom of action within its territory compatible with respect for the sovereign equality of other States;
2. the protection of the rights and interests of other States requires the adoption of measures of prevention and reparation for injury; and
3. the innocent victim should not be left to bear his [*sic*] own loss.[22]

In 2001, after more than 30 years of work, the ILC adopted 19 draft articles entitled 'Prevention of Transboundary Harm from Hazardous Activities', followed by the adoption in 2006 of eight draft principles on the allocation of loss in the case of transboundary harm arising out of hazardous activities.[23] The 2001 articles apply to activities which involve a 'risk of causing significant transboundary harm through their physical consequences,[24] which is defined as encompassing 'a high probability of causing significant transboundary harm and a low probability of causing disastrous transboundary harm'.[25]

An opportunity was missed to consolidate an obligation not to cause harm to the environment per se because the definition of 'transboundary harm' is not expressed to apply to areas beyond the jurisdiction of affected States. The term is defined as 'harm caused in the territory of or in other places under the jurisdiction or control of a State other than the State of origin, whether or not the States concerned share a common border'.[26] However, this does not negate existing duties of 'Flag States', principally under LOSC, where vessels on their registries conduct activities on the high seas.[27] For example, a flag State is obliged to ensure that a ship flying its flag is appropriately equipped and regularly inspected so that it can navigate safely, and has qualified crew who 'are fully conversant with and

22 Boyle, above n 17, 6.

23 The Draft Articles are available at the ILC website: www.un.org/law/ilc/.

24 Art 1.

25 Art 2.

26 Art 2.

27 See International Law Commission, *Draft Articles on Prevention of Transboundary Harm from Hazardous Activities, with Commentaries 2001* (United Nations, 2008) 151, Alfred Rest, 'State Responsibility/Liability: *Erga Omnes* Obligations and Judicial Control' (2010) 40 *Environmental Policy and Law* 298, 303 and John N K Mansell, *Flag State Responsibility: Historical Development and Contemporary Issues* (Springer, 2009).

required to observe' applicable international rules (such as those adopted by the International Maritime Organization) concerning the prevention, reduction and control of marine pollution.[28]

The 2001 draft articles emphasize the need to act diligently to prevent or reduce the risk of significant transboundary harm[29] using methods such as EIA:

> Article 7: Assessment of risk
> Any decision in respect of the authorization of an activity within the scope of the present articles shall, in particular, be based on an assessment of the possible transboundary harm caused by that activity, including any environmental impact assessment.

Although a convention on the topic is yet to eventuate (and is unlikely to do so), the ILC's 2001 and 2006 draft articles are critically important in consolidating and refining international environmental law principles. They remain non-binding yet, due to the painstaking, detailed, consultative and comprehensive nature of their development, they are constructive for States which wish to adopt best practice in oversight and regulation of activities under their jurisdiction which pose environmental threats to other States.

The Duty to Prevent Harm to 'the Environment' Principle 21 of the 1972 Stockholm Declaration is a concise reformulation of the general principles emanating from *Trail Smelter* and subsequent jurisprudence. It is binding on all States as customary law, as evidenced by the 1996 statement of the ICJ in an advisory opinion that the prevention of transboundary harm arising from hazardous activities has become a central obligation of international law. In its statement, the ICJ made a significant observation on the future direction of international environmental law:

> The environment is not an abstraction but represents the living space, the quality of life and the very health of human beings, including generations unborn. The existence of the general obligation of States to ensure that activities within their jurisdiction and control respect the environment of other States or of areas beyond national control is now part of the corpus of international law relating to the environment.[30]

Principle 21 of the Stockholm Declaration contains the most elemental statement relating to the obligation on States to protect the environment. The Principle sought to balance the 'sovereign right' of States 'to exploit their own resources

---

28 LOSC art 94(4).

29 Art 3.

30 *Legality of the Threat or Use of Nuclear Weapons*, Advisory Opinion, ICJ Reports 1996, pp. 241–2, [29].

pursuant to their own environmental policies' with the responsibility to ensure that activities within their jurisdiction or control do not cause damage to the environment of other States or of ABNJ.

Not only did Principle 21 effectively codify the *Trail Smelter* doctrine, it also went further than the decision in that case in so far as it recognized the responsibility States have to adopt suitable measures to prevent harm outside their jurisdiction. The duty to prevent harm is often expressed in a way which requires States to take all 'practicable' steps to avoid harm. An example is Article 194 of LOSC which provides that:

> States shall take, individually or jointly as appropriate, all measures consistent with this Convention that are necessary to prevent, reduce and control pollution of the marine environment from any source, using for this purpose the best practicable means at their disposal and in accordance with their capabilities, and they shall endeavor to harmonize their policies in this connection.

This suggests that States must make all reasonable efforts to avoid causing environmental harm. However, the most important aspect of the Principle as articulated by the ILC and the Stockholm Declaration is its reference to the broad obligation States have to ensure that activities within their jurisdiction do not cause harm to 'the environment'. Thus it can be seen that since the early 1970s, international environmental law has dispensed with the need to establish direct and tangible injury to the territory of another State. This means that ABNJ, such as the high seas, benefit from the general obligation all States have to not cause harm to the environment. However, while there is an obligation not to cause damage to the environment in ABNJ, including the high seas, there is uncertainty about what is compensable damage and which entities are entitled to claim compensation. The ILC, in its 2001 draft Articles on State Responsibility, proposed that any State, irrespective of whether it is injured, is entitled to invoke the responsibility of another State if the obligation breached 'is owed to a group of States including that State, and is established for the protection of a collective interest of the group' or the obligation breached 'is owed to the international community as a whole'.[31] This view was supported by ITLOS in 2011.[32]

The Duty to Cooperate A broad duty on States to cooperate with each other is found in many international environmental treaties, as well as other international environmental instruments.[33] Indeed, Boyle opined that '[i]t is undoubtedly true that co-operation in the control of environmental risks is one of the central elements

31 Art 48. The Draft Articles are available at the ILC website: www.un.org/law/ilc/.

32 *Responsibilities and Obligations of States Sponsoring Persons and Entities with Respect to Activities in the Area* (Advisory Opinion) (2011) ITLOS Case no 17, [180].

33 See, eg, Rio Declaration Principles 7, 9, 12–14, 18, 19, 27 and ILC 2001 Draft Articles.

of general international law on environmental protection.'[34] A duty to cooperate is arguably most notable in LOSC. It is found in 70 of the 320 articles, covering a range of issues including protection and preservation of the marine environment.[35] ITLOS in the 2001 *Mox Plant case* considered that the duty to cooperate 'is a fundamental principle in the prevention of pollution of the marine environment' under LOSC and general international law.[36]

The duty to cooperate is not an easy concept to define (and indeed it is a contested concept)[37] nor is it easy to determine in detail what specific actions (and in what circumstances) must be taken to fulfil the duty. Treaties such as LOSC do not provide a definition of cooperation nor prescribe consequences for States which do not engage in the required level of cooperation. Nevertheless, the duty to cooperate can be seen as underpinning and complementing the duty States have to not cause significant harm or the risk of significant harm to other States or to ABNJ. In circumstances where the activities of one State potentially threaten the environment of another, the duty to cooperate could be seen as requiring at minimum the provision of information to the potentially affected State and continual notification of proposed remedial measures.[38]

The Duty to Conduct Transboundary EIA Notwithstanding the difficulty of establishing liability for transboundary harm, new norms of environmental behaviour have emerged that focus on avoiding harm by requiring States to act prior to harm occurring. These norms can in time harden into enforceable rules of international law, such as what has recently occurred in relation to EIA. An obligation to conduct EIA has been derived from the jurisprudence which followed the *Trail Smelter* decision. A corollary of the duty a State has not to knowingly cause harm to other States is the duty it has to monitor the environmental impacts of activities as facts and knowledge progress. Monitoring contributes to

---

34 Alan Boyle, 'The Environmental Jurisprudence of the International Tribunal for the Law of the Sea' (2007) 22 *International Journal of Marine and Coastal Law* 369–381, 379.

35 See arts 197, 199, 200, 201, 211, 217, 226 and 235.

36 *MOX Plant case* (Ireland v United Kingdom) (Provisional Measures, Order of 3 December 2001) ITLOS case no 10, [82]; *Case Concerning Land Reclamation by Singapore in and around the Straits of Johor* (Malaysia v Singapore) (Provisional Measures, Order of 8 October 2003) ITLOS Case No 12, [92].

37 See, eg, Kenneth A Oye, 'Explaining Cooperation under Anarchy: Hypothesis and Strategies' (1985) 38 *World Politics* 1–24; Oran R Young, *Governance in World Affairs* (Cornell University Press, 1999); Rüdiger Wolfrum and Nele Matz, *Conflicts in International Environmental Law* (Springer, 2003); Alan E Boyle, 'The Principle of Co-operation: The Environment' in Vaughan Lowe and Colin Warbrick (eds), *The United Nations and the Principles of International Law: Essays in Memory of Michael Akehurst* (Routledge, 1994) 120–136.

38 See ILC 2001 Draft Articles Prevention of Transboundary Harm from Hazardous Activities, arts 8–9, 12.

baseline knowledge of ecosystems and is also necessary to determine if a State is complying with specific emission standards contained in conventions. Writing in 1992, Robinson considered that 'it is becoming a norm of customary international law that nations should engage in effective EIA before taking action that could adversely affect either shared natural resources, another country's environment, or the Earth's commons'.[39] A State likely to be affected by a harmful activity should be consulted and furnished with sufficient information to enable it to make an assessment of the probable effects of the proposed activities.[40] This necessitates some form of environmental assessment and notification to potentially affected States of proposed activities which foreseeably involve risk of harm. Support for this proposition can be found in the 1997 decision of the ICJ in the *Gabcíkovo-Nagymaros* case in which it was noted that environmental risks need to be evaluated and 'assessed on a continuous basis'.[41] This suggests that it is appropriate – if not obligatory – for a State to conduct some form of EIA for a project or activity which is likely to cause significant transboundary harm.

The most recent development in international jurisprudence regarding transboundary EIA is the 2010 judgment of the ICJ in the *Pulp Mills* case. The Court opined that it was now

> a requirement under general international law to undertake an environmental impact assessment where there is a risk that the proposed industrial activity may have a significant adverse impact in a transboundary context, in particular, on a shared resource. Moreover, due diligence, and the duty of vigilance and prevention which it implies, would not be considered to have been exercised, if a party ... did not undertake an environmental impact assessment on the potential effects of [the project].[42]

Thus it can be seen that there is an international law obligation to conduct EIAs for projects with the potential to cause significant transboundary harm. However, the key issue is the minimum content requirements of the international obligation to conduct EIA. The ICJ noted that there was no specification in international

39 Robinson, above n 8, 602. See also Jonas Ebbesson, *Compatibility of International and National Environmental Law* (Kluwer Law International, 1996) 47. Cf John H Knox, 'The Myth and Reality of Transboundary Environmental Impact Assessment' (2002) 96 *American Journal of International Law* 291–319.

40 See Montreal Rules of International Law Applicable to Transfrontier Pollution (1982) art 7.

41 ICJ, Judgment in the *Case Concerning the Gabcíkovo-Nagymaros Project*, 25 September 1997, para 112, 37 ILM 162 (1998). See, however, Preiss for argument that the ICJ's opinion was misguided in terms of it failing to establish that EIA is a customary principle of international law: Erika L Preiss, 'The International Obligation to Conduct an Environmental Impact Assessment: The ICJ Case Concerning the Gabcikovo-Nagymaros Project' (1999) 7 *New York University Environmental Law Journal* 307–351.

42 *Case concerning pulp mills on the River Uruguay* (Argentina v Uruguay) [204].

law of the scope and content of EIA. Rather, in the ICJ's opinion, States have wide ranging discretion regarding how they conduct EIA, depending on the nature of the activity in question and likely seriousness of potential transboundary environmental impact. It opined:

> it is for each State to determine in its domestic legislation or in the authorization process for the project, the specific content of the environmental impact assessment required in each case, having regard to the nature and magnitude of the proposed development and its likely adverse impact on the environment as well as to the need to exercise due diligence in conducting such an assessment. The Court also considers that an environmental impact assessment must be conducted prior to the implementation of a project.[43]

It has also been argued that the law has evolved from the *Trail Smelter* preventative principle to require the preparation of EIAs as a technical implementation of the duty to implement the precautionary principle.[44] This responsibility also offers increased opportunity to consider cumulative, distant or uncertain transboundary environmental effects of activities for which compensation at international law would be unlikely to flow. Another obligation includes conducting continuing EIA which is derived from the 'duty to continuously monitor the environmental impacts of development projects as facts and knowledge progress', as well as exchange of information.[45]

Treaty Law and Other Specific Instruments

As far back as 1978, the United Nations Environment Programme recommended that: 'States should make environmental assessments before engaging in any activity with respect to a shared natural resource which may create a risk of significantly affecting the environment of another State or States sharing that resource.'[46] A number of international instruments have adopted EIA processes. Numerous international conventions dealing with specific subject matters or the

43 Ibid [205].

44 The ILC (1998: ch 4, para 47) considered international EIA as part of the procedural obligations contained within the general duty to prevent injurious consequences, together with the precautionary principle as a substantive obligation under this head. See Principle 3 of the ILC draft principles of international law: 'States shall take all appropriate measures to prevent, or to minimize the risk of, significant transboundary harm.'

45 Stephen Stec and Gabriel E Eckstein, 'Of Solemn Oaths and Obligations: The Environmental Impact of the ICJ's Decision in the *Case Concerning the Gabíkovo-Nagymaros Project*' (1997) 8 *Yearbook of International Environmental Law* 41–50, 48.

46 *Environmental Law Guidelines and Principles on Shared Natural Resources*, Principle 4, (1978) 17 ILM 1097.

general transboundary context require some form of EIA.[47] Transboundary EIA agreements have also appeared. This section briefly reviews the most prominent international agreements regarding transboundary EIA as well as the less specific obligations contained in LOSC.

EU EIA Directive The EU EIA Directive, adopted by the European Commission Council in 1985, was the first attempt to generate a regional EIA framework. It supports the harmonization of the main principles of EIA among member States although its provisions lack detail and it places relatively few procedural demands on States.[48] The Directive, which was substantially amended in 1997,[49] applies to public and private projects which are 'likely to have significant effects on the environment by virtue, inter alia, of their nature, size or location'.[50] These are defined in two categories. First, Annex I provides that the provisions of the Directive shall apply to the type of projects listed therein.[51] Second, States shall determine by case by case examination or according to thresholds or criteria set by them, whether projects listed in Annex II shall be made subject to EIA.[52]

An EIA procedure is provided which must be completed prior to the granting of project consent,[53] and must be taken into consideration in final decision-making.[54] This covers standard EIA elements including the identification, description and assessment of 'the main effects which the project is likely to have on the environment'.[55] There needs to be consultation with other member States

47 See, eg, Climate Change Convention Article 4(1)(f), Biodiversity Convention Article 14(1)(a), and treaties dealing with the global commons such as the Convention on the Conservation of Antarctic Marine Living Resources Article XV(2)(d) and the Antarctic Treaty System.

48 See Howard L Brown, 'Expanding the Effectiveness of the European Union's Environmental Impact Assessment Law' (1997) 22 *Boston College International and Comparative Law Review* 313–334.

49 Council Directive 85/337/EEC of 27 June 1985 on the assessment of the effects of certain public and private projects on the environment, OJ 1985, L75, p. 40. See also Council Directive 97/11/EC of 3 March 1997 amending Directive 85/337/EEC on the assessment of the effects of certain public and private projects on the environment, OJ 1997, L73, p 5. See Simon Marsden, 'Transboundary Environmental Impact Assessment in European Law' in Simon Marsden and Timo Koivurova (eds), *Transboundary Environmental Impact Assessment in the European Union: The Espoo Convention and its Kiev Protocol on Strategic Environmental Assessment* (Earthscan, 2011) 39–56.

50 Art 2(1).

51 These generally apply to land-based activities although some are applicable to marine activities, such as petroleum and natural gas extraction works, and large gas and oil pipelines.

52 Art 4(2).

53 Art 2(1).

54 Art 8.

55 Arts 3 and 5.

in addition to the public and authorities.[56] The Directive requires developers to provide information on alternatives to the intended project that they choose to study,[57] although it does not require that project approval be balanced against the relative merits of each project option.

The Directive is not intended to displace domestic EIA processes, but rather harmonize member States' EIA procedures to reduce competition and misallocation of resources.[58] The absence of exacting standards in the Directive has led to criticism that it merely formalizes procedures already in existence in member States and does little to advance standards and practice in EIA.[59] However, the Directive offers guidance to ensure transboundary EIA is conducted effectively across jurisdictions. It reiterates that European Commission environmental policy is based on the precautionary principle[60] and aims to promote the consideration of environmental issues in planning and design.

Espoo Convention on EIA in a Transboundary Context The most significant advance in transboundary environmental impact assessment is the 1991 UN Convention on Environmental Impact Assessment in a Transboundary Context (adopted at Espoo, Finland under the auspices of the United Nations Economic Commission for Europe (ECE), and hereafter referred to as the Espoo Convention).[61] The Convention entered into force on 10 September 1997 upon the ratification of 16 States. At present, 45 States have ratified, accepted, approved or acceded to the Convention. It provides that EIA procedures must be undertaken for certain activities which are likely to have significant transboundary impacts within an area under the jurisdiction of another State party.

The Convention defines EIA as 'a national procedure for evaluating the likely impact of a proposed activity on the environment'.[62] It is therefore envisaged that all States will adopt minimum EIA procedures. The Convention does not provide for the conduct of EIAs separate from domestic procedures. Rather, it seeks the harmonization of them. Similar to the EU EIA Directive, the Convention provides that EIA shall be undertaken prior to a decision to authorize or undertake proposed activities listed in Appendix I that are likely to cause significant adverse

56 Arts 6 and 7.

57 Preamble and art 5(3).

58 Preiss, above n 41, 316.

59 See, e.g., Paul D McHugh, 'The European Community Directive: An Alternative Environmental Impact Assessment Procedure?' (1994) 34 *Natural Resources Journal* 589–628, 605; Simon Dresner and Nigel Gilbert, 'Decision-making Processes for Projects Requiring EIA: Case Studies in Six European Countries' (1999) 1 *Journal of Environmental Assessment Policy and Management* 105–130, 106; Preiss, above n 41, 316 and Knox, above n 40, 302.

60 Preamble.

61 United Nations Convention on Environmental Impact Assessment in a Transboundary Context, (conducted at Espoo, Finland, 25 February 1991).

62 Art 1(vi).

transboundary impacts. Many of the activities listed are well defined. However, qualifying words such as 'major', 'integrated' and 'large' appear to alter the threshold, thus meaning that the provisions of the Convention only apply to a subset of all possible activities under consideration. The significance of the likely transboundary impacts can only be considered once a determination is made that the activity in question falls within the projects listed in Appendix I. The determination of the 'significance' of a transboundary environmental impact is to a certain degree a value judgment. This is to be determined by comprehensive consideration of the characteristics of the activity and its possible impact. EIAs may also be conducted for activities that are not listed in Appendix I by agreement of the parties, and depending upon the size, location, and potential effects of the project.[63] Relatively brief content requirements are provided in Appendix II which state that EIAs must include, at a minimum:

- a description of the proposed activity and its purpose;
- a description, where appropriate, of reasonable alternatives to the proposed activity including the no-action alternative;[64]
- a description of the environment likely to be significantly affected by the proposed activity and its alternatives;
- a description of the potential environmental impact of the proposed activity and its alternatives and an estimation of significance;
- a description of mitigation measures;
- where appropriate, an outline for monitoring and management systems and any plans for post-project analysis; and
- a non-technical summary.

The Convention also requires an 'explicit indication of predictive methods and underlying assumptions', as well as an 'identification of gaps in knowledge, and uncertainties encountered in compiling the required information'. The Convention's main requirements relate to notifying potentially affected States about a proposed activity likely to cause a significant adverse transboundary impact and inviting their participation in the EIA procedure. There is also a requirement of participation from the public that may be affected.[65] In accordance with EIA theory, the Convention emphasizes the importance of considering alternatives to the proposed project. It requires a description of the potential impacts of 'reasonable alternatives', including the no-action alternative. However, similar to other processes and NEPA, the Espoo Convention does not require proponents

63 Art 2(5).

64 Appendix II, paras (b) and (d).

65 Art 2(6).

of projects to choose the least environmentally harmful alternative. It is simply necessary that the environmental assessment be completed.[66]

In 2003 a Protocol to the Espoo Convention was adopted, known as the Kiev Protocol, which concerns strategic environmental assessments. It facilitates the extension of the Espoo Convention's environmental assessment arrangements to legislation and official plans, programs and policies.[67] The Protocol entered into force on 11 July 2010.

North American Transboundary EIA Agreement The North American Free Trade Agreement (NAFTA) concluded between Canada, the United States and Mexico in 1993 generated considerable criticism concerning predicted negative environmental impacts arising as a consequence of its implementation. These objections led to a series of separate negotiations which resulted, in 1994, in a 'side-agreement' to NAFTA entitled The North American Agreement on Environmental Cooperation (NAAEC).[68] The Commission of Environmental Cooperation (CEC) was created by the Agreement. It soon undertook work with the aim of concluding another agreement between the three States on transboundary EIA. [69] This stems from Article 10(7) of the NAAEC which states:

> Recognizing the significant bilateral nature of many transboundary environmental issues, the Council [of the CEC] shall … consider and develop recommendations with respect to:
>
> (a) assessing the environmental impact of proposed projects subject to decisions by a competent government authority and likely to cause significant adverse transboundary effects, including a full evaluation of comments provided by other Parties and persons of other Parties;
>
> (b) notification, provision of information and consultation between Parties with respect to such projects; and

---

66 Art 6. See Kevin R Gray, 'International Environmental Impact Assessment: Potential for a Multilateral Environmental Agreement' (2000) 11 *Colorado Journal of International Environmental Law and Policy* 83, 103.

67 See Simon Marsden and Timo Koivurova, *Transboundary Environmental Impact Assessment in the European Union: The Espoo Convention and its Kiev Protocol on Strategic Environmental Assessment* (Earthscan, 2011).

68 See Jameson Tweedie, 'Transboundary Environmental Impact Assessment under the North American Free Trade Agreement' (2006) 63 *Washington and Lee Law Review* 849–910 and Joseph F DiMento and Pamela M Doughman, 'Soft Teeth in the Back of the Mouth: The NAFTA Environmental Side Agreement Implemented' (1998) 10 *Georgetown International Environmental Law Review* 651–752.

69 Marc Paquin, 'Environmental Impact Assessment: Law and Practice in North America' (1999) *North American Environmental Law and Policy*, Winter: 3–4, 3.

(c) mitigation of the potential adverse effects of such projects.

In 1997, a Draft North American Agreement on Transboundary EIA was produced, yet negotiations for an enforceable transboundary EIA agreement between Canada, the United States and Mexico soon stalled, resulting in attention being focused on the identification of uniform standards among the three States and provincial jurisdictions.[70] Negotiators faced difficulties in concluding an agreement because of differences in environmental management systems in the three States. In light of these difficulties, in 1999, the Council members of the CEC agreed to work with their respective negotiators and individual border states and provinces to build 'good neighbour' agreements based on reciprocity. The Parties have since pursued bilateral discussions and have reached a number of agreements on the conduct of EIAs at a lower administrative level, such as between British Columbia in Canada and Washington State in the United States. Both Canada and the United States (although not Mexico) have signed the Espoo Convention by virtue of them being member States within the EC (although the United States is yet to ratify Espoo).

Law of the Sea Convention The most significant treaty pertaining to the marine environment is the LOSC. Its text was settled in 1982 following nine years of negotiations. It entered into force in 1994 although many States did not ratify or accede to it until much later (for example, Canada 2003, Kiribati 2003; and notably the United States is yet to accede). Among its achievements is that it clarified, or otherwise established, various zones of jurisdiction adjacent to coastal States (namely internal waters, archipelagic waters, territorial sea, contiguous zone, exclusive economic zone (EEZ) and continental shelf) as well as clarifying rights and obligations in areas beyond the jurisdiction of any State. These are the high seas (located beyond the outer limit of States' EEZ) and areas of the deep seabed and ocean floor and subsoil, known as 'The Area' (located beyond the outer limit of States' EEZ or continental shelf).[71]

The LOSC is largely a framework convention which was aimed at facilitating the subsequent creation of more detailed subject-specific international agreements. It contains a number of assertive provisions aimed at enhancing protection of the marine environment, principally from pollution. These provisions reflect some aspects of the development of customary international environmental law principles as well as providing some more specific measures. Most of the relevant provisions are contained in Part XII of LOSC, entitled 'Protection and Preservation of the Marine Environment'. It provides an overarching general obligation on all State parties 'to protect and preserve the marine environment'[72] which, as noted above, is immediately balanced by the declaration that 'States have the sovereign right to exploit their natural resources pursuant to their environmental policies and

70 See Tweedie, above n 68.

71 Art 1.

72 Art 192.

in accordance with their duty to protect and preserve the marine environment'.[73] The focus is on States ensuring that they do not cause 'pollution of the marine environment',[74] an obligation which extends to all marine areas (namely within the State's zones of jurisdiction or those of other States, as well as ABNJ).

Separate from a specific provision regarding EIA (Article 206, discussed below), there are a number of provisions in LOSC which place obligations on States to take various measures to avoid marine pollution, parts of which could be given effect by utilizing EIA procedures. For example, a noble objective is set in Article 194, entitled 'Measures to prevent, reduce and control pollution of the marine environment':

> States shall take, individually or jointly as appropriate, all measures consistent with this Convention that are necessary to prevent, reduce and control pollution of the marine environment from any source, using for this purpose the best practicable means at their disposal and in accordance with their capabilities, and they shall endeavour to harmonize their policies in this connection.

LOSC also recognizes the need to avoid causing transboundary pollution in Article 195 ('Duty not to transfer damage or hazards or transform one type of pollution into another'):

> In taking measures to prevent, reduce and control pollution of the marine environment, States shall act so as not to transfer, directly or indirectly, damage or hazards from one area to another or transform one type of pollution into another.

Various provisions also encourage cooperation between States, either on a global or regional basis, to protect and preserve the marine environment. For example, Article 200 ('Studies, research programmes and exchange of information and data'):

> States shall cooperate, directly or through competent international organizations, for the purpose of promoting studies, undertaking programmes of scientific research and encouraging the exchange of information and data acquired about pollution of the marine environment. They shall endeavour to participate actively in regional and global programmes to acquire knowledge for the assessment of

---

73 Art 193.

74 The expression 'pollution of the marine environment' is defined in LOSC art 1(4) as meaning 'the introduction by man, directly or indirectly, of substances or energy into the marine environment, including estuaries, which results or is likely to result in such deleterious effects as harm to living resources and marine life, hazards to human health, hindrance to marine activities, including fishing and other legitimate uses of the sea, impairment of quality for use of sea water and reduction of amenities'.

> the nature and extent of pollution, exposure to it, and its pathways, risks and remedies.[75]

States are also required to cooperate to implement this obligation in order to establish 'appropriate scientific criteria for the formulation and elaboration of rules, standards and recommended practices and procedures for the prevention, reduction and control of pollution of the marine environment'.[76]

Although not specifically mentioning 'EIA', LOSC envisages the adoption of at least analogous processes. Three articles are included in a section entitled 'Monitoring and environmental assessment' which provides an obligation on State parties to conduct environmental assessments for activities that might result in marine pollution or significant changes to the marine environment, in particular, Article 206:

> When states have reasonable grounds for believing that planned activities under their jurisdiction or control may cause substantial pollution of or significant harmful changes to the marine environment, they shall, as far as practicable, assess the potential effects of such activities on the marine environment and shall communicate reports of the results of such assessments.[77]

The expression 'under their jurisdiction or control' has the effect of extending this obligation to activities undertaken by States in the marine environment outside their various zones of jurisdiction such as the EEZ. Notwithstanding the clear obligation to conduct environmental assessments in the circumstances envisaged, identifying and enforcing the standard for application is difficult due to subjective elements, namely when States have 'reasonable grounds for believing' and the words 'substantial' and 'significant', as well as 'as far as practicable'.[78] Some guidance is provided in Article 204 ('Monitoring of the risks or effects of pollution'):

> 1. States shall, consistent with the rights of other States, endeavour, as far as practicable, directly or through the competent international organizations, to observe, measure, evaluate and analyse, by recognized scientific methods, the risks or effects of pollution of the marine environment.

---

75 See also arts 197–199.

76 Art 201.

77 Art 206.

78 See further Neil Craik, *The International Law of Environmental Impact Assessment: Process, Substance and Integration* (Cambridge University Press, 2008) 98, 116. For discussion of the subjective adjective 'significant' in the context of transboundary harm, see Economic Commission for Europe, *Current Policies, Strategies and Aspects of Environmental Assessment in a Transboundary Context* (UN, 1996) 48–50.

> 2. In particular, States shall keep under surveillance the effects of any activities which they permit or in which they engage in order to determine whether these activities are likely to pollute the marine environment.

LOSC also established a specific regime to protect and manage 'The Area'. Responsibility for the Area is entrusted to the International Seabed Authority.[79] In 2011, ITLOS delivered a lengthy advisory opinion on the responsibilities and obligations of States sponsoring activities in the Area.[80] Exploitation of the Area is complicated due to its depth and distance offshore, and the existence of many undelimited boundaries with adjacent areas of States' continental shelf. Nevertheless, interest in exploiting deep seabed resources is increasing. Future exploitation is set to occur only in accordance with environmental assessments.[81]

Finally, LOSC declares areas of responsibility and liability of State parties in Article 235:

> 1. States are responsible for the fulfilment of their international obligations concerning the protection and preservation of the marine environment. They shall be liable in accordance with international law.
>
> 2. States shall ensure that recourse is available in accordance with their legal systems for prompt and adequate compensation or other relief in respect of damage caused by pollution of the marine environment by natural or juridical persons under their jurisdiction.
>
> 3. With the objective of assuring prompt and adequate compensation in respect of all damage caused by pollution of the marine environment, States shall cooperate in the implementation of existing international law and the further development of international law relating to responsibility and liability for the assessment of and compensation for damage and the settlement of related disputes, as well as, where appropriate, development of criteria and procedures

79 Art 156.

80 *Responsibilities and Obligations of States Sponsoring Persons and Entities with Respect to Activities in the Area* (Advisory Opinion) (2011) ITLOS Case no 17. See Duncan French, 'From the Depths: Rich Pickings of Principles of Sustainable Development and General International Law on the Ocean Floor – the Seabed Disputes Chamber's 2011 Advisory Opinion' (2011) 26 *International Journal of Marine and Coastal Law* 525–568.

81 Gwénaëlle Le Gurun, 'EIA and the International Seabed Authority' in Kees Bastmeijer and Timo Koivurova (eds), *Theory and Practice of Transboundary Environmental Impact Assessment* (Martinus Nijhoff, 2008) 221–263. See also Michael W Lodge, 'Environmental Regulation of Deep Seabed Mining' in Andrée Kirchner (ed), *International Maritime Environmental Law* (Kluwer, 2003) 49–59 and environmental provisions in Agreement Relating to the Implementation of Part XI of the United Nations Convention on the Law of the Sea of 10 December 1982 of 28 July 1994 (in force 28 July 1996).

for payment of adequate compensation, such as compulsory insurance or compensation funds.

Notwithstanding the assertive declarations in LOSC of mandatory obligations on States to protect the marine environment, their effect in practice is muted. This is because of difficulties in bringing international proceedings to settle disputes, a distinct lack of detail in LOSC as to what are the standards of the various elements,[82] as well as the existence of other legal regimes with which to deal with various incidents (in particular, civil liability provisions under the 1973 International Convention for the Prevention of Pollution From Ships for dealing with pollution from ships). Nevertheless, LOSC provides obligations on States to conduct environmental assessments for a range of activities which would be best implemented through domestic EIA regimes.

Summary of International Legal Context for Transboundary EIA

States have obligations under customary international law to conduct environmental assessments of developments and activities likely to cause significant transboundary environmental harm. Many States are also obliged to conduct environmental assessments under various treaties. Although there is a lack of specificity in the international legal framework regarding virtually all aspects of transboundary EIA (including when it is triggered, how it should be conducted, and what the outcome should be), there are sufficient legal rules and emerging State practice to conclude that transboundary EIA is both a legal obligation and best environmental practice of States when engaging in activities that might have environmental consequences to other States or ABNJ. However, the effectiveness of these developments in the rules of international environmental law and improving State practice is limited due to a lack of specificity in the rules which limit options for enforcing the obligation to conduct transboundary EIA. Yet, a review of a handful of ICJ cases, in the context of the regular inclusion of environmental assessment provisions in environmental treaties, indicates that over time the increasing acceptance of EIA at the international level will result in further refinement of the circumstances in which EIA is to be conducted and how it is to be conducted. The most likely forum for this elucidation is the ICJ, as seen from the *Pulp Mills case*, unless there is further use of provisional measures applications under LOSC.[83] If a State were to have concerns about the potential transboundary environmental consequences of an activity it plans to undertake, consideration will need to be given to whether

82 See Boyle, above n 34, 377–378.

83 LOSC art 290 provides that where a dispute has been submitted to a court of tribunal which considers that it has jurisdiction under either Part XI or XV of the Convention, the court or tribunal 'may prescribe any provisional measures which it considers appropriate under the circumstances to preserve the respective rights of the parties to the dispute or to prevent serious harm to the marine environment, pending the final decision'.

any provisions of international treaties are triggered. The general principles of international environmental law would inform the minimum standards needed to fulfil treaty obligations. Thus the international legal framework for transboundary EIA in a given case is likely to be an amalgam of specific treaty obligations and general law principles. States should consider applying best practice international standards rather than rely on overly discretionary domestic EIA processes.

Transboundary EIA in the Marine Context

The foregoing discussion reveals the expectation that States engaging in developments or activities that might cause significant harm to the marine environment of other States or ABNJ will engage in EIA prior to approving the proposed developments or activities. These obligations are sourced in general, hardening rules of international law, supplemented by more specific obligations for those largely European States which have become parties to the Espoo Convention. Relying on the general rules of international environmental law, the difficulty is that we are yet to see elucidation of detailed content requirements for transboundary EIA. Development of standards is likely to evolve slowly. An absence of detailed content requirements can be expected for some time due to the nature of the way in which the obligation to conduct transboundary EIA is formed, standing in contrast with detailed domestic legislative EIA regimes (especially so in the United States where countless judicial cases have elucidated the content requirements of NEPA).[84] Further difficulties arise when the principles of international environmental law, as formed by the various international cases such as the *Trail Smelter* arbitration, are sought to be applied to the marine environment. The complexity and different circumstances of activities undertaken at sea means that it is not a simple task to transplant the rules to the marine context.[85]

In the continuing absence of a treaty specifying in detail the requirements for transboundary EIA, the implementation of the general international obligation to conduct transboundary EIA takes place under domestic EIA regimes. As noted above, there is wide variance in domestic EIA procedures. One aspect of variance is the manner in which domestic procedures are equipped to deal with potential transboundary environmental harm. For example, Australia's EIA legislation does not contain a specific requirement to assess transboundary harm.[86] It is the

84 Preiss, above n 41, 314.

85 Stuart Kaye, 'The Impact of the *Trail Smelter* Arbitration on the Law of the Sea' in Rebecca M Bratspies and Russell A Miller (eds), *Transboundary Harm in International Law: Lessons from the* Trail Smelter *Arbitration* (Cambridge University Press, 2006) 209–221.

86 EPBC Act. There is no doubt that the Australian Parliament has legislative competence to enact laws with effect outside the outer limit of the EEZ: Warwick Gullett and Gregory Rose, 'Australia's Marine Jurisdictions Under International and Domestic

same situation in the United States under NEPA, although a limited discretionary provision is included in Canada's EIA legislation.[87] Attention now turns to illustrative examples of marine activities or developments and the role of EIA.

Development Projects

EIA traditionally only applied to large scale development projects. It is ideally suited to new discrete activities because it has the ability to inform and improve all aspects of a project's design and operation prior to the making of a determination to proceed with the development. Opportunities can exist through EIA to relocate projects in more suitable locations or to modify project design or monitor environmental performance.

A number of projects with transboundary and multi-jurisdiction marine implications have now undergone EIA or another form of environmental assessment, under a range of legal regimes. These include the:

- Baltic Sea Gas Pipeline[88]
- Tourism activities in Antarctica[89]
- Denmark–Sweden Øresund Fixed Link[90]

EIA is appropriate for a wide range of marine projects, including offshore hydrocarbon exploitation in various locations around the world, deep seabed mining, dumping of wastes at sea, coastal nuclear facilities, geo-engineering, ocean fertilization and offshore windfarms.

Law' in Warwick Gullett, Clive Schofield and Joanna Vince (eds), *Marine Resources Management* (LexisNexis Butterworths, 2011) 25–40, 38.

87 *Canadian Environmental Assessment Act* (1992) s 47. See Neil Craik, 'Transboundary Environmental Assessment in Canada: International and Constitutional Dimensions' (2010) 21 *Journal of Environmental Law and Practice* 107–138, 124–128.

88 See Timo Koivurova and Ismo Pölönen, 'Transboundary Environmental Impact Assessment in the Case of the Baltic Sea Gas Pipeline' in Simon Marsden and Timo Koivurova (eds), *Transboundary Environmental Impact Assessment in the European Union: The Espoo Convention and its Kiev Protocol on Strategic Environmental Assessment* (Earthscan, 2011) 184–214.

89 See Kees Bastmeijer and Ricardo Roura, 'Environmental Impact Assessment in Antarctica' in Kees Bastmeijer and Timo Koivurova (eds), *Theory and Practice of Transboundary Environmental Impact Assessment* (Martinus Nijhoff, 2008) 175–219.

90 See Warwick Gullett, 'Environmental Decision-making in a Transboundary Context: Principles and Challenges for the Denmark–Sweden Øresund Fixed Link' (2000) 2 *Journal of Environmental Assessment Policy and Management* 503–533.

Fisheries

Fishing – one of the most ancient and enduring uses of the seas – is an activity that extends almost throughout the world's marine waters and has become so extensive, intensive and efficient that it needs to be regulated wherever it occurs. The Food and Agricultural Organization (FAO) of the United Nations classifies most of the world's major fisheries as either fully exploited or overexploited. In 2008, it estimated that 52 per cent of marine stocks were being exploited at their maximum sustainable level and that 24 per cent were already overexploited or depleted.[91] Although there have been inroads into the traditional high seas freedom of fishing, especially through the establishment of regional fisheries management organizations (RFMOs), the scale of commercial fishing in EEZs and high seas areas means that commercial fishing has the potential to have significant transboundary implications. This may be in terms of depletion of targeted species, consequences for the abundance of predator and prey species, and alterations to wider ecosystem dynamics (eg, impacts to benthic environments caused by bottom fishing activities). For these reasons, there is the potential for improvements in fishing regulation and practices by utilizing EIA procedures to assess the range of environmental impacts of fishing, especially if new fisheries are proposed. Support for this approach can be found in the 1995 UN Fish Stocks Agreement, which requires, for straddling and highly migratory fish stocks, that fishing States should 'assess the impacts of fishing, other human activities and environmental factors on target stocks and species belonging to the same ecosystem or associated with or dependent upon the targeted stock'.[92] Further discussion on this topic has taken place through the FAO, which, for example, in 2009 adopted guidelines for managing deep sea fisheries in high seas areas.[93] A difficulty, as noted by Oude Elferink, is that fisheries management has tended to focus on impacts on target and associated species rather than on wider ecosystem dynamics, and fishing, as largely an ongoing activity, differs from traditional EIA in which there is assessment of predicted environmental impacts of new activities.[94] The 1992 UN Convention on Biological Diversity[95] may also have relevance to States' obligations regarding the management of their commercial fishing vessels in EEZs or the high seas.

91 Food and Agricultural Organization of the United Nations, *The State of the World Fisheries and Agriculture* (2008) 7.

92 United Nations Agreement for the Implementation of the Provisions of the United Nations Convention on the Law of the Sea of 10 December 1982 relating to the Conservation and Management of Straddling Fish Stocks and Highly Migratory Fish Stocks of 4 August 1995, art 5(d).

93 International Guidelines for the Management of Deep Sea Fisheries in the High Sea (FAO, 2009).

94 AG Oude Elferink, *Environmental Impact Assessment in Areas Beyond National Jurisdiction* (Utrecht University report, 2011) 18.

95 United Nations Convention on Biological Diversity, opened for signature 5 June 1992, 1760 UNTS 79 (entered into force 29 December 1993).

The objectives of the convention include conservation of biological diversity and sustainable use of its components.[96] Article 3 of the convention provides that States have the responsibility to ensure that activities within their jurisdiction or control do not cause damage to the environment of other States or of areas beyond the limits of national jurisdiction.

ABJN

The large ocean areas that are ABNJ present additional problems when seeking to ensure the conduct of environmental assessments of human activities. Although there is no legal impediment to a State to extend its domestic EIA provisions to activities conducted from a ship or offshore platform flying its flag, ensuring the conduct of EIA for appropriate activities whichever the State of the vessel or nationals concerned requires a cooperative multilateral approach. While the environmental provisions in LOSC discussed above provide strong yet amorphous obligations, they do not go far enough in ensuring the conduct of EIA for the range of non-fishing activities that can take place. Attention has only recently shifted to the issue of environmental assessments in ABNJ.[97]

Conclusion

EIA is an established and effective process for assessing potential environmental effects of human activities, providing opportunities to minimize environmental harm. Its relevance to projects with transboundary marine impacts is axiomatic. However, the circumstances in which EIA needs to be conducted at sea require consideration not just of domestic law but also international treaty and customary law. This includes analysing competing rights of Coastal and Flag States in various international maritime zones in which relevant activities are proposed to take place, and considering the appositeness of EIA processes to a variety of marine activities, ranging from discrete projects such as offshore drilling to more geographically extensive activities such as commercial fishing. It can be concluded that international environmental law has developed to the point where an obligation to conduct transboundary EIA exists, yet the challenge of ensuring its implementation is bedevilled by lack of specificity in international rules and difficulties in pursuing enforcement options. It is submitted that the most appropriate approach for improving international standards and practice is for States intending to conduct similar activities in offshore regions, or different activities in regions of shared interest, to reach consensus about EIA procedures, formalized in regional or activity-specific EIA agreements. In the absence of such

96 Art 1.

97 Robin Warner, *Protecting the Oceans Beyond National Jurisdiction: Strengthening the International Law Framework* (Martinus Nijhoff, 2009) 51.

agreements, States aggrieved at the causation of environmental harm in their domestic maritime areas or in ABNJ will likely need to rely on difficult options to enforce general obligations under LOSC or customary international law.

Chapter 12
Conserving Marine Biodiversity beyond Boundaries: Developing Environmental Assessment Frameworks

Robin Warner

Introduction

The focal point of the international law framework for the protection of the marine environment is Part XII of the 1982 United Nations Convention on the Law of the Sea (LOSC)[1] on the Protection and Preservation of the Marine Environment, complemented by a burgeoning variety of instruments on international environmental law and an evolving body of customary international law principles. Substantial implementation of this framework has occurred in marine areas within national jurisdiction with some transboundary collaboration between States in different regions to protect their marine environment across national boundaries. The regulatory framework for environmental protection in marine areas beyond national jurisdiction (ABNJ) is at a much earlier stage of development as States grapple with the broader institutional and legal challenges posed by high seas governance.

Environmental impact assessment (EIA) is acknowledged as a key element in the suite of tools for environmental protection, and its application to activities affecting the marine environment has been endorsed in a wide array of international law instruments and policy statements. Since the LOSC was adopted in 1982, there has been a gradual evolution and deepening of EIA for marine areas through a mix of treaty obligations and soft law principles.[2] The LOSC imposes a general obligation on States Parties to assess the potential effects of activities under their jurisdiction or control that may cause substantial pollution of, or significant and harmful changes to the marine environment.[3] This obligation has been implemented

---

1 *United Nations Convention on the Law of the Sea*, opened for signature 10 December 1982, 1833 UNTS 3 (entered into force 16 November 1994).

2 K Gray, 'International Environmental Impact Assessment: Potential for a Multilateral Environmental Agreement' (2000) 11(1) *Colorado Journal of International Environmental Law and Policy* 91–92.

3 *UN Convention on the Law of the Sea*, opened for signature 10 December 1982, 1833 UNTS 3 (entered into force 16 November 1994) ('*LOSC*').

and elaborated through regional and sectoral instruments that contain more specific provisions on environmental assessment in different contexts such as the regional seas conventions, the 1991 Protocol on Environmental Protection to the Antarctic Treaty (Madrid Protocol), the UN Fish Stocks Agreement and the International Seabed Authority's Regulations on Exploration for Polymetallic Nodules and Polymetallic Sulphides.[4] For transboundary impacts, including those across adjacent marine areas within national jurisdiction, EIA has been further developed through the 1991 Convention on Environmental Impact Assessment in a Transboundary Context (Espoo Convention).[5] The more recent concept of strategic environmental assessment (SEA) refers to the formal systematic and comprehensive process of identifying and evaluating the significant environmental implications of proposed plans, programmes, policies, and in some cases legislation to ensure that they are fully considered and addressed at the earliest stage of decision making.[6] SEA is a more overarching concept than EIA and allows for more holistic, comprehensive and long-term consideration of environmental considerations at the policy, planning and implementation levels.[7] While EIA is often site-specific and limited in time, SEA processes broaden the spatial and temporal range of environmental assessment often being applied to whole sectors of activity or geographic areas as an institutionalized part of decision making on a long-term basis. For maximum efficacy, SEA and EIA need to be vertically integrated or tiered with environmental considerations being taken into account at the policy and programme level and then flowing down to the project level.[8] At the global level, SEA for all components of the environment, including the marine environment, is still at an embryonic phase, with the 2003 Protocol on Strategic Environmental Assessment to the Convention on Environmental Impact Assessment in a Transboundary Context (Kiev Protocol)

4 The text of the regional seas conventions can be found at <http://www.unep.ch/regional seas/main/conlist.html>; *Protocol on Environmental Protection to the Antarctic Treaty*, opened for signature 4 October 1991, 30 ILM 1455 (entered into force 14 January 1998) ('*Madrid Protocol*'); *Agreement for the Implementation of the Provisions of the United Nations Convention on the Law of the Sea of 10 December 1982 relating to the Conservation and Management of Straddling Fish Stocks and Highly Migratory Fish Stocks*, opened for signature 4 August 1995, 2167 UNTS 3 (entered into force 11 December 2001); the text of the ISA Regulations can be found at <http://www.isa.org.jm/en/documents/mcode>.

5 *Convention on Environmental Impact Assessment in a Transboundary Context*, opened for signature 25 February 1991, 30 ILM 802 (entered into force 14 January 1998) ('*Espoo Convention*').

6 Sadler B and R Verheem, *Strategic Environmental Assessment Status, Challenges and Future Directions*, Ministry of Housing, Spatial Planning and the Environment, Publication number 54, The Hague 1996) 1.

7 N Craik, *The International Law of Environmental Impact Assessment* (Cambridge University Press, 2008) 155–156.

8 Ibid, 156.

being the key instrument for this process.[9] This chapter examines the scope of the current legal and institutional framework for EIA and SEA as it applies to ABNJ and its implementation in sectoral and regional contexts. Gaps in the legal and institutional framework to implement EIA and SEA for activities affecting ABNJ are discussed as well as the initiatives being taken and the options available for the international community to develop a more comprehensive legal and institutional framework for EIA and SEA in these extensive areas of the ocean.

The International Law Framework for EIA of Activities Affecting Marine Areas beyond National Jurisdiction (ABNJ)

The Customary International Law Status of the Obligation to Conduct EIA

The customary international law status of the obligation on States to conduct EIAs of activities with the potential to significantly affect the environment in ABNJ, including its marine components, has been steadily crystallizing in the recent jurisprudence of the International Court of Justice (ICJ) and the International Tribunal for the Law of the Sea (ITLOS). In the *Gabcikcovo-Nagymaros* case the court considered assessment, notification and consultation, effectively the elements of an EIA process, to be a necessary step in a State's implementation of the duty to prevent transboundary harm and the concept of sustainable development.[10] In the *Pulp Mills Case*, the ICJ found that 'it may now be considered a requirement under general international law to undertake an environmental impact assessment where there is a risk that the proposed industrial activity may have a significant adverse impact in a transboundary context, in particular, on a shared resource'.[11]

In the Mox Plant Case, ITLOS made provisional orders for the parties, Ireland and the United Kingdom, to improve their transboundary environmental cooperation including carrying out an adequate assessment of the potential impacts of a nuclear fuel reprocessing plant in Cumbria on the marine environment of the Irish Sea.[12] The advisory opinion of ITLOS on the Responsibilities and Obligations of States Sponsoring Persons and Entities with Respect to Activities in the Area,

9 *Protocol on Strategic Environmental Assessment to the Convention on Environmental Impact Assessment in a Transboundary Context*, opened for signature 21 May 2003 text at <http://www.unece.org/env/pp/prtr/docs/prtrtext.html> (entered into force 8 October 2009) ('*Kiev Protocol*'); Craik, above note 7, 29.

10 *Gabcikovo-Nagymaros Project (Hungary/Slovakia)* (1997) ICJ Rep 7, para 141; Alan Boyle, 'The Gabcikovo-Nagymaros Case: New Law in Old Bottles' (1997) 8 *Yearbook of International Environmental Law* 18; Craik, above note 7, 114.

11 *Pulp Mills on the River Uruguay Case (Argentina/Uruguay)(Provisional Measures)* (2006) ICJ Rep, para 204.

12 *Mox Plant Case (Provisional Measures)* ITLOS No 10 (2001) para 82; Alan Boyle, 'Environmental Jurisprudence of the International Tribunal for the Law of the Sea' (2007) 22(3) *International Journal for Marine and Coastal Law* 377; Marie Cordonnier

has also acknowledged the customary international law status of the obligation to conduct EIAs for activities with the potential for significant impacts on the marine environment, including for ABNJ, specifically the Area.[13]

Global Instruments

United Nations Convention on the Law of the Sea (LOSC) The LOSC provides for prior and ongoing assessment of activities likely to pollute or cause significant and harmful changes to the marine environment. Article 206 specifies that where States have reasonable grounds for believing that planned activities under their jurisdiction or control may cause substantial pollution of, or significant and harmful changes to, the marine environment, they shall, as far as practical, assess the potential effects of such activities on the marine environment. The obligation to conduct such an assessment is not limited to effects on areas within national jurisdiction and therefore includes the potential effects on ABNJ. States must also keep under surveillance the effects of any activities they engage in or permit, to determine whether these activities are likely to pollute the marine environment (Article 204(2)). Articles 206 and 205 of the LOSC provide that States should publish reports of the results obtained at appropriate intervals to the competent international organizations, which should then make them available to all States. This procedural obligation complements an earlier obligation in Article 198 of the LOSC which requires a State that becomes aware of cases in which the marine environment is in imminent danger of being damaged or has been damaged by pollution, to immediately notify other States it deems likely to be affected by such damage as well as the competent international organizations. These general obligations to conduct environmental assessments in the LOSC must be read in conjunction with the more specific EIA principles and procedural provisions that have been developed in international environmental law instruments and associated guidelines.

United Nations Environment Programme (UNEP) Goals and Principles of EIA One of the earliest global elaborations of the objectives and fundamental procedures encompassed in EIA is found in the 1987 United Nations Environment Programme Goals and Principles of EIA (UNEP Principles).[14] Principle 1 specifies that an EIA should include, at a minimum:

Segger, Marcus Gehring and Andrew Paul Newcombe, *Sustainable Development in World Investment Law* (Kluwer Law International, 2011) 152.

13 *International Tribunal of the Law of the Sea, Advisory Opinion on Responsibilities and Obligations of States Sponsoring Persons and Entities with Respect to Activities in the Area*, 1 February 2011, <http://www.itlos.org/fileadmin/itlos/documents/cases/case_no_17/adv_op_010211.pdf>, p 44, para 145.

14 UNEP, United Nations Environment Programme Goals and Principles of EIA (UNEP Principles), <http://www.unep.org/Documents.Multilingual/Default.asp?Documen

- a description of the proposed activity;
- a description of the potentially affected environment, including specific information necessary for identifying and assessing the environmental effects of the proposed activity;
- a description of the practical alternatives, as appropriate;
- an assessment of the likely or potential environmental impacts of the proposed activity and alternatives, including the direct, indirect, cumulative, short-term and long-term effects;
- an identification and description of measures available to mitigate adverse environmental impacts of the proposed activity and alternatives, and an assessment of those measures;
- an indication of gaps in knowledge and uncertainties that may be encountered in compiling the required information; and
- an indication whether the environment of any other State or of areas beyond national jurisdiction are likely to be affected by the proposed activity or alternatives.

From the perspective of ABNJ, this overarching statement of minimum requirements is significant as it highlights the need to include in EIAs an indication of whether proposed activities will affect these areas. ABNJ are also mentioned in Principle 11 which specifies that States should endeavour to conclude bilateral, regional or multilateral arrangements so as to provide reciprocal notification, exchange of information and agreed upon consultation on the potential environmental effects of activities under their control or jurisdiction likely to significantly affect other States or ABNJ. The UNEP Principles also list some of the mechanisms States can use to determine whether an activity is likely to significantly affect the environment, including:

- lists of categories of activities that by their nature are, or are not, likely to have significant effects;
- lists of areas that are of special importance or sensitivity (such as national parks or wetland areas), so that any activity affecting such areas is likely to have significant effects;
- lists of categories of resources (such as water, tropical rain forests, etc.) or environmental problems (such as increased soil erosion, desertification, deforestation) which are of special concern, so that any diminution of such resources or exacerbation of such problems is likely to be significant;
- an initial environmental evaluation, i.e., a quick informal assessment of the proposed activity to determine whether its effects are likely to be significant; and
- criteria to guide determinations on whether the effects of a proposed activity are likely to be significant.

---

tsID=1008ArticleID=1658>.

The general obligation to consult with interested stakeholders on an EIA before a decision is made to proceed with an activity is recognized in Principle 7 which provides that '... government agencies, members of the public, experts in relevant disciplines and interested groups should be allowed appropriate opportunity to comment on the EIA'. For activities affecting ABNJ, this immediately raises the question of who qualifies as an interested stakeholder and which organization is responsible for administering and responding to such consultation.

In relation to decisions or actions taken by the proponent following an EIA, the UNEP Principles adopt a due diligence approach requiring the proponent to fully examine the potential environmental impacts of a particular project or activity and give due consideration to the interests of affected parties but not imposing a particular decision path on the proponent. Principle 9 contains a requirement for justification specifying that the decision on any proposed activity subject to an EIA should be in writing, state the reasons, and include the provisions, if any, to prevent, reduce or mitigate damage to the environment. It should be made available to interested persons or groups as well. Although the UNEP Principles do not extend the proponent's obligations beyond this due diligence approach, it could be argued that if an EIA concludes that significant harm is likely to ABNJ, under the international law duty to prevent transboundary harm set out in Principle 21 of the Stockholm Declaration and Principle 2 of the Rio Declaration and confirmed by the ICJ in their Advisory Opinion on the Legality of the Threat or Use of Nuclear Weapons, the State conducting such an EIA would be under a positive obligation to mitigate that harm or refrain from the activity.[15]

Convention on Biological Diversity (CBD) The 1992 Convention on Biological Diversity (CBD) links Contracting Parties' obligations to conduct EIAs more directly to the conservation of biodiversity in both marine and terrestrial environments.[16] Under its provisions, Contracting Parties must introduce appropriate procedures requiring EIA of proposed projects that are likely to have significant adverse effects on biodiversity with a view to avoiding or minimizing such effects (Article 14(1)(a)). Having identified processes and categories of activities that have or are likely to have significant adverse impacts on the conservation and sustainable use of biodiversity, Contracting Parties must then monitor their effects through sampling and other techniques (Article 7(c)). This

15 *Declaration of the United Nations Conference on the Human Environment*, Stockholm, 16 June 1972 (1972) 11 ILM 1416; *Rio de Janeiro Declaration on Environment and Development*, Rio de Janeiro, 3 to 14 June 1992, UN Doc A/CONF.151/5/REV.1 (1992) 31 ILM 876; International Court of Justice, Advisory Opinion on Legality of the Threat or Use of Nuclear Weapons, 8 July 1996, <http://www.icj-cij.org/docket/fi les/95/7495.pdf PH PSESSID=244d61421d993dcdd51859ee9c657b1b>, 241–242, para 29; Craik, above note 7, 67.

16 *Convention on Biological Diversity*, opened for signature 22 May 1992, 31 ILM 822 (entered into force 29 December 1993)('*CBD*').

obligation applies to processes and activities, regardless of where their effects occur, carried out under the jurisdiction or control of Contracting Parties in areas under their national jurisdiction or in ABNJ (Article 4(b)). The critical importance of collaboration between States in minimizing adverse impacts to biodiversity in ABNJ is emphasized in Article 14(1)(c). This section requires Contracting Parties to promote reciprocal notification, exchange of information and consultation on activities under their jurisdiction or control that are likely to significantly affect adversely the biodiversity of other States or ABNJ. In the case of imminent or grave danger or damage, originating under their jurisdiction or control, to biodiversity under the jurisdiction of other States or in ABNJ, Contracting Parties must notify immediately the potentially affected States as well as initiate action to prevent or minimize such danger or damage.

These broadly conceived EIA obligations in the CBD have been augmented by the CBD Voluntary Guidelines on Biodiversity-Inclusive Impact Assessment (CBD Guidelines), which emphasize the importance of including biodiversity-related criteria in the screening process.[17] The CBD Guidelines specify the following questions related to biodiversity impacts that should be asked:

- Would the intended activity affect the biophysical environment directly or indirectly in such a manner or cause such biological changes that it will increase risks of extinction of genotypes, cultivars, varieties, populations of species, or the chance of loss of habitats or ecosystems?
- Would the intended activity surpass the maximum sustainable yield, the carrying capacity of a habitat/ecosystem or the maximum allowable disturbance level of a resource, population, or ecosystem, taking into account the full spectrum of values of that resource, population or ecosystem?
- Would the intended activity result in changes to, and/or rights over, biological resources?[18]

Instead of using negative or positive lists of types of activities that should be subject to EIA, the CBD Guidelines promote lists identifying those geographical areas where important biodiversity is found as a basis for determining which projects require an EIA.[19] They also recommend that biodiversity expertise be included in expert teams assessing whether particular activities should be subject to EIA.[20] The Guidelines elaborate on the types of impacts and alternatives that should be identified and examined in a biodiversity-inclusive EIA report.

---

17 *Biodiversity in Impact Assessment. Background Document to Decision VIII/28 of the Convention on Biological Diversity. Voluntary Guidelines on Biodiversity-Inclusive Impact Assessment*, <http://www.cbd.int/doc/publications/pubcbd-ts-26-en.pdf>.

18 Ibid, 23, para 5.3(a).

19 Ibid, 24–26.

20 Ibid.

The CBD Guidelines reflect a best practice standard for EIAs of activities with the potential to significantly affect all aspects of biodiversity, including those components situated in ABNJ. They depend on a detailed level of knowledge of species, habitats and ecosystems and their interconnections in a particular marine area. A later section of this chapter will examine the process currently being undertaken in the CBD to define the special considerations to be taken into account in EIAs of activities with the potential to significantly affect biodiversity in marine and coastal areas, including ABNJ.

Convention on the Conservation of Migratory Species of Wild Animals (CMS) The objective of the 1979 Convention on the Conservation of Migratory Species of Wild Animals (CMS) is to conserve migratory species of wild animals, including certain marine species that migrate through marine areas within and beyond national jurisdiction.[21] In its Resolution 7.2 on Impact Assessment and Migratory Species of 8 September 2002, the Conference of Parties (COP) of the CMS urged States to include in EIAs and SEAs 'as complete a consideration as possible of effects involving impediments to migration, of transboundary effects on migratory species, and of impacts on migratory patterns or migratory ranges'. Obligations to conduct EIAs and SEAs are reflected in subsidiary agreements to the CMS relevant to species migrating through the marine environment.

The 2006 Agreement on the Conservation of Albatross and Petrels provides in Annex 3 that the Parties shall assess the potential impact on albatrosses and petrels of policies, plans, programmes and projects that they consider likely to affect the conservation of albatrosses and petrels before any decision on whether to adopt such policies, plans, programmes and projects is made and to make the results of these assessments publicly available.[22] The 1996 Agreement on the Conservation of Cetaceans of the Black Sea, Mediterranean Sea and Contiguous Atlantic Area (ACCOBAMS) is even more rigorous, requiring Parties to carry out EIAs in order to provide a basis for either allowing or prohibiting the continuation or the future development of activities that may affect cetaceans or their habitat in the Agreement area.[23] These activities include fisheries, offshore exploration and exploitation, nautical sports, tourism, and cetacean watching, as well as establishing the conditions under which such activities may be conducted. In Resolution No. 4, Adverse Effects of Sound, Vessels and other Forms of Disturbance on Small Cetaceans of 12 December 2006 to the 1991 Agreement on Small Cetaceans of the

21 *Convention on the Conservation of Migratory Species of Wild Animals*, opened for signature 23 June 1979, 19 ILM 15 (entered into force 1 November 1983)('*CMS*').

22 *Agreement on the Conservation of Albatross and Petrels*, opened for signature 19 June 2001, <http://www.acap.aq/Instruments> (entered into force 1 February 2004) ('*ACAP*').

23 *Agreement on the Conservation of Cetaceans of the Black Sea, Mediterranean Sea and Contiguous Atlantic Area*, opened for signature 24 November 1996, <http://www.cms,int/species/accombams/acc_text.htm> (entered into force 1 June 2001)('*ACCOBAMS*').

Baltic and North Seas (ASCOBANS), the Parties called for the development, with military and other relevant authorities, of effective mitigation measures, including EIAs and relevant standing orders, to reduce disturbance of and potential physical damage to small cetaceans.[24]

Regional Instruments

Regional Seas Conventions There are broad obligations on EIA in some of the regional seas agreements. Parties to these conventions are typically responsible for developing EIA guidelines, legislation and processes that prevent or minimize harmful effects on the Convention Area with the assistance of competent global, regional and sub-regional organizations. In most cases, the Convention Area is limited to marine areas within the national jurisdiction of the Parties, although there are some regional seas conventions that include ABNJ in their scope of application.[25] The conventions do not, however, incorporate scoping and content prescriptions for EIA, leaving this responsibility to the more detailed legislative enactments of their member States. Different versions of the duty to notify and consult on EIAs with other parties and the relevant regional seas organization appear in many of the conventions, but most are relatively loose prescriptions urging rather than obligating States to disseminate results of EIAs and consult with affected parties.[26]

The 1995 Barcelona Convention for the Protection of the Marine Environment and Coastal Region of the Mediterranean makes specific mention of notification and consultation among Contracting Parties where activities are likely to have a significant adverse effect on ABNJ.

Article 4(3)(c) provides that:

> the Contracting Parties shall promote cooperation between and among States in environmental impact assessment procedures related to activities under their jurisdiction or control which are likely to have a significant adverse effect on the marine environment of other States or *areas beyond the limits of national jurisdiction* on the basis of notification, exchange of information and consultation.

---

24 *Agreement on Small Cetaceans of the Baltic and North Seas*, opened for signature 13 September 1991, <http://www.cms.int/species/ascobans/asc_text.htm (entered into force 29 March 1994)(*'ASCOBANS'*).

25 The scope of application of the 1986 *Convention for the Protection of the Natural Resources and Environment of the South Pacific Region* (Noumea Convention), the 1992 *Convention for the Protection of the Marine Environment of the North-east Atlantic* (OSPAR Convention) and the 1995 *Convention for the Protection of the Marine Environment and the Coastal Region of the Mediterranean* (Barcelona Convention) extend to ABNJ.

26 Craik, above note 7, 145.

This provision recognizes the mandatory responsibility of Contracting States to protect and preserve the marine environment beyond national jurisdiction in their region.

The OSPAR Commission established to implement the 1992 Convention for the Protection of the Marine Environment of the North-east Atlantic (OSPAR Convention) is moving towards more collaborative arrangements between competent regional and global authorities for EIA and SEA of activities, plans, programmes and policies affecting marine protected areas beyond national jurisdiction within the convention's area of responsibility. The OSPAR Ministerial Meeting in 2010 established six marine protected areas (MPAs) in ABNJ encompassing four seamounts, an area of the deep seabed beyond national jurisdiction in the southern area of the Charlie Gibbs Fracture Zone and an area to the north of the Azores Islands in the Atlantic.[27] A collective arrangement between OSPAR and global and regional organizations with responsibilities for managing activities such as fisheries, deep seabed mining and ships routeing in these MPAs including the North East Atlantic Fisheries Commission, the International Seabed Authority and the International Maritime Organization is in the course of negotiation. Under this arrangement, joint management plans will be prepared for each of the six MPAs including provisions for cooperation on EIAs and SEAs.[28]

Protocol on Environmental Protection to the Antarctic Treaty (Madrid Protocol) The test applied for screening activities for EIA under the Madrid Protocol to the Antarctic Treaty is more complex and multi-layered than many other international instruments and clearly applies to ABNJ, although there are significant exceptions to its application to certain activities. The screening process has three levels – the preliminary assessment, initial environmental evaluation (IEE) and comprehensive environmental evaluation (CEE).[29] A preliminary assessment is carried out at the national level for all activities subject to the Protocol with less than a minor or transitory impact. If an activity has no more than a minor or transitory impact, an IEE must be carried out, and if it has more than a minor or transitory impact, a CEE must be carried out. All activities, both governmental and non-governmental, in the Antarctic treaty area (south of 60° south latitude)

27 OSPAR Commission, *OSPAR Network of Marine Protected Areas*, <http:www.ospar.org/content/content.asp?menu=00700300100011_000000_000000>.

28 'Designation and Management of OSPAR MPAs Beyond National Jurisdiction in the North-East Atlantic', Presentation by Dr Henning von Nordheim and Tim Packeiser, IUCN/German Federal Agency for Nature Conservation Seminar on the Conservation and Sustainable Use of Marine Biodiversity beyond National Jurisdiction, 3–6 December 2011, Bonn, Germany.

29 Madrid Protocol, Article 8(1); K Bastmeijer and R Roura, 'Environmental Impact Assessment in Antarctica,' in K Bastmeijer and T Koivurova (eds), *Theory and Practice of Transboundary Environmental Impact Assessment* (Martinus Nijhoff Publishers, 2008) 182.

are subject to these provisions, except for fishing, sealing, whaling and emergency operations, since these are covered by other international instruments.[30]

Guidelines for Environmental Impact Assessment in the Arctic (Arctic EIA Guidelines) The Arctic EIA Guidelines, although not legally binding on Arctic States, suggest that they be applied across jurisdictional boundaries and in different EIA processes.[31] They recommend that EIA should be applied to activities associated with the exploitation of both renewable and non-renewable natural resources, public use, military activities and the development of infrastructure for different purposes that may cause significant environmental impacts.[32] They note that the two main approaches adopted by Arctic States for deciding on the application of EIA procedures are mandatory assessment based on lists of environmentally harmful projects and case-by-case decisions.[33] The Guidelines also note that the sensitivity of Arctic areas may justify the application of lower threshold levels for EIA that recognize the sensitivity of Arctic areas and the potential for cumulative impacts.[34] Sensitivity criteria in the marine context can be based on factors such as: time period of the project, the status of marine species, habitats and ecosystems in particular marine areas, the level of production or quantities of emissions involved in a particular project, and the scientific and cultural significance of particular marine areas. The example is given of an EIA being undertaken for the first scientific expedition in Arctic waters of the Swedish icebreaker *Oden* in 1991 because of concerns about the effects of underwater noise, interference with marine mammals and exhaust emissions.[35]

Convention on Environmental Impact Assessment in a Transboundary Context (Espoo Convention) The Espoo Convention is the only specific international instrument on EIA and provides a detailed template for implementing transboundary assessment in marine areas. For its Parties, it steps beyond the softer obligations found in the regional seas conventions to a more fully fledged implementation of EIA for transboundary activities and projects. It employs a combination of mechanisms to determine whether a proposed activity is likely to have a significant adverse transboundary impact and should therefore be subject to an EIA. Parties must establish an EIA procedure for activities listed in Appendix I that are likely to cause significant adverse transboundary impact.[36] Of the activities listed in Appendix I, large-diameter oil and gas pipelines and offshore

30 Madrid Protocol, Article 8(2).

31 Arctic Environment Protection Strategy, *Guidelines for Environmental Impact Assessment in the Arctic*, 1997, <http://ceq.hss.doe.gov/nepa/eiaguide.pdf>, 5.

32 Ibid, 11.

33 Ibid.

34 Ibid, 12.

35 Ibid.

36 Espoo Convention, Article 2(2).

hydrocarbon production are relevant for their potential to affect biodiversity beyond national jurisdiction (both the high seas water column and the deep seabed beyond national jurisdiction). Appendix III sets out the following general criteria to assist in determining whether an activity is likely to have a significant adverse transboundary impact:

- Size: proposed activities that are large for the type of activity.
- Location: proposed activities that are located in or close to an area of special environmental sensitivity or importance (such as wetlands designated under the Ramsar Convention, national parks, nature reserves, sites of special scientific interest, or sites of archaeological, cultural or historical importance); also, proposed activities in locations where the characteristics of the proposed development would be likely to have significant effects on the population.
- Effects: proposed activities with particularly complex and potentially adverse effects, including those giving rise to serious effects on humans, valued species or organisms, those which threaten the existing or potential use of an affected area, and those causing additional loading that cannot be sustained by the carrying capacity of the environment.

The Espoo Convention does not currently require EIAs to be conducted for activities with the potential for significant impacts on ABNJ, although the possibility of negotiating a protocol to the Convention, which provides for such assessments, would be open to the Parties.[37] At the sub-regional level, the Espoo Convention has prompted the ongoing negotiation of the draft Protocol on Environmental Impact Assessment in a Transboundary Context in the Caspian Sea Region to the 2003 Framework Convention on the Protection of the Marine Environment of the Caspian Sea.[38] This instrument, using the threshold of significant adverse effect on the marine environment, lists activities in Appendix I that are recognized as being likely to cause significant adverse transboundary environmental impacts. These include oil, gas and petrochemical industry exploration and extraction activities, the laying at the bottom of the sea of oil and gas pipelines, construction of artificial islands, spits and reefs in the coastal zone, introduction of species alien to natural ecological systems, and plans, programmes, concepts, and other documents aimed at the solution of global environmental problems, such as preservation of the ozone layer and biodiversity, which are likely to affect the marine environment of the Caspian Sea.

37 See Timo Koivurova's Chapter 13 in this book.

38 Caspian Sea Protocol, <http://live.unece.org/env/eia/subregions/caspian1.html>.

Protocol on Strategic Environmental Assessment to the Espoo Convention (Kiev Protocol) The key regional instrument on strategic environmental assessment is the 2003 Protocol on SEA to the Espoo Convention (Kiev Protocol) which focuses on SEA in a domestic context. It requires Parties to carry out SEAs for specified plans and programmes that are likely to have significant environmental and health effects and to endeavour to ensure that environmental, including health, concerns are considered and integrated in the preparation of proposals for policies and legislation that are likely to have significant effects on the environment. For plans and programmes, the Kiev Protocol imports some of the same procedural stages as EIA into its definition of SEA. Article 2(6) of the Protocol defines SEA as:

> the evaluation of the likely environmental effects, including health effects, which comprises the determination of the scope of an environmental report and its preparation, the carrying out of public participation and consultations and the taking into account of the environmental report and the results of public participation and consultations in a plan or programme.

The ambit of the Kiev Protocol is wide, with SEAs being required for plans and programmes that are prepared for agriculture, forestry, fisheries, energy, and industry, including mining, transport, regional development, waste management, telecommunications, tourism, town and country planning and land use and for other projects listed in Annex II which require an EIA under national legislation.[39] The Kiev Protocol's provisions are not limited to plans and programmes with transboundary environmental effects such as the Espoo Convention, but apply to environmental effects wherever they occur, as the focus is within a State. Projects listed in Annexes I and II that could have the potential for significant effects on marine biodiversity beyond national jurisdiction include offshore hydrocarbon production, intensive fish farming, the laying of pipelines for transport of gas, oil or chemicals and installations for the harnessing of wind power for energy production. For plans and programmes setting the framework for future development consent, other than those specified for automatic application of SEA in the Protocol, Parties must assess, using either a case-by-case examination or specific listing or a combination of both methods, whether they are likely to have significant environmental effects, including health effects. Annex III to the Protocol provides criteria to be taken into account in this assessment.

Some of the criteria contained in Annex III would be particularly relevant if States were conducting SEAs for plans and programmes likely to have significant environmental effects on marine biodiversity beyond national jurisdiction. These include:

---

39 The Kiev Protocol is open to all members of the United Nations however the Espoo Convention is yet to be amended to allow this. See Timo Koivurova's chapter in this book.

- the transboundary nature of effects;
- the degree to which the plan or programme will affect valuable or vulnerable areas, including land/seascapes with a recognized national or international protection status; and
- the nature of the environmental and health effects, such as probability, duration, frequency, reversibility, magnitude and extent (such as geographical area or size of population likely to be affected).

The scoping provisions of the Kiev Protocol are very comprehensive, requiring Parties to prepare an environmental report on plans and programmes subject to SEA that identifies, describes and evaluates the likely significant environmental and health effects of implementing the plan or programme and its reasonable alternatives. Annex IV to the Protocol prescribes the information required in this report which, in addition to the typical content of an EIA, includes a description of the likely significant transboundary environmental effects of plans and programmes and the environmental objectives established at international, national and other levels that are relevant to the plan or programme and the ways in which these have been taken into account during its preparation. Parties to the Kiev Protocol must provide early, timely and effective opportunities for public participation in the SEA of relevant plans and programmes. The public for these purposes is defined in Article 8(3) of the Protocol as including relevant non-governmental organizations. Parties must consult with other States Parties likely to be affected by significant transboundary environmental effects of a plan or programme (Article 10).

Sectoral Instruments

UN Fish Stocks Agreement In the fisheries sector, the UN Fish Stocks Agreement is a ground breaking instrument focusing on ecosystem based management of fisheries. It requires Parties to assess the impacts of fishing, other human activities and environmental factors on target stocks and species belonging to the same ecosystem or associated with or dependent upon the target stocks, to develop data collection and research programmes to assess the impact of fishing on non-target and associated or dependent species and their environment, and to adopt plans that are necessary to ensure the conservation of such species and to protect habitats of special concern.[40] This obligation has been further elaborated in the 2009 FAO International Guidelines for the Management of Deep Sea Fisheries in the High Seas (Deep Sea Fishing Guidelines), which were developed to help States and regional fisheries management organizations and arrangements, implement a call from the United Nations General Assembly (UNGA) to prevent significant adverse impacts on vulnerable marine ecosystems or not to authorize the bottom

40 UN Fish Stocks Agreement, Articles 5(d) and 6(3)(d).

fishing activity to proceed (UNGA Resolution 61/105 paragraphs 80–91).[41] In the Guidelines, significant adverse impacts are defined as those that compromise ecosystem integrity (i.e., ecosystem structure or function) in a manner that:

1. impairs the ability of affected populations to repair themselves;
2. degrades the long-term natural productivity of habitats; and
3. causes, on more than a temporary basis, significant loss of species richness, habitat or community types.[42]

The Guidelines also specify that impacts should be evaluated individually, in combination and cumulatively.[43] They call for States to conduct assessments of individual bottom fishing activities and to adopt measures to prevent significant adverse impacts on vulnerable marine ecosystems (VMEs). These procedures include identifying areas or features where VMEs are known or likely to occur, identifying the location of fisheries in relation to these areas and features, and then developing data collection and research programmes to assess the impact of fishing on target and non-target species and their environment.[44] The Guidelines list the characteristics of VMEs that should be subject to assessments and give examples of potentially vulnerable species groups, communities and habitats, as well as features that potentially support them.[45]

Convention on the Prevention of Marine Pollution by Dumping of Wastes and Other Matter (London Convention) and 1996 Protocol to the Convention on the Prevention of Marine Pollution by Dumping of Wastes and other Matter (London Protocol) The dumping of waste from ships in ABNJ is subject to risk and environmental assessment processes under the London Convention and the later London Protocol. For Parties to the London Convention, dumping of non-prohibited substances is only allowed subject to the requirements of prior EIA, permitting, and ongoing monitoring set out in Annex III of the Convention.[46] For Parties to the London Protocol, dumping of all waste and other matter is prohibited, except for five listed categories of substances, the dumping of which is nevertheless subject to the stringent assessment, permitting, and ongoing monitoring requirements of Annex 2 to the Protocol.[47] Any application for a permit to dump these listed

41 FAO, *International Guidelines for the Management of Deep Sea Fisheries in the High Seas*, 2009, <http://www.fao.org/docrep/011/0816t/0816t00.htm>.

42 Ibid, 4, para 17.

43 Ibid.

44 Ibid, 9–11.

45 Ibid, 4, paras 14–16.

46 *Convention on the Prevention of Marine Pollution by Dumping of Wastes and Other Matter*, opened for signature 29 December 1972, 11 ILM 1294 (entered into force 30 August 1975) (*'London Convention'*), Article IV and Annex III.

47 *Protocol to the Convention on the Prevention of Marine Pollution by Dumping of Wastes and Other Matter*, opened for signature 7 November 1996, 36 ILM 1 (entered into

substances must be accompanied by an assessment of the sea disposal options, including information on waste characteristics, conditions at the proposed dump site, fluxes and proposed disposal techniques and also specify the potential effects on human health, living resources, amenities and other legitimate uses of the sea. These assessments can apply to dumping of wastes in ABNJ as well as to areas within national jurisdiction.

In May 2007, the Parties to the London Convention and London Protocol were faced for the first time with proposals for large scale commercial ocean iron fertilization projects. Some U.S. and Australian companies were promoting ocean fertilization as a tool to buffer ocean acidity, replenish the marine food chain and sequester CO_2, while inviting investors and green cosponsors to finance their activities in return for the provision of carbon credits to offset investors' CO_2 emissions. A 'statement of concern' adopted by the Scientific Groups of the London Convention and London Protocol in July 2007 'noted with concern the potential for [ocean fertilization] activities to have negative impacts on the marine environment and human health' and recommended that the Parties to the London Convention and London Protocol consider the issue with a view to its regulation.[48] This 'statement of concern' was endorsed by the Parties during their joint annual meeting in November 2007 where they agreed that while it was within the purview of each State to consider proposals for ocean fertilization projects on a case-by-case basis in accordance with the Convention and/or Protocol, knowledge about the effectiveness and potential environmental impacts of open ocean fertilization was currently insufficient to justify large scale projects. They also agreed that ocean fertilization fell within their regulatory competence and that they would 'further study this issue from scientific and legal perspectives with a view to its regulation'.[49]

The ongoing discussions in the London Convention/London Protocol Scientific Groups concerning ocean fertilization prompted the Conference of the Parties of the Convention on Biological Diversity (COP CBD) at their 9th meeting in May 2008 to request Parties and urge other governments

> in accordance with the precautionary approach to ensure that ocean fertilization activities do not take place until there is an adequate scientific basis on which to justify such activities, including assessing associated risks, and a global transparent and effective control and regulatory mechanism is in place for those

force 24 March 2006) ('*London Protocol*'), Article 4 and Annex 2.

48 LC/LP Scientific Groups, 'Statement of Concern Regarding Iron Fertilization of the Ocean to Sequester CO_2,' Doc. LC-LP.1/Circ.14, 13 July 2007.

49 International Maritime Organization, *Report of the 29th Consultative Meeting of the Contracting Parties to the Convention on the Prevention of Marine Pollution by Dumping of Wastes and Other Matter, 1972 and 2nd Meeting of the Contracting Parties to the 1996 Protocol thereto*, IMO Doc. LC29/LP2 (2007).

> activities; with the exception of small scale scientific research within national jurisdiction.[50]

An exception was noted in the case of 'small scale scientific research studies within coastal waters', which 'should only be authorized if justified by the need to gather specific scientific data, and should also be subject to a thorough prior assessment of the potential impacts of the research studies on the marine environment, and be strictly controlled, and not be used for generating and selling carbon offsets or any other commercial purposes'.[51]

In October 2008, the Parties to the London Convention and London Protocol adopted a non-binding resolution agreeing that 'given the present state of knowledge ocean fertilization activities other than legitimate scientific research should not be allowed' and that 'ocean fertilization activities other than legitimate scientific research, should be considered as contrary to the aims of the Convention and Protocol and not currently qualify for any exemption from the definition of dumping'.[52] They identified the need for preparatory work on technical and scientific issues and agreed to further consider a potentially legally binding resolution or an amendment to the London Protocol at their 2009 session. An intersessional Technical Working Group on Ocean Fertilization was established to develop an Assessment Framework for Scientific Research Involving Ocean Fertilization to provide a mechanism for assessing, on a case-by-case basis, whether proposals for ocean fertilization activities represent legitimate scientific research.[53] The draft Assessment Framework[54] was reviewed by the Scientific Groups in June 2009 and adopted as a work in progress.[55] The draft was tabled again during an extraordinary session of the Scientific Groups in October 2010[56] where further revisions were made, and it was adopted, by consensus, in a non-binding resolution at the October 2010 meeting of the Parties.[57]

---

50 COP 9 Decision XI/16 on Biodiversity and Climate Change (presented at the Ninth Meeting of the States Parties to the Convention on Biological Diversity (COP 9), Bonn, 19–30 May 2008) Section C, <http://www.cbd.int/decisions/cop9/?m=COP-09&id=11659&lg=0>, 27 August 2008.

51 Ibid.

52 Resolution LC/LP.1 (2008), *Report of the 30th Consultative Meeting of the Contracting Parties to the Convention on the Prevention of Marine Pollution by Dumping of Wastes and Other Matter, 1972 and 3rd Meeting of the Contracting Parties to the 1996 Protocol thereto*, IMO Doc LC30/16, 9 December 2008, paras 4.1–4.18 and Annexes 2 and 5.

53 LC.30/16, para 2.3.

54 LC/SG-CO2 3/5, annex 2.

55 LC/SG 32/15, paras 2.18–2.29.

56 See Draft Assessment Framework for Scientific research Involving Ocean Fertilization Doc LC/SG/ES.2, 30 July 2010.

57 32nd Consultative Meeting of Contracting Parties to the Convention on the Prevention of Marine Pollution by Dumping of Wastes and Other Matter, 1972 (London Convention) and 5th Meeting of Contracting Parties to the 1996 Protocol thereto (London

The Assessment Framework (AF) describes itself as a 'tool … to determine if the proposed activity constitutes legitimate scientific research that is not contrary to the [LC/LP] aims'. It sets out a two-stage process involving an initial assessment and an environmental assessment. The purpose of the initial assessment is to determine whether the proposed ocean fertilization activity constitutes legitimate scientific research. To qualify as such, the proposed activity must have 'proper scientific attributes', which means:

1. The proposed activity should be designed to answer questions that will add to the body of scientific knowledge. Proposals should state their rationale, research goals, scientific hypotheses and methods, scale, timings and locations with clear justification for why the expected outcomes cannot reasonably be achieved by other methods.
2. Economic interests should not influence the design, conduct and/or outcomes of the proposed activity. There should not be any financial and/or economic gain arising directly from the experiment or its outcomes. This should not preclude payment for services rendered in support of the experiment of the future financial impacts of patented technology.
3. The proposed activity should be subject to scientific peer-review at appropriate stages in the assessment process. The outcomes of the scientific peer review should be taken into consideration by the Contracting Parties. The peer review methodology should be stated and the outcomes of the peer review of successful proposals should be made publicly available together with the details of the project.
4. The proponents of the proposed activity should make a commitment to publish the results in peer-reviewed scientific publications and include a plan in the proposal to make the data and outcomes publicly available in a specified time frame.

Proposals that meet these criteria may then proceed to the next stage, the environmental assessment that includes requirements of risk management and monitoring. The environmental assessment stage entails a number of components including the problem formulation, a site selection and description, an exposure assessment, an effects assessment, risk characterization and risk management sections.[58] Only after completion of the environmental assessment is a decision made on whether the proposed activity constitutes legitimate scientific research that is not contrary to the aims of the London Convention and/London Protocol. If so, the activity is permitted to proceed.

Protocol) Assessment Framework for Scientific Research Involving Ocean Fertilization, Resolution LC-LP.2 (2010).

58 Assessment Framework for Scientific Research Involving Ocean Fertilization, LC 32/15, Annex 6, pp. 5–19, <http://ww.imo.org/SharePoint/blastDataHelper.asp/data_id%3D30641/AssessmentFramework-annex6-LC-32-15.pdf>.

Deep Seabed Mining Instruments under the LOSC Part XI Deep seabed mining exploration activities in ABNJ are subject to a well-developed framework of EIA obligations. An exploration contractor must submit an assessment of the potential environmental impacts of proposed activities with an application for approval of a plan of work together with a description of a programme for oceanographic and baseline environmental studies in accordance with the rules, regulations and procedures adopted by the International Seabed Authority (ISA).[59] This obligation is reiterated in Regulation 18(c) and (d) of the ISA's Regulations for the Prospecting and Exploration of Polymetallic Nodules (Polymetallic Nodules Regulations) which provides that applicants for exploration contracts must submit a preliminary assessment of the possible impact of the proposed exploration activities on the marine environment and a description of proposed measures for the prevention, reduction and control of possible impacts on the marine environment to the ISA.[60] The Recommendations for the Guidance of Contractors for the Assessment of the Possible Environmental Impacts Arising from Exploration for Polymetallic Nodules in the Area, issued by the Authority's Legal and Technical Commission in revised form in 2010, specify the particular activities of exploration contractors that are subject to EIA.[61] The sponsoring State for an exploration contractor is under a due diligence obligation to ensure that an exploration contractor fulfils all these obligations.[62]

Gaps in the International Law Framework for EIA in ABNJ

Although there is an established customary international law obligation and many conventional international law obligations to conduct EIAs of activities with the potential for significant impacts on the marine environment and some obligations at the regional level to conduct SEAs of plans, programmes and policies with the potential for significant impacts on the marine environment, implementation of these obligations for ABNJ is still at a nascent stage. There is no overarching international agreement which develops in more specific terms the obligation contained in Article 206 of the LOSC to assess the potential effects of planned

59 *Agreement Relating to the Implementation of Part XI of the United Nations Convention on the Law of the Sea of 10 December 1982*, opened for signature 28 July 1994, 33 ILM 1309 (entered into force 28 July 1996) (*'Part XI Implementation Agreement'*), Annex, para 7.

60 Regulations for Prospecting and Exploration of Polymetallic Nodules (Polymetallic Nodule Regulations), <http://www.isa.org.jm/files/documents/EN/Regs/PN-en.pdf>, Regulation 18(c) and (d).

61 Recommendations for the Guidance of Contractors for the Assessment of the Possible Environmental Impacts Arising from Exploration for Polymetallic Nodules in the Area, <http://www.isa.org.jm/files/documents/EN/7Sess/LTC/isba_7ltc_1Rev1.pdf>, para 10.

62 ITLOS Advisory Opinion, above note 13, 43–44, paras 141–143; Polymetallic Nodules Regulation 31(6) and Polymetallic Sulphides Regulation 33(6).

activities under States' jurisdiction or control that may cause substantial pollution of or significant and harmful changes to the marine environment. Similarly institutional coverage for ABNJ is far from comprehensive with no global body having overarching responsibility for protection and preservation of the marine environment or conservation of marine biodiversity beyond national jurisdiction and only a few regional seas programmes having specific environmental protection responsibilities for these areas.[63] The ISA has comprehensive environmental protection powers for activities affecting the Area, but this advanced environmental governance situation for the deep seabed beyond national jurisdiction is not matched by a global institution with comparable environmental protection powers for the high seas water column.

With the increasing variety of sectoral activities in ABNJ, the establishment of a global instrument and institutional infrastructure to protect the marine environment and conserve the marine biodiversity of these areas is becoming increasingly urgent. In the fisheries sector, the FAO's Deep Sea Fishing Guidelines apply only to bottom fishing activities rather than all high seas fishing and aquaculture activities and rely on the variable standards inherent in flag State implementation either by individual flag States or through regional fisheries management organizations. While dumping at sea and small-scale ocean fertilization experiments are subject to risk and environmental assessment processes for Parties to the London Convention and London Protocol, there are many other activities involving ships in ABNJ such as oil and gas exploration, bio-prospecting, marine scientific research, survey activities, marine geo-engineering, deep-sea tourism and military activities that are not subject to any EIA process. In most cases the EIA obligations in regional seas conventions do not require member States to assess the impact of their activities on the marine environment beyond national jurisdiction because the geographic scope of the conventions do not extend to these areas.

The complex and fragmentary nature of environmental governance in ABNJ is also highlighted by the array of international instruments applicable in these areas, many with overlapping mandates. Antarctica is a case in point with the Antarctic Treaty system conventions, the LOSC, the CBD, the CMS and the International Convention on the Regulation of Whaling (ICRW) all applying to ABNJ below 60° south latitude. A more comprehensive environmental governance framework for these areas could develop EIA and SEA processes for new and emerging activities in ABNJ and coordinate existing sectoral EIA and SEA processes. It could also perform the role of prescribing and monitoring best practice standards for EIA and SEA in ABNJ.

---

63 See above note 27.

Global Initiatives to Develop the International Law Framework for EIA in ABNJ

United Nations General Assembly (UNGA) Initiatives

In the five meetings since its inception in 2005, the United Nations General Assembly (UNGA) Ad Hoc Open-ended Informal Working Group, created to study issues related to the conservation and sustainable use of marine biological diversity beyond areas of national jurisdiction (BBNJ Working Group), has consistently identified EIA for activities affecting marine areas beyond national jurisdiction as an important component of its work. At the first meeting of the Working Group, the Co-Chairpersons noted that the conservation and sustainable use of marine biological diversity beyond areas of national jurisdiction should be based on the precautionary and ecosystem approaches using the best available science and prior EIAs.[64] In 2008, the Co-Chairpersons of the Working Group provided further endorsement for EIA as a significant element in the conservation of marine biodiversity beyond national jurisdiction, commenting that the UNGA may wish to refer the development and implementation of effective EIAs as a tool for improving ocean management to the Working Group for further study.[65] In 2010, the Co-Chairpersons of the Working Group identified as a key issue requiring more background studies, the review of approaches to EIAs, including in the context of the ISA and the regional seas programmes, and determining commonalities and best practices.[66] In 2011, the Co-Chairpersons recommended to the UNGA that a process be initiated, by the General Assembly, with a view to ensuring that the legal framework for the conservation and sustainable use of marine biodiversity in ABNJ effectively addresses those issues by identifying gaps and ways forward. These issues would be dealt with through the implementation of existing instruments and the possible development of a multilateral agreement under the LOSC. In particular, it was recommended that the process address, inter alia, measures such as EIA.[67] The UNGA in the annual Oceans and Law of

---

64 Report of the Ad Hoc Open-ended Informal Working Group to study issues relating to the conservation and sustainable use of marine biodiversity beyond areas of national jurisdiction, 20 March 2006, <http://daccess-dds-ny.un.org/doc/UNDOC/GEN/N06/277/50/PDF/NO627750.pdf ?Open Element>, Annex I, para 5.

65 Letter from the Co-Chairpersons of the Ad Hoc Open-ended Informal Working Group to study issues relating to the conservation and sustainable use of marine biodiversity beyond areas of national jurisdiction addressed to the President of the General Assembly, 16 May 2008, <http://daccess-dds-ny.un.org/doc/UNDOC/GEN/N08/344/16/PDF/NO834416.pdf ?Open Element>, para. 54 c).

66 Letter from the Co-Chairpersons of the Ad Hoc Open-ended Informal Working Group to the President of the General Assembly, 17 March 2010, <http://daccess-dds-ny.un.org/doc/UNDOC/GEN/N10/277/20/PDF/N1027720.pdf ?Open Element>, para 80(g).

67 Letter from the Co-Chairs of the Ad Hoc Open-ended Informal Working Group to the President of the General Assembly, 30 June 2011, <http://daccess-dds-ny.un.org/

the Sea Resolution on 24 December 2011 endorsed the BBNJ Working Group recommendations.[68] The fifth meeting of the BBNJ Working Group in May 2012 recommended that two intersessional workshops be held in the first half of 2013, one of which would be to discuss and provide expert advice to the Working Group on conservation and management tools in ABNJ, including area-based management and environmental impact assessments.[69] The UN Conference on Sustainable Development (Rio + 20) meeting in June 2012 supported the urgent taking of a decision on whether to develop an international instrument under the LOS Convention on the conservation and sustainable use of marine biodiversity in areas beyond national jurisdiction.[70]

CBD Initiatives

In support of the BBNJ Working Group's study of issues related to the conservation and sustainable use of marine biodiversity beyond areas of national jurisdiction and, in particular its focus on EIA, the COP CBD convened an Expert Workshop on Scientific and Technical Elements of CBD Voluntary Biodiversity Inclusive EIA Guidelines for Marine Areas beyond National Jurisdiction in Manila in November 2009.[71] This workshop highlighted ecological, governance and practical differences related to the implementation of EIA and SEA for activities with the potential for significant impacts on marine biodiversity beyond national jurisdiction. Key ecological differences noted in the Workshop Report included the following:

- the great depth of many ocean areas beyond national jurisdiction creates extreme conditions for biodiversity-pressure changes, lower temperatures and lack of oxygen;
- most ocean areas beyond national jurisdiction have lower primary and secondary productivity meaning that populations and communities can sustain lower levels of perturbation without serious adverse impacts;

---

doc/UNDOC/GEN/N11/397/64/PDF/N1139764.pdf ?OpenElement>, Annex, Section I, paras(a) and (b).

68 Oceans and the Law of the Sea; Resolution adopted by the UNGA on 24 December 2011 (A/RES/66/231 of 28 November 2011), para 167.

69 Letter from the Co-Chairs of the Ad Hoc Open-ended Informal Working Group to the President of the General Assembly, 13 June 2012, http://daccess-dds-ny.un.org/doc/UNDOC/GEN/N12/372/82/PDF/N1237282.pdf?OpenElement, Annex, Section I, para (b) and Appendix, para 8(2),

70 UN Conference on Sustainable Development – Rio + 20, *The Future We Want* , paragraph 162 at http://www.uncsd2012.org/content/documents/727The%20Future%20We%20Want%2019%20June%201230pm.pdf.

71 Report of the Expert Workshop on Scientific and Technical Aspects relevant to Environmental Impact Assessment in Marine Areas beyond National Jurisdiction, UNEP/CBD/EW-EIAMA/2, 20 November 2009, <http://www.cbd.int/doc/?metting=EWEIAMA-01>.

- recovery from perturbations for most species and ecosystems in marine areas beyond national jurisdiction is longer than for coastal and terrestrial ecosystems;
- connectivity of coastal to deepwater ecosystems is likely to be much looser than between ecosystems along shore; and
- not as much is known about the migratory and dispersal characteristics of benthic species beyond national jurisdiction.[72]

The Workshop Report emphasized the practical difficulties associated with conducting EIAs including the following:

- the industry proposing the activity and the national flag State jurisdiction are often far from the marine area affected;
- the conduct of EIA and management, control, monitoring, surveillance and follow-up activity were likely to be more costly and may be less effective for a given budget; and
- capacity building needs for EIA in marine areas beyond national jurisdiction would be greater as customs of practice are less established, methodologies less mature, and multiple assessment cultures may converge in the same area.[73]

In relation to the international framework for EIA of activities affecting ABNJ, the Workshop Report highlighted its complex and fragmentary characteristics referring to the following factors:

- different legal framework for marine areas beyond national jurisdiction – high seas (UNCLOS Part VII) and deep seabed beyond national jurisdiction – the Area (Part XI UNCLOS and Part XI Implementation Agreement);
- the different institutional framework for marine areas beyond national jurisdiction including global and regional organizations as well as flag State jurisdiction and that cooperation is required between all these components to conserve the biodiversity of these areas;
- the UNGA has a central role in matters relating to conserving marine biodiversity beyond national jurisdiction;
- stakeholders are harder to define for marine areas beyond national jurisdiction because communities do not have immediate proximity to these areas; and
- international conventions contain certain obligations relating to EIA and SEA but there are variable standards of compliance among States.[74]

---

72 Ibid, Annex II, paras 3–6.
73 Ibid, Annex II, paras 10–14.
74 Ibid, Annex II, paras 7–9.

The Workshop Report identified the need for:

- global and, where appropriate, regional standards for acceptable perturbation;
- compilation of global experiences on how oceanic ecosystems have responded to past human impacts and natural forces, and how effective mitigation measures have been;
- a better understanding of the connectivity between impacts and ecosystem processes within and beyond national jurisdictions.[75]

For SEA, the Workshop reviewed the CBD's Guidance Document on Biodiversity Inclusive SEA adopted by the eighth meeting of the COP CBD in 2006 (Decision VIII/28) and identified elements that were lacking in this guidance in relation to marine ABNJ as well as specific characteristics and ecosystems that must be considered in undertaking SEA in these areas.[76] The Workshop Report highlighted a number of direct and indirect drivers of biophysical and non-biophysical changes to ecosystems that should trigger the conduct of SEAs for plans, programmes and policies affecting marine areas beyond national jurisdiction. These included commercial activities such as trade and shipping patterns, fisheries, extraction of non-living resources, bioprospecting, climate change mitigation activities, the laying of pipelines and cables on the seabed, waste disposal and technological improvements to navigation, fishing equipment, mapping and visualization capabilities.[77]

The Workshop's Report was considered by the tenth COP CBD in 2010. The relevant decision in the COP 10 report requested the Executive Secretary of the CBD to facilitate the development of voluntary guidelines for the consideration of biodiversity in EIAs and SEAs in marine and coastal areas using the guidance in Annexes II, III and IV to the Manila Workshop Report, to provide for technical peer review of the guidelines and to submit them for consideration to a future meeting of the Subsidiary Body on Scientific, Technical and Technological Advice (SBSTTA) prior to the eleventh meeting of COP CBD in 2012.[78] The decision impliedly recognized the existence of some sectoral EIA processes for activities affecting marine ABNJ by acknowledging the guidelines would be most useful for activities that are currently unregulated with no process for assessing impacts. It also requested that the guidelines be developed for all marine and coastal areas rather than simply for marine ABNJ, emphasizing the interconnections between

75 Ibid, Annex II, paras 16–18.

76 Ibid, Annex IV, paras 8–9.

77 Ibid, Annex IV, para 14.

78 Report of the Tenth Meeting of the Conference of the Parties to the Convention on Biological Diversity, UNEP/CBD/COP/10/27, 20 January 2011, Annex, Decision X/29, para 50, <http://www.cbd.int/cop10/doc/>.

ocean ecosystems across jurisdictional boundaries. The draft Guidelines are still under development within the CBD.[79]

Conclusion

There is an established obligation to conduct EIAs of activities with the potential for significant impacts on the marine environment in both customary international law and many conventional international law instruments. There are also recognized customs of practice for implementing this obligation in the majority of marine areas within national jurisdiction supported by national legislation and policy. In addition, there is emerging regional and national practice relating to transboundary EIA and the conduct of SEA of plans, programmes and policies with the potential for significant impacts on the marine environment. This chapter has explored the basis in international law for the obligation to conduct EIA of activities with the potential to significantly affect marine biodiversity beyond national jurisdiction and its implementation in limited sectoral contexts including deep-sea fishing, dumping of wastes at sea, ocean fertilization experiments and deep seabed mining. Propelled by the impetus of increasing human impacts on the oceans including ABNJ, the global community, through the BBNJ Working Group with the scientific and technical support of the COP CBD, has supported the development of Voluntary Guidelines on Biodiversity-Inclusive EIA and SEA for Marine and Coastal Areas including ABNJ. The Guidelines take into account the specific ecological, governance and practical differences associated with conducting EIAs and SEAs of activities, plans, programmes and policies affecting marine biodiversity beyond national jurisdiction. This initiative represents an important step in articulating the peculiar characteristics of EIAs and SEAs related to activities affecting ABNJ and should provide a catalyst for more comprehensive implementation of these important tools in such areas across all regions and sectors. Beyond this soft law initiative, a number of options are available to the international community for a legally binding instrument on EIA and SEA in ABNJ including a stand-alone instrument, relevant provisions in a potential implementation agreement under the LOSC for the conservation of marine biodiversity in ABNJ and a supplementary protocol to existing instruments such as the Espoo Convention and the Kiev Protocol for ABNJ.[80] All these options are likely to be canvassed in future meetings of the BBNJ Working Group, which has emerged as the political centre of gravity for discussions on ABNJ governance.

79 Report of the Sixteenth Meeting of Subsidiary Body on Scientific, Technical and Technological Advice (SBSTTA), UNEP/CBD/COP/11/3, 21 June 2012, paragraph 99, http://www.cbd.int/sbstta16/documents/.

80 On the last option see the chapter by Timo Koivurova in this volume.

Chapter 13
Could the Espoo Convention Become a Global Regime for Environmental Impact Assessment and Strategic Environmental Assessment?

Timo Koivurova*

Introduction

The Convention on Environmental Impact Assessment (EIA) in a Transboundary Context (the Espoo Convention) is now 20 years old.[1] It was negotiated under the auspices of the United Nations Economic Commission for Europe (UNECE) and signed in Espoo, Finland, in 1991.[2] Following six meetings of the signatories, the Convention entered into force in 1997 and the first meeting of the parties (MoP) took place in Oslo in 1998. Four MoPs have been held since, at approximately

* The author would like to thank Professor Simon Marsden for his encouragement to think beyond the existing transboundary environmental impact assessments. The article is based on a keynote the author made in the seminar organized by the Australian National Centre for Ocean Resources and Security, University of Wollongong, NSW titled 'Perspectives on Transboundary Environmental Governance in Australia and Beyond'. Part of the research for this article was done during the time the author was a visiting professorial fellow in the Faculty of Law of the University of New South Wales.

1 The Convention on Environmental Impact Assessment in a Transboundary Context, 25 February 1991, ILM, vol. 30, 1991, 800 [hereinafter Espoo Convention]. The Convention entered into force on 10 September 1997. There is an increasing body of literature on transboundary EIA; see, e.g., the special issue on transboundary EIA, (2008) 26 *Impact Assessment And Project Appraisal* (IAPR); Bastmeijer Kees and Koivurova Timo (eds.), *Theory and Practise of Transboundary Environmental Impact Assessment* (2008); Neil Craik, *The International Law of Environmental Impact Assessment, Process, Substance and Integration* (2008); S. Marsden and T. Koivurova (eds.), *Transboundary Environmental Impact Assessment in the European Union: The Espoo Convention and its Kiev Protocol on Strategic Environmental Assessment* (2011). The Review of European Community and International Environmental Law (RECIEL) will publish soon its special issue marking the 20th anniversary of the Espoo Convention.

2 For an overview of the negotiations, see Robert Connelly, 'The UN Convention on EIA in a Transboundary Context: A Historical Perspective' (1999) 19 *Environmental Impact Assessment Review* 37.

three-year intervals: in 2001 in Sofia, Bulgaria; in 2004 in Cavtat, Croatia; in 2008 in Bucharest, Romania; and in Geneva, Switzerland in 2011.[3] At present, there are 45 parties to the Convention.[4] The Strategic Environmental Assessment (SEA) Protocol to the Convention was signed in 2003 as part of the Environment for Europe process and has been signed by 37 states as well as the EC.[5]

Following the 20th anniversary of the adoption of the Espoo Convention, it is appropriate to ponder the future directions of the Espoo regime ('regime' being the Convention, the Protocol, decisions by the MoP and the associated subsidiary body decisions[6]), especially in view of the fact that the Espoo parties have expressed their willingness to open the membership of the Convention to all the United Nations (UN) member states:

> Any other State, not referred to in paragraph 2 of this Article, that is a Member of the United Nations may accede to the Convention upon approval by the Meeting of the Parties. The Meeting of the Parties shall not consider or approve any request for accession by such a State until this paragraph has entered into force for all the States and organizations that were parties to the Convention on 27 February 2001.[7]

The SEA Protocol can already be joined by all UN member states.[8] Hence, the main question evaluated in this chapter is whether the Espoo regime could have global application and whether this would also be a desirable development from the viewpoint of environmental protection.

One important sub-set of this question is whether the Espoo regime could expand into a new realm of covering EIA and SEA in relation to impacts to the environment in areas beyond national jurisdiction (ABNJ).[9] The main focus of

---

3 See the Espoo Convention website, at http://live.unece.org/env/eia/mop.html.

4 See at http://treaties.un.org/Pages/ViewDetails.aspx?src=TREATY&mtdsg_no=XXVII-4&chapter=27&lang=en.

5 Available at http://treaties.un.org/Pages/ViewDetails.aspx?src=TREATY&mtdsg_no=XXVII-4-b&chapter=27&lang=en (1 June 2009). There are currently 23 parties. The Protocol entered into force on 11 July 2010.

6 Subsidiary bodies are organs created by the meeting of the parties to implement the regime in various ways. Examples include bodies tasked to review the compliance of the parties with their obligations.

7 Article 17(3) of the Convention includes here the first amendment to the Convention, adopted as Decision II/14, at http://live.unece.org/env/eia/about/amendment.html.

8 Article 23(3) reads: 'Any other State, not referred to in paragraph 2 above, that is a Member of the United Nations may accede to the Protocol upon approval by the Meeting of the Parties to the Convention serving as the Meeting of the Parties to the Protocol', at http://live.unece.org/env/eia/about/sea_text.html.

9 These are marine areas beyond national jurisdiction including the high seas beyond 200 nautical miles from the coastal states' territorial sea baselines and the deep seabed beyond national jurisdiction known as the Area.

this part of the chapter is to examine one possible legal approach to EIA/SEA over development activities possibly having an impact on the environment of the ABNJ, given that so far policy development has resulted in principally soft regulation. It is important to commence discussion on this, given that there is practically no scholarly research or policy proposals in relation to these questions.

Before moving to examining the main questions of this chapter, it is important to provide further explanation as to why the questions related to the expanding scope of membership of the Espoo regime should be addressed now. It is also useful to examine how the Espoo Convention is meant to function and how it in fact operates. This evaluation will be made partly on the basis of a recent study the author has conducted with Dr. Neil Craik and researcher Minna Torkkeli over how the Finnish EIA procedure has in practice been able to comply with the obligations of the Espoo Convention.[10] Moreover, one case study will be taken up – transboundary EIA (TEIA) over the Baltic Sea Gas Pipeline (BSGP). This case illustrates well how the Espoo Convention regime has become more ambitious in its approach to TEIA.

Distinguishing TEIA from Domestic EIA

EIA is a fairly simple regulatory tool and has spread throughout the globe. The first national EIA procedures appeared at the end of the 1960s and especially in the beginning of the 1970s, the most well known being the US National Environmental Policy Act (NEPA) of 1969.[11] In many cases the spread of national EIAs has been explained by other states borrowing the NEPA model but its expansion has not been that straightforward.[12] Many inter-governmental organizations – and later multinational development banks – have promoted EIA as a national policy tool from the mid 1970s onwards.[13]

---

10 Timo Koivurova, Neil Craik ja Minna Torkkeli, YVA-lain toimivuus valtioiden rajat ylittäviä ympäristövaikutuksia koskevien velvoitteiden näkökulmasta, 14.4.2011. Evaluation commissioned by the Finnish Ministry of the Environment. On file with the author.

11 National Environmental Policy Act, 42 USC §§ 4321–4370(f).

12 See, e.g., Tsaming Yang and Robert V. Percival, 'The Emergence of Global Environmental Law' (2009) 34 *Yale Journal of International Law* 615–664, at 627–630. They use the term 'legal transplantation' as 'deliberate copying and adaptation of significant portions of statutes or particular doctrines of law by one country from another' (p. 626).

13 Some of the relevant instruments can be found in Harald Hohmann (ed.), *Basic Documents of International Environmental Law, Vol. 1: The Important Declarations* (1992). The main international organizations in this field have been the United Nations General Assembly (UNGA), the United Nations Environment Programme (UNEP), the Organisation for Economic Co-operation and Development (OECD), the United Nations Economic Commission for Europe (UNECE) and the Council of Europe. See, e.g., the following UN instruments: United Nations General Assembly Resolution 2995 (XXVII), Co-operation Between States in the Field of the Environment; 1974 Charter of Economic

EIA can be defined as a governmentally controlled procedure by which scientific assessments are made – together with public participation – of the proposed activity the impacts of which may be harmful. Its goals include improving the quality of information to enable decision-makers to make better decisions from the viewpoint of the environment and to raise in general the level of public participation in environmental decision-making. It was the spread of national EIA procedures that made it possible to conclude legally relevant instruments and treaties on TEIA. Since TEIA functions to integrate foreign impacts and foreign actors into the operation of a domestic EIA procedure of the origin state in cases where transboundary impact is likely, this is best done by an international treaty, given that states' jurisdiction is confined mainly to their national territory.

Treaties or other instruments that try to organize a TEIA procedure must take into account the basic fact that states have differing domestic EIA procedures. From the viewpoint of the functioning of a TEIA procedure, the ideal situation would obviously be one in which all the contracting states had an identical EIA procedure, for the potentially affected state and its public would then know when and how to participate in the EIA procedure taking place in accordance with the EIA procedure of the origin state. Yet in many instances the domestic EIA procedure differs to quite some extent, making the organization of TEIA a complicated task.

TEIA is often perceived only as an extended EIA procedure between territorial states to include also transboundary impacts and foreign actors into the domestic EIA of the origin state in relation to the proposed projects, plans and programmes. Yet today the concept has enlarged in many ways. Questions have been raised as to whether countries are required to conduct EIA even if there are no transboundary impacts, in line with the goal of sustainable development.[14] Common concerns of

---

Rights and Duties of States (Art. 3); 1987 UNEP Goals and Principles of Environmental Impact Assessment; Provisions for Co-operation Between States in Weather Modification. For the OECD, see, e.g., 1979 OECD Recommendation on the Assessment of Projects with Significant Impact on the Environment; 1974 OECD Recommendation on the Analysis of Environmental Consequences of Significant Projects; 1974 OECD Principles Concerning Transfrontier Pollution (paras. 6, 8); Equal Right of Access in Relation to Transfrontier Pollution in Relation to Implementation; Strengthening International Co-operation on Environmental Protection in Transfrontier Regions; Provision of Information to the Public and Public Participation in Decision-making Processes Related to the Prevention of, and Response to Accidents Involving Hazardous substances. See, e.g., the following UNECE instruments: Declaration of Policy on Prevention and Control of Water Pollution, Including Transboundary Pollution; Decision on International Co-operation on Shared Water Resources; Decision on Principles Regarding Co-operation in the Field of Transboundary Waters, 1987. A relevant instrument concluded by the Council of Europe is the Air Pollution in Frontier Areas. See also Chapter 8 of Agenda 21, especially Section 8 (5b).

14 The former vice-president of the International Court of Justice, Christopher Weeramantry, articulates this well – even if with fairly unique legal methodology – in his separate opinion to the case concerning the Gabcíkovo–Nagymaros Project (Hungary/Slovakia), Judgment, I.C.J. Reports 1997, at http://www.icj-cij.org/docket/files/92/7383.pdf.

humankind, chief among them climate change and biodiversity loss, are required by their respective treaties to be evaluated as part of a state's EIA procedure.[15] EIA procedures designed to evaluate the likely impacts of human activities on the environment in ABNJ are the most recent development in EIA/SEA since they are now being actively developed as one of the tools to tackle problems of biodiversity loss beyond national jurisdiction.[16]

Why This Question and Why Now?

Why should we ask whether the Espoo regime could become a global treaty regime for EIA/SEA? There are high normative expectations from the spread of EIA to various levels of governance. Currently, there are several processes trying to evaluate how EIA/SEA should be conducted to include common concerns of humankind, when proposed activities may impact the environment in ABNJ or how multilateral financial institutions and other lending institutions should perform EIA/SEA. There is moreover increased attention being given to whether the only developed international EIA/SEA regime, Espoo, could spread to become a global one and fulfil the normative expectations that there are for environmental assessment.

Why is this question topical now? In 2011, as noted, the Espoo Convention celebrated the 20th anniversary of its adoption. Even though the Convention did not enter into force until 1997, meetings of the signatories and pilot studies

15 Article 14(1) of the Convention on Biological Diversity expresses it in this way: 'Each Contracting Party, as far as possible and as appropriate, shall: (a) Introduce appropriate procedures requiring environmental impact assessment of its proposed projects that are likely to have significant adverse effects on biological diversity with a view to avoiding or minimizing such effects and, where appropriate, allow for public participation in such procedures; (b) Introduce appropriate arrangements to ensure that the environmental consequences of its programmes and policies that are likely to have significant adverse impacts on biological diversity are duly taken into account; (c) Promote, on the basis of reciprocity, notification, exchange of information and consultation on activities under their jurisdiction or control which are likely to significantly affect adversely the biological diversity of other States or areas beyond the limits of national jurisdiction, by encouraging the conclusion of bilateral, regional or multilateral arrangements, as appropriate …'. See at http://www.cbd.int/convention/articles/?a=cbd-14.

16 The most recent outcome of the United Nations Ad Hoc Open-ended Informal Working Group to study issues relating to the conservation and sustainable use of marine biological diversity beyond areas of national jurisdiction is the Report on the work of the United Nations Open-ended Informal Consultative Process on Oceans and the Law of the Sea at its twelfth meeting, at http://daccess-dds-ny.un.org/doc/UNDOC/GEN/N11/431/39/PDF/N1143139.pdf?OpenElement. The recommendations of the fourth meeting of the UNGA BBNJ Working Group in 2011 at http://daccess-dds-ny.un.org/doc/UNDOC/GEN/N11/397/64/PDF/N1139764.pdf?OpenElement and CBD COP 10 Decision X/29 paragraph 50http://www.cbd.int/cop10/doc/ are also relevant.

started almost immediately when the Convention was signed in 1991.[17] The 20th Anniversary of the Convention offers its parties an opportunity to look back and into the future, following the fifth MoP in June 2011 (together with the first MoP to the SEA Protocol).[18]

The Espoo regime continues to expand although a few states still need to ratify it for the 1st amendment to enter into force and open the Convention for all UN members (Iran has already expressed interest in becoming a party).[19] The SEA Protocol is already open to all UN members since it entered into force on 11 July 2010. Hence, when the Espoo Convention's 1st amendment enters into force, the Espoo regime seems likely to expand further. Moreover, international courts have given very recent normative signals that TEIA is binding on all states under general international law, making it very timely to ask how to operationalize TEIA. In the 2010 decided *Pulp Mills* case between Uruguay and Argentina the International Court of Justice (ICJ) unequivocally stated the following:

> In this sense, the obligation to protect and preserve, under Article 41 (a) of the Statute, has to be interpreted in accordance with practice, which in recent years has gained so much acceptance among States that it may now be considered a requirement under general international law to undertake an environmental impact assessment where there is a risk that the proposed industrial activity may have a significant adverse impact in a transboundary context, in particular, on a shared resource. Moreover, due diligence, and the duty of vigilance and prevention which it implies, would not be considered to have been exercised, if a party planning works liable to affect the régime of the river or the quality of its waters did not undertake an environmental impact assessment on the potential effects of such works.[20]

The ICJ thus made clear that TEIA is both an independent normative principle of general international law as well as part of the no-harm principle. Consequently, all states are expected to perform TEIA as an international legal obligation. Yet, the Court also said that the scope and content of TEIA remain under the discretion of states although it argued that it needs to be conducted diligently. This likely means that the discretion of states on how to regulate and apply TEIA is fairly broad, even if constrained by the requirement of due diligence.[21] Argentina invoked the

17 These meetings of the signatories are studied in T. Koivurova, *Environmental Impact Assessment in the Arctic: A Study of International Legal Norms* (2002) 298–300.

18 See at http://live.unece.org/env/eia/meetings/mop_5.html.

19 See at http://treaties.un.org/Pages/ViewDetails.aspx?src=TREATY&mtdsg_no=XXVII-4-a&chapter=27&lang=en.

20 Case Concerning Pulp Mills on the River Uruguay (Argentina v. Uruguay) (20 April 2010, Judgment), para. 204, at http://www.icj-cij.org/docket/files/135/15877.pdf.

21 Ibid., para. 205 provides: '… it is the view of the Court that it is for each State to determine in its domestic legislation or in the authorization process for the project, the specific content of the environmental impact assessment required in each case, having

Espoo Convention to support its legal argument, but the ICJ could not apply the Convention as neither of the disputants were parties to it.[22]

In a similar vein, the recent advisory opinion of the International Tribunal for the Law of the Sea (ITLOS) Sea-Bed Disputes Chamber first relied on the above-quoted paragraph from the *Pulp Mills* case and then continued that:

> Although aimed at the specific situation under discussion by the Court, the language used seems broad enough to cover activities in the Area even beyond the scope of the Regulations. The Court's reasoning in a transboundary context may also apply to activities with an impact on the environment in an area beyond the limits of national jurisdiction; and the Court's references to 'shared resources' may also apply to resources that are the common heritage of mankind. Thus, in light of the customary rule mentioned by the ICJ, it may be considered that environmental impact assessments should be included in the system of consultations and prior notifications set out in article 142 of the Convention with respect to 'resource deposits in the Area which lie across limits of national jurisdiction'.[23]

Even if the Sea-Bed Disputes Chamber did not provide a clear-cut answer as to whether EIA/SEA needs to be conducted prior to authorization of an activity likely to have adverse impacts to the environment in ABNJ, it does contemplate that possibility in a serious manner. The duty to evaluate impacts to the environment of ABNJ seems already included in the no-harm principle as articulated in the Stockholm and Rio Declarations[24] and in numerous international treaties and other instruments; it is also affirmed to be part of the corpus of international law relating to the environment by the ICJ.[25] The principle, as articulated in Rio Declaration's principle 2 stipulates that:

---

regard to the nature and magnitude of the proposed development and its likely adverse impact on the environment as well as to the need to exercise due diligence in conducting such an assessment. The Court also considers that an environmental impact assessment must be conducted prior to the implementation of a project. Moreover, once operations have started and, where necessary, throughout the life of the project, continuous monitoring of its effects on the environment shall be undertaken.'

22 Ibid., para. 205.

23 Responsibilities and obligations of States sponsoring persons and entities with respect to activities in the Area (Request for Advisory Opinion submitted to the Seabed Disputes Chamber), Case No. 17, para. 148, at http://www.itlos.org/fileadmin/itlos/documents/cases/case_no_17/adv_op_010211.pdf.

24 Article 21 of the Stockholm Declaration and Article 2 of the Rio Declaration of 1992. The Stockholm Declaration can be found from 11 I.L.M. 1416 (1972) and the Rio Declaration from 31 I.L.M. 874 (1992).

25 The ICJ first stated this view in its Advisory Opinion in the *Legality of the Threat or Use of Nuclear Weapons*, Advisory Opinion, I.C.J. Reports 1996, p. 226, para. 29. The

> States have, in accordance with the Charter of the United Nations and the principles of international law, the sovereign right to exploit their own resources pursuant to their own environmental and developmental policies, and *the responsibility to ensure that activities within their jurisdiction or control do not cause damage to the environment* of other States or *of areas beyond the limits of national jurisdiction.* (author's emphasis)

The Espoo Convention – How is it Supposed to Function?

The Espoo Convention differs from domestic approaches to TEIA and also inter-state procedures. By 'domestic approaches' is meant domestic EIA and permitting procedures that are formally open for foreign impacts and foreign actors. With this approach, it is however practically impossible to include transboundary impacts and actors in any meaningful way, given that the mere opening of domestic procedures to foreign impacts and actors does not guarantee that these can be effectively included in the operation of domestic EIA and authorization procedures; international treaties are needed to ensure that domestic procedures can be extended to the territory of other states. By 'inter-state procedures' is meant nation-states preventing or at least minimizing transboundary pollution and using TEIA only as a trigger. In the UN International Law Commission's Preventive Draft Articles[26] the focus is on nation-states negotiating how to prevent and minimize transboundary pollution on the basis of TEIA results. The practical problem faced by this approach is that it is very difficult to operationalize rules that expect states to shoulder each and every transboundary case anew.[27] The Espoo Convention builds on the regular functioning of domestic EIA and domestic authorization procedures to which foreign impacts and foreign actors can then be integrated via an international treaty. This type of approach can be called a 'transnational EIA procedure'[28] in the sense that it avoids as much as possible interference by the nation-states and rather builds on the regular functioning of domestic legal and administrative systems, into which foreign impacts and foreign actors can be integrated.

Court also repeated this passage in the case concerning the *Gabcíkovo-Nagymaros Project (Hungary/Slovakia)*, Judgment, I.C.J. Reports 1997, p. 7, para. 53.

26 Draft articles on Prevention of Transboundary Harm from Hazardous Activities, with commentaries, 2001, at http://untreaty.un.org/ilc/texts/instruments/english/commentaries/9_7_2001.pdf.

27 See John Knox, 'Assessing the Candidates for a Global Treaty on Transboundary Environmental Impact Assessment' (2003–2005) Vol. XII *New York University Environmental Law Journal* 153–168, at 159–161.

28 See T. Koivurova, 'The Transnational EIA procedure of the Espoo Convention' (1997) Vol. VIII *Finnish Yearbook of International Law* 161–199.

The Espoo Convention expects the States Parties to establish national EIA and authorization procedures for Appendix 1 activities ('screening').[29] It also lays down minimum requirements for the Environmental Impact Statement (EIS)[30] and expects EIA to include public participation. The Convention's system is very much built on the functioning of domestic EIA and permitting procedures, since it is to these procedures that the foreign impacts and foreign actors are integrated. Consequently, the way each TEIA is conducted depends on what kind of domestic EIA and authorization procedure exists in a given state. Here, the Finnish national EIA procedure will be used to illustrate how TEIA is organized when a national system (that of Finland's) acts as the framework for Espoo TEIA.

Under Article 3 the Espoo Convention obliges the origin state to initiate the TEIA procedure as early as possible but no later than when it informs its own public of a proposed development activity.[31] Different states will thus commence the TEIA procedure when their national systems require the authorities to inform the public. Finland's domestic EIA procedure contains a 'scoping' stage, in which the proponent (who submits the first draft of the scoping document and is responsible for making the impact assessments), together with the public and expert authorities, discuss what should be studied in the actual impact assessment stage. Since the public is notified in the scoping phase, Finland is obligated by the Espoo Convention to commence the TEIA very early on with the affected state and its public. During the scoping stage, the affected state and its public must be informed and given an opportunity to comment on the scoping document. This is of importance from the viewpoint of studying the transboundary impacts, given that it is the affected state and its public that will likely place most emphasis on how transboundary impacts are studied. The emphasis on studying transboundary impacts carefully is further reinforced by Article 3(6), which requires the affected state to deliver information on the environmental conditions on its side of the border to the origin state, if the latter so requests.

When the final EIS has been completed by the proponent, the responsible authorities organize consultation of the public on both sides of the border: the affected state's public has equal rights to be informed and to comment on the proposed activity as the origin state's public.[32] The Convention requires the origin

29 Article 2 (2 and 3) of the Convention reads: 'Each Party shall take the necessary legal, administrative or other measures to implement the provisions of this Convention, including, with respect to proposed activities listed in Appendix I that are likely to cause significant adverse transboundary impact, the establishment of an environmental impact assessment procedure that permits public participation and preparation of the environmental impact assessment documentation described in Appendix II … The Party of origin shall ensure that in accordance with the provisions of this Convention an environmental impact assessment is undertaken prior to a decision to authorize or undertake a proposed activity listed in Appendix I that is likely to cause a significant adverse transboundary impact'.

30 See Appendix II of the Convention.

31 Article 3(1) of the Convention.

32 Article 2(6) of the Convention.

state to immediately commence consultations with the potentially affected state in order to discuss possible mitigation measures etc.[33] The final EIS is thus commented on differently by the affected state and its public: the former will discuss the proposed activity via inter-state consultations with the origin state whereas the members of the public of the affected state channel their comments directly to the domestic EIA authorities of the origin state under the same conditions as the origin state's public. The Convention expects the origin state's permit authority to take due account of the comments made by the affected state and its public, which are of crucial importance in deciding how the proposed activity's transboundary impacts will be mitigated.[34] The final decision must be delivered to the affected state and its public. Post-project analysis – a phase where the concerned states would monitor what impacts will result from the activity – will be undertaken if concerned states agree on its necessity.

The Espoo Regime – How it Functions in Practice?

Recently, the present author conducted an evaluation of the Finnish TEIA capacity together with Dr. Neil Craik from Canada and researcher Minna Torkkeli.[35] Overall it was found that the Finnish TEIA system had performed effectively. There had been quite a number of TEIA's where Finland had been an origin state (21 cases) and an affected state (17). In comparison with other Member States of the European Union (EU), Finland was a little over the average in terms of how many TEIAs had been completed.[36]

One of the surprises found in the study was the way Finland had interpreted Article 5 of the Espoo Convention. Article 5 reads as follows:

> The Party of origin shall, after completion of the environmental impact assessment documentation, without undue delay enter into consultations with the affected Party concerning, inter alia, the potential transboundary impact of the proposed activity and measures to reduce or eliminate its impact. Consultations may relate to:
>
> (a) Possible alternatives to the proposed activity, including the no-action alternative and possible measures to mitigate significant adverse transboundary impact and to monitor the effects of such measures at the expense of the Party of origin;

---

33 See Article 5 of the Convention.

34 Article 6 of the Convention.

35 See above, note 101.

36 2009 European Commission, DG ENV Study concerning the report on the application and effectiveness of the EIA Directive Final report, June 2009, table 6.8.

> (b) Other forms of possible mutual assistance in reducing any significant adverse transboundary impact of the proposed activity; and
>
> (c) Any other appropriate matters relating to the proposed activity.
>
> The Parties shall agree, at the commencement of such consultations, on a reasonable time-frame for the duration of the consultation period. Any such consultations may be conducted through an appropriate joint body, where one exists.

Article 5 accords the affected state a right to convey its views directly to the origin state, and enables it to raise possible mitigation measures to be taken to reduce transboundary harm on the basis of the EIS. As mentioned above, the public of the affected state has a right to comment on the impacts of the proposed activity on an equal footing with the public of the origin state. Yet when Finland is an origin state, the standard procedure (with a couple of exceptions) is to not commence inter-state consultations but to merge the affected state's comments as part of all the comments from the affected state into Finland's domestic EIA. Another surprise was that this was fairly common practice amongst the Espoo parties. This was found from the cases where Finland had been an affected state. Of all the cases where Finland had been an affected state (with the exception of the BSGP), none of the origin states had felt it necessary to organize inter-state consultations with Finland.[37]

This misinterpretation of Article 5 begs the question: what procedures does the Convention have in place for non-compliance? Such matters fall to the Implementation Committee, which is now also in charge of scrutinizing the state reports, and which has collated and published its previous opinions on matters related to the Convention.[38] This is a document consisting of the major findings of the Implementation Committee between the years 2001–2010, enabling the committee to signal how the Convention should be interpreted by the states parties in the future. In this document, the Implementation Committee urges the parties to separate inter-state consultations under Article 5 from the way the public of the affected state is entitled to participate under Article 4.2:

> The Committee reminded Parties that consultations under article 5 were bilateral or multilateral discussions between authorities that had been authorized by the concerned Parties, and should not be confused with public participation under

---

37 Above, note 10.

38 Opinions of the Implementation Committee, 2001–2010, note by the Implementation Committee, ECE/MP.EIA/IC/2011/INF.1. There is an interesting parallel here to the way the human rights treaty monitoring mechanisms issue General Comments.

> article 3, paragraph 8, and article 4, paragraph 2, or with consultation of the authorities under article 4, paragraph 2, in the areas likely to be affected.[39]

Case-Study: Baltic Sea Gas Pipeline

The Espoo regime has also had to confront ever more challenging projects, of which the most difficult has been the BSGP, that is, TEIA over two gas pipelines from Russia to Germany to be laid in the seabed of the Baltic Sea, traversing the EEZs and territorial seas of five states (the Russian Federation, Finland, Sweden, Denmark and Germany). Here it is useful to only highlight some aspects of the case that relate to the marine environment and emphasize how quickly the Espoo regime is becoming more ambitious and collective in its approach.[40]

A pipeline traversing the EEZs and territorial seas of five states does not fit easily within the system of the Espoo Convention. The Convention requires each and every state to determine for itself whether there are likely significant adverse transboundary impacts from the proposed projects within its jurisdiction to other states' environments. During the initial stages of the BSGP project, some states were of the view that there would be no significant adverse transboundary impacts from the BSGP, hence no need to apply the Espoo Convention to the pipeline project. This would have meant that the company developing the project, Nord Stream, would have undergone EIA and permitting procedures in regard to each portion of the pipeline in each of the five origin states. This is known as 'salami slicing', a practice which has been condemned by the European Court of Justice (ECJ)[41] in relation to the EIA Directive.[42]

Yet, as a sign of how far the Espoo regime has evolved based on experience in the EU, the Espoo contact points got together in 2006 and required the company to perform an EIA over the entire gas pipeline(s), not only the individual portions of it. They also decided that each of the Baltic Sea littoral states can and must be seen as affected states of the BSGP, meaning that nine states and their publics could participate in any of the five national EIA systems as well as comment on the EIA done by the company over the entire pipeline(s). This type of community approach illustrates well the changes in the way the Espoo Convention can handle very complex and challenging projects; the BSGP case involved all nine Baltic Sea littoral states and their publics even though there was no clear evidence at the beginning that significant adverse transboundary impact would ensue. Similar types of development have recently commenced with nuclear energy-related

39 Ibid, para. 69.

40 For a more extensive treatment, see T. Koivurova and I. Pölönen, 'Transboundary Environmental Impact Assessment in the Case of the Baltic Sea Gas Pipeline'(2010) 25 *International Journal of Marine and Coastal Law* 151–181.

41 After the Treaty of Lisbon entered into force in December 2009, it is now named 'Court of Justice of the European Union'.

42 See Case C 205/08.

projects, some states notifying each and every party to the Espoo Convention, just to make sure that all states that want to participate in the TEIA have the opportunity to do so. For this reason, the Secretariat prepared a background note to the fifth meeting of the parties as to how to apply the Convention to nuclear energy-related activities.[43]

Could the Espoo Convention Become a Global Treaty on TEIA?

Since the Espoo parties have signalled their willingness to open the Espoo regime to all the UN member states, it is pertinent to ask whether: (a) this is the best way to move forward and (b) it is politically viable. We may ponder whether the requirements the Convention sets out for domestic EIA, studied above, are too ambitious for e.g. many developing nations. On the other hand, the Convention only expects a minimum standard for domestic EIAs: that they are established for appendix I activities, with no ambition to harmonize the national EIAs to any great measure.

It might also be questioned whether there is enough emphasis in the Espoo Convention on preventing or at least minimizing transboundary pollution along the lines of the UN International Law Commission produced Preventive Draft Articles – articles that have already been cited by judicial bodies.[44] These Draft Articles expect states to be key actors in preventing and mitigating transboundary pollution, which in itself, as pointed out above, can be seen as a problem. It is very difficult to foresee that the ILC's Preventive Draft Articles could serve as a basis for a regime that functions on a day-to-day basis, given that the Articles expect central governments to act on TEIA; they are too large actors for such procedures. The Espoo Convention does not contain strong substantive guidance: Article 2(1) expresses more of a goal than a substantive standard.[45] The Convention relies intensely on scientific information influencing decision-making, which in many cases seems to have at the very least the possibility to modify project planning.

We might also ask whether it makes sense at all to have global MoPs to scrutinize situations of transboundary pollution that take place largely between immediate neighbours only. This question is usefully answered by pointing to increasing sub-regionalization of the Espoo regime. The Espoo parties now work with their neighbours via different sub-regions, which are created and sustained

43 Background note on the application of the Convention to nuclear energy-related activities, at http://live.unece.org/fileadmin/DAM/env/documents/2011/eia/ece.mp.eia.2011.5.e.pdf.

44 See e.g. para. 116 of the Seabed Disputes Chamber's advisory opinion, above note 23.

45 It reads: 'The Parties shall, either individually or jointly, take all appropriate and effective measures to prevent, reduce and control significant adverse transboundary environmental impact from proposed activities.'

either via legally binding agreements or just by regular meetings.[46] Hence, sub-regionalization of the Espoo regime makes possible both taking into account of (a) regional realities and, importantly, (b) assistance from the community of states. Many developing nations do need financial support and capacity building in order to organize as complex a procedure as TEIA.[47]

Moreover, since the Espoo regime is the only really functioning multilateral TEIA regime (with 20 years of experience), it is evident that the experience garnered throughout its life-cycle is of extreme importance to be disseminated to other regions and countries. And its parties are not only EU states. In fact, the Espoo Convention's 45 parties range from Canada and Western European states to Eastern Europe and Caucasus and even to Central Asia. The regime thus already possesses a wide diversity of developing and developed states as parties. Very recently, Russian President Dimitri Medvedev announced Russia's intention to ratify both the Espoo and the UNECE Convention on Access to Information, Public Participation in Decision-making and Access to Justice in Environmental Matters[48] (Aarhus Convention).[49] Russia is a Central and East Asian state as well as a European one. Furthermore, the last meeting of the parties adopted a decision to accelerate the globalization of the Espoo regime:

> 1. Request any State that wishes to accede to the Convention or to the Protocol, and that is a Member of the United Nations but that is not a member of UNECE, to address a letter to the Executive Secretary of UNECE from its Minister of Foreign Affairs expressing the State's desire to accede to the Convention or to the Protocol;
>
> 2. Also request a State referred to in paragraph 1, which wishes to accede to the Convention, to provide a copy of its legislation in one of the official languages of the United Nations, establishing clear, transparent and effective procedures for environmental impact assessment in a transboundary context in accordance with the provisions of the Convention;
>
> 3. Further request a State referred to in paragraph 1, which wishes to accede to the Protocol, to provide a copy of its legislation in one of the official languages of the United Nations, establishing clear, transparent and effective procedures

46 See the sub-regions website at http://live.unece.org/env/eia/subregions.html.

47 See Simon Marsden's chapter 6 in this volume.

48 The text is reproduced in 38 I.L.M. 517 (1999).

49 See at UNECE website at http://www.unece.org/press/pr2011/11env_p26e.html. This is in line with another recent development, namely that Russia's nuclear power company agrees to consult with neighbours on environmental impacts within the framework of UNECE's Espoo Convention, see at http://www.unece.org/press/pr2011/11env_p21e.htm.

for strategic environmental assessment in accordance with the objective and provisions of the Protocol;

4. Expect to consider the information referred to in paragraphs 1, 2 and 3, when deciding whether to approve the accession of a State that is a Member of the United Nations but that is not a member of UNECE;[50]

Is the Espoo Regime's Globalization Politically Viable?

The only significant problem standing in the way of the Espoo Convention becoming a globally applicable TEIA regime is that it was commenced as a regional regime, with core countries being Member States of the EU. There are very few treaties that have become global treaty regimes if they have started as regional ones. Yet, in the case of the Espoo regime, there are good prospects for globalizing a regionally initiated regime. First of all, the Espoo regime is functioning under the auspices of the universal UN system, in one of its Economic Commissions (UNECE). Another reason for possible globalization of the Espoo Convention was taken up by John Knox in an article where he discussed which of the two possible global TEIA regimes have better chances of realization, ending up favouring the Espoo Convention rather than the ILC Preventive Draft Articles. As pointed out by Knox, the Espoo regime can very well induce a type of ripple effect:

> Espoo originally addressed the third obstacle – countries' preference for agreements on transboundary harm that include their neighbors – simply by limiting its scope to European and North American countries. Now that most of those countries have joined, they might create a kind of snowball effect, in which the membership of Espoo naturally expands as countries along the borders of the existing parties decide that it is in their interest to join an agreement that includes their neighbors. In addition, existing parties have an incentive to convince their neighbors to join. For example, Russia is not yet a party to Espoo, but several of its neighbors are, including Finland, Kazakhstan, and Ukraine. Those countries have presumably already done much of the work necessary to bring themselves into compliance with Espoo's obligations. They now have an incentive to convince Russia to join so that they have the benefits of receiving transboundary EIA of projects in Russia. If Russia joined, it would then have a similar incentive to bring in non-UNECE countries that neighbor it, such as China and Japan. In this way, Espoo could gradually ripple across the globe.[51]

Even if the Convention is not yet opened for parties outside of the UNECE, it already involves non-parties in its practical work, especially in sub-regions, which

50 See MoP decisions V/8 and I/8, at http://live.unece.org/fileadmin/DAM/env/documents/2011/eia/ece.mp.eia.2011.L.2_ece.mp.eia.sea.2011.L.2.e.pdf.

51 See Knox, above note 27, 165–166.

likely paves the way for a speedier ripple effect when the Convention opens up for all UN members. Already now there are signs that states are perceiving TEIA as a global institution. In December 2009, the Federated States of Micronesia requested initiation of a TEIA to examine the expansion and life-extension of the Prunéřov II coal-fired power plant in the Czech Republic. Micronesia – a state that is particularly vulnerable to impacts of rising sea levels – was concerned about the climate change impacts of this expansion and hence requested TEIA from the Czech Ministry of the Environment.[52]

On balance, there do seem to be good prospects for the Espoo Convention to spread as obstacles are lifted by the States Parties when the 1st amendment enters into force. This is very much related to the design of the Espoo regime, which builds both on sub-regional bottom-up practical co-operation but also on the treaty community being able to address issues related to capacity building and financial support, which are of vast importance for the developing world. And it does seem desirable that this will take place. The Espoo Convention has 20 years' experience of how to conduct TEIAs, which certainly should find its way to the practice of states throughout the globe, especially now that the ICJ has also affirmed that all states are required to carry out TEIA.

Projects and Strategies Likely to Have an Impact on the Environment of ABNJ – Any Role for the Espoo Regime?

A much more challenging question for the Espoo regime is whether it could cover EIA/SEA over impacts to ABNJ. This is a reasonable question for the Espoo parties, given that they have intentionally opened the regime for the global community of states. It is also an important question to resolve for at least some of the concerns related to ABNJ management. The Espoo regime is already the main EIA/SEA international regime, and if its membership extends further, it is only natural to ask whether the Espoo regime would cover, as perhaps the primary example of an ABNJ, those parts of high seas governance that relate to EIA/SEA.

Even if EIA/SEA over proposed activities likely to have an impact on high seas biodiversity is one of the cutting-edge issues – being discussed both in the UN[53] and under the Convention on Biological Diversity regime[54] – it is puzzling

---

52 Two documents stating what has taken place so far (received from Sini Harkki, on file with the author).

53 This is done in the United Nations Ad Hoc Open-ended Informal Working Group to study issues relating to the conservation and sustainable use of marine biological diversity beyond areas of national jurisdiction, at http://www.un.org/Depts/los/biodiversityworkinggroup/marine_biodiversity.htm.

54 See, e.g., Report of the Expert Workshop on Scientific and Technical Aspects Relevant to Environmental Impact Assessment in Marine Areas beyond National Jurisdiction, UNEP/CBD/SBSTTA/14/INF/5, 8 March 2010.

why there have been no scholarly proposals as to how legal EIA/SEA for activities likely to have an adverse impact on the environment of the ABNJ could be created. There is one research article, published in 2004, contemplating the possibility of negotiating an implementing agreement to the United Nations Convention on the Law of the Sea (UNCLOS) on EIA, but not even this article looks into the impacts on ABNJ.[55]

One reason for this scholarly inattention is likely the ongoing processes to produce rules – or even an implementing agreement – for activities that have an adverse impact on high seas biodiversity. The UN informal working group has convened four times since 2006 to study the issue, and has confronted significant problems, in particular the one relating to the legal status of marine genetic resources in ABNJ. Developing states argue that such resources should be part of the common heritage of mankind and thus fall under the mandate of the International Sea-Bed Authority; developed states have opposed this approach and pointed to the clear provisions in UNCLOS,[56] which includes only non-living resources of the Area under the common heritage of mankind, resulting in marine living resources including marine genetic resources being part of the open access high seas regime. Aside from these difficult political controversies, there is a lot of consensus on certain aspects governing the biodiversity issues related to ABNJ, in particular the use of EIA/SEA. The CBD Expert Workshop on Scientific and Technical Elements of CBD Voluntary Biodiversity Inclusive EIA Guidelines for Marine Areas beyond National Jurisdiction held in Manila in November 2009 developed some guidance on EIA/SEA over activities that may impact ABNJ biodiversity, which will likely be adopted as soft-law guidelines at some point in time.[57] Yet it seems obvious that soft-law guidance is not enough, especially in an area where compliance is very difficult to monitor.[58]

It remains to be seen what comes out of these ABNJ biodiversity processes as the issues are difficult, and concern the mandates of many state and non-state institutions.[59] Hence, one possibility might be to 'isolate' EIA/SEA from the

---

55 M. Tanaka, 'Lessons from the Protracted MOX Plant Dispute: A Proposed Protocol on Marine Environmental Impact Assessment to the United Nations Convention on the Law of the Sea' (2004) 25 *Michigan Journal of Environmental Law* 337. There is a forthcoming article in the *International Journal of Marine and Coastal Law* (2012) 27(2), in which Alex Oude Elferink and Petra Drankier will look into these issues.

56 The 1982 United Nations Convention on the Law of the Sea (the 1982 LOSC). The text is reproduced in 21 I.L.M. 1261 (1982).

57 See the interesting 2009 expert meeting report, at http://www.cbd.int/doc/meetings/mar/eweiama-01/official/eweiama-01-02-en.pdf. This guidance is being incorporated in Draft CBD Guidelines on Biodiversity Inclusive EIA/SEA for Marine and Coastal Areas which are likely to be considered by the 11th meeting of the Conference of the Parties (COP 11) of the CBD in 2012.

58 See Robin Warner's chapter 12 in this volume.

59 For a comprehensive overview, see R. Warner, *Protecting the Oceans beyond National Jurisdiction: Strengthening the International Law Framework* (2009), in particular

overall agenda for biodiversity protection and use in ABNJ, given that such a broad and ambitious regulatory agenda is not easily solved. Yet there is a lot of consensus on the need for developing EIA/SEA frameworks for ABNJ,[60] which might present an opportunity for the Espoo regime to provide hard-law guidance.

Projects and Strategies Likely to Have an Impact on the Environment of ABNJ – Possible Problems for the Role of the Espoo Regime?

The Espoo regime is not a natural 'nesting' place for EIA/SEA rules for activities having a likely impact on the environment in ABNJ. Since UNCLOS regulates in its Articles 204–206 EIA for all activities having an impact on the marine environment, it would be this convention where such an EIA/SEA implementing agreement would most naturally be located. Yet the current processes envisage measures geared towards regulating, in ambitious and overarching manner, protection and use of biodiversity in ABNJ; the EU has already made a proposal to move forward with an implementing agreement to realize this, and the UN process is moving in this direction.[61] One component of such an implementing agreement could be EIA/SEA. Yet, as there currently are only few positive signals that such an implementing agreement would receive political support, it is important to study possible hard-law alternatives, such as the Espoo regime taking over the EIA/SEA component.

It has to be noted that the Espoo regime has not much expertise and experience in the maritime domain. The Convention and the Protocol cover only land-based (some offshore) stationary activities. They do not cover vessel source pollution or fisheries activities, which are of course the root cause of many problems for the

pp. 207–235.

60 See Robin Warner's chapter 12 in this volume.

61 Recommendations of the Ad Hoc Open-ended Informal Working Group to study issues relating to the conservation and sustainable use of marine biological diversity beyond areas of national jurisdiction and Co-Chairs' summary of discussions took this up after its most recent meeting from 31 May to 3 June 2011. They provide the following: '… recommends that: (a) A process be initiated, by the General Assembly, with a view to ensuring that the legal framework for the conservation and sustainable use of marine biodiversity in areas beyond national jurisdiction effectively addresses those issues by identifying gaps and ways forward, including through the implementation of existing instruments and the possible development of a multilateral agreement under the United Nations Convention on the Law of the Sea; (b) This process would address the conservation and sustainable use of marine biodiversity in areas beyond national jurisdiction, in particular, together and as a whole, marine genetic resources, including questions on the sharing of benefits, measures such as area-based management tools, including marine protected areas, and environmental impact assessments, capacity-building and the transfer of marine technology; (c) This process would take place: (i) in the existing Working Group; and (ii) in the format of intersessional workshops aimed at improving understanding of the issues and clarifying key questions as an input to the work of the Working Group …'. See at http://daccess-dds-ny.un.org/doc/UNDOC/GEN/N11/397/64/PDF/N1139764.pdf?OpenElement.

biodiversity and the environment of the marine areas in ABNJ. On the other hand, it is important to note that that the Espoo parties have already shown the ambition to develop the regime to new regulatory fields, as exemplified by the adoption of the SEA Protocol, which focused on harmonizing SEA procedures (only one provision on transboundary SEA) rather than regulating what the Convention does, namely transboundary pollution. Hence, we know that the Espoo parties are ready to extend the regime to new horizons if regulatory need can be shown to exist. It is also useful to note that there is an increasing experience in the Espoo regime over performing collective EIAs protecting the rights of the whole treaty community, for instance in nuclear energy-related activities.

A Second Protocol to the Espoo Convention?

It is possible to envisage a process whereby globalizing the Espoo regime triggers negotiations for a second Protocol to the Convention aimed at preventing and minimizing impacts to the environment in ABNJ (possibly also including specified forms of vessel source pollution to the marine environment in general). It would be important to base the second Protocol on the already existing customary international law principle of no-harm, which explicitly requires states to prevent harm to the environment in ABNJ from the activities under their jurisdiction and control, in particular activities of their flag vessels.

A possible sketchy model for EIA/SEA in ABNJ should build on the strengths of the Espoo regime. Only activities, plans and programmes of the origin state would need to be evaluated by it, if they were likely to have a significant adverse impact on the environment of ABNJ. If such impacts were likely, the origin state would be under an obligation to notify all states parties to the second protocol and other interested parties other than nation-states, including international and regional organizations such as the International Sea-Bed Authority, regional fisheries management organizations and some regional seas organizations. It might be asked how third states can be excluded from such notification, given that they also have rights and interests in protecting the ABNJ environment.[62] Yet this can also serve as an incentive for third states (and possibly some inter-governmental institutions) to become parties to the second protocol since second protocol parties could respond that they are only trying to create a procedure whereby the no-harm principle is really put into practice in a legally effective manner. They could make an argument that if the third states and other institutions are serious in applying the no-harm principle in practice and thus protecting the environment of the ABNJ, they should become parties to the second protocol. This type of collective notification procedure is already increasingly taking place

62 It has to be admitted, however, that if third states would e.g. invoke their UNCLOS or general international law guaranteed rights, it would be difficult for the origin state to reject notifying them.

in the Espoo Convention as regards the nuclear energy-related projects and has manifested itself at least to some extent in the BSGP case.[63]

As in the Espoo regime in general, TEIA is operationalized via the functioning of the domestic EIA system and this type of approach would also be suitable in terms of evaluating impacts to the environment of ABNJ. When the origin state had completed the assessment of impacts to the environment of ABNJ, it would need to notify all those states that have informed the origin state that they wanted to participate in the domestic EIA/SEA and their publics. All these affected states and their civil societies would have a right to comment on the results of the assessments by sending these to the domestic EIA authorities. Thereafter, all this information would be delivered, as is standard practice in the Espoo regime, to the permitting authority, which would be obliged to take due account of the information from the affected states and their publics.[64] Moreover, the permitting authority would be obligated to send the final decision to the authorities of all the affected states, which in turn would need to deliver it to their own publics.

Conclusion: Is an Espoo Regime the Solution?

There seems to be no clear-cut reason why the Espoo regime could not become the global regime on EIA/SEA. The Espoo parties have intentionally opened the regime for all UN members, it contains the best standards in this field of international relations and is the only regime that has experience and continues to learn how to better conduct EIA/SEA in an international context. If a second protocol on impacts to the environment on ABNJ were negotiated, this would likely place further incentives on states to join the globalizing Espoo regime, given that this protocol would deal with impacts to the global commons – a development that should be of interest to the whole international community. Even if the Espoo regime has not garnered experiences in evaluating impacts of vessel source pollution, this is no obstacle for adopting the kind of second protocol considered above, even if one has to admit that this latter development is less likely than global spread of the Espoo Convention in terms of TEIA/SEA between states.

Yet as also pointed out in this chapter, it may also happen that the Espoo regime will not spread throughout the world and remains (only) an important regional regime on EIA/SEA. It is very difficult to predict the way states and other actors will come to perceive the best and most viable solution for EIA/SEA in an international context. If they choose the Espoo regime, one single regime would be in charge of evaluating the likely significant environmental impacts from activities, plans and programmes to various components of the environment. From the perspective of environmental protection, this option would certainly have its benefits.

63 See above, section entitled 'Case-Study: Baltic Sea Gas Pipeline'.

64 Article 6 of the Convention.

Bibliography

Abdulrazzak, Dalal and Stephen Trombulak, 'Classifying Levels of Protection in Marine Protected Areas' (2011) 36 *Marine Policy* 576

Adedayo Ayoade, Morakinyo, *Disused Offshore Installations and Pipelines: Towards Sustainable Decommissioning* (Kluwer Law International, 2002)

Agardi, Tundi, Giuseppe Notarbartolo di Sciara and Patrick Christie, 'Mind the Gap: Addressing the Shortcomings of Marine Protected Areas through Large Scale Marine Spatial Planning' (2011) 36 *Marine Policy* 226

Alexander, Lisa, 'Stakeholder Participation in New Governance: Lessons from Chicago's Public Housing Reform Experiment' (2009) 16 *Georgetown Journal on Poverty Law and Policy* 117

Allchin, R and J Davidson, *Whitsundays Case Study Background Report, Changing Currents in Marine Biodiversity Governance and Management: Responding to Climate Change* (School of Geography and Environmental Studies, University of Tasmania, 2012)

ARC Centre of Excellence, Coral Reef Studies, 'What is the Coral Triangle Initiative?' http://www.coralcoe.org.au/events/ctiworkshop/ctiinfo.html

Arctic Environment Protection Strategy, *Guidelines for Environmental Impact Assessment in the Arctic*, 1997, http://ceq.hss.doe.gov/nepa/eiaguide.pdf

Ashe, John and Simon Marsden, 'SEA in Australia' in Barry Sadler et al, (eds), *Strategic Environmental Assessment Handbook* (Earthscan, 2011) 26

Asian Development Bank, *Safeguard Policy Statement* (Asian Development Bank, 2009)

Australian Fisheries Management Authority, *Heard Island and McDonald Islands Fishery Management Plan* (Australian Fisheries Management Authority, 2002)

Axelrod, Robert, *The Evolution of Cooperation* (Basic Books, 1984)

Badenoch, Nathan, *Transboundary Environmental Governance – Principles and Practice in Mainland Southeast Asia* (World Resources Institute, 2002)

Baker, Susan and Katarina Eckerberg (eds), *In Pursuit of Sustainable Development: New Governance Practices at the Sub-national Level in Europe* (Routledge, 2008)

Bala, G et al, 'Impact of Geoengineering Schemes on the Global Hydrological Cycle' (June 3 2008) 105 *PNAS* 7664

Barrett, Scott, 'The Incredible Economics of Geo-engineering' (2008) 39 *Environ. Resource Econ.* 45

Bastmeijer, Kees and Timo Koivurova (eds), *Theory and Practice of Transboundary Environmental Impact Assessment* (Martinus Nijhoff, 2008)

Bastmeijer, Kees and Ricardo Roura, 'Environmental Impact Assessment in Antarctica' in Kees Bastmeijer and Timo Koivurova (eds), *Theory and Practice of Transboundary Environmental Impact Assessment* (Martinus Nijhoff, 2008) 175

Bates, Gerry, *Environmental Law in Australia*, 7th edn (LexisNexis Butterworths, 2010)

Bauer, Steffan, Per-Olf Busch and Bernd Siebenhüner, 'Treaty Secretariats in Global Environmental Governance' in Frank Bierman, Bernd Siebenhüner and Anna Schreyögg, *International Organisations in Global Environmental Governance* (Routledge, 2009) 174

Beckman, Robert, 'China, UNCLOS and the South China Sea' (2011) *Asian Society of International Law Third Biennale Conference*, Beijing, China 27–28 August 2011, 11 [32] http://cil.nus.edu.sg/wp/wp-content/uploads/2009/09/AsianSIL-Beckman-China-UNCLOS-and-the-South-China-Sea-26-July-2011.pdf

Beeton, RJS, CD Buxton, GC Cutbrush, PG Fairweather, EL Johnston and R Ryan, *Report of the Independent Scientific Audit of Marine Parks in New South Wales* (NSW Department of Primary Industries and Office of Environment and Heritage, 2012)

Bickel, J Eric and Lee Lane, 'Climate Engineering' in Bjørn Lomborg, *Smart Solutions to Climate Change. Comparing Costs and Benefits* (Cambridge University Press, 2010) 9

Biermann, Frank et al, 'Earth System Governance: A Research Framework' (2010) 10(4) *International Environmental Agreements: Politics, Law and Economics* 277

Bishop, K, A Phillips and LM Warren, 'Protected Areas for the Future: Models from the Past' (1997) 40 *Journal of Environmental Planning and Management* 81

Blain, S, 'Effect of Natural Iron Fertilization on Carbon Sequestration in the Southern Ocean' (2007) 446 *Nature* 1070

Blomgren Bingham, Lisa, 'The Next Generation of Administrative Law: Building the Legal Infrastructure for Collaborative Governance' (2010) *Wisconsin Law Rev* 297

Blomquist, William, Brian Haisman, Ariel Dinar, Anjali Bhat, *Institutional Policy Analysis of River Basin Management: The Murray Darling River Basin, Australia* (World Bank Policy Research Working Paper No 3527, World Bank, February 2005)

Bodansky, Daniel, 'May We Engineer the Climate?' (1996) 33 *Climate Change* 301

Bonnell, Joseph E and Tomas M Koontz, 'Stumbling Forward: The Organizational Challenges of Building and Sustaining Collaborative Watershed Management' (2007) 20 *Society & Natural Resources* 153

Boyd, P et al, 'A Mesocale Phytoplankton Bloom in the Polar Southern Ocean Stimulated by Iron Fertilization' (2000) 407 *Nature* 695

Boyle, Alan, 'Marine Pollution under the Law of the Sea Convention' (1985) 79 *American Journal of International Law* 356

Boyle, Alan, 'State Responsibility and International Liability for Injurious Consequences of Acts not Prohibited by International Law: A Necessary Distinction?' (1990) 39 *International and Comparative Law Quarterly* 1

Boyle, Alan, 'The Gabcikovo-Nagymaros Case: New Law in Old Bottles' (1997) 8 *Yearbook of International Environmental Law* 18

Boyle, Alan, 'The Principle of Co-operation: The Environment' in Vaughan Lowe and Colin Warbrick (eds), *The United Nations and the Principles of International Law: Essays in Memory of Michael Akehurst* (Routledge, 1994) 120

Boyle, Alan, 'The Environmental Jurisprudence of the International Tribunal for the Law of the Sea' (2007) 22 *International Journal of Marine and Coastal Law* 369

Brels, Sabine, David Coates and Flavia Loures, *Transboundary Water Resources Management: The Role of International Watercourse Agreements in Implementation of the CBD*, CBD Technical Series No. 40 (Secretariat of the Convention on Biological Diversity, 2008)

Breu, Thomas and Hans Hurni, 'High Mountain Areas: A Wildlife Habitat' in Thomas Breu and Hans Hurni (eds), *The Tajik Pamirs – Challenges of Sustainable Development in an Isolated Mountain Region* (2003) 28

Brodie, JE, J Binney, K Fabricius, I Gordon, O Hoegh-Guldberg, H Hunter, P O'Reagain, R Pearson, M Quirk, P Thorburn, J Waterhouse, I Webster, S Wilkinson, *Synthesis of Evidence to Support the Scientific Consensus Statement on Water Quality in the Great Barrier Reef* (Intergovernmental Operations Committee and the RWQP Management Committee, 2008)

Brown, Howard L, 'Expanding the Effectiveness of the European Union's Environmental Impact Assessment Law' (1997) 22 *Boston College International and Comparative Law Review* 313

Bruch, Carl, Mikiyasu Nakayama, Jessica Troell, Lisa Goldman and Elizabeth Marunma Mrema, 'Assessing the Assessments: Improving Methodologies for Impact Assessment in Transboundary Watercourses' (2007) 23 *Water Resources Development* 391

Brumfiel, Geoff, 'Climate Control Plans Scrutinized' (September 2009) 461 *Nature* 19

Buesseler, K et al, 'The Effects of Iron Fertilization on Carbon Sequestration in the Southern Ocean' (2004) 304 *Science* 417Burdekin Dry Tropics NRM (BDTNRM), *Burdekin Dry Tropics Natural Resource Management Plan 2005–2010* (BDTNRM, 2005)

Byron, Helen and Joanna Treweek, 'Guest Editorial: Strategic Environmental Assessment – Great Potential for Biodiversity?' (2005) 7 *Journal of Environmental Assessment Policy and Management* v

Caldeira, K and P Duffy, 'The Role of the Southern Ocean in Uptake and Storage of Anthropogenic Carbon Dioxide' (2000) 287 *Science* 620

Camacho, Alejandro, 'Can Regulation Evolve? Lessons from a Study in Maladaptive Management' (2007) 55 *UCLA Law Review* 293

Camacho, Alejandro, 'Beyond Conjecture: Learning about Ecosystem Management from the Glen Canyon Dam Experiment' (2008) 8 *Nevada Law Journal* 942

Cardone, John V, 'Substantive Standards and NEPA: Mitigating Environmental Consequences with Consent Decrees' (1991) 18 *Boston College Environmental Affairs Law Review* 159

Carter, J and J Howe, 'The Water Framework Directive and the Strategic Environmental Assessment Directive: Exploring the Linkages' (2006) 26 *Environmental Impact Assessment Review* 287

Carter, JG, CM Wood and M Baker, 'The Environmental Appraisal of National Park Management Plans in England and Wales' (2003) 46 *Journal of Environmental Planning and Management* 271

Cassar, Angela Z and Carl E Bruch, 'Transboundary Environmental Impact Assessment in International Watercourse Management' (2003) 12 *New York University Environmental Law Journal* 169

Cedeño, Marianela, 'Assessment of Transboundary Environmental Impacts in Developing Countries: The Case of Central America' in Bastmeijer, Kees and Timo Koivurova (eds), *Theory and Practice of Transboundary Environmental Impact Assessment* (Martinus Nijhoff, 2008) 119

Charlebois, P et al, 'Steering the Course towards Safer Shipping and Cleaner Seas' (2010) 16 *Tropical Coasts* 8

Chircop, Aldo, 'Regional Cooperation in Marine Environmental Protection in the South China Sea: A Reflection on New Directions for Marine Conservation' (2010) 41(4) *Ocean Development and International Law* 334

Churchill, RR and AV Lowe, *The Law of the Sea* (3rd edition) (Manchester, 1999)

Cicin-Sain, B and S Belfiore, 'Linking Marine Protected Areas to Integrated Coastal and Ocean Management: A Review of Theory and Practice' (2005) 48 *Ocean and Coastal Management* 847

Clark, Sandford, 'The River Murray Question: Part 1 – Colonial Days' (1971) 8(1) *Melbourne University Law Review* 11

Clark, Sandford, 'The River Murray Question: Part II – Federation, Agreement and Future Alternatives' (1971–1972) 8(1) *Melbourne University Law Review* 215

Codling, Rosamunde, 'Aspects of Environmental Planning in the Antarctic' (2001) 44 *Journal of Environmental Planning and Management* 129

Commonwealth of Australia, *National Strategy for Ecologically Sustainable Development* (Council of Australian Governments, 1992)

Commonwealth of Australia, *National Strategy for the Conservation of Australia's Biological Diversity* (Department of Environment, Sport and Territories, 1996)

Commonwealth of Australia, *Australia's Oceans, New Horizons, Oceans Policy Consultation Paper* (Australian Government Publishing Service, 1997)

Commonwealth of Australia, *Australia's Ocean Policy* (Environment Australia, 1998)

Commonwealth of Australia, *Guidelines for Establishing the National Representative System of Marine Protected Areas* (Australian and New Zealand

Environment and Conservation Council Task Force on Marine Protected Areas, Environment Australia, 1998)
Commonwealth of Australia, *Our Vital Resources: A National Action Plan for Salinity and Water Quality* (Council of Australian Governments, 2000)
Commonwealth of Australia, *Australian IUCN Reserve Management Principles for Commonwealth MPAs* (Environment Australia, 2002)
Commonwealth of Australia, *Australia's Strategy for the National Reserves System 2009–2030* (National Reserves System Task Force convened under the Natural Resource Policies and Program Committee, 2009)
Commonwealth of Australia, *Caring for our Country Outcomes* (Australian Government, 2010)
Commonwealth of Australia, *Plain English summary of the Proposed Basin Plan – including explanatory notes* (Murray Darling Basin Authority, November 2011)
Commonwealth of Australia, *Proposed Basin Plan – a draft for consultation* (Murray Darling Basin Authority, November 2011)
Conca, Ken, *Governing Water* (MIT Press, 2006)
Conley, Alexander and Margaret A Moote, 'Evaluating Collaborative Natural Resource Management' (2003) 16 *Society & Natural Resources* 371
Connell, Daniel, 'The Role of the Commonwealth Environmental Water Holder' in Crabb, Peter, 'Straddling Boundaries: Inter-governmental Arrangements for Managing Natural Resources' in Stephen Dovers and Su Wild River (eds), *Managing Australia's Environment* (The Federation Press, 2003) 229
Connell, Daniel, *Water Politics in the Murray Darling Basin* (Federation Press, 2007)
Connell, Daniel and R Quentin Grafton, *Basin Futures: Water Reform in the Murray-Darling Basin* (ANU E-Press, 2011)
Connelly, Robert, 'The UN Convention on EIA in a Transboundary Context: A Historical Perspective' (1999) 19 *Environmental Impact Assessment Review* 37
Cordonnier Segger, M and A Khalfan, *Sustainable Development Law: Principles Practices and Prospects* (Oxford University Press, 2004)
Cordonnier Segger, M, Marcus Gehring and Andrew Paul Newcombe, *Sustainable Development in World Investment Law* (Kluwer Law International, 2011)
Craik, Neil, *The International Law of Environmental Impact Assessment: Process, Substance and Integration* (Cambridge University Press, 2008)
Craik, Neil, 'Transboundary Environmental Impact Assessment in North America: Obstacles and Opportunities' in Bastmeijer, Kees and Timo Koivurova (eds), *Theory and Practice of Transboundary Environmental Impact Assessment* (Martinus Nijhoff, 2008) 93
Craik, Neil, 'Transboundary Environmental Assessment in Canada: International and Constitutional Dimensions' (2010) 21 *Journal of Environmental Law and Practice* 107
Crawford, Adam, *The Local Governance of Crime* (Clarendon Press, 1997)

Crofts, Robert, 'Linking Protected Areas to the Wider World: A Review of Approaches' (2004) 6 *Journal of Environmental Policy and Planning* 143

Crowley, Kate, 'Effective Environmental Federalism? Australia's Natural Heritage Trust' (2001) 3 *Journal of Environmental Policy & Planning* 255

Crutzen, Paul J, 'Albedo Enhancement by Stratospheric Sulfur Injections: A Contribution to Resolve a Policy Dilemma?' (2006) 77 *Climatic Change* 211

Curtis, Allan, 'The Landcare Experience' in Stephen Dovers and Su Wild River (eds), *Managing Australia's Environment* (Federation Press, 2003)

Daniell, Katherine, 'Enhancing Collaborative Management in the Basin' in Daniell Connell and R Quentin Grafton (eds), *Basin Future: water reform in the Murray-Darling Basin* (ANU E-Press, Canberra 2011) 413

Davenport, Tara, 'Joint Development in Asia: Lessons for Sustainable Peace in the South China Sea' (2011) *Asian Journal of Comparative Law* 11

Davis, W, 'What Does Green Mean? Anthropogenic Climate Change, Geoengineering and International Law' (2009) 43 *Georgia Law Review* 901

Davison, Graeme, John Hirst and Stuart Macintyre (eds), *The Oxford Companion to Australian History* (Oxford University Press, 2001)

De Búrca, Gráinne and Joanne Scott, 'Introduction: New Governance, Law and Constitutionalism' in Gráinne De Búrca and Joanne Scott (eds), *Law and New Governance in the EU and the US* (Hart Publishing, 2006) 1

De Freitas, DM, *The Role of Public Participation, Spatial Information and GIS in Natural Resource Management of the Dry Tropical Coast, Northern Australia*, PhD thesis (James Cook University, 2010)

De Mulder, Jan, 'Case Note' (2010) 19 *Review of European Community and International Environmental Law* 263

Department of Natural Resource Management (DNRM), *Options for Future Community Engagement in Regional Natural Resource Management* (Queensland State Government, 2005)

Department of Sustainability, Environment, Water, Population and Communities, *Heard Island and McDonald Islands: Marine Reserve Amendment Proposal* (Australian Government, 2011)

Department of Sustainability, Environment, Water, Population and Communities, *Solitary Island Marine Reserve (Commonwealth waters)* (DSEWPC, 2011)

Department of the Environment, Water, Heritage and the Arts, *Independent Review of the Environment Protection and Biodiversity Conservation Act 1999* (DEWHA, 2009)

Dickinson, Robert E, 'Climate Engineering: A Review of Aerosol Approaches to Changing the Global Energy Balance' (1996) 33 *Climatic Research* 279

Di Leva, Charles E, 'Transboundary Management of Natural Resources: A Brief Overview of World Bank Policies and Projects' in Sharelle Hart (ed), *Shared Resources: Issues of Governance* (IUCN, 2008) 50

DiMento, Joseph F and Pamela M Doughman, 'Soft Teeth in the Back of the Mouth: The NAFTA Environmental Side Agreement Implemented' (1998) 10 *Georgetown International Environmental Law Review* 651

Dinar, Ariel et al, 'Case Study 4: The Aral Sea Basin' in Ariel Dinar et al (eds), *Bridges Over Water – Understanding Transboundary Water Conflict, Negotiation and Cooperation*, World Scientific Series on Energy and Resource Economics (World Scientific Publishing, 2007) Vol 3, 291

Doelle, Meinhard, 'The Role of Strategic Environmental Assessments in Energy Governance: A Case Study of Tidal Energy in Nova Scotia's Bay of Fundy' in Timo Koivurova, Aldo Chircop, Eric Franckx, Eric Molenaar and David VanderZwaag (eds), *Understanding and Strengthening European Union-Canada Relations in Law of the Sea and Ocean Governance* (University of Lapland, 2009)

Douvere, Fanny, 'The Role of Marine Spatial Planning in Implementing Ecosystem-Based, Sea Use Management' (2008) 32 *Marine Policy* 762

Dresner, Simon and Nigel Gilbert, 'Decision-making Processes for Projects Requiring EIA: Case Studies in Six European Countries' (1999) 1 *Journal of Environmental Assessment Policy and Management* 105

Dudley, N (ed), *Guidelines for Applying Protected Areas Management Categories* (IUCN, 2008)

Dukhovny, Viktor and Vadim Sokolov, 'Lessons on Cooperation Building to Manage Water Conflicts in the Aral Sea Basin' (Scientific-Information Center of the Interstate commission for Water Coordination in Central Asia, 2003) http://unesdoc.unesco.org/images/0013/001332/133291e.pdf

Dunlap, RE, KD Van Liere, A Mertig and RE Jones, 'Measuring Endorsement of the New Ecological Paradigm: A Revised NEP Scale' (2000) 56 *Journal of Social Issues* 428

Ebbesson, Jonas, *Compatability of International and National Environmental Law* (Kluwer Law International, 1996)

Economic Commission for Europe, *Current Policies, Strategies and Aspects of Environmental Assessment in a Transboundary Context* (UN, 1996)

European Commission, *Study Concerning the Report on the Application and Effectiveness of the SEA Directive (2001/42/EC)* Final Report (European Commission, 2009)

Ewing, Sarah, 'Catchment Management Arrangements' in Stephen Dovers and Su Wild River (eds), *Managing Australia's Environment* (Federation Press, 2003) 405

FAO (Food and Agriculture Organization of the United Nations), 'Review of the State of the World Marine Capture Fisheries Management: Pacific Ocean' (2007) *FAO fisheries technical paper* T488/1

Farrelly, Megan, 'Regionalisation of Environmental Management: A Case Study of the Natural Heritage Trust, South Australia' (2005) 43 *Geographical Research* 393

Fischer, Thomas, *Theory and Practice of SEA – Towards a More Systematic Approach* (Earthscan, 2007)

Fisher, D, 'The impact of international law upon the Australian environmental legal system' (1996) 16 *Environmental and Planning Law Journal* 372

Fisher, Douglas, *The Law and Governance of Water Resources: The Challenge of Sustainability* (Edward Elgar, 2009)

Fitzmaurice, Malgosia, 'International Responsibility and Liability' in Daniel Bodansky, Jutta Brunnée and Ellen Hey (eds), *The Oxford Handbook of International Environmental Law* (Oxford University Press, 2007) 1010

Fleming, JR, 'The Climate Engineers' (2007) 31 *The Wilson Quarterly* 46

Fleming, JR, *Fixing the Sky: The Checkered History of Weather and Climate Control* (Columbia University Press, 2010)

Floress, K et al, 'Constraints to Watershed Planning: Group Structure and Process' (2009) 45(6) *JAWRA* 1352

FNQ NRM Ltd & Rainforest CRC, *Sustaining the Wet Tropics: A Regional Plan for Natural Resource Management 2004–2008* (FNQ NRM, 2004)

Freeman, Jody and Daniel A Farber, 'Modular Environmental Regulation' (2005) 54 *Duke Law Journal* 795

French, Duncan, 'From the Depths: Rich Pickings of Principles of Sustainable Development and General International Law on the Ocean Floor – the Seabed Disputes Chamber's 2011 Advisory Opinion' (2011) 26 *International Journal of Marine and Coastal Law* 525

Furhman, J and D Capone, 'Possible Biogeochemical Consequences of Ocean Fertilization' (1991) 36 *Limnology & Oceanography* 1951

Fung, Archon and Erik Olin Wright, 'Thinking about Empowered Participatory Governance' in Archon Fung and Erik Olin Wright (eds), *Deepening Democracy* (Verso, 2003) 3

Gaines, Sanford E, 'Reflexive Law as a Legal Paradigm for Sustainable Development' (2002/2003) 10 *Buffalo Environmental Law Journal* 1

Gao, Zhiguo, *Environmental Regulation of Oil and Gas* (Kluwer Law International, 1998)

Gao, Zhiguo, 'Environmental Regulation of the Oil and Gas Industries' (2000) 2(11) *Journal for the Centre for Energy, Petroleum and Mineral Law and Policy* http://www.dundee.ac.uk/cepmlp/journal/html/vol2/article2-11.html

Gardner, Alex, Richard Bartlett and Janice Gray, *Water Resources Law* (LexisNexisButterworths, 2009)

Garrison, Tom, *Essentials of Oceanography* (5th edition) (Brooks/Cole Cengage Learning, 2009)

Gehring, Thomas and Markus Jachtenfuchs, 'Liability for Transboundary Environmental Damage: Towards a General Liability Regime?' (1993) 4 *European Journal of International Law* 92

Gehring, Thomas and Sebastian Oberthür, 'Interplay: Exploring Institutional Interaction' in Oran Young, Leslie A King and Heike Schroeder (eds), *Institutions and Environmental Change: Principal Finds, Applications and Research Frontiers* (MIT Press, 2008) 187

Gilbey, P. (2002) *Rights and Duty of Care: A Queensland Perspective*, http://www.clw.csiro.au/lbi/publications/ANCID2002paper-Gilbey.pdf

Gillespie, Alexander, *Protected Areas and International Environmental Law* (Martinus Nijhoff, 2007)

Glaser, John A, 'Climate geo-engineering' (2010) 12 *Clean Technologies and Environmental Policy* 91

Goodell, Jeff, *How to Cool the Planet: Geoengineering and the Audacious Quest to Fix Earth's Climate* (Houghton Mifflin Harcourt, 2010)

Govindasamy, B et al, 'Impact of Geoenginnering Schemes on the Terrestrial Biosphere' (2002) 29 *Geophysical Research Letters* No. 22

Gray, Barbara, *Collaborating: Finding Common Ground for Multiparty Problems* (Jossey-Bass, 1989)

Gray, Kevin R, 'International Environmental Impact Assessment: Potential for a Multilateral Environmental Agreement' (2000) 11 *Colorado Journal of International Environmental Law and Policy* 83

Great Barrier Reef Marine Park Authority, *Great Barrier Reef Outlook Report* (GBRMPA, 2009)

Great Barrier Reef Marine Park Authority, *Strategic Assessment of the Impacts of Actions on the Values of the Great Barrier Reef World Heritage Area, Other Relevant Matters of National Environmental Significance, and the Management Arrangements to Deal with such Impacts under the Jurisdiction of the GBRMPA* (Great Barrier Reef Marine Park Authority, 2011)

Gullett, W, 'Environmental Decision-making in a Transboundary Context: Principles and Challenges for the Denmark–Sweden Øresund Fixed Link' (2000) 2 *Journal of Environmental Assessment Policy and Management* 503

Gullett, W, *Fisheries Law in Australia* (LexisNexis Butterworths, 2008)

Gullett, W and G Rose, 'Australia's Marine Jurisdictions under International and Domestic Law' in Warwick Gullett, Clive Schofield and Joanna Vince (eds), *Marine Resources Management* (LexisNexis Butterworths, 2011) 25

Gullett, W and C Schofield, 'Pushing the Limits of the Law of the Sea Convention: Australian and French Cooperative Surveillance and Enforcement in the Southern Ocean' (2007) 22 *International Journal of Marine and Coastal Law* 545

Hahn, T, P Olsson, C Folke and K Johansson, 'Trust-building, Knowledge Generation and Organizational Innovations: The Role of a Bridging Organization for Adaptive Co-management of a Wetland Landscape around Kristianstad, Sweden' (2006) 34 *Human Ecology* 573

Hamilton, Clive, *The Return of Dr Strangelove: The Politics of Climate Engineering as a Response to Global Warming* (June 2010) available online at: http://www.clivehamilton.net.au/cms/media/documents/articles/dr_strangeloves_return.pdf

Hardin, Garrett, 'Tragedy of the Commons' (1968) 162 (3859) *Science* 1243

Harris, Jane, Marcus Haward, Julia Jabour and Eric J Woehler, 'A New Approach to Selecting Marine Protected Areas (MPAs) in the Southern Ocean' (2007) 19 *Antarctic Science* 189

Harvey, L, 'Mitigating the Atmospheric CO_2 Increase and Ocean Acidification by Adding Limestone Powder to Upwelling Regions (2008) 113 *Journal of Geophysical Research* 113

Hassan, Daud, 'Environmental Impact Assessment in the Bay of Bengal Sub Region of South Asia' in Bastmeijer, Kees and Timo Koivurova (eds), *Theory and Practice of Transboundary Environmental Impact Assessment* (Martinus Nijhoff, 2008)

Haward, Marcus, 'The Ocean and Marine Realm' in Stephen Dovers and Sue Wild River (eds), *Managing Australia's Environment* (Federation Press, 2003) 38

Haward, Marcus, 'Australian Marine Resources and Environmental Policy and Politics' in Warwick Gullett, Clive Schofield and Joanna Vince (eds), *Marine Resources Management* (Lexis Nexis Butterworths, 2011)

Haward, Marcus, Rob Hall and Aynsley Kellow, 'Setting and Implementing the Agenda: Australian Antarctic Policy' in Lorne Kriwoken, Julia Jabour, and Alan Hemmings (eds), *Looking South: Australia's Antarctic Agenda* (Federation Press, 2007)

Haward, MG, 'The Australian Offshore Constitutional Settlement' (1989) 13 *Marine Policy* 334

Haward, MG and J Davidson, *Scenarios (Phase 1), Report Number 2, Changing Currents in Marine Biodiversity Governance and Management: Responding to Climate Change* (School of Geography and Environmental Studies, University of Tasmania, 2012)

Head, Brian, 'Participation or Co-Governance? Challenges for Regional Natural Resource Management' in R Eversole and J Martin (eds), *Participation and Governance in Regional Development* (Ashgate, 2005)

Head, Brian, 'Assessing Network-Based Collaborations' (2008) 10(6) *Public Management Review* 733

Heikkila, Tanya and Andrea Gerlak, 'The Formation of Large-scale Collaborative Resource Management Institutions: Clarifying the Roles of Stakeholders, Science, and Institutions' (2005) 33(4) *Policy Studies Journal* 583

Heinen, Joel T, Emil Shukurov and Chinara Sadykova, 'Legislative and Policy Initiatives in Biodiversity Conservation in The Kyrgyz Republic' (2001) 42 *Post-Soviet Geography and Economics* 519

Hess, David, 'Social Reporting and New Governance Regulation: The Prospects of Achieving Corporate Accountability through Transparency' (2007) 17(3) *Business Ethics Quarterly* 453

Hirsch, Philip and Kurt Mørck Jensen *with* Ben Boer, Naomi Carrard, Stephen FitzGerald and Rosemary Lyster, *National Interests and Transboundary Water Governance in the Mekong* (Australian Mekong Resource Centre, University of Sydney, Danish International Development Assistance, 2006)

Hobday, AJ, JW Young, C Moeseneder and JM Dambacher, 'Defining Dynamic Pelagic Habitats in Oceanic Waters off Eastern Australia' (2011) 58(5) *Deep Sea Research Part II: Topical Studies in Oceanography* 734

Hoegh-Guldberg, O, *Likely Ecological Impacts of Global Warming and Climate Change on the Great Barrier Reef by 2050 and Beyond* (Queensland Land and Resources Tribunal, 2007)

Hohmann, Harald (ed.), *Basic Documents of International Environmental Law, Vol. 1: The Important Declarations* (Graham & Trotman Ltd, 1992)

Holley, Cameron, 'Aging Gracefully? Examining the Conditions for Sustaining Successful Collaboration in Environmental Law and Governance' (2009) 26(6) *Environmental and Planning Law Journal* 457

Holley, Cameron, 'Facilitating Monitoring, Subverting Self-Interest and Limiting Discretion: Learning from "New" Forms of Accountability in Practice' (2010) 35 *Columbia Journal of Environmental Law* 127

Holley, Cameron, 'Removing the Thorn from New Governance's Side: Examining the Emergence of Collaboration in Practice and the Roles for Law, Nested Institutions and Trust' (2010) 40(7) *Environmental Law Reporter* 10654

Holley, Cameron, 'International Environmental Law and Australia and New Zealand' in Shawkat Alam, Jahid Hossain Bhuiyan, Tareq MR Chowdhury and Erika J Techera (eds), *Routledge Handbook of International Environmental Law* (Routledge, 2012)

Holley, Cameron and Neil Gunningham, 'Environment Improvement Plans: Facilitative Regulation in Practice' (2006) 23 *Environmental and Planning Law Journal* 448

Holley, Cameron and Neil Gunningham, 'Natural Resources, New Governance and Legal Regulation: When Does Collaboration Work?' (2011) 24 *New Zealand Universities Law Review* 309

Holley, Cameron, Neil Gunningham and Clifford Shearing, *New Environmental Governance* (Earthscan, 2011)

Holley, Cameron and Darren Sinclair, 'Collaborative Governance and Adaptive Management: (Mis)Applications to Groundwater, Salinity and Run-Off' (2011) 14(1) *Australasian Journal of Natural Resources Law and Policy* 37

Hong Thao, Nguyen, 'Joint Development in the Gulf of Thailand' 1999 (Autumn), *IBRU Boundary and Security Bulletin* 79

Hornstein, Donald, 'Complexity Theory, Adaptation, and Administrative Law' (2005) 54 *Duke Law Journal* 913

House, K et al, 'Electrochemical Acceleration of Chemical Weathering as an Energetically Feasible Approach to Mitigating Anthropogenic Climate Change' (2007) 41 *Environ. Sci. Technol.* 8464

Intergovernmental Oceanographic Commission, *Marine Spatial Planning – A Step by Step Approach towards Ecosystem-Based Management* (UNESCO, 2009)

International Centre for Environmental Management, Strategic Environmental Assessment in the Greater Mekong Subregion – Status Report, Greater Mekong Subregion (GMS) Core Environment Program (Asian Development Bank, 2006)

International Centre for Environmental Management, Strategic Environmental Assessment of Hydropower on the Mekong Mainstream: Final Report (Mekong River Commission, 2010)

International Law Commission, *Draft Articles on Prevention of Transboundary Harm from Hazardous Activities, with Commentaries 2001* (United Nations, 2008)

IPCC, *Asia. Climate Change 2007: Impacts, Adaptation and Vulnerability* (Cambridge University Press, 2007)

IPCC, *Climate Change 2007: Synthesis Report* (Cambridge University Press, 2007)

IUCN, *Guidelines for Protected Area Management Categories* (IUCN, 1994)

John, DeWitt, 'Civic Environmentalism' in Robert F Durant, Daniel J Fiorino and Rosemary O'Leary (eds), *Environmental Governance Reconsidered* (MIT Press, 2004) 219

Johns, F, B Saul, P Hirsch, T Stephens and B Boer, 'Law and the Mekong River Basin: A Socio-Legal Research Agenda on the Role of Hard and Soft Law in Regulating Transboundary Water Resources' (2010) 11 *Melbourne Journal of International Law* 154

Johnston, Douglas M, 'Fishery Diplomacy and Science and the Judicial Function' (1999) 10 *Yearbook of International Environmental Law* 33

Karkkainen, Bradley, 'Collaborative Ecosystem Governance: Scale, Complexity, and Dynamism' (2002) 21 *Virginia Environmental Law Journal* 189

Karkkainen, Bradley, 'Marine Ecosystem Management & "Post-Sovereign" Transboundary Governance' (2004) 6 *San Diego International Law Journal* 113

Karkkainen, Bradley, '"New Governance" in Legal Thought and in the World: Some Splitting as Antidote to Overzealous Lumping' (2004) 89 *Minnesota Law Review* 471

Karkkainen, Bradley, 'Toward Ecologically Sustainable Democracy?' in Archon Fung and Erik Olin Wright (eds), *Deepening Democracy* (Verso, 2003)

Karkkainen, Bradley, 'Post-Sovereign Environmental Governance' (2004) 4(1) *Global Environmental Politics* 72

Karkkainen, Bradley, 'Information – Forcing Regulation and Environmental Governance' in Gráinne De Búrca and Joanne Scott (eds), *Law and New Governance in the EU and the US* (Hart Publishing, 2006) 293

Karkkainen, Bradley, 'Managing Transboundary Aquatic Ecosystems: Lessons from The Great Lakes' (2006) 19 *Pacific McGeorge Global Business and Development Law Journal* 209

Kashubsky, M, 'Marine Pollution from the Offshore Oil and Gas Industry: Review of Major Conventions and Russian Law (Part I) (2006) *Maritime Studies* 151

Katerere, Yemi, Ryan Hill and Sam Moyo, *A Critique of Transboundary Natural Resource Management in Southern Africa*, IUCN Series on Transboundary Natural Resource Management (2001)

Kaye, Stuart, *Australia's Maritime Boundaries* (Centre for Maritime Policy, University of Wollongong, 2nd edn, 2001)

Kaye, Stuart, 'The Impact of the *Trail Smelter* Arbitration on the Law of the Sea' in Rebecca M Bratspies and Russell A Miller (eds), *Transboundary Harm in International Law: Lessons from the* Trail Smelter *Arbitration* (Cambridge University Press, 2006) 209

Keessen, Andrea, Jasper van Kempen and Helena van Rijswick, 'Transboundary River Basin Management in Europe Legal Instruments to Comply with European Water Management Obligations in Case of Transboundary Water Pollution and Floods' (2008) 4(3) *Utrecht Law Review* 35

Keith, David W, 'Geoengineering the Climate: History and Prospect' (2000) 25 *Annu. Rev. Energy Environ.* 245.

Kelly, Nicholas, 'A Bridge? The Troubled History of Inter-State Water Resources and Constitutional Limitations on State Water Use' (2007) 30 *University of New South Wales Law Journal* 639

Kelly, R, 'Getting the Balance Right: Why the Murray Darling Basin Plan can implement the "triple bottom line" approach' (2011) 10(3) *Canberra Law Review* 178

Kersten, Charles, 'Rethinking Transboundary Environmental Impact Assessment' (2009) 34 *Yale Journal of International Law* 173

Keyuan, Zou, 'The Sino-Vietnamese Agreement on Maritime Boundary Delimitation in the Gulf of Tonkin' (2005) 36(1) *Ocean Development and International Law* 13

Keyuan, Zou, 'Cooperative Development of Oil and Gas Resources in the South China Sea' in Sam Batement and Ralf Emmers (eds), *Security and International Politics in the South China Sea: Towards a Cooperative Management Regime* (Routledge, 2009)

Kheng-Lian, Koh and Nicholas A Robinson, 'Strengthening Sustainable Development in Regional Intergovernmental Governance: Lessons from the ASEAN' (2002) 6 *Singapore Journal of International and Comparative Law* 640

Kheshgi, H, 'Sequestering Atmospheric Carbon Dioxide by Increasing Ocean Alkalinity' (1995) 20 *Energy – The International Journal* 915

Kildea, Paul and George Williams, 'The Constitution and the management of water in Australia's rivers' (2010) 32 *Sydney Law Review* 595

Kildea, Paul and George Williams, 'The *Water Act* and the Murray Darling Basin Plan' (2011) 22 *Public Law Review* 3

Klein-Chesivoir, Carole, 'Avoiding Environmental Injury: The Case for Widespread Use of Environmental Impact Assessments in International Development Projects' (1990) 30 *Virginia Journal of International Law* 517

Kheng-Lian, Koh and Nicholas A Robinson, 'Streghtening Sustainable Development in Regional Intergovernmental Governance: Lessons from the ASEAN' (2002) 6 *Singapore Journal of International and Comparative Law* 640

Klein, Natalie, 'Whales and Tuna: The Past and Future of Litigation between Australia and Japan' (2009) 21 *Georgetown International Environmental Law Review* 143
Knox, John, 'The Myth and Reality of Transboundary Environmental Impact Assessment' (2002) 96 *American Journal of International Law* 291
Knox, John H, 'Assessing the Candidates for a Global Treaty on Transboundary Environmental Impact Assessment' 12 (2003) *New York University Environmental Law Journal* 153
Knox, John, 'Assessing the Candidates for a Global Treaty on Transboundary Environmental Impact Assessment' (2003–2005) Vol. XII *New York University Environmental Law Journal* 153
Koivurova, Timo, 'The Transnational EIA procedure of the Espoo Convention' (1997) Vol. VIII *Finnish Yearbook of International Law* 161
Koivurova, Timo, *Environmental Impact Assessment in the Arctic: A Study of International Legal Norms* (Ashgate, 2002)
Koivurova, Timo and Ismo Pölönen, 'Transboundary Environmental Impact Assessment in the Case of the Baltic Sea Gas Pipeline' (2010) 25 *International Journal of Marine and Coastal Law* 121
Koivurova, Timo and Ismo Pölönen, 'Transboundary Environmental Impact Assessment in the Case of the Baltic Sea Gas Pipeline' in Simon Marsden and Timo Koivurova (eds), *Transboundary Environmental Impact Assessment in the European Union: The Espoo Convention and its Kiev Protocol on Strategic Environmental Assessment* (Earthscan, 2011) 184
Koontz, Thomas M and Craig W Thomas, 'What Do We Know and Need to Know about the Environmental Outcomes of Collaborative Management' (2006) 66 *Public Administration Review* 111
Koskenniemi, Martii, 'Peaceful Settlement of Environmental Disputes' (1991) 60 *Nordic Journal of International Law* 73
Kosugi, Takanobu, 'Role of Sunshades in Space as a Climate Control Option' (2010) 67 *Acta Astronautica* 241
Kraska, James, 'Sustainable Development is Security: the Role of Transboundary River Agreements as Confidence Building Measure (CBM) in South Asia' (2003) 28 *Yale Journal of International Law*
Krever, V, O Pereladova, M Williams and H Jungius (eds), *Biodiversity Conservation in Central Asia* cited in Joel T Heinen, Emil Shukurov and Chinara Sadykova, 'Legislative and Policy Initiatives in Biodiversity Conservation in the Kyrgyz Republic' (2001) 42 *Post-Soviet Geography and Economics* 519
Kriwoken, L, 'Australian Biodiversity and Marine Protected Areas' (1996) 33 *Ocean and Coastal Management* 113
Kriwoken, L, 'Charting a Course for Marine Protected Areas' in W Gullett, C Schofield and J Vince (eds), *Marine Resources Management* (LexisNexis Butterworths, 2011) 171
Kriwoken, L, L Fallon and DR Rothwell, 'Australia and the Precautionary Principle: Moving from International Principles to Domestic and Local

Implementation' in DR Rothwell and D VanderZwaag (eds), *Towards Principled Oceans Governance: Australian and Canadian Approaches and Challenges* (Routledge, 2006) 181

Kriwoken, L and Nick Holmes, 'Emerging Issues of Australia's Sub-Antarctic Islands: Macquarie Island and Heard Island and McDonald Islands' in Lorne Kriwoken, L, Julia Jabour and Alan Hemmings (eds), *Looking South: Australia's Antarctic Agenda* (Federation Press, 2007)

Kriwoken, L and DM Rootes, 'Tourism on Ice: Environmental Impact Assessment and Antarctic Tourism' (2000) 18 *Impact Assessment and Project Appraisal* 138

Lackner, KS, 'Capture of Carbon Dioxide from Ambient Air' (2009) 176 *The European Physical Journal, Special Topics* 93

Lane, Marcus, *Critical issues in Regional Natural Resources Management* (prepared for the Australian State of the Environment Committee, 2006)

Lane, Marcus, Bruce Taylor and Cathy Robinson, 'Introduction: Contested Country – Regional Natural Resource Management in Australia' in M Lane, C Robinson and B Taylor (eds), *Contested Country* (CSIRO, 2009) 1

Lane, Marcus et al, 'Will Regionalisation Achieve Integrated Natural Resource Management? Insights from Recent South Australian Experience' in Marcus Lane, Cathy Robinson and Bruce Taylor (eds), *Contested Country* (CSIRO, 2009)

Last, PR, WT White, DC Gledhill, AJ Hobday, R Brown, GJ Edgar and G Pecl, 'Long-term Shifts in Abundance and Distribution of a Temperate Fish Fauna: A Response to Climate Change and Fishing Practices' (2011) 20(1) *Global Ecology and Biogeography* 58–72

Latham, John et al, 'Global Temperature Stabilization via Controlled Albedo Enhancement of Low-level Maritime Clouds' (2008) 366 *Phil. Trans. R. Soc. A* 3969

Lausche, Barbara and Francoise Burhenne, *Guidelines for Protected Areas Legislation* (IUCN, 2011)

Lawrence, M, 'Side-effects of Ocean Iron Fertilization' (2002) 297 *Science* 1993

Lefeber, René, *Transboundary Environmental Interference and the Origin of State Liability* (Kluwer Law International, 1996)

Le Gurun, Gwénaëlle, 'EIA and the International Seabed Authority' in Kees Bastmeijer and Timo Koivurova (eds), *Theory and Practice of Transboundary Environmental Impact Assessment* (Martinus Nijhoff, 2008)

Leitmann, J, 'Options for Managing Protected Areas: Lessons from International Experience' (1998) 41 *Journal of Environmental Planning and Management* 129

Lewis, SE, JE Brodie, ZT Bainbridge, KW Rohde, AM Davis, BL Masters, M Maughan, MJ Devlin, JF Mueller and B Schaffelke, 'Herbicides: A New Threat to the Great Barrier Reef' (2009) 157(8–9) *Environmental Pollution* 2470

Libecap, Gary, *Contracting for Property Rights* (Cambridge UP, 1994)

Lobel, Orly, 'The Renew Deal: The Fall of Regulation and the Rise of Governance in Contemporary Legal Thought' (2004) 89 *Minnesota Law Review* 342

Lobel, Orly, 'Beyond Experimentation: Governing Occupational Safety in the United States' in Gráinne De Búrca and Joanne Scott (eds), *Law and New Governance in the EU and the US* (Hart Publishing, 2006)

Lockwood, M, GL Worboys and A Kothari (eds), *Managing Protected Areas: A Global Guide* (Earthscan, 2006)

Lockwood, Michael et al, 'Multilevel Environmental Governance: Lessons from Australian Natural Resource Management' (2009) 40(2) *Australian Geographer* 169

Lockwood, Michael et al, 'Governance Principles for Natural Resource Management' (2010) 23(10) *Society and Natural Resources* 986

Lodge, Michael W, 'Environmental Regulation of Deep Seabed Mining' in Andrée Kirchner (ed), *International Maritime Environmental Law* (Kluwer, 2003) 49

Loke Ming, Chou and COBSEA Secretariat (eds), *State of the Marine Environment Report for the East Asian Seas 2009* (UNEP/COBSEA, 2010)

Lovelock, J and C Rapley, 'Ocean Pipes Could Help the Earth to Cure Itself' (27 September 2007) 449 *Nature* 403

Lubell, Mark et al, 'Watershed Partnerships and the Emergence of Collective Action Institutions' (2002) 46(1) *American Journal of Political Science* 146

Lugten, Gail L, 'Net Gain or Net Loss? Australia and Southern Ocean Fishing' in Lorne Kriwoken, Julia Jabour, and Alan Hemmings (eds), *Looking South: Australia's Antarctic Agenda* (Federation Press, 2007) 100

Lundquist, Carolyn J and Elise F Granek, 'Strategies for Successful Marine Conservation: Integrating Socioeconomic, Political and Scientific Factors' (2005) 19 *Conservation Biology* 1771

Lunt, DJ et al, '"Sunshade World": A Fully Coupled CGM Evaluation of the Climatic Impacts of Geoengineering' (2008) 35 *Geophysical Research Letters* L12710

Lyons, Youna, 'Offshore Oil and Gas in the SCS and the Protection of the Marine Environment – Part 1 A Review of the Context and Profile of Offshore Activities' (2011) 25[5.2.3] 28[5.3.5] http://cil.nus.edu.sg/wp/wp-content/uploads/2010/10/OOG_SCS-YounaLyons-Part1.pdf

Madin, EMP, NC Ban, ZA Doubleday, TH Holmes, GT Pecl and F Smith, 'Socio-economic and Management Implications of Range-shifting Species in Marine Systems' (2011) 22 *Global Environmental Change* 137–146

Maes, Frank, 'The International Legal Framework for Marine Spatial Planning' (2008) 32 *Marine Policy* 797

Mahon, R, L Fanning, P McConney and R Pollnac, 'Governance Characteristics of Large Marine Ecosystems' (2010) 34(5) *Marine Policy* 919

Majchrzak, Ann, 'Focus of Information Inquiry' in her *Methods for Policy Research* (Sage Publications, 1984) 24

Makino, Mitsutaku, Hiroyuki Matsuda and Yasunori Sakurai, 'Expanding Fisheries Co-Management to Ecosystem-Based Management: A Case in the Shiretoko World Natural Heritage Area, Japan' (2009) 33 *Marine Policy* 207

Malcolm, HA, SDA Smith and A Jordan, 'Using Patterns of Reef Fish Assemblages to Refine a Habitat Classification System for Marine Parks in NSW, Australia' (2010) 20(1) *Aquatic Conservation: Marine and Freshwater Ecosystems* 83

Manheim, Bruce S, 'NEPA's Overseas Application' (1994) 36 *Environment* 43

Mansell, John N K, *Flag State Responsibility: Historical Development and Contemporary Issues* (Springer, 2009)

Mansfield, Bill, 'The Southern Bluefin Tuna Arbitration: Comments on Professor Kwiatkowska's Article' (2001) 16 *International Journal of Marine and Coastal Law* 361

Marchetti, C, 'On Geo-engineering and the CO_2 Problem' (1977) 1 *Climate Change* 59

Margerum, Richard, 'Overcoming Locally Based Collaboration Constraints' (2007) 20 *Society and Natural Resources* 135

Margerum, Richard, 'A Typology of Collaboration Efforts in Environmental Management' (2008) 41(4) *Environmental Management* 487

Margoulis, R, C Stem, N Salafsky and M Brown, 'Using Conceptual Models as a Planning and Evaluation Tool in Conservation' (2009) 32 *Evaluation and Program Planning* 138

Marsden, Simon, 'Strategic Environmental Assessment in Australia: An Evaluation of Section 146 of the *Environment Protection and Biodiversity Conservation Act 1999*' (1999) 8 *Griffith Law Review* 394

Marsden, Simon, 'An International Overview of Strategic Environmental Assessment, with Reference to World Heritage Areas Globally and in Australian Coastal Zones' (2002) 4 *Journal of Environmental Assessment Policy and Management* 31

Marsden, Simon, 'Strategic Environmental Assessment and Fisheries Management in Australia: How Effective is the Commonwealth Legal Framework?' in Simon Marsden and Stephen Dovers (eds), *Strategic Environmental Assessment in Australasia* (Federation Press, 2002) 47

Marsden, Simon, *Strategic Environmental Assessment in International and European Law: A Practitioner's Guide* (Earthscan, 2008)

Marsden, Simon, 'Environmental Impact Assessment in Hong Kong: An Evaluation of Principles, Procedures and Practice Post-1997' (2010) 13 *Asia Pacific Journal of Environmental Law* 115

Marsden, Simon, 'Transboundary Environmental Impact Assessment in European Law' in Simon Marsden and Timo Koivurova (eds), *Transboundary Environmental Impact Assessment in the European Union: The Espoo Convention and its Kiev Protocol on Strategic Environmental Assessment* (Earthscan, 2011) 39

Marsden, Simon, 'Assessment of Transboundary Environmental Effects in the Pearl River Delta Region: Is There a Role for Strategic Environmental Assessment?' (2011) 31 *Environmental Impact Assessment Review* 593

Marsden, Simon, 'Developing Approaches to Transboundary Environmental Impact Assessment in China: Cooperation through the Greater Tumen Initiative and in the Pearl River Delta Region' (2011) 9 *Chinese Journal of International Law* 393

Marsden, Simon, 'Introducing Strategic Environmental Assessment to the Madrid Protocol: Lessons from International Experience' (2011) 1 *The Polar Journal* 36

Marsden, Simon and John Ashe, 'Strategic Environmental Assessment legislation in Australian States and Territories (2006) 13 *Australasian Journal of Environmental Management* 205

Marsden, Simon and Timo Koivurova (eds), *Transboundary Environmental Impact Assessment in the European Union: The Espoo Convention and its Kiev Protocol on Strategic Environmental Assessment* (Earthscan, 2011)

Marshall, Graham R, 'Can Community-based NRM Work at the Scale of Larger Regions? Exploring the Roles of Nesting and Subsidiarity' in M Lane, C Robinson and B Taylor (eds), *Contested Country* (CSIRO, 2009) 50

Martin, John H, 'Glacial-Interglacial CO_2 Change: The Iron Hypothesis' (1990) 5 *Paleoceanography* 1

Martin, Paul V et al, 'Developing a Good Regulatory Practice Model for Environmental Regulations Impacting on Farmers' (Australian Farm Institute, 2007)

Matthews, H Damon et al, 'Sensitivity of Ocean Acidification to Geoengineered Climate Stabilization' (2009) 36 *Geophysical Research Letters* L10706

Mayo-Ramsay, J, 'Environmental, Legal and Social Implications of Ocean Urea Fertilization; Sulu Sea Example' (2010) 34 *Marine Policy* 831

McGinnis, Michael (ed), *Polycentric Governance and Development* (University of Michigan Press, 1999)

McGregor Tan Research, *Solitary Islands Marine Park Community Survey Final Report* (NSW Marine Parks Authority, 2008)

McHugh, Paul D, 'The European Community Directive: An Alternative Environmental Impact Assessment Procedure?' (1994) 34 *Natural Resources Journal* 589

McInnes, CR, 'Space-based Geoengineering: Challenges and Requirements' (2010) 224 *Proc. IMechE Vol. 224 Part C: J. Mechanical Engineering Science* 571

McIntyre, Owen, 'Analysis: The Proceduralisation and Growing Maturity of International Water Law' (2010) 22 *Journal of Environmental Law* 475

McKinney, Daene C, 'Cooperative Management of Transboundary Water Resources in Central Asia' in D Burghart and T Sabonis-Helf (eds), *In the Tracks of Tamerlane – Central Asia's Path into the 21st Century* (National Defence University Press, 2003)

McManus, John W, Kwang-Tsao Shao and Szu-Yin Lin, 'Towards Establishing a Spratly Islands International Marine Peace Park: Ecological Importance and Supportive Activities with an Emphasis on the Role of Taiwan' (2010) 41(3) *Ocean Development and International Law* 270

Menkel-Meadow, Carole, 'Getting to "Let's Talk": Comments on Collaborative Environmental Dispute Resolution Processes' (2008) 8 *Nevada Law Journal* 835

Mercier, Jean-Roger, 'The World Bank and Environmental Impact Assessment', in Bastmeijer, Kees and Timo Koivurova (eds), *Theory and Practice of Transboundary Environmental Impact Assessment* (Martinus Nijhoff, 2008)

Meyer, L, A Constable and R Williams, *Conservation of Marine Habitats in the Region of Heard Island and McDonald Islands* (Australian Antarctic Division, Department of the Environment and Heritage, 2000)

Michaelson, J, 'Geoengineering: A Climate Change Manhatten Project' (1988) 17 *Stanford Environmental Law Journal* 73

Miclat, Evangeline FB and Romeo B Trono, 'One Vision, One Plan, Common Resources, Joint Management Conserving the Sulu-Sulawesi Sea' (2008) 15(1) *Tropical Coasts* 4

Mohamed-Katerere, Jennifer, *Review of the Legal and Policy Framework for Transboundary Natural Resource Management in Southern Africa*, The IUCN-ROSA Series on Transboundary Natural Resources Management (IUCN Regional Office for Southern Africa, 2001)

Molle, François, Tira Foran and Mira Käkönen (eds), *Contested Waterscapes in the Mekong Region: Hydropower, Livelihoods and Governance* (Earthscan, 2009)

Moore, Cameron, 'Maritime Regulation and Enforcement', in Rachel Baird and Donald R Rothwell (eds), *Australian Coastal and Marine Law* (The Federation Press, 2011) 331

Moore, Susan A and Susan F Rockloff, 'Organizing Regionally for Natural Resource Management in Australia: Reflections on Agency and Government' (2006) 8 *Journal of Environmental Policy and Planning* 259

Murphree, Marshall W (ed), *Communities as Resource Management Institutions*, Gatekeeper Series No. 36 (Sustainable Agriculture and Rural Livelihoods Programme, International Institute for Environment and Development, London, 1991)

National Natural Resource Management Taskforce (NNRMTF), *Managing Natural Resources in Rural Australia for a Sustainable Future* (DAFF, 1999)

Natural Resource Management Ministerial Council (NRMMC), *Framework for the Extension of the Natural Heritage Trust* (NRMMC, 2002)

Natural Resource Management Ministerial Council, *Australia's Biodiversity Conservation Strategy 2010–2030* (Australian Government, 2010)

Nazari, Mehrdad M, 'The Transboundary EIA Convention in the Context of Private Sector Operations Co-Financed by an International Financial Institution: Two

Case Studies from Azerbaijan and Turkmenistan' (2003) 23 *Environmental Impact Assessment Review* 441

Negri, AP, F Flores, T Röhig and S Uthicke, 'Herbicides Increase the Vulnerability of Corals to Rising Sea Surface Temperature' (2011) 56(2) *Limnology and Oceanography* 471

Nursey-Bray, M, 'Learning and Local Government: The Local Government Coastal Management Strategy, South Australia, *20th NSW Coastal Conference* (2011)

NSW Marine Parks Authority, Cape Byron Marine Park Operation Plan (NSW Marine Parks Authority, 2010)

Oberthür, Sebastian, 'Clustering of Multilateral Environmental Agreements: Potentials and Limitations' (2002) 2 *International Environmental Agreements: Politics, Law and Economics* 317

Oberthür, Sebastian, 'Interplay Management: Enhancing Environmental Policy Integration among International Institutions' (2009) 9 *International Environmental Agreements: Politics, Law and Economics* 371

Oberthür, Sebastian and Thomas Gehring, 'Conceptual Foundations of Institutional Interaction' in Sebastian Oberthür and Thomas Gehring (eds), *Institutional Interaction in Global Environmental Governance: Synergy and Conflict among International and EU Policies* (MIT Press, 2006) 19

Okereke, Chukwumerije, Harriet Bulkeley and Heike Schroeder, 'Conceptualizing Climate Governance Beyond the International Regime' (2009) 9(1) *Global Environmental Politics* 58

O'Leary, Rosemary, Tina Nabatchi and Lisa B Bingham, 'Environmental Conflict Resolution' in Robert F Durant, Daniel J Fiorino and Rosemary O'Leary (eds), *Environmental Governance Reconsidered* (MIT Press, 2004) 338

Olson, Mancur, *The Logic of Collective Action Public Goods and the Theory of Groups* (Harvard UP, 1965)

Ong, David M, 'From "International" to "Transnational" Environmental Law? A Legal Assessment of the Contribution of the "Equator Principles" to International Environmental Law' (2010) 79 *Nordic Journal of International Law* 35

Open Lines Environmental Consulting, *A Guide to Undertaking Strategic Assessments* (Department of Sustainability, Environment, Water, Population and Communities, 2011)

Opie, Hayden, 'Commonwealth power to regulate industrial pollution' (1976) 10 *Melbourne University Law Review* 577

Organisation for Security and Cooperation in Europe/UNECE, Environmental Impact Assessment in a Transboundary Context: Pilot Project in Central Asia Project Report (Vienna, 2009)

Ornstein, Leonard, Igor Aleinov and David Rind, 'Irrigated Afforestation of the Sahara and Australian Outback to End Global Warming' (2009) 97 *Climatic Change* 409

Orts, Eric and Cary Coglianese, 'Collaborative Environmental Law: Pro and Con, Debate' (2007) 156 *University of Pennsylvania Law Review* 289

Osborne, Matthew, 'Commonwealth and State Marine Environmental Management' in Rachel Baird and Donald R Rothwell (eds), *Australian Coastal and Marine Law* (The Federation Press, 2011) 89

Ostrom, Elinor, *Governing the Commons: The Evolution of Institutions for Collective Action* (Cambridge UP, 1990)

Ostrom, Elinor, 'The Danger of Self Evident Truths' (2000) 33(1) *Political Science and Politics* 33

Ostrom, Elinor, 'Beyond Markets and States: Polycentric Governance of Complex Economic Systems' (2010) 100 *American Economic Review* 641

Ostrom, Vincent et al, 'The Organization of Government in Metropolitan Areas: A Theoretical Inquiry' (1961) 55(4) *American Political Science Review* 831

Oye, Kenneth A, 'Explaining Cooperation under Anarchy: Hypothesis and Strategies' (1985) 38 *World Politics* 1

Paquin, Marc, 'Environmental Impact Assessment: Law and Practice in North America' (1999) *North American Environmental Law and Policy*, Winter: 3

Peipei, Phua, 'China's Collaboration with Indochina Countries in Hydropower Development in the Mekong Region: How Far Can It Go?' in Mingjiang Li and Chong Guan Kwa (eds), *China–ASEAN Sub-Regional Cooperation* (World Scientific/Imperial College Press, 2011)

Pétursson, Jón Geir, Pål Vedeld and John Kaboggoza, *Transboundary Biodiversity Management Challenges: Case Of Mt. Elgon in Uganda And Kenya* http://www.landbunadur.is/landbunadur/wgsamvef.nsf/0/a3a279aa3fd7b53900257102005467cb/$FILE/83.pdf

Phillips, Freedom-Kai, 'Ocean Renewable Energy in the European Union: Understanding and Strengthening EU–Canada Relations in Law of the Sea and Oceans Governance' in Timo Koivurova, Aldo Chircop, Eric Franckx, Eric Molenaar and David VanderZwaag (eds), *Understanding and Strengthening European Union-Canada Relations in Law of the Sea and Ocean Governance* (University of Lapland, 2009)

Pielke, Roger A Jr, 'Climate Engineering: Alternative Perspective' in Bjørn Lomborg, *Smart Solutions to Climate Change. Comparing Costs and Benefits* (Cambridge University Press: 2010) 52

Pink, Brian, *Water and the Murray Darling Basin – A statistical profile 2000–01 to 2005–06* (ABS Catalogue No 4610.0.55.007, Australian Bureau of Statistics, 2008)

Pittock, Jamie, Max Finlayson, Alex Gardner and Clare McKay, 'Changing character: the Ramsar Convention on Wetlands and climate change in the Murray Darling Basin, Australia' (2010) 27 *Environmental and Planning Law Journal* 401

Polat, Necati, *Boundary Issues in Central Asia* (Transnational Publishers, 2002)

Poloczanska, ES, RC Babcock, A Butler, AJ Hobday, O Hoegh-Guldberg, TJ Kunz, R Matear, DA Milton, TA Okey and AJ Richardson, 'Climate Change and Australian Marine Life' (2007) 45 *Oceanography and Marine Biology: An Annual Review* 407–478

Preiss, Erika L, 'The International Obligation to Conduct an Environmental Impact Assessment: The ICJ Case Concerning the Gabcikovo-Nagymaros Project' (1999) 7 *New York University Environmental Law Journal* 307

Pushkina, Darya, 'EU Crisis Management Role in Water Conflict in Central Asia: Open Opportunities or Lost Causes?' (2009) 7–8 *Historical Processes and Peace Politics* 105

Putnam, Robert, Robert Leonardi and Raffaella Nanetti, *Making Democracy Work: Civic Traditions in Modern Italy* (Princeton UP, 1993)

Queensland Government, *South East Queensland Regional Plan 2009–2031* (Queensland Government, 2009)

Rakhmatullaev, Shavkat et al, 'Facts and Perspectives of Water Reservoirs in Central Asia: A Special Focus on Uzbekistan' (2009) 2(2) *Water* 1

Ramachandran, Pavit and Lothar Linde, 'Integrating Spatial Support Tools into Strategic Planning – SEA of the GMS North–South Economic Corridor Strategy and Action Plan' (2011) 31 *Environmental Impact Assessment Review* 602

Raymond, Leigh, 'Cooperation without Trust: Overcoming Collective Action Barriers to Endangered Species Protection' (2006) 34 *Policy Studies Journal* 37

Razzaque, Jona, 'Public Participation in Water Governance' in JW Dellapenna and J Gupta (eds), *The Evolution of the Law and Politics of Water* (Springer, 2009) 353

Renard, Ian, 'The River Murray Question: Part III – New Doctrines for Old Problems' (1971–1972) 8 *Melbourne University Law Review* 625

Rest, Alfred, 'State Responsibility/Liability: *Erga Omnes* Obligations and Judicial Control' (2010) 40 *Environmental Policy and Law* 298

Rhodes, RAW, 'Understanding Governance: Ten Years On' (2007) 28 *Organization Studies* 12431

Ridgway, K and K Hill, 'The East Australian Current' in ES Poloczanska, AJ Hobday and AJ Richardson (eds), *A Marine Climate Change Impacts and Adaptation Report Card for Australia 2009* (NCCARF Publication, 2009)

Robins, L and S Dovers, 'Community-based NRM Boards of Management: Are they Up to the Task?' (2007) 14 *Australasian Journal of Environmental Management* 111

Robins, L and P Kanowski, '"Crying for our Country": Eight Ways in Which "Caring for our Country" has Undermined Australia's Regional Model for Natural Resource Management' (2011) 18(2) *Australasian Journal of Environmental Management* 88

Robinson, Nicholas A, 'International Trends in Environmental Impact Assessment' (1992) 19 *Boston College Environmental Affairs Law Review* 591

Robock, Alan et al, 'Regional Climate Responses to Geoengineering with Tropical and Arctic SO_2 Injections' (2008) 113 *Journal of Geophysical Research* D16101

Roll, Gulnara et al, 'Aral Sea – Experiences and Lessons Learned Brief' (IW: Science, United Nations University-Institute for Water, Environment and Health (UNU-INWEH), 2006)

Rose, Greg, 'Australian Approaches to International Environmental Law during the Howard Years' (2008) 27 *Australian Year Book of International Law* 115

Rothwell, Donald, 'Conservation and Management Frameworks for Sub-Antarctic International Waters' (2007) 141 *Papers and Proceedings of the Royal Society of Tasmania* 1

Rothwell, Donald, 'Environmental Integration and Coastal and Marine Law' in Rachel Baird and Donald R Rothwell (eds), *Australian Coastal and Marine Law* (The Federation Press, 2011) 356

Roura, Ricardo M and Alan D Hemmings, 'Realising Strategic Environmental Assessment in Antarctica' (2011) 13 *Journal of Environmental Assessment Policy and Management* 483

Ruhl, JB, 'The Pardy-Ruhl Dialogue on Ecosystem Management, Part IV: Narrowing and Sharpening the Questions' (2007) 24 *Pace Environmental Law Review* 25

Sabatier, Paul et al, *Swimming Upstream: Collaborative Approaches to Watershed Management* (MIT Press, 2005)

Sainsbury, K, M Haward, LK Kriwoken, M Tsamenyi and T Ward, *Multiple Use Management in the Australian Marine Environment: Principles, Definitions and Elements: Issues Paper 1* (Environment Australia, 1997)

Salman, Salman, *The World Bank Policy for Projects on International Waterways: An Historical and Legal Analysis* (The World Bank, 2009)

Sandwith, T et al, *Transboundary Protected Areas for Peace and Co-operation*, Best Practice Protected Area Guidelines Series No. 7 (IUCN, 2001)

Sandwith, T and M Lockwood, 'Linking the Landscape' in M Lockwood, GL Worboys and A Kothari (eds), *Managing Protected Areas: A Global Guide* (Earthscan, 2006) 574

Scanlon, John, 'A hundred years of negotiations with no end in sight: Where is the Murray Darling Basin Initiative leading us? (2006) 23 *Environmental and Planning Law Journal* 386

Schäfer, N, 'Maritime Spatial Planning: About the Sustainable Management of the Use of Our Seas and Oceans' in Timo Koivurova, Aldo Chircop, Eric Franckx, Eric Molenaar and David VanderZwaag (eds), *Understanding and Strengthening European Union-Canada Relations in Law of the Sea and Ocean Governance* (University of Lapland, 2009)

Schiermeier, Q, 'The Oresmen' (2003) 421 *Nature* 109

Schrage, Wiecher, 'The Convention on Environmental Impact Assessment in a Transboundary Context' in Bastmeijer, Kees and Timo Koivurova (eds),

Theory and Practice of Transboundary Environmental Impact Assessment (Martinus Nijhoff, 2008)

Schrage, Wiek and Nick Bonvoisin, 'Transboundary Impact Assessment: Frameworks, Experiences and Challenges' (2008) 26 *Impact Assessment and Project Appraisal* 234

Scott, Joanne and David Trubek, 'Mind the Gap: Law and New Approaches to Governance in the European Union' (2002) 8 *European Law Journal* 1

Scott, Karen N, 'International Environmental Governance: Managing Fragmentation through Institutional Connection' (2011) 12 *Melbourne Journal of International Law* 177

Seitz, Russell, 'Bright Water: Hydrosols, Water Conservation and Climate Change' (2011) 105 *Climatic Change* 365

Serge, Ngendakumana et al, *Transboundary Landscape Management to Improve Livelihoods and Biodiversity Conservation: Case of Guinea and Sierra Leone* (USAID, The World Agroforestry Centre and The Centre for International Forestry research, 2009) http://www.worldagroforestry.org/downloads/publications/PDFs/RP16486.PDF

Shanazarov, AS et al, 'Strategy and Action Plan for Sustainable Land Management in the High-Pamir and Pamir-Alai Mountains' (GEF/UNEP/UNU Project, 'Sustainable Land Management in the High Pamir and Pamir-Alai Mountains – Integrated and Transboundary Initiative in Central Asia', 2011)

Sheate, William, Helen Byron, Suzan Dagg and Lourdes Cooper, *The Relationship between the EIA and SEA Directives: Final Report to the European Commission* (Imperial College Consultants, 2005)

Shutterhelm, R, *Diomede Crossroads: Saving the North Pole? Thoughts on Plausibility* http://www.cleverclimate.org/art/uploads/Diomede_Crossroads(1).pdf

Sievers, Eric W, 'Water, Conflict and Regional Security in Central Asia' (2002) 10 *New York University Environmental Law Journal* 356

Skjaeseth, JB, 'Protecting the Northeast Atlantic: One Problem, Three Institutions' in Sebastian Oberthür and Thomas Gehring (eds), *Institutional Interaction in Global Environmental Governance: Synergy and Conflict among International and EU Policies* (MIT Press, 2006) 103

Slater, Stephen, Graham Sortino and John Latham, 'Sea-going Hardware for the Cloud Albedo Method of Reversing Global Warming' (2008) 366 *Phil. Trans. R. Soc. A* 3989

Smetacek, V and SWA Naqvi, 'The Next Generation of Iron Fertilization Experiments in the Southern Ocean' (2008) 366 *Phil. Trans. R. Soc. A.* 3947

Smith, Elizabeth, 'Implementing the Espoo Convention: An International Financial Institutions Perspective' in Bastmeijer, Kees and Timo Koivurova (eds), *Theory and Practice of Transboundary Environmental Impact Assessment* (Martinus Nijhoff, 2008)

Solomon, Jason, 'Law and Governance in the 21st Century Regulatory State' (2008) 86(4) *Texas Law Review* 819

Spackman, Alan, 'Environmental Standards for Offshore Drilling', *Touch Oil and Gas* (online) (2003) http://www.touchoilandgas.com/environmental-standards-offshore-drilling-a101-1.html

Sprinz, Detlef and Tapani Vaahtoranta, 'The Interest-Based Explanation of International Environmental Policy' (1994) 48 *International Organization* 77

State of Queensland (Department of the Premier and Cabinet), *Reef Water Quality Protection Plan 2009* (RWQPP Secretariat, 2009)

Stec, Stephen and Gabriel E Eckstein, 'Of Solemn Oaths and Obligations: The Environmental Impact of the ICJ's Decision in the *Case Concerning the Gabíkovo-Nagymaros Project*' (1997) 8 *Yearbook of International Environmental Law* 41

Steinzor, Rena I, 'The Corruption of Civic Environmentalism' (2000) 30(10) *Environmental Law Reporter* 909

Stephens, Tim, *International Courts and Environmental Protection* (Cambridge University Press, 2009

Stephens, Tim and Ben Boer, 'Enforcement and Compliance in the Australian Antarctic Territory: Legal and Policy Dilemmas' in Lorne Kriwoken, Julia Jabour, and Alan Hemmings (eds), *Looking South: Australia's Antarctic Agenda* (Federation Press, 2007)

Stern, P and T Dietz, 'The Value Basis of Environmental Concern' (1994) 50(3) *Journal of Social Issues* 65

Stewart, Jenny and Grant Jones, *Renegotiating the Environment* (Federation Press, 2003)

Storey, Ian, 'China and the Philippines: Implications of the Reed Bank Incident', *Institute of Southeast Asia China Brief* 11(8), 6 May 2011

Strand, S and G Benford, 'Ocean Sequestration of Crop Residue Carbon: Recycling Fossil Fuel Carbon Back to Deep Sediments' (2009) 43 *Environ. Sci. Technol.* 1001

Strong, A, 'Ocean Fertilization: Time to Move On' (2009) 461 *Nature* 347

Strong, A et al, 'Ocean Fertilization: Science, Policy and Commerce' (2009) 22 *Oceanography* 236

Susskind, Lawrence, Alejandro E Camacho, and Todd Schenk, 'Collaborative Planning and Adaptive Management in Glen Canyon: A Cautionary Tale' (2010) 35(1) *Columbia Journal of Environmental Law* 1

Sutton, SG, *Recreational Fishers' Perceptions about the Costs and Benefits of the 2004 Great Barrier Reef Marine Park Zoning Plan* (Reef and Rainforest Research Centre Limited, 2008)

Tanaka, M, 'Lessons from the Protracted MOX Plant Dispute: A Proposed Protocol on Marine Environmental Impact Assessment to the United Nations Convention on the Law of the Sea' (2004) 25 *Michigan Journal of Environmental Law* 337

Tarlock, A Dan, 'Changing Currents: Perspectives on the State of Water Law and Policy in the 21st Century: Four Challenges for International Water Law' (2010) 23 *Tulane Environmental Law Journal* 369

Tarlock, A Dan and Patricia Wouters, 'Are Shared Benefits of International Waters an Equitable Apportionment?' 18 *Colorado Journal of International Environmental Law & Policy* 523

Therrien-Richards, Suzanne, 'SEA of Parks Canada Management Plans' in MR Partidario and R Clark (eds), *Perspectives on Strategic Environmental Assessment* (CRC-Lewis, 2000)

Thompson, A and A Dolman, 'Coral Bleaching: One Disturbance too many for Near-shore Reefs of the Great Barrier Reef' (2010) 29(3) *Coral Reefs* 637

Timagenis, CG, *The International Control of Marine Pollution* (Oceana Publications, 1979)

Timoshenko, Alexandre S, 'The Problem of Preventing Damage to the Environment in National and International Law: Impact Assessment and International Consultations' (1988) 5 *Pace Environmental Law Review* 475

Triggs, Gillian and Dean Bialek, 'Australia Withdraws Maritime Disputes from the Jurisdiction of the ICJ and ITLOS' (2002) 17(3) *International Journal of Marine and Coastal Law* 423

Trombitcaia, Iulia et al, *River Basin Commissions and Other Institutions for Transboundary Water Cooperation – Capacity for Water Cooperation in Eastern Europe, Caucasus and Central Asia* (Economic Commission for Europe – Convention on the Protection and Use of Transboundary Watercourses and International Lakes, United Nations, 2009)

Trubek, David and Louise Trubek, 'New Governance and Legal Regulation' (2006) 13 *Columbia Journal of European Law* 540

Tsutsumi, Rie and Kristy Robinson, 'Environmental Impact Assessment and the Framework Convention for the Protection of the Marine Environment of the Caspian Sea' in Bastmeijer, Kees and Timo Koivurova (eds), *Theory and Practice of Transboundary Environmental Impact Assessment* (Martinus Nijhoff, 2008)

Turner, M and GN Batianoff, 'Vulnerability of Island Flora and Fauna in the Great Barrier Reef to Climate Change' in JE Johnson and PA Marshall (eds), *Climate Change and the Great Barrier Reef: A Vulnerability Assessment* (Great Barrier Reef Marine Park Authority and Australian Greenhouse Office, 2007)

Tweedie, Jameson, 'Transboundary Environmental Impact Assessment under the North American Free Trade Agreement' (2006) 63 *Washington and Lee Law Review* 849

Twomey, A, 'Aspirational Nationalism or Opportunistic Federalism?' *Quadrant* (October 2007) 40

Twomey, Brian, 'Study Assesses Asia-Pacific Offshore Decommissioning Costs' (2010) 15 March, *Oil and Gas Journal* 51–55

UNECE, Resource Manual to Support Application of the UNECE Protocol on Strategic Environmental Assessment (United Nations and Regional Environment Centre for Central and Eastern Europe, 2012, 2nd edition)

UNEP, *Atlas of International Freshwater Agreements* (UNEP, 2002)

UNEP and Caspian Environment Programme, *Guidelines on Environmental Impact Assessment in a Transboundary Context in the Caspian Sea Region: Step by Step Procedures* (UNEP, 2003)

UNEP, UNECE, UNDP, NATO, REC, OSCE, *Environment and Security in Europe, Transforming Risks into Cooperation: The Case of the Eastern Caspian Region* (2008)

Vaughan, Naomi E and Timothy M Lenton, 'A Review of Climate Geoengineering Proposals' (2011) 109 *Climatic Change* 745

Verlaan, Philomene, 'Geo-engineering, the Law of the Sea, and Climate Change' (2009) 4 *Carbon and Climate Law Review* 446

Victor, David G, 'On the Regulation of Geo-engineering' (2008) 24 *Oxford Review of Economic Policy* 322

Victor, David G et al, 'The Geoengineering Option: A Last Resort against Global Warming?' (2009) 88 *Foreign Affairs* 64

Vince, J, 'Managing Australia's Oceans through the Oceans Policy Process' in W Gullett, C Schofield and J Vince (eds), *Marine Resources Management* (LexisNexis Butterworths, 2011) 77–89

Vinogradov, Sergei and Vance PE Langford, 'Managing Transboundary Water Resources in the Aral Sea Basin: in Search of a Solution' (2001) 1(3/4) *International Journal of Global Environmental Issues* 345

Virgo, J, 'International Governance of a Possible Geo-engineering Intervention to Combat Climate Change' (2009) 95 *Climate Change* 103

Walker, BH, LH Gunderson, AP Kinzig, C Folke, SR Carpenter and L Schultz, 'A Handful of Heuristics and some Propositions for Understanding Resilience in Social-ecological Systems' (2006) 11(1) *Ecol. Soc.*

Walker, Neil, 'EU Constitutionalism and New Governance' in Gráinne De Búrca and Joanne Scott (eds), *Law and New Governance in the EU and the US* (Hart Publishing, 2006) 15

Wallington, Tabatha, Geoffrey Lawrence and Barton Loechel, 'Reflections on the Legitimacy of Regional Environmental Governance: Lessons from Australia's Experiment in Natural Resource Management' (2008) 10(1) *Journal of Environmental Policy and Planning* 1

Warner, R, 'Preserving a Balanced Ocean: Regulating Climate Change Mitigation Activities in Marine Areas beyond National Jurisdiction' (2007) 14 *Australian International Law Journal* 99

Warner, Robin, *Protecting the Oceans beyond National Jurisdiction: Strengthening the International Law Framework* (Martinus Nijhoff, 2009)

Waugh, SM, GB Baker, R Gales and JP Croxall, 'CCAMLR Process of Risk Assessment to Minimise the Effects of Longline Fishing Mortality on Seabirds' (2008) 32 *Marine Policy* 442

WCPA, *Guidelines for Applying the IUCN Protected Area Management Categories to Marine Protected Areas (supplementary to the 2008 Guidelines)* (IUCN, 2011)

Wegerich, Kai, 'Water Resources in Central Asia: Regional Stability or Patchy Make-up' (2011) 30(2) *Central Asian Survey*, 275

Wescott, G, 'The Long and Winding Road: The Development of a Comprehensive, Adequate and Representative System of Highly Protected Marine Protected Areas in Victoria, Australia' (2006) 49 *Ocean and Coastal Management* 905

Wiersema, Annecoos, 'A Train without Tracks: Rethinking the Place of Law And Goals In Environmental And Natural Resources Law' (2008) 38 *Environmental Law* 1239

Wilkinson, CR, *Status of Coral Reefs of the World: 2008* (Australian Institute of Marine Science, 2008)

Wilkinson, Michael, 'Three Conceptions of Law: Towards A Jurisprudence Of Democratic Experimentalism' (2010) *Wisconsin Law Review* 673

Williams, John M and Adam Webster, 'Section 100 and State water rights' (2010) 21 *Public Law Review* 267

Wolfrum, Rüdiger and Nele Matz, *Conflicts in International Environmental Law* (Springer, 2003)

Wondolleck, Julia and Steven Yaffee, *Making Collaboration Work: Lessons from Innovation in Natural Resource Management* (Island Press, 2000)

Wu, Shicun and Hong Nong, 'The Energy Security of China and Oil and Gas Exploitation in the South China Sea' in Myron H Nordquist, John Norton Moore and Kuen-Chen Fu (eds), *Recent Developments in the Law of the Sea and China* (Martinus Nijhoff Publishers, 2005) 149

Wyatt, Andrew B and Ian G Baird, 'Transboundary Impact Assessment in the Sesan River Basin: The Case of the Yali Falls Dam' (2007) 23 *International Journal of Water Resources Development* 427

Yang, Tsaming and Robert V. Percival, 'The Emergence of Global Environmental Law' (2009) 34 *Yale Journal of International Law* 615

Yool, A et al, 'Low Efficiency of Nutrient Translocation for Enhancing Oceanic Uptake of Carbon Dioxide' (2009) 114 *Journal of Geophysical Research* 114

Young, Mike, 'Improving the Basin Plan: Options for consideration' in Daniell Connell and R Quentin Grafton (eds), *Basin Future: Water reform in the Murray-Darling Basin* (ANU E-Press, 2011) 439

Young, Oran, 'Institutional Linkages in International Society: Polar Perspectives' (1996) 2 *Global Governance* 1

Young, Oran, *Governance in World Affairs* (Cornell University Press, 1999)

Young, Oran, 'Institutions and the Growth of Knowledge: Evidence from International Environmental Regimes' (2004) 4 *International Environmental Agreements: Politics, Law and Economics* 215

Yu, Xia, 'Transboundary Water Pollution Management: Lessons Learned from River Basin Management in China, Europe and the Netherlands' (2011) 7(1) *Utrecht Law Review* 188

Zammit, Charles et al, *A Review of the NRM Arrangements in Queensland* (Department of Natural Resources and Mining, 2004)

Zhou, S and P Flynn, 'Geoengineering Downwelling Ocean Currents: A Cost Assessment' (2005) 71 *Climatic Change* 203

Index

Note: Figures are in *italic* and tables in **bold**.

For Product Safety Concerns and Information please contact our EU representative GPSR@taylorandfrancis.com
Taylor & Francis Verlag GmbH, Kaufingerstraße 24, 80331 München, Germany

www.ingramcontent.com/pod-product-compliance
Ingram Content Group UK Ltd.
Pitfield, Milton Keynes, MK11 3LW, UK
UKHW020023200926
475702UK00014B/2022
* 9 7 8 1 1 3 8 1 1 8 5 3 9 *